VOICES FROM THE PAST

By the same author, with Bruce Carrick

365: Great Stories From History for Every Day of the Year
(Icon Books, 2004)

366: A Leap Year of Great Stories From History
(Icon Books, 2007)

*Tales of War: Great Stories From Military History
for Every Day of the Year* (Icon Books, 2010)

VOICES FROM THE PAST

W. B. Marsh

ICON

Published in the UK and USA in 2020 by
Icon Books Ltd, Omnibus Business Centre,
39–41 North Road, London N7 9DP
email: info@iconbooks.com
www.iconbooks.com

Sold in the UK, Europe and Asia
by Faber & Faber Ltd, Bloomsbury House,
74–77 Great Russell Street,
London WC1B 3DA or their agents

Distributed in the UK, Europe and Asia
by Grantham Book Services, Trent Road,
Grantham NG31 7XQ

Distributed in the USA
by Publishers Group West,
1700 Fourth Street, Berkeley, CA 94710

Distributed in Canada by Publishers Group Canada,
76 Stafford Street, Unit 300
Toronto, Ontario M6J 2S1

Distributed in Australia and New Zealand by
Allen & Unwin Pty Ltd, PO Box 8500,
83 Alexander Street, Crows Nest, NSW 2065

Distributed in South Africa by
Jonathan Ball, Office B4, The District,
41 Sir Lowry Road, Woodstock 7925

Distributed in India by Penguin Books India,
7th Floor, Infinity Tower – C, DLF Cyber City,
Gurgaon 122002, Haryana

ISBN: 978-178578-663-1

Typeset in Adobe Garamond by Marie Doherty

Printed and bound in Great Britain by
Clays Ltd, Elcograf S.p.A.

For Ingrid, without whom little would have been possible and even less worth doing.

About the author

A graduate of Princeton University, W.B. Marsh spent two years as an officer in the US Marine Corps, followed by a career in international advertising. He and his wife live in London.

Author's note

Before writing this book I co-authored three similar books – *365*, *366* and *Tales of War* – with my lifelong friend, Bruce Carrick. We would both write parts of the books and then edit what the other had written. In 2016 we agreed to work together again on the book that you now hold in your hands, but almost before we could do any writing, tragedy struck. Bruce was brought down by cancer, which ended his life on 27 December 2017.

It goes without saying that this book would have been far better had Bruce been able to work on it with me. Even more important for me, writing it would have been more fun. So, Bruce, if you're looking down from wherever you are, I hope you think this book is as good as it could be without you. You are missed on every level – as a writer, as an editor, and most of all as a friend.

A note on copyright

Contents

CONTENTS

CONTENTS

CONTENTS

CONTENTS

CONTENTS

CONTENTS

CONTENTS

CONTENTS

CONTENTS

CONTENTS

CONTENTS

CONTENTS

CONTENTS

CONTENTS

CONTENTS

CONTENTS

CONTENTS

CONTENTS

CONTENTS

CONTENTS

CONTENTS

CONTENTS

CONTENTS

CONTENTS

CONTENTS

Preface

This book is dedicated to the idea that history is a feast to be enjoyed every day and that memorable quotations are like glasses of fine Bordeaux that bring out the flavour of a three-star meal.

In this book, every date has a story from history, each headlined with a quotation related to that event. The text itself contains hundreds more quotes – in all, there are about 1,200. Even so, there are still dozens that I love but couldn't find a way to include.

Some pose profound questions: in the 6th century Boethius queried: 'If there is a God, whence proceed so many evils? If there is no God, whence cometh any good?' Others are more sceptical, like Alfonso the Wise of Castile in the 13th century: 'Had I been present at the Creation, I would have given some useful hints for the better ordering of the universe.' In the 19th century Lord Melbourne was simply dismissive: 'Things have come to a pretty pass when religion is allowed to invade the sphere of private life.'

Many memorable quotations come from commanders in the field. In the 1st century BC, when the defenders of a besieged city cried outrage at being unlawfully attacked by the Romans, Pompey the Great told them: 'Stop quoting laws, we carry weapons!' In the early 19th century, Napoleonic marshal François Joseph Lefebvre told the inhabitants of a conquered town: 'We come to give you liberty and equality, but don't lose your heads about it – the first person who stirs without permission will be shot.' And for pure bravado, little could beat American Marine General Chesty Puller's dictum: 'Pain is weakness leaving the body.'

Another of my favourites is '*In vino veritas*' ('In wine lies the truth'), but I was surprised to learn in researching it that originally it was coined in Greek by Alcaeus of Mytilene in the 6th century BC, that Pliny the Elder gave us the Latin version and numerous others have elaborated on it, like Charles Dickens in *Nicholas Nickleby* – 'Wine in, truth out'.

Another favourite is German statesman Otto von Bismarck's answer, when asked what was the greatest political fact of modern times: 'The inherited and permanent fact that North America speaks English.'

Political insult is another fertile field, including the perhaps apocryphal exchange in Parliament between John Wilkes and John Montagu. When Montagu told his adversary, 'Sir, I do not know whether you will die on the gallows or of the pox!', Wilkes retorted: 'That, sir, depends on whether I first embrace your Lordship's principles or your Lordship's mistresses.'

Another master of quotable insults was Winston Churchill. He attacked one Labour opponent, 'An empty cab pulled up to Downing Street. Clement Attlee got out', and had this to say about Stanley Baldwin: 'He occasionally stumbled over the truth, but hastily picked himself up and hurried on as if nothing had happened.' Less elegantly, former Democratic president Lyndon Johnson said this about Republican Gerald Ford, a noted athlete at university: 'He's a nice guy, but he played too much football with his helmet off.' The 19th-century American senator Simon Cameron gave this acerbic view: 'An honest politician is one who when he is bought will stay bought.' The American writer P.J. O'Rourke would agree: 'Giving money and power to government is like giving whiskey and car keys to teenage boys.' And here is Lloyd George's take: 'A politician is a person with whose policies you don't agree; if you agree with him he is a statesman.' On a gentler note, Hillary Clinton once described her errant husband Bill as 'a hard dog to keep on the porch'. One step removed from politics is royalty, and I particularly like Disraeli's comment: 'Everyone likes flattery; and when it comes to Royalty, you should lay it on with a trowel.'

Then there are those quotations that simply make me smile, like movie mogul Louis B. Mayer's telegram after screen-testing Ava Gardner: 'She can't sing, she can't act, she can't talk, she's terrific!' Or American senator Barry Goldwater's comment about a verbose opponent: 'Hubert Humphrey talks so fast that listening to him is like trying to read *Playboy* magazine with your wife turning the pages.' Or Mark Twain's defence of Wagner: 'Wagner's music is better than it sounds.'

Clearly my choice of favourite quotations is erratic, but in defence I can only quote Ralph Waldo Emerson: 'A foolish consistency is the hobgoblin of little minds.'

I could continue but I will stop, my final quotation from that unlucky French poet/philosopher Paul Valéry, who was nominated twelve times for the Nobel Prize in Literature but never won it. His comment on poetry could equally apply to my preface: 'A poem is never finished, only abandoned.'

W.B. Marsh, April 2020

1 January

'Hail, Caesar! They who are about to die salute you.'

404 AD According to tradition, as they paraded into the arena, Roman gladiators would face the emperor and shout in unison: '*Ave, Caesar, morituri te salutant!*' It was the opening ritual in the bloodiest entertainment ever devised, one that had been part of Roman life since the 3rd century BC. But today in Rome, the savage spectacle of man killing man for sport made its last appearance, its final victim not a gladiator but a Christian monk.

Fights between gladiators had been staged in Rome since 264 BC, when Decimus Junius Brutus Scaeva had three pairs of slaves fight to the death in the Forum Boarium to honour his dead father. In this he was adopting earlier Etruscan rites of sacrifice for the dead, appeasing their spirits with blood offerings.

At first the games (*munera*) were presented by aristocratic families, not only to honour their dead but increasingly to display status and wealth. Over the centuries they were transformed into one of the essential ingredients of what Juvenal termed 'bread and circuses' (*panem et circenses*) to distract the masses.

The combatants were called gladiators after the Roman sword they carried, the *gladius*, a double-edged blade good for both stabbing and cutting. *Gladius* itself derived from the Latin '*gulam dividere*' ('separates the throat'). The ground where gladiators fought was customarily strewn with sand (*harena*) to absorb the blood; hence our word 'arena'.

Most gladiators were slaves, prisoners of war or criminals condemned to death; but, as gladiatorial contests became increasingly popular, gladiators became professionals. Sometimes enthusiastic amateurs, including Roman senators and even women, fought in the games, either for the money or for the pure adventure.

Many Roman rulers sponsored gladiatorial fights, including Julius Caesar, who, according to Pliny, once staged a contest of 320 pairs. Almost two centuries later, to celebrate his conquest of Dacia (today's Romania), the Emperor Trajan ordered 123 days of games in the Coliseum that included a record 5,000 pairs, as well as the slaughter of 11,000 animals. A few emperors actually fought in the arena, including Caligula, Titus, Hadrian and Lucius Verus, but they invariably arranged their participation so that they faced no real risk. Undoubtedly the

1

most 'gladiatorial' of the emperors was Commodus (180–192 AD), who not only organised bizarre contests such as those between women and dwarfs but also dressed himself as Hercules, wearing a lion-skin cloak and wielding a club, and fought in over 700 contests against both men and animals.

By the beginning of the 4th century, however, these bloody spectacles were diminishing in number, partly under the disapproving eye of the Christian Church. In 325 Constantine (who had legalised Christianity eight years before) formally prohibited them. Although his ban was widely flouted, in 399 Honorius closed any remaining gladiatorial schools. Still, however, fights occasionally took place – until this day in 404.

In Rome at the time was the monk Telemachus, an ascetic from the East (probably Syria) who believed he had been called by God to come to the city on pilgrimage. On the first day of January he joined crowds thronging to a stadium (possibly the Coliseum). Inside, he saw two gladiators locked in grisly combat. Horrified, he jumped down onto the sands and imposed himself between the two, crying out, 'In the name of Christ, forbear!'

The gladiators separated, but the crowd, incensed at his interference, seized rocks, debris and bits of fallen masonry and stoned him to death.

When Honorius heard of Telemachus' lynching, he proscribed all future gladiatorial contests, bringing to an end the gory spectacles that had so enthralled the Roman world for almost seven centuries.

1660 Samuel Pepys makes the first entry in his diary: 'Jan. 1 (Lord's Day). This morning (we living lately in the garret) I rose, put on my suit with great skirts, having not lately worn any other clothes but them. Went to Mr Gunning's chapel at Exeter House, where he made a very good sermon …' * **1863** After Abraham Lincoln issues the Emancipation Proclamation on 22 September 1862, today it comes into force: 'All persons held as slaves within any State or designated part of a State, the people whereof shall then be in rebellion against the United States, shall be then, thenceforward, and forever free.'

2 January

*'You do well to weep like a woman for what
you could not defend like a man.'*

1492 For 280 years the Nasrid dynasty had ruled Andalusia, their capital Granada, their palace the fabled Alhambra. Now the emir was Abu Abdallah Muhammad XII, known by the Spanish as Boabdil. He was the 23rd of his dynasty to hold power – and he would be the last.

Back in 711 the Berber chieftain Tariq ibn Ziyad had crossed from Morocco to start the Moorish invasion of the Iberian peninsula, and within a decade the Moors had conquered almost all of today's Spain and Portugal. But the fight back – the *Reconquista* – started only eleven years later when the Asturians scored the first Christian victory against the Muslims.

Since then, in fits and starts, Spain's Christian kingdoms had been slowly regaining territory. Finally, in 1482, Spain's joint monarchs Ferdinand and Isabella resolved to complete the Christian reconquest. They were particularly determined to take Granada, the last Moorish stronghold, since its ruler Boabdil had once been a refugee in their court and later their vassal, but had launched a rebellion.

In the spring of 1491 the Catholic Monarchs set out with an army of 80,000 and soon reached the walls of Granada. Fighting was at first restricted to occasional sallies by the besieged Moors, but in July a few daring Spaniards slipped into the city by night and attached a copy of a Christian prayer to the door of a mosque. The next day a Moor named Yarfe stormed out of the gates and galloped back and forth before the Spanish positions with the prayer tied to his horse's tail.

Smarting from the insult, a Spanish knight challenged Yarfe to single combat. The two knights charged each other, first on horseback and then on foot, until Yarfe was slain. While the knights were fighting, both Spaniards and Moors had watched the struggle but refrained from attack, abiding by the rules of chivalry. But when Yarfe was defeated, the Moorish garrison rushed out, only to be shattered by the Spanish cavalry; they left 2,000 casualties outside the walls before scurrying back inside.

It looked like a victory for Christ, but that night Allah seemingly took a hand when a candle set fire to Queen Isabella's tent and the conflagration burned most of the Spanish camp. The following day Ferdinand marched his army around the city walls to show that despite the fire, he still controlled the siege. Boabdil once more sent his soldiers on the attack, but after a few skirmishes they were forced to retreat. Eventually lack of food and the hopelessness of his position drove Boabdil to capitulate.

On this day Ferdinand and Isabella rode out to a clearing on the Genil river about a mile from the city's walls. There, with the royal banners and the cross of Christ plainly visible on the red walls of the Alhambra, they received Boabdil's surrender. Then the gates of Granada were thrown open and Ferdinand entered, bearing the great silver cross he had carried throughout his ten-year crusade.

Mortified by his defeat, Boabdil rode away with his entourage, never to return. Reaching a lofty spur of the Alpujarras, he stopped to gaze back at the fabulous city he had lost. As he turned to his mother who rode at his side, a tear escaped him. But instead of the sympathy he expected, his mother addressed him with contempt: 'You do well to weep like a woman for what you could not defend like a man.' The rocky ridge from which Boabdil had his last look at Granada has henceforth been called El Ultimo Suspiro del Moro (The Last Sigh of the Moor).

1882 When Oscar Wilde arrives in New York, he tells the customs officer: 'I have nothing to declare except my genius.' * **1900** When an equerry tells an improper story at dinner at Windsor Castle, Queen Victoria responds: 'We are not amused.'

---

3 January

'Ich liebe Deutschland! Heil Hitler! and farewell.'

1946 Half a mile south of the Thames squats an ungainly group of 19th-century buildings called Wandsworth Prison. There at a little after nine this morning, Lord Haw-Haw was hanged. From the surge in blood pressure that occurred when he dropped from the gallows, the long scar that ran down the right side of his face split open, a ghastly finish for one of Britain's most notorious traitors.

Lord Haw-Haw was born William Joyce in Brooklyn, New York in 1906 and moved to Ireland with his family when he was three. Twelve years later they settled in England.

At seventeen Joyce joined the British Fascisti, which aped Mussolini's Partito Nazionale Fascista that had just gained power in Italy. He devoted his talents to street brawling, and at eighteen, as he led a squad of thugs to attack communist agitators, he was slashed by a razor, resulting in the ugly scar that ran from his right ear to the corner of his mouth.

When Oswald Mosley founded the British Union of Fascists in 1932, Joyce rushed to join. Eventually, however, his aggression and virulent antisemitism alarmed even Mosley, who eased him out of the party. With about twenty followers, Joyce formed the British National Socialist League, which rejoiced in violence, admiration for Hitler and hatred of Jews.

With Europe on the brink of war, the British government was preparing to intern Nazi sympathisers, but six days before Hitler invaded Poland, Joyce fled to Berlin with his wife, fearing (correctly) that he would be detained.

Joyce joined German propaganda radio in Berlin and started his infamous broadcasts aimed at undermining British morale. Each transmission began with 'Germany calling, Germany calling, Germany calling' and then continued with Joyce's brand of Nazi disinformation: Jews had started the war; Churchill 'is the servant, not of the British public, or of the British Empire, but of International Jewish finance'; Hitler is invincible; a Nazi Fifth Column will undermine Britain. Joyce also gave fatherly advice on how to treat bombing wounds. His broadcasts drew 18 million occasional listeners, almost as many as the BBC.

Joyce's marked nasal drawl prompted a *Daily Express* journalist to write: 'He speaks English of the haw-haw, damit-get-out-of-my-way variety, and his strong suit is gentlemanly indignation.' From then on Joyce was known as Lord Haw-Haw.

Even when Allied bombing forced Joyce to move near Hamburg, he continued to broadcast, and a grateful German government awarded him the Cross of War Merit 1st Class with a certificate signed by Hitler. But the growing likelihood of German defeat began to take its toll; Joyce's marriage collapsed and he turned increasingly to drink.

Lord Haw-Haw made his final broadcast on 30 April 1945, the day that Hitler shot himself in his Berlin bunker. Drunk and maudlin, his speech slurred, he ranted that now Communist Russia would rule Europe, while Great Britain would shrivel and die, having squandered her power and wealth during a foolish war. His final words were, '*Ich liebe Deutschland! Heil Hitler!* and farewell.'

A few days after the German surrender, some British soldiers came across a forlorn figure in a forest near Hamburg. When Joyce reached for a forged passport in his pocket, the soldiers thought he was pulling a gun and shot him in the buttocks.

Joyce was flown back to England to face trial. While newspapers bayed for his blood, the court debated his nationality: born an American and raised in Ireland, he had become a German citizen in 1939, and, he asserted, could not betray a country that was not his own. But Joyce had also held a British passport, and he had remained British until it had expired in July 1940. On 19 September the court condemned him to death by hanging, a sentence carried out on this day.

Lord Haw-Haw died unrepentant, claiming at the last: 'In death as in life, I defy the Jews who caused this last war, and I defy the powers of darkness they represent.' He was buried in an unmarked grave inside the prison grounds.

1777 After defeating the British at the Battle of Princeton, George Washington reflects: 'It was a glorious day, and I would not have been absent from it for all the money I ever expect to be worth.'

---

4 January

'Basically, at the very bottom of life, which seduces us all, there is only absurdity, and more absurdity.'

1960 Who can forget Henri Cartier-Bresson's iconic black and white photograph of Albert Camus? Coat collar turned up against the cold, he glances half left into the camera, a stub of cigarette in the corner of his mouth, reminding you of Humphrey Bogart – masculine, careworn and wary. As Camus himself wrote, 'after a certain age every man is responsible for his face'.

Camus was born in Algeria to a Pied-Noir family, but he lost his father when he was less than a year old, killed in the Battle of the Marne. His mother was an illiterate cleaning woman. Nonetheless, he won a scholarship to the University of Algiers. He had also been a keen football player, before tuberculosis forced him to quit the game. A strikingly attractive man, he married twice and indulged in numerous affairs.

Although never a true communist, Camus joined the French Communist Party when he was 21, only to be kicked out two years later when he joined the independent Algerian People's Party. During the Second World War he moved to Paris, where he witnessed the

Wehrmacht marching in. By 1942 he had fled to Bordeaux and enlisted in the Resistance, taking the *nom de guerre* Beauchard.

Earlier, Camus had written to a friend: 'Basically, at the very bottom of life, which seduces us all, there is only absurdity, and more absurdity.' Now in Bordeaux he published his first existentialist novel, *The Stranger*, and *The Myth of Sisyphus*, a philosophical essay on the absurdity of the human condition.

In the Greek myth, Sisyphus is condemned eternally to roll a boulder up a hill, only for it to roll back down again as he approaches the summit. But in Camus' essay, Sisyphus ultimately finds meaning in his task, simply by continually applying himself to it. Camus believed that there is no meaning in life beyond what we give it, and in a world without meaning, 'there is only one truly serious philosophical problem, and that is suicide'.

Camus returned to Paris in time to witness its liberation, and he became a prominent member of the intellectual Left, frequenting the Café de Flore and the Deux Magots with other thinkers like Jean-Paul Sartre (although Camus' criticisms of communism eventually alienated Sartre).

In 1947 Camus published *The Plague* and over the next decade produced *The Fall*, essays like *The Rebel* and several plays. In 1957 he was awarded the Nobel Prize in Literature.

In early 1960, when Camus was 46, he was staying at his house in the Provençal town of Lourmarin with his publisher Michel Gallimard. Since he hated driving, he had bought train tickets to Paris, but Gallimard owned a smart new Facel-Vega, a fashionable French car powered by a huge Chrysler engine. He persuaded Camus to come with him by car. Early on the morning of 4 January they set out for Paris with their wives.

At lunch they stopped in Sens, where they enjoyed *boudins noirs* and a bottle of burgundy, then headed north in a slight drizzle. Impatient to reach Paris, Gallimard pushed the Facel-Vega to over 100 miles an hour. The car suddenly veered off the road, bounced off one tree and then wrapped itself around another. The two wives, sitting in the back seat, survived unscathed, but Camus died instantly of a broken neck. Gallimard died of a brain haemorrhage five days later. In the wreckage the police found the unused train tickets and 144 pages of handwritten manuscript for an unfinished novel, *The First Man*.

Earlier, Camus had written that there can be 'nothing more absurd than to die in a car accident'. Newspapers everywhere commented on the irony – a man who confronted death and the absurdity of existence was killed by chance in a car crash, when he had planned to take the train.

In 1967 the town where Camus died raised a fountain in his memory, inscribed with a sentence from *The Myth of Sisyphus*: 'The struggle toward the summit itself suffices to fill a man's heart.'

---

46 BC During Rome's civil war, Caesar's one-time subordinate Titus Labienus swears: 'There can be no peace until Caesar's head is brought back to us.' ('*Nam nobis nisi Caesaris capite relato pax esse nulla potest.*') He then defeats Caesar at the Battle of Ruspina, but the next year Caesar triumphs at Munda, and Labienus' head is brought to Caesar instead.

---

5 January

'Before Grandson, lost treasure. Before Morat, lost heart. Before Nancy, lost life.'

1477 In the last ten months of his life Charles the Bold, Duke of Burgundy, besieged three cities and failed three times. The last failure today at Nancy left him dead on the field of battle.

A century earlier, Charles's great-grandfather Philip the Bold had made Burgundy virtually independent, with only spasmodic control from France. This enormously rich duchy included present-day Belgium and Luxembourg as well as Burgundy and Picardy, and its ruler was a king in everything but title.

But Charles dreamt of resurrecting the ancient kingdom of Lotharingia, one of the three parts of Charlemagne's empire. Since coming to power in 1465, he had been at loggerheads with neighbouring France and Switzerland, and often with his own vassals. Initially he was brutally successful – for example, he punished an uprising in Dinant by throwing 800 burghers into the River Meuse and setting fire to the city, killing every man, woman and child within.

In 1475 the Swiss Confederation occupied Grandson Castle on the shores of Lake Neuchâtel, but the following March Charles besieged the castle with a large army. The garrison quickly surrendered after he promised clemency, but he hanged or drowned all 412 defenders.

Four days later the vanguard of the Swiss army approached, but the Burgundians mistook it for the main force. Knowing battle was imminent, the Swiss knelt to pray for victory, which Charles's men mistook for a sign of submission. In no mood to accept surrender, Charles ordered his artillery to fire. But suddenly the main body of Swiss troops charged from the forest, routing the Burgundians and capturing Charles's treasury, seizing his gold dinnerware, an incredible collection of jewels that included a 139-carat diamond and an even more tempting prize, 2,000 Burgundian *filles de joie*. Although there were few casualties, the Swiss had humiliated the greatest duke in Europe.

Despite this fiasco, fifteen weeks later Charles began another siege 50 kilometres east, at Morat. When no relief had arrived after two weeks, he stood his army down so that his treasurer could pay his men. But just at that moment a Swiss force from Berne emerged from the nearby woods, catching the Bungundians totally unprepared. In the slaughter that followed, Charles's army suffered 10,000 dead.

Charles himself escaped back to Burgundy, where he stayed for months in deep depression, disheartened by his failures. Despite the pleas of his captains, however, by December he was heading toward the walled city of Nancy, which its ruler, René of Lorraine, had retaken a year earlier.

The 6,000-strong Burgundian army encircled Nancy, Charles hoping for a swift victory, but on this Sunday, René arrived with 10,000 Lorrainers plus 10,000 Swiss mercenaries. Charles must have known he stood little chance against a vastly superior enemy in the bitter cold of winter, but his famed obstinacy prevented him from retreat.

Hidden by snow-covered trees, René sent 2,000 cavalry and 7,000 Swiss infantry around Charles's left flank. After two hours of slogging, the Swiss charged from the woods on the Burgundians' rear, blowing their alpine horns. Stunned and overwhelmed by superior numbers, Charles's troops began to flee.

Charles was swept along until his party was surrounded. A Swiss soldier named Claude de Bauzémont approached the duke, brandishing his halberd. Charles pleaded, '*Sauvez le duc de Bourgogne!*' ('Save the Duke of Burgundy!'), but Bauzémont failed to recognise him and mistook his words for a defiant '*Vive le duc de Bourgogne!*' ('Long live the Duke of Burgundy!') and savagely struck him down.

For three days no one knew what had become of the great duke. Then a captured Burgundian page was led to the barren and frozen battlefield, where he identified Charles's naked body, his face opened from ear to jaw and his body pierced by two lance thrusts. Wolves had gnawed the bloody remains.

With the death of Charles the Bold, France annexed Burgundy. From Charles's three sieges and three defeats came an old Swiss saying, 'Before Grandson, lost treasure. Before Morat, lost heart. Before Nancy, lost life.' (*Devant Granson, perdit ses possessions. Devant Morat, le coeur brisa. Devant Nancy, perdit la vie.*)

1066 On his deathbed, Edward the Confessor warns Harold Godwinson (Harold II) about William the Conqueror: 'Harold! take it [the crown], if such be thy wish; but the gift will be thy ruin. Against the Duke and his baronage no power of thine can avail thee!' * **1933** On hearing that the passive and taciturn President Calvin Coolidge has died, Dorothy Parker asks, 'How could they tell?'

---

6 January

'Rise not – obey my commands and do not presume to wet the edge of my robe.'

1017 Today a young Dane of about 23 was crowned in St Paul's Cathedral. He was Cnut (or Canute), the king who commanded the tide not to come in (or did he?).

Cnut came from some colourful forbears; his great-grandfather was Gorm the Languid, his grandfather Harald Bluetooth, his father Sweyn Forkbeard and his stepmother the terrifying Sigrid the Haughty, who, according to legend, had once had two suitors burned to death following a feast to discourage other admirers.

Cnut had first come to England with his father's conquering army in 1013. Sweyn had chased the hapless Aethelred the Unready into exile in Normandy and taken over the kingdom. But less than a year later he died, and Cnut was forced to flee back to Denmark as English barons recalled Aethelred.

In the summer of 1015, Cnut gathered a fleet of 200 longships and set sail with an army of 10,000 Vikings from all over Scandinavia. Over the next few months he conquered much of England, despite sporadic resistance from Aethelred and his son Edmund Ironside. On 23 April 1016 Aethelred died, leaving Edmund to fight on, but six months later Cnut routed Edmund's small army at the Battle of Assandun, where Edmund was wounded. The two claimants to the throne met to negotiate terms and agreed that all of England north of the Thames was to be held by Cnut, while Edmund would keep the south as well as London, with the entire realm passing to the survivor if one of them died. Only a month later Edmund conveniently dropped dead (some reports said he was shot with a crossbow while sitting on the toilet), leaving Cnut master of the land.

At first Cnut ruthlessly eliminated any who resisted him, but over time he slowly eased out his Danish ministers to replace them with English ones. His rule was fair and effective; he even became a strong supporter of the Church and made a pilgrimage to Rome. By modern standards, however, he might be considered somewhat stern; his Law 53 ruled that if a woman committed adultery, her husband was entitled to all her property and 'she is to lose her nose and ears'.

Cnut inherited the Danish throne in 1019 and Norway's in 1028, making him one of the most powerful sovereigns in Europe, but despite this worldly success, he remains best known for commanding the tide not to rise.

According to the almost contemporary English historian Henry of Huntingdon, Cnut set his throne by the seashore and commanded: 'Ocean! The land where I sit is mine, and you are part of my dominion. Therefore rise not – obey my commands and do not presume to wet the edge of my robe.'

While his retainers waited for the sea to comply, it obstinately continued to roll in, finally forcing Cnut to leap backwards when waves had wet his shoes. He then addressed his sycophantic courtiers: 'Let all men know how empty and worthless is the power of kings, for there is none worthy of the name, but He whom heaven, earth, and sea obey by eternal laws.' He then hung his gold crown on a crucifix and never wore it again, 'to the honour of God the almighty King'.

After a reign of eighteen years, eleven months and eleven days, Cnut died at Shaftesbury in Dorset in 1035, and his immense empire of England, Denmark and Norway was split into three pieces, with his illegitimate son Harold Harefoot taking control of England. He was buried in the old Anglo-Saxon cathedral at Winchester, but during the English Civil War, marauding Roundhead soldiers used his bones as missiles to shatter stained glass windows and left them scattered on the floor. They were scooped up and mixed with those of some Saxon kings and bishops and the Norman King William Rufus and placed in various mortuary chests, where they remain to this day.

1991 Saddam Hussein tells the people of Iraq: 'The battle in which you are locked today is the mother of all battles.'

7 January

*'When I am dead and opened, you shall find
"Philip" and "Calais" engraved on my heart.'*

1558 The port of Calais is the closest French town to England, a meagre
30 miles from the English coast and so near that the White Cliffs of
Dover can easily be seen on a clear day. Unsurprisingly, it has long
played a part in English history. Way back in 54 BC Julius Caesar and
his legions embarked at Calais for his second invasion of Britain. More
than a millennium later, in 1189, Richard the Lionheart landed there
with his army on his way to the Third Crusade. Then, on 4 August 1347,
after thrashing the French at Crécy, England's Edward III captured the
city after an eleven-month siege as he launched the Hundred Years' War.

During the next two centuries Calais grew in importance and
wealth, and its population reached some 12,000 people. It became
England's main gateway for the wool trade, and its customs revenues
amounted at times to a third of the English government's revenue.

Despite numerous French attempts to retake it, Calais remained
English, the last English possession in France, until on this day
211 years of English rule finally came to an end during the reign of
Queen Mary I.

In 1554 Mary, then a 38-year-old spinster, married and became
besotted by Philip II of Spain. Two years later Philip persuaded his
compliant bride to join him in his ongoing war with France. This gave
France's Henri II just the excuse he needed to throw the English out
of Calais for good.

Henri selected his greatest general, François de Lorraine, second
duc de Guise, and ordered him to besiege Calais. A robust and athletic
warrior of 39, Guise had been fighting for French kings all his adult
life. His face carried a deep scar from a battle wound suffered when he
was 26, resulting in his nickname, *Le Balafré* (Scarface).

On 1 January 1558 Guise and his army of 30,000 men launched
a lightning assault against Calais, which was garrisoned by a mere
2,500 defenders. He struck swiftly across the frozen marshes on the town's
seaward side, capturing an English strongpoint that protected the sluice
gates, which if opened could have flooded the attackers. After only six days
of fighting, the English were forced to yield, and so on this day the English
lost Calais and were swept clean out of France. The French proudly named
the area around Calais *le Pays Reconquis* (the Reconquered Country).

Just eleven months later, on 17 November, Mary died during an influenza epidemic that was sweeping London. During her final painful hours she lamented: 'When I am dead and opened, you shall find "Philip" and "Calais" engraved on my heart.' (Philip's grief was more subdued; 'I felt a reasonable regret for her death', he wrote to his sister.)

On 3 April of the following year, Henri II signed the Peace of Cateau-Cambrésis with England and Spain, which officially gave Calais to France. Three months later Henri, too, was dead from a wound suffered during a jousting tournament.

Since the 16th century Calais has been used twice more for attempts to reach England. In 1805 Napoleon gathered his fleet there for his aborted invasion, and until 2016 migrants in the 'Calais Jungle' refugee camp waited for a chance to dodge the guards to slip across the Channel.

> **1536** As Henry VIII's discarded first wife Catherine of Aragon is dying, she writes a last letter to Henry, ending: 'Lastly, I make this vow, that mine eyes desire you above all things.'

8 January

*'In painting Cimabue thought that he/
Should hold the field, now Giotto has the cry,/
So that the other's fame is growing dim.'*

1337 Today the painter credited with being the father of the Renaissance died in Florence. He was Giotto di Bondone, known to most of us simply as Giotto.

So little is known for certain about Giotto's life that his biography must be a series of guesses, but almost everyone agrees that he was once a student of Cimabue. Here is his legend, mostly sourced from Giorgio Vasari's *Lives of the Most Excellent Painters, Sculptors, and Architects*, written in the mid-16th century.

The son of a blacksmith named Bondone, Giotto was born in a hilltop farmhouse in Colle Vespignano, a hamlet 35 kilometres north of Florence, in 1266 or 1267. Vasari relates: 'When he had reached the age of ten years ... Bondone gave him the care of some sheep. As he was leading them for pasture ... he was constantly driven by his natural inclination to draw on the stones or the ground some object in nature ... One day Cimabue, going on business from Florence to

Vespignano, found Giotto, while his sheep were grazing, drawing a sheep from nature upon a smooth and solid rock with a pointed stone, having never learnt from anyone but nature. Cimabue, marvelling at him, stopped and asked him if he would go and be with him. And the boy answered that if his father were content he would gladly go. Then Cimabue asked Bondone for him, and he gave him up to him, and was content that he should take him to Florence.'

While he was an apprentice in Cimabue's studio, Giotto learned to paint. Vasari says he was a merry and intelligent child who once, when Cimabue was away, painted a fly on the nose of a figure in one of his master's unfinished paintings. When Cimabue returned he repeatedly tried to brush it away, before he realised that it was just one of Giotto's practical jokes.

At that time Cimabue was considered Florence's greatest artist, but, according to Vasari, he was vain of his abilities and 'so haughty and proud that if someone pointed out to him any mistake or defect in his work, or if he had noted any himself ... he would immediately destroy the work, no matter how precious it might be'.

After leaving his apprenticeship, Giotto had no trouble finding patrons, as his art was recognised as more natural than the Byzantine-style work of his contemporaries, with a new, convincing sense of pictorial space.

In the late 1290s Pope Boniface VIII sent to Giotto for a sample of his work. Instead of sending a painting, he drew a perfect circle with a single continuous stroke and sent that to the Pope, who was so impressed that he agreed to patronise him. During his career Giotto decorated chapels in Rome, Padua, Florence, Naples and most famously Assisi.

From 1288 to 1292 Cimabue had worked in the great Basilica of San Francesco in Assisi. He died about 1302, and four years later Giotto began painting the cycle of 28 scenes from the life of St Francis of Assisi in the upper church and other works in the lower church.

Even in his own day Giotto was considered the greater painter. A close friend was the poet Dante Alighieri, who completed the *Divine Comedy* in 1320. In *Purgatorio* he places Cimabue among the proud, with the words:

> In painting Cimabue thought that he
> Should hold the field, now Giotto has the cry,
> So that the other's fame is growing dim.

(Credette Cimabue ne la pittura
tener lo campo, e ora ha Giotto il grido,
sì che la fama di colui è scura.)

Cimabue had died almost 30 years before the *Divine Comedy* was published, but Giotto is one of the few living people included in Dante's work. Over two centuries later Vasari echoed Dante's judgement: 'Giotto truly eclipsed Cimabue's fame just as a great light eclipses a much smaller one.'

1790 George Washington addresses both houses of Congress: 'To be prepared for war is one of the most effectual means of preserving peace.' * **2008** Barack Obama at the New Hampshire Democratic primary: 'When we have faced down impossible odds; when we've been told we're not ready, or that we shouldn't try, or that we can't, generations of Americans have responded with a simple creed that sums up the spirit of a people: Yes we can.'

---

9 January

'I am not ordering you to attack. I am ordering you to die.'

1916 Before dawn on this cold January morning, as British ammunition dumps erupted and boats carried off the last 200 British soldiers from the Gallipoli peninsula, the Ottoman Empire celebrated its only major victory of the First World War. Yet what would emerge from this triumph was not a stronger Ottoman state but a republican Turkey.

After the Ottomans had entered the war on the side of the Central Powers in October 1914, First Lord of the Admiralty Winston Churchill proposed an attack to seize the Dardanelles in order to capture the Ottoman capital, Constantinople (now Istanbul), and knock the Ottoman Empire out of the war.

In February 1915 British and French warships bombarded Ottoman positions along the Gallipoli peninsula, which forms the northern edge of the Dardanelles, but after three battleships had been sunk and three others damaged, the naval attack was abandoned, to be replaced by a major land invasion. The Turks were certain that a land attack was imminent but argued over where the enemy would come ashore. One of their officers, a 34-year-old lieutenant colonel named Mustafa Kemal, knew the Gallipoli peninsula from fighting in the Balkan Wars and correctly predicted that Cape Helles and Gaba Tepe (now known as Anzac Cove) were the likely landing areas.

On 25 April 40,000 British, French, Australian and New Zealand troops began the greatest amphibious operation the world had yet seen. Opposing them was the Ottoman Fifth Army, including units commanded by Mustafa Kemal.

Vastly outnumbered by the attackers, the Turks could not prevent the Allies from establishing beachheads, but they inflicted heavy casualties. Soon low on ammunition and with only small arms and bayonets to meet the attackers, Kemal ordered the 57th Infantry Regiment: 'Men, I am not ordering you to attack. I am ordering you to die. In the time which passes until we die, other forces and commanders can come forward and take our place.' And the Turks held, with every man of the regiment either killed or wounded.

After two days of desperate defence, Kemal ordered an attack by the full 19th Division, reinforced by six battalions from the 5th Division. Now it was the Allies who were desperate, holding off the Turks only with the help of naval gunfire.

The situation at Gallipoli now became a battle of attrition. Despite fierce attacks and counter-attacks over the next seven months, the Allies failed either to get their warships though the straits or to advance their army up the well-defended peninsula.

By holding their ground the Turks had destroyed any possibility of an Allied victory, and in December the British began a massive evacuation which finished on 9 January 1916. The Turks had suffered 250,000 casualties, but the Allies had lost even more. Furthermore, the Ottoman Empire had been saved – at least temporarily.

Although the empire survived the war, it did not survive the peace. It was partly broken up in 1920, and Constantinople was occupied, although the sultan remained. But this humiliation led to a Turkish national movement under the leadership of Mustafa Kemal, the only Turkish general in the war never to suffer a defeat. After three years of desultory fighting in the Turkish War of Independence, the Allies left Anatolia, and the Grand National Assembly of Turkey established the Republic of Turkey, with the sultanate dissolved and Kemal at its head. He would be known as Atatürk, the father of Turkey, and would shake Turkey out of centuries of Ottoman lethargy to create a secular, Western state.

1770 Pitt the Elder in the House of Lords: 'Unlimited power is apt to corrupt the minds of those who possess it.'

10 January

'Let the die be cast.'

49 BC Three days ago the Roman Senate had ordered Julius Caesar to hand over his ten well-trained legions to a new governor of Gaul and return to Rome as an ordinary citizen. Caesar was in Ravenna when he received the command, and now he had to make one of history's most momentous decisions.

For the past nine years Caesar had ruled Gaul and Transalpine Gaul, most of today's France and Belgium. There he had waged ferocious war on the primitive local tribes, subduing them in the name of Rome. Plutarch writes that he conquered 800 towns while defeating enemy armies totalling 3 million men, of whom a third were killed and another third sold into slavery.

But now the Senate, jealous of Caesar's success and fearful of his ambitions, were determined to bring him to heel. Caesar knew that, despite his enormous achievements, a small clique of senators was not willing to concede to him the honours he thought he deserved, even wanted to destroy him. He believed, almost certainly correctly, that once he had relinquished his power, his enemies would trump up charges against him and then ruin or even execute him. His answer would be to lead the 13th Legion into Italy, treasonously breaking the Lex Cornelia Majestatis, the law that forbade a general from bringing an army out of the province to which he was assigned.

Most historians agree that he had no desire to start a civil war, let alone create a dictatorship, but his *amour propre* demanded that the ungrateful senators recognise his achievements and reward him as they had so many other great generals in the past. The 1st-century Greek historian Plutarch tells us what happened next:

> [Caesar] took the road to Rimini. When he came to the river (it is called the Rubicon) which forms the frontier between Cisalpine Gaul and the rest of Italy he became full of thought; for now he was drawing nearer and nearer to the dreadful step, and his mind wavered as he considered what a tremendous venture it was upon which he was engaged. He began to go more slowly and then ordered a halt. For a long time he weighed matters up silently in his own mind, irresolute between the two alternatives ... He thought of the sufferings which his crossing the river would

bring upon mankind and he imagined the fame of the story of it which they would leave to posterity. Finally, in a sort of passion, as though he were casting calculation aside and abandoning himself to whatever lay in store for him, making use of the expression which is frequently used by those who are on the point of committing themselves to desperate and unpredictable chances, 'Let the die be cast,' he said, and with these words hurried to cross the river.

For this fateful act Caesar was quoting the 4th-century BC Greek poet Menander: 'Ἀνερρίφθω κύβος', in English: 'Let the die be cast.' When the Roman historian Suetonius wrote his famous *The Twelve Caesars* in 121 AD, he mistranslated it to '*iacta alea est*', the more familiar 'the die is cast'.

But by whatever phrase you prefer, when Caesar crossed the Rubicon, the die really was cast. Not only did his action initiate a three-year civil war, it also led to the end of the Republic, which had lasted 460 years, and to the age of Roman emperors, which would last 503 more. One man, armed only with a few legions, his own military genius and what Pliny the Elder called 'the fiery quickness of his mind', took over the largest and most advanced empire the world had known.

1776 Thomas Paine publishes *Common Sense*: 'Society is produced by our wants, and government by our wickedness; the former promotes our happiness POSITIVELY by uniting our affections, the latter NEGATIVELY by restraining our vices.'

---

11 January

*'A custome lothsome to the eye, hatefull to the Nose,
harmefull to the braine, dangerous to the Lungs, and in
the blacke stinking fume thereof, neerest resembling the
horrible Stigian smoke of the pit that is bottomelesse.'*

1964 So had King James I railed against smoking in 1604. Today, over three centuries later, the Surgeon General of the United States took a more scientific approach in publishing a ground-breaking report on the dangers of cigarettes. It was a major step in improving the nation's health while triggering a long campaign of obfuscation and evasion by corporate interests.

Cigarettes were probably invented in South America in the 9th century, and smoking, long practised by American Indians, was introduced to Europe by Christopher Columbus. Walter Raleigh is said to have brought tobacco to England from Virginia in 1586, and in 1609 at Jamestown John Rolfe became the first in America successfully to grow tobacco commercially. (Despite this, Rolfe is far better known for his Indian bride – Pocahontas.)

In 17th-century Spain cigarettes evolved into their current form – minced tobacco wrapped in paper. Around 1830 the French invented the word 'cigarette', suggesting a small and dainty cigar. Hand-rolled cigarettes were expensive, but that changed dramatically in 1880 when the American James Bonsack invented the cigarette rolling machine, which increased hourly production thirteen-fold.

At the start of the 20th century annual per capita consumption in the United States was still only 54 cigarettes, but by 1964 – the year of the Surgeon General's report – it had risen to over 4,000.

Ever since King James's diatribe, there had been concern about smoking. In America in the 1880s cigarettes were called 'coffin nails', but there was no known causal connection between smoking and health until German doctors in the 1930s linked smoking to lung cancer. (Today's anti-smoking crusaders may be surprised to learn they are following in the footsteps of Adolf Hitler, who ordered the first modern anti-tobacco campaign in 1941.)

In 1950, when more than half of British adults smoked, the *British Medical Journal* associated smoking with lung cancer and heart disease. Similar assertions were made by the then US Surgeon General in 1957.

In 1962 President John Kennedy requested Surgeon General Luther Terry to study the problem. His Advisory Committee analysed over 7,000 scientific papers before concluding: 'Cigarette smoking is associated with a 70 per cent increase in the age-specific death rates of males, and to a lesser extent with increased death rates of females.'

Now US and British governments began banning cigarette advertising and sport sponsorship, raising cigarette taxes and demanding health warnings on packages, but the tobacco industry fought back, obscuring their knowledge of cigarettes' harmful effects. (In the UK, an internal memo from Gallaher Limited in 1970 concluded: 'the Auerbach work [research conducted on beagles] proves beyond reasonable doubt that fresh whole cigarette smoke is carcinogenic to dog lungs and therefore it is highly likely that it is carcinogenic to human lungs', but no report was made public.)

The most egregious example of manufacturer duplicity was on 14 April 1994, when eight tobacco industry executives falsely testified to a Congressional committee that their companies did not 'manipulate nicotine to addict smokers' and denied the link between smoking and disease, even though their own company scientists recognised its existence.

The tobacco companies may have convinced themselves but nobody else. They were sued by 46 American states, and in November 1998, Philip Morris, R.J. Reynolds, Brown & Williamson and Lorillard agreed to pay $206 billion over 25 years.

Despite manufacturer stonewalling, cigarette consumption has plummeted since the Surgeon General's report. In America smoking among adults has dropped from 43 per cent to 16 per cent, and nearly half of all living adults who ever smoked have quit. In the UK adult smoking has declined from 50 per cent to 16 per cent.

You would think every smoker would quit, as it is now known that smoking can cause heart attacks, strokes, emphysema, bronchitis and cancers of the larynx, mouth, bladder, pancreas and especially the lung. Each cigarette you smoke is said to shorten your life by eleven minutes. But smoking continues to plague both countries. In the US, 45 million adults still smoke, and about 438,000 die prematurely each year as a result (by comparison, the opioid epidemic in America kills about 65,000 people annually).

---

630 AD Muhammad conquers Mecca and declares: 'God has made Mecca a sanctuary since the day He created the Heavens and the Earth, and it will remain a sanctuary by virtue of the sanctity God has bestowed on it until the Day of Resurrection.'

---

12 January

'Lies, lies!'

1519 Today in the Spanish colony at Acla in modern-day Panama, the explorer who discovered the Pacific Ocean was brutally executed after a drumhead trial. He was Vasco Núñez de Balboa.

Balboa was raised in the Extremadura region of western Spain, that flat, arid province whose very name means 'extremely hard'. He was the first of the tough and uncompromising conquistadors from that area, a list that includes Cortés, de Soto and Pizarro.

At 25 Balboa first came to the New World on a voyage of exploration to Colombia. Later he tried to settle down in Hispaniola (current Haiti), but by the time he was 35 he was mired in debt and fled the island as a stowaway, hiding inside a barrel with his dog. He landed at Darién on the north coast of Panama, and there at last he began to prosper, soon taking command of the Spanish settlement.

Balboa was shortly leading expeditions into the interior in search of gold and slaves. Although he never resorted to the wholesale slaughter of the Indians as some of his Spanish contemporaries did, he used bribes, force where necessary, and occasionally terror, once having 40 Indians torn to pieces by Spanish war dogs because they were homosexual.

In 1513 Balboa set out to find a vast cache of gold rumoured to be somewhere in the interior. With 190 men and several hundred Indian guides and bearers, he trudged for a month through virtually impenetrable jungle and foetid swamp, before climbing a mountain peak to see the ocean shimmering in the distance. Four days later he reached the ocean and plunged into the water in full armour, brandishing his sword, thus becoming the first European to reach the Pacific from the New World.

In 1514 Balboa was superseded as governor of Darién by an elderly Spanish nobleman called Pedrarias. Jealous of Balboa's accomplishments and popularity, Pedrarias turned against him and tried to have him arrested. Fortunately for Balboa, the local bishop and the town's mayor persuaded Pedrarias to drop the charges. Now feigning friendship, Pedrarias offered Balboa his daughter (who was in a Spanish convent) for his wife and gave him permission for an expedition to explore the Mar del Sur.

Pedrarias proved to be an incompetent tyrant as governor; his soldiers provoked Indian attacks on Spanish settlements because of their disdain and theft of Indian gold. Many settlers died of disease and starvation since most of the food brought from Spain spoiled in the humid climate and the hostile natives refused to supply more. Over a hundred colonists returned to Cuba, out of fear for their lives.

While Balboa was away exploring, discontented settlers sent a stream of complaints to King Ferdinand of Spain, claiming that Pedrarias was unfit to be governor. Ferdinand ordered a judicial review and dispatched a replacement to take over the colony. Desperate to keep the popular Balboa from testifying against him, Pedrarias ordered him back from his exploration and had him arrested on trumped-up charges of rebellion, high treason and mistreatment of Indians.

Balboa's trial was brutally short and final. He and four of his comrades were sentenced to death by decapitation. On this day the five men were led to the block in Acla's main square, as the town crier labelled them as traitors. In fury Balboa cried out, 'Lies, lies! Never have such crimes held a place in my heart, I have always loyally served the King, with no thought in my mind but to increase his dominions.'

As Pedrarias secretly watched from behind some scaffolding, the executioner dispatched the five victims with an axe. For several days their heads remained on public display, but their bodies were fed to vultures.

1833 When fabled chef Antonin Carême dies in Paris at 48, the poet Laurent Tailhade writes that he was 'burnt out by the flame of his genius and the charcoal of the roasting pit'. * **1919** French Prime Minister Georges Clemenceau at the Paris Peace Conference: 'War is a series of catastrophes that results in a victory.'

---

13 January

'J'Accuse ... !'
LETTRE AU PRÉSIDENT DE LA RÉPUBLIQUE
Par ÉMILE ZOLA

1898 This afternoon the newspaper *L'Aurore* carried this shocking headline across its front page as 300,000 copies hit the Paris newsstands with the force of an explosion. The inflammatory article beneath it, written by one of France's greatest authors, accused the leaders of the French army of framing an innocent army captain on a charge of treason, and, four years later, of covering up their crime by arranging the acquittal of a second officer whom they knew to have been the guilty party.

The unlucky captain was Alfred Dreyfus, the only Jew on the French army's general staff. Convicted as a spy who had given French artillery secrets to Germany, on 22 December 1894 he had been sentenced to life imprisonment on Devil's Island. Two years later, evidence of Dreyfus' innocence surfaced, but army top brass suppressed it. Zola's letter excoriated the military for concealing its mistaken conviction.

'*J'Accuse*' provoked national outrage on both sides of the issue, among political parties, religious organisations, and the general public.

When supporters of the military sued Zola for libel, he was found guilty and sentenced to a year in prison. Seeing that his appeal would fail, he fled to the safety of England.

Zola was not the first Dreyfusard, but the Dreyfus case – *l'affaire*, as it became known in France – gained enormous publicity when he took it up so dramatically. With him were men like Georges Clemenceau (who was *L'Aurore*'s publisher), Jean Jaurès and Anatole France. But they faced a public sentiment laced with anti-Semitism that believed in the army's rectitude and the captain's guilt.

In 1898 evidence surfaced that another officer, Ferdinand Walsin Esterhazy, was the true spy who had sold information to Germany. He was eventually tried by a closed military court, only to be found not guilty in another military cover-up.

Dreyfus was granted a second trial in 1899 but was convicted once again. Because of 'extenuating circumstances' he was sentenced to just ten years in prison, but many in France now understood that what was extenuating in the case was Dreyfus' innocence. In a nation divided to its very core, public turmoil had become so great that French President Émile Loubet offered him a pardon, which Dreyfus, already in poor health, accepted so that he would not be returned to Devil's Island. It was a compromise that saved face for the military, although Dreyfus remained a traitor to half the public. On his release he pronounced: 'The government of the Republic has given me back my freedom. It is nothing for me without my honour.'

Émile Zola returned to France shortly after Dreyfus' pardon but died in 1902, asphyxiated by fumes from a faulty chimney (some maintained that anti-Dreyfusards had stuffed the flue). But by then the cause he championed had gained great strength.

For two years after being pardoned Dreyfus lived under house arrest, but on 12 July 1906 he was finally cleared of all charges by a military commission. Restored to the army, he served in the First World War as a lieutenant colonel and earned the Legion of Honour.

Back in September 1898 the real spy, Ferdinand Walsin Esterhazy, had shaved off his moustache, fled to England and settled in the village of Harpenden, just north of London. There he lived under a pseudonym until his peaceful death in 1923.

Dreyfus died in Paris on 12 July 1935, at the age of 75. Two days later, his funeral cortège passed through the ranks of troops assembled for Bastille Day in the Place de la Concorde.

1583 When Philip II's ferocious general, Fernando Álvarez de Toledo, 3rd Duke of Alba, dies in Lisbon after having taken Portugal, he tells those around him: 'If the king asks me for an account, I will make him a statement of kingdoms preserved or conquered, of signal victories, of successful sieges, and of sixty years' service.' * **1943** US Marine Captain Henry P. 'Jim' Crowe, at the Battle of Guadalcanal, to his men: 'Goddamn it, you'll never get the Purple Heart hiding in a foxhole! Follow me!'

14 January

'The whole world is three drinks behind.'

1957 Humphrey Bogart appeared in over 70 films and was killed on screen seventeen times, mostly shot, but once, in *The Wagons Roll at Night*, mauled to death by a circus lion. Today he died for real, brought down by cancer at 57.

Bogart was born on Christmas Day 1899 in a wealthy New York family. He was sent to Andover, one of America's most prestigious boarding schools, but expelled for illicit smoking and drinking, two vices that he enjoyed for the rest of his life.

After a stint in the Navy he began to dabble in the theatre. He loved the late hours and Manhattan's speakeasies. 'I was born to be indolent and this was the softest of rackets', he recalled. He married actress Helen Menken, but the marriage lasted only a year and a half. Seventeen months later he started another short-lived marriage. 'Long drinks and short marriages', said his friends.

In 1928 Bogart made his first movie, *The Dancing Town*, but his big break came in 1935, when he played an escaped murderer in *The Petrified Forest* on Broadway. When Warner Bros. bought the screen rights, the play's star Leslie Howard refused to perform unless Bogart was also cast.

The Petrified Forest cemented Bogart's place in Hollywood, but his place was playing gangsters in a string of B movies, in most of which he was bumped off. In 1938 he married the alcoholic actress Mayo Methot, a relationship so turbulent that they were called 'the battling Bogarts'.

In 1941 Bogart's drinking buddy John Huston directed the *film noir*, *The Maltese Falcon*, with Bogart playing private eye Sam Spade, a tough and cynical but vulnerable loner with a code of honour. He would reprise this persona for the rest of his career.

Then came *Casablanca* with Ingrid Bergman. With his wife there to chaperone, there was no off-screen romance, although Bogart remembered, 'when the camera moves in on that Bergman face, and she's saying she loves you, it would make anybody feel romantic'. Bergman shrugged: 'I kissed him but I never knew him.'

Two years later Bogart, now 44, made the film that would transform his personal life, *To Have and Have Not*. He played opposite a tawny-haired nineteen-year-old model named Betty Perske who had adopted the stage name of Lauren Bacall. Within weeks the two were enmeshed in a passionate affair.

Next, Bogart and Bacall shot another *film noir, The Big Sleep*. By that time he had become Hollywood's most highly paid actor. In February 1945, he filed for divorce from Mayo Methot and three months later married Bacall, with whom he made *Dark Passage* and *Key Largo*.

In 1947 Bogart and Bacall led a group of Hollywood stars to Washington to protest against the House Un-American Activities Committee's harassment of Hollywood screenwriters and actors. Although liberal, Bogart was far from being a communist, but he privately had his own solution: 'The whole world is three drinks behind … If Stalin, Truman and everybody else in the world had three drinks right now, we'd all loosen up and we wouldn't need the United Nations.'

In 1951 Bogart made *The African Queen*, for which he won his only Oscar. Meanwhile he and Bacall were palling around with a group of hard-drinking friends such as Frank Sinatra, Judy Garland, David Niven, Katharine Hepburn, Spencer Tracy and Rex Harrison. One evening, after seeing her husband and his friends return from a night in Las Vegas, Bacall cracked: 'You look like a goddamn rat pack.' And so the original Rat Pack was named.

A heavy drinker who smoked three packs of Chesterfields a day, Bogart developed throat cancer. By 1956, after two operations and chemotherapy, he weighed only 80 pounds and was too weak to walk upstairs. But he never complained or lost his sense of humour. 'I should never have switched from scotch to Martinis', he allegedly explained. On 13 January 1957 he fell into a coma and died the next day.

In 1999, the American Film Institute ranked him the greatest male movie star of all time.

1766 Pitt the Elder replies in the Commons to the First Lord of the Treasury, who has just passed the Stamp Act that would so infuriate the American colonies: 'Is this your boasted peace? Not to sheathe the sword in its scabbard, but to sheathe it in the bowels of your countrymen?' *

1963 When Charles de Gaulle rejects the UK bid to join the Common Market because 'the nature, the structure, the situation, which are peculiar to England, differ from those of continental states', Harold Macmillan responds: 'I think this man has gone crazy – absolutely crazy. He is inventing any means whatever to knock us out and the simple thing is he wants to be the cock on a small dunghill instead of having two cocks on a larger one.'

15 January

'After the tattooed prisoners had been examined, the ones with the best and most artistic specimens were kept in the dispensary, and then killed by injections.'

1951 Today a West German court sentenced a blowsy 44-year-old redhead named Ilse Koch to life behind bars for crimes she had committed when she was the commandant's wife at the Buchenwald concentration camp during the Second World War.

Once a librarian, when she was 30 Ilse Köhler, as she was then, married an SS colonel named Karl Otto Koch, who was the commandant of the Sachsenhausen concentration camp. In 1939 he was transferred to Buchenwald, and there the Kochs settled down to enjoy the war. Karl Otto had an indoor riding hall built by prisoners, so now Ilse could enjoy a ride while thrashing inmates with her riding crop. She also forced prisoners to have sex with her, to Karl Otto's indifference. Meanwhile Karl Otto was running a profitable line of embezzlement from prisoners while murdering anyone unwise enough to get in his way.

In 1941, however, the Nazi general overseeing Buchenwald recognised the name on the camp's death list of a hospital orderly who had previously treated him. An investigation revealed that the orderly had treated Karl Otto for syphilis, who had then arranged for his killing to seal his lips. Soon more evidence emerged of murdered prisoners, embezzlement, fraud and sexual offences. Karl Otto was brought to trial, convicted and shot in the Buchenwald courtyard on 5 April 1945, thus saving the American army the trouble of doing it, as they liberated the camp just a week later.

The Nazis had tried Ilse Koch with her husband but then released her for lack of evidence, but she was rearrested in June 1945, this time by the Americans. Put before the military court at Dachau, she was charged with 'participating in a criminal plan for aiding, abetting and participating in the murders at Buchenwald'. Witness after witness told of her misdeeds, referring to her as '*Die Hexe von Buchenwald*' ('The Witch of Buchenwald'). Meanwhile she had been enlivening her imprisonment by having sex with another prisoner. In the midst of her trial she announced that she was eight months pregnant.

But the biggest sensation at Ilse's trial came when one witness testified: 'all prisoners with tattooing on them were ordered to report to the dispensary. No one knew what the purpose was. But after the tattooed prisoners had been examined, the ones with the best and most artistic specimens were kept in the dispensary, and then killed by injections … the desired pieces of tattooed skin were detached from the bodies and treated. The finished products were turned over to SS Standartenführer Koch's wife, who had them fashioned into lampshades and other ornamental household articles.' With a fine ear for alliteration, American newspapers renamed the Witch of Buchenwald the Bitch of Buchenwald.

Ilse was sentenced to life imprisonment, but the military governor of the occupied zone, General Lucius Clay, subsequently reduced her sentence to four years. 'There was absolutely no evidence in the trial transcript', he wrote, 'other than she was a rather loathsome creature, that would support the death sentence.' He also pointed out that the lampshades submitted at the trial had been shown to be made from goatskin.

Ilse Koch may have been free, but not for long. She was arrested once again in 1949 and tried before a West German court. Again, witnesses claimed that they had seen her select tattooed prisoners to be murdered or had themselves been forced to make lampshades and gloves from human skin. And once again this most sensational of charges was dropped when the prosecution could not prove that any of the items were actually made from human skin.

Nonetheless, on this day in 1951 the German court put Ilse away for life, convicted of incitement to murder, to attempted murder and to committing grievous bodily harm. She mouldered away in prison until 1 September 1967 when, at the age of 60, she hanged herself with bed sheets in her cell at the women's prison in Aichach.

1965 Nine days before he dies, Winston Churchill complains, 'I'm bored with it all', just before slipping into a coma.

---

16 January

'We have ascended the throne by the bidding of God.'

1547 Today in Moscow a sixteen-year-old boy was proclaimed the Tsar of all the Russias. He was Ivan IV, whose murderous rule would earn him the nickname of Ivan the Terrible.

In 1462 Ivan's grandfather Ivan III had become Grand Prince of Moscow nine years after the Byzantine Empire had succumbed to the Turks. With the imperial throne vacant (or non-existent), Ivan III had hubristically appropriated the imperial title of 'Caesar', which mutated into 'Tsar'. But his grandson was the first Russian to be crowned with the title, so becoming Russia's first official tsar.

Born in 1530, Ivan revealed his brutal side while still a child by torturing small animals for amusement. From the moment he became tsar he was certain he was fulfilling God's plan, a notion shared by most European monarchs of the time. 'We have ascended the throne by the bidding of God', he claimed. He professed to be highly religious and demanded that his subjects follow suit. 'To shave the beard', he said, 'is a sin that the blood of all the martyrs cannot cleanse. It is to deface the image of God.'

Despite his professed piety, Ivan became ever more tyrannical. By the time he was 30 he was enjoying unfettered personal rule. In his paranoia, he instituted a reign of terror and established a bodyguard of 6,000 men, known as the Oprichniki, to suppress those he thought opposed him. Wearing black and riding black horses, these fanatically loyal 'children of darkness' could kill anyone they wished, operating beyond the law.

One of Ivan's worst excesses was his massacre of the citizens of Novgorod, whom he suspected of planning rebellion. Without confirmation of the charge, in January 1570 he led his army into the city and slaughtered 60,000 men, women and children.

Prone to fits of insane rage, Ivan saw conspiracy everywhere. His answer was torture and death, and his means included disembowelment, burning at the stake, impalement, drowning and burial alive, punishments that he often supervised personally. He once had his own doctor roasted alive on a spit on suspicions of treachery, and some victims were fed to wild bears.

Ivan's contempt for others reached an artistic peak on the completion of St Basil's Cathedral in Moscow. So taken was he by its splendour that he ordered blinded the architect who had designed it to ensure that no other building so beautiful could ever be built.

Ivan married seven times. Three of his wives died, three were dispatched to monasteries and one outlived him. He caught his sixth wife, Vasilisa Melentyeva, in a liaison with a Russian prince and forced her to watch her lover being impaled before confining her to life in a nunnery.

One of the few people Ivan trusted was his son and heir, also named Ivan. But on one occasion his son's pregnant wife came to court wearing what the tsar thought was immodest clothing. Furious, he subjected his daughter-in-law to a beating. When his son remonstrated, Ivan became so incensed that he beat him to death with an iron-tipped rod.

During his last days Ivan's body became swollen and racked with pain. When his doctors could find no cure he turned to clairvoyants and astrologers, but they helped no more than his physicians. He died on 18 March 1584, just a few days after telling the English ambassador that his enemies had poisoned him.

Ivan's demise has been variously attributed to dysentery, syphilis and other diseases, but four centuries later his tomb was opened for tests on his desiccated corpse. His body contained toxic levels of arsenic and mercury, suggesting that indeed Russia's first tsar had died at the hands of a poisoner, proving the old adage that even a paranoid can have real enemies.

1605 'In a place of La Mancha whose name I do not want to remember.' The first line of Cervantes' *Don Quixote*, which goes on sale in Madrid today. Also from *Don Quixote*: 'The pen is the tongue of the soul.' *
1809 The last words of General John Moore, who is killed at the Battle of Corunna: 'I hope the people of England will be satisfied. I hope my country will do me justice.'

---

17 January

'The throne is a glorious sepulchre.'

532 AD Today one of the most remarkable women in history stood firm in the face of bloody insurrection and saved her husband's control of the Byzantine Empire.

The Empress Theodora was hardly born to the purple. The daughter of a bear-keeper in Constantinople and by all accounts exceptionally beautiful, in her teens she had become an actress, virtually synonymous at the time with prostitute. By the time she met future emperor

Justinian at twenty, she had already been kept and discarded by several lovers, by one of whom she bore an illegitimate child.

Justinian persuaded his uncle, the Emperor Justin, to change the law that prohibited a noble from marrying an actress and took Theodora as his wife. She was, however, far more than just an accomplished lover; she was possessed of both an acute intelligence and nerves of steel. After Justinian became emperor in 527, he treated her as a full partner in ruling his realm.

Justinian's greatest challenge came five years after his accession, when rioting broke out between the Green and Blue factions at the chariot races in Constantinople's Hippodrome. A city prefect had ordered seven hooligans hanged, but during the execution the scaffolding had broken, saving two, who fled to sanctuary in a nearby church. When both Greens and Blues petitioned the emperor for clemency, his refusal provoked a week of chaos, the two factions combining forces under the slogan 'Nika' ('Conquer'), the catchword usually shouted during the races. They freed the condemned men, conducted a burning and looting spree throughout the city and demanded that the emperor dismiss two of his senior officials.

At dawn on Saturday, 17 January, Justinian publicly agreed to the rioters' conditions, but it was too late. The hostile mob continued its wanton destruction, proclaimed an unwilling noble named Hypatius as emperor and drove Justinian into his royal palace in full retreat.

The terrified Justinian called together his panicky counsellors, who urged him to flee the city on the ships that were waiting at the garden stairs of the palace. But Theodora addressed her husband with a ringing call to defy the rioters: 'If flight were the only means of safety, yet should I disdain to fly. Death is the condition of our birth, but they who have reigned should never survive the loss of dignity and dominion. I implore Heaven that I may never be seen, not a day, without my diadem and purple; that I may no longer behold the light when I cease to be saluted with the name of queen. If you resolve, O Caesar! to fly, you have treasures; behold the sea, you have ships; but tremble lest the desire of life should expose you to wretched exile and ignominious death. For my own part, I adhere to the maxim of antiquity, that the throne is a glorious sepulchre.'

Inspired by her courage, Justinian regained his nerve and sent the eunuch general Narses to face the murderous mob armed only with a bag of gold coins, with which he bribed the Blues to leave.

The emperor then sent his general Belisarius with the Imperial Guard to the Hippodrome, where they slaughtered over 30,000 rebels.

Justinian wanted to spare Hypatius' life, but Theodora prevailed upon him to have him executed, his body thrown into the sea.

Without Theodora's stirring call to action, Justinian's reign would have ended in shameful flight. As it was, he ruled for another 33 years.

1925 President Calvin Coolidge tells the Society of American Newspaper Editors: 'The chief business of the American people is business.' Commonly quoted as: 'The business of America is business.' * **1961** President Dwight Eisenhower delivers a televised farewell address to the nation three days before leaving office, in which he warns: 'In the councils of government, we must guard against the acquisition of influence, whether sought or unsought, by the military-industrial complex.'

18 January

'This is not a peace, it is an armistice for twenty years.'

1919 Today in the sumptuous Salle d'Horloge on the Quai d'Orsay in Paris, diplomats from 32 countries met to set the peace terms following the First World War. For defeated Germany, although not allowed to attend, it was a day with huge historical resonance.

On the same date, 18 January, in 1701, Frederick of Hohenzollern finally attained the title he yearned for. He was already Margrave of Brandenburg and Duke of Prussia, but the laws of the Holy Roman Empire barred him from becoming a king. But Frederick persuaded Holy Roman Emperor Leopold I to permit his elevation in exchange for his support against Louis XIV in the War of the Spanish Succession. Frederick thus became the first King of Prussia.

On 18 January in 1871, with nearby Paris still burning under Prussian siege and bombardment, Frederick's great-great-grandson King Wilhelm of Prussia was crowned Kaiser (Emperor) of the Germans in the Palace of Versailles at the tail end of the Franco-Prussian War.

Now, on 18 January 1919, France was among the victors, and the greatest loser was the Germany of Frederick's great-great-great-great-grandson, Kaiser Wilhelm II. The French had never forgotten the shame of 1871, and the choice of 18 January was not coincidence – France's Prime Minister Georges Clemenceau had specially chosen the date to humiliate the Germans in their turn.

The Paris Peace Conference lasted one year and three days. The major decisions were taken by the four most powerful victors, Great Britain, France, Italy and the United States. Although there were important developments such as the establishment of the League of Nations, the most controversial result was the Treaty of Versailles, signed in the Hall of Mirrors in the Palace of Versailles on 28 June 1919, the fifth anniversary of the assassination of Archduke Franz Ferdinand that had triggered the war. It forced Germany to 'accept the responsibility of Germany and her allies for causing all the loss and damage' and return Alsace and Lorraine to France. In addition, Germany was to pay the gigantic sum of 132 billion marks (equal to almost a trillion dollars today) in reparations and lose 25,000 square miles – 13 per cent – of her territory and 10 per cent of her people.

Now, a century later, many believe that the huge reparations demanded of Germany were a major contributor to the rise of Hitler and the Second World War. At the time, however, there were many who thought that Germany's punishment was too light, among them French Marshal Ferdinand Foch, Supreme Commander of the Allied Armies, who thought Germany should have been broken up into separate countries so that it could never again threaten France. 'This is not a peace', he said, 'it is an armistice for twenty years.' Exactly twenty years and 65 days later, Germany marched into Poland to start the Second World War.

1865 During a speech in Birmingham, Liberal MP John Bright says: 'With scarcely any intervening period, Parliaments have met constantly for 600 years, and there was something of a Parliament before the Conquest. England is the mother of Parliaments.'

---

19 January

'Does your Majesty want to kill me?'

1568 Early this morning Spain's Philip II entered the chambers of his 22-year-old son Don Carlos. Seeing the king with several attendants, Carlos mockingly asked, 'Are we having a meeting of the Council of State?' No, Philip demurred; he was there, he said, to supervise the incarceration of his son, who was dangerously and incurably mad.

'I am not crazy', Carlos responded. 'I am desperate. Does your Majesty want to kill me?'

Paying no heed, the king ordered all doors and windows to be nailed shut and commanded that no one but his jailers be allowed to speak to the prince. Carlos was never seen in public again.

Most accounts say that Carlos had been a fairly normal boy until at the age of eighteen he fell down a staircase, sustaining serious head injuries. For several days he lay blind and delirious, his head swollen to enormous size, and all despaired for his life.

One legend maintains that, in a desperate attempt to save him, Carlos' family and doctors called on the intervention of God. From the nearby monastery of Jesús María they took the mummified body of the holy Fray Diego, who had died a century before, and placed it beside Carlos in his bed for a night, relying on Fray Diego's holy spirit to cure the young prince.

Other (more likely) sources say that a prominent doctor saved his life by a trepanation of the skull. What is certain, however, is that from this time forward Carlos descended into madness. He revelled in sadism and suffered periods of manic and murderous fury. He tried to stab the Duke of Alba and to strangle his own uncle, Don Juan of Austria, Philip II's illegitimate half-brother. Stories circulated of him torturing horses, whipping nubile girls and cooking rabbits alive. He once tried to force a shoemaker to eat some shoes that didn't fit, and, far worse, he attempted to escape to the Spanish Netherlands, then in revolt against his father's rule. He even contemplated murdering his father.

The true causes of Carlos' madness will never be known with certainty, but one theory is that the fall down the stairs simply triggered his inherent insanity, which was the result of the infamous Habsburg interbreeding. Carlos had only four great-grandparents instead of eight, and six great-great-grandparents, instead of sixteen. The net result was that his parents were as closely related by blood as if they had been half-brother and sister.

During Carlos' imprisonment he repeatedly attempted suicide, trying everything from self-starvation to lying naked on blocks of ice to setting his bed on fire. Then, on 24 July, six months after his incarceration, the Court announced that he had died. There were rumours that he had been poisoned on Philip's orders in order to prevent him eventually inheriting the throne, and even more lurid accounts that Philip had him killed on learning of Carlos' passion for his queen, young Elizabeth of Valois, a theory embraced with more gusto than historical probability by Schiller and Verdi. In all likelihood Carlos died of natural causes, exacerbated by his insanity and his imprisonment.

> **1971** National Security Advisor and future Secretary of State Henry Kissinger: 'Power is the great aphrodisiac.'

20 January

'It is the curse of the great man to have to step over corpses.'

1942 Today in a Berlin suburb at a handsome villa at 56–58 Am Grossen Wannsee, Germany's picture-postcard Nazi Reinhard Heydrich opened a conference of Nazi bigwigs to set in motion the *Endlösung der Judenfrage* (Final Solution to the Jewish Problem).

Pogroms were nothing new to Germany; back in the 11th century, entire communities of Jews were murdered in towns like Trier, Worms, Mainz, and Cologne. During the Black Death three centuries later, Jews were accused of poisoning wells and slaughtered en masse. Indeed, as recently as 1819 Jews in Bavaria had been attacked, their property destroyed. But Nazi Germany's *Endlösung* was different; its aim was not the killing of some Jews but the extermination of all 11 million Jews in Europe, about half of whom were in German-occupied territory.

The initial impetus came from Adolf Hitler, who in *Mein Kampf* had suggested that Jews should be eliminated, a sentiment reinforced in his speech of 30 January 1939: 'Today I will once more be a prophet: If the international Jewish financiers in and outside Europe should succeed in plunging the nations once more into a world war, then the result will not be the Bolshevization of the earth, and thus the victory of Jewry, but the annihilation of the Jewish race in Europe!'

Equally vicious was Reichsführer-SS Heinrich Himmler, Reinhard Heydrich's long-time boss and mentor, who had been responsible for assembling *Einsatzgruppen* (death squads) to eliminate communists and Jews in Russia during Operation Barbarossa. After watching the execution of 200 Jews near Minsk, Himmler sententiously remarked: 'It is the curse of the great man to have to step over corpses.'

Heydrich was chosen to orchestrate the *Endlösung* because he had form in the assault on Jews. He had sent thousands to concentration camps during Kristallnacht in 1938, and in Poland he had crammed over 2 million into ghettos, where half a million had died from starvation and disease.

He was blond, arrogant, intelligent and totally ruthless. He claimed to have killed his first man at fifteen, fighting communists in the streets of his home town of Halle. Later, in Russia, he took unauthorised flights over enemy territory, was shot down and survived for two days on his own before being rescued. According to German intelligence chief Walter Schellenberg, 'His unusual intellect was matched by the ever-watchful instincts of a predatory animal'.

After running the combined SD (the intelligence agency of the SS), Gestapo, and Criminal Police, in 1941 he was appointed Reichsprotektor (read military dictator) of Bohemia and Moravia (roughly, Czechoslovakia), but now he had taken a few days off to chair the Wannsee conference, a task he welcomed because it magnified his role in the Nazi hierarchy. (According to SS-Sturmbannführer Wilhelm Höttl of the SD, 'Truth and goodness had no intrinsic meaning for him; they were instruments to be used for the gaining of more and more power'.)

At Wannsee Heydrich led a group of fifteen top officials, including Adolf Eichmann. They pondered various gruesome ways to eliminate the Jews, including mass sterilisation and deportation to Madagascar. Then Heydrich proposed a simpler solution: moving all Jews to concentration camps 'in the East' and working them to death. When it was pointed out that some might take a long time to die, he agreed that those who survived would be 'treated accordingly' by the SS.

The Wannsee conference marked a turning point in Nazi policy towards the Jews. Although the final protocol never explicitly mentioned extermination, within a few months, the first gas chambers were installed in Polish extermination camps. Before the conference, over 439,800 Jews had already been murdered, but with Heydrich's more systematic approach, the total rose to some 6 million by the war's end.

The conference lasted only 90 minutes, and at the close the participants relaxed with snifters of cognac. Perhaps they should not have been so nonchalant. Heydrich was assassinated by Czech partisans less than six months later, one attendee was killed in an American air raid and another was killed in action. After the war three were executed, two were imprisoned and one committed suicide.

1936 When his doctor tries to soothe a dying George V with the thought that he could convalesce at Bognor Regis, the king responds (his last words): 'Bugger Bognor!' * **1961** President John Kennedy concludes his inaugural address: 'And so, my fellow Americans, ask not what your country can do for you – ask what you can do for your country. My fellow citizens of the world: ask not what America will do for you, but what together we can do for the freedom of man.'

21 January

'The king must die so that the country may live.'

1793 Today the well-meaning but fat and bumbling Louis XVI mounted the scaffold amid the roars of the Paris mob.

Louis had been imprisoned in the Temple since August 1792, and in September the monarchy had been abolished and Louis stripped of his titles, becoming simply Citoyen Louis Capet. Then in December Robespierre had defined the course of Louis' trial by telling the National Convention: 'It is with regret that I pronounce the fatal truth: the king must die so that the country may live.' He was convicted of treason on 18 January and sentenced to death the next day.

On this grey, wet morning Louis was brought through the streets of Paris in a carriage surrounded by troops in a cavalcade that lasted two hours. Riding with him was his trusted confessor, l'Abbé Edgeworth de Firmont. At every corner were citizens armed with pikes or guns, a precaution against any demonstration in favour of the king. L'Abbé Edgeworth describes the event:

> The carriage arrived ... in the greatest silence, at the Place Louis XV [the pre-Revolutionary name for the Place de la Concorde], and came to a halt in the middle of a large empty space that had been left around the scaffold. This space was bordered with cannon; and beyond, as far as the eye could reach, was a multitude in arms. ...
>
> As soon as the king descended from the carriage, three executioners surrounded him and wished to take off his coat. He repulsed them with dignity and took it off himself. The executioners, whom the proud bearing of the king had momentarily disconcerted, seemed then to resume their audacity and, surrounding him again, attempted to tie his hands.
>
> 'What are you trying to do?' asked the king, withdrawing his hands abruptly. 'Tie you,' replied one of the executioners. 'Tie me!' returned the king in an indignant tone. 'No, I will never consent; do what you are ordered to do, but I will not be tied; renounce that idea.' The executioners insisted, they lifted their voices, and seemed about to call for help in order to use force. ...
>
> 'Sire,' I said to him with tears, 'in this new outrage I see only a final resemblance between Your Majesty and the Saviour who

is to reward you.' At these words he lifted his eyes to heaven with a sorrowing look that I cannot describe … and, turning to the executioners, said: 'Do what you wish; I will drain the cup to the dregs.'

The steps that led to the scaffold were extremely steep in ascent. The king was obliged to hold to my arm, and by the pains he seemed to take, I feared that his courage had begun to weaken; but what was my astonishment when, upon arriving at the last step, I saw him escape, so to speak, from my hands, cross the length of the scaffold with firm step to impose silence, by a single glance, upon ten or fifteen drummers who were in front of him, and with a voice so strong that it could be heard at the Pont-Tournant, distinctly pronounce these words forever memorable: 'I die innocent of all the crimes imputed to me. I pardon the authors of my death, and pray God that the blood you are about to shed will never fall upon France.'

The executioners seized him, the knife struck him, his head fell at fifteen minutes after ten. The executioners seized it by the hair, and showed it to the multitude, who cried 'Long live the Republic!'

As Louis' remains were whisked away to the cemetery of the Church of the Madeleine, members of the crowd ran forward to dip their handkerchiefs in his blood. His body was put in a pauper's coffin, his severed head between his legs. While two state priests chanted the Office of the Dead, the coffin was placed in a pit six feet square and covered with quicklime.

1932 Last words of English critic and biographer Lytton Strachey: 'If this is dying, I don't think much of it.' * **1950** Last entry in George Orwell's working notebook: 'At fifty, everyone has the face he deserves.'

---

22 January

'March slowly, attack at dawn and eat up the red soldiers.'

1879 Today at Isandlwana in what is now South Africa, the British army suffered its most humiliating defeat, caused by arrogance, complacency and greed.

In 1877 Sir Bartle Frere was made High Commissioner for Southern Africa. Despite objections from South Africans, British, Afrikaans and tribal chiefs, Frere was determined to unite the jumble of British colonies, Boer republics and independent black states into a British Confederation. The only snag was the Zulu Kingdom's King Cetshwayo, who kept an army of 40,000 warriors. Calling the Zulus 'a bunch of savages armed with sticks', Frere planned to invade.

After failing to persuade the British government to sanction a war, in December 1878 Frere started one on his own, sending Cetshwayo an unacceptable ultimatum: disband your army or face invasion – even though the Zulus were British allies.

In command of British forces in South Africa was Frere's close friend, Lieutenant General Lord Chelmsford, whom Frere ordered into Zululand. 'My only fear is that the Zulu will not fight', commented the complacent Chelmsford.

At 6.00am on 11 January 1879, Chelmsford's army – 4,500 soldiers, 300 wagons and 1,600 transport animals – crossed the Buffalo River from Natal into Zululand. The British were armed with Martini-Henry rifles, two field guns and a Hale rocket battery, while their foe carried only *assegai* (spears), cowhide shields and a few antique rifles.

Hearing of the British incursion, Cetshwayo ordered his warriors to halt the invaders, commanding: 'March slowly, attack at dawn and eat up the red soldiers.'

By 20 January Chelmsford's troops had advanced to Isandlwana, a huge rock outcrop dominating the landscape. There he made his first fatal blunder, failing to fortify his camp because of his contempt for the enemy's fighting abilities. Then, thinking that the main Zulu force was to the south-east, today he made the second one, taking two-thirds of his force off to find them, leaving only 1,700 British soldiers and native auxiliaries at Isandlwana, when 20,000 Zulu warriors were lying concealed only five miles away.

At 11.00 that morning British scouts stumbled across the mass of the Zulu army, sitting in total quiet. Discovered, the Zulus instantly attacked in their classic 'horns of the beast' formation, in which the 'chest' attacks the centre while the two 'horns' sweep around the sides to encircle the enemy.

The British fought bravely but were overwhelmed, the battle ending by 2.30 that afternoon, when the Zulus captured their camp just as an eclipse darkened the battlefield. Some 1,350 British and allies lay dead on the blood-soaked field, including 52 officers (more than at Waterloo). Alongside were perhaps 2,000 Zulus.

The few surviving British fled to Rorke's Drift six miles away, where they joined a small garrison left there by Chelmsford. There, about 150 British and colonial troops fought off attacks by 3,000 to 4,000 Zulu warriors in a twelve-hour battle that continued into the next day. By a miracle of courage (eleven Victoria Crosses were awarded), the British held off the attackers, inflicting about 800 casualties at a cost of seventeen killed and fifteen wounded.

Back in Natal, Lord Chelmsford asked London for reinforcements and, with British prestige on the line, the government gave him everything he asked for. In late March, he began a second invasion against a weakened enemy with 23,000 British and native troops. Reaching the Royal Kraal of Ulundi, the Zulu capital, he utterly destroyed what was left of the Zulu army and burnt the capital to the ground.

Cetshwayo was captured, deposed and exiled, but Frere, the war's instigator, continued with disastrous policies that helped ignite the Boer and the Basotho Gun wars. He was recalled for censure but died before he could be disciplined. Chelmsford returned to London where he recounted the heroics of Rorke's Drift and the victory at Ulundi while blaming the Isandlwana debacle on an officer killed in the battle. With the blessing of Queen Victoria, he was promoted to full general, weighted down with honours. The man who had cost so many needless deaths passed away peacefully in 1905, playing billiards at his club.

> **1901** When Queen Victoria dies at Osborne House on Isle of Wight, American expatriate writer Henry James writes: 'We all feel a bit motherless today. Mysterious little Victoria is dead and fat vulgar Edward is King.'

23 January

'England has saved herself by her exertions, and will, as I trust, save Europe by her example.'

1781 Today a new Member of Parliament walked onto the floor of the House of Commons for the first time. He was only 21 and had been elected in the pocket borough of Appleby, controlled by a friend of a friend. As the new MP had predicted, 'The Election will be made without my having any trouble, or even visiting my constituents'. He was William Pitt, the son of the late William Pitt (the Elder), 1st Earl of Chatham, who had been Prime Minister in the 1750s and 60s. A month later, when the younger Pitt made an eloquent maiden speech to the House, Edmund Burke commented: 'He is not a chip off the old block, he is the old block itself.'

Pitt was reserved, withdrawn and arrogant except with a few close friends. He never married and was indifferent to women, perhaps a latent homosexual. His only known vice was an inordinate fondness for port, of which he consumed more than a quart a day. He was also extraordinarily insular. He hardly travelled in England, never went to Ireland or Scotland and visited France only once. He showed little interest in either the arts or science.

But in Parliament Pitt was incisive, astute and forceful, a brilliant orator with a comprehensive knowledge of the issues of the day. When George III chose him as Prime Minister, he was still only 24, the youngest person ever to hold that office.

Pitt's elevation was received in the House of Commons with derisive laughter; little did the mocking MPs realise that he would serve as Prime Minister for the next seventeen years and, after three years on the sidelines, return for another nineteen months, longer than any other PM in history.

Pitt is usually considered the founder of the Tory party because he believed in slow, evolutionary change. Indeed, he failed at the more progressive causes that he backed. He wanted to lift restrictions on Catholics in Ireland and to permit Catholic Members of Parliament, but he was steadfastly opposed by George III. He supported his friend William Wilberforce's efforts to ban the slave trade, but it was finally outlawed only after Pitt's death.

The great test during Pitt's time as Prime Minister was war with France. On 1 February 1793 Republican France declared war, a conflict that was to last 22 years, well beyond Pitt's lifetime. After six years of war, Pitt was forced to introduce Britain's first income tax to pay for it. (By modern standards, it was modest; the highest rate was 10 per cent.)

In 1805 the British overwhelmed the French at the Battle of Trafalgar. In celebrating the victory, Pitt was toasted at the Lord Mayor's banquet as 'the Saviour of Europe', to which he demurred: 'Europe is not to be saved by any single man. England has saved herself by her exertions, and will, as I trust, save Europe by her example.'

But just two months after Trafalgar, Napoleon's crushing victory at

Austerlitz prompted Pitt's despairing but accurate remark: 'Roll up that map [of Europe], it will not be wanted these ten years.'

The war had consumed much of Pitt's time and most of his energy and by now too much port was taking its toll. A month after Austerlitz he became seriously ill, and by mid-January 1806 he was so weak that he took to his bed in his house on Putney Heath. For several days he received visits from leading politicians and generals, including the future Duke of Wellington. He then lapsed into periods of delirium in which he imagined he was debating in Parliament. On the morning of 23 January, 25 years to the day since he first took his seat in Parliament, he died at the age of 46.

Shortly after his death English hagiography established Pitt's last words to have been an anguished 'Oh, my country! How I leave my country!' But Disraeli insisted that an aged servant had once told him that his last thoughts were somewhat less high-minded. 'I think', he said, 'I could eat one of Bellamy's veal pies.'

> **1931** The last words of famed Russian ballerina Anna Pavlova as she dies in the Hotel des Indes in the Hague: 'Get my Swan costume ready.'

24 January

'Let them hate, so long as they fear.'

41 AD Today in Rome, history's prototype monster of despotic cruelty, the Emperor Caligula, was murdered by his own guards.

Born to the purple in 12 AD, Caligula was related to the most powerful figures of the empire. Two great-grandfathers were Augustus and Mark Antony, and Augustus' foremost general, Marcus Agrippa, was his grandfather. Tiberius, who became emperor when Caligula was two, was his great-uncle.

When Caligula was three, his father Germanicus took him on campaign, where adoring legionaries nicknamed him Caligula ('Little Boots') because of his miniature soldier's uniform and tiny military boots. But in 19 AD Germanicus died in Syria, many believed poisoned on orders from Tiberius, who was jealous of his reputation for bravery, generosity and military leadership.

During the next twelve years Caligula was shuttled between relations while his mother and brothers were banished, imprisoned and eventually killed by the emperor on charges of treason. When Caligula was nineteen, Tiberius brought him to his royal villa on Capri. There he lived for six years and became the emperor's heir, docile and obsequious in the court of the tyrant who had caused the deaths of three of his family.

In early 37, the sick and decrepit Tiberius lapsed into a coma. Believing him dead, Caligula slipped the seal ring from the imperial finger to show himself to the public as the new emperor. But suddenly Tiberius awoke and demanded food. Caligula stood petrified with terror, but the quick-thinking commander of the Praetorian Guard rushed in and stifled the old emperor with a blanket. Caligula now became Rome's third emperor.

The first seven months of his rule were both just and generous, but he then fell severely ill, emerging from the sickness as the ogre of legend. He enjoyed wholesale executions for imagined offences or to seize rich men's property; a notorious sadist, he often witnessed the killings, telling the executioner to kill his victim slowly in order to 'make him feel that he is dying'. Hated by Rome's senators as well as the public, he disdainfully remarked: 'Let them hate, so long as they fear.' ('*Oderint dum metuant.*')

Even Caligula's family were not safe from his vindictive cruelty; he forced his father-in-law to cut his own throat and probably poisoned his grandmother Antonia. He had sex with boys and women alike, including his own sisters.

Most famously, Caligula housed his horse Incitatus in an ivory stall, adorned him with a collar of precious stones and said he would make him consul (but never did). Eventually he concluded that he was a god, and ordered the Senate to treat him as such. He even built a temple for himself on the Palatine Hill.

After four years in power Caligula had created enemies everywhere, even in his Praetorian Guard. A special target was the military tribune Cassius Chaerea, whom Caligula mocked for his supposed femininity. Unable to bear the constant taunting, Chaerea conspired with the Guard's commander Cornelius Sabinus. On this day, while Caligula was walking through a secluded passageway at the Palatine games, they struck. The near-contemporary historian Suetonius tells us that there are two versions of what happened:

Some say, that ... Chaerea came behind him, and gave him a heavy blow on the neck with his sword, first crying out, 'Take this!', that then a tribune, by name Cornelius Sabinus, another of the conspirators, ran him through the breast. Others say, that the crowd being kept at a distance by some centurions who were in the plot, Sabinus came, according to custom, for the [pass] word, and that Caius gave him 'Jupiter', upon which Chaerea cried out, 'Be it so!' and then, on his looking round, clove one of his jaws with a blow. As he lay on the ground, crying out that he was still alive, the rest dispatched him with thirty wounds. For the word agreed upon among them all was, 'Strike again'. Some likewise ran their swords through his privy parts.

Chaerea's murder of Caligula brought the feeble Claudius to power. But instead of rewarding Chaerea, Claudius ordered him put to death. At Chaerea's own request, he was executed with the sword he had used to despatch Caligula.

1899 In a speech at Mansion House, American diplomat and envoy to the Court of St James, Edward John Phelps, says: 'The man who makes no mistakes does not usually make anything.'

---

25 January

'A monstrosity of a human being, one that Nature began and never finished.'

41 AD He stammered and slobbered, his nose ran when he was excited, his head shook and he occasionally suffered fits of uncontrollable laughter. His knees were so weak that he limped, and the philosopher Seneca said that his voice belonged to 'no land animal'. Even his mother called him 'a monstrosity of a human being, one that Nature began and never finished'. Yet on this day the Roman Senate formally invested him with all the powers of *princeps* – first citizen – a euphemism for dictator. He was Claudius, Rome's fourth emperor.

Although Claudius came from an illustrious background, his infirmities (today believed to have been cerebral palsy) kept him out of the line of succession, as first his uncle Tiberius and then his nephew Caligula mounted the imperial throne. Although intelligent and perceptive, Claudius had spent his life in the shadows, studying history under the tutelage of Livy and composing almost 30 books on the Etruscans and Carthaginians, all written in Greek.

In the chaos after the Praetorian Guard murdered Caligula, the guards cut down several uninvolved noblemen and bystanders. Terrified, Claudius fled to the palace. A Praetorian named Gratus found him there, cowering behind a curtain, but instead of slaying him, he took him to the guards' camp, where the Praetorians hailed him as emperor. Rome's senators realised that they were powerless against several thousand armed Praetorians and hurried off to congratulate the new emperor.

Claudius immediately added the family name 'Caesar' to his name, the first step in the transformation of 'Caesar' from a family name to a royal title, one that evolved over the centuries into 'czar' (or 'tsar') and 'kaiser'. To everyone's surprise, he became one of Rome's better rulers.

He added Mauretania (North Africa), Thrace (the Balkans) and Lycia (part of Turkey) to the empire, and in 43 AD visited Britain for sixteen days, captured Colchester and returned to Rome in triumph. Britain remained a Roman province for the next four centuries.

Although Claudius seems to have shared Rome's bloodlust (he revelled in gladiatorial games and enjoyed the odd execution), he allowed conquered people to become citizens and decreed that masters who killed slaves could be charged with murder. A widespread practice of slave owners was to abandon sick slaves on an island in the Tiber, then reclaiming them if they survived. Claudius ruled that slaves who recovered would be free.

Claudius' major weakness was his judgement on wives. He divorced his first wife for scandalous behaviour and suspicion of murder, his second for what the historian Suetonius calls 'minor offences'. Then, three years before he became emperor, he married the infamous Messalina, whose adulteries ranged from minor actors to prominent senators. To destroy her enemies and rivals, Messalina persuaded Claudius that they were plotting against him. Some 35 senators, over 300 knights and Claudius' own niece were put to death. Finally, in 48 AD, Messalina openly married one of her lovers although still wed to the emperor. Claudius had them both executed.

Within a year of disposing of Messalina, Claudius married his niece Agrippina, who had been accused of poisoning her husband only a few months before. She persuaded him to give her son (the future emperor Nero) precedence over his own son Britannicus, but she soon became apprehensive on hearing Claudius' claim that it was 'his destiny to suffer and finally to punish the infamy of his wives'.

Claudius kept an official poisoner named Locusta on the palace payroll. On the evening of 12 October 54, Agrippina bribed Locusta to spice some fresh mushrooms with a delicate poison and then enlisted the aid of Halotus, the official taster, to offer them to the emperor. When Claudius was seized with diarrhoea but showed no signs of dying, Agrippina brought on Xenophon, the court doctor. On the pretence of making Claudius vomit, Xenophon put a poisoned feather down the emperor's throat.

In the small hours of the following morning Claudius died in agony at the age of 63, after almost fourteen years as the most powerful man in the world.

1947 American gangster Al Capone's (supposed) last words: 'You can get more with a kind word and a gun than you can get with a kind word alone.'

---

26 January

'Without exception the finest Harbour in the World.'

1788 A week earlier, Captain Arthur Phillip's fleet of eleven ships had arrived at Botany Bay off the south-eastern coast of Australia. But the bay suffered from poor soil and little water, and Phillip thought it would make a poor harbour. Taking a longboat and two cutters, he sailed ten miles up the coast and landed in Port Jackson, where he found (as described in his first dispatch back to England): 'Without exception the finest Harbour in the World, in which a thousand sail of the line may ride in the most perfect security.' On this day he established there the first colony in Australia. Around it would grow the city of Sydney.

Although without European settlements and inhabited by only 300,000 Aborigines, Australia was hardly *terra incognita*. Back in the 2nd century Romans had hypothesised a continent in the southern hemisphere that they called Terra Australis – 'southern land'. (In 1814 the English navigator and cartographer Matthew Flinders suggested shortening it to 'Australia'.)

The first Europeans to sight the continent were Portuguese navigators in 1528, followed by the Spanish in 1605, the same year that Dutchman Willem Jansz reached Cape Keerweer in the far north. Twenty-nine other Dutch navigators continued intermittent explorations for the next half century, calling the continent New Holland. The most prominent was Abel Tasman, who discovered Tasmania in 1642.

The first Englishman to visit Australia was the buccaneer William Dampier, who spent almost three months on the north-western coast in 1688, returned to England and wrote a book about his adventures that so captivated the English that William III commissioned him to captain a 26-gun warship on an exploratory mission around Shark Bay in 1699.

Later the British Admiralty sent Captain James Cook on another voyage of discovery in HMS *Endeavour*. After a crewman sighted Australia's south-eastern coast on 20 April 1770, Cook landed several times and claimed the land for the British crown. (Cook seemed to agree with his contemporary Jean-Jacques Rousseau about the 'noble savage'. 'The Natives of New-Holland', he wrote in his journal, 'may appear to some to be the most wretched people upon Earth, but in reality they are far more happier than we Europeans; being wholly unacquainted not only with the superfluous but the necessary Conveniences so much sought after in Europe, they are happy in not knowing the use of them.')

When Captain Phillip came to Australia in 1788, his purpose was not to explore but to settle. In Great Britain the prisons and prison ships were full to overflowing, particularly since after the start of the American Revolution in 1776 the British could no longer ship their felons to America. Therefore the government decided to offload these undesirables by planting a convict colony on Australia.

When Phillip's fleet arrived off the Australian coast, they had been sailing for 252 days and had covered more than 15,000 miles. On board were about 1,400 people, including four companies of marines, 570 free men, women and children, and 730 convicts, mostly male. (There would have been more but about 50 had died during the voyage.)

During the next four years over 4,000 more convicts were landed at Sydney, and by the middle of the 19th century some 162,000 had arrived. After expertly steering the colony during its first difficult years, Phillip left for England on 11 December 1792, became an Admiral of the Blue and died in 1814 at 74.

Back in 1788 the British government had spent £84,000 in outfitting and despatching the First Fleet, equal to about £10 million today. Not a bad investment for a country that now boasts over 25 million citizens (including 800,000 Aborigines) with a gross domestic product of about £1.2 trillion. Much has been said about today's Australians, many of whom are descendants of the original convict pioneers – independent, irreverent, casual, exuberant, laid-back, straightforward, sporty, but not noticeably thirsting for culture. The 20th-century American poet Phyllis McGinley neatly summed it up: 'In Australia, not reading poetry is the national pastime.'

1998 President Bill Clinton tells the American public on television: 'I did not have sexual relations with that woman, Miss Lewinsky.'

---

27 January

'Arbeit macht frei'

1945 Ten days earlier Warsaw had fallen to the Russians, and Hitler's armies were now desperately battling to stem the Russian tide before it flowed into Germany itself. Less than 200 miles to the south-west stood a few nondescript buildings at Auschwitz, the scene of more murders than any other spot on earth. There, on the orders of Reichsführer-SS Heinrich Himmler, records were being destroyed and buildings burned, while 58,000 detainees were being evacuated, driven on foot on a death march west, in a futile effort to disguise the appalling crimes carried out there.

On this day, the soldiers of the 322nd Rifle Division of Marshal Konev's First Army of the Ukrainian Front reached Auschwitz, an area of approximately five miles by three where the main buildings were clustered, now abandoned by Wehrmacht troops. As they neared the building designated Auschwitz I, the Russians came upon a black cast-iron sixteen-foot sign that seemed to wave like a banner across the entrance: *Arbeit macht frei* ('Work makes [you] free'). It was the Nazi equivalent to Dante's 'Abandon all hope, ye who enter here' at the gates of Hell. Of the concentration camp's once vast population of detainees, just 7,000 remained alive when the Russians arrived, all too sick or too weak to walk in the death march.

In May 1940 the first prisoners, Poles, were sent to Auschwitz, but by September of the next year the camp found its true avocation: the extermination of its inmates, largely Jews. The killing process was greatly speeded up that month with the introduction of the cyanide-based gas Zyklon B. According to historian Max Hastings, of the 1.1 million Jews who were sent to Auschwitz, about 1 million perished. In addition, 70,000 Poles, 21,000 gypsies, 12,000 political prisoners and 15,000 Russian POWs also died. In all, about 85 per cent of those brought there did not survive. Auschwitz was also the home of the Nazis' most loathsome doctor, Josef Mengele, who performed lethal experiments on its inmates.

Although *Arbeit macht frei* is now seen as one of the most sinister and cynical of all the slogans in history, the phrase was first coined by a pastor and librarian named Lorenz Diefenbach, who used it in 1873 in the title of a book about the redemption of a conman through hard work. The phrase was later picked up by the Weimar government to promote its public works programme. The Nazis first employed it when they came to power in 1933 in the Oranienburg concentration camp (rebuilt and renamed Sachsenhausen in 1936) for communists, socialists and homosexuals. Other detention camps like Dachau and Theresienstadt followed suit. But because of the number of innocent people put to death there, Auschwitz has become the most closely associated with the slogan, which was cast in iron and erected by the camp commandant SS Obersturmbannführer Rudolf Höss.

At the war's conclusion Höss evaded capture for a year, but was eventually turned in by his wife in order to keep their son from being sent to almost certain death in the Soviet Union. Convicted of murder by a Polish court, Höss was hanged on 2 April 1947 next to one of Auschwitz's crematoria.

The *Arbeit macht frei* sign remained over the gate at Auschwitz as a grim reminder of the horrors within until 2009, when it was stolen and cut into three pieces by a Swedish neo-Nazi and two Polish accomplices. All three thieves were jailed, and the repaired sign is now in the Auschwitz-Birkenau State Museum.

1837 After being shot in a duel by a man he suspects of having an affair with his wife, Russian poet Alexander Pushkin tells his wife: 'Try to be forgotten. Go live in the country. Stay in mourning for two years, then remarry, but choose somebody decent.' Pushkin dies two days later.

---

28 January

'Vous êtes de la merde dans un bas de soie!'

1809 Today in Paris Emperor Napoleon spewed vitriol on his elegant but traitorous Grand Chamberlain, Charles-Maurice de Talleyrand-Périgord, in one of French history's most famous confrontations.

In 1799 Talleyrand was already Foreign Minister under the Directorate, but he knew and admired Napoleon and helped him gain power in his coup d'état of 9 November of that year (18 Brumaire). Eleven days later Napoleon appointed him Foreign Minister, later writing: 'I needed an aristocrat, and an aristocrat who knew how to handle things with an entirely princely insolence.' Talleyrand entirely agreed. 'A monarchy', he wrote, 'should be governed by democrats and a republic by aristocrats.'

Talleyrand came from an ancient and aristocratic Parisian family. Both his father and his uncle were generals, but, barred from the military by his withered left foot, he entered the Church, eventually becoming a bishop. During the French Revolution, however, he was excommunicated for helping the government appropriate Church property and supporting the revolutionaries' anti-clericalism.

Talleyrand was brilliant, ambitious and virtually clairvoyant in his understanding of the great events of his time, but his immense abilities were surpassed only by the cynicism by which he lived. 'You must guard yourself against your first impulse', he said. 'It is almost always honest.' In 1806 Napoleon made Talleyrand Prince de Bénévent, mocked by his detractors as *'Prince de bien au vent'* – 'Prince who blows with the wind'.

In 1807 Napoleon's armies invaded Spain, but Spanish guerrillas mauled the French, and only Napoleon's personal intervention saved the day. Now other European powers – Austria, Russia, Prussia and Britain – seemed ready to turn on him.

Talleyrand now began to plot for France's – and his own – future without Napoleon. He resigned as Foreign Minister in 1807, but Napoleon kept him on in the Council of State. In September the next year he travelled to Erfurt and secretly persuaded Tsar Alexander II not to ally Russia with Napoleon's France. Hearing of Talleyrand's scheming, the emperor summoned him to a meeting on this day and launched his famous diatribe.

In front of his cabinet and his leading marshals, Napoleon ranted at Talleyrand for half an hour: 'You are a thief, a coward, a man without faith. You don't believe in God. You have, all your life, failed in your duty, you have cheated and betrayed everyone. For you, nothing is sacred. You would sell your father. I have loaded you with honours but there is nothing against me that you are not capable of.'

The emperor continued: 'For the past ten months, when you wrongly thought my affairs in Spain were going badly, you have had the impudence to tell anyone who will listen that it is all my fault, while you were the first to give me the idea and have ceaselessly pushed me on … What are your plans? What do you want? What do you hope for? … You deserve that I should break you like a glass, I have the power but I hold you in too much contempt to take the trouble. Why didn't I hang you on the Carrousel gates?' Then came Napoleon's scornful summing up of this conniving aristocrat: '*Vous êtes de la merde dans un bas de soie!*' ('You are a shit in a silk stocking!')

Napoleon stalked out of the room, and Talleyrand coldly told the others, 'Pity that so great a man should have been so badly brought up!'

From this point onwards, Talleyrand became in effect an Austrian spy, betraying Napoleon's secrets. When the emperor rashly invaded Russia, Talleyrand began surreptitiously negotiating for the restoration of France's Bourbon kings, and when Napoleon's first abdication led to the occupation of Paris, Tsar Alexander stayed at Talleyrand's luxurious town house. On Napoleon's fall, Talleyrand was elected president of the provisional government and led the Senate's deposition of the emperor. At the Congress of Vienna, when Tsar Alexander criticised those who 'betrayed the cause of Europe', Talleyrand replied: 'Treason, Sire, is a question of dates.'

In exile Napoleon brooded: 'I have two faults with which to reproach myself regarding Talleyrand. The first was not to have followed the wise advice he gave me; the second was not to have hanged him.'

1547 After 38 years on the throne, Henry VIII dies defiant, calling for a bowl of white wine and shouting, 'All is lost! Monks, Monks, Monks! So, now all is gone – Empire, Body, and Soul!' * **1986** After Space Shuttle *Challenger* breaks apart 73 seconds into its flight, killing all seven crew members, President Ronald Reagan tells the nation: 'The future doesn't belong to the faint-hearted but to the brave … We will never forget them nor the last time we saw them, this morning, as they prepared for their journey and waved goodbye, and slipped the surly bonds of Earth to touch the face of God.'

---

29 January

'She has miscarried of her saviour.'

1536 Today at Peterborough Abbey Henry VIII's first wife Catherine of Aragon was laid to rest. Only 50, she had succumbed to cancer. Three years earlier, to her bitter resentment, Catherine had been stripped of her title as queen and Anne Boleyn crowned in her place. The Holy Roman Empire ambassador Eustace Chapuys remarked: 'It is rumoured that the king … means to increase [Anne's] train and exalt her position. I hope it may be so, and that no scorpion lurks under the honey.'

But scorpion there was. On the very day of Catherine's interment, Anne, three months pregnant, miscarried.

For three years of marriage Anne had failed to deliver that *sine qua non* of dynastic unions, a son and heir to the throne. (Her daughter Elizabeth, now two, of course didn't count; she was merely a girl.) And Anne knew that Henry was tiring of her, a wife grown shrewish and no longer the only magnet for the king's great lust.

Earlier that day Anne had entered a room unexpectedly and found one of her maids-in-waiting, proper, pleasant Jane Seymour, snuggling in Henry's lap. Anne reacted so violently that she lost the child within her, which was in fact the baby boy she and Henry so craved. When he heard the news, Ambassador Chapuys presciently commented: 'She has miscarried of her saviour.'

Henry reacted with fury, declaring that he had been tricked into the marriage in the first place. His interest in Anne now vanished entirely, and he moved Jane Seymour into royal quarters. On 2 May, just three months after losing her child, Anne was arrested and incarcerated in the Tower of London. She was charged with adultery, an indictment that most historians consider a convenient fiction to release the king from his marriage. Henry's chief minister Thomas Cromwell assured Henry that it was equivalent to treason, for which the only penalty was death.

To commit adultery one requires a partner, but in a capital case five would be even better. Anne's friends Francis Weston and William Brere were members of her Privy Chamber, Henry Norris a courtier, and Mark Smeaton a court musician. The fifth accused, astonishingly, was Anne's brother George, thus enabling the courts to add incest to the charges.

On 15 May the five accused paramours were brought to trial. Although only Smeaton admitted the adultery (under torture), all were condemned and two days later went to the block, perhaps a merciful punishment for treason, which usually was rewarded with hanging, drawing and quartering. Possibly Henry had taken into account the fact that they were innocent. On the same day Anne was tried, convicted and condemned to death.

On the morning of 19 May Anne was taken to Tower Green for execution. As a special kindness, instead of turning her over to the public axeman, Henry had imported an expert executioner from Calais who employed a sharp French sword instead of a common axe, which often required several chops to decapitate the victim. When told of this signal favour, Anne commented bitterly: 'He shall not have much trouble, for I have a little neck.'

Wearing a dark gown trimmed in fur, her mahogany hair bound up under her head-dress, Anne knelt upright before her executioner, not required to place her neck on the block. One of her ladies in waiting removed the head-dress and blindfolded her. Then, in a small act of kindness intended to make her think she still had a few moments left to live, the executioner said, with feigned confusion, 'Where is my sword?' He then deftly decapitated her with one sideways blow.

The next day Henry became betrothed to Jane Seymour and married her ten days after that. Nineteen months later Queen Jane gave birth to the heir Henry so desperately wanted, the future Edward VI. Within two weeks, however, Jane died of the after-effects of the delivery, probably of puerperal fever.

With Jane's demise, three of the king's wives had died in the space of 21 months. But not to worry, Henry still had three more wives to go.

1956 American journalist H.L. Mencken dies, having written some years before his death: 'If, after I depart this vale, you ever remember me and have thought to please my ghost, forgive some sinner and wink your eye at some homely girl.'

---

30 January

'A subject and a sovereign are clear different things.'

1649 During the 24 years that Charles I had been King of England, there was not a day when he doubted his divine right. 'Princes are not bound to give account of their actions', he wrote, 'but to God alone.' Even today, as he faced the executioner's axe, he insisted that he alone should rule, not subject to the will of his people or Parliament.

Self-righteous and arrogant, just six weeks after he became king, Charles had married the French princess Henrietta Maria, despite strong opposition to his marrying a Catholic. (She was so stubborn in her faith that she refused to attend Charles's coronation because it was a

Protestant ceremony.) In August the same year he dissolved Parliament in a contest of wills over customs revenue. In 1629 he dissolved it again and ruled without it for eleven years. He also brooked no criticism of his private life, ordering a Puritan lawyer's ears sliced off when he denounced court dancing as immoral.

By 1642 relations between Charles and Parliament were so strained that he gathered an army and sent his wife to Holland to pawn the crown jewels to pay for it. On 22 August he raised the royal standard at Nottingham.

The civil war that followed was long and brutal – 300,000 people, 6 per cent of the population, perished. Despite frequent setbacks, Charles refused to accept Parliament's demands for a constitutional monarchy. He was captured, escaped and captured again. His war against Parliament and his endless duplicity led to his trial.

Charles was indicted for 'all the treasons, murders, rapines, burnings, spoils, desolations, damages and mischiefs to this nation', but he refuted the legitimacy of the court and refused to enter a plea, insisting that 'a king cannot be tried by any superior jurisdiction on earth'. The court found him guilty of high treason and pronounced that 'his head should be severed from his body'.

Today, just three days after the trial ended, Londoners shivered in the bitter cold. Charles donned two heavy shirts, explaining: 'The season is so sharp as probably may make me shake, which some observers will imagine proceeds from fear. I would have no such imputation; I fear no death. I bless my God that I am prepared.'

At ten o'clock the king walked across from St James's to Whitehall, where a scaffold had been erected outside the Banqueting House. At two he stepped from a window upon the scaffold, which was surrounded by ranks of soldiers.

Addressing the watching crowd, he insisted to the last on his divine right as king. He desired the liberty and freedom of the people, he said, but 'liberty and freedom consists in having government ... It is not their having a share in the government; that is nothing appertaining unto them. A subject and a sovereign are clean different things.'

Charles faced death with courage. Turning to the masked executioner, he said: 'I shall say but very short prayers, and when I thrust out my hands—' After murmuring a few words to himself, he stooped and laid his neck on the block. Then, according to an eyewitness: 'After a very short pause, his Majesty stretching forth his hands, the executioner at one blow severed his head from his body; which, being held up and showed to the people, was with his body put into a coffin covered with black velvet and carried into his lodging. His blood was taken up by divers persons for different ends: by some as trophies of their villainy; by others as relics of a martyr.'

Through his insistence on unconstrained royal power, Charles had triggered a civil war that led to his own death and the dissolution of the monarchy. But by 1660 the country had tired of the constrictions of Puritanism and restored Charles's son, Charles II, to the throne. In a grisly demonstration of the fate of regicides, on this day in 1661 – the twelfth anniversary of Charles's execution – the corpses of four long-dead Parliamentarian leaders, including Oliver Cromwell, were disinterred and formally hanged in chains at Tyburn.

1933 When President Hindenburg appoints Hitler as Chancellor, General Erich Ludendorff tells him: 'I solemnly prophesy that this accursed man will cast our Reich into the abyss and bring our nation to inconceivable misery. Future generations will damn you in your grave for what you have done.' * **1948** After a disgruntled Hindu shoots Indian leader Mohandas Gandhi, Jawaharlal Nehru laments: 'The light has gone out of our lives and there is darkness everywhere.'

---

31 January

'I don't think anybody should write his autobiography until after he's dead.'

1974 Today at his home in Los Angeles pioneering movie producer Samuel Goldwyn died in his sleep. In one of the 'Goldwynisms' for which he was famous, he had once said: 'I don't think anybody should write his autobiography until after he's dead.' Goldwyn didn't write his autobiography at all.

Goldwyn came from the poorest of backgrounds; born Szmuel Gelbfisz in Warsaw in a Jewish Hasidic household, his father a pedlar. At nineteen he left for New York and anglicised his name to Samuel Goldfish.

Goldfish's start in showbusiness came through his wife Blanche's brother, the vaudeville producer Jesse Lasky. He and Lasky and a failing play producer named Cecil B. DeMille founded the Jesse Lasky Feature Play Company to make movies. Their first production was the western,

The Squaw Man, in 1914. (Could that have been when Goldfish supposedly said: 'We can get all the Indians we need at the reservoir.'?)

Three years later Goldfish left the company (perhaps that's when he said 'Include me out') and set up a new venture with Broadway producers Edgar and Arch Selwyn, calling it the Goldwyn Pictures Corporation. Goldfish liked the name so much he changed his own to Goldwyn. But Goldwyn was a difficult man. In 1922 he left to become an independent producer. (In 1924 Goldwyn Pictures merged with two other companies to create Metro-Goldwyn-Mayer, but Goldwyn had nothing to do with the company that still bears his name.)

In 1926 Goldwyn joined United Artists. During the late 20s he was considering filming a book called *The Well of Loneliness*, but was warned it would never get through the censor's code because it was about lesbians. 'That's all right', he said, 'we'll make them Hungarians.'

After thirteen years he resigned once more, this time because of a falling out with a company founder, actress Mary Pickford. (Perhaps this was when he claimed: 'I'm willing to admit that I may not always be right, but I am never wrong.') He now developed Samuel Goldwyn Productions into the most financially and critically successful independent production company in Hollywood's Golden Age.

Goldwyn was a demanding boss, once saying: 'I hate a man who always says "yes" to me. When I say "no" I like a man who also says "no."' When an accountant asked him if he could destroy old paperwork that was no longer needed, he responded: 'Certainly. Just be sure to keep a copy of everything.'

Goldwyn always tried to choose the best talent, commenting about a famous actor: 'We're overpaying him, but he's worth it.' He also insisted: 'Give me a smart idiot over a stupid genius any day.'

Goldwyn produced a stream of fine movies, with Oscar nominations for *Dodsworth, Dead End, Wuthering Heights* and *The Little Foxes*. In 1947 he won for *The Best Years of Our Lives*. Always conscious of the need for box office success, he told his team: 'We want a story that starts out with an earthquake and works its way up to a climax.'

Goldwyn made outstanding films such as *Guys and Dolls* until 1959, when he produced his last, *Porgy and Bess*. Along the way he added to his Goldwynisms with comments like: 'I can answer you in two words: im-possible!' and 'I had a monumental idea this morning, but I didn't like it.' Once, when told that a script was full of old clichés, he responded: 'Let's have some new clichés.' He praised a singer with the comment: 'Can she sing? She's practically a Florence Nightingale.'

Goldwyn remained in Los Angeles with his second wife for the last years of his life. ('Monogamy is OK in the office, but at home I prefer white', he said.) Famed for his relentless ambition, bad temper and genius for publicity, he had become Hollywood's leading independent producer – largely because none of his partners could tolerate him for long. He had once opined: 'If I could drop dead right now, I'd be the happiest man alive.' On this day he did at the age of 94.

1943 As German Generalfeldmarschall Friedrich Paulus is surrendering to the Russians at Stalingrad, Hitler, unaware of the capitulation, sends him a message: 'You and your soldiers ... should enter the New Year with the unshakeable confidence that I and the whole German Wehrmacht will do everything in our power to relieve the defenders of Stalingrad.'

1 February

'I lived that Bohème, *when there wasn't yet any thought stirring in my brain of seeking the theme of an opera.'*

1896 The son of a tailor and a concierge, Henri Murger was an undistinguished French poet who often lived in poverty with deteriorating health. Most people knew nothing of his work, but he achieved some notoriety with his mantra, 'the first duty of wine is to be red. Don't talk to me of your white wines.' Enthralled by the romance and gaiety of 19th-century Paris, in his early twenties he started writing serialised stories about the Bohemian life he led in the Latin Quarter.

His tales began to be published in the mid-1840s. They told of Paris's radicals, rebels and artists who rejected bourgeois values to follow a life of independence, work and pleasure, choosing the path of artistic creation and the suffering and privation that often went with it. He called this unconventional existence *'la préface de l'Académie, de l'Hôtel-Dieu ou de la Morgue'* (the foreword to the [French] Academy, the hospital or the morgue).

Murger's pieces became so popular that he pulled them together in a book, *Scènes de la vie de bohème*, and into a successful play. Although celebrated by Victor Hugo, lauded by Louis Napoleon and awarded the Légion d'honneur, Murger enjoyed fame and fortune only briefly, falling back into penury and dying at 38. The French government paid for his funeral.

If you are an opera fan, however, one of Murger's stories will sound familiar: 'During that time, the great philosopher Gustave Colline, the great painter Marcel, the great musician Schaunard, and the great poet Rudolphe, as they referred to each other among themselves, regularly frequented the Café Momus.' Rudolphe, of course, was a portrait of Murger himself, but more importantly, 35 years after his death this tale became the basis for one of the world's best loved operas, *La bohème*.

Two years before Murger died, Giacomo Puccini was born in Lucca. Although from an accomplished musical family, during his early years he, like Murger, lived in relative poverty, often short of money for food, clothing and to pay the rent, and frequently relied on pawnbrokers. When he was 34, however, his opera *Manon Lescaut* established him as a major composer, called by the Turin newspaper *La Stampa* 'a young man among the few for whom great hopes are not optimistic illusions'.

For his next major project Puccini created an opera around Murger's *Scènes de la vie de bohème*, a natural choice since 'I had lived that *Bohème*, when there wasn't yet any thought stirring in my brain of seeking the theme of an opera'.

On this day in 1896 Puccini's *La bohème* opened at the Teatro Regio in Turin. Conducting was another young Italian, 28-year-old Arturo Toscanini, who had been born in Parma, just a hundred miles south of Lucca. As a cellist rather than conductor, Toscanini had already played in the premiere of Verdi's *Otello* and then had conducted the first performance of *Pagliacci* by Leoncavallo. (A famously demanding conductor and, like Puccini, a Lothario, Toscanini once berated his orchestra, 'Can't you read? The score demands '*con amore*,' and what are you doing? You are playing it like married men!')

La bohème quickly became a huge international success, cementing Puccini's reputation as well as Toscanini's. But after thirty years of high living and heavy smoking, Puccini succumbed to a heart attack following surgery for throat cancer on 29 November 1924. In one of those coincidences seemingly contrived by fate, the news of his death reached Rome during a performance of *La bohème*. The opera was immediately stopped, and the orchestra played Chopin's *Marche funèbre* for the stunned audience.

1979 After the Ayatollah Khomeini returns to Iran after fifteen years in exile, he spells out his policies: 'All those against the revolution must disappear and quickly be executed.' * **1908** After republicans gun down Portuguese King Carlos and his son Luís Filipe in an open carriage while riding through a city square in Lisbon, England's indignant Edward VII gets his priorities right in telling a friend: 'They murdered two gentlemen of the Order of the Garter in the street like dogs!'

---

2 February

'The head that used to lie in Queen Catherine's lap would now lie in the executioner's basket.'

1461 Today at Mortimer's Cross in Herefordshire the forces of York routed the Lancastrians during the Wars of the Roses. One of the doomed Lancastrian commanders was the Welshman Owen Tudor, a knight with a special place in England's history – the founder of the Tudor dynasty.

In 1422 England's Henry V had died while extending his conquests in France, leaving behind his queen, Catherine of Valois, daughter of France's mad King Charles VI.

Queen Catherine – now dowager queen at the age of twenty – moved to Windsor Castle. In her entourage was the keeper of her wardrobe (i.e. chamberlain) the handsome Owen Tudor, the same who would later fight at Mortimer's Cross.

Owen was just a year older than Catherine, and it was said that she liked to hide behind the bushes on the banks of the Thames to watch him bathe naked in the river. There may be truth in the tale, because she bore him six children, of whom the eldest was named Edmund. Historians still debate whether Catherine and Owen were ever married; royalists insist they were secretly wed in 1429.

Catherine died in 1437, and in 1455 the Wars of the Roses broke out, a bitter struggle to determine whether the House of Lancaster or the House of York would hold the throne of England. That same year Edmund, Catherine's son by Owen, married Lady Margaret Beaufort. A year later Edmund was captured by the Yorkists and died of plague, but three months after his death, on 28 January 1457, Lady Margaret gave birth to his posthumous son, Henry Tudor.

Four years later came today's battle at Mortimer's Cross. Owen Tudor, now 60, was marching east from Wales with about 4,000 inexperienced Lancastrian troops when they encountered a superior enemy force under Edward of York, the pretender to the throne.

The battle was a crushing defeat for the Lancastrians, and at its conclusion Owen Tudor was captured. A vindictive Edward of York ordered his execution.

As he awaited the fatal axe, the insouciant Owen pondered the fate that had carried him so high and now brought him so low: 'The head that used to lie in Queen Catherine's lap would now lie in the executioner's basket.' He was duly decapitated in the Hereford marketplace, his head set up on the market cross. It is said that a mad woman combed the hair and washed the face of this one-time lover of a queen, and set lighted candles around it.

The condemned Owen had probably given little thought to his four-year-old grandson Henry, but over the years other claimants fell by the wayside, so by 1483 this grandson was the leading Lancastrian – and the Lancastrians had never given up their claim to the English throne. Henry Tudor's right to be king was tenuous at best – his grandmother Catherine had been married to Henry V, and his mother,

Lady Margaret Beaufort, could trace her lineage four generations back to Edward III. But it was enough.

In 1485 Henry Tudor, who had been living in exile, landed in Wales with a small French and Scottish force, where he was joined by disaffected English nobles. On 22 August 1485 his army defeated and slew Richard (III) of York at Bosworth Field, and Owen Tudor's grandson took the throne as Henry VII, the first monarch of the Tudor dynasty that would last until 1603 and include Henry VIII, Bloody Mary and Queen Elizabeth.

1884 English novelist James Payn publishes in *Chamber's Journal*: 'I never had a piece of toast/Particularly long and wide,/But fell upon the sanded floor,/And always on the buttered side.' * **1913** American poet Joyce Kilmer writes the first two lines of a new poem in his notebook: 'I think that I shall never see/A poem lovely as a tree.'

---

3 February

'Because there were no bounds to his malice, Divine Vengeance did not allow the blasphemer to live any longer.'

1014 On this Sunday the Viking marauder-king Sweyn Forkbeard died at Gainsborough, Lincolnshire, only 41 days after having seized the throne of England. Could his death have been celestial retribution for the havoc and destruction he wreaked in conquering the country?

Sweyn Forkbeard had a history of unscrupulous power grabbing. In 986 he had rebelled against his own father, the Danish king Harald Bluetooth, and had driven him into exile and death.

Despite occasional forays against England, Sweyn might have been content to remain in Denmark had not England's Aethelred the Unready unleashed the St Brice's Day massacre on 13 November 1002, when some 40 young Danes, including Sweyn's sister Gunhilde and her husband, were brutally slaughtered at St Frideswide's Priory in Oxford. Sweyn swore revenge.

Between 1003 and 1007 Sweyn led several punitive expeditions that ravaged England. He was the first Scandinavian king to command the raids in person. Despite his success, six years later he was again short of money, and in August 1013 he came with his fleet to Sandwich in Kent, launching a full-scale invasion. He conquered Northumbria and the East Midlands, then Oxford, Winchester, Bath and finally London. Aethelred fled to the Isle of Wight, and on Christmas Day 1013 Sweyn was declared King of England, making him ruler of a North Sea empire that also included Denmark and Norway.

Sweyn promptly began extorting money from conquered towns, one of which was Bury St Edmunds, where in 869 East Anglia's pious King Edmund the Martyr had been interred. (Heathen Danish invaders had beaten him with rods, tied him to a tree and shot him dead with arrows.)

According to the early 12th-century monk John of Worcester, Sweyn's demands on Bury St Edmunds led to his death:

> After many cruel atrocities, which he perpetrated both in England and in other lands, the tyrant Sweyn filled up the measure of his damnation by daring to demand enormous tribute from the town where the incorrupt body of the precious martyr Edmund lay ... He very frequently threatened that if it were not speedily paid he would destroy utterly the martyr's church, and he would torture the clergy in various ways ... Because there were no bounds to his malice, Divine Vengeance did not allow the blasphemer to live any longer ...
>
> At the general assembly which he held at Gainsborough, he repeated the same threats. At a time when he was surrounded by Danish troops crowded together, he alone saw St Edmund, armed, coming towards him. When he had seen him, he was terrified and began to shout very noisily, saying 'Help, fellow-warriors, help! St Edmund is coming to kill me!' And while he was saying this he was run through fiercely by the saint with a spear, and fell from the stallion on which he sat, and, tormented with great pain until twilight, he ended his life with a wretched death on 3 February.

The manner of Sweyn's demise is corroborated by the Canterbury monk Osbern, who in the 1080s wrote that he was 'killed in a terrible manner by Almighty God'. Less reverent accounts agree at least that Sweyn was killed falling from his horse.

Sweyn Forkbeard was succeeded in Denmark by his elder son Harald, but his army in England hailed his younger son Cnut (or Canute) as king.

Cnut also had a difficult brush with a saint, this time the formidable St Edith, who had died in 984. According to the medieval historian

William of Malmesbury, Cnut demanded to see for himself if Edith's body had remained inviolate. When her tomb was opened, the veiled corpse sat up and struck the insolent king, who fell backwards to the floor and lay for several moments unbreathing.

Deeply humbled, Cnut, who had converted to Christianity, endowed a shrine to St Edith near Canterbury. Knowing of St Edmund's vengeance on his father, he also rebuilt the abbey at Bury St Edmunds. In 1020 he made a pilgrimage there and offered his own crown upon the shrine as atonement for the sins of his pagan forefathers.

1557 When Holy Roman Emperor Charles V retires to the monastery of San Jeronimo at Yuste, he apologises: 'I have done what I could and am sorry that I could not do better. I have always recognised my insufficiency and incapacity.'

---

4 February

'Be united, enrich the soldiers, and despise all others.'

211 AD According to the contemporary historian Cassius Dio, Roman Emperor Septimius Severus 'lived sixty-five years, nine months, and twenty-five days … Of this he had ruled seventeen years, eight months and three days.' Today he died in Eboracum (modern-day York), while preparing a campaign against the Caledonians, aka Scots.

Although his reign was successful, it was bloody from the start. On the last day of 192 AD the paranoiac Emperor Commodus had been strangled in his bath in a plot orchestrated by his favourite concubine. The next day the Praetorian Guard proclaimed the general Pertinax emperor, but he lasted only 86 days, cut down by a contingent of his own soldiers over a pay dispute. Hearing of the murder, two Roman legions stationed in modern-day Austria declared for Septimius Severus, their local governor. Soon they were marching for Rome.

Before Severus and his army could arrive, however, the Praetorian Guard began to auction off the imperial throne to the highest bidder, who turned out to be the proconsul Didius Julianus. Although Julianus paid every Guard member 6,250 denarii, he reigned for a mere 66 days; when Severus neared Rome with his army, the apprehensive Senate chose him as emperor and sentenced Julianus to death. A soldier quickly cut Julianus down in his royal palace.

During the next four years Severus defeated his two remaining rivals, killing one while the other committed suicide. He ordered their wives and children to be executed as well. Since his power rested on military might, he ignored the Senate, gave his soldiers a year's pay and raised their annual salary from 300 to 400 denarii. He also permitted them to marry.

During his years in power Severus took over swathes of territory in Mesopotamia and North Africa and in 208 marched through Roman Britain with the intention of conquering Caledonia. Although the Scots killed thousands of his soldiers with their hit-and-run tactics, Severus forced them to sue for peace. When they revolted he ordered: 'Let none escape utter destruction at our hands. Yea, whatsoever is found in the womb of the mother, child unborn though it be, let it not escape utter destruction!' When not off killing foreigners, Severus kept the Senate docile by executing a large number of its members for corruption or conspiracy.

In 198, after Severus had ruled for five years, he elevated his two sons Caracalla and Geta to joint emperors when they were only ten and nine, in order to prepare them for shared authority on his death. But, as Gibbon puts it: 'The fond hopes of the father, and of the Roman world, were soon disappointed by these vain youths, who displayed the indolent security of hereditary princes and a presumption that fortune would supply the place of merit and application.' The brothers hated each other, and each was committed to the other's destruction. So bitter was their rivalry that each tried to poison the other.

In 211 Severus and his sons were about to attack the Caledonians again when he fell ill and withdrew to his base at Eboracum. As he lay dying he counselled his sons: 'Be united, enrich the soldiers, and despise all others.' Caracalla followed the last two of these directives but energetically rejected the first. He killed his brother Geta with his own hands while he was cowering in their mother's arms in the imperial palace. Caracalla then threw himself under the protection of the Praetorian Guard and informed a powerless Senate that it was all in self-defence.

Caracalla conducted a murderous reign for six years, a tyrant who commanded mass slaughter in Germany and Alexandria and killed his own wife. But he, too, came to a bloody end. On 8 April 217, while he was campaigning in Parthia (modern Iran), he was struck by dysentery. As he stepped behind some shrubs to relieve himself, a disgruntled officer in the imperial bodyguard killed him with a single thrust of his sword.

> **1716** After a futile 44 days invading Scotland, James Francis Edward Stuart, the Pretender, retreats to France. Abandoning Scotland for ever, he promises: '*Nous reculons pour mieux sauter.*' ('We pull back in order to jump forward better.') He never returned. * **1830** Six months before King Charles X is overthrown, Adolphe Thiers writes in *Le National*: '*Le roi n'administre pas, ne gouverne pas, il règne.*' ('The king does not administer, does not govern, he reigns.')

5 February

*'The Congo Free State is unique in its kind.
It has nothing to hide and no secrets and is not
beholden to anyone except its founder.'*

1885 At the end of the 19th century, colonialism was every European nation's favourite sport. In the 'Scramble for Africa', Great Britain, France, Germany, Portugal, Spain and Italy manoeuvred with each other to colonise an entire continent. In the midst of this carve-up, King Leopold II of Belgium today wolfed down the Congo. He would treat the natives like slaves and with appalling irony call the territory the Congo Free State.

Born in 1835, Leopold had inherited the throne at 30. He belittled his own country for its insignificance, could hardly speak Flemish and usually wintered on the Côte d'Azur at Les Cèdres, an astonishing villa in Saint-Jean-Cap-Ferrat that sold in 2019 for $220 million. One of his principal hobbies was teenaged girls – at 64 he would start a liaison with a sixteen-year-old French prostitute that lasted until his death.

Leopold had long wished to establish a colony, but the Belgian government refused to agree. His response was extraordinary in its hubris – he would do it himself, acting as a private citizen.

European powers had long greedily eyed the Congo River basin, but in 1884 German chancellor Otto von Bismarck convened a conference in Berlin to avert an armed clash. Small, neutral Belgium seemed the perfect compromise, especially when Leopold presented himself as a philanthropist eager to bring the natives the benefits of Christianity and Western civilisation. Today the conference awarded a million square miles of Congo territory to Leopold's 'philanthropic' Association Internationale Africaine, an institution with but a single shareholder, Leopold himself.

To protect his new colony Leopold formed the Force Publique, a 19,000-man private army with white officers and black soldiers. Initially he used his Congo Free State mainly as a source for ivory, but the invention of inflatable rubber bicycle tubes and the growing popularity of the automobile heated up the world market for rubber – and his colony was flush with wild rubber trees.

Leopold had earlier nationalised all 'uninhabited' land in the Congo and dished it out to private companies, keeping a large amount for himself. Soon the companies were using forced labour and violent coercion to collect the rubber, creating a slave society with the Force Publique as enforcer. Natives who refused to work were whipped or even shot, hostages were taken to ensure prompt collection and punitive expeditions were dispatched to burn recalcitrant villages. In a measure of grisly parsimony, Force Publique soldiers had to account for every shot they fired by bringing back the hands of their victims. Even children could lose their hands if their parents performed badly. Soon baskets of severed hands were piling up. A junior officer described a raid on an intractable village: '[We were] ordered to cut off the heads of the men and hang them on the village palisades ... and to hang the women and children on the palisade in the form of a cross.'

Leopold never once visited his colony, but when he heard of the atrocities, he remarked: 'Cut off hands – that's idiotic. I'd cut off all the rest of them, but not hands. That's the one thing I need in the Congo.'

When Great Britain and the United States were pressuring Leopold to renounce his ownership of the Congo, he blithely responded: 'The Congo Free State is unique in its kind. It has nothing to hide and no secrets and is not beholden to anyone except its founder.' Eventually, however, in 1908 the Belgian government annexed the country, thirteen months before Leopold died.

In addition to the barbarism of its rulers, the Congo Free State was also beset with a series of pandemics – smallpox, swine influenza, and amoebic dysentery, plus the most virulent, African sleeping sickness. In 1919 the Belgian government estimated that during Leopold's ownership the Congo population had declined from 20 million to 10 million.

1750 Lord Chesterfield in a letter to his son: 'Take care of the pence, and the pounds will take care of themselves.'

---

6 February

'The angels shall come forth,
and sever the wicked from among the just,
And shall cast them into the furnace of fire.'

1481 Today in Seville six men were burned at the stake in the first *auto-da-fé* of the Spanish Inquisition.

In 1469 Ferdinand of Aragon had married Isabella of Castile, beginning a reign that would eventually unite all of Spain, but their hold on the country was still fragile. The *Reconquista* would not be completed until 1492, and, in addition to Moors (Arabs), there were still some 200,000 *conversos* – Jews who had converted to Christianity – living in Spain. Of these, many were thought to be *marranos*, Jews who were forced to convert to Christianity yet continued to practise Judaism in secret while trying to proselytise *conversos* and even good Catholics.

The Catholic Monarchs, as Ferdinand and Isabella are called, considered these *marranos* heretics, and since God had sanctified the Monarchs' kingship, heresy was not only a sin but also an inherent challenge to royal authority.

At the request of Ferdinand and Isabella, on 1 November 1478 Pope Sixtus IV issued a bull allowing the crown to form the Tribunal del Santo Oficio de la Inquisición (Tribunal of the Holy Office of the Inquisition). The first court was set up in Seville, where Judaising was alleged to be most flagrant.

The establishment of this fearful tribunal was enough to cause hundreds to escape the city, afraid they might be seized. But in an atmosphere where suspicion replaced proof, the inquisitors took their flight as evidence of guilt. Soon, six of the fleeing *conversos* were lodged in the Convent of St Paul, which did double duty as a prison, and were brought to trial. Convicted of heresy and apostasy, they were delivered up to the secular authorities for punishment.

And what a terrible punishment it would be. Had not the Bible itself described what should happen to sinners? According to Matthew 13: 41–42: 'The angels shall come forth, and sever the wicked from among the just, And shall cast them into the furnace of fire: there shall be wailing and gnashing of teeth.'

Surrounded by guards and wearing yellow sack clothes, the barefoot victims were paraded through the crowded streets, led by a black-robed Dominican holding the green cross of the Inquisition, now swathed in black crêpe. In their wake came the inquisitors with their attendants and a group of Dominicans from the convent, headed by their prior.

First the condemned men were treated to a sermon at the Seville cathedral and then marched to a meadow on the city's outskirts where stakes had been erected. Fire was set to the faggots, and the six men perished in agony.

This first *auto-da-fé* (a bizarre euphemism meaning 'act of faith') was followed on 26 March when another seventeen supposed *marranos* were burnt. But the Inquisition really got going in 1483 when the Dominican Tomás de Torquemada was made the first Grand Inquisitor of Spain. During his doleful fifteen years in power he encouraged the use of torture to extract confessions, including such Spanish delicacies as the *toca*, in which water is forced down your throat, and the *potro*, a form of the rack. Some 2,000 were condemned to the stake.

The Spanish Inquisition endured for over three centuries, until Napoleon's brother Joseph abolished it in 1808 when he was King of Spain, but on Napoleon's fall it was reconstituted. In 1826 the school teacher Cayetano Ripoll became its last fatality, executed for insisting that the only necessary religious teaching was the keeping of the Ten Commandments. The institution itself was finally suppressed in 1834, although its offspring, the Inquisition in Mexico, lived on, with the last *auto-da-fé* taking place in 1850.

All told, the Spanish Inquisition prosecuted 150,000 people for various offences, of whom perhaps 5,000 were put to death.

1685 As Charles II lies dying, he tells his courtiers: 'I have been a most unconscionable time dying; but I hope you will excuse it.'

---

7 February

'I have seen man's infinite misery, the rapes, the adulteries, the robberies, the pride, the idolatry, the vile curses, all the violence of a society that has lost all capacity for good.'

1497 Today in Florence it was Martedì grasso, the last festive day of Carnivale before the beginning of Lent. But instead of a joyous celebration, Florence's de facto ruler, the joyless monk Girolamo Savonarola, had ordered a penitential bonfire in the Piazza della Signoria.

Piled high were what Savonarola considered 'occasions of sin' – that is, anything that might entice people to transgress his stern moral code. Included were richly decorated clothing, cosmetics, jewellery and mirrors. Also consigned to the flames were ancient sculptures, musical instruments, tapestries and 'immoral' books by writers such as Ovid, Dante and Boccaccio. Among the great works of art destroyed were ancient paintings and those of the flowering Renaissance. Sandro Botticelli delivered some of his own work depicting mythological nudes. This holy cleansing came to be known as *il Falò delle vanità* – the bonfire of the vanities.

As the flames grew higher before Florence's sombre citizens, no one would have guessed that only 407 days later Savonarola himself would be hanged and his body burned where the bonfire now raged.

Born in Ferrara in 1452, Savonarola was already despairing of this world by the time he was 22, when he entered the Convent of San Domenico in Bologna. 'I choose religion', he wrote to his father, 'because I have seen man's infinite misery, the rapes, the adulteries, the robberies, the pride, the idolatry, the vile curses, all the violence of a society that has lost all capacity for good … I could not stand the great wickedness of the blind people of Italy, especially when I saw that virtue had been completely cast down and vice raised up.'

Savonarola moved to Florence in 1489 and within two years was the most controversial figure in the city. Now prior of the monastery of San Marco, this ascetic monk was a striking figure with the death's head of a fanatic: hollow cheeks beneath a great beak of a nose, full, rubbery lips and piercing green eyes that were said to glow with inner zeal. In his sermons he castigated the gentry for corruption, pleasure-seeking and vanity and singled out Lorenzo the Magnificent as a promoter of pagan art and frivolous living.

Savonarola's influence grew when he predicted Lorenzo's death and interpreted Charles VIII of France's invasion of Tuscany in 1494 as the scourge of God he had so long foreseen. The power vacuum when Charles left Tuscany thrust Savonarola into de facto control of Florence, and the next four years were filled with grim religiosity. 'I am the hail-storm that shall break the heads of those who do not take shelter', he threatened. But as his authority grew, so did his list of enemies. The most dangerous was Alexander VI, the dissolute and calculating Borgia pope who was determined to bring the friar to heel. Alexander particularly objected to Savonarola's claim to direct communication with God, thereby putting himself above the Pope himself.

Finally in May 1497 Alexander excommunicated him, but Savonarola merely advised the Pope to look to his own salvation and continued to harangue the Florentine crowds.

The monk's intransigence led Alexander to threaten to place all of Florence under interdict, meaning that there could be no Mass, weddings, baptisms or funerals. This was the moment his enemies were waiting for. Florence's Franciscan monks, long jealous of the Dominicans' predominance, challenged his supremacy, and the rich and powerful families, longing for a return to more civilised days, stirred up the mob. On Palm Sunday in 1498, Savonarola was chased from his pulpit and arrested by the civil government. Torture soon led to confession and confession to conviction for heresy and promoting schism in the True Church.

On 23 May three scaffolds were erected in the Piazza della Signoria, and on them Savonarola and his two most faithful followers were hanged, then their bodies burned. The ashes were scattered in the Arno so that no trace of Savonarola could ever be found.

1807 The start of the inconclusive two-day Battle of Eylau between Napoleon and the Russians and Prussians in which both sides suffer over 20,000 casualties. After the battle Marshal Michel Ney says to Napoleon: '*Quel massacre! Et sans résultat!*' ('What a massacre! And without a result!')

---

8 February

'The Queen entered the room full of grace and majesty, just as if she were coming to a ball.'

1587 With little likelihood that Queen Elizabeth would produce an heir, Mary, Queen of Scots was next in line to the crown of England (she was the great-granddaughter of Henry VII). For the past nineteen years, however, she had been a prisoner in England. Today she would die.

Mary was a fiery and beautiful woman, proud and brave but vain and astonishingly foolish. On 14 December 1542, six days after her birth, she became Queen of Scots on the death of her father. At five she was sent to France, the bride presumptive of the French Dauphin, the future François II, whom she married in April 1558.

Seven months later her cousin Elizabeth inherited the English throne, but many Catholics considered Elizabeth illegitimate because the 'true' English queen, Catherine of Aragon, had been put aside in favour of Elizabeth's mother, Anne Boleyn. Mary, they claimed, should be queen, rather than Elizabeth. The fact that Mary was Catholic while Elizabeth Protestant (i.e. a heretic) strongly underpinned their views.

King François died on 5 December 1560, and Mary returned to Scotland. In 1565 she married the vain, stupid, indolent and drunken Henry, Lord Darnley, but she soon fell for the Scottish adventurer James Hepburn, Earl of Bothwell. On 9 February 1567 a tremendous explosion was heard throughout Edinburgh. Bothwell had placed a barrel of gunpowder in the room directly below Darnley's bedroom and set it off. Darnley was found naked and dead in the street outside. Three months later Mary married Bothwell.

An outraged Scottish nobility forced Mary to abdicate in favour of her one-year-old son, James, and imprisoned her in Loch Leven Castle. The following year Mary escaped and raised a small army, but she was defeated at Langside and fled to England, hoping that Queen Elizabeth would help her regain the Scottish throne. Elizabeth imprisoned her instead.

From now on Mary would be moved from castle to castle, living in luxury with a large household, but never free. She never ceased scheming to regain her freedom and to seize the English throne, and royal councillors urged Elizabeth to execute her. '*Mortui non mordent*' ('A dead woman bites not'), intoned Lord Gray, but Elizabeth rejected their advice.

In 1586 one of Mary's letters was intercepted; it was proof that she was plotting to assassinate Elizabeth. Moved to Fotheringhay Castle, she was convicted of treason and sentenced to death. Elizabeth dithered, but on 1 February 1587, she finally signed the death warrant. On 8 February Mary faced her execution.

An eyewitness, Pierre de Bourdeille, seigneur de Brantôme, relates that at Fotheringhay Castle 'the scaffold had been erected in the middle of a large room. It measured twelve feet along each side and two feet in height, and was covered by a coarse cloth of linen. The Queen entered the room full of grace and majesty, just as if she were coming to a ball. There was no change on her features as she entered.' Mary was dressed entirely in black, her dark red hair impeccably coiffed. Crucifix in hand, she signalled for her cloak to be removed. The 300 nobles in attendance gasped as they saw that underneath she was clad entirely in velvet the colour of blood.

'One of [her attendants] then tied the handkerchief over her eyes. The Queen quickly, and with great courage, knelt down, showing no signs of faltering … The Queen repeated in Latin the Psalm beginning *In te, Domine, speravi; non confundar in aeternum.* When she was through she laid her head on the block, and as she repeated the prayer, the executioner struck her a great blow upon the neck, which was not, however, entirely severed. Then he struck twice more.' The axeman picked up the severed head, but suddenly it slipped from his grasp, and he was left holding a dark red wig. Mary's real hair was short-clipped and grey, that of an old woman. According to another eyewitness, Robert Wynkfielde, 'Her lips stirred up and down a quarter of an hour after her head was cut off'.

1601 Robert Devereux, Earl of Essex, rides through London with 200 followers in revolt against Queen Elizabeth, forgetting her warning: 'Those who touch the sceptres of princes deserve no pity.' His revolt fails and he is beheaded seventeen days later.

---

9 February

'I have here in my hand a list of 205 that were known to the Secretary of State as being members of the Communist Party.'

1950 Today at the Women's Republican Club of Wheeling, West Virginia, an unscrupulous American senator made a startling claim. 'The State Department is infested with communists', he said. Flourishing a piece of paper, he continued: 'I have here in my hand a list of 205 that were known to the Secretary of State as being members of the Communist Party, and who nevertheless are still working and shaping the policy in the State Department.'

He was Joseph McCarthy, a 41-year-old senator who in 1946 had become the Republican candidate in Wisconsin by falsely intimating that the incumbent, Robert La Follette, had been a war profiteer. He then easily gained the Senate seat.

This was during the opening stages of the Cold War. The Soviet Union held Eastern Europe in an iron grip and groped to extend its tentacles further. In America the first anti-communist witch hunts had already begun, like the notorious 1947 House Un-American Activities Committee hearings into the motion picture industry. When the USSR detonated its first atomic bomb in 1949, American fears and suspicions were brought to a boil, many suspecting espionage (later proved correct). In 1950 a former State Department heavyweight named Alger Hiss, thought to be a Soviet mole, was convicted for perjury, and the atomic scientist Klaus Fuchs was unmasked as a Russian spy.

During his first years in the Senate, 'Joe' McCarthy had remained a minor figure, distrusted by his colleagues for his lack of principle. But now, as anti-communist hysteria swept across the nation, he began his demagogic crusade.

McCarthy's allegation that the State Department knowingly harboured communists set off a media frenzy, leading him to repeat the accusations, but each time changing the number and steadfastly refusing to show anyone the list. Only a month after he had levelled his sensational claim, the *Washington Post* cartoonist Herbert Block coined the word 'McCarthyism', denoting baseless defamation, mud-slinging and demagoguery.

As newspapers across the country reported on McCarthy's charges, the Senate set up a subcommittee to investigate. Although many were intent on bringing McCarthy to account, the publicity served only to encourage him, and he hurled false denunciations at eminent figures, including General George Marshall and Secretary of State Dean Acheson.

By 1953 McCarthy had become the most famous (and feared) 'Red-hunter' in America. With a flair for the dramatic and a penchant for wild allegations, he ruined careers, cowed opponents into silence, and made the United States an object of derision abroad. In all of the hysteria, however, few noticed that he never exposed a single communist, in or out of the US government.

In 1954 McCarthy overreached himself when, during televised hearings, he accused the US Army of protecting communist traitors. The senior counsel for the Army, a shrewd Boston lawyer named Joseph Welch, showed that McCarthy was nothing but an arrogant bully. When McCarthy attacked one of Welch's young law partners, Welch interrupted, asking, 'Have you no sense of decency, sir?'

The hearings destroyed McCarthy's credibility, and public figures such as journalist Edward R. Murrow attacked his use of intimidation and lies. One courageous senator claimed: 'Were he in the pay of the Communists he could not have done a better job for them.'

On 2 December 1954 the Senate formally censured him, and McCarthy, shunned by his colleagues and deserted by the media, retreated into drink and self-pity. On 2 May 1957 he died of alcoholism in the Bethesda Naval Hospital, still only 48.

The final irony is that, since the collapse of the Soviet Union, evidence has come to light confirming the penetration of the American government by communist agents. But, as William Bennett, the Secretary of Education under Ronald Reagan, wrote: 'McCarthy addressed a real problem: disloyal elements within the US government. But his approach to this real problem was to cause untold grief to the country he claimed to love … Worst of all, McCarthy besmirched the honourable cause of anti-communism. He discredited legitimate efforts to counter Soviet subversion of American institutions.'

1450 As Agnès Sorel, official mistress of King Charles VII, lies dying, she laments the human condition: '*C'est peu de chose, et orde et fétide, de nostre fragilité.*' ('It's a trifling thing, just filth, foulness and frailty.')

---

10 February

'*I mak sikker.*'

1306 Today a murder in a small church cleared the path for Robert the Bruce to take the throne of Scotland.

In 1296 England's Edward I had defeated the Scots at Dunbar and exiled its king, John Balliol. Now two of Scotland's most powerful nobles, Robert the Bruce, Earl of Carrick, and John the Red Comyn, were waiting for Balliol to resume power. But Balliol, held in Castle Gaillard in Normandy, was falling into blindness and would never return.

The Red Comyn came from Scotland's most important family and was related to Balliol. His rival, Robert the Bruce, also had a claim to the crown, as a fourth great-grandson of King David, who had reigned more than half a century before.

Bruce had a chequered history of fighting both for and against the English. But now, with power almost within his grasp, he had become a fervent Scot. Perhaps his commitment stemmed from an incident after one of the battles that he had helped England to win. As he sat down to eat with his hands still stained with the blood of the Scots he had slain, an English soldier remarked: 'Look at the Scotchman eating his own blood.' Filled with shame, he resolved to fight only for the Scots.

To gain Scotland's throne, however, Bruce needed to defeat the Red Comyn. In 1299 Bruce, Bishop Lamberton, and the Red Comyn had been elected guardians for Scotland, but during the meeting, Comyn 'leaped on Robert Bruce, Earl of Carrick, and took him by the throat'. Only the intervention of others stopped the scuffle.

Despite this animosity, Bruce realised that he could not overthrow the English on his own and secretly offered Comyn a bargain: 'Give me your lands, and I will help you to win the crown for yourself; or take my lands, and help to make me king.' Comyn agreed to take Bruce's estates and to help him to the Scottish throne.

On this Thursday in 1306, something brought the two men together at a place of sanctuary, the Greyfriars Church in Dumfries. Did they meet to finalise their agreement, did Bruce suspect Comyn of treachery, or was Bruce laying a trap for his foe? We do not know.

Leaving their swords outside, the two men moved to the church's high altar to talk in private. Soon a quarrel broke out, and Comyn shouted 'You lie!' Bruce instantly drew his dagger and plunged it into Comyn, who fell to the floor, his life blood draining away.

The shouts of horrified monks sent Bruce and his supporters running from the church, where his ally Roger de Kirkpatrick was waiting. 'I must be off, for I doubt I have slain the Red Comyn', shouted Bruce. 'You doubt?' Kirkpatrick answered. 'I mak sikker.' ('I make sure.') He dashed back into the church and finished Comyn off with his own dagger.

Outside the church a bloody running sword fight broke out, but Bruce and Kirkpatrick leapt onto their horses and fled.

Six weeks later Bruce was crowned King of Scotland, but his troubles were far from over. In June, King Edward utterly crushed his army at Methven, and Bruce fled into hiding. He had been reduced to a hunted fugitive within his own kingdom, his castles captured and his Scottish enemies swearing to avenge the Red Comyn's murder.

In May of 1307, however, Bruce routed an English force at Loudoun Hill and began a highly successful guerrilla war against the English, while simultaneously defeating his Scottish foes.

On 7 July 1307 Edward died, but his son Edward II carried on the war. Finally, in 1314, Bruce destroyed the younger Edward's army at Bannockburn, which gave substance to the Scots' claim of independence and to Bruce's leadership of his nation. It did not end the fighting, which dragged on until 1328, when Edward III signed the Treaty of Northampton, the main clause of which read: 'Scotland shall remain to Robert, King of Scots, free and undivided from England, without any subjection, servitude, claim or demand whatsoever.'

1741 At the Battle of Mollwitz, when the Austrians start to take the upper hand, Prussian Field Marshal Kurt Christoph von Schwerin is asked if his men should fall back; he replies: 'We'll retreat over the bodies of our enemies.' He won the battle.

11 February

'I never lose. Either I win or I learn.'

1990 Today Nelson Mandela stepped out of prison a free man. Four years later he was elected president of the country that had incarcerated him for 27 years, and his house at the prison was declared a national monument.

Originally named Rolihlahla, Mandela was born into a royal family of the Thembu tribe in South Africa's Eastern Cape in 1918. He attended a local missionary school, about which he later wrote: 'On the first day of school my teacher, Miss Mdingane, gave each of us an English name … Miss Mdingane told me that my new name was Nelson. Why this particular name I have no idea.'

After school, where he excelled in boxing and athletics as well as his studies, he entered the blacks-only University of Fort Hare, but he was suspended for joining a protest against the quality of the food. Returning home, he discovered his family had arranged a marriage for him, and to escape it, he fled to Johannesburg where he took up odd jobs, completed his law degree and joined the African National Congress (ANC).

There had long been a huge legal, social and economic gulf between blacks and whites in South Africa, but apartheid became official government policy after the National Party came to power in 1948. Mandela became increasingly involved in fighting racial injustices and was increasingly punished. But, as he famously said: 'I never lose. Either I win or I learn.'

Initially Mandela favoured peaceful protest, but that changed after 69 people were killed when police opened fire on black demonstrators at Sharpeville in 1960. He became one of the founders of the clandestine Umkhonto we Sizwe (Spear of the Nation), the military wing of the ANC, and now encouraged blacks to sabotage the apartheid regime. He went underground to evade capture and for a while lived in Rivonia masquerading as a gardener and cook, occasionally disguising himself as a chauffeur to travel around the country. In 1962 he went to Algeria for training in sabotage and guerrilla warfare. On his return, however, he was captured at a roadblock and jailed.

While still in prison, in 1963 Mandela and twelve others were tried for sabotage, treason, and conspiracy to foment revolution. In defence, Mandela justified sabotage and guerrilla warfare against the repressive apartheid regime, concluding: 'I have fought against white domination, and I have fought against black domination. I have cherished the ideal of a democratic and free society in which all persons will live together in harmony and with equal opportunities. It is an ideal which I hope to live for. But if needs be, it is an ideal for which I am prepared to die.'

On 12 June 1964, Mandela was sentenced to life behind bars, narrowly escaping the death penalty. But now he was becoming a symbol of black South Africans' fight for justice and his imprisonment a *cause célèbre* around the world. He was held in a small cell without a bed or plumbing and forced to work in a quarry at Robben Island, where he was held for eighteen years. He was then moved to Pollsmoor Prison and finally to Victor Verster Prison, a minimum-security facility from which he was finally released on orders from South African president F.W. de Klerk.

Despite his incarceration, Mandela emerged without rancour, later writing: 'As I walked out the door toward the gate that would lead to my freedom, I knew if I didn't leave my bitterness and hatred behind, I'd still be in prison.' He was determined to work with his former oppressors to create a free South Africa – later he would even invite to dinner Percy Yutar, the prosecutor who had demanded the death penalty during Mandela's trial.

During the next four years Mandela and de Klerk worked together to find a peaceful end to apartheid, work for which they were jointly awarded the Nobel Peace Prize in 1993. The next year the ANC won the country's first fully free election and on 10 May Mandela became president of what Archbishop Desmond Tutu called 'the rainbow nation'.

1851 Benjamin Disraeli in a speech in the House of Commons: 'Justice is truth in action.'

12 February

'The crown is not my right and pleases me not.'

1554 Today in the Tower of London a beautiful sixteen-year-old girl was beheaded for treason. She was Lady Jane Grey, the granddaughter of Henry VIII's sister. She was a pawn manipulated by her weak but ambitious father and her power-hungry and devious father-in-law, the Duke of Northumberland, because they thought she should be – and could be – queen.

By early 1553 it was clear that Jane's cousin, the sickly fifteen-year-old Edward VI, could not long survive. A firm Protestant, he feared his half-sister Mary's morbid Catholicism and was determined to prevent her from succeeding him. Northumberland and his allies persuaded the dying boy-king that if he put Mary aside he must do the same with his other half-sister, Elizabeth, even though she was Protestant. This left Lady Jane: a devout Protestant with Tudor blood in her veins. On 21 June Edward named her as his heir.

Edward died on 6 July, and the next day Northumberland and his allies gathered before Lady Jane to recognise her as queen. To their astonishment, Jane was aghast. 'The crown is not my right and pleases me not', she said. 'The Lady Mary is the rightful heir.'

Despite Jane's reluctance, on 10 July Northumberland and his followers proclaimed her queen, while Mary Tudor fled to Norfolk. But it was immediately clear that the country would not support this substitution – Mary was Edward's sister and the legitimate daughter of Henry VIII. Jane's support soon withered away, and she was easily persuaded to abandon her 'reign' after a mere nine days. She and her father were incarcerated in the Tower of London, but he was soon pardoned.

On 1 October Mary Tudor was crowned in Westminster Abbey. Now 37, she began the search for a suitable husband. A Parliamentary delegation begged her to choose an Englishman, or at least a Protestant, but Mary was resolved to restore Catholic supremacy and insisted on Philip II of Spain, eleven years her junior but another fanatical Catholic. It was a fatal choice – for Lady Jane Grey.

On 3 February 1554, an aristocratic soldier named Thomas Wyatt, who had seen the Spanish Inquisition at first hand while fighting on the Continent, gathered 3,000 rebels, including Lady Jane's father, and advanced on London to depose Queen Mary and eliminate the possibility of Philip II becoming king. London's citizens, however, bolted their doors and refused to join the uprising, and Wyatt's plot collapsed.

Princess Elizabeth was imprisoned in the Tower but quickly released. Although Lady Jane had nothing to do with the rebellion, Mary condemned her to death, believing that she could always be a focus for revolt, especially since her father had joined Wyatt's attempted coup.

On 12 February Jane watched from her window in the Tower as first Northumberland was led to the block, and then her young husband Guildford. One hour later she was taken to the scaffold. Bravely and willingly she went; five days earlier she had written to her father: 'Yet can I patiently take it, that I yield God more hearty thanks for shortening my woeful days.'

She recited the 51st Psalm and then asked the executioner, 'I pray you dispatch me quickly'. She then blindfolded herself but lost her composure as she could not find the block. 'What shall I do? Where is it?' she asked. The Tower's Deputy Lieutenant gently guided the floundering girl. Her last words were 'Lord, into thy hands I commend my spirit!' The executioner decapitated her with a single blow.

Lady Jane was the third Tudor woman beheaded, after Anne Boleyn and Katherine Howard. There would be a fourth yet to come, Mary, Queen of Scots.

1789 As American Revolutionary War general Ethan Allen lies dying, a clergyman hoping for a few last words of piety whispers: 'The angels are waiting for you, General Allen.' The belligerent Allen responds: 'They are, are they? Well, God damn 'em, let 'em wait!' But a few minutes later he is dead.

---

13 February

'Few, if any, ladies now at court would henceforth aspire to such an honour.'

1542 When King Henry VIII sent his fifth bride Catherine Howard to the block today, his rage was that of the ridiculous old cuckold, as she had betrayed him to acquire that which he could rarely now provide.

Only nineteen months earlier it had been a June and December wedding when Henry, already 49, took seventeen-year-old Catherine to the altar at Oatlands Palace. The king was enamoured, calling her his 'rose without a thorn', but Catherine may have been revolted – with a 52-inch waist, he was grossly overweight, with a suppurating ulcer on his leg, the result of a riding accident that had never properly healed.

Catherine had first come to Henry's notice as a maid of honour for his previous wife, Anne of Cleves. Henry had married Anne in January 1540 but had found her repulsive and was soon pursuing Catherine, who was prettier and sexier than his queen. Just six months after his wedding, he divorced Anne, having never consummated the marriage. He then dashed off to marry Catherine eighteen days later.

Catherine had first-hand knowledge of the perils of the job. Her first cousin was Anne Boleyn, who had lost her head only four years earlier. Furthermore, on the very day that Catherine married Henry, Thomas Cromwell, for nine years Henry's closest advisor, was beheaded for treason, in reality for pushing the king into his doomed marriage to Anne of Cleves.

Before coming to court Catherine had led an adventurous life. At thirteen she had embarked on an affair with her music teacher, Henry Manox, and two years later she took up with her cousin Francis Dereham.

Shortly after her marriage to Henry, Catherine noticed a handsome 26-year-old courtier named Thomas Culpeper with whom she began an affair. Their late-night meetings were arranged by Catherine's lady-in-waiting, Lady Rochford, who also must have understood the danger – she was Anne Boleyn's sister-in-law.

To make matters worse, the insouciant queen made her former lover Francis Dereham her private secretary, although most historians doubt they resumed their liaison.

Soon, rumours of Catherine's adventures reached the ear of the Archbishop of Canterbury, Thomas Cranmer, who chose All Saints' Day to slip a message to Henry during Mass that described her crimes. The king immediately ordered an investigation.

During his inquest, Cranmer not only confirmed Catherine's pre-marital affair with Dereham but also discovered a suggestive letter from Catherine to Culpeper in which she called him 'my little, sweet fool'. According to historian Lacey Baldwin Smith: 'When Henry stood before his council listening to the story of his wife's infidelities, the tears trickled down his cheeks as the illusions and obsessions of his life shattered around him. The king could never forgive Catherine for what she had taken from him – the image of youth.'

Catherine was stripped of her title as queen, formally indicted for leading an 'abominable, base, carnal, voluptuous and vicious life' and imprisoned in Syon Abbey. Meanwhile Culpeper and Dereham were arraigned for high treason. Culpeper was decapitated and Dereham hanged, drawn and quartered, their severed heads placed on spikes on top of London Bridge.

The next February Parliament passed an Act of Attainder that made it treason for a woman whose previous life had been unchaste to wed the king. Upon learning of this new law, the Imperial ambassador Eustace Chapuys summed up the situation: 'Few, if any, ladies now at court would henceforth aspire to such an honour.' Catherine was found guilty of adultery and sentenced to death.

At seven this morning at the Tower of London a large crowd gathered around the black-clad scaffold, which stood on the same spot as that used for Anne Boleyn. Catherine was beheaded with a single stroke of the executioner's axe.

Next, an addled Lady Rochford was brought to the block now soaked in Catherine's blood. She had suffered a nervous breakdown so severe that the king had been forced to push a bill through Parliament allowing the execution of the medically insane for the first time in English history.

1883 On hearing that Wagner has died, Johannes Brahms stops a choral rehearsal with the comment: 'A master is dead. Today we sing no more.' *
1945 The Dresden bombing begins that will kill 25,000 Germans, mostly civilians, and wound many more. British Air Chief Marshal 'Bomber' Harris justifies indiscriminate bombing: 'When you destroy a fighter factory it takes the Germans six weeks to replace it. When I kill a workman it takes 21 years to replace him.'

---

14 February

'Ambition leads me not only farther than any other man has been before me, but as far as I think it possible for man to go.'

1779 Two and a half centuries earlier Ferdinand Magellan had been caught up in a minor skirmish with a local tribe on the beach of the tiny island of Mactan in the Philippines. Overwhelmed, he had tried to cover the retreat of his men, but the natives cut him down with bamboo spears and poison arrows. Today Captain James Cook would suffer a similar fate, slain by the tribesmen of Hawaii.

Cook made three historic voyages of discovery. First, in 1768 when he was still a lieutenant, he led an expedition to Tahiti. By the time he returned to England three years later he had explored the coasts of New Zealand and Australia and sailed around the globe. He set sail again in 1772 to the South Pacific, a voyage in which he discovered New Caledonia and explored 'the Great Southern Land' (the Antarctic). While making his way among the dangerous icebergs, he noted in his journal that 'Ambition leads me not only farther than any other man has been before me, but as far as I think it possible for man to go'.

With this spirit of ambitious adventure driving him on, he set sail on his third voyage in 1776, this time as commander of two ships, HMS *Resolution* and *Discovery*. On 18 January 1778 he reached what we now call the Hawaiian Islands, probably the first European ever to visit them. As a gesture to his superiors, he named the archipelago the Sandwich Islands after the First Lord of the Admiralty, John Montagu, 4th Earl of Sandwich (who is much better remembered today for supposedly inventing the sandwich).

Initially the Hawaiians treated Cook and his crew as gods, but when one of the crew died, they realised that these strange white men were simply human. On the night of 13 February 1779 some Hawaiians stole one of Cook's longboats. Normally Cook would have taken hostages among the natives until the stolen item was returned. Today, however, he made the fatal error of choosing Kalani'ōpu'u, the island's chief, for his prisoner.

Accompanied by some of his ship's marines, Cook went to the royal enclosure where Kalani'ōpu'u was sleeping. Holding the chief by the arm, Cook led him from the town toward the beach near his anchored ship. It was only when his wife began to beg him to remain that Kalani'ōpu'u realised that he was not being invited aboard Cook's ship but forced. His response was simply to sit down in the sand and refuse to budge.

By now a large crowd of angry natives were gathering on the beach, and the marines began to raise their guns as Cook tried to force the chief to stand. Then a strong young sub-chief named Kana'ina approached the captain, who hit him with the flat of his sword. Kana'ina grabbed Cook, lifted him off the ground and dropped him. As he was trying to get up, another islander stabbed him in the back with a knife. The marines fired their muskets, killing several natives, including Kana'ina, but the incensed mob killed four marines.

The remaining English leaped aboard their boats and fled back to the *Resolution*. There, a young officer named William Bligh (who would later find notoriety in the mutiny on HMS *Bounty*) put a telescope to his eye and saw the Hawaiian natives dragging Cook's body back to the town and tearing it to pieces.

1797 Before Sir John Jervis attacks the Spanish at the Battle of Cape St Vincent, one of his ships' captains tells him there are 27 enemy sail-of-the-line approaching. Jarvis replies: 'Enough, sir, no more of that, sir … the die is cast, and if there are fifty sail I will go through them.' * **1929** After Al Capone's hitmen machine-gun seven members of Bugs Moran's rival gang in a Chicago warehouse during the St Valentine's Day Massacre, the mortally wounded Frank Gusenberg keeps the Mafia code of silence, telling the police: 'No one, nobody shot me.'

---

15 February

'The unexamined life is not worth living.'

399 BC The accused was 70, an ugly man with a snub nose going to fat, dressed in shabby old clothes and barefoot. His uncombed hair was receding over his high forehead, his beard unkempt. Today a jury in Athens sentenced him to death. He was the great Greek philosopher Socrates.

Socrates had long been an honoured citizen, but he claimed he was the gadfly of Athens which, like a lazy horse, needed to be awakened by his stinging. He asked awkward questions that made prominent Athenians look foolish and openly espoused the undemocratic view that the most successful government would be one in which the few people with professional competence and genuine knowledge should determine policy, rather than the masses. It was not a popular opinion in a city-state that prided itself on its democracy (albeit one in which none of the women or 80,000 slaves could vote).

In 405 BC the Athenian fleet had been utterly destroyed at Aegospotami, ending the Peloponnesian War, with oligarchic Sparta triumphant over democratic Athens. In the war's wake the so-called 'Thirty Tyrants' took over the Athenian government. Although the Tyrants ruled for only about a year before being overthrown, during their time in power they summarily executed 1,500 of Athens' most prominent democrats and drove others into exile and confiscated their property. One of the leading Tyrants was the greedy and brutal Critias, who had once been Socrates' pupil.

Once democracy had been restored, an amnesty was declared, but many Athenians blamed Socrates for inspiring the Tyrants with his teachings. Because of the amnesty, he was tried on the trumped-up charges of 'not believing the Gods of the city, introducing new Gods, and corrupting the youth'.

Socrates' trial was held in the People's Court in the agora, with a mammoth jury of 500 male citizens, chosen by lot. (One was Socrates' 27-year-old student, Plato.) The jurors sat on wooden benches separated from a large crowd of spectators.

During the one-day trial Socrates addressed the jurors with an unapologetic speech. Instead of humility and contrition, he told them that he had tried to save Athens' soul, urging its citizens to lead an ethical life. 'Men of Athens', he said, 'I honour and love you, but ... while I have life and strength I shall never stop the practice and teaching of philosophy.'

It seemed that he was almost willing the jurors to send him to his death, telling them 'the unexamined life is not worth living'. By this he meant that a life lived according to the values of others, without examining what you believe and actually want out of it, is not worth having.

The jury found Socrates guilty by fewer than 30 votes. When he was asked to propose his own punishment, he waggishly suggested that the government give him free dinners for the rest of his life in recompense for the time he had spent teaching Athenians. The jurors had other views; they voted for death by drinking hemlock.

Socrates spent his final hours in a cell in the Athens jail. There his friends pleaded with him to escape, confident that they could bribe the jailer, but he refused to flout the law and thought that fleeing would indicate a fear of death, which he believed no true philosopher has.

'All of philosophy is training for death', he said, explaining that in death the soul is released from the impure body and 'only when we are dead, can we attain that which we desire and of which we claim to be lovers, namely, wisdom.'

According to Plato's description, after drinking the hemlock Socrates was told to walk around until his legs felt numb. Then he lay down and 'the numbness crept up his body until it reached his heart' (actually his respiratory muscles, causing death from oxygen deprivation). His last words were addressed to his lifelong friend Crito: 'We owe a cock to

Asclepius. Pay it and do not neglect it.' When Crito saw that Socrates' eyes were fixed, he closed his mouth and eyes.

1942 After Winston Churchill sententiously orders the British on Singapore, 'There must at this stage be no thought of saving the troops or sparing the population ... Commanders and senior officers should die with their troops ... The honour of the British Empire and of the British Army is at stake', British commander Lieutenant General Arthur Percival surrenders to the Japanese at five o'clock that afternoon.

---

16 February

'The most bold and daring act of the Age.'

1804 It should have been an action movie with Errol Flynn in the lead, but on this day it really happened on the coast of Libya. At seven in the evening under the ghostly light of a crescent moon, a small two-masted ketch that appeared to be a Maltese merchant ship sailed slowly into Tripoli harbour. When guards challenged the ship, one of the crew answered in Arabic that they had lost their anchor in a storm and had come to Tripoli to seek repairs.

The ketch drifted near the captured American 36-gun frigate, the USS *Philadelphia*, that looked forlorn and bedraggled, without a foremast and her lower yards strewn across her deck. Suddenly the ketch's captain shouted 'Board!' and 60 American sailors and marines disguised as Maltese sailors emerged from below decks armed with boarding pikes and swords and swarmed aboard *Philadelphia*. Within ten minutes the boarders had killed twenty of the Tripolitan crew who were manning the moribund *Philadelphia* and forced the others to jump overboard.

Now the attackers, after loading some of *Philadelphia*'s cannon, set the ship ablaze and then leapt back onto the ketch. As the fire swept through the warship, its overheated guns began firing willy-nilly, some into Tripoli and its shore batteries. Now the flames engulfed its rigging and tops, and when the mooring ropes gave way, the burning ship drifted onto the rocks on shore and exploded when its store of gunpowder was touched off. Despite a tardy response from Tripolitan gunboats and shore guns, the ketch weaved its way out of the harbour and made it unscathed to the open sea.

This nifty bit of derring-do was led by a 25-year-old lieutenant in the US Navy named Stephen Decatur. During this period, corsairs from the Barbary states – Morocco, Algeria, Tunisia, and Tripolitania – were raiding ships from all nations, capturing booty, sailors and passengers and demanding tribute from each nation to leave their ships in peace.

In 1801 Yusuf Karamanli, Pasha of Tripoli, had asked for an annual payment of $225,000 (a huge amount at that time) from the United States, which had been paying tribute for several years. President Thomas Jefferson's answer was to send American warships.

In October 1803 the American frigate *Philadelphia* was chasing a pirate ship when she ran aground on a reef two miles off Tripoli harbour. The crew jettisoned anchors, water barrels and some cannon and sawed off the foremast to make the ship light enough to refloat, but all failed and they were seized by the pirates. They had been too impatient – after their capture, a high tide lifted the ship off the reef, and the Tripolitans towed her into the harbour.

The American government now feared that the corsairs would convert the powerful frigate into a pirate ship and copy its design to build more. This led to Lieutenant Decatur's spectacular night-time raid in the ketch USS *Intrepid*, with the American brig USS *Syren* providing covering fire when the *Intrepid* was dodging out of the harbour. All of Decatur's 74 men had been volunteers, and he had brought them through safely, without losing a man.

At the time British Vice Admiral Horatio Nelson was blockading the French in Toulon. On hearing of Decatur's audacious attack, he declared it 'the most bold and daring act of the Age'. Pleased as he must have been by praise from the great admiral, Decatur was no doubt even happier when, after another display of heroics during the Battle of the Gunboats six months later, he was made a captain, the youngest ever in the US Navy, before or since.

Continued American aggression paid off fifteen months later when Pasha Yusuf signed a peace treaty and traded 300 American prisoners (including the unfortunate crew of *Philadelphia*) for the 100 Tripolitans being held by the Americans for 'the sum of sixty thousand dollars, as a payment for the difference between the prisoners herein mentioned'. With typical governmental casuistry, the US agreed to pay this ransom, as distinct from tribute, which was never paid again.

1923 English archaeologist Howard Carter opens the sealed doorway of Tutankhamun's burial chamber. He later writes: 'Details of the room within emerged slowly from the mist, strange animals, statues and gold – everywhere the glint of gold.' * **1939** American comedian Leo Rosten, in a speech at a Masquers' Club dinner in Hollywood, about the guest of honour, the curmudgeonly actor W.C. Fields: 'Any man who hates dogs and babies can't be all bad.'

17 February

'We hold these truths to be self-evident,
that all men are created equal.'

1801 This opening of the Declaration of Independence is said to be the most famous line ever written by an American. The man who wrote it – Thomas Jefferson – was today elected America's third president. In one of history's greatest ironies, he owned black slaves all his life.

Before becoming president at 57, Jefferson had been a member of the Second Continental Congress, Governor of Virginia, Minister to France, Secretary of State and Vice President. But his interests ranged far beyond politics. According to the Marquis de Chastellux, he was 'a Musician, Draftsman, Surveyor, Astronomer, Natural Philosopher, Jurist, and Statesman'.

He also designed his own house at Monticello and many of the buildings at the University of Virginia, which he founded. He was an ingenious inventor, played the violin and was an oenophile, historian and farmer.

Jefferson ran for president against the incumbent John Adams and the New York banker and political fixer Aaron Burr in a bitter campaign featuring slanderous accusations in partisan newspapers. Jefferson and Burr each received 73 electoral votes, Adams coming third. Then the highly influential Alexander Hamilton, who hated Burr, persuaded the House to vote against Burr, giving Jefferson the presidency, with Burr as Vice President. (This was a factor leading to the Burr–Hamilton duel in 1804 where Burr shot Hamilton dead.)

Jefferson served two terms, championing limited federal government and an agrarian economy. 'When we get piled upon one another in large cities, as in Europe, we shall become as corrupt as Europe', he wrote. He suppressed the Barbary pirates, backed the Lewis and Clark expedition that opened the West, and purchased the Louisiana Territory from France – 828,000 square miles, more than ten times the size of Great Britain – for a bargain $15 million, doubling the size of the country.

Despite his passionate views about equality, Jefferson had less conviction about certain sub-groups. The business of women, he said, is 'to soothe and calm the mind of their husbands', and, although he philosophised against the evils of slavery, he made no effort to have it banned and kept many slaves himself.

At 28 Jefferson married Martha Wayles Skelton. A year later Martha's father died, leaving the couple 135 black slaves, including an infant named Sally Hemings, who was in fact Martha's father's daughter, that is, her half-sister.

The Jefferson marriage was happy but blighted by the death of four of their six children under seven. Then, weakened by her last pregnancy, Martha died in 1782.

Two years later Jefferson went to Paris as America's representative, taking his eldest daughter Patsy with him. Three years later he brought his other daughter Polly to France, accompanied by Sally Hemings, by then fourteen.

Sally Hemings was actually more white than black – her father was white, her mother half-white. According to the duc de La Rochefoucauld-Liancourt, all the Hemingses 'neither in point of colour nor features, shewed the least trace of their original descent'. But they were still slaves. While in Paris, Sally became Jefferson's concubine at about age sixteen. After they returned to Virginia, she bore him four children that survived, the last during his second term as president.

Jefferson had once written: 'Whenever you do a thing, act as if all the world were watching.' Apparently having a slave concubine was not included, just as blacks had not been included in 'all men are created equal'. It was only in 1998, after some extensive DNA testing, that the public learned of his second family.

By the time Jefferson died in 1826, he had already freed two of Sally's children, and the other two were freed on his death. The rest of his 250 slaves were sold with his estate, except Sally, who, valued at $50 on the slave inventory, was freed by his daughter Patsy.

Before he died, Jefferson had written his own epitaph, listing the things for which 'I wish most to be remembered' – 'author of the Declaration of American Independence, of the Statute for Virginia for Religious Freedom, and Father of the University of Virginia'. He did not mention that he had been President of the United States.

1843 After British general Charles Napier conquers the province of Sindh (now in Pakistan), he reports his triumph to headquarters with a single word: '*Peccavi!*' (Latin for 'I have sinned [Sindh]'.) * **1856** German poet Heinrich Heine dies, having remarked to a friend the previous day: '*Dieu me pardonnera. C'est son métier.*' ('God will pardon me. It is his trade.')

18 February

'*I make war on the living, not on the dead.*'

1546 The Augustinian monk Martin Luther gained enduring fame through his confrontations with the Vatican, most famously nailing 95 theses criticising the Catholic Church to a church door in Wittenberg. His attacks on papal indulgences, corruption in the Holy See, and the Pope himself – 'how openly and shamelessly the Pope and the cardinals in Rome practice sodomy', was one of his accusations – led Leo X to excommunicate him.

Leo's successor, Adrian VI, demanded that Luther be punished for heresy. After Adrian came Clement VII, Leo's Medici cousin but born illegitimate. Luther claimed that 'next to Satan there is no greater rascal than the Pope. He has plotted evil things against me … He is a Florentine bastard.' Even though Clement's successor Paul III made attempts at Church reform, Luther mocked his efforts as half-hearted and insufficient.

That should have been enough conflict for any monk, but Luther also confronted the strongly Catholic Holy Roman Emperor Charles V at the Diet of Worms in 1521. Only the emperor's refusal to withdraw the safe conduct he had promised saved Luther's skin, but he did brand him an outlaw with a price on his head. But nothing, it would seem, would stem Luther's tirades against Church corruption, for which he became a secular saint across northern Europe.

During the last thirteen years of his life, Luther was dean of theology at the University of Wittenberg. He suffered from arthritis, heart problems and digestive disorders and the emotional strain of being a fugitive. He became short-tempered and highly critical even of his closest followers, one of whom lamented: 'Hardly one of us can escape Luther's anger and his public scourging.'

In 1543 Luther published two treatises, one entitled *Against the Jews and their Lies* and the other *Vom Schem Hamphoras*, in which he equated Jews with the Devil. (Not surprisingly, four centuries later this anti-Semitic German was much quoted by Heinrich Himmler.) In 1545 he exploded again against the Church of Rome in a tract entitled *Against the Papacy established by the Devil.*

Perhaps the strain of all the years of defying rulers temporal and clerical – plus most of the Christian world – became unbearable for Luther. When the Dowager Electress of Saxony wished him many years of long life, he replied: 'Madame, rather than live another forty years I would give up my chance of Paradise.' (Luther was not always so morose, once remarking: 'When I die I want to be a ghost and pester the bishops, priests, and godless monks so that they have more trouble with a dead Luther than they could have had before with a thousand living ones.')

During a snowy winter in early 1546 Luther travelled to Eisleben. Already elderly and frail, he contracted a chill, and at about three o'clock in the morning on this day he died of a heart attack at the age of 62 in the town where he was born. He was buried in the Schlosskirche in Wittenberg, where he had nailed his theses to the door 29 years before.

The year after Luther died, Emperor Charles V crushed the rebellious Protestant princes of Germany at the Battle of Mühlberg. Afterwards he took possession of Wittenberg and stopped at the church and contemplated Luther's tomb. There, one of his lieutenants suggested that they have Luther's remains exhumed and publicly burned. Charles instantly rebuked the man, saying: 'Let him repose in peace. He has already found his judge. I make war on the living, not on the dead.'

Through his protestations and strength of belief, Luther gave the world Protestantism, as well as several centuries of religious war. But, according to legend, he also gave us a most joyful tradition, the Christmas tree. The story goes that one Christmas Eve he took a walk in a nearby forest where he was profoundly moved by the snowy fir trees shimmering in the starlight. To remind local children of the beauty of God's creation, he brought a tree indoors and decorated it with candles to simulate the stars.

1861 President of the Confederacy (the South) Jefferson Davis in his inaugural address: 'All we ask is to be left alone.'

---

19 February

*'The successful prosecution of the war requires every possible
protection against espionage and against sabotage.'*

1942 In December 1941 Japan had launched a surprise attack on the
American base at Pearl Harbor, branded by US president Franklin
Roosevelt 'a date which will live in infamy'. On this day ten weeks
later, Roosevelt issued Executive Order 9066 that read in part: 'Whereas
the successful prosecution of the war requires every possible protection
against espionage and against sabotage to national-defense material,
national-defense premises, and national-defense utilities … I hereby
authorize and direct the Secretary of War … to prescribe military areas
in such places and of such extent as he … may determine, from which
any or all persons may be excluded.' In other words, Secretary of War
Henry Stimson could now designate certain areas in the United States
as military zones and then kick out any undesirables living there.

Roosevelt's order opened the door to one of the greatest injustices
perpetrated by the United States during the war – the incarceration of
American citizens of Japanese, German or Italian ancestry in internment camps.

A month later Congress turned Roosevelt's directive into law by
passing Public Law 503. Lieutenant General John L. DeWitt, the commander responsible for coordinating the defence of the Pacific coast,
created military zones in a 50- to 60-mile-wide area up and down the
entire west coast. These were in Oregon, Washington and California –
those states closest to Japan but also those with large Japanese-American
populations. Then the US military began building ten internment
camps in remote areas in Arkansas, Arizona, Wyoming, Utah, Idaho
and inland California.

After encouraging voluntary evacuation, the Western Defense
Command started gathering up 'undesirable' west coast residents. During
the next six months, 120,000 men, women and children of Japanese
origin were moved first to assembly centres and then on to isolated,
fenced, and guarded internment camps. There they stayed for the next
two and a half years. The government made no charges against them,
but in 1944 the Supreme Court ruled that the need to protect against
espionage outweighed the rights of Americans of Japanese descent.

About 60 per cent of those locked up were American citizens,
while the others were merely residents, some of whom had lived in

the States for decades. In addition, about 5,000 German-Americans and 300 Italian-Americans were rounded up. (There were of course far more Americans of German or Italian ancestry than of Japanese, but about 95 per cent of those relocated to camps were of Japanese origin. A great majority of German-Americans and Italian-Americans had been in the US for many generations, and it was Japan of course that had attacked Pearl Harbor.)

The US was not alone in this egregious violation of civil liberties; Canada relocated 21,000 Japanese residents from its west coast, and several South American countries – Peru, Brazil, Chile and Argentina – sent 2,500 people of Japanese descent to the US for internment.

Although the war against Japan lasted until August 1945, in December 1944 Roosevelt suspended Executive Order 9066, and, effective on 2 January 1945, evacuees could start returning home. Many, however, had lost their homes, businesses, property, and savings. Finally, in 1988 President Ronald Reagan issued tax-free payments of $20,000 to each surviving evacuee plus a formal apology from the American government.

In spite of the internment, during the war almost 33,000 Japanese-Americans served in the army, and of the ten American citizens convicted of spying for Japan, not one was of Japanese ancestry.

---

197 AD Before defeating the usurper Clodius Albinus in the Battle of Lugdunum (Lyon), Roman Emperor Septimius Severus gives an early example of fake news by telling his troops: 'Who does not know Albinus' effeminate nature? Who does not know that his way of life has prepared him more for the chorus than for the battlefield?'

---

20 February

'In the end, there was just a tiny insignificant pop.'

1944 On this cold Sunday, resistance fighters blew up the ferry SF *Hydro* on Lake Tinn in western Norway. Sunk with the ship were 40 steel drums of irreplaceable heavy water that Nazi Germany urgently needed to build an atomic bomb. This was the fifth attempt to deny the Germans the heavy water from the nearby Vemork power plant – the only heavy water plant in occupied Europe.

The first operation was mounted by the French Deuxième Bureau (military intelligence) two months before Germany invaded Norway in February 1940. French agents flew in under false passports, bought the Vemork plant's supply of heavy water and flew back out again with canisters loaded with the entire stock of 185 kilos. But the factory was still capable of producing more, and on 9 April the Wehrmacht marched into Norway, giving Hitler control.

Germany already had expertise in nuclear fission – two German scientists, Otto Hahn and Fritz Strassmann, had discovered it in 1938. In February 1942, the Norwegian resistance alerted the Allies that the Nazis were now trying to develop a nuclear bomb.

In November the British mounted the second attempt to halt the Vemork heavy water production: gliders would land 34 British demolition experts, who, guided by Norwegian scouts, would blow up the factory. They took off from Scotland, but two tow planes and three gliders crashed over occupied Norway, killing or injuring twenty of the attackers, while all the others were captured – and shot.

The Vemork plant was built on a rocky promontory 1,000 feet above a river, accessible only by a single bridge. The Germans now ramped up their defences, stretching cables across the valley against air attacks and positioning a machine-gun to guard the bridge.

The third attempt was in February 1943, when eleven Norwegian commandos flew in from Scotland, parachuted onto a plateau 35 miles from Vemork, skied across country, descended into a ravine, crossed an icy river and, just after midnight, followed an unguarded railroad track into the plant. Helped by an accomplice inside, they placed explosive charges and fled. One of the saboteurs, Knut Haukelid, later wrote: 'In the end, there was just a tiny insignificant pop … Sure, the windows broke, and there was a flash of light in the night, but it wasn't much.'

But it was – they had destroyed the entire inventory of heavy water as well as the electrolysis chambers used to make it. All the commandos escaped; five skied 250 miles to neutral Sweden while the others joined the Norwegian resistance.

The raid temporarily stopped production of heavy water, but by April the Germans had rebuilt the facilities. The fourth attack came in November when 143 American B-17 bombers dropped several tons of bombs, but most missed the factory, while killing 21 civilians. Despite the raid's disappointing results, the Germans were convinced that future air attacks might demolish the plant and decided to move remaining stocks to Germany. The first step was to transport the heavy water across Lake Tinn by the SF *Hydro* ferry.

When Knut Haukelid, one of the Norwegian commandos from the third attempt, learned of the enemy's plan, he recruited two resistance fighters to make a fifth attempt to stop the Germans. On the evening of 19 February 1944, the three saboteurs cut through a fence to break into the quay and slipped aboard the ferry. There they hid eight kilos of explosives in the hold, with two alarm-clock fuses that were set to sink the ship at the deepest part of the lake, but close enough to shore to allow any survivors a hope of rescue.

The next morning the SF *Hydro* peacefully left the pontoon dock and began crossing the lake. After a few minutes the charges exploded, and the ferry sank to the bottom to a depth of 1,400 feet. Fourteen Norwegian crew and passengers and four German soldiers were killed, while 29 others were rescued by farmers from across the lake. By their courageous final act of sabotage the Norwegian resistance had finally achieved their mission: Nazi Germany would never develop the atomic bomb.

1962 American astronaut John Glenn goes into orbit; he later reflects: 'As I hurtled through space, one thought kept crossing my mind – every part of this rocket was supplied by the lowest bidder.'

---

21 February

*'No! You should not have offered my son
such a dangerous responsibility.'*

1598 & 1613 Russia's Time of Troubles began on this date in 1598, when the Zemsky Sobor (National Assembly) elected the cold and ruthless Boris Godunov as tsar. He was beset by pretenders seeking power, and during his reign Russia suffered a devastating famine that killed a third of the population. After Godunov's death in 1604, his sixteen-year-old son was proclaimed tsar, but he was strangled two months later. More pretenders claimed the throne, civil uprisings broke out and the Polish army invaded, briefly even occupying Moscow.

Desperate for a single strong hand to restore order and evict the Poles, on this day exactly fifteen years after Godunov's election, the Zemsky Sobor chose an unlikely candidate as the new tsar, sixteen-year-old Michael (Mikhail) Romanov.

Michael was a cousin of the last legitimate tsar before Boris Godunov and the son of a leading aristocrat or *boyar*, but his father had been forced to become a monk, which disqualified him from ever becoming tsar. And, although his father had become the Patriarch of Moscow (i.e. head of the Russian Orthodox Church), he was now in Polish captivity. Michael's mother, who had been compelled to become a nun, had taken her son to the Ipatiev monastery on the Volga River about 200 miles north-east of Moscow.

Having elected Michael, the Zemsky Sobor now had to persuade him to accept the crown. A group of *boyars* set off for the monastery, but when they arrived, the religious and unworldly Michael burst into tears of fear and despair at the prospect of becoming tsar. His mother was equally afraid. 'No!' she cried out, 'you should not have offered my son such a dangerous responsibility.'

At length, however, the *boyars'* pleas and prayers brought Michael and his mother around, and he became Russia's first Romanov tsar.

Tsar Michael was barely literate, sickly, unintelligent and pious. But because the *boyars* knew the country needed an honoured leader, they presented him to the public as a god-like figure – no one was allowed to look him in the eye and his subjects had to prostrate themselves before him. In reality he was weak – when his father returned from exile in 1618, Michael tamely allowed him take over most of the reins of power. But Michael (or his advisors) could also be ruthless. One rebel Cossack leader was captured with his wife and her four-year-old son. The Cossack was impaled in Red Square, his wife starved to death and her son hanged from the Kremlin walls.

Michael died in July of 1645 after a reign of 32 years, longer than any other tsar except Peter the Great (43 years) and Catherine the Great (34 years). The Romanovs continued to rule until the forced abdication (and then murder) of Nicholas II in 1918. In all, the dynasty produced nineteen monarchs (or twenty if you include Ivan VI, who reigned for a year when he was two years old), of whom four were women. The Romanovs ruled Russia for 304 years and 22 days.

1965 Two days after telling his followers, 'It is a time for martyrs now, and if I am to be one, it will be for the cause of brotherhood', firebrand black-rights activist Malcolm X is gunned down before 400 people in a New York auditorium by three killers from the rival activist group, Nation of Islam.

22 February

'Long live freedom!'

1943 At five o'clock this afternoon, a brother and sister who had defied the Nazis were guillotined at Stadelheim Prison in Munich.

In May 1942, twenty-year-old Sophie Scholl enrolled at Munich University, where her elder brother Hans was studying medicine. Both had once belonged to the Hitler Youth, but by now they were so disillusioned that they joined a clandestine resistance cell of about fifteen members, mostly students. They adopted the name 'The White Rose', a symbol of innocence in the face of evil.

In June the conspirators wrote their first leaflet attacking the regime, which would be secretly handed to other students or mailed to carefully chosen professors, intellectuals, libraries and doctors around the country. It asked: 'Who among us has any conception of the dimensions of shame that will befall us and our children when one day the veil has fallen from our eyes and the most horrible of crimes – crimes that infinitely outdistance every human measure – reach the light of day?' The message was signed 'The White Rose'.

The White Rose supporters' abhorrence of Hitler's government was intensified that summer when several medical student members were sent to the Eastern front for training. There they witnessed atrocities against Russian prisoners and the civilian population, including a group of naked Jews being shot in a pit.

Now five more leaflets followed, each urging Germans to recognise the evil in their midst. 'The German people slumber on in dull, stupid sleep and encourage the fascist criminals', accused the second leaflet. The fourth concluded: 'We are your bad conscience. The White Rose will not leave you in peace!' The fifth demanded 'freedom of speech, freedom of religion and protection of the individual citizen from the arbitrary action of criminal dictator-states'.

In February 1943, after the German army's catastrophic defeat at Stalingrad, the White Rose issued a sixth leaflet that claimed 'the day of reckoning [has come for] the most contemptible tyrant our people has ever endured ... The dead of Stalingrad command us!' Meanwhile Hans Scholl and another conspirator painted university walls: 'Hitler the slaughterer of the masses! Down with Hitler!'

So far, the Gestapo had failed to identify the agitators, but on 18 February a janitor saw Hans and Sophie distributing leaflets in empty university classrooms for the students to find, and called the police. They were immediately turned over to the Gestapo, while other members of the cell were rounded up.

Three days later Sophie, Hans and a confederate, Christoph Probst, were tried before the notorious Nazi judge Roland Freisler, president of Germany's Volksgerichtshof, an extra-judicial court with jurisdiction over political offences such as 'defeatism'. So keen was he to punish the offenders that he had come from Berlin to try the case himself.

None of the accused denied their guilt. During the trial, Sophie challenged Freisler: 'You know as well as we do that the war is lost. Why are you so cowardly that you won't admit it?'

On the trial's second day Freisler found the Scholls and Probst guilty of treason and sentenced them to death. Sophie told the judge: 'I did the best that I could for my country. I therefore do not regret my conduct and will bear the consequences.'

At five o'clock that same afternoon the condemned were led to the guillotine. According to her cellmate, Sophie's last words were: 'It is such a splendid sunny day, and I have to go … But what does my death matter if by our acts thousands are warned and alerted?' Before he died, Hans told his executioners: 'Your heads will fall as well.' Just before the blade swished down he shouted: 'Long live freedom!' (*'Es lebe die Freiheit!'*)

Two more White Rose trials sentenced most of the other members either to immediate death by execution or slow death in concentration camps. But the White Rose's sixth leaflet was smuggled out of Germany, and in July British planes dropped copies of it, retitled *The Manifesto of the Students of Munich*, in cities all over Germany. Two years later the malignant Judge Freisler was crushed to death by a falling column when American bombers attacked Berlin.

1946 American Moscow-based diplomat George Kennan sends the 5,500-word 'Long Telegram' to Secretary of State James Byrnes that posits that at the 'bottom of the Kremlin's neurotic view of world affairs is the traditional and instinctive Russian sense of insecurity', that the Soviet leadership is 'impervious to the logic of reason … [and] highly sensitive to the logic of force', and that Marxist-Leninist doctrine 'is the justification for the Soviet Union's instinctive fear of the outside world, for the dictatorship without which they did not know how to rule … the fig leaf of their moral and intellectual respectability'. Kennan's analysis leads to the successful American policy of 'containment' of the Soviet Union.

23 February

'The script was very neat and legible, not at all difficult to follow – your grace would be able to read it without effort, and indeed without glasses.'

1455 Today in Germany Johannes Gutenberg published his Bible, the first major book printed in Europe from movable type. According to the American Library of Congress: 'Gutenberg's invention of the mechanical printing press made it possible for the accumulated knowledge of the human race to become the common property of every person who knew how to read – an immense forward step in the emancipation of the human mind.'

Before Gutenberg's printing press, a few European books were produced by woodblock printing, a process that the Chinese had been using since at least 868 AD, when the earliest printed book, known as the 'Diamond Sutra', first appeared. But woodblock printing is onerously labour-intensive, as the block is painstakingly hand-carved in relief in a mirror-image of the desired end result. Furthermore, inks used in woodblock printing tend to 'bleed' on paper, making it difficult to print fine details – such as letters. But in 15th-century Europe, the vast majority of books were still copied by hand, a lengthy and laborious process. It has been estimated that hand-copying Gutenberg's 1,286-page Bible would take about two years, but even with his relatively primitive press, Gutenberg produced 180 copies in less than three.

Gutenberg also developed an oil-based varnish to replace the water-based inks then in use, and cast his letters from moulds rather than carving them by hand. This was a critically important innovation, given the number of letters, both upper- and lower-case, needed to print a single page, let alone the full text. It took Gutenberg's workers two years to cast the needed letters.

At the time, most important books were made on parchment, but Gutenberg used paper for the most practical of reasons. The skin from one goat or sheep yields only about eight parchment pages. Thus you would need 159 sheepskins for a single Bible, or about 29,000 for the full run of 180 copies.

Gutenberg lived and worked in Mainz, in the midst of a wine-growing region. In constructing his printing press, he looked to the familiar wine press. According to historian Neil MacGregor: 'The screw could be turned to exert very strong but equal pressure across the page, and this was what allowed him to print all the different lines with such regularity and clarity.'

Gutenberg displayed his Bibles at the 1455 Frankfurt Book Fair, where they were seen by Enea Silvio Piccolomini, who one day would reign as Pope Pius II. After the fair Piccolomini wrote to Cardinal Carvajal: 'All that has been written to me about that marvellous man seen at Frankfurt is true. I have not seen complete Bibles but only a number of quires of various books of the Bible. The script was very neat and legible, not at all difficult to follow – your grace would be able to read it without effort, and indeed without glasses.'

In the mid-1400s there were only around 30,000 books in all of Europe, but in spite of Gutenberg's efforts to keep his technique a secret, the printing press spread rapidly; within 50 years some 2,500 European towns had acquired presses. Gutenberg's invention can be credited not only for a revolution in the production of books, but also for fostering rapid development in the sciences, arts and religion through the transmission of texts. It was, as one historian put it, 'the transition from the Middle Ages to the modern world'.

Given that Gutenberg's press is widely regarded as the most important invention of the second millennium, we know surprisingly little about the man himself. We don't know when he was born, whether he married or had children, where he is buried or even what he looked like. The numerous drawings, statues and paintings of him were all inventions of the artists who created them, as he was never portrayed in his lifetime.

1821 John Keats dies in Rome. His last request is to be placed under a tombstone bearing no name or date, only the words: 'Here lies one whose name was writ in water.'

---

24 February

'Man is descended from a hairy, tailed quadruped, probably arboreal in its habits.'

1871 Back in 1859 Charles Darwin had landed the first punch; he published *On the Origin of Species* in which he asserted that living species evolve over the course of generations. 'I have called this principle, by which each slight variation, if useful, is preserved, by the term of

Natural Selection', he wrote. Although the book elicited admiration from scientists, it caused dismay among God-fearing Christians and fury from the Church hierarchy, enraged by its denial of the story of Genesis and the creation of the world in seven days. But in this work Darwin focused primarily on the evolution of animals, only lightly touching on the implications for humans.

Most people in mid-19th-century Britain were doggedly conformist in their faith that God had created the world for man. Even the president of the prestigious Geological Society averred that the length of the night had been fixed by God to fit man's sleeping patterns.

Against this background, today Darwin landed his second, knock-out blow against traditional beliefs – he published *The Descent of Man, and Selection in Relation to Sex*, which filled out his theory of evolution, asserting: 'We thus learn that man is descended from a hairy, tailed quadruped, probably arboreal in its habits, and an inhabitant of the Old World.' Indeed, he wrote, 'the difference in mind between man and the higher animals, great as it is, certainly is one of degree and not of kind'. He ended the book with the claim that man 'still bears in his bodily frame the indelible stamp of his lowly origin'. The Church was hostile in the extreme, for, in positioning humans as descendent from other primates rather than created separately in God's image, the book specifically refuted the biblical account of man's origin.

In spite of his conviction that his books revealed nature's truth, Darwin always felt somewhat guilty for his heretical theory, referring to himself as 'the Devil's Chaplain'. He declined to comment publicly on his own views on a Christian God, writing to a friend: 'I feel most deeply that the whole subject is too profound for human intellect. A dog might as well speculate on the mind of Newton.'

Darwin's angst about his own ideas manifested itself in extreme poor health. As he grew older he suffered from nausea, heart palpitations and insomnia and became a semi-invalid. No specific cause was ever diagnosed, and many believe his illnesses were psychosomatic, brought on by the stress of developing ideas totally in conflict with the religious teachings with which he had been raised.

Darwin continued to write at his house in Kent, his last work the rather less controversial *The Formation of Vegetable Mould through the Action of Worms*. He died at home on 19 April 1882 at 73, a national icon who was buried in Westminster Abbey.

The publication of *The Descent of Man* not only changed our view of humankind, but it also unknowingly gave birth to a germ that half a century later would become a raging disease. In his theory of 'the survival of the fittest' (a term coined by his contemporary, Herbert Spencer), Darwin wrote: 'Because modern medicine saves "weak members" of society from death, they propagate their kind ... this must be highly injurious to the race of man ... excepting in the case of man himself, hardly any one is so ignorant as to allow his worst animals to breed.' This concept was central to Adolf Hitler's euthanasia programme.

1981 The day after machine-gun-toting Lieutenant Colonel Antonio Tejero leads 200 armed Guardia Civil officers into the Spanish Cortes, King Juan Carlos goes live on television, telling the nation: 'The Crown, symbol of the permanence and unity of the nation, will not tolerate, in any degree whatsoever, the actions or behaviour of anyone attempting through use of force to interrupt the democratic process of the Constitution.' The coup fails.

---

25 February

'The King of Heaven has ordained that, through me, you will be anointed and crowned in Reims.'

1429 The castle of Chinon still rises rugged and formidable near the Loire, as it did six centuries ago when on this day Charles VII first met a seventeen-year-old peasant girl who would save his kingdom.

Although his father, mad King Charles VI, had died seven years before, the Dauphin Charles had never been crowned because the cathedral at Reims, the traditional venue for the investiture of French kings, was in the hands of the English and their Burgundian allies. Charles reigned only in south-central France and was derisively called 'the little king of Bourges'.

But was France his country anyway? In 1420, with his father incapacitated by insanity, his dissolute mother Isabeau of Bavaria had signed the shameful Treaty of Troyes with England's Henry V that made Henry and his successors heirs to the French throne. Isabeau justified the treaty by announcing that Charles was not the king's son but the product of one of her extramarital affairs. Isabeau's daughter Catherine married Henry and gave birth to a son, another Henry. When Henry V died in August 1422, this infant became nominal King of France.

Thus Charles's hold on the crown was exceptionally fragile. Since October 1428 the English had been besieging Orléans. If it fell, nothing below the Loire would be secure. Thinking that only a miracle could save him, he had agreed to see a girl who said God had chosen her.

The girl was Jeanne Darc. (When her family was ennobled, they would change it to the more aristocratic d'Arc. In English we call her Joan of Arc.)

Since the age of twelve, Joan had been hearing the 'voices' of saints Michael, Marguerite and Catherine of Alexandria telling her 'to oust the English from all of France' and to restore Charles as the legitimate king. When she was sixteen, she travelled from her home in Domrémy to Vaucouleurs to ask the garrison commander Robert de Baudricourt to take her to Chinon to see the king. At first he refused, but, on her third attempt, after she had miraculously predicted a French defeat (the Day of the Herrings), he relented. After cropping her dark hair and donning a page's costume to disguise her from men she might encounter along the way, she left, accompanied by her brother Pierre and six men-at-arms.

Travelling mostly by night, the small band embarked on an eleven-day journey to Chinon through 300 miles of enemy territory, arriving on 23 February. Joan was greeted with scepticism by the king's bemused courtiers, and for two days Charles refused to see her. But he then orchestrated a simple test. He stood among his courtiers, clad in modest dress, and had Joan brought into the room. Although she had never seen him before, she instantly picked him out. 'Gentle Dauphin', she said. 'My name is Joan the Maid [*Jeanne la Pucelle*]; the King of Heaven has ordained that, through me, you will be anointed and crowned in Reims. Give me people so that I can raise the siege of Orléans and lead you to be anointed at Reims.'

Charles chose to believe this illiterate teenaged mystic. After she passed examinations for virginity and heresy, in one of the most improbable decisions in history, he equipped her with armour, gave her an escort with pages and a herald and sent her to join a French force near Blois. From there she marched on Orléans. By 8 May the English had abandoned their siege, turning the tide of the war, and on 17 July Charles was crowned at Reims with Joan in attendance.

Joan's triumph of course ended in tragedy; captured by the Burgundians at Compiègne, she was sold to the English in one of history's most sordid deals and burned at the stake on 30 May 1431. Charles did nothing to try to save her, even though he probably could have negotiated her release.

Charles recaptured Paris from the English in 1436 and then virtually all of France over the next twenty years, with the exception of Calais.

1723 British architect Christopher Wren dies; he is buried in St Paul's Cathedral, where beneath the great dome graven on the floor is his epitaph: '*Lector, si monumentum requiris, circumspice.*' ('Reader, if you seek his monument, look around you.')

26 February

'Five marks a week you must put aside,/
If in your own car you want to ride.'

1936 Who would have thought that Adolf Hitler was inspired by Henry Ford? In 1908, when Hitler was an impoverished art student in Vienna, Ford first began producing the Model T. A year later Hitler was broke and living in homeless shelters, just when Ford's fame was spreading around the globe. By 1913 Ford was selling half of the world's automobiles. Imagine Hitler's growing admiration when Ford's anti-Semitic rant, *The International Jew*, was translated into German in 1922 (a typical sentiment: 'The finances of the world are in the control of Jews.').

In 1924, when he was in prison for his failed Beer Hall Putsch, Hitler read Ford's autobiography, *My Life and Work*, and wrote his own, *Mein Kampf*, in which Ford was the only American mentioned. He then began dreaming of creating a Teutonic version of the Model T.

In January 1933, President Hindenburg appointed Hitler Chancellor in dire economic circumstances. In 1929, over 20 million Germans had been in work; now just 11.5 million had jobs. But, just as Franklin Roosevelt was establishing the Public Works Administration in America to build dams, hospitals and schools to revive the economy, Hitler was ordering the construction of 7,300 miles of four-lane Autobahnen. But super-highways need cars, and only one German in 50 owned one, compared to one in five in the United States. Hitler's answer was a 'people's car' or '*Volkswagen*'.

Hitler signed up noted automotive designer Ferdinand Porsche to create the Volkswagen, giving him some of his own drawings of a small, rounded vehicle that looked something like a beetle. Then, on this day in 1936, in Fallersleben, 50 miles east of Hanover, he inaugurated a new factory in which to build it.

Hitler told Porsche to design a basic car that could carry two adults and three children and cruise at 100 kilometres an hour. He specified an air-cooled engine because most people would keep it on the street during Germany's cold winters. By the end of 1937 Porsche had finished his design for a prototype '*Käfer*' ('Beetle'), as it would soon be known.

For the needed capital, Hitler raided the huge *Kraft durch Freude* ('Strength through Joy', abbreviated KdF) state-operated leisure organisation for 50 million marks. The KdF's leader Robert Ley found a novel way to pass these costs on to those who wanted a car. In a sort of hire purchase plan in reverse, Germans were invited to pay five Reichsmarks a week. When the buyer had accumulated 750 Reichsmarks, he would be entitled to a car as soon as it was built. To encourage sales, KdF ran a spirited advertising campaign centring on the catchy couplet:

> 'Five marks a week you must put aside,
> If in your own car you want to ride.'

> (*'Fünf Mark die Woche musst Du sparen,*
> *willst Du im eigenen Wagen fahren.'*)

Response was huge, as 330,000 Germans applied to buy a Volkswagen.

Sadly for the applicants, no Volkswagens were made until mid-1938, when a few were put on show and Hitler gave one to his girlfriend Eva Braun as a birthday present. But in September 1939 Hitler launched the Second World War, and production at Fallersleben was switched to *Kübelwagen* (comparable to the American Jeep) that were manufactured mostly by a slave workforce drawn from concentration camps. Not one of those 330,000 who had paid their money ever got a car.

After the war the British army took over the Volkswagen factory, which was offered to Britain's motor manufacturers, but they turned it down. An official British report found that 'the vehicle does not meet the fundamental technical requirement of a motor-car ... it is quite unattractive to the average buyer ... To build the car commercially would be a completely uneconomic enterprise.' So the Germans started churning out Beetles instead.

How proud Hitler would have been. On 17 February 1972 the Volkswagen Beetle passed Ford's Model T as the most highly produced car in history. Finally, on 30 July 2003 the last Beetle (number 21,529,464) rolled off the assembly line at Puebla, Mexico, accompanied by the celebratory sounds of a mariachi band.

1815 When Napoleon escapes from Elba, police minister Joseph Fouché predicts: 'This man has come back even crazier than when he left. His case is settled, he won't last four months!' The Battle of Waterloo was three months, 22 days later.

---

27 February

'Give us back our husbands!'

1943 The German government codenamed it *Die Fabrikaktion*, a business-like name meaning simply 'The Factory Action'. It was supposed to be just a little tidying up – the round-up of the last German Jews for deportation to extermination camps in the East.

A year earlier SS-Obergruppenführer Reinhard Heydrich had given orders for the *Endlösung* – the Final Solution – at a conference at Wannsee, and well over a million European Jews had already been massacred. Today in Berlin the Gestapo arrested some 8,000 more, including 1,800 classified as *Mischehen* – Jewish men married to women of 'pure German race' – as well as male children called *Mischlinge* (mongrels) of these mixed marriages.

At 6.00 this morning SS troops carrying whips stormed into factories across Berlin shouting 'All Jews out!' Other Jews were picked up as they walked to work or as they lined up for their bus passes. As bystanders looked the other way or clapped their hands in approval, trucks packed with Jews drove through the streets of Berlin, delivering their catch to an impromptu detention centre at Rosenstrasse 2–4 in central Berlin that once was a Jewish community building. But now something unparalleled in Nazi Germany was about to take place; the prisoners' desperate wives would form a public protest, calling for the release of their husbands.

The first evening about two hundred women gathered in Rosenstrasse, a crowd that swelled each day, despite the glacial cold. A jeep with four men from the Waffen-SS arrived and ordered them to go home, but they declared that they would not leave until their husbands had been freed. As the bemused soldiers looked on, the women marched back and forth in front of the building chanting in chorus, 'Give us back our husbands! Give us back our husbands!' The detention centre guards called the Berlin police for reinforcements as the crowd continued to grow, but even the police had no effect.

On 1 March a bombing raid by the Royal Air Force forced the women to leave the street, but the Berlin authorities, expecting the protests to stop, were stunned when the crowd returned even larger than before. So it continued, with the women refusing to be cowed.

Finally on 5 March the SS sent in trucks with machine-gun-toting troops. The gunners trained their weapons on the crowd and shouted 'Clear the streets or we'll shoot!' – but even then the women refused to budge, and it was the soldiers who backed down.

At the time the sinister Joseph Goebbels was Gauleiter of Berlin, but he realised that there was no way he could order the machine-gunning of thousands of unarmed women in the centre of the capital and keep the massacre secret. He also feared that if news of the slaughter got out, it would severely damage German morale and undermine the *Volksgemeinschaft* (people's community), that mystical unity to which all Germans supposedly belonged. And the timing couldn't have been worse – the surrender of the Sixth Army at Stalingrad just a month before had already provoked pessimism and gloom throughout the Fatherland.

On 6 March Goebbels ordered all of the prisoners held at Rosenstrasse 2–4 released, recording in his diary: 'I am giving the SD the order not to continue the Jewish evacuation at such a critical time. We would rather think about it for a few more weeks; then we can carry it all the more thoroughly.'

That day the Rosenstrasse Jewish detainees were freed and allowed to join their families. But, fearful of more protests, Goebbels never did reinstate the order. Although the German police returned the next day to pick up the *Mischehen* and teenage boys, and the Gestapo sent them to forced-labour camps in Berlin and elsewhere in the Reich, all those imprisoned in Rosenstrasse survived the Holocaust.

---

274 AD The three reigning Roman emperors, Theodosius, Gratian and Valentinian II, issue the Edict of Thessalonica that sets Catholic Christians above others such as Arians: 'Let us believe in the one deity of the Father, the Son and the Holy Spirit, in equal majesty and in a holy Trinity. We authorise the followers of this law to assume the title of Catholic Christians; but as for the others, since, in our judgement they are foolish madmen, we decree that they shall be branded with the ignominious name of heretic.'

28 February

*'Many Germans feel guilty about the war. But they
don't explain the real guilt we share – that we lost.'*

1944 Ever since the Greek King Leonidas led his men to certain death
at Thermopylae in 480 BC, innumerable warriors have deliberately laid
down their lives for their country. In the Second World War we think first
of Japanese Kamikaze pilots. Far less known is that the Germans almost
beat them to it – on the initiative of a woman, the aviatrix Hanna Reitsch.

Today in Hitler's outpost at Berchtesgaden in the Bavarian Alps,
Reitsch, a diminutive blonde of 31, proposed to the Führer the creation
of a corps of pilots 'who were ready to sacrifice themselves in the conviction that only by this means could their country be saved'. Although
Hitler was lukewarm about the idea, a suicide squadron was formed
and the V-1 guided missile (the 'doodlebug') was adapted to be flown
by a pilot. Hanna Reitsch became the pilots' instructor.

Ultimately, however, no suicide flights ever took place because high-
ranking Nazis thought that the idea was 'un-German'. As Reitsch recorded
in her post-war memoirs, 'the decisive moment had been missed'.

Hanna Reitsch, a fervent backer of Hitler, was a flyer extraordinaire
who had been a glider pilot, a stunt flyer, the first woman to fly a
helicopter, and a test pilot for the Luftwaffe. In 1942 Reichsmarschall
Göring had awarded her a Gold Medal for Military Flying because
of the horrific crash she had barely survived while testing a rocket-
propelled Messerschmitt. Her jaws were misaligned, her skull fractured
in four places and her nose nearly sliced off. But after five months in
the hospital and much plastic surgery, she emerged still looking attractive and ready to fly.

By April 1945 the Third Reich was crumbling, with Russian
forces in the outskirts of Berlin. Hitler appointed Generaloberst
Robert von Greim as head of the Luftwaffe, replacing Göring who
had been accused of attempting a coup d'état. On 26 April Reitsch
flew Greim into Berlin in a flimsy Fieseler Storch to meet Hitler in
the Führerbunker, landing on an improvised airstrip in the Berlin
zoo. During the meeting Hitler gave Reitsch two cyanide capsules for
herself and Greim, then ordered them to abandon the city. On the
28th Reitsch took off with Greim from the same airstrip, dodging heavy
Russian anti-aircraft fire. It was the last plane to escape from Berlin.
Hitler shot himself two days later.

The day after Germany surrendered, the Americans took Reitsch and Greim into custody. After fifteen months in prison, she was released, despite having told her interrogators that 'it was the blackest day when we could not die at our Führer's side'. Greim was not so lucky; he swallowed a cyanide capsule when he heard that he was going to be turned over to the Russians.

After her release Reitsch settled in Frankfurt. In 1952 she won a bronze medal in the World Gliding Championships and became German champion in 1955. Over her lifetime she set more than 40 world records flying gliders and planes.

She then began lecturing around Europe, opened a gliding school in Ghana and visited the United States where she met Neil Armstrong and President Kennedy.

Despite her success, Reitsch never relinquished her belief in the Third Reich, saying: 'And what have we now in Germany? A land of bankers and car-makers. Even our great army has gone soft. Soldiers wear beards and question orders. I am not ashamed to say I believed in National Socialism. I still wear the Iron Cross with diamonds Hitler gave me … Many Germans feel guilty about the war. But they don't explain the real guilt we share – that we lost.'

In August 1979 Reitsch wrote enigmatically to her friend, Royal Navy test pilot Eric 'Winkle' Brown: 'It began in the bunker, there it shall end.' On 24 August, at the age of 67, she died, officially of a heart attack, but many believe she had at last used the potassium cyanide capsule Hitler had given her in his bunker.

1916 Henry James dies in London. His last words: 'So here it is at last, the Distinguished Thing.'

---

29 February

'Even the stars now obey Caesar in his commands.'

45 BC Since his return to Rome after defeating Pompey in the Civil War, Julius Caesar had ordered a raft of changes and reforms to state laws and institutions, and on 1 January 45 BC the new calendar he had decreed went into effect. Sixty days later, on this day, the world celebrated its first Leap Year. So bemused was the great statesman Cicero that he famously commented: 'Even the stars now obey Caesar in his commands.'

Of all Caesar's achievements, the new calendar would be the most long-lasting. The western world would define the year by it for the next 1,537 years.

Legend has it that the first Roman calendar was instituted by Romulus in 738 BC, but it had only ten months. Then, in the 7th century BC, the Roman King Numa Pompilius added January and February to create a twelve-month year, and the Roman world lived with it for six centuries, even though it totalled only 355 days, leading to calendrical chaos.

Then Caesar stepped in, basing his new calendar on the calculations of Sosigenes of Alexandria, who had worked out that a year should have 365 and a quarter days.

But how to account for that last quarter day? Cleverly, Sosigenes added an additional day at the end of February every fourth year. Back then, however, they didn't call it a Leap Year but *bis-sexto-kalendae*. Luckily, centuries later the Scandinavians coined the term Leap Year, derived from the Old Norse *hlaupa* ('to leap'). This was based on the observation that during a Leap Year any fixed event leaps forward an extra day, falling two days after the day of the week it fell on the previous year, rather than only one day later as in normal years.

If the number of days, the number of months and a *bis-sexto-kalendae* weren't change enough, Caesar also changed the name of one of the months, or at least the Roman Senate did, when it renamed Quintilis 'July' in his honour. (Later another obsequious Senate renamed Sextilis in honour of Caesar's successor, Augustus, calling it 'August'.) The Senate also paid homage to the (by now dead) Julius by choosing 1 January in 42 BC to deify him.

One thing Caesar forgot was the week – there were none in his calendar. But in the 4th century the first Christian emperor Constantine introduced the seven-day week, based on the Book of Genesis. And while Caesar's calendar looked accurate, in fact it overestimated the length of the year by eleven minutes and fourteen seconds, so that it gained a day about every 134 years. This problem was resolved only in 1582 when Pope Gregory XIII adjusted Caesar's calendar and re-baptised it the Gregorian calendar. Even then, Caesar's decree remained in force in some countries for centuries; Russia moved to the Gregorian calendar in 1918 and Greece only in 1923.

1868 When Benjamin Disraeli becomes Prime Minister for the first time, he tells his friends: 'I have climbed to the top of the greasy pole.'

---

1 March

'Never flinch, never weary, never despair.'

1955 On 18 February 1901 Winston Churchill made his maiden speech in the House of Commons at the age of 26. During the next half century he would become renowned for his inspiring addresses and stirring rhetoric (although his friend Lord Birkenhead once commented, 'He has devoted the best years of his life to preparing his impromptu speeches.'). Here are some examples:

After Neville Chamberlain signed the Munich Agreement with Hitler (1 October 1938): 'Britain and France had to choose between war and dishonour. They chose dishonour. They will have war.'

The day Churchill replaced Chamberlain as Prime Minister (13 May 1940): 'I have nothing to offer but blood, toil, tears, and sweat ... You ask, what is our policy? I will say: It is to wage war, by sea, land and air, with all our might and with all the strength that God can give us: to wage war against a monstrous tyranny, never surpassed in the dark, lamentable catalogue of human crime. That is our policy. You ask, what is our aim? I can answer in one word: It is victory, victory at all costs, victory in spite of all terror, victory, however long and hard the road may be; for without victory, there is no survival.'

The day the last British troops were evacuated from Dunkirk (4 June 1940): 'We shall not flag or fail. We shall go on to the end, we shall fight in France, we shall fight on the seas and oceans, we shall fight with growing confidence and growing strength in the air, we shall defend our island, whatever the cost may be, we shall fight on the beaches, we shall fight on the landing grounds, we shall fight in the fields and in the streets, we shall fight in the hills; we shall never surrender.'

To inspire his countrymen for the struggle to come (18 June 1940): 'Let us therefore brace ourselves to our duties, and so bear ourselves that, if the British Empire and its Commonwealth last for a thousand years, men will still say, "This was their finest hour."'

Six weeks after the start of the Battle of Britain (20 August 1940): 'Never in the field of human conflict was so much owed by so many to so few.'

Reporting on armaments discussions with US President Roosevelt on a BBC radio broadcast (9 February 1941): 'Here is the answer which I will give to President Roosevelt: Put your confidence in us. ... We shall not fail or falter; we shall not weaken or tire. Neither the sudden shock of battle, nor the long-drawn trials of vigilance and exertion will wear us down. Give us the tools and we will finish the job.'

Speaking to Allied delegates in St James's Palace (12 June 1941): 'We cannot see how deliverance will come or when it will come, but nothing is more certain that every trace of Hitler's footsteps, every stain of his infected, corroding fingers will be sponged and purged and, if need be, blasted from the surface of the earth.'

Speech at the Mansion House after the British victory at El Alamein (10 November 1942): 'Now this is not the end. It is not even the beginning of the end. But it is, perhaps, the end of the beginning.'

Attacking the opposition in the House of Commons (22 October 1945): 'The inherent vice of capitalism is the unequal sharing of blessings. The inherent virtue of Socialism is the equal sharing of miseries.'

On this day, four months after his 80th birthday, Churchill gave his last great speech in the House of Commons, ending with these lines: 'The day may dawn when fair play, love for one's fellow-men, respect for justice and freedom, will enable tormented generations to march forth serene and triumphant from the hideous epoch in which we have to dwell. Meanwhile, never flinch, never weary, never despair.'

It was a fittingly eloquent capstone for a parliamentary career that had begun more than a half century before. Churchill would resign his office 35 days later, after being partially paralysed by a stroke.

1815 After landing at Golfe-Juan on escaping from Elba, Napoleon proclaims: 'The eagle, with the national colours, will fly from steeple to steeple until it flies from the towers of Notre-Dame.'

---

2 March

'We are on the march; we will stop only when the French flag waves from Strasbourg Cathedral.'

1941 It had been eight long months since France had ignominiously fallen to the invading Germans. Today at last the Free French celebrated their first victory, with the help of Britain's Long Range Desert Group (LRDG), at Kufra, an isolated oasis 750 miles south of Benghazi in the Libyan desert.

At the beginning of December, a Free French major named Philippe Leclerc had arrived in Chad, then a French colony, planning to attack Italian positions in Libya. The day he arrived he started preparations for an assault on the Kufra oasis, over 1,000 miles to the north, where an Italian garrison was stationed, reinforced by a motorised company, the Compagnia Sahariana di Cufra. It was the southernmost post occupied by the German–Italian alliance.

Leclerc set out across the desert with about 100 French soldiers and 250 *tirailleurs* (riflemen) and camel cavalry from Chad and Cameroon. This small force was equipped with whatever makeshift equipment they could find, dressed in a variety of mismatched uniforms and transported on a couple of dozen old vehicles. Supporting his advance was the LRDG, which was assigned to neutralise the Sahariana, 120 Italians and Libyans who patrolled the region in six armoured cars and utility tractors. The British unit, however, was spotted by an enemy plane, which directed the Sahariana assault. With superior firepower backed up by air support, the Italians drove off the LRDG, capturing many of its men.

On 7 February Leclerc's troops came in view of the fortress at Kufra. Leclerc's first task was to neutralise the Sahariana, which was forced to withdraw when the Italian garrison at Kufra, hunkered down inside the fort, failed to come to their assistance.

Leclerc now besieged Kufra, although his artillery consisted of only one 75mm gun and a few mortars. He positioned the gun 3,500 yards from the fort, beyond the range of the enemy machine-guns, and, to make the Italians believe his force was stronger than it was, he moved it from place to place in an old Chevrolet van, firing 20 to 30 rounds a day, while French patrols periodically tested the enemy defences. The inexperienced Italian commander overestimated the attackers' strength and entered into surrender negotiations.

The next day the Italians left the fort under flag of truce, ready to surrender if they could do so with honour. But when the verbal wrangling seemed as if it would continue interminably, Leclerc ordered the Italians back into their vehicles – and then sat down beside them and commanded them to drive back into the fort. There he imposed his demands on the wilting commandant, who signed the surrender. The defending garrison of eleven officers, eighteen NCOs and 273 Libyan soldiers marched out of the fort under the gaze of the French, leaving all their armaments behind. They had suffered only three killed and four wounded, fewer than the French.

The next day – 2 March – Leclerc assembled his men in the fortress courtyard. After hoisting the colours, he told his men: 'We are on the march; we will stop only when the French flag waves from Strasbourg Cathedral.'

This must have appeared a grandiose claim – the French had only just gained their first small victory after almost two years of defeat. But three and a half years later, on 23 November 1944, the French 2nd Armoured Division – led by Leclerc, now a general – liberated Strasbourg as he had promised.

1917 'We have thought it well to renounce the Throne of the Russian Empire and to lay down the supreme power.' Nicholas II abdicates, bringing to an end the Romanov dynasty and the monarchy in Russia. * **1977** President Ronald Reagan at a conference in Los Angeles: 'Politics is supposed to be the second oldest profession. I have come to realise that it bears a very close resemblance to the first.'

---

3 March

'Bolsheviks are tigers, round them up and shoot them!'

1918 The Soviet government of Russia had been in power for only four months, but today a delegation led by Foreign Minister Leon Trotsky signed a peace treaty with the Central Powers, led by Imperial Germany, in the Polish city of Brest-Litovsk. After three years of conflict, warfare on the Eastern Front of the First World War came to an end.

Negotiations had followed a December ceasefire, after Russia's new government, its army defeated and in disarray, announced its withdrawal from the war. By that time, German forces had penetrated deeply into Russian territory, and Soviet leader Vladimir Lenin was far more interested in putting down internal opposition than in fighting Germans.

For Germany, a peace treaty brought permanent access to the enormous territory it had invaded, land rich in agriculture, industry, and mining. Beyond that, a treaty would allow the transfer of large numbers of its troops to the Western Front, where in the spring the High Command intended to launch a war-winning offensive.

Speed was of the essence for Germany, but not for Russia, whose leaders were seeking a peace 'without annexations or indemnities'. They saw the negotiation process as a highly visible propaganda showcase that would persuade the European proletariat that the time was ripe for world revolution. In the meantime, negotiations furnished the Soviet government with breathing space in which to consolidate its rule at home.

As the meetings dragged on through January with much debate but little progress, the German military became increasingly aggravated. But on 10 February Russia unilaterally declared an end of hostilities as Trotsky, proclaiming 'No war, no peace', withdrew the Soviet delegation and left for Petrograd.

Frustrated and enraged, the German High Command persuaded Kaiser Wilhelm to renew the fighting against Russia. When his Foreign Minister objected, the Kaiser informed him: 'Bolsheviks are tigers, round them up and shoot them.' On 18 February, the German army resumed its attack, coming close to Petrograd. Fearing that if the German advance continued the Soviet regime would be overthrown, Lenin sent the Russian delegation back to Brest-Litovsk to agree enemy terms, but Trotsky could not face the humiliation and had a subordinate sign the treaty for him.

It was a victor's peace, and the terms were severe. Germany and Austria gained sovereignty over Poland, Lithuania, and the Baltic provinces. Turkey gained territory in the Caucasus. Russia was also forced to recognise the independence of Finland, the Ukraine, and Georgia. Russia lost a third of her population, a third of her agricultural land, 54 per cent of her industrial undertakings, and 89 per cent of her coal production. Moreover, Russia eventually had to pay 120 million gold rubles in reparations.

But the treaty revealed to the Allies what they could expect if Germany won the war. President Woodrow Wilson, who had recently issued his Fourteen Points calling for 'peace without victory', denounced the treaty as evidence of Germany's true war aims. 'There is, therefore, but one response possible from us,' he said, 'force, force to the utmost, force without stint or limit ...'

But by the summer of 1918 the realities of the war had changed. The view of the German High Command that peace in the east would allow them to bolster their strength in the west proved an illusion, as a million troops were needed to hold the vast conquered territories. By autumn defeat was a certainty, and Germany renounced the treaty just six days before surrendering to the Allies. On 13 November 1918 the treaty of Brest-Litovsk was abrogated, which at least saved Russia from some of its worst consequences, though Poland, the Baltic states and Finland were not recovered in the peace settlement at Versailles in 1919.

1861 Five years previously, Tsar Alexander II has told the Marshals of the Nobility: 'The present order of owning souls cannot remain unchanged'; today Russia's serfs are finally emancipated.

---

4 March

'Go and take my shroud through the streets and cry loudly, "Behold all that Saladin, who conquered the East, bears away of his conquests".'

1193 Saladin, the sultan of Egypt and Syria who recaptured Palestine from the Crusaders, died today in Damascus at about age 55. A formidable warrior who destroyed Crusader power in the East, Saladin was known among his Christian enemies as a man of honour and chivalric virtue.

Saladin was born around 1138 in Tikrit in what was then Mesopotamia, today's Iraq. Although he is best known in the West for his battles against Christians, his first wars were against smaller Muslim states, as he expanded his power. Indeed, fellow Muslims came closer to killing him than Christians ever did. In 1176 during the siege of Aleppo, hired killers from the Hashashin twice tried to assassinate him, once wounding him in the process.

Although the Christians failed to conquer Saladin, they defeated him several times, most notably in 1177 when Baldwin IV of Jerusalem and Raynald of Châtillon overwhelmed him at the Battle of Montgisard. Of Saladin's army of 30,000, some 27,000 were slain, and Saladin escaped only by vaulting onto the back of a camel and fleeing the field.

Saladin was a devout Muslim, totally committed to the idea of jihad against the Christians, but he was famed for his chivalry in war. While he was besieging the great Christian fortress at Kerak in 1183, a royal wedding was taking place. The half-sister of Jerusalem's King Baldwin IV was to marry Humphrey IV of Toron. As the wedding ceremonies continued, Saladin instructed his troops to avoid bombarding the newlyweds' quarters.

Saladin's ultimate goal was the recapture of Jerusalem. In July 1187 he completely routed a Crusader army at Hattin and then marched on the holy city. After a protracted siege, it fell on 2 October. To the delighted astonishment of the conquered Christians, Saladin and his men treated them with kindness and courtesy rather than the indiscriminate slaughter that had followed the Crusaders' capture of the city 88 years before. He agreed to a low ransom for the city's inhabitants and allowed many families who could not afford the ransom to leave. Nonetheless, most of the captured foot soldiers were sold into slavery.

Jerusalem's fall sent a shock wave through Christian Europe, triggering the Third Crusade led by England's Richard the Lionheart. The chivalrous Saladin sent Richard and his captains chilled wine, pears and grapes from Damascus to ease their life in camp. During the Battle of Arsuf, Richard's horse was killed under him. Rather than ordering his men to finish him off, Saladin sent him a fresh horse instead (a gallant act Saladin may have regretted, since a re-horsed Richard led the final charge that shattered the Muslims).

After his victory at Arsuf, Richard came within sight of the walls of Jerusalem but was forced to abandon his crusade in October 1192 because he had neither the men to take the city nor enough to garrison it if he had. Saladin died of fever only five months later, on this day in 1193. Before he died, he gave away his great wealth to his poorer subjects, retaining only one piece of gold and 47 pieces of silver, not enough even to pay for his funeral. As death closed in, he saw the ephemeral nature of all his triumphs. His last instructions to his followers were: 'Go and take my shroud through the streets and cry loudly, "Behold all that Saladin, who conquered the East, bears away of his conquests".'

1536 The House of Commons passes the bill for the dissolution of the monasteries after Henry VIII threatens Lord Chief Justice Sir Edward Montagu: 'Have my bill passed by tomorrow, or else tomorrow this head of yours will be off!' * **1933** President Franklin Delano Roosevelt in his First Inaugural Address: 'Let me assert my firm belief that the only thing we have to fear is fear itself.'

5 March

'Facts are stubborn things.'

1770 On this moonlit winter evening in Boston, British soldiers fired on a mob of two to three hundred angry but unarmed American colonists, killing five of them. What became known as 'the Boston Massacre' was one of the first signs of the full-scale revolution that would break out five years later. But when the soldiers were tried for murder, a future American president put the principles of justice above the clamour for revenge.

Boston had become the hotbed of defiant behaviour in North America, provoked by British efforts to extract more revenues from its colonies. The Stamp Act of 1765 incited mob violence, including the ransacking of the home of the colony's lieutenant governor, and further British actions stirred up even more.

So the situation was already tense on 1 October 1768, when two British regiments arrived. Boston was now a garrison town, or, to the Americans, an occupied city. Seventeen months later, colonial tempers reached boiling point on this day.

The confrontation had begun on the previous Friday, when 40 British soldiers had tangled with colonists at Hancock's Wharf. The brawl was quelled only when a British colonel ordered his men back to barracks. Peace settled over the city during the two-day Puritan Sabbath, but on Monday evening it began again.

Guarding the Customs House, a lone sentry was soon being taunted by a crowd of unruly colonists. As the mob grew, eight more Redcoats reinforced the sentry, and Captain Thomas Preston assumed command, ordering them to fix bayonets as he unsheathed his sword. Now the mob cursed the soldiers, hurling snowballs, chunks of ice, oyster shells and stones. 'Fire!' they taunted, daring the troops.

An innkeeper named Richard Palms asked Preston if the soldiers' muskets were loaded. Preston said they were, but he had no intention to fire, since he was standing in front of them.

Then one of the soldiers – Hugh Montgomery – fell to the ground. Or, some claim, was cudgelled to the ground by Palms. Whatever the truth, Montgomery regained his feet and pulled the trigger. Instantly, other soldiers fired. Captain Preston ordered his men to cease fire, but two colonists had been killed outright, with nine more wounded, three of whom eventually died. The first to fall was Crispus Attucks, a runaway slave and sailor, who was shot twice. He is often considered the first fatality of the American Revolution.

The next day Preston and his soldiers were arrested for murder. Desperate to find a defence attorney, they approached a short, stocky 34-year-old lawyer named John Adams, who accepted the task despite knowing how unpopular it would make him in Boston.

On the trial's first day, Adams spoke to establish basic principles: 'It is of more importance to the community that innocence should be protected than it is that guilt should be punished.' 'Facts are stubborn things,' he told the jury, 'and whatever may be our wishes, our inclinations, or the dictums of our passions, they cannot alter the state of facts and evidence.' He asserted that the riot was the inevitable result of billeting British troops in the city. 'Soldiers quartered in a populous town will always occasion two mobs where they prevent one,' he said. 'They are wretched conservators of the peace.' But, he insisted, the soldiers had acted in self-defence.

Preston was found innocent of giving the order to fire (two centuries later a scientific reconstruction demonstrated that, even had he given the order, he could not have been heard above the roar of the crowd since he was facing away from his troops). Of the soldiers, none was convicted of murder, but two were held for manslaughter, for which they were branded on their thumbs.

The Boston Massacre made colonists consider the legitimacy of British power in America and took the people closer to open revolt. John Adams, who 27 years later would become the country's second president, claimed that 'On that night the foundation of American independence was laid'.

1827 Last words of French scientist and polymath Pierre-Simon, Marquis de Laplace: 'Man pursues nothing but chimeras.' * **1957** The Duke of Windsor (formerly Edward VIII): 'The thing that impresses me most about America is the way parents obey their children.'

---

6 March

'Remember the Alamo!'

1836 Today in a dilapidated former Franciscan mission in what is now San Antonio, Texas, a Mexican army commanded by President

Antonio López de Santa Anna utterly crushed a meagre force of about 185 'Texians' after a thirteen-day siege. The defenders were killed to a man, either during the final assault or shot by firing squad in its aftermath. But their heroic but futile resistance created one of the enduring legends of American history.

Although Texas was then part of Mexico, most of its inhabitants were immigrants from the United States who objected to Santa Anna's dictatorial rule (as well as to a Mexican prohibition against slaveholding). By the end of 1835 the Texians were in full revolt, and a detachment of volunteers ousted a Mexican force from San Antonio and occupied an abandoned mission there called the Alamo. Some Texas leaders like Sam Houston warned that the Alamo would be impossible to defend, but the headstrong volunteers were determined to stay put.

Soon more volunteers were drifting in to bolster the small Texian force. The legendary pioneer and knife-fighter Jim Bowie arrived with 30 men, and on 3 February a 36-year-old lieutenant colonel named William Travis entered the improvised fort and took command. Five days later another American legend, the frontiersman Davy Crockett, joined the defenders with about 60 volunteers from Texas and Tennessee.

The Texians did not have long to wait. At dawn on 23 February they noted feverish activity among the Mexican villagers, many of whom were preparing to flee. That afternoon Santa Anna appeared with about 1,500 soldiers and 5,000 conscripted peasants and surrounded the Alamo. He refused all negotiation and began to bombard the Alamo in an effort to reduce its protective walls to rubble. He also ordered a red flag to be raised, a warning that the defenders would be given no quarter.

The next day Travis composed a letter addressed 'To the People of Texas and All Americans in the World' beseeching them 'to come to our aid, with all dispatch'. Writing that 'I shall never surrender or retreat', he sent the letter in an envelope dramatically labelled 'VICTORY or DEATH'.

But it was too late. The Mexicans continued to batter the walls until before dawn on 6 March, Santa Anna launched a massive frontal assault. The defenders repulsed two attacks but were then overwhelmed in vicious hand-to-hand fighting until all but a handful were killed. Tradition has it that Jim Bowie, who was laid up with illness, was slaughtered in his bed after emptying his pistols into several enemy soldiers. William Travis was also cut down in the fighting.

By 6.30 that morning the battle was over. Mexican soldiers inspected the fallen enemy, bayoneting anyone who moved, and the five to ten

Texians who had surrendered were summarily shot. Some accounts say that Davy Crockett was among those executed, while another maintains that his body was found surrounded by 'no less than sixteen Mexican corpses'.

The toll among the Mexicans was huge, somewhere between 500 and 600 killed (although Santa Anna initially reported that his men had killed 600 Texians while suffering only 70 killed and 300 wounded).

The Battle of the Alamo was a pyrrhic victory for Santa Anna not just in the number of men he lost; the defenders' heroism inspired further Texian revolt, sparked by the rallying cry, 'Remember the Alamo!', that swelled the ranks of the Texian army. Just a month later the Texians defeated the Mexicans at the Battle of San Jacinto, capturing Santa Anna and forcing him to lead his troops back across the Rio Grande. Now the independence of Texas was assured, and finally, on 29 December 1845 the Texians got what they really wanted when Texas became the 28th state of the United States.

1566 'I shall be your wife no longer, and shall never rest till I give you as sorrowful a heart as I have at this present.' Mary, Queen of Scots' threat to her husband Lord Darnley after he murders her confidant Riccio.

---

7 March

'If there is among you a soldier who wants to kill his emperor, here I am.'

1815 The ex-emperor Napoleon had escaped from Elba after nine months and 22 days of regal confinement. After a night in Cannes, he started his advance towards Paris, almost 600 miles away, with a small corps of 1,200 soldiers.

Knowing that troops loyal to Louis XVIII were to the west in Marseille and the Rhône valley, he headed straight north through Grasse and, following small trails and mule tracks, climbed into the foothills of the Alps, past Séranon and through the Clue de Taulanne in heavy snow. By nightfall on 4 March he was at the Château de Malijai.

The next day, while Napoleon was lunching in Sisteron, at the royal palace of the Tuileries in Paris, King Louis received the news of his escape. Frantically, he summoned his generals and sent word to block Napoleon's progress. (Not all royalists were as concerned as the king;

the optimistic newspaper *Moniteur* called Napoleon's escape 'an act of madness which can be dealt with by a few rural policemen'.)

When Napoleon reached the hamlet of Laffrey on 7 March, he found that the 5th Battalion of the Royal French Army was waiting there, ready to capture or kill him. On a meadow at the south end of the Lac de Laffrey, the ex-emperor's soldiers nervously faced the royalist troops, all with rifles at the ready. But Napoleon had already seen (and caused) enough French blood spilt. Dismounting from his horse, he directed his guard to raise the Tricolore and play the Marseillaise, which had been outlawed by the monarchy.

Now he sent 100 of his Polish lancers forward in a slow advance. When the opposing soldiers pulled back, he ordered the lancers to wheel and return. He then stepped forward alone, a proud figure in his grey battle coat and black bicorn hat, and moved within pistol range of the enemy line.

'Fire!' cried out a royalist officer, but there was only silence. 'Fire!' he cried again, but still with no result. Then Napoleon called out: 'Soldiers of the 5th, I am your emperor. Recognise me.'

Another moment of hush, and then Napoleon dramatically opened his coat to expose his breast: 'If there is among you a soldier who wants to kill his emperor, here I am.' ('*S'il est parmi vous un soldat qui veuille tuer son empereur, me voilà.*') The response was an immediate roar of '*Vive l'Empereur!*' as the royalist ranks broke and men ran towards him, acclaiming and touching him. Their desperate commander broke into tears and offered his sword to Napoleon, who embraced him.

The same day Napoleon trekked a further seventeen miles to Grenoble, his force now doubled in size, joined by the royalist soldiers from Laffrey. Then north through Lyon and on to Paris, picking up more reinforcements in every town he passed. He reached Paris the day after Louis XVIII had scuttled off to Belgium. Arriving at the Tuileries at nine in the evening, Napoleon found himself cheered by 20,000 Parisians. He was emperor once more.

Napoleon had covered a 40-day journey in twenty days, converted opposing troops through a magnificent display of personal courage and regained his throne without a trace of violence or a single shot being fired.

AD 161 '*Aequanimitas*' ('peace'), last word of Roman Emperor Antoninus Pius.

---

8 March

'An evil empire'

1983 Today Ronald Reagan, two years into his first term as president, addressed the National Association of Evangelicals in Orlando, Florida. The first half of his 30-minute speech dealt largely with moral issues that would please the Evangelicals. He said that he favoured 'a constitutional amendment to restore prayer to public schools' (in 1963 the US Supreme Court had ruled that prayer in state-supported schools was an unconstitutional violation of separation of Church and State). He called abortion 'infanticide', and attacked bigotry, saying, 'there is no room for racism, antisemitism, or other forms of ethnic and racial hatred in this country'.

So far, so uncontentious – at least for an Evangelical audience (and of course Reagan failed either to curtail abortion or reinstitute prayer in public schools). But at the time the US Congress was debating a nuclear freeze, favoured by the Soviet Union, that would have prevented the deployment of American missiles in Europe, so then Reagan segued from quasi-religious questions to his real focus – the Cold War, the immorality of the Soviet Union and the folly of the recommended freeze.

He cited Lenin, 'who said in 1920 that they [communists] repudiate all morality that proceeds from supernatural ideas – that's their name for religion ... Morality is entirely subordinate to the interests of class war. And everything is moral that is necessary for the annihilation of the old, exploiting social order and for uniting the proletariat.'

Reagan then spoke strongly against the proposed freeze, calling it 'a dangerous fraud' that 'would remove any incentive for the Soviets to negotiate seriously ... and reward the Soviet Union for its enormous and unparalleled military build-up.'

He then attacked the leaders in 'that totalitarian darkness': 'While they preach the supremacy of the state, declare its omnipotence over individual man, and predict its eventual domination of all peoples on the Earth, they are the focus of evil in the modern world.' He concluded by damning 'the aggressive impulses of an evil empire' and calling communism 'another sad, bizarre chapter in human history whose last pages even now are being written'.

Reagan's speech succeeded in its first objective, to prevent the National Association of Evangelicals from passing a nuclear freeze resolution, as both the Catholic bishops and the National Council of Churches had already done. But elsewhere it brought denunciation. The Russians claimed it showed his intent to dominate the world and that Reagan 'can think only in terms of confrontation and bellicose, lunatic anti-communism'. Liberal opinion in the United States and Europe also condemned Reagan as a Cold War warrior with a holy war mentality. Conservatives, on the other hand, welcomed Reagan's straight talking and saw his speech as a necessary signal in confronting Soviet aggression.

Eventually American missiles were installed in Europe and used as bargaining chips in arms talks with the USSR's new leader Mikhail Gorbachev, and in 1987 Reagan and Gorbachev agreed to eliminate intermediate- and short-range nuclear missiles. In the early 1990s the Soviet Union collapsed, far more quickly than even Reagan had imagined.

Reagan's 'evil empire' speech has been debated ever since, as has Ronald Reagan himself. Although many argue that the Soviet Union would have disintegrated with or without Reagan's initiatives, many in power at the time believed his role in ending the Cold War was fundamental. Gorbachev called him 'a man who was instrumental in bringing about the end of the Cold War', and Margaret Thatcher said: 'Ronald Reagan had a higher claim than any other leader to have won the Cold War for liberty and he did it without a shot being fired.'

1702 After William of Orange, the only Dutchman to become King of England, dies from pneumonia after severely injuring himself falling from his horse, his sister-in-law Anne becomes Queen of England, promising Parliament: 'I know my heart to be entirely English.'

---

9 March

'In France a woman will not go to sleep until she has talked over affairs of state with her lover or her husband.'

1661 Tormented by gout, his legs covered with ulcers treated with poultices of horse dung, Cardinal Jules Mazarin passed away at 2.30 this morning in the Château de Vincennes.

Mazarin had governed France for the past eighteen years, initially as First Minister to Louis XIII and then during the regency of Louis' widow,

Anne of Austria, while Louis XIV was still under-age. He amassed an immense fortune, built a magnificent palace with a 58-metre-long library, and acquired one of history's greatest art collections.

This was an extraordinary achievement for the grandson of a Sicilian fisherman and son of a Roman steward who was born Giulio Mazzarino, neither titled nor rich. Furthermore, Mazarin was never ordained, becoming a cardinal without being a priest, and he ruled France although born Italian. ('My heart is French, though my language is not', he said.)

Mazarin served Pope Urban VIII as both diplomat and papal infantry captain. When he was 29, he was part of a diplomatic corps sent to negotiate with France's First Minister, Cardinal Richelieu. Impressed by his brilliance, Richelieu said he 'took to him by instinct'.

After ten more years in the papal service (some spent in Paris), Mazarin entered the service of France and made himself so valuable that Richelieu brought him into the council of state.

Mazarin was a passionate gambler. One evening at the gaming table he built up an enormous pile of gold *écus* that attracted a crowd as well as Anne of Austria. As she watched, Mazarin risked all his winnings on a single throw of the dice – and won. Attributing his good fortune to the queen's presence, he gave her 50,000 *écus*. Several days later he received even more in return, affirming that he was now in the favour of the king and the queen.

On 16 December 1641, at Richelieu's urging, Urban VIII created Mazarin a cardinal, and when Richelieu was dying a year later, he won King Louis' promise that Mazarin would take over as First Minister.

Within six months Louis, too, was dead, leaving Anne of Austria as regent for four-year-old Louis XIV. Mazarin had written, 'In France a woman will not go to sleep until she has talked over affairs of state with her lover or her husband' – and now he became Anne's lover (some say they married in secret). He would be France's First Minister for the rest of his life.

Between 1648 and 1653 France was riven by the Fronde, a series of revolts by the nobility (and sometimes the Parlement) against their loss of privilege, as Mazarin and Anne of Austria centralised their power. Even the people of Paris rose up to protest against increased taxes, using children's slingshots (*frondes*) to hurl stones at the windows of Mazarin's associates. Mazarin and Anne were forced to flee the capital, but in the end, through compromise and military force, royal authority was reimposed.

After Louis XIV was crowned in 1654, Mazarin continued as First Minister but increasingly involved the young sovereign in government and introduced him to ministers like Colbert and Fouquet who would become so important during his reign.

During his years in power Mazarin had brought France's fractious nobility to heel, created a stable peace in Europe, with France as arbiter, and reduced the power of the clergy, but by the beginning of 1661 he was worn by work and feeble with illness. When he learned from his doctor that he had only months to live, he took to wandering the corridors of his vast palace admiring his art collection, exclaiming, 'Must I quit all these?' He died four months short of his 59th birthday.

Between them, Mazarin and Richelieu had ruled France for 37 years, but the day after Mazarin's death his subordinates asked Louis XIV from whom they should now take their orders. 'From me', he told them curtly. For the next 30 years he was his own First Minister.

1513 After Giovanni de' Medici is elected Pope Leo X, he tells his brother Giuliano: 'Since God has given us the papacy, let us enjoy it.'

---

10 March

'Mr Watson, come here, I want you.'

1876 Today in Boston a 29-year-old man with a handsome full beard accidentally spilled battery acid on his hand. Calling out to his assistant, he said: 'Mr Watson, come here, I want you.' Although Watson was in another room, he heard the words loud and clear through a receiver he was working on. The first telephone call in history had just been made.

The caller was Alexander Graham Bell, a transplanted Scot who had moved to the United States only five years before, after a one-year stay in Canada. His research into hearing and speech was in part spurred by his mother's deafness. When he moved to Boston in 1870, he founded a school to train teachers of the deaf, and in 1873 he became a professor at Boston University. There one of his students was Mabel Hubbard, who had lost her hearing at age five because of scarlet fever. Four years later they would marry.

In 1874 Bell met Thomas A. Watson, a young electrical designer and mechanic, whom he hired to construct the devices he was designing to turn electricity into sound. As Bell explained: 'If I could make a current of electricity vary in intensity precisely as the air varies in density during the production of sound, I should be able to transmit speech telegraphically.'

After two years of experimentation, on 7 March 1876 Bell was granted a patent. Three days later the battery acid accident prompted the first successful transmission of the human voice.

From this point Bell and Watson made rapid progress. At the 1876 Centennial Exposition in Philadelphia, when he recited a Hamlet soliloquy into his phone, Emperor Pedro II of Brazil heard it on another phone 50 feet away. 'My God, it talks!' exclaimed the emperor. Later that year Bell and Watson spoke to each other over a two-mile wire stretched between Cambridge and Boston.

On 9 July 1877 they created the Bell Telephone Company, with Mabel Hubbard's father, Gardiner Greene Hubbard, who had backed the company, as president. Two days after the company was launched, Bell married Mabel, with whom he lived contentedly for the rest of his life. For a wedding present he gave her 1,487 of his 1,497 shares.

The proliferation of telephones around the world was rapid. In 1879 President Rutherford Hayes had the first phone installed in the White House, and the next year the Bell Telephone Company morphed into the American Telephone and Telegraph Company (AT&T), which by the middle of the 20th century would become the world's largest company.

In January 1915, Bell and Watson spoke for the last time when they made the first transcontinental telephone call. Calling from New York, Bell joked: 'Mr Watson, come here, I want you.' Watson was 3,400 miles away in San Francisco.

Bell was always a visionary, predicting in 1906 that 'The day will come when the man at the telephone will be able to see the distant person to whom he is speaking.' Only four years after the Wright brothers' first flight, he prophesied: 'It will not be long until a man can take dinner in New York and breakfast the next morning in Liverpool.' He also foresaw '[using] the roofs of our houses to install solar apparatus to catch and store the heat received from the sun'. In 1917 he anticipated that the unchecked burning of fossil fuels 'would have a sort of greenhouse effect'.

Alexander Graham Bell's image as the inventor of the telephone – brainy, bearded and boring – is far from the truth. To friends he was simply Alec. He also developed a hydrofoil, with which he set a world water speed record (70 miles per hour) in 1919 – when he was 72.

When Bell died at his summer home on Cape Breton Island, Nova Scotia on 2 August 1922, millions of telephones all across America went silent for one minute in his honour.

1740 Thirty-one-year-old William Pitt the Elder retorts to Robert Walpole in Parliament: 'I am accused of the atrocious crime of being a young man.'

---

11 March

*'Here, in a scant piece of earth, lies he
whom all the world feared.'*

1507 Today died the infamous Cesare Borgia, the ambitious, energetic, murderous and totally unscrupulous son of Pope Alexander VI. He was considered the handsomest man in Italy and fathered at least eleven bastards.

During his lifetime – and since – there have been numerous accusations of Cesare's foul crimes, most of them true. Through his father he became Captain General of the papal forces and later was created a duke by Louis XII of France. He was a brilliant general who reduced many an enemy fortress, sometimes aided by his military engineer, Leonardo da Vinci. But he also conquered by guile and treachery. Once he invited four enemy captains to truce talks, disarmed them and then had them publicly garrotted. For this perfidious act he was venerated by his friend Niccolò Machiavelli, who travelled with his army as Florence's ambassador. Cesare is said to be Machiavelli's model for *The Prince*.

Cesare was not beyond assassination to further his ambitions. Historians still debate whether he arranged the murder of his brother Juan, although he inherited many of his titles and estates. Regarding the murder of his brother-in-law, however, there is no doubt. His sister Lucrezia had married Alfonso de Bisceglie, bastard son of the King of Naples and heir to the throne. It soon became apparent, however, that instead of a help, Naples was becoming a hindrance to Cesare's plan to make himself ruler of the Romagna in middle Italy.

In July 1500 assassins set upon Alfonso as he left the Vatican. He escaped, badly wounded, but as he refused to die, Cesare sent his notorious henchman Michelotto to the room in the Vatican where he lay recovering. After shooing Lucrezia and Alfonso's sister away with threats, Michelotto strangled the wounded man, demonstrating Cesare's single-minded determination to succeed at all costs, as suggested by his motto, '*Aut Caesar, aut nihil*' ('Either Caesar or nothing').

Cesare's plans of conquest now moved forward. Leading troops borrowed from his other brother-in-law, Jean d'Albret, King of Navarre, and the papal army, he captured large swathes of Romagna. But he never achieved his ambition to carve out an independent Borgia state and make himself its prince. When Alexander VI died in 1503, he found himself without political support in an area where he was both feared and detested because of his vicious military campaigns. Imprisoned in Spain by Pope Julius II, he escaped after two years and enlisted as a military commander in the services of Jean d'Albret. By then this once dashing *condottiere* must have been a fearful presence, a leather mask covering half his face disfigured probably by syphilis.

Leading a force of 5,000 troops against the Castilians, Cesare captured Viana but not its castle. Amidst heavy rain, at dawn today a group of enemy knights fled from the castle. Cesare immediately gave chase with 70 cavalry but in his rage outran his men. Seeing their enemy virtually alone, the knights dragged him off his horse and hacked him to death, piercing his body with 25 wounds. It is said that his last words were: 'I die unprepared.' Stripped of armour and clothing, his naked corpse was left with just a red cloth covering his crotch.

Cesare was buried in a marble tomb in Viana. The inscription reads: 'Here, in a scant piece of earth, lies he whom all the world feared, he who peace and war held in his hand.' (A philosophical epitaph but hardly original. As Shakespeare wrote of Hotspur, killed in 1403, 'A kingdom for [his body] was too small a bound,/But now two paces of the vilest earth/Is room enough.' Even earlier, just before he died in 211, Roman Emperor Septimius Severus apostrophised, 'Little urn, you will soon hold all that will remain of him whom the world could not contain.')

Cesare was still only 31 when he was killed. He had pursued an unusually bloody career for a man who had been a cathedral canon at seven, a bishop at fifteen, an archbishop at sixteen and a cardinal at eighteen.

1867 After having defeated Denmark and Austria and almost completing the unification of Germany, Prussian leader Otto von Bismarck tells the Parliament of the German Federation: 'Let's put Germany, so to speak, in the saddle. You'll see that she can ride.' * **1942** General MacArthur leaves the Philippines under Japanese attack, promising: 'I shall return.'

12 March

'Ein Volk, ein Reich, ein Führer'

1938 It was an inauspicious omen: precisely five years earlier German President Paul von Hindenburg had replaced the traditional red, black and gold flag of the German Republic in favour of the swastika flag of the Nazi Party. From today that menacing banner would fly over an extra 6.5 million people as Adolf Hitler marched into Austria.

At 5.30 this Saturday morning the Eighth Army of the German Wehrmacht crossed the border, paving the way for Hitler's triumphant drive this afternoon over a bridge across the Inn River at the town of Braunau, where he had been born almost 49 years earlier. The streets were jammed with expectant crowds who cheered the imposing motorcade of a 4,000-man bodyguard and the great man himself. *'Ein Volk, ein Reich, ein Führer'* ('One people, one nation, one leader') they chanted, in celebration of what they hoped the Führer would engineer the next day: the union – *Anschluss* – of their nation with Nazi Germany.

Hitler could hardly have remembered Braunau, for he was only two when his father moved the family to Bavaria. Nevertheless, he managed to turn it to good use in 1924 when, in an effort to construct destiny out of chance, he opened *Mein Kampf* with these words: 'Today it seems to me providential that Fate should have chosen Braunau on the Inn as my birthplace. For this little town lies on the boundary between the two German states, which we of the younger generation at least have made it our life work to reunite by every means possible.'

Since becoming German chancellor, it had taken Hitler five years to bring about the Anschluss, during which he used every means at his disposal, including subversion, agitation, provocation, intimidation, and assassination. Within Austria itself his efforts enjoyed the active and disruptive support of the illegal Austrian Nazi party.

Even so, it had been a slow process that required the murder of one Austrian chancellor and the intimidation of his successor. Hoping to prevent Austria being swallowed by Germany, in 1933 Chancellor Engelbert Dollfuss abolished the Austrian Parliament, banned the Austrian Nazi party and assumed dictatorial powers, preferring his own 'Austrofascism' to Hitler's German version. On 25 July 1934 a group of Austrian Nazis, probably on Hitler's instigation, seized the Chancellery, attempted to proclaim a government and shot Dollfuss dead.

The coup failed, and Dollfuss was replaced by Kurt von Schuschnigg, who publicly declared, 'An absolute abyss separates Austria from Nazism.' In 1938, however, Hitler summoned him to Berchtesgaden and bullied him into accepting a greater Nazi presence. But then, returning to Vienna, the chancellor reneged and instead announced his intention to call a plebiscite on 13 March, allowing Austrian voters to determine their nation's future. This unexpected recalcitrance, and the fear that the Austrians might declare their independence by a public vote, forced an impatient Hitler to play his last and strongest card, one threatened but never dealt: invasion.

And so it was that on 12 March Hitler crossed into Austria in the wake of his troops, who had invaded on the pretence of 'restoring order'. The next day Austria was officially absorbed into Germany and then on the glorious spring morning of 14 March, the Führer motored to Vienna, his progress marked by massive demonstrations of public approval (enforced by savage treatment for dissenters). In the Heldenplatz at midday he addressed 200,000 delirious listeners, proclaiming 'the entry of my homeland into the German Reich' and later echoing the lie that despots have used throughout the ages: 'Not as tyrants have we come, but as liberators.' The following evening he flew back to Germany, master of a greater Germany, his eyes now on Czechoslovakia.

---

604 AD Pope Gregory I (Saint Gregory) dies in Rome, having previously displayed some unsaintly *schadenfreude*: 'The bliss of the elect in heaven would not be perfect unless they were able to look across the abyss and enjoy the agonies of their brethren in eternal fire.'

---

13 March

'It is too early to thank God.'

1881 Next time you are in St Petersburg, be sure to visit the Church of the Saviour on Spilled Blood facing the Catherine Canal. Unlike the neoclassical architecture of most of the city, it features colourful onion domes reminiscent of St Basil's Cathedral in Moscow, even though it was built three centuries later. Its construction was started by Tsar Alexander III to commemorate his father Alexander II, who was assassinated on this day on the very spot where the church now stands.

Alexander II inherited the throne at 36 in 1855. During his long reign he was a progressive force in a reactionary country, curtailing some of the nobility's privileges, fostering university education, abolishing corporal punishment and, most importantly, freeing Russia's serfs. Despite these reforms, however, Alexander was convinced both of his duty to maintain his God-given autocratic power and of his country's unreadiness for democracy, so Russia remained one of the most backward and repressed nations in Europe.

The first attempt on Alexander's life came in 1866, when a revolutionary named Dmitry Karakozov tried to shoot him because 'the tsar ... never holds out his hand to the people because he is himself the people's worst enemy'. During the next fifteen years there were four more unsuccessful attempts, two by pistol, two by bomb. The closest call came in February 1880 when a terrorist set off a bomb directly below the tsar's dining room in the Winter Palace, killing eleven people and wounding 30 others but not the tsar, who was late for dinner.

The most dangerous terrorist group was Narodnaya Volya (People's Will), which had been responsible for both of the failed bombings. On this Sunday morning they were finally to succeed.

To start the day, Tsar Alexander had sex with his wife of eight months on top of a table and then left for his customary appearance at a military parade at the Mikhailovsky riding academy. As usual, he was strongly protected, travelling in a bomb-proof carriage accompanied by six mounted Cossacks and followed by two sleighs carrying the chief of police and the head of his guards.

The parade was exemplary, but on the return journey the cavalcade unknowingly passed members of Narodnaya Volya waiting near the Catherine Canal. The first terrorist, twenty-year-old Nikolai Rysakov, took a bomb hidden beneath a handkerchief and hurled it under the tsar's coach. The explosion killed a Cossack and a passer-by, while a policeman and another passer-by were seriously wounded. The armoured carriage, however, protected Alexander, who jumped down to check on the wounded while his guards apprehended the bomb-thrower. No one noticed that another terrorist was leaning on a fence only yards away.

When asked if he had been hurt, Alexander replied, 'Thank God, I'm untouched.' 'It is too early to thank God', called out the second terrorist, throwing a bomb that exploded at the tsar's feet. As the police chief later wrote: 'His Majesty was half-lying, half-sitting, leaning on his right arm. Thinking he was merely wounded heavily, I tried to lift him but the tsar's legs were shattered, and the blood poured out of them. Twenty people, with wounds of varying degree, lay on the sidewalk and on the street. Some managed to stand, others to crawl, still others tried to get out from beneath bodies that had fallen on them. Through the snow, debris, and blood you could see fragments of clothing, epaulets, sabres, and bloody chunks of human flesh.'

The bomb-thrower had been killed in the blast, but Alexander was still alive. Rushed back to his study in the Winter Palace, he succumbed to his wounds at 3.30 that afternoon. Just before he died he exclaimed: 'I am sweeping through the gates, washed in the blood of the lamb.' Among those who witnessed his death were his son, Alexander III, and his twelve-year-old grandson, Nicholas II. Having seen terror at first hand, both suppressed civil liberties still further and used the police to enforce their will, guaranteeing the final dénouement of the tsars 36 years later.

---

624 '*Yā manṣūr amit!*' ('O thou whom God hath made victorious, slay!') – the cry of Muhammad's Muslim soldiers as they attack the Quraish at Badr, a victory that overnight transformed Muhammad from a Meccan outcast into a major leader.

---

14 March

'Pour encourager les autres'

1757 Today, in Portsmouth harbour in the midst of a howling gale, all hands were called on deck of the British warship HMS *Monarch*, while boats carrying the captains of all the warships in port surrounded the *Monarch*. They had been summoned to witness the execution of a British admiral.

In May 1756, on the eve of the Seven Years' War against France, the British had dispatched Vice Admiral Sir John Byng with a small fleet of ten sail of the line to defend their base on the Mediterranean island of Minorca. By the time he arrived, however, the French had already taken much of the island. After an inconclusive encounter with a larger enemy fleet, Byng concluded that he could neither defeat the French ships nor relieve the British garrison and set sail for the British base at Gibraltar without further attempts to accomplish his mission. Ironically, on 4 June he was promoted to full admiral.

But when the news of Minorca's fall reached London, both the press and the public exploded with indignation, aimed largely at the British Prime Minister, the Duke of Newcastle, for leaving the island unprepared. To deflect the blame, Newcastle charged Byng with dereliction of duty and guaranteed a biased court-martial by announcing publicly that 'he shall be tried immediately; he shall be hanged directly'.

Brought back to Portsmouth, Byng was tried on board HMS *St George* before a jury of fellow admirals. The court acquitted him of cowardice and most other charges but convicted him of 'not having done his utmost'. Although the draconian 1749 Naval Act forced them to condemn him to death, they unanimously voted to petition George II for mercy. But the king, embroiled in his own political problems, refused to pardon him. So it was that on this day Admiral Byng went to meet his fate aboard his own flagship, the *Monarch*.

On the quarterdeck a squad of nine marines in scarlet uniforms lined up in three rows, their muskets fixed with bayonets. Dressed in a pale coat and white breeches and wearing a white wig, just before noon the admiral walked from his cabin to the quarterdeck, apparently serene. There he tied a blindfold over his eyes, having been persuaded that it would not be fair to the marines to have to look him in the eyes when they fired.

Now Byng knelt upon a cushion that had been placed there, while the six marines in the first two rows raised their muskets, the third row in reserve. In his right hand the admiral held a white handkerchief that, after a long moment's hesitation, he dropped as a signal to fire. The muskets belched smoke and one shot went wide, but Byng fell dead on the deck, one bullet in his heart and four others in his chest.

No other British admiral had ever been executed for such a crime, and all of Europe was bemused by the news. Two years later, Voltaire published his masterpiece *Candide*, which includes the celebrated observation: '*Dans ce pays-ci il est bon de tuer de temps en temps un amiral pour encourager les autres.*' ('In this country [England] it's good to kill an admiral from time to time to encourage the others.')

1590 'My friends, you are Frenchmen, I am your king, there is the enemy: let us charge! If you lose your ensigns, rally to my white plume; you will always find it in the path of honour and victory.' Henri IV's call to his troops as he defeats the Catholic League at the Battle of Ivry. * **1883** 'Go on, get out! Last words are for fools who haven't said enough.' Karl Marx's final words to his housekeeper who asked if he had a last message to the world.

15 March

'I am ready to die for what I have done,
and I know I shall die for it.'

1921 Today Ottoman Turkey's Minister of the Interior Talaat Pasha would pay the ultimate price for the crime against the Armenians he had instigated six years before.

At the beginning of the 20th century the Ottoman Empire's population included 2 million Armenians, about 5 per cent of the total. Although Armenians had lived in the empire for centuries, the nation's Muslims looked on them with contempt because they were Christians; they could not testify in court against Muslims, and their houses could not overlook those of Muslims. Even the ringing of church bells was forbidden. Infraction of these rules could result in huge fines or even execution. Many Turks wanted to exclude Armenians from Anatolia altogether.

In November 1914, Turkey allied itself with Germany to become embroiled in the First World War. In December, however, the Russians badly routed their army at the Battle of Sarikamish, inflicting over 100,000 casualties.

The beleaguered Ottoman government now feared that their Armenian subjects would join forces with the Russians, who were Christians like themselves, so, on 24 April 2015, Talaat Pasha ordered the deportation from Constantinople of 250 Armenian community leaders and intellectuals. Arrested that night, they were transported to Ottoman-controlled Syria. Most never returned, slaughtered by Turkish soldiers or executed for 'crimes against the state'. Armenians would call this 'Red Sunday' (*Garmir Giragi*), the start of Turkey's Armenian genocide.

Having dealt with Constantinople's Armenian leaders, Talaat Pasha now introduced the infamous Tehcir Law, which authorised the deportation of the empire's entire Armenian population.

The army and police forced Armenians into long convoys of cattle cars headed for Aleppo in Syria. When they arrived, they were marched to concentration camps in the desert, under a scorching summer sun, without food, drink or shelter, menaced by Kurdish tribesmen who were happy to rob and kill. The only ones spared were young women (especially the pretty ones), who were enslaved, forced to convert to Islam and married off to Muslims.

This 'resettlement' caused perhaps 1,500,000 deaths. As the *New York Times* reported, 'the roads and the Euphrates are strewn with corpses of exiles, and those who survive are doomed to certain death'. Theodore Roosevelt called it 'the greatest crime of the war'. Yet Talaat Pasha defended the slaughter: 'I am here on this earth to think of my people and not of my sensibilities … I am ready to die for what I have done, and I know I shall die for it.'

Brave words, but Talaat did his best to avoid his fate. On 30 October 1918 Turkey quit the war, and four days later he escaped from Constantinople in a German submarine. The new sultan, Mehmed VI, had Talaat tried *in absentia* and condemned to death, but he was in hiding in Berlin, plotting to organise Muslim countries against the Allied powers.

Alarmed by Talaat's intrigues and determined to bring him to justice, the British and Soviet intelligence services collaborated to hunt him down and recruited some Armenian revolutionaries led by Soghomon Tehlirian, a member of the Armenian Revolutionary Federation. (His mother, three sisters and two brothers had been among Talaat's victims.)

Learning that Talaat was holed up in the Berlin suburb of Charlottenburg, Tehlirian and his associates kept him under surveillance for three months and then, on the morning of 15 March 1921, they shot him dead with a single bullet as he left his house.

Tehlirian readily admitted his guilt, but after a cursory two-day trial, he was found innocent on the grounds of temporary insanity due to the traumatic experience he had gone through when his family had been slaughtered.

When Kemal Atatürk came to power in Turkey, he wanted to prosecute Turks guilty of the Armenian slaughter, but he put it aside in his attempts to consolidate his battered country, and the entire Turkish nation entered into a state of collective amnesia. In 1939, just before he ordered the euthanasia of Germany's handicapped, Adolf Hitler recalled how the guilty had escaped, remarking, 'Who remembers anymore the extermination of the Armenians?'

---

44 BC The augur Spurinna warns Julius Caesar, 'Beware the Ides of March!', on the day of Caesar's assassination. * **1936** After successfully reoccupying the Rhineland, Hitler tells the Germans in a speech in Munich: 'I go the way that Providence dictates with the assurance of a sleepwalker.'

16 March

'The Babylonian king marched to the land of Hatti,
besieged the City of Judah and on the second day of the
month of Adar took the city and captured the king.'

597 BC According to the Old Testament, Saul founded the 'United Monarchy of Israel' in the late 11th century BC. Then, in about 930 BC, the country split into the Kingdom of Israel in the north and the Kingdom of Judah in the south. But around 720 BC, the Assyrians swallowed up the Kingdom of Israel and deported the population, and the Kingdom of Judah became a vassal state of Egypt.

But in 605 BC Nebuchadnezzar II, the new king of Babylonia, the Middle East's new superpower, first routed the Egyptians at the Battle of Carchemish and then marched on the Kingdom of Judah, capturing Jerusalem and deporting many of its citizens. Judah's King Jehoiakim wisely changed allegiances, and now started paying tribute to Babylonia instead of Egypt.

Then in 601 BC, Nebuchadnezzar was repulsed with heavy losses when he tried to invade Egypt, and Jehoiakim, thinking that Babylonia was no longer to be feared, foolishly cut off his payments.

But Nebuchadnezzar was far from finished, and, if we believe the Old Testament, he was not of a forgiving nature. When three young Jewish officials refused to worship a golden idol that he had erected, according to the Book of Daniel, 'he ordered the furnace heated seven times hotter than usual and commanded some of the strongest soldiers in his army to tie up Shadrach, Meshach and Abednego and throw them into the fiery furnace'.

Shadrach, Meshach and Abednego survived their test by fire without a scorch, but King Jehoiakim would not be so fortunate. Nebuchadnezzar besieged Jerusalem, sent raiders to kill Jehoiakim and captured the new king, Jehoiakim's son Jeconiah, as recorded on the tablets of the Nebuchadnezzar Chronicle, which states: 'the Babylonian king marched to the land of Hatti [Syria], besieged the City of Judah [Jerusalem] and on the second day of the month of Adar [16 March] took the city and captured the king.'

Jeconiah's reign had lasted just 108 days; on Jerusalem's fall Nebuchadnezzar exiled him, his court and 3,000 Jews to Babylon.

Nebuchadnezzar now installed Jeconiah's uncle Zedekiah as Judah's new king. Despite the prophet Jeremiah's dire warning that the Babylonian army would return to conquer Jerusalem, Zedekiah revolted against Babylon and formed an alliance with Egypt, which triggered Nebuchadnezzar's third invasion. After another siege, this one lasting over two years, Jerusalem fell once again. King Zedekiah escaped through a breach in the city wall but was captured near Jericho and taken to Rablah on the Syrian coast. There he was forced to watch his sons being put to death and then was blinded, loaded with chains and thrown into a dungeon where he died.

After the fall of Jerusalem, the city was plundered and razed to the ground, and Solomon's Temple was destroyed. Most of the occupants were exiled to Babylon, and only a small number of farmers were permitted to remain in the land. Israel lost its independence for the next 2,500 years (excepting a short period under the Maccabees in the 2nd century BC) until its resurrection on 14 May 1948, when the State of Israel was formed.

1923 Kemal Atatürk in a speech: 'Unless a nation's life faces peril, war is murder.'

---

17 March

'All is lost save honour!'

1526 Today France's King François I reached French soil after 362 days as a prisoner of Holy Roman Emperor Charles V in Madrid. Although elated to be back, his return was touched by anguish – as his boat crossed the River Bidassoa that formed the boundary between Spain and France, another boat carrying his eight- and seven-year-old sons passed him in midstream; they were now hostages, taken to ensure François followed the terms of his release. He would not see them again for over three years.

François' reign had started so well. The 24th king in an unbroken line of Capetians since 987, he had inherited the throne on New Year's Day 1515. In 1516, two days after his 22nd birthday, he had triumphed at the Battle of Marignano, taking control of Milan.

François brought the Renaissance to France, even enticing Leonardo to spend his last years there. He created a fabled court full of poets and musicians and loved archery, falconry, hunting, jousting, real tennis and wrestling, but his favourite sport was women. According to a Venetian envoy, 'He gets up at eleven o'clock, hears Mass, has dinner, passes two or three hours with his mother, then goes whoring or hunting and finally wanders here and there throughout the night.' Among his many conquests was Anne Boleyn's sister Mary, before her entanglement with Henry VIII.

But things started to go wrong in 1523 when Imperial and Papal forces pushed the French out of Lombardy. Determined to recoup his losses, in 1525 François brought his army over the Alps, reoccupied Milan and marched twenty miles south to Pavia, defended by Charles V's mercenaries.

After a failed assault on the walls, François began a siege, but soon a large Imperial relief force was approaching, commanded by Charles de Lannoy.

Before dawn on 24 February, Lannoy's infantry attacked. François led a spirited counter-attack, but in the *mêlée* he was wounded in the hand, arm and forehead and cornered by Imperial pikemen. Then an enemy *condottiere* killed his horse, forcing him to surrender.

In the catastrophic defeat, François had suffered 12,000 casualties against 500 for the enemy and was now an Imperial prisoner. (He was the third French monarch to be captured in battle – Louis IX (Saint Louis) was taken by the Mamluks at Al Mansurah in 1250 and Jean II (The Good) by the English at Poitiers in 1356. One more was to come; the Prussians captured Napoleon III at Sedan in 1870.)

François was taken to Madrid, en route writing melodramatically to his mother, 'All is lost save honour!' ('*Tout est perdu fors l'honneur!*')

To end his imprisonment, in 1526 François agreed to renounce his claims in Italy, surrender Burgundy, send two of his sons as hostages and marry Charles's sister Eleanor. Once back in France, however, he declared that an imprisoned knight's promise was valueless and that it was beyond his power to dismember his kingdom, thus instigating another war in which he was allied with the Pope. Now a furious Charles marched on Italy and his troops sacked Rome. Finally, in 1529 François agreed the Treaty of Cambrai to get his children back, but he had to pay Charles 2 million crowns.

Although the young François had been a carefree *galant*, as he grew older, he was plagued by illness and perhaps syphilis and suffered from bouts of melancholy and remorse. He let his beard grow, his hair was thinning and he was losing most of his teeth.

During his last weeks he moved incessantly from château to château, finally to Rambouillet, so ill that he had to be carried in a litter.

There he died on 31 March 1547, apparently penitent, refusing to see his distraught mistress during his final hours. Pious as he may have been at the end, François is better remembered for his love of women, a reputation enhanced three centuries later with Victor Hugo's drama, *Le roi s'amuse*, which in turn inspired Verdi's opera *Rigoletto*.

1931 After being savaged by press barons Lords Rothermere and Beaverbrook, future British PM Stanley Baldwin retorts: 'Power without responsibility – the prerogative of the harlot throughout the ages.'

---

18 March

'No worse deed than this was done to the English race, since they first sought out the land of Britain.'

978 AD The Anglo-Saxon Dowager Queen Elfrida was no stranger to murder, as she had been the cause of one herself fifteen years before. Today she murdered her stepson King Edward in order to place her own son on the throne.

Elfrida was the ravishing daughter of a high-ranking official in the West Country. When tales of her beauty reached England's King Edgar, he sent one of his nobles to see if the reports of her beauty were true, and if so, to ask for her hand in marriage on the king's behalf. But the nobleman was so smitten by her pulchritude that he told the king that she was ugly and dull – and then married her himself.

When Edgar learned of this deception, he feigned disappointment and said that he would come to see this poor sad creature. Alarmed, the nobleman instructed Elfrida to make herself as plain as possible. But she did exactly the opposite, to such good effect that Edgar murdered her husband during a hunt, married her and made her his queen.

In Edgar's household was a boy of about two named Edward, the by-blow of an earlier liaison, who was treated like a legitimate son. In 968 Elfrida gave birth to a son of her own, to be named Aethelred.

Edgar's sudden death in July 975 triggered intense wrangling about who should be his successor. Elfrida backed her son Aethelred, hoping to rule in his name, but the barons who supported Edward proved to be more powerful, and Edward was duly installed as the new monarch.

From this moment Elfrida hated Edward because he wore the crown that she had hoped for her son. Living in a sullen state with her son at Corfe in Dorset, she searched for a way of putting Aethelred on the throne. Today, she found it.

Now sixteen, Edward had been hunting in the woods near Corfe. Tired and thirsty, he rode off from his hunting party to call on them. After Elfrida greeted him affectionately, without dismounting, Edward asked for something to drink, and Elfrida ordered one of her servants to bring some wine. As the king raised his arms to bring the cup to his lips, the servant stepped forward and stabbed him in the chest.

Crying in pain, Edward spurred his horse for the safety of the woods, but, weak from loss of blood, he tumbled from the saddle and entangled his foot in a stirrup. He was dragged behind his mount, his head banging on the ground. By the time the horse finally stopped, he was dead.

His corpse was carried to the solitary cottage of a poor blind woman, where it remained until Elfrida ordered the body buried without ceremony in a nearby churchyard.

Everyone knew that the young king had been unjustly and cruelly murdered. As the contemporary *Anglo-Saxon Chronicle* relates, 'No worse deed than this was done to the English race, since they first sought out the land of Britain.'

As Elfrida had planned, her ten-year-old son Aethelred became king. Elfrida was now regent, so no one was ever charged with the crime.

Despite official silence, rumours soon began to spread – and miracles began to happen. The blind woman who had sheltered Edward's body suddenly regained her sight. A heavenly light appeared over his humble grave, and a spring bubbled up there, whose water effected miraculous cures. Two years later Edward's body was moved to Shaftesbury Abbey, where the healings continued, and his tomb became the object of devotion and pilgrimage. In 1008 the Archbishop of Canterbury canonised him as St Edward the Martyr.

Elfrida served as regent for Aethelred until he came of age six years later. (As king he acquired the famous sobriquet of Aethelred the Unready.) Perhaps Elfrida had some regrets for the murder she had instigated, for just two years after relinquishing her regency she founded a Benedictine nunnery, where late in life she retired and died.

1922 Mahatma Gandhi in a speech: 'Non-violence is the first article of my faith. It is also the last article of my creed.'

19 March

'God will avenge our death.'

1314 Today Jacques de Molay, the last Grand Master of the Templars, was burned at the stake in Paris, his eyes fixed on Notre-Dame in the distance.

A French knight from Champagne named Hugues de Payns had founded the Order of the Temple in 1128, becoming its first Grand Master. The Templars' mission was to guard the passage of pilgrims en route to the Holy Land.

Two centuries later the Templars had grown immensely wealthy, and Jacques de Molay had the misfortune to be in charge when France's King Philip (IV) the Fair, greedy for the Templars' riches, decided on the wholesale destruction of the order.

Arrested in 1307 with all the other Templar knights in France, Molay kept a hard silence of seven long years in prison in Paris, strenuously denying any wrongdoing, even after the order was suppressed in 1312. He was determined to take his defence to the only man who could save him, the Pope. Unfortunately for Molay, however, Pope Clement V was virtually a household pet of King Philip's. (It was this same Clement, a Frenchman by birth, who moved the Holy See from Rome to Avignon.) So when the day came for Grand Master Molay to be judged, the Pope dispatched three cardinals to do the job, keeping himself well clear.

Convicted on torture-induced confessions, Molay was on the point of being condemned to life imprisonment, and he realised that he would have only this one chance to defend himself and the Order. 'The Order is pure, it is holy', he said. 'The confessions are absurd lies.' As for himself, his only crime was basely betraying the Order to save his own life.

The cardinals were thrown into confusion by Molay's eloquent defence, and decided to take the issue back to Pope Clement. But Philip the Fair would not wait. The same day a royal council was convoked, and the Grand Master was condemned once more, this time to the stake.

As the sun set, guards took Jacques de Molay to the place of execution on l'Île aux Juifs, a few hundred metres from the massive towers of Notre-Dame. Dressed only in a cloth shirt, he was chained to the stake. Addressing his executioners, he spoke for the last time: 'God knows who is wrong and who has sinned, and tribulation will befall those who wrongly condemn us. God will avenge our death. Philip, thy life is condemned. I await thee within a year at the Tribune of God.' He then asked to be turned on the stake to face the cathedral.

Just 31 days later Pope Clement suddenly died near Avignon. While his body was lying in state, lightning struck the church, igniting a fire that reduced his corpse to a blackened shell. Then, on 29 November of that same year, Philip the Fair suffered a fatal stroke while hunting. The last curse of the last Templar had been fulfilled.

1945 Hitler issues the Nero Decree: 'All military transport and communication facilities, industrial establishments and supply depots, as well as anything else of value within Reich territory, which could in any way be used by the enemy immediately or within the foreseeable future for the prosecution of the war, will be destroyed.' Reich minister of armaments and war production Albert Speer ignores the order.

---

20 March

'I did not write it. God wrote it. I merely did his dictation.'

1852 Today a Boston firm, John P. Jewett & Co., published an author's first novel. In its first year, the book would sell over 300,000 copies in America, and elsewhere around the world, in English and in translations, another 2,000,000. In the 19th century no book except the Bible sold as many copies.

The novel was *Uncle Tom's Cabin*, subtitled *Life Among the Lowly*. The author, Harriet Beecher Stowe, raised in New England in a strict clerical family, was the daughter, sister, and eventually wife of Presbyterian ministers. In 1832, at the age of 21, she accompanied her father to Cincinnati. There she worked as a schoolteacher, married, bore seven children, and began writing sketches, essays, and stories. Living across the Ohio River from slave-state Kentucky, she encountered at close hand many aspects of slavery and the growing abolitionist sentiment.

In 1850 the US Congress passed the Fugitive Slave Law that required all escaped slaves to be returned to their masters, even if they had escaped to 'free' states. Stowe's sister-in-law urged her, 'Hattie, if I could use a pen as you can, I would write something that will make this whole nation feel what a cursed thing slavery is.' In 1851 she began writing instalments that were published serially over some 40 issues of the abolitionist weekly *The National Era*. The book was published the following year.

Uncle Tom's Cabin was, in Alfred Kazin's phrase, 'the book that really awoke the middle-class conscience to the horrors of slavery'. Its publication broke a silence that had surrounded, in Stowe's words, 'a subject of such delicacy that no discussion of it could be held in the free states without impinging upon the sensibilities of the slave states, to whom alone the management of the matter belonged'.

Despite its enormous success, the book found many dissenters. Radical abolitionists felt the book's message too mild to further their cause. In the South, detractors denounced it as a distortion of an institution sanctioned in the Bible. But elsewhere millions of readers found the book a compelling narrative whose characters put a human face on the practice of slavery. The Afro-American writer Frederick Douglass, who had himself escaped from slavery, described it as 'a flash to light a million camp fires in front of the embattled hosts of slavery'.

During the American Civil War, organisations like the Protestant Episcopal Society gave thousands of copies of *Uncle Tom's Cabin* to Union Army troops. In 1862 Stowe went to Washington, wishing to add her voice to those hoping to persuade President Lincoln to issue an emancipation proclamation. Lincoln greeted her with, 'So this is the little woman who wrote the book that caused this great war.'

Overseas the book's reception was enthusiastic. Tolstoy called it an example 'of the highest art flowing from love of God and man'. George Sand said its author 'has the genius which humanity has the most need of – the genius of good!' Charles Dickens wrote: 'I admire more than I can express to you both the generous feelings which inspired [your book], and the admirable power with which it is executed.'

Even after the war the characters Stowe created – Eliza, Uncle Tom, Topsy, Eva, Simon Legree – lived on for years in numerous stage dramatisations. These 'Tom Shows' caricatured and greatly debased what Stowe had created, in particular turning her Christ-like Uncle Tom into a servile, boot-licking figure. The book went out of print in the early 20th century, not to be reprinted until 1948.

Stowe wrote many other books after *Uncle Tom's Cabin*, including nine novels. None of her later works enjoyed even remotely the success of her first. But then, as she said of that effort, 'I didn't write it. God wrote it. I merely did his dictation.'

1413 Usurper King Henry IV dies in the Jerusalem Chamber of Westminster Abbey repenting his traitorous act: 'God alone knows by what right I took the crown.' * **1815** As Napoleon Bonaparte enters Paris during the 100 Days, he chastises those who had acquiesced to his abdication: 'There are two kinds of fidelity – that of dogs and that of cats; and you, gentlemen, have the fidelity of cats, who never leave the house.'

21 March

'This is the hand that wrote it, therefore shall it suffer first punishment.'

1556 Five months earlier, bishops Hugh Latimer and Nicholas Ridley had been burned at the stake just outside Oxford's city walls. Today their friend and one-time Archbishop of Canterbury Thomas Cranmer met the same fate on the same spot.

On 30 March 1533, when Henry VIII's pursuit of Anne Boleyn was reaching the boiling point, Cranmer had been consecrated as archbishop. Although still married to Catherine of Aragon, Henry secretly wed the pregnant Anne in January of the next year. On 23 May Cranmer declared Henry's marriage to Catherine contrary to the laws of God (she had previously been married to Henry's brother) and proclaimed that Henry's daughter Mary was therefore a bastard. On 28 May he validated Henry's marriage to Anne. Twenty-three years later Mary, now queen, would take her bloody revenge.

Thomas Cranmer sincerely believed in royal power. To Henry VIII he was the perfect minister, promulgating the Treason Laws, generally increasing the king's authority and helping him with the annulment not only of his marriage with Catherine of Aragon but also with that of Anne of Cleves. He was also a strong supporter of reform in the Church, intervening in religious disputes and supporting other reformers who wanted to break the link with Rome.

When Henry died in 1547, Cranmer retained his influence during the brief reign of Edward VI. Then, on Edward's death in 1553, Cranmer followed the dying monarch's wish and backed Lady Jane Grey to succeed. But Lady Jane was executed and Mary Tudor gained the throne. Within four months Cranmer had been tried and convicted of treason.

For seventeen months Cranmer was locked up in Bocardo Prison in Oxford and then was tried again, this time for heresy. Cranmer denied all charges but was found guilty and sentenced to death by fire. By October 1555 bishops Latimer and Ridley had been convicted and burnt, and Cranmer was forced to witness their execution. Then, on 4 December, the Pope gave permission to the secular authorities to carry out the death sentence on Cranmer.

In a last bid to save his life, Cranmer started to backtrack about his religious beliefs. Six times he repudiated the reformed Church, saying that now he fully accepted Catholic dogma, including papal supremacy and transubstantiation, and stated that there was no salvation outside the Catholic Church. He even participated in a Catholic mass.

Having recanted his heresy, under Canon Law Cranmer should have been reprieved. But Queen Mary had never forgotten his humiliation of her mother and branding her a bastard all those years ago. Despite his repentance, she was determined that he should die, telling Edmund Bonner, Bishop of London, that 'his iniquity and obstinacy was so great against God and your Grace that your clemency and mercy could have no place with him'.

On this day, a Saturday, Cranmer was brought to the pulpit in Saint Mary Magdalen Church in Oxford so that he might repent his sins in public before his execution. But instead of repudiating his past, he stunned the zealous crowd by renouncing 'things written in my hand, contrary to the truth which I thought in my heart, and written for fear of death, and to save my life'. He concluded with: 'As for the pope, I refuse him, as Christ's enemy and antichrist, with all his false doctrine.'

Cranmer's infuriated executioners bustled him to the place of execution a few yards from the church and bound him to the stake. As the flames leapt up, Cranmer held out his right hand that had signed his recantations, saying: 'This is the hand that wrote it, therefore shall it suffer first punishment.' Then, to the horror of the onlookers, he thrust it into the fire. And so in unspeakable agony died the archbishop who, more than any other man, built the Church of England.

1646 After being captured at the Battle of Stow-on-the-Wold, Cavalier Sir Jacob Astley to his captors: 'Now you have done your work and may go play, unless you fall out among yourselves.' * **1804** After the royalist pretender, the duc d'Enghien, is abducted and shot on Napoleon's orders, Talleyrand comments: '*C'est plus qu'un crime; c'est une faute.*' ('It's more than a crime; it's a blunder.')

---

22 March

'Paris is well worth a mass.'

1594 Paris, the heart of France, was the goal, but for Henri de Navarre, born in Pau in the deepest south-west corner of the country, it remained a distant aspiration, a city that refused to accept him as king.

At eighteen, Henri experienced first-hand the dangers of Paris. In August 1572, he barely escaped with his life when Catholics ignited the Saint Bartholomew's Day Massacre against the country's Huguenots (Protestants), of which Henri was one.

In 1589, after Henri III had been stabbed to death by a frenzied monk, Henri de Navarre inherited the throne, becoming Henri IV, France's first Bourbon king – but he spent the first four years of his reign trying to conquer his own country. Ranged against him were the Catholic League, largely supported by that fanatical Catholic, Philip II of Spain, and much of the French population, particularly in Paris, which Henri had been unable to capture or control.

Taking the field, Henri prevailed at Arques and Ivry, but then was stymied at Paris. Lacking artillery to break through the city walls, he attempted to starve the Parisians into submission, but after four months a Spanish-Catholic army broke the siege, during which 40,000 people had died of hunger.

Paris remained defiantly independent – and Catholic. Realising that his Protestantism remained an insuperable barrier, Henri at last agreed to join the Church of Rome.

On 25 July 1593, Henri converted in the old basilica at St Denis – not in Paris but just outside. His true objective can be inferred from his famous comment just before he entered the cathedral: 'Paris is well worth a Mass.' (*'Paris vaut bien une messe.'*)

That evening Henri galloped to the top of Montmartre to look down on the city he so longed to rule and saw the crowded streets lit with bonfires to celebrate his conversion. Perhaps the tide was beginning to turn.

Even though officially a Catholic, Henri continued to face resistance from the Catholic League, and the Pope (Clement VIII) dragged his heels in accepting his abjuration. Finally, five years after he had inherited the throne, he was crowned, but at Chartres rather than Reims, which was still held by the League. Nineteen months after that, Clement at last recognised him as 'Christian King of France'.

Paris was still in hostile hands, defended by 4,000 Spanish troops, but by now Parisians were sick of warfare and Spanish intervention and increasingly wanted Henri as king.

At 4.00am on this day, Henri sent his soldiers to the walls of the city, not in attack but in orderly formation. Met at the Porte Neuve by the Provost of Paris, they marched along the bank of the Seine until they reached the Île de la Cité. The Spaniards remained in their barracks. Two hours later Henri himself arrived, wearing full armour and accompanied by his archers and 400 cavalry. As he rode to Notre-Dame, the cathedral bells rang out and the people of Paris rushed into the streets with a delirious welcome for the king they had shunned for so long.

Although now master of Paris, Henri's troubles were far from over. During the next sixteen years his enemies tried to assassinate him thirteen times, finally succeeding in May 1610. But he proved to be one of France's greatest kings. In 1598, he issued the Edict of Nantes, granting substantial rights to his nation's Huguenots and ending 30 years of religious war. He also signed a peace treaty with Philip II, under which Spain withdrew their troops from France and recognised him as king.

Henri cared deeply about the French people, advancing trade and agriculture. 'If God keeps me,' he said, 'I will make sure that no peasant in my realm will lack the means to have a chicken in the pot [the famous *poule au pot*] on Sunday!'

The king also restored the Paris that had for so long rejected him, including the construction of the Grande Galerie of the Louvre, the Pont Neuf and the Place Royale (today the Place des Vosges). Paris had indeed been well worth a mass, not just to Henri but also to the Parisians themselves.

1832 '*Mehr Licht!*' ('More light!'), Johann Wolfgang von Goethe's last words.

---

23 March

'*Smite my womb.*'

59 AD If ever a woman was born to power, it was Julia Agrippina, known as Agrippina the Younger. She was the great-granddaughter of Rome's first emperor, Augustus (and also of his rival, Mark Antony), the great niece of the second emperor, Tiberius, the brother of the third, Caligula, and the niece (and eventually wife) of the fourth, Claudius.

But Agrippina had also seen Rome's brutal side. At four, her father died, probably poisoned by a political rival. At fourteen, Tiberius exiled her mother Agrippina the Elder and two of her brothers for meddling with the imperial succession. Four years later her mother and one brother were starved to death, while the other brother committed suicide.

In 28 AD, when Agrippina was thirteen, she had married Gnaeus Domitius Ahenobarbus, but her ascent to power began when Tiberius died in March 37, leaving the throne to her surviving brother, Caligula. In December she gave birth to the future emperor Nero.

Initially Caligula granted Agrippina substantial power, but in 39 he discovered that Agrippina and her sister Julia Livilla were having an adulterous affair with their brother-in-law Marcus Lepidus and were plotting to murder Caligula and put Lepidus in his place. Lepidus was summarily executed, and Agrippina and her sister were exiled.

In January 40 Agrippina's husband died, and twelve months later Caligula was murdered, making her uncle Claudius the new emperor. Agrippina returned from exile and married the fabulously wealthy Passienus Crispus. But when Crispus died in 47, rumours spread that she had poisoned him to inherit his fortune.

In 48, when Agrippina was 33, Emperor Claudius ordered the execution of his wife, the predatory and sexually insatiable Messalina. It was an opportunity not to be missed; Agrippina seduced her 59-year-old uncle and married him on New Year's Day 49, despite the scandal of what was considered an incestuous union. She was now the most powerful woman in the Roman Empire.

Now Agrippina began to plot for her son Nero to succeed Claudius, ordering several of his rivals murdered. She persuaded Claudius to adopt Nero and replace his own son Britannicus as heir, but after three years of marriage, Claudius began to repent his decision and started grooming Britannicus as the next emperor. Agrippina's power and her son's future were threatened, but she had a solution in hand. On the evening of 12 October 54, she served her husband some poisoned mushrooms. He died in agony at dawn the next morning.

Nero duly became emperor, still only sixteen. Initially Agrippina controlled both him and the empire, but soon a titanic power struggle began.

Nero became involved with a freed slave named Claudia Acte, greatly reducing Agrippina's sway over her son and therefore over the empire. Her unrelenting efforts to separate Nero from his mistress served only to increase his infatuation, and Nero expelled Agrippina from the palace to live in Misenum on the Bay of Naples, depriving her of all powers and even removing her bodyguards.

For the next two years Nero and his mother sparred for power, with occasional meetings of feigned affection. But as Nero became increasingly megalomaniac, he was tormented by Agrippina's continued popularity and influence.

In mid-March 59, mother and son met at the festival of Minerva at Baiae, three miles up the coast from Misenum. After an evening of filial love and reconciliation, Nero escorted Agrippina to her boat. She retired to her cabin, but suddenly the ceiling came crashing down, stopped from crushing her only by the high sides of her couch. Nero had ordered the boat booby-trapped in order to kill his mother.

As Agrippina extricated herself from the cabin, the crew capsized the boat. One of her handmaidens tried to escape by calling out that she was Agrippina, but she was bludgeoned to death by the crew who could not see in the dark. Meanwhile Agrippina slipped into the sea, swam to shore and returned to Misenum. As soon as Nero learned that she was still alive, he sent three assassins to finish the job.

On this day the assassins broke into her house, and one struck her with a club. Then, according to Tacitus, as another 'bared his sword for the fatal deed, presenting her person, she exclaimed, "Smite my womb" and with many wounds she was slain.'

1775 American revolutionary Patrick Henry tells the Second Virginia Convention: 'I know not what course others may take; but as for me, give me liberty or give me death.' * **1801** After assassinating the feckless Tsar Paul I, one of the conspirators, General Nikolay Zubov, tells Paul's son and heir Alexander I, 'Time to grow up! Go and rule!'

---

24 March

'All my possessions for a moment of time!'

1603 'Nature's common work is done, and he that was born to die hath paid his tribute', once wrote Elizabeth I of England in a letter of condolence. Now as the shadows of age closed in, it was her turn to pay her tribute after 45 years as queen.

Elizabeth had been a strong-minded leader who once scorned her enemies with the comment: 'I am more afraid of making a fault in my

Latin than of the kings of Spain, France, Scotland and the House of Guise and all their confederates.' As a Protestant she was abhorred by the Church of Rome, but even Pope Sixtus V said admiringly, '[She is] only mistress of half an island, and yet she makes herself feared by Spain, by France, by the Empire, by all.' Her chief minister Sir Robert Cecil had said that she was 'more than a man but sometimes (by troth) less than a woman'.

Earlier in her reign Elizabeth had told Parliament: 'As for me, I see no such great cause why I should either be fond to live or fear to die. I have had good experience of this world, and I know what it is to be subject and what to be a sovereign.' But as she grew older, doubts began to enter her mind. She was, according to Sir Walter Raleigh, 'a lady surprised by time'.

Her last years were sombre. Always vain, she wore a tawny wig to hide her grey and thinning hair, and by her decree her palace at Richmond contained not a single mirror. The friends and counsellors of her youth were gone, and she knew her time was near. It was rumoured that her gloomy ghost wandered the palace corridors, anticipating her demise.

During March 1603 for four days she refused to go to bed, remaining seated on her cushions at Richmond Palace. One day she spent all the daylight hours in silence, her finger in her mouth. Yet she was not senile, but seemingly contemplating her life and past and what was to come. Even at the end she had not lost her authority or her bite; when Sir Robert Cecil told her that she must go to bed, she snapped: 'Must! Is must a word to be addressed to princes? Little man, little man!'

On 23 March Elizabeth announced: 'I wish not to live any longer, but desire to die.' Was this resignation – or bravado? By the early hours of the next morning it may have been fear, as her last reported words were, 'All my possessions for a moment of time!'

At three o'clock the greatest queen that England (and perhaps any nation) would ever know drifted away, the Archbishop of Canterbury at her side in prayer. Legend asserts that her coronation ring could be removed only by cutting off her finger, symbolising her union with her country. She had lived for 69 years, six months and fourteen days.

The queen's coffin was carried down the Thames at night to Whitehall, on a barge lit with torches. At her funeral, the coffin was taken to Westminster Abbey on a hearse drawn by four horses hung with black velvet. The contemporary chronicler John Stow reported that vast crowds thronged the streets and 'there was such a general sighing, groaning and weeping as the like hath not been seen or known in the memory of man'.

1603 James VI of Scotland succeeds to the English throne as James I. In his first speech in England he asserts that Scotland and England form a single realm: 'I am the husband and the whole isle is my lawful wife; I am the head and it is my body; I am the shepherd and it is my flock. I hope therefore that no man will think that I, a Christian King under the Gospel, should be a polygamist and husband to two wives; that I being the head should have a divided or monstrous body or that being the shepherd to so fair a flock should have my flock parted in two.' But it still takes 104 years for the Kingdom of Great Britain to be legally formed.

---

25 March

'I forgive you my death
and will exact no revenge.'

1199 Today King Richard the Lionheart received a mortal wound in the insignificant village of Châlus, but at his death he showed the knightly chivalry for which he was famed.

About twenty miles south-west of Limoges, Châlus is dominated by a small castle, where its owner, a knight named Achard, lived with about fifteen soldiers. Early in 1199 a local farmer had found buried nearby a treasure of golden coins, probably Roman, and took it to Achard, his lord. When King Richard heard about the find, he declared he would have half of it by right, since he was overlord of the Limousin. Unwisely, Achard decided to resist.

Soon Richard was riding toward Châlus with a troop of mercenaries led by the Provençal freebooter Mercadier, a soldier of fortune who had already served Richard for fifteen years and had accompanied him on the Third Crusade.

In March Richard laid siege to this insignificant fortress, and even when Achard offered to surrender if he and his men were allowed to leave unharmed, Richard refused, swearing he would take the castle by storm and hang all its defenders.

On the evening of 25 March, the king decided to inspect the progress his sappers were making in undermining the castle's walls, ignoring the occasional arrow fired by Achard's men. Protected by a shield but without his armour, he was so nonchalant that he even applauded the efforts of an enemy bowman.

Suddenly through the twilight sped a crossbow bolt, striking the king in his unprotected left shoulder. Richard quickly retreated to his quarters, summoning Mercadier and his surgeon. But the bolt had penetrated deep and was at last recovered only by the excruciating torment of laying open the flesh.

Even without Richard, Mercadier's mercenaries soon reduced the fortress and, in the process, captured a youth named Pierre Basile who had fired the shot. But by now Richard's wound showed unmistakable signs of gangrene, and the Lionheart knew he would soon die. Perhaps because it was the Lenten season, he performed one last chivalrous act.

Summoning the terrified Basile, Richard demanded, 'What harm have I done to you that you should kill me?' The young man replied, 'Because you killed my father and brother. Do with me as you want. I have no regrets for the vengeance I have taken.'

'Go forth in peace', said Richard. 'I forgive you my death and will exact no revenge.'

Twelve days later, on 6 April, the great troubadour-knight-crusader-king was dead, at the age of 41. Ignoring Richard's forgiveness, Mercadier had Basile flayed alive and hanged.

1963 Christine Keeler tells a journalist: 'The trouble is I am 21 ... I have lived in the West End of London and frequently been to parties with well-known people present. Presumably if I had been 52 and a housewife from Surbiton there would have been none of this trouble.'

---

26 March

'I shall hear in heaven.'

1827 Today, in the midst of a violent thunderstorm, Ludwig van Beethoven died in Vienna at 56.

Born in Bonn, Beethoven was a child prodigy at the piano, giving his first public performance at age seven. At twelve he published his first composition, a set of keyboard variations. Four years later he visited Vienna, apparently in the hope of enrolling Mozart as his teacher. He may have seen Mozart (who is said to have presciently remarked,

'He will give the world something worth listening to'), but it is uncertain that they actually met.

When he was 21, Beethoven moved permanently to Vienna, where he studied under Joseph Haydn and quickly gained a reputation as a virtuoso pianist. As well as performing, he now increasingly dedicated himself to composing. At 25 he gave his first public concert, playing one of his own piano concertos. About this time, however, he started losing his hearing. Despite this affliction, he continued to perform and to compose. On 2 April 1800 he premiered his First Symphony at Vienna's Burgtheater.

Unlike Mozart, who lived and died on the edge of penury for lack of sponsors, Beethoven was recognised and supported throughout his career. Although never rich, he was comfortable. In December 1808 he held the premieres of both his Fifth and Sixth Symphonies at the Theater an der Wien, but the concert was not a critical success (a verdict disputed ever since; the writer E.M. Forster maintained that 'Beethoven's Fifth Symphony is the most sublime noise that has ever penetrated into the ear of man').

Beethoven's hearing continued to decline, so he tried a variety of hearing aids and ear horns, but by 1818 he was reduced to communicating with conversation notebooks. His personal appearance also deteriorated, as did his manners in public, especially when dining. He became a solitary and cantankerous man totally devoted to his music. He remained a bachelor, in spite of several attempts to marry. After his death, three letters were found locked in his cabinet, all including declarations of love and addressed to his 'Immortal Beloved'. The letters are undated and had never been sent, and the identity of his 'Immortal Beloved' has never been discovered.

On 7 May 1824 Beethoven conducted the premiere of his final symphony, the Ninth, which he had been working on for six years. At the symphony's conclusion the audience shook the concert hall with thunderous applause – but the stone-deaf composer, facing the orchestra, was completely unaware of the ovation until one of the soloists made him turn to face the cheering crowd.

During his last years, Beethoven's health had been in steady decline. In December 1826 he suffered episodes of vomiting and diarrhoea and was bedridden for the final three months of his life. On this stormy afternoon he died. Controversy continues over his last words. One version has him histrionically murmuring the classical ending to Roman plays: '*Plaudite, amici, comoedia finita est.*' ('Applaud, my friends, the comedy is over.') Another account describes him receiving a shipment of Rhine wine which he had ordered months before. Taking a sip, he mumbled, 'Pity, pity ... Too late!' But in the story we'd like to believe, he ended his life with the hope: '*Ich werde im Himmel hören!*' ('I shall hear in heaven.')

Sitting by Beethoven's bedside was his friend the Austrian composer Anselm Hüttenbrenner, who reported: 'At this startling, awful peal of thunder, the dying man suddenly raised his head from [my] arm, stretched out his own right arm majestically – like a general giving orders to an army. This was but for an instant; the arm sunk back; he fell back. Beethoven was dead.' Retrospective diagnosis suggests he died of cirrhosis of the liver.

Three days later the great composer was buried in Währing church-yard in Vienna, after a funeral attended by 20,000 people. In the apocalyptic words of the near-contemporary Russian anarchist Mikhail Bakunin, 'Everything will pass, and the world will perish but the Ninth Symphony will remain.'

1766 Voltaire writes to M. Mariott: 'It is amusing that a virtue is made of the vice of chastity; and it's a pretty odd sort of chastity at that, which leads men straight into the sin of Onan, and girls to the waning of their colour.'

---

27 March

'You can't make an omelette without breaking eggs.'

1793 In January Louis XVI had been fed to the guillotine, but all over France there was resistance to the bloody republicanism now gripping the nation, none more dogged than that in the Vendée, a *département* south of Brittany on the Atlantic coast.

Vendéan peasants had initially supported the Revolution, but Republican excesses, the shackling of the Catholic Church and new conscription demands had caused major unrest in this isolated and highly conservative region. By March there were riots, before long followed by bloodshed, as rebels ambushed and murdered local may-ors and judges. Soon, however, soldiers from the new Republican government invaded the region, slaughtering at will to bring anti-revolutionaries and royalists to heel.

In late March 1793 the Republicans crushed some 4,000 Vendéans at Pornic and summarily executed 250 prisoners after the battle. Four days later, on the 27th, the rebels headed for the nearby town of Fonteclose to entreat a 29-year-old French aristocrat named François-Athanase Charette de La Contrie to become their leader. Charette was a noted royalist soldier who had defended Louis XVI and Marie Antoinette during the revolutionary attack on the Tuileries on 10 August the previous year. Yet he had no desire to join the Vendéan insurgents and had hidden under his bed in the hope they would go away. Discovered, he told them: 'So be it, but I order and they obey.' On the same day, the rebels recaptured Pornic under his leadership. From that day he would be a major royalist chief in the Vendée.

During the counter-revolution he fought in 24 battles against the Republican government. A flamboyant commander, he had his scarf embroidered in gold letters: '*Combattu: souvent. Battu: parfois. Abattu: jamais.*' ('Fought: often. Defeated: sometimes. Downcast: never.')

In the summer of 1795, a group of royalist *émigrés* landed in Quiberon Bay to take on the Republicans, but even with Charette fighting beside them, they were comprehensively crushed, with most of those captured executed. After this defeat Charette had all his Republican prisoners shot and committed other bloody reprisals. Two months later Charette was defeated once again in a failed assault on the fortified town of Saint-Cyr-en-Talmondais, where he was wounded in the head and body.

Now on the run with only 32 remaining followers, Charette was hunted in the woods like a wild beast. He was considered so dangerous that the Republican general Hoche offered him a large bribe plus free passage to England, but Charette refused to go.

On 23 March 1796 he was finally captured outside La Chabotterie and taken to Nantes for a trial. Today, when the judges accused him of causing the deaths of so many people, he shrugged, 'You can't make an omelette without breaking eggs.' ('*On ne saurait faire d'omelette sans casser des œufs.*') This expression may have been employed since about 1750, but this is its first recorded use.

Condemned to death, on 29 March he was marched to the Place Viarme for a public execution. Charette himself commanded the firing squad. Refusing a blindfold, he ordered: 'When I close my eyes, shoot straight to the heart.' Then, with a last effort, as the soldiers fired, he threw himself forward into the bullets.

1306 Robert the Bruce's wife warns her husband before meeting the English in battle: 'You are indeed a summer king, but you will scarce be a winter one.' * **1775** Dr Johnson declares: 'There are few ways in which a man can be more innocently employed than in getting money.'

28 March

'Dearest, I feel certain that
I am going mad again.'

1941 Today one of England's greatest writers filled her pockets with stones and threw herself into the freezing waters of the River Ouse. She was Virginia Woolf, who was tormented by visions and preferred death to the demons of insanity.

Woolf (*née* Stephen) was born in London in an affluent, literate and well-connected household, but she was sexually abused by her two half-brothers when she was six. At thirteen she lost her mother and at fifteen her half-sister, after which she had her first nervous breakdown. By the time she was eighteen, however, Woolf was already writing professionally, initially with the *Times Literary Supplement*.

When she was 22, her father also died, provoking a collapse so alarming that she was institutionalised. For the rest of her life she would suffer from intense periods of depression, spending short periods in mental hospitals.

After her second breakdown Woolf moved to the Bloomsbury area of London with her brother and sister. There she mixed with the intellectual circle of writers and artists known as the Bloomsbury Group, which included E.M. Forster, Lytton Strachey, Rupert Brooke, John Maynard Keynes and, most significantly, Leonard Woolf, who had been a civil servant in Ceylon but had returned to London to take up writing. In August 1912 Leonard and Virginia married. They would remain devoted to each other until her death, despite her affair with the writer Vita Sackville-West.

In 1915 Woolf published her first novel, *The Voyage Out*, which she had been working on for three years. She would write eight more novels that secured her place among the greats of modernist literature, including *To the Lighthouse*, *Mrs Dalloway* and *Orlando*, a book inspired by her relationship with Sackville-West. She also penned an extended essay called *A Room of One's Own*, which included her famous dictum, 'a woman must have money and a room of her own if she is to write fiction'.

In 1919 she and Leonard purchased an 18th-century cottage called Monk's House in Rodmell in East Sussex. After their London flat was bombed in September 1940 during the Blitz, they moved to it full-time. There she continued to write in a small wooden lodge at the bottom of the garden.

Woolf had first attempted suicide in 1913, and for the remainder of her life depression was never far away; her last work published in her lifetime had been *The Years* in 1937, and now, at 59, she felt unable to work. Moreover, as Britain braced itself for German invasion, she feared what would happen to her husband (who was Jewish) if he fell into Nazi hands. On this day she wrote a last note to Leonard:

> Dearest, I feel certain that I am going mad again. I feel we can't go through another of those terrible times. And I shan't recover this time. I begin to hear voices, and I can't concentrate. So I am doing what seems the best thing to do. You have given me the greatest possible happiness. You have been in every way all that anyone could be. I don't think two people could have been happier till this terrible disease came. I can't fight any longer. I know that I am spoiling your life, that without me you could work. And you will I know. You see I can't even write this properly. I can't read. What I want to say is I owe all the happiness of my life to you. You have been entirely patient with me and incredibly good. I want to say that – everybody knows it. If anybody could have saved me it would have been you. Everything has gone from me but the certainty of your goodness. I can't go on spoiling your life any longer. I don't think two people could have been happier than we have been. V

She then put on her overcoat, loaded its pockets with stones and walked to the river less than a mile away. Her body was not found until three weeks later.

1710 Lady Mary Wortley Montagu writes in a letter to her husband: 'General notions are generally wrong.' * **1960** Gloria Steinem in *Newsweek*: 'A liberated woman is one who has sex before marriage and a job after.' In the same issue Zsa Zsa Gabor says: 'A man in love is incomplete until he has married. Then he's finished.'

29 March

'I am just going outside and may be some time.'

1912 The South Pole sits on a barren, windswept plateau of polar ice 9,000 feet thick in Antarctica. In 1910 British Navy captain Robert Scott set out with his team, determined to be the first ever to reach the Pole, but as he was preparing for his expedition, he learned that the Norwegian explorer Roald Amundsen was organising a team for the same purpose. The race was on – who would get there first?

Scott's ship *Terra Nova* set sail from New Zealand and after much turmoil (it nearly sank in a storm and was trapped in pack ice for twenty days) finally reached their base on the Ross Sea, 858 miles of frozen terrain from the Pole. Amundsen was camped 200 miles to the east.

On 19 October 1911 Amundsen and four teammates started the overland trek to the Pole, and on 1 November Scott began his march on a route 60 miles longer than Amundsen's.

By 4 January 1912 Scott had traversed almost 700 miles and now selected the group to make the final push – Edward Wilson, Henry Bowers, Lawrence 'Titus' Oates, Edgar Evans and Scott himself. After two weeks of temperatures of –45°F, nearly impassable terrain, blinding blizzards or blinding sunshine, they came within three miles of the Pole, only to find Norwegian sledge tracks – Amundsen and his team had reached the Pole on 14 December. The disappointed Scott wrote in his journal: 'Great God! This is an awful place.'

The next day Scott's team trudged the last few miles to the Pole itself and then began the daunting return journey. As Scott recorded, 'Well, we have turned our back now on the goal of our ambition and must face our 800 miles of solid dragging – and good-bye to most of the day-dreams!' By then Amundsen was just a week from his return to base without having lost a man.

Already weakened by the eleven-week slog to the Pole, the Scott team was now faced with exceptionally adverse weather, diminishing food supplies and the effects of scurvy and frostbite.

On 4 February Edgar Evans fell into a crevasse, injuring his head. When he dropped behind, the team were forced to ski back to find him. As Scott wrote, 'he was on his knees with clothing disarranged, hands uncovered and frostbitten, and a wild look in his eyes'. He died on 17 February.

The next casualty was Titus Oates, who was suffering from scurvy and whose feet were severely frostbitten. On 15 March, Scott wrote: 'poor Titus Oates said he couldn't go on; he proposed we should leave him in his sleeping-bag. That we could not do …' Three days later he recorded in his journal: '[Oates] slept through the night before last, hoping not to wake; but he woke in the morning – yesterday. It was blowing a blizzard. He said, "I am just going outside and may be some time." He went out into the blizzard and we have not seen him since.' It was Oates's 32nd birthday.

On 22 March the remaining men were within eleven miles of their next food depot, but Scott recorded their desperation: 'Blizzard bad as ever – Wilson and Bowers unable to start – to-morrow last chance – no fuel and only one or two of food left.'

For over a week freezing storms prevented the men from venturing out of their tents. A despairing Scott wrote: 'outside the door of the tent it remains a scene of whirling drift … We shall stick it out to the end, but we are getting weaker, of course, and the end cannot be far.'

Scott, Wilson and Bowers are presumed to have died on 29 March; the positions of their bodies when they were discovered eight months later suggested that Scott was the last to succumb.

After a century of storms and snow, the frozen corpses of the three explorers now lie under about 75 feet of ice in the Ross Ice Shelf, which is inching towards the sea. In about 275 years the bodies should reach the sea, and perhaps float away inside an iceberg.

1951 A jury in New York unanimously convicts spies Julius and Ethel Rosenberg of treason for giving atomic secrets to the Soviet Union. A week later Judge Irving Kaufman sentences them to the electric chair, saying: 'I consider your crime worse than murder.'

---

30 March

'Honey, I forgot to duck.'

1981 At half past two this afternoon the newly elected president Ronald Reagan, still robust at 70, walked from the Washington Hilton Hotel where he had given a speech. From a crowd of admirers waiting behind a rope fifteen feet away lurked a balding man wearing a dark jacket over a striped shirt. He was there to kill the president.

The aspirant assassin was John Hinckley Jr, a 25-year-old college dropout who had seen the film *Taxi Driver* fifteen times and had become fixated with Jodie Foster, who played a child prostitute. Although only eighteen, Foster was already a celebrated actress. Hinckley came to believe that if he, too, could become famous she would return his love, even though he had never met her.

Pulling a Röhm .22 calibre revolver from his pocket, Hinckley fired six wild shots in less than two seconds. The first caught White House Press Secretary James Brady in the head, another hit a police officer in the neck, while a third hit a Secret Service agent as he spread his body over Reagan to shield him. Two bullets went wide, one smashing into the window of the presidential limousine, another hitting a window of a building across the street. But by a fluke of luck the sixth bullet ricocheted off the limousine and hit Reagan in his left underarm, grazing a rib and lodging in his lung, only an inch from his heart.

A brave union official in the crowd knocked Hinckley to the ground, and Secret Service agents piled on. Meanwhile another agent whipped a submachine-gun from his briefcase to deter other possible attackers.

In great pain from the bullet wound, Reagan was bundled into the limousine, which raced for George Washington University Hospital, only four minutes away. When he arrived at the hospital, he spurned a stretcher and insisted on walking, but once inside his knees buckled and he went down on one knee and had to be assisted to the emergency room. There, much to his annoyance, the medical team cut off his custom-made suit.

Reagan was still bleeding and deep in shock, a condition that in itself could kill a man of his age, but he remained composed while the medical team treated him with intravenous fluids, oxygen and an anti-tetanus shot. When his wife Nancy reached the emergency room, he cracked with a smile, 'Honey, I forgot to duck'. (At the time many credited the quip to Reagan's wit, not realising that he was quoting boxer Jack Dempsey's line to his wife the night he was beaten by Gene Tunney in 1927.)

Just before the doctors operated to remove the bullet, Reagan removed his oxygen mask to joke, 'I hope you are all Republicans'. The operation lasted almost two hours; by the time it was over Reagan had lost over half his blood. Unknown to the public, he had come very close to dying.

Within a month Reagan had returned to the White House, although initially his workload was limited to two hours a day. The wounded police officer and Secret Service agent soon recovered, but Press Secretary James Brady was partially paralysed and required a wheelchair for the rest of his life. When he died in 2014, his death was ruled a homicide, a consequence of the shooting.

The assassination attempt had a great impact on Jodie Foster. She rarely spoke about it, once explaining: 'I never wanted to be the actress who was remembered for that event. Because it didn't have anything to do with me. I was kind of a hapless bystander.'

Hinckley was found not guilty by reason of insanity. To prove the point, after the trial he wrote that the shooting was 'the greatest love offering in the history of the world'. He was locked up in St Elizabeth's psychiatric hospital in Washington until September 2016, when he was released to live with his mother, with mandatory psychiatric treatment.

Ronald Reagan successfully ran for re-election in 1984 and completed his eight years in the White House a month short of his 79th birthday, a record among American presidents.

1867 When Russia sells Alaska to the United States for $7.2 million, the *New York Tribune* fulminates against the purchase of a frigid wilderness: 'The treaty had been secretly prepared, and signed and foisted upon the country at one o'clock in the morning. It was a dark deed done in the night.' But this enormous territory (almost seven times the size of Great Britain) holds $500 billion worth of oil and now has a median family income of $73,000 a year.

---

31 March

'Judas sold Jesus Christ for thirty pieces of silver. You would sell Him again for three hundred thousand ducats.'

1492 Just three months earlier, Spain's Catholic monarchs Ferdinand and Isabella had ousted the Moors from Granada to complete the *Reconquista*. On this day in Granada they turned from conquering Muslims to banishing Jews, issuing the infamous Alhambra Decree that ordered all Jews to convert to Christianity or leave the country no later than 31 July or face summary execution.

The Decree followed almost immediately upon the appointment of the ascetic Francisco Jiménez de Cisneros as Isabella's confessor, and he may have been a strong influence on her decision. Her husband

Ferdinand also backed the Decree, or at least did not oppose it. But the prime mover was the Dominican monk Tomás de Torquemada, who had been the Grand Inquisitor of the Spanish Inquisition since its inception in 1483.

In his ongoing persecution of the Jews, Torquemada was a chilling forerunner of the Nazis half a millennium later. His ultimate goal was to establish nothing less than *sangre limpia* (pure blood) in Spain – that is, Christian blood.

Torquemada's concern was not just the Jews living in Spain but particularly the so-called *marranos*, Jews who claimed to have converted to Christianity but who secretly still followed the Jewish faith. He was convinced they were furtively trying to convert Christians to Judaism. He made detected *marranos* forfeit their property, forced them to wear a yellow shirt sewn with crosses, and had them flogged in public at the entrance to a church. He even issued a set of tell-tale signs by which good Christians could detect these crypto-Jews, e.g. 'If on Saturday your neighbours wear clean clothes, they are Jews.'

After ten years of pursuing *marranos*, Torquemada exhorted King Ferdinand and Queen Isabella to expel all the Jews from Spain. But then some wealthy Jews offered 300,000 ducats if the Jews could remain, and the king and queen were sorely tempted.

On hearing of the offer, Torquemada hurried to the palace and, holding his crucifix before him, confronted the royal pair. 'Judas sold Jesus Christ for thirty pieces of silver', he admonished. 'You would sell Him again for three hundred thousand ducats. Here, take Him and sell Him, and I will leave my office and you will explain your agreement to God.' He then turned and left the room.

In the face of such holy intransigence, Ferdinand and Isabella issued the Alhambra Decree. Approximately 50,000 Jews received Christian baptism in order to remain in Spain, some of them no doubt becoming *marranos* in their turn. But somewhere between 40,000 and 100,000 fled with only their personal possessions. They were forbidden to take 'gold or silver or minted money or other things prohibited by the laws of our kingdoms'. The Jews had to sell anything they couldn't carry with them – their land and their houses. But the Spanish market was soon awash with property for sale, and prices dropped to rock bottom, so many Jews left the country with only a fraction of their former wealth.

The banished Jews ended up not only throughout Europe but also in Turkey, North Africa and the Arab world, where they were known as Sephardic Jews – *Sefarad* being the Hebrew name for Spain. (Although rarely enforced after the great expulsion of 1492, the Alhambra Decree remained technically in force for another 476 years, finally overturned on 16 December 1968.)

Many have wondered what drives a man like Torquemada to such extremes of relentless persecution. Some believe that, like Hitler's notorious SS officer Reinhard Heydrich, Torquemada was compelled by the knowledge of his own tainted bloodline: his grandmother had been a converted Jew.

1987 Ronald Reagan tells an interviewer for the *Guardian*: 'It's true hard work never killed anybody, but I figure why take the chance?'

---

1 April

'It is a womb that I am marrying.'

1810 Today in a civil ceremony at St Cloud, the 40-year-old Emperor Napoleon married Austrian archduchess Marie-Louise, 21 years his junior and daughter of the Austrian Emperor Franz I. Marie-Louise was Napoleon's second bride and a striking contrast to his first.

Twenty-four years earlier a youngish general still spelling his name Buonaparte had wed an erotic 32-year-old widow named Joséphine de Beauharnais, whose first husband had been guillotined during the Terror. Joséphine had been introduced to Napoleon by her lover of the moment, Paul Barras, and their marriage was passionate from the start. Two days after the wedding he left Paris to lead the army into Italy, and just before his return he famously wrote to her: '*Ne te lave pas, j'accours et dans huit jours je suis là.*' ('Do not wash yourself, I am coming and in eight days I will be there.') (A century and a half later Coco Channel offered French women complementary advice: '*Parfumez-vous là où vous voulez être embrassée.*' ('Perfume yourself where you want to be kissed.'))

Within weeks of Napoleon's departure, however, Joséphine had started a liaison with another army officer, almost causing divorce. Eventually Napoleon forgave her, but he embarked on the first of his 22 affairs. But infidelity did not break down the marriage – in 1809 it was given the *coup de grâce* for reasons of state. In August Napoleon had impregnated his mistress Marie Walewska, proving he might sire an heir. He told Josephine that – in the interest of France – he must find a new wife. 'I love you still,' he said, 'but in politics there is no heart, only head.'

He dissolved his sixteen-year marriage and began the hunt for a bride. 'It is a womb that I am marrying,' he said. Then the shrewd Austrian statesman Klemens von Metternich suggested Archduchess Marie-Louise, persuading her father that the marriage would consolidate his hold on the Austrian throne at a time when Napoleon was master of Europe. When Metternich informed the bland Marie-Louise, she replied, 'I wish only what my duty commands me to wish'. Napoleon was heartened by the news that Marie-Louise's mother had borne thirteen children, her grandmother seventeen and her great-grandmother 26.

The couple were wed by proxy on 11 March, and two weeks later Marie-Louise left for Paris. Knowing her route, Napoleon intercepted her carriage at Courcelles, rode with her to Compiègne and whisked her off to consummate the marriage. Later he wistfully recalled, 'She liked it so much she asked me to do it again.'

At St Cloud the proxy-weds were welcomed with a 100-gun salute. On the morning of 1 April hundreds of onlookers waited in a cold, heavy rain while inside the palace civil and ecclesiastical dignitaries and a pride of foreign ambassadors watched Napoleon and Marie-Louise be pronounced man and wife.

Just six weeks later Napoleon received news that he had a child at last – by Marie Walewska, who had given birth to a healthy son. But Marie-Louise proved equally fertile and gave Napoleon a second son in March 1811.

Although it was a political marriage rather than a love match, at first all went smoothly, but when Napoleon abdicated in 1814, Marie-Louise returned to Vienna. Ignoring his pleas to join him on Elba, she entered an entrenched affair with Adam Adalbert, Count von Neipperg. She never saw her husband again, refusing to come to him even after he escaped from Elba.

While in Elba Napoleon learned that Joséphine had died of pneumonia a month before her 51st birthday. In his grief he stayed locked alone in his room for two days.

When incarcerated on St Helena the ex-emperor brooded about Marie-Louise, bitterly commenting: 'With her I stepped onto an abyss covered with flowers.' But perhaps in the end he forgave her. Just before he died, he directed that his heart be offered to her – a gift she declined, perhaps because by that time she was living openly with Neipperg and had already borne him two children. At the end, it was his first wife that Napoleon yearned for. His last words were '*Tête d'armée! France! France! Joséphine!*'

1895 On his 80th birthday, Bismarck observes: 'The first eighty years of a man's life are sure to be the happiest.'

---

2 April

'I have the right to be blind sometimes …
I really do not see the signal.'

1801 Horatio Nelson had suffered his first serious battle wound in 1794 when his squadron was besieging Corsica. Then a 35-year-old captain, he was in charge of the naval guns brought ashore to pound the enemy fortress at Calvi when a French shell exploded, showering the attackers with sand and broken rock. Something struck him in the right eye, permanently clouding his vision. Although a serious wound, it would add to his legend on this day seven years later.

In their fight against Napoleon, in 1800 the Royal Navy began cavalierly searching neutral nations' ships for contraband in an attempt to cut off military supplies and other trade from France. Russia's response was to form the League of Armed Neutrality with Prussia and the Scandinavian countries to protect their shipping, but the British regarded the League not as neutral, but as a covert alliance with France.

Today British admiral Hyde Parker led his fleet to attack the Danish navy anchored at Copenhagen to force the Danes to renounce the Russian alliance. Leading the British van was Vice Admiral Nelson in the 74-gun warship HMS *Elephant*. With him were eleven other ships of the line, five frigates and thirteen smaller British vessels.

The Danish ships and hulks were moored along the shore as a line of floating batteries, reinforced by the powerful guns in the Danish fortress on land. At about ten o'clock Nelson attacked in what might be called a full-frontal naval assault. Each British ship anchored about a cable's length (608 feet) from a Danish ship and opened fire. Broadside after broadside crashed into the Danes, who returned fire in kind. After almost four merciless hours both sides were badly battered, and three British warships had been grounded.

Aboard his flagship Admiral Parker could see little of the battle owing to gun smoke, but he could make out the distress signals flying from the grounded British ships. It was clear only that the Danes were still vigorously returning fire. Fearing that the enemy might be getting the upper hand, Parker signalled to his fleet to discontinue the action.

Seeing Parker's signal, Nelson growled, 'Now, damn me if I do!' He turned to his flag captain Thomas Foley and said, 'You know, Foley, I have only one eye – and I have the right to be blind sometimes.' He then raised his telescope to his blind eye and said, 'I really do not see the signal.'

During the next half hour Nelson's ships continued to trade fire with the enemy, making more and more Danish ships cease firing because they were so badly damaged, some forced to surrender. Nelson now sent a message to the Danish regent, Crown Prince Frederick, who had been watching the battle from the ramparts of the fortress:

To the Brothers of Englishmen, the Danes

Lord Nelson has directions to spare Denmark when she is no longer resisting, but if firing is continued on the part of Denmark, Lord Nelson will be obliged to set on fire the floating batteries he has taken, without having the power of saving the brave Danes who have defended them.

Nelson

Although the British fleet was probably in as much danger as the Danish one, Nelson's confident letter worked. By late afternoon the Danes had agreed a ceasefire.

The next day Nelson went ashore and negotiated an indefinite armistice with Prince Frederick, but the Danes initially refused to abandon Russia and the League of Armed Neutrality. Nelson then threatened to bombard Copenhagen itself. In the meantime, dramatic news had reached the Danes: the Russian Tsar Paul had been murdered on 23 March by a band of dismissed officers. On 9 April the Danes left the League, and the following October they signed a final peace treaty with Great Britain.

1791 Just before he dies, French moderate revolutionary Honoré Gabriel Riqueti, Count of Mirabeau prophetically tells Talleyrand: 'I take away with me the last shreds of monarchy.' * **1917** President Woodrow Wilson asks Congress to declare war against Germany: 'The world must be made safe for democracy.'

---

3 April

'Murdered by a traitor and a coward whose name is not worthy to appear here'

1882 Today Jesse James, America's most famous outlaw, was shot in the back by one of his own gang.

Born in Missouri in 1847, James was only fifteen when he and his brother Frank joined William Quantrill's notorious Confederate guerrilla band during America's Civil War. The next year they participated in one of the war's most brutal slaughters when 450 Quantrill Raiders attacked the abolitionist town of Lawrence, Kansas, looting the banks and stores and slaughtering 150 mostly unarmed men.

The James brothers then joined a guerrilla group led by Quantrill's former lieutenant, Bloody Bill Anderson. These bushwhackers carried out another massacre at Centralia, Missouri, first executing 22 unarmed Union soldiers and then killing 123 more during the subsequent one-sided battle. Jesse James himself shot the Union commander.

When the war ended, the James brothers teamed up with other guerrillas-turned-outlaw to use their military raiding skills for armed robbery. Although still just nineteen and four years younger than Frank, Jesse became the gang's leader. The next February they robbed their first bank, stealing $60,000 (about $500,000 today) and killing a bystander on the street outside.

During the next sixteen years Jesse's gang raided and murdered throughout the Midwest, in July 1873 committing their first train robbery. Despite these depredations, the press in Missouri began portraying Jesse as a loyal Son of the South, a modern-day Robin Hood who was driven to crime by unscrupulous bankers and landowners. His crimes were widely reported, and he occasionally telegraphed newspaper editors to give his version of published reports. In reality, he was just a ruthless killer who stole only for himself.

Jesse's bank-robbing career almost ended after a bank raid in September 1876 when two members of his gang were gunned down and others captured. Only Jesse and Frank escaped. But by now the brothers were so harried by the law (including the famous Pinkerton Detective Agency) that they moved to Nashville, Tennessee, where they lived anonymously for three years.

Jesse hankered for the old days of plunder and formed a new gang, but its members were mostly thugs and adventurers rather than hardened Confederate guerrilla fighters. After a few error-strewn robberies, Jesse and Frank fled back to Missouri. Soon Frank decamped for Virginia, but Jesse, now sporting a dark beard and calling himself Thomas Howard, recruited Bob and Charlie Ford to help with another bank job. But the Ford brothers had no intention of robbing a bank; they planned to collect the $5,000 bounty Missouri governor Thomas Crittenden had placed on Jesse's head.

Today in a one-storey white wood cottage at 1318 Lafayette Street in St Joseph, Missouri, Jesse had just finished breakfast when the Ford brothers came in from the stable behind the house. Because of the unseasonal heat, he had removed his jacket and now laid his pistols on a sofa because he didn't want a passer-by to look through the window and see him carrying a gun. Picking up a feather duster, he stood on a chair to clean a dusty picture. The Fords moved between him and his guns and drew their revolvers. Just as Jesse started to turn his head, Bob Ford fired a single bullet into the back of his skull.

First buried on his family property, James was moved to a cemetery in Kearney, Missouri. On his tombstone are the words written by his mother Zerelda:

Devoted husband and father
Jesse Woodson James
Sept. 5, 1847
MURDERED
Apr. 3, 1882
BY A TRAITOR
AND COWARD WHOSE NAME
IS NOT WORTHY
TO APPEAR HERE

Bob and Charlie Ford were sentenced to hang for murder but were pardoned that same afternoon by Governor Crittenden. Capitalising on their notoriety, they began a stage career re-enacting their famous murder, Bob styling himself 'the man who shot Jesse James'. Two years later Charlie, suffering from terminal tuberculosis, shot himself, and then in 1892 a man named Edward O'Kelley emptied two barrels of a shotgun into Bob Ford's back in a saloon in Colorado, thus earning for himself the title of 'the man who killed Robert Ford'.

1721 Robert Walpole becomes First Lord of the Treasury – effectively Britain's first Prime Minister, although the term was never officially used; later he famously tells his opponents in Parliament: 'I know the price of every man in this house except three', popularly rendered as: 'Every man has his price.' * **1948** In a speech at Harvard the previous June, Secretary of State George Marshall had said: 'The United States should do whatever it is able to do to assist in the return of normal economic health to the world, without which there can be no political stability and no assured peace. Our policy is not directed against any country, but against hunger, poverty, desperation and chaos.' Today President Truman signs the Marshall Plan into law that will transfer almost $13 billion (about $130 billion currently) to seventeen countries, of which Great Britain receives over a quarter, the largest amount of any country.

4 April

'Why did you usurp the universal Roman
See in such a spirit of ambition?'

896 AD Today a contentious pope died in Rome, having reigned a mere four and a half years. On his election he had chosen the papal name Formosus – 'handsome' – despite his advanced age of 76. By now he would be long forgotten, except for his grisly trial – he was exhumed, tried and punished after he was dead.

Formosus' troubles had begun even before he ascended the papal throne. In 876 he was excommunicated by Pope John VIII for 'conspiring with certain iniquitous men and women for the destruction of the papal see', pope-speak for 'plotting to take my job'. In 882, however, one of John's greedy relatives tried to poison him, hoping to seize his treasures, but when the poison proved too slow, he bashed his head in with a hammer, making John the first pope ever to be murdered. John's demise cleared the way for Formosus' rehabilitation and return to Rome.

Early in his reign Formosus became embroiled with Lambert of Spoleto, whom he had been forced to crown Holy Roman Emperor in 892. Fearful of the ambitions of the House of Spoleto, Formosus implored King Arnulf of the East Franks to invade Italy and become Holy Roman Emperor himself. In February 896 Arnulf marched on Rome, where Formosus greeted him with joy, crowned him emperor in St Peter's and saluted him as Augustus. But just 41 days later Formosus died, and a few months after that Arnulf suffered a stroke that forced him to return home, leaving Rome under the thumb of Lambert of Spoleto and the new pope whom he had backed, Stephen VI.

Probably at Lambert's bidding, in January 897 – nine months after Formosus had been buried – Stephen had the dead Formosus put on trial in what has become known as the Cadaver Synod. Formosus' mouldering corpse was dragged from his tomb, dressed in papal robes and propped up in a chair in the Basilica San Giovanni Laterano, the Pope's official church as Bishop of Rome. Stephen himself took the role of prosecutor, delegating the defence to a junior and obedient deacon.

In a demented rant, Stephen accused Formosus' rotting cadaver of perjury, violating canon law and illegally seizing the papal crown. Gesticulating wildly, Stephen screamed his hatred and hurled insults, demanding, 'Why did you usurp the universal Roman See in such a spirit of ambition?' To which the junior deacon answered in Formosus' place, 'Because I was evil.'

At one point an earthquake shook the basilica, but Stephen ploughed on, pronouncing Formosus guilty of all charges and his papacy retroactively declared null. The corpse was stripped of its papal vestments, and the three fingers which the dead pope had used in consecrations were severed from his right hand. The body was buried in a graveyard for foreigners, but Stephen ordered it dug up again, dragged through the streets and cast into the Tiber.

This macabre trial caused tumult in Rome, and that very summer a mob threw Stephen in prison, where he was strangled in his cell.

Formosus' trials were now over but not his tribulations. In December Pope Theodore II had his body, which a monk had drawn from the Tiber, dressed once more in pope's clothing and reinterred with full honours in St Peter's. But in January 904 one of Stephen's allies, the reprehensible Sergius III, gained the papal throne. (Sergius has the distinction of being the only pope who murdered another pope, Leo V. He is also the only pope whose illegitimate son also became pope, John XI.) Sergius held another synod that reaffirmed the dead Formosus' conviction and had his much-abused corpse exhumed once more, tried, found guilty again, and beheaded.

1814 Cornered by his enemies, Napoleon tells his officers that his army will follow him, but when Marshal Ney responds, 'The army will follow its generals', Napoleon abdicates.

---

5 April

'Show my head to the people, it's worth seeing.'

1794 Prior to the French Revolution Georges Danton had been a successful Parisian lawyer. Despite his bloated and unattractive face, he was a powerful speaker who could sway a mob (or seduce a lady). He became a member of the Legislative Assembly in 1791 when only 32.

From then on, his actions became increasingly demagogic – and dangerous, as he practised his own preaching for '*de l'audace, encore de l'audace, toujours de l'audace*'. In 1792 he instigated the September Massacres in which imprisoned suspects were given mock trials and then turned over to the mob for slaughter.

Danton became a prominent member of the Committee for Public Safety that instigated the Terror in September 1793. Within a year, however, he was trying to lead the revolution toward a more moderate path, but the Committee, led by Robespierre, turned on him, jealous of his power and fearful of his ambitions. He was arrested on 30 March, and his trial began four days later.

Danton's two-day trial was a political lynching; after the charges were levelled, he was removed from the courtroom, refused permission to defend himself or to call defence witnesses. The public prosecutor, Fouquier-Tinville, then entered the jury room and threatened the jurors with death if they failed to convict. Predictably, Danton was found guilty and condemned to the guillotine, with the sentence to be carried out the same day. On hearing his punishment, he grandly announced, 'My dwelling-place will soon be nothingness. My name is written in the Pantheon of history.'

That same afternoon Danton, along with fourteen other condemned men, was carried to the scaffold in a horse-drawn tumbrel. As they passed Robespierre's house, he shook his fist and called out, 'You will appear in the cart in your turn, Robespierre, and the soul of Danton will howl with joy!'

Stopping to embrace another victim at the bottom of the steps that led to the guillotine, he grandly asked, 'Why should I regret to die? I have enjoyed the Revolution. Let us go to slumber.'

The playwright Antoine-Vincent Arnault witnessed the scene:

I arrived at the gate that opens onto Place Louis XV [now Place de la Concorde]. From there I saw the condemned men appear in turn on the fatal theatre, to disappear immediately, lying on the plank or the bed on which eternal rest was about to begin for them … Danton appeared last in this theatre, inundated with the blood of all his friends. Daylight was falling. I saw this scaffold standing, half lit by the dying sun. Nothing could be more courageous than the face of the athlete of the Revolution; nothing more formidable than this profile which defied the axe, for the expression of this head which, ready to fall, still seemed to dictate laws. What a frightful pantomime! Time cannot erase it from my memory. I find in it all the feelings that inspired Danton's last words [to his executioner], terrible words which I could not hear, but which people repeated, trembling with horror and admiration: 'Above all, do not forget. Show my head to the people, it's worth seeing.' ('*Tu montreras ma tête au peuple, elle en vaut la peine.*')

Danton's persecutors did not long survive him; Robespierre was guillotined less than four months later, and Fouquier-Tinville followed him nine months after that. But Danton himself gradually came to be seen as a national hero. The street where he lived in Paris's Left Bank is named after him, and in 1891 his statue was erected on the site of his house.

1242 After warning all comers that 'Whoever will come to us with a sword, from a sword will perish', Rus leader Alexander Nevsky destroys the Teutonic Livonian Order of warrior monks at the Battle of the Ice.

---

6 April

'The course of history is always being altered by something or other – if not by a horseshoe nail, then by an intercepted telegram.'

1917 Today the US Congress voted for war against Germany, despite President Woodrow Wilson's deep-held desire to keep his country out of the conflict already raging in Europe. One of the key factors in bringing around the president's and American opinion was a clandestine interception of a German telegram by British Naval Intelligence.

On 16 January a coded telegram left Berlin and made its way westward over the Atlantic cable. Addressed to the German ambassador in Washington, it began: 'Most secret. For Your Excellency's information and to be handed on to the Imperial Ministry in Mexico.' It closed with the sender's name, 'Zimmermann'. In between lay a message with fateful consequences.

By the end of 1916 Imperial Germany had concluded that to win the war it would have to resume unrestricted submarine warfare to cut the Allies' maritime supply lines. But torpedoing ships of neutral nations might arouse public opinion in the United States sufficiently to bring that nation into the war on the side of the Allies. What could Germany do to make sure the Americans stayed on their own side of the Atlantic?

On 31 January Germany informed the world that from the next day 'all sea traffic will be stopped with every available weapon and without further notice'. President Wilson promptly broke relations with Germany. But in informing Congress of his decision, he said: 'I refuse to believe that it is the intention of the German authorities to do in fact what they warned us they will feel at liberty to do ... only overt acts on their part can make me believe it even now.'

Meanwhile the telegram had been retransmitted to the German embassy in Mexico City, but it had been intercepted and decoded by Room 40, an office of British Naval Intelligence in London. The British government was sure its content would bring the United States into the war.

To cover their breaking of the German code, Room 40 arranged to have a decoded copy of the telegram stolen from the German embassy in Mexico. The full text was then sent to Washington, and four days after reading it, Wilson released it to the press.

On Thursday, 1 March 1917, the front page of the *New York Times* bore this eight-column headline:

GERMANY SEEKS AN ALLIANCE AGAINST U.S.
ASKS JAPAN AND MEXICO TO JOIN HER.
FULL TEXT OF HER PROPOSAL MADE PUBLIC.

And what a proposal it was: the telegram, sent by the German Foreign Secretary Arthur Zimmermann to his ambassador in Mexico, stated that should the United States enter the war, the ambassador was to propose to President Carranza of Mexico a military alliance with Germany against the United States, a move that would allow Mexico to 'reconquer the lost territory in Texas, New Mexico, and Arizona'. Furthermore, the ambassador should suggest to Carranza that he invite Japan to join the new alliance. War with Mexico, and perhaps also with Japan, the German government was sure, would keep the Americans too embroiled to send troops to Europe.

The telegram caused a great public outcry across the country. Some called it an act of war, others a forgery perpetrated by British agents. However, the latter charge was almost immediately dispelled when Zimmermann at a Berlin press conference confirmed that he had sent the telegram.

On 18 March German submarines sank three American ships. On 2 April Wilson addressed a joint session of Congress, declaring: 'the day has come when America is privileged to spend her blood and her might for the principles that gave her birth and happiness and the peace which she has treasured. God helping her, she can do no other.' On 6 April Congress voted to take the country into the war.

Some years later, Winston Churchill observed: 'The course of history is always being altered by something or other – if not by a horseshoe nail, then by an intercepted telegram.'

1529 When Renaissance painter Raphael dies on his 46th birthday, his last word is 'Happy'. * **1958** Former president Harry Truman: 'It's a recession when your neighbour loses his job; it's a depression when you lose your own.'

---

7 April

'Abandon all hope, ye who enter here.'

1300 On this day, the eve of Good Friday, Dante Alighieri entered a 'dark woods' ('*una selva oscura*'), or so he says in the opening of Canto I of the *Divine Comedy*.

Dante sets the date for his trip into the underworld in 1300, two years before he was banished from Florence by the pro-pope Black Guelphs, whom he opposed. During his exile he wrote the *Divine Comedy*, which was published in 1320, the year before he died.

Now remembered almost exclusively as a great poet (T.S. Eliot declared, 'Dante and Shakespeare divide the world between them. There is no third.'), in truth he was much more than that – the precursor of the versatile Renaissance Men who were to spring forth from Florence a century after his death. Philosopher, councilman, servant of princes and ambassador, he had even been a dashing cavalryman (at 24 he fought for Florence at the Battle of Campaldino).

The *Divine Comedy* is an epic of 100 cantos split into three sections, *Inferno*, *Purgatorio* and *Paradiso*, of which *Inferno* is the best known and the most fun. Guided by Virgil, Dante approaches the entrance to Hell, and sees 'written upon the summit of a gate' the most famous line of the 14,233 in the poem: 'Abandon all hope, ye who enter here.' ('*Lasciate ogne speranza, voi ch'intrate.*')

The Hell Dante visits is constructed of nine downward-spiralling circles, with Satan at its bottom. In Limbo he encounters pre-Christian worthies, including Aristotle, Socrates, Plato and Cicero. He also sees Julius Caesar, 'falcon-eyed and fully armed'. But not all the ancients are spared Hell's torments. In the Seventh Circle are 'tyrants who indulged in blood and rapine', notably Alexander the Great.

Dante was particularly unforgiving toward wayward popes. In the antechamber to Hell he recognises 'the shade of him/who due to cowardice made the great refusal', probably Celestine V, who resigned the papacy after five months in 1294. Dante condemns Pope Nicholas III (1244–80) for simony – he had promoted his brother and nephew to the cardinalate on the same day. Placed head-first in a hole, he has flames burning on the soles of his feet. Another notorious simoniac whom Dante consigns to Hell is Boniface VIII, who created cardinal three nephews and an uncle – and who had connived to get Dante exiled from Florence. A third Hell-bound pope is Clement V, 'a lawless shepherd, of ugly deeds' who moved the papacy to Avignon in 1309. (Don't think that Dante assigns only sinful Christians to Hell; Muhammad is in the Eighth Circle as a 'sower of discord'. 'Cleft from crotch to chin', he walks in a circle as his wounds heal, only for sword-bearing demons endlessly to open them again.)

The worst fate is reserved for betrayers, all trapped in the ice of a large frozen lake, and at the very bottom of Hell, frozen mid-breast in the ice, is a giant Satan with three faces and a pair of bat-like wings under each chin. In his three mouths he savagely chews the three ultimate traitors, Brutus, Cassius and Judas Iscariot.

After leaving Hell, Dante visits Purgatory, a mountain with seven terraces dedicated to the seven deadly sins of pride, envy, wrath, sloth, avarice, gluttony and lust. Here he sees ancient Rome's richest man, Crassus, and two more popes, Adrian V, condemned for his worldly ambitions, and Martin IV, who died after a gluttonous feast of eels and wine.

Finally, Dante ascends to Paradise, where gruesome punishment is replaced by ethereal enlightenment. There he is guided by his unrequited love, Beatrice Portinari, who had died in 1290. *Paradiso* is based on seven virtues – prudence, justice, temperance, fortitude, faith, hope and charity. Here Dante sees a few righteous leaders like Solomon, Justinian, Charlemagne and Trajan, but spends most of his time with the souls of more saintly folk like Thomas Aquinas, Boethius and Saint Bonaventure.

As another Florentine, Niccolò Machiavelli, commented two and a half centuries later: 'I would rather go to hell than to heaven. There I will enjoy the company of popes, kings and princes, while in the other place are only beggars, monks and apostles.'

1775 Dr Johnson: 'Patriotism is the last refuge of a scoundrel.'

8 April

'If it is the Lance of the Lord, I will pass through the fire unhurt.'

1099 Today – Good Friday – a French monk named Peter Bartholomew (Pierre Barthélemy) undertook a trial by fire, holding what he claimed to be the Holy Lance with which a Roman soldier had stabbed Christ at the end of his crucifixion.

Bartholomew was a mystic from Provence who had joined the First Crusade in 1096 under the banner of Raymond IV, Count of Toulouse. In October the next year the crusaders attacked Antioch (in southern Turkey), besieging it for seven months before it fell due to the treachery of an Armenian guard. But a large Muslim force arrived almost immediately, and now the Christians were besieged, starving and dying of disease.

At this desperate moment Bartholomew solemnly told Raymond: 'Christ Jesus, our blessed Saviour, and Saint Andrew his holy disciple will reveal to me the resting place of the Holy Lance, which pierced our Saviour's side upon the cross. And he commands you to go to Bishop Adhémar [the apostolic legate leading the crusade] and tell him of this, that we may search for it. For with its help alone we can be saved from the danger that threatens us, and our army will proceed in triumph to Jerusalem.' Saint Andrew, he said, had revealed that the Holy Lance was buried in Antioch's cathedral.

A few days later Raymond, Adhémar and Bartholomew entered the cathedral, where the monk pointed to a spot below the high altar, claiming that the Holy Lance lay hidden there. Several knights pulled away the paving stones and dug a trench but found nothing. Bartholomew shook himself as if roused from a dream and said: 'Digging cannot bring it to light, prayer can.' He then jumped into the trench and pulled out a head of a lance protruding from the earth.

This miraculous find caused jubilation and wild excitement among the crusading army, and Raymond decided to harness this enthusiasm for an attack.

The crusaders charged from Antioch's main gate, a knight carrying the Holy Lance before them. Cheered by St George, St Demetrius and St Maurice riding alongside, the knights shattered the Muslim force to break the siege and save the crusade.

Bartholomew continued to report miraculous visions from St Andrew and even some from Jesus Christ himself. When Adhémar died six weeks after the battle, Bartholomew became the de facto spiritual leader of the crusade and began issuing orders to the army.

There were many, however, who resented Bartholomew's assumption of power, doubted his visions and believed the Holy Lance was a fraud. Finally, during a council of leaders, Bartholomew defied his detractors, declaring: 'I wish and beg that a very large fire be built; and I will pass through the midst of it with the Lance of the Lord. If it is the Lance of the Lord, I will pass through the fire unhurt, but if it is not, I will be burned in the fire.'

On this day the crusader army circled around two large fires built side by side, the flames leaping 50 feet. Wearing only a tunic, Bartholomew briefly knelt in prayer and then stepped between the two massive piles of blazing wood, holding the Holy Lance. Miraculously, he emerged on the other side, still alive and claiming to be unhurt. The joyous soldiers crowded around him, certain they were in the presence of a saint.

In fact, Bartholomew had been badly burnt and six days later he died of his injuries, so the soldiers began to doubt the authenticity of the lance, but Count Raymond continued to treat it with great reverence. Soon the crusaders were again on the march for Jerusalem. On 15 July, after a two-day siege, Jerusalem fell and the First Crusade reached its triumphant conclusion, just as Peter Bartholomew had predicted.

No one is quite certain what happened to the Holy Lance. It is said to have been in Constantinople and later in the possession of Louis IX of France. Some believe it is the same lance that to this day is preserved beneath the dome of Saint Peter's Basilica in Rome.

1915 Adjutant Péricard of the French 95th Infantry Regiment inspires his wounded to fight off a German attack at Woëvre with the command: '*Debout les morts!*' ('On your feet, dead men!')

---

9 April

'I have nothing, I owe a great deal, and the rest I leave to the poor.'

1553 The great French writer François Rabelais died today, aged around 63. Like Dickens, Orwell, Kafka and de Sade, he is one of the very few novelists whose name has become an adjective in our everyday speech.

The *Oxford Dictionary* defines 'Rabelaisian' as 'marked by exuberant imagination and language, coarse humour, and satire'.

Born in the Loire Valley, Rabelais was initially intended for the priesthood and joined the Franciscans, but he was bemused by the credulity of the local villagers who gathered at his abbey to kneel in awe before a statue of St Francis. This prompted Rabelais to don a Franciscan habit and take the place and pose of the statue. He then moved his head back and forth as the peasants shouted with joy that they had seen a miracle. Needless to say, this earned Rabelais a stern reprimand from the abbot.

The Franciscans also confiscated all Rabelais' books in Greek because they thought a knowledge of Greek could lead to a liberal interpretation of the New Testament. After appealing to Pope Clement VII, Rabelais was able to transfer to the more lenient Benedictines.

Eventually, however, Rabelais found even Benedictine life too confining and left to study medicine, first in Poitiers and then Montpellier. He mastered not only Greek and Latin but also Italian, Spanish, German, English and Hebrew, and even had some Arabic.

In 1532 Rabelais moved to Lyon to practise medicine. In his spare time, he wrote humorous pamphlets critical of established authority and published the first part of his pentalogy of novels, *The Life of Gargantua and of Pantagruel*, using the pseudonym Alcofribas Nasier (an anagram of François Rabelais). These five extravagant, satirical works packed with scatological humour show Rabelais' positive view on life. In his introduction he writes: 'Seeing how sorrow eats you, defeats you, I'd rather write about laughing than crying, for laughter makes men human, and courageous. BE HAPPY!' (Not everyone appreciated them – his first three volumes were banned until he successfully appealed to King François I, who became a friend.)

Another instance of Rabelais' ready wit happened when he found himself in Lyon but had run out of money to return to Paris. Taking an assumed name, he called together some of the city's leading doctors, telling them of miraculous cures he had discovered. He then suddenly closed the doors to the room and said that he had a secret to share. Placing a flask on the table, he announced: 'Look, this is a very subtle poison I brought from Italy to free you from the king and his son. Yes, I intend to kill this tyrant, who drinks the blood of the people and is devouring France.'

The stunned doctors fled the room, and a few moments later city magistrates surrounded the hotel, took Rabelais prisoner and sent him to Paris under guard, but at no expense to Rabelais. Informed of the arrest of a great criminal, King François asked to see him, and Rabelais was brought before him, whereupon the king broke into a great laugh, and, after thanking the guards for delivering his friend, he invited Rabelais to dinner.

In the 1530s Rabelais joined the entourage of Cardinal Jean du Bellay, moving with him briefly to Turin in 1540, the same year that Bellay successfully petitioned the Pope to legitimise Rabelais' two children. Between 1545 and 1547 Rabelais lived in Metz, then a semi-independent city in the Holy Roman Empire, to escape condemnation by the University of Paris.

Rabelais finished his life as curate of an abbey at Meudon just outside Paris. It was in Paris, at his house in rue des Jardins Saint-Paul (on the Right Bank, north of the Île de la Cité), where he died.

Shortly before his death, Rabelais penned a one-sentence will: 'I have nothing, I owe a great deal, and the rest I leave to the poor.' The great writer's last words are supposed to have been: '*Je m'en vais chercher un grand peut-être; tirez le rideau, la farce est jouée.*' ('I am going to seek a great perhaps. Draw the curtain, the farce is over.')

1865: Confederate General Robert E. Lee tells his officers, 'There is nothing left for me to do but go and see General Grant, and I would rather die a thousand deaths', before surrendering to Union General Ulysses S. Grant at Appomattox, ending the American Civil War.

---

10 April

'It is better to die on your feet than to live on your knees.'

1919 The Mexican revolutionary Emiliano Zapata had spent his life refusing to bow to those who oppressed his nation, inspiring his followers with his declaration, 'It is better to die on your feet than to live on your knees'. (*'Es mejor morir de pie que vivir toda una vida arrodillado.'*) Today he literally died on his feet, gunned down by government soldiers as he arrived for lunch.

Zapata was born in 1879 in the agricultural town of Anenecuilco, about 60 miles south of Mexico City. At eighteen he was already involved in revolutionary activity, arrested for protesting with the *campesinos* (poor farmers) of his village against the appropriation of their lands by the *hacendados* (large landowners). From that time forward

Zapata became a champion of land redistribution, hoping to strip the *hacendados* of much of their land to re-establish the *ejidos*, the system of communal land ownership previously used by the Indians.

When Zapata was 31, the Mexican Revolution broke out, and he backed one faction or another against the government, often leading guerrilla bands with weapons captured from government soldiers. Photographs show a swarthy man (witness to his mestizo heritage) with cold black eyes and a large drooping moustache. He is frequently portrayed wearing a huge Mexican sombrero, with bandoliers crisscrossed over his chest.

In effect Zapata became the ruler of Morelos, the state in southern Mexico where he was born. His methods were direct and often brutal. With no government willing to redistribute land, Zapata did it himself, sometimes burning haciendas of the rich and ordering summary executions.

In 1914 a moderate politician named Venustiano Carranza rose up against the reigning dictator Victoriano Huerta. Allied with Zapata and Pancho Villa, he forced Huerta into exile, but he was not radical enough for Zapata, who turned against him. In November of that year Zapata's army – now grown to 25,000 men – occupied Mexico City. To the surprise of its inhabitants, Zapata's *campesinos* neither looted the city nor raped the women but humbly went from door to door asking for food and drink.

The civil war continued, but in 1917 Carranza's generals defeated Villa and isolated Zapata. Carranza then established a constitutional convention from which Zapata was excluded, and the convention elected him as president. But the war carried on almost unabated, with both Zapata and Carranza scoring victories at various moments. At one point pressure from government armies forced Zapata to retreat to the hills to organise guerrilla resistance.

In early 1919 Zapata tried to persuade a disgraced government colonel named Jesús Guajardo to change sides, but when the attempt was discovered, Guajardo was pressured into pretending to defect to Zapata while all the while planning his death.

On 10 April Guajardo asked Zapata to come to a secret lunch at the hacienda of Chinameca in Morelos, where he would defect to the revolutionaries. Ignoring warnings from his own officers, Zapata arrived at two o'clock, to be met by two ranks of Guajardo's soldiers standing at attention, presenting arms. As he stepped forward to greet Guajardo, the soldiers lowered their guns and riddled him with bullets.

Zapata's revolutionaries briefly fought on, encouraged, it is said, by seeing his ghost riding in the hills, but eventually the government brought the whole country under control. The land reforms that Zapata so desperately wanted were finally instituted in part in the late 1930s. Today Zapata is still considered a hero in Mexico and an inspiring example elsewhere. During the Spanish Civil War *La Pasionaria* Dolores Ibárruri galvanised the Republicans with his creed: 'It is better to die on your feet than to live on your knees.'

1899 Future president Theodore Roosevelt in a speech to the Hamilton Club in Chicago: 'I wish to preach not the doctrine of ignoble ease, but the doctrine of the strenuous life.'

---

11 April

'I didn't fire him because he was a dumb son of a bitch, although he was, but that's not against the laws for generals.'

1951 Douglas MacArthur – brilliant, arrogant, unbending – was one of America's most celebrated generals. Today, in the midst of the Korean War, his career ended in bitterness and controversy.

MacArthur graduated top of his class at West Point in 1903. During the First World War he was wounded twice and highly decorated, and by 1930 he had risen to Chief of Staff. In 1937 he retired, but in 1941 President Franklin Roosevelt appointed him commander of American forces in the Far East. Four years later, after a brilliant series of operations, Japan was forced to capitulate under the hammer blows of atomic bombs. On 2 September 1945 MacArthur accepted Japan's surrender aboard the USS *Missouri* and brilliantly oversaw the American occupation of Japan, effectively the nation's ruler.

When North Korea invaded South Korea in 1950, President Harry Truman called on him to command the United Nations forces defending the South, despite his advanced age of 70. In September, with UN forces facing almost certain annihilation, MacArthur executed a brilliant amphibious landing at Inchon that forced the Communist invaders out of South Korea.

Incipient disaster had been turned to what seemed like victory, but it did not end the war. When UN forces pursued the retreating North Koreans, they suddenly encountered half a million Chinese

Communist 'volunteers', a threat MacArthur had not foreseen and then underestimated.

In Washington, Truman was desperately trying to find a way to stop the Communist advance without attacking mainland China and possibly triggering a vastly wider war, but MacArthur wanted to bomb Chinese troops grouping north of the Korean–Chinese border and have the authority to use atomic weapons. He infuriated Truman by telling reporters that restrictions against these actions were 'an enormous handicap, unprecedented in military history'.

UN forces then started to drive the Chinese back, inflicting huge casualties and recapturing Seoul. But MacArthur torpedoed Truman's efforts to reach a negotiated settlement when he issued a 'military appraisal' that denigrated China's military competence and threatened 'an expansion of our military operations to its coastal areas and interior bases [that] would doom Red China to the risk of imminent military collapse'.

Truman later stated that 'I was ready to kick him into the North China Sea ... It was an act totally disregarding all directives to abstain from any declarations on foreign policy. It was in open defiance of my orders as President and as Commander-in-Chief.'

Then a congressman read on the floor of the House a letter from MacArthur that criticised Truman's priorities, concluding: 'We must win. There is no substitute for victory.' As historian William Manchester wrote: 'Brave, brilliant and majestic, he was a colossus bestriding Korea until the nemesis of his hubris overtook him. He simply could not bear to end his career in checkmate. It would [be] ... an acknowledgement that MacArthur was imperfect.'

That was it for Truman; feeling that 'I could no longer tolerate his insubordination', on 11 April 1951 he relieved MacArthur of duty.

MacArthur's firing ignited a storm of controversy, with most of the public disagreeing with Truman's decision. Then, on 19 April MacArthur addressed the US Congress, histrionically concluding, 'I still remember the refrain of one of the most popular barrack ballads ... which proclaimed most proudly that "old soldiers never die; they just fade away". And like the old soldier of that ballad, I now close my military career and just fade away, an old soldier who tried to do his duty.'

Although still a national hero but bruised by events, MacArthur declined to bid for the 1952 Republican presidential nomination – and Truman, equally damaged, also declined to run.

Years later, Truman recalled: 'I fired him because he wouldn't respect the authority of the President ... I didn't fire him because he was a dumb son of a bitch, although he was, but that's not against the laws for generals. If it was, half to three-quarters of them would be in jail.' And MacArthur, looking back, commented: 'The little bastard had the guts to fire me and I like him.'

1918 During the German Georgette offensive, General Douglas Haig tells his troops: 'Every position must be held to the last man; there must be no retirement. With our backs to the wall, and believing in the justice of our cause, each one of us must fight to the end.' * **1919** Winston Churchill tells the House of Commons: 'Of all the tyrannies in history, the Bolshevik tyranny is the worst, the most destructive, the most degrading.'

---

12 April

'Dieu le volt!'

1096 Peter the Hermit was a small, middle-aged priest with a dark, unsmiling face almost as long and lugubrious as that of his donkey. According to the contemporary historian Guibert of Nogent, 'He wore a wool shirt, and over it a mantle reaching to his ankles; his arms and feet were bare. He lived on wine and fish; he hardly ever, never, ate bread.'

A native of Amiens in northern France, Peter had travelled to Jerusalem in 1095. There he had been manhandled by the ruling Seljuk Turks and saw first-hand the miseries of the Christians and the sacrilegious insults offered to the city's Christian shrines. Back in Europe, he claimed that Jesus had appeared to him in the Church of the Holy Sepulchre and commanded him to tell the world about the sufferings of Christians in Jerusalem. His mystic vision helped inspire Pope Urban II to unite the faithful into a crusade.

In November 1095 outside Clermont Cathedral, Urban harangued Europe's Christians to go to Jerusalem's aid, 'to bathe your hands in the blood of infidels'. The crowd was so roused that they broke forth into loud cries of '*Dieu le volt! Dieu le volt!*' ('God wills it! God wills it!') 'It is, indeed, His will', said the Pope, 'and let these words be your war-cry when you meet the enemy.'

Peter the Hermit now began to recruit volunteers for what came to be known as the Peasants' Crusade, a prelude to the First Crusade that Urban had called for. At Cologne about 40,000 mostly French and

German peasants joined Peter. According to the 12th-century historian Albert of Aix, the horde included 'the chaste as well as the sinful, adulterers, homicides, thieves, perjurers, and robbers ... also, women and those influenced by the spirit of penance'. Most were untrained in fighting and some were unarmed, but Peter promised that the Holy Ghost would protect them. Without waiting for the more professional army that was assembling at Puy, on this day this rag-tag force departed for the Holy Land.

In spring 1096 Peter's motley crusaders marched through the Balkans, but many starved or returned home, while a substantial number were taken and sold into slavery by Slavic robber barons. Now desperate for food, the remainder pillaged and burned Belgrade. Then on 3 July some of Peter's German peasants set fire to some mills in Niš in Serbia, igniting a full-scale battle against the Byzantine army. The peasants were overwhelmed, with many killed or captured.

On 1 August Peter and about 30,000 followers finally reached Constantinople. Although Emperor Alexius I Comnenus at first welcomed these fellow Christians, he was soon anxious to be shed of them, for they pillaged local farms, forcing him to provide them with food.

On 6 August Alexius shipped them across the Bosporus to the Asiatic shore, with promises of guards and passage through the Turkish lines. He warned the peasants to await his orders, but they zealously marched into Turkish territory. When the Turks began attacking, Peter returned in desperation to Constantinople, seeking the emperor's help.

In his absence, the peasants were ambushed by the Turks at the Battle of Civetot. Despite Peter's promises of divine protection, the vast majority were slaughtered or enslaved. Perhaps 3,000 returned to Constantinople, the only survivors of the Peasants' Crusade.

The Peasants' Crusade might have been finished, but Peter the Hermit's role was not. When the First Crusade's army set siege to Jerusalem in June 1099, he led processions around the walls to summon divine aid. On 15 July Jerusalem fell to the Crusaders.

1945 President Franklin Roosevelt dies, causing German propaganda minister Joseph Goebbels to write in his diary: 'This was the Angel of History! We felt its wings flutter through the room.' Goebbels commits suicide nineteen days later.

---

13 April

'L'État, c'est moi.'

1655 In 1638 Queen Anne of France was 37 and had already suffered four stillbirths. Therefore, when she was delivered of a healthy baby boy that year, the court saw it as a miracle, and her infant son was called Louis-Dieudonné – Louis the God-given. Thus from his earliest years Louis would have seen himself as exceptional, placed on earth by the express will of heaven.

When his father Louis XIII died, the young boy was only four, and he inherited the throne as Louis XIV. His coronation necessarily had to wait until he came of age, but on 7 June 1654, when he was still just sixteen, he was crowned at Reims. In the words of historian Philippe Erlanger, Louis was 'raised once and for all above the level of common humanity. The Lord's Anointed, clothed in sacerdotal dignity, was God's representative in his realm. Only to God did Louis owe any account of the power which it was a crime for a Frenchman to evade, and he remained fully conscious of that prerogative until his dying day.'

On this day ten months later, Louis was hunting in the woods around Vincennes when he heard that members of the government were challenging some of his proclamations on fiscal matters. He galloped to the Parlement of Paris on the Île de la Cité (where the present Palais de Justice stands) and strode into the assembly chamber, booted and spurred, whip in hand. Pointing his finger directly at the counsellors, he said in a cold and commanding voice: 'I have come here expressly to forbid you to continue, and to forbid you, Monsieur le Président, to grant or to suffer any resumption of these debates …' Then – according to tradition – he staked his claim to absolute authority with the haughty declaration, '*L'État, c'est moi.*' ('*I* am the State.')

Six years later Louis' Prime Minister, the great Cardinal Mazarin, died. Louis declined to appoint a successor and from then on reigned without one.

Louis never for an instant relinquished his supreme self-belief. In his *Memoires* he wrote: 'Kings are absolute masters, and as such have a natural right to dispose of everything belonging to their subjects', and he once declared that 'it is legal because I wish it'.

1598 Henri IV issues the Edict of Nantes that gives France's Huguenots freedom of worship: 'We herewith permit those of the said religion called

Reformed to live and abide in all the cities and places of this our kingdom and countries of our sway, without being annoyed, molested, or compelled to do anything in the matter of religion contrary to their consciences.'

14 April

'I have the mould to make more!'

1488 With her auburn hair and sultry looks, Caterina Sforza was considered one of the most beautiful women in Italy – and one of the toughest.

Born in 1463, she was the illegitimate daughter of Galeazzo Maria Sforza, Duke of Milan, and granddaughter of Francesco Sforza, a renowned mercenary leader or *condottiere*. She was raised in luxury in the refined Milanese court but at ten was betrothed to Girolamo Riario, the 30-year-old nephew of Pope Sixtus IV. Some sources say the marriage was consummated four years later, while others claim she immediately agreed with the demands of her husband. (She eventually bore him six children.)

Coming from Savona's leading family, Girolamo Riario became even more powerful when Pope Sixtus gave him the seignory of Imola to celebrate his marriage. An overbearing man who had once had a political enemy tortured to death, he was also a key figure in the Pazzi conspiracy of 1478 against Lorenzo the Magnificent.

In 1480 the Pope gave his nephew the lordship of Forlì, but four years later Sixtus died. Although seven months pregnant, Caterina rode into the Castel Sant'Angelo and trained its guns on the Vatican to persuade the cardinals to elect a Riario-friendly pope. In this she failed, as the new pope was Innocent VIII.

Soon it was Riario's turn to be the object of a murder plot, this one by the Orsi, a noble family from Forlì, backed by Innocent, who wanted to replace Riario with his own illegitimate son, and by Lorenzo de' Medici, who wanted revenge for the Pazzi conspiracy.

When Checco and Ludovico Orsi came to Forlì's ducal palace today, they found Riario leaning out of a window talking with his chancellor in the square outside. As Riario welcomed Checco by raising his arms for an embrace, Checco stabbed him twice. After throwing the corpse into the piazza, the Orsi captured Caterina and her children, but the castellan of the Rocca di Ravaldino (the town's fortress) refused to surrender.

In his *Discorsi*, Machiavelli (who was then sixteen) reports that Caterina offered to persuade the castellan to lay down his arms, leaving her children as hostages. But once inside the fortress, she let loose a volley of threats and promises of vengeance. When the Orsi threatened to kill her children, she climbed on the fortress wall, faced her enemies, lifted her skirt and showed them '*le membra genitali*' while shouting, 'Do it if you want: hang them in front of me, too. I have the mould to make more!' ('*Fatelo, se volete: impiccateli pure davanti a me. Ho con me lo stampo per farne degli altri!*')

Taken aback by Caterina's nerve – and knowing that she was backed by her uncle Ludovico il Moro, the powerful Duke of Milan – the Orsi dared not touch the children. Shortly word came from Florence: now that Riario, his brother's murderer, was dead, Lorenzo de' Medici would take no further part in the coup. Soon the Pope followed suit, and the Orsi departed, allowing Caterina to regain her domains.

Caterina married again in 1488, but her new husband was slain in another intrigue in 1495. She avenged this murder by summarily torturing and executing not only the conspirators but also their wives and children.

Two years later Caterina, now 34, married for the third time, to Giovanni il Popolano, a dashing Florentine four years her junior, but he died of fever after only a year.

Caterina's adventures were still not over. After fighting off an attack by the Venetians, in 1499 she came into conflict with the Pope, now the Borgia Alexander VI, who invalidated her claim to Imola and Forlì so that his son Cesare could rule the Romagna. After a long siege, Cesare captured her and locked her up in the Castel Sant'Angelo. She was released after sixteen months even though she had tried to kill Alexander with a poisoned letter.

Caterina spent the rest of her life in Florence, dying of pneumonia on 28 May 1509 at the age of 46. Towards the end of her life, she confided to a monk: 'If I could write everything that happened, I would amaze the world.'

1865 John Wilkes Booth cries out '*Sic semper tyrannus!*' ('As always to tyrants!' – Brutus' words to Caesar) just before shooting Abraham Lincoln in the back of the head at Ford's Theater in Washington.

15 April

'A writer of dictionaries; a harmless drudge'

1755 Today Samuel Johnson published *A Dictionary of the English Language*, a massive tome of 2,300 pages weighing some twenty pounds that defined 42,773 words. The remarkable clarity of Johnson's definitions was enhanced by over 114,000 quotations from more than 500 authors, following his principle that a word means what it is used to mean by the best writers in the language. It was not the first English dictionary but the pre-eminent one until the first part of the *Oxford English Dictionary* was published more than a century later.

In June 1746 Johnson had signed a contract with a group of booksellers to write a dictionary, for which he would receive a fee of 1,500 guineas, equal to £200,000 today. It was a godsend for him since, at 46, he was penniless, almost unknown and in imminent danger of debtors' prison. (Nineteen years later, Johnson confirmed his pecuniary motivation, saying, 'No man but a blockhead ever wrote except for money'.)

With his fee in hand, Johnson rented a house at 17 Gough Square, off Fleet Street in London, and settled down to a task that would require over eight years. Remarkably, he wrote almost his entire *Dictionary* himself, although he engaged six assistants who functioned primarily as secretaries to copy out the quotations that he had marked in books.

Johnson's definitions were all articulate, many arresting and some amusing. He defined 'Oats' as 'a grain, which in England is generally given to horses but in Scotland supports the people'. And surely he had his tongue firmly in his cheek with his definition of 'network': 'Anything reticulated or decussated at equal distances, with interstices between the intersections.'

Prior to his assignment from the booksellers, Johnson had approached the 4th Earl of Chesterfield for support. Chesterfield eventually backed out of the sponsorship that Johnson thought he had promised. In the *Dictionary* Johnson described 'Patron' as 'one who countenances, supports or protects. Commonly a wretch who supports with insolence, and is paid with flattery.'

But Johnson could also be self-deprecating in his humour, as in: 'Lexicógrapher. *n.s.* [λεξικὸν and γράφω; *lexicographe*, French.] A writer of dictionaries; a harmless drudge, that busies himself in tracing the original, and detailing the signification of words.'

A Dictionary of the English Language received huge critical success on its publication, and he came to be known as 'Dictionary Johnson'. However, at a price of 4 pounds, 10 shillings (perhaps £500 today), only a few thousand copies were sold during its first decade, and Johnson was soon again in money troubles, forced to relinquish his house in Gough Square. But in 1762 King George III granted him a pension of £300 a year, and three years later Johnson received an honorary Doctor of Laws degree from Trinity College, Dublin, thus gaining the title 'Dr'.

In spite of his renown, Johnson suffered from frequent depression and was in severe physical discomfort for most of his life, plagued by a constant swelling of his legs and chronic bronchitis. In 1783, when he was 74, he suffered a stroke, while still in continual distress from his other illnesses. On 13 December the next year he died, according to his biographer Boswell, 'with so little apparent pain that his attendants hardly perceived when his dissolution took place'. He is buried in Westminster Abbey.

---

73 AD Elazar ben Yair tells his followers: 'Let our wives die before they are abused, and our children before they have tasted of slavery, and after we have slain them, let us bestow that glorious benefit upon one another mutually', before the mass suicide of Jewish resistors as Roman soldiers attack their stronghold at Masada. * **1912** As the *Titanic* is sinking, Captain Edward Smith tells his crew: 'Well, boys, do your best for the women and children, and look out for yourselves.'

---

16 April

'They transported Lenin in a sealed truck like a plague bacillus from Switzerland into Russia.'

1917 Just before midnight today at the Finland Station in Petrograd, Vladimir Ilyich Lenin arrived from exile in a closed one-carriage train. As he stepped onto the platform, a crowd of workers, sailors and soldiers waving red flags broke into the Marseillaise. Looking vaguely unfamiliar – he had shaved off his trademark goatee as a disguise – he turned to address them: 'Sailors, comrades, we have to fight for a socialist revolution, to fight until the proletariat wins full victory! Long live the worldwide socialist revolution!'

Lenin had been working for the destruction of Russia's monarchy and the capitalist system ever since his elder brother had been hanged for plotting to blow up the tsar in 1887. Banished to Siberia in 1895, he had gone into exile in Europe in 1900, where he remained until today, except briefly during the Revolution of 1905. While abroad, he had established the Russian Social-Democratic Workers' Party, organised the underground newspaper *Iskra* (*The Spark*) and published *Materialism and Empirio-criticism*, a philosophic foundation for Marxism-Leninism. When the First World War broke out, he called on Russian soldiers to turn their guns on capitalist leaders rather than the enemy.

Lenin's return to Russia was the culminating effort by German intelligence to cripple Russia, a plan fomented by another exiled intriguer, a militant Marxist named Israel Gelfand, who went by the *nom de guerre* of Alexander Parvus.

In 1915 Parvus had approached the German ambassador to Turkey with a scheme to sabotage tsarist Russia through internal revolution. 'The interests of the German government', he claimed, 'are identical with those of the Russian revolutionaries.' The ambassador arranged for Parvus to present his ideas to the German Foreign Ministry in Berlin.

In January 1916 Parvus' programme of Bolshevik propaganda, massive strikes and civil unrest was put into action in Petrograd, but workers in Moscow and the provinces refused to join, and the attempt collapsed. Now the German security services, together with Parvus, hatched a more deadly plot, the return to Russia of Lenin, who was living in Switzerland.

As Winston Churchill wrote in *The World Crisis*: 'In the middle of April the Germans took a sombre decision ... They were in the mood which had opened unlimited submarine warfare with the certainty of bringing the United States into the war against them. Upon the Western front they had from the beginning used the most terrible means of offense at their disposal. They had employed poison gas on the largest scale and had invented the '*Flammenwerfer*' [flamethrower]. Nevertheless it was with a sense of awe that they turned upon Russia the most grisly of all weapons. They transported Lenin in a sealed truck like a plague bacillus from Switzerland into Russia.'

So Lenin and 30 other revolutionaries were sent back to destabilise Russia, along with 250,000 goldmarks (then worth more than £12 million).

At first it looked as if the German scheme had failed, as Lenin was forced to flee again in July (this time by the Russian Provisional

Government – the tsar had abdicated a month before Lenin's clandestine train ride). But in October he secretly returned, and on 7 November the Red Guards under his direction deposed the Provisional Government, and Lenin became virtual dictator. Then, in March 1918, Russia withdrew from the First World War.

Thus it was that the Germans' devious plan had succeeded – the Bolsheviks had taken over Russia and Russia had quit the war. By then, however, it was too late for Germany, forced just over a year later to surrender, and, in another sense, too late for Russia, forced to live for the next 73 years in a state more tyrannical than even the tsars had imagined.

1687 As archetypal Restoration rake George Villiers, Duke of Buckingham, dies from a chill caught while hunting, he complains: 'Oh, what a prodigal have I been of that most valuable of all possessions – Time.'

---

17 April

'Marin Falier of the beautiful wife;/
Others enjoy her, he maintains her.'

1355 At 70, Marin Falier had capped an exceptional military career by attaining the highest of all ranks in Venice, that of doge. The other great trophy of his declining years was his beautiful wife Aluycia, 40 years his junior.

In 1354 Falier was living in Avignon as ambassador to the Pope, but in September Venice's reigning doge Andrea Dandolo had died and Venice's aristocracy elected Falier to replace him.

Falier's return to Venice was marked by a sinister omen. Lost in the fog, his ship docked not before the entrance to the Doges' Palace but in front of the columns of Saint Mark and Saint Theodore, Venice's traditional place of execution.

Now Falier settled into his role as ruler, but the beautiful Aluycia cared little for affairs of state. She had already enjoyed an adventurous love life and now became entangled with a 23-year-old aristocrat named Michiel Sten.

Somehow Doge Falier learned of their affair, and when Sten made the mistake of coming to a court ball at the Doges' Palace, Falier ordered his removal, a deep humiliation in Venetian society. Passing through the palace's throne-room, Sten scratched this couplet on the marble Chair of State:

> 'Marin Falier of the beautiful wife;
> Others enjoy her, he maintains her.'

> (*'Marin Falier, da la bea mugier,*
> *tutti i la gode e lu la mantien.'*)

Sten's verse was a gross insult to the sacred person of the doge and to his wife. Livid with anger – and jealousy – Falier denounced him to Venice's governing Council, expecting him to be sentenced to death. But Sten had many supporters, and he was condemned to a mere month's imprisonment and a fine of 100 gold ducats.

Humiliated by the Council's verdict and enraged by those who would favour a young reprobate over a reigning doge, Falier now conspired with other malcontents to massacre Venice's principal aristocrats and seize dictatorial power. The plan was to strike down the nobility when the great bell of San Marco rang to summon the Council members to the palace. However, a traitor in Falier's camp told the Council of the conspiracy.

Falier and some 30 plotters were arrested and brought to trial the same day. Falier disdained to deny the charges. Laying his hand upon his sword-hilt, he exclaimed: *'Il Doxe nol seppe ingane!'* ('The Doge never lies!') He was allowed to make his will and confess to God, but not to see Aluycia or any member of his family.

At dawn on 17 April San Marco's great bell gave forth the funeral peal as if for the burial of a doge. Clothed in his state robes, Falier was led into the courtyard of the Doges' Palace, where, at the bottom of the great stairway, he bravely and contemptuously stepped forth to death. Stripped of his emblems of office, the old man knelt on the hard stones and bared his neck for the executioner.

One quick blow was enough; Falier's grey-bearded head rolled to the feet of the leader of the Council, who picked it up and hurried to the piazza outside. There he showed it and the bloody executioner's sword to a huge crowd, proclaiming, 'Look! – All of you! – Look! – Justice hath been done to the traitor!'

That night under cover of darkness, Falier's remains were taken in a covered barge and buried in the church of San Zanipolo. His portrait, which had been hanging in the Doges' Palace, was removed, the empty space painted over with a black shroud, with the inscription, '*Hic est locus Marini Faletro decapitati pro criminibus*' ('This is the space reserved for Marin Falier, beheaded for his crimes'). It can still be seen there today.

The Dogaressa Aluycia was stripped of her possessions and reduced to absolute poverty, an object of aversion and suspicion. Unhinged by her ordeal, she died in a madhouse 30 years later, forgotten by the world.

Michiel Sten was the only one to prosper. On 1 December 1400 he was elected as Venice's 63rd doge, an office he held until his death thirteen years later.

1790 Benjamin Franklin dies; 56 years earlier he had written his own epitaph: 'The body of Benjamin Franklin, Printer (Like the cover of an old book, its contents torn out and stript of its lettering and gilding), Lies here, food for worms; But the work shall not be lost, for it will (as he believed) appear once more in a new and more elegant edition, revised and corrected by the author.'

---

18 April

'*Here I stand. I can do no other.*'

1521 The Diet of Worms is remembered for the clash of wills between two of history's most strong-willed men. Sitting in judgement was Holy Roman Emperor Charles V, only 21 but already Europe's most powerful monarch in the long millennium between Charlemagne and Napoleon. Testifying to his faith was a 38-year-old German monk who defied the True Church, Martin Luther.

Appalled by the corruption in Rome, Luther had refused to accept the Church's authority, bowing only to 'scripture and plain reason'. Four years earlier he had dramatically nailed his 95 theses to the door of the Schlosskirche in Wittenberg and subsequently published several religious tracts attacking the Church. But Emperor Charles, a strong Catholic, could not tolerate that 'a single monk, deluded by his own judgement' could presumptuously conclude 'that all Christians up till now are wrong'.

On 3 January 1521 the Medici pope Leo X had excommunicated Luther for his heretical beliefs. 'Arise, O Lord', said the bill, 'Protect yourself, because a wild boar of the forest is seeking to destroy your vineyard.' When Luther received the written censure, he hurled it into a bonfire.

Luther's patron, Prince Frederick the Wise of Saxony, had persuaded Charles V to hear the monk's views at Worms rather than ordering his arrest. But, Charles insisted, 'A single friar who goes counter to all Christianity for a thousand years must be wrong.' Luther was eager to state his case and to defend himself from accusations of heresy, in spite of warnings from friends that Worms was a town 'where his death had already been decided upon'.

He was certainly well aware of the fate of Jan Hus a century before, who was burned at the stake for heresy at the Council of Constance, despite promises of safe conduct. But Luther was adamant. Even when begged by a supporter to stay away, he replied: 'I am resolved to enter Worms although as many devils should set at me as there are tiles on the housetops.'

The prosecution demanded that Luther renounce all his heretical opinions and writings, but he refused. 'I cannot and will not recant anything, since it is neither safe nor right to go against conscience', he said. Finally, on this day, he concluded his defence with the famous words, 'Here I stand. I can do no other. God help me. Amen.' ('*Hier stehe ich. Ich kann nicht anders. Gott helfe mir, Amen!*')

On 25 May the emperor issued the Edict of Worms, which declared Luther an outlaw, banned his writings and concluded, 'we want him to be apprehended and punished as a notorious heretic, as he deserves'. But Charles, who had previously promised him safe conduct, refused to have him arrested. Luther now departed from Worms, but to ensure that no over-zealous churchman might seize him anyway, Prince Frederick intercepted him on his way home and hid him in Wartburg Castle.

A year later Luther returned to the University of Wittenberg, now a hero to many and the most famous man in Europe. He wrote more tracts and married an ex-nun he had helped to escape from a convent. Until he died in 1546 he continued to preach the same 'heresy' for which he had been tried. Charles V spent the remaining 37 years of his life unsuccessfully trying to undo what Luther had started.

1791 In a speech against slavery, William Wilberforce tells the House of Commons: 'Never, never will we desist till we have wiped away this scandal from the Christian name, released ourselves from the load of guilt, under which we at present labour, and extinguished every trace of this bloody traffic, of which our posterity, looking back to the history of these enlightened times, will scarce believe that it has been suffered to exist so long a disgrace and dishonour to this country.'

19 April

'He is neither a man nor a beast, but a statue.'

1314 France's King Philip the Fair (IV) may have been handsome, but he was also known as *le Roi de fer* (the Iron King) for his relentless pursuit of his own ends. Nothing showed this more clearly than his implacable punishment of two of his daughters-in-law.

Philip had three sons, Louis, Philippe and Charles. Louis married Marguerite, Philippe married Jeanne d'Artois and Charles married Jeanne's sister Blanche. The young princesses gave the court an air of gaiety, in contrast to the austerity of pious King Philip, but courtiers whispered that Marguerite and Blanche seemed far too close to the Norman knights Gautier and Philippe d'Aunay. No one dared breathe a word to the king.

In 1314, however, the king's daughter Isabelle, wed to England's Edward II, came to visit her family. When she noticed that the Aunay brothers were carrying embroidered purses that she had given to Marguerite and Blanche, she accused her sisters-in-law of adultery. The king ordered an inquest, which found that Blanche and Marguerite had been entertaining their lovers in an old guard tower next to the Seine, the Tour de Nesle. The third sister-in-law, Jeanne, although faithful, had known of the two affairs.

Earlier Bernard Saisset, the Bishop of Pamiers, had said of Philip: 'He is neither a man nor a beast, but a statue.' Now this cold king remorselessly let 'justice' take its course.

Gautier and Philippe d'Aunay were tortured and sentenced to death for *lèse-majesté*, an offence against the dignity of the sovereign. On this day the brothers were flayed alive, burned with hot lead and sulphur, emasculated, their genitals thrown to the dogs, and finally decapitated. But the real cause of the king's wrath was not his dignity but his dynasty. What would have been the authority of the royal line if the paternity of future monarchs lay open to question?

Now Philip turned to his daughters-in-law. Tried before the Parlement de Paris, Jeanne was cleared, but Marguerite and Blanche were condemned for adultery.

The two princesses were stripped of their fine clothes and dressed in coarse robes, their heads shaven, and taken to the Château Gaillard, a forbidding fortress in Normandy. There Blanche, still only eighteen, was confined in an underground cell, while Marguerite, the eldest at 24, was locked in the top of the keep, exposed to the wind and the rain.

Just months after the trial, Philip died of a stroke, leaving his son Louis as king. The next summer Louis' wife Marguerite – now Queen of France – was found dead at the Château Gaillard, probably strangled on orders from Louis, who was eager to remarry and sire an heir. It is said that her ghost still haunts the château.

Blanche remained in prison for eight years and was then confined to a nunnery, where she died the next year, her health broken from the years spent underground. But what of Philip's daughter Isabelle, who had instigated the investigation into the princesses' adultery? It seems she was worse than her sisters-in-law. Back in England she not only started her own adulterous affair (with Roger Mortimer) but also connived in her husband's barbarous murder, earning herself the nickname the She-wolf of France.

This sad, gruesome story became known as the scandal of the Tour de Nesle, where Marguerite and Blanche conducted their affairs. Its salacious details gave rise to a legend that became as famous as the scandal itself – that Marguerite was so depraved that she would watch from her window for handsome young men passing by. When she spotted one to her taste, her soldiers would bring him to her chamber, where she would ravish him. Afterwards the soldiers would sew the discarded lover in a sack and throw him into the Seine. One lucky victim, however, was a professor who escaped his doom when he was dropped into a boat full of hay positioned by his students under the tower window. This legend became so famous that the great 15th-century poet François Villon referred to it in his classic *Ballade des dames du temps jadis*.

1775 As British regulars approach Lexington in the first battle of the American Revolution, American Captain John Parker tells his militia: 'Don't fire unless fired upon; but if they mean to have war, let it begin here.'
* **1881** Benjamin Disraeli dies; when his rival William Gladstone learns that he had refused a state funeral to be buried alongside his wife, he grumbles: 'In death he remains as he was in life. All show with no substance.'

---

20 April

'Soldiers of my Old Guard: I bid you farewell.'

1814 Napoleon had been master of 70 million people, including 30 million French, and his empire had extended to Belgium, Holland, Spain, Portugal, most of Italy and Germany and parts of Poland and Yugoslavia. But then, in 1812, he made the fatal blunder of invading Russia and was forced into a humiliating retreat, with most of his Grande Armée left dead on the Russian steppes. Since then, disaster had followed disaster.

In June 1813 the Duke of Wellington liberated Spain, forcing the French to retreat back into France. Then, in October, the emperor had been crushed by a massive allied force at Leipzig.

Despite a string of minor victories at the beginning of 1814, Napoleon was now cornered by his enemies, who marched through Paris on 31 March, the first time the city had been occupied by a foreign army since the time of Joan of Arc.

Two days later the French Senate passed the Acte de déchéance de l'Empereur, deposing him, and finally, on 11 April his own marshals forced him to abdicate, fourteen years, two months and nineteen days after his famous coup d'état of 18 Brumaire (9 November 1799).

Now Napoleon waited at the royal château at Fontainebleau, hoping that his wife Marie-Louise and their son would join him, but they were already on the road to her native Austria. Many of his veterans had left him to join the Comte d'Artois (the future Charles X) while even his loyal chief-of-staff Marshal Berthier was transferring command of the army to the provisional government in Paris.

'La vie m'est insupportable!' he exclaimed to his aide Armand de Caulaincourt, and on the night of 12 April he stirred a small sachet of opium into a glass of water and drank it. But the dose was not enough, causing painful vomiting but failing to kill.

Now resigned to his capture and whatever fate his enemies might dictate, on this day Napoleon summoned the remaining faithful officers of the Old Guard (la Garde impériale) to the courtyard at Fontainebleau. These were the renowned *grognards* (gripers) who had served with him since his first campaigns. They were the elite of the elite, imposing men, mostly over six foot tall, veterans of battles like Lodi, Wagram, Austerlitz and Dresden. Now it was time to say adieu:

Soldiers of my Old Guard: I bid you farewell. (*Soldats de ma Vielle Garde, je vous fais mes adieux.*)

For twenty years I have constantly accompanied you on the road to honour and glory. In these latter times, as in the days of our prosperity, you have invariably been models of courage and fidelity. With men such as you our cause could not be lost; but the war would have been interminable; it would have been civil war, and that would have entailed deeper misfortunes on France.

I have sacrificed all of my interests to those of the country; I go, but you, my friends, will continue to serve France.

Her happiness was my only thought. It will still be the object of my wishes. Do not regret my fate; if I have consented to survive, it is to serve our glory. I intend to write the history of the great achievements we have performed together. Adieu, my friends. I wish I could press you all to my heart; let me at least embrace your flag!

With a tear in his eye, the ex-emperor then hugged one of his generals, kissed the tricolour and finished: 'Goodbye again, my old companions! May this last kiss remain in your hearts.'

Within a month Napoleon was in exile in Elba, but in February the next year he escaped back to France. Accompanied by a thousand men from the Old Guard he marched toward Paris and his famous 100 Days. The Old Guard played a prominent role at Waterloo, but even their passionate loyalty could not save Napoleon.

1653 Oliver Cromwell tells the Rump Parliament, 'In the name of God, go!' * **1968** At the Midland Hotel in Birmingham, Enoch Powell tells his audience, 'As I look ahead, I am filled with foreboding; like the Roman, I seem to see "the River Tiber foaming with much blood."'

21 April

'I am growing old from the feet upwards, but I know someone it is happening to just as fast from the head downwards.'

1736 Small in stature with a narrow, horsy face, Prince Eugene of Savoy came from the same noble house that would one day provide the kings for a united Italy. He was born and brought up in Paris but achieved his greatness serving Austria, which he did for almost 40 years.

Eugene was a charismatic leader who was made a field marshal at 29. He fought in 24 battles and was wounded thirteen times, including a musket ball to his knee when he was 23 and another above his left eye at 45.

Eugene received his baptism of fire at the most important battle of his lifetime, the siege of Vienna in 1683, when the Turks threatened to overrun central Europe. Among his great victories were the Battle of Zenta, where he inflicting 30,000 Turkish casualties at the cost of 300 dead, and the battles of Blenheim, Oudenarde and Malplaquet against the French, where he teamed up with the Duke of Marlborough. (Malplaquet was seen as a victory because the French withdrew at the end, but Eugene and Marlborough suffered 22,000 casualties against only 12,000 for the French. After the battle the beaten French commander, the duc de Villars, wrote to Louis XIV: 'If God should grant us another such defeat, our enemies would be destroyed.')

Eugene's greatest triumph was when he was besieging Belgrade in 1717. Under cover of darkness and a thick fog, he launched an attack with just 40,000 men against a 150–200,000-strong Turkish relief force, crushing the enemy and compelling Belgrade to surrender.

When Eugene reached his 70s, he was considered the greatest general of his age; he had crushed the Ottoman advance into central Europe and liberated many of its peoples after 150 years of Turkish rule, and he and Marlborough had stymied the ambitions of Louis XIV, preventing France from dominating Europe.

Now Eugene was failing both physically and mentally, but when the War of Polish Succession broke out in 1733, he was confirmed as the commander-in-chief of the army of the Holy Roman Empire. Although he managed to conduct an intelligent campaign, his memory was so poor that his subordinates did much of the work, and one observer noted that Eugene 'only gives orders, and the rest of the time he is seen to play trictrac [a form of backgammon], smiling from time to time, saying very little, afraid that it will be noticed that his memory is gone and that his spirit is depressed'. Among Eugene's entourage was 22-year-old Prince Frederick of Prussia (the future Frederick the Great), sent by his father to learn the art of war. Frederick was horrified by Eugene's condition, writing, 'his body was still there but his soul had gone'.

In October 1735, Eugene returned to Vienna. One of the ladies at the court wrote: 'Everyone tried to keep him happy with masques and children's games, which were more appropriate to the feebleness of his age than to his character.' His old subordinate and rival, the 77-year-old Guido Starhemberg, maliciously commented: 'I am growing old from the feet upwards, but I know someone it is happening to just as fast from the head downwards.'

On 20 April of the next year, Prince Eugene, now 72, lunched with friends, briefly played cards and returned to his town palace in Vienna's Himmelpfortgasse. Fatigued, he postponed a conference, saying, 'That's enough for today. We'll save the rest for tomorrow … If I live that long.' A premonition? He retired early, and the following morning his servants found him dead in bed, having died of apparent pneumonia.

As is fitting for a prince of the House of Savoy, Eugene's heart was removed and sent for burial with his ancestors in Turin. His meagre body, made lighter still by death, was interred in the Kreuzkappel of Vienna's St Stephen's Cathedral.

1946 Economist John Maynard Keynes' last words: 'I wish I'd drunk more Champagne.'

---

22 April

'You have captured the Napoleon of the Western world.'

1836 Admiring countrymen saw Mexican general Antonio López de Santa Anna as brave and charismatic, while his detractors called him vainglorious, corrupt, and murderous. Whatever the truth, he had an extraordinary career that culminated in victory over the Spanish at Tampico in 1829, after which he styled himself as 'The Saviour of the Motherland'. His primary loyalty was to himself, as he changed sides countless times in the chaos that was Mexico in the early 19th century, becoming president on eleven different occasions.

By 1836 Santa Anna was effectively Mexico's dictator, having voided the country's constitution. At the time what is now Texas was still a Mexican province, but it was peopled largely by immigrant Americans. These Texians, as they were called, had been fulminating – and occasionally fighting – against the Mexican government since October 1835, furious at increased taxes and unwilling to give up their slaves, as the Mexican constitution demanded. To quell the Texian unrest, Santa Anna gathered his army.

After a few minor setbacks, Santa Anna's forces crushed ill-advised Texian resistance at the Alamo, a rundown mission outside San Antonio. Shortly afterwards at Goliad, on Santa Anna's orders 342 prisoners were shot or bayoneted to death.

Now Santa Anna set out to destroy the main Texian army, commanded by Sam Houston, a Virginia-born veteran of the War of 1812. For six weeks Santa Anna pursued the Texians, unable to bring this force of fewer than 1,000 men to battle. Then he unwisely detached 1,500 of his men to speed up his pursuit.

When Houston learned of the reduced Mexican force, he decided the time was ripe for battle. Setting out with 783 men, he positioned his troops with their backs to the San Jacinto River.

After a light skirmish on 20 April, the overconfident Santa Anna thought he had the Texians cornered and decided to rest his men. The next day the general retired for an afternoon siesta while his soldiers dozed away the afternoon. So sure was he that he failed to post pickets or run patrols.

At three that afternoon Houston formed his men in two ranks in a line 900 yards long facing the enemy but out of sight due to a ridge between them. The Texians moved forward in silence, rifles at the ready, until they topped the ridge, only 200 yards from the Mexican camp.

Now the Mexicans spotted the advancing enemy, but it was far too late. As they scrambled for their guns, the Texian band of a drummer and three fifers broke the silence and the Texians charged to the cry of 'Remember the Alamo!'

Mexican resistance collapsed in eighteen minutes, as the soldiers threw down their weapons, but the Texians showed little mercy. When the firing stopped an hour later, 630 Mexicans lay dead, with another 730 captured, while only nine Texians had perished, plus 23 wounded, including Sam Houston with a musket ball in his ankle.

But where was Santa Anna? Not among the dead and not among the captured.

The next day Houston sent out scouts to find the elusive general. A search party discovered a Mexican private hiding in the high grass. When they brought their captive back to the Texian camp, other prisoners saluted and called him 'El Presidente'. The lowly private was in fact Santa Anna, who had shed his baroque uniform to pose as a common soldier.

Santa Anna was brought before Houston, who was sprawled beneath a tree nursing his shattered ankle. In a display of fawning self-aggrandisement, the Mexican addressed his captor: 'You, sir, are born to no common destiny, for you have captured the Napoleon of the Western world.'

Despite pressure from his men to execute Santa Anna because of his massacre of Texian prisoners, Houston spared his life because the general was the only man who could end the hostilities and withdraw Mexican troops. Within six months of the battle, Texas had established the first Texas Congress as an independent country.

1509 Henry VIII becomes king the day after the death of his father, Henry VII, whose passing was celebrated by Thomas More: 'This day is the end of our slavery, the beginning of our freedom, the end of sadness.' Twenty-six years later Henry VIII has More beheaded.

---

23 April

'Honi soit qui mal y pense.'

1348 How the Order of the Garter gained its name and motto – '*Honi soit qui mal y pense*' – has been a matter of debate ever since the order was founded. So here is the (best) story.

In 1346, during the Hundred Years' War, France enlisted the help of King David (II) of Scotland, who led a foray into England. In his path lay Wark Castle, on the south bank of the River Tweed. The castle was defended by only a few knights, twenty archers and servants and the castle's chatelaine, the ravishing Catherine, Countess of Salisbury, whose husband was a prisoner in France.

Catherine marshalled her small force to such good effect that she held the invaders at bay until the castle was relieved by the English army, led by King Edward III himself. In gratitude, Catherine invited him to stay the night. But when the king approached her with seduction in mind, she rebuffed him with the words, 'I hope, gracious liege, that the good Lord in heaven would drive from your noble heart such villainous designs … I am, and ever shall be, ready to serve you, but only in what is consistent with my honour, and yours.' So impressed was Edward by Catherine's virtue that he immediately ransomed her husband.

For some time Edward had planned to create a noble order based on the Round Table of King Arthur, but he had yet to find the proper name for it. Nonetheless he appointed several members, and on this day held a grand ball at Windsor Castle to inaugurate the order. The date – 23 April – was chosen because it was Saint George's Day, honouring the patron saint of England.

According to the contemporary chronicler Jean Froissart, Edward 'expressly ordered the Earl of Salisbury to bring the lady, his wife'. But Catherine had not forgotten the king's attempt at seduction. Froissart tells us: 'All the ladies and damsels who assisted at this first convocation of the Order of the Garter came superbly dressed, excepting the Countess of Salisbury, who attended the festival dressed as plainly as possible.'

The story goes that during the dancing Catherine inadvertently lost a blue silk garter. Gallantly, Edward picked it up and attached it to his own sleeve. Then, thinking of the lady's reputation, he remarked to his guests, *'Honi soit qui mal y pense. Tel qui s'en rit aujourd'hui, s'honorera de la porter.'* ('Ashamed be he who thinks evil of it. Those who laugh at this today, tomorrow will be proud to wear it.') The incident gave Edward the inspiration he needed; he named the new order the Order of the Garter, with its motto *'Honi soit qui mal y pense'*.

The Order had 25 founding members, plus the king. Today the maximum is 24, plus two ex-officio members, Queen Elizabeth and the Prince of Wales. Most have come from Britain's highest aristocratic or political levels. Not all, however, have been faithful to their trust, as 36 have been beheaded. The order has been refused twice.

In 1790 George III offered William Pitt the Younger the Order, which then included a significant financial payment, but Pitt refused, requesting that it might be given to his less well-off brother. In 1945 Winston Churchill turned it down because he had just been defeated in an election. As he told a friend, 'I can hardly accept the Order of the Garter from the king after the people have given me the Order of the Boot.' Eight years later, however, after he had been re-elected, Churchill accepted the honour.

A few members have been unceremoniously dumped; Austrian Emperor Franz Joseph and German Kaiser Wilhelm II both had their appointments annulled in 1915, while Japanese Emperor Hirohito was elected in 1929, thrown out in 1941 and restored in 1971.

Although the exact origins of the Order of the Garter have long been debated, the Order has always held to one tradition: new appointments are always announced on 23 April, the anniversary of the first official ceremony.

> **1868** When asked on his deathbed if he forgave his enemies, Spanish general and sometime prime minister Ramón María Narváez, 1st Duke of Valencia, replies: 'I have none. I had them all shot.'

24 April

'O Lord, give me chastity and continence, but not yet.'

387 AD Today was Sabbatum Sanctum – the Saturday before Easter. In Milan's main church, the city's famous bishop Ambrose led a 33-year-old man and his young son to a sunken octagonal pool twenty feet in diameter, built to look like a big tomb – the church's huge baptismal font. After Ambrose had immersed them, the father and son rose from the water, having ritually 'drowned' and 'risen up' in imitation of Christ's death and resurrection.

The man was a Roman citizen from today's Algeria named Aurelius Augustinus Hipponensis; he would become one of the most important Christian theologians of the early Church, the writer of *The City of God* and *Confessions*. He is known today as Saint Augustine of Hippo.

Although Augustine's father was a pagan, his mother was a Christian, so he was raised in the Christian faith. At seventeen, he went to Carthage to study and there he became a libertine, enjoyed numerous affairs, acquired a mistress and fathered a son. As he later admitted in his *Confessions*, he was sorely tempted by sins of the flesh. He is reputed to have said: 'Women should not be enlightened or educated in any way. They should, in fact, be segregated as they are the cause of hideous and involuntary erections in holy men.' He famously prayed, 'O Lord, give me chastity and continence, but not yet.' ('*Da mihi castitatem et continentiam, sed noli modo.*')

Augustine became a convert to Manichaeism (a sect that believed the universe was ruled by the powerful, though not omnipotent power of good (God) and the power of evil (Satan)). For nine years he followed this sect, while becoming a brilliant professor of rhetoric. He then moved first to Rome and when he was 30 to Milan. Nagged by his mother, he finally ended his long relationship with his mistress and prepared to marry a ten-year-old heiress, but the marriage would never take place; while waiting for the girl to reach the then marriageable age of twelve, he opted instead for the celibacy of priesthood.

According to his *Confessions*, one day in his garden he heard a neighbour's young boy calling, 'Take it and read!' Glancing at a book held by a friend, his eyes fell on a passage by Saint Paul which instructed, 'As one dresses in new clothes, let us clothe ourselves in Christ and care no more about our bodies.' This inspired him to renounce Manichaeism and return to Christianity. The following year he was baptised by Ambrose. (After the ceremony Ambrose gave him some practical counsel. 'When I am at Rome', he said, 'I fast on a Saturday; when I am at Milan, I do not. Follow the custom of the church where you are.' His advice has remained in the English language as 'When in Rome, do as the Romans do'.)

The year after his baptism, Augustine's mother died, and he returned to Algeria, where his son also died. After three years in monastic seclusion in a villa outside Hippo, he entered the priesthood and was made Bishop of Hippo in 396.

During the next three years he wrote the autobiographical *Confessions*. After the Visigoths had sacked Rome in 410, he wrote *The City of God* (*De civitate Dei*) to restore the confidence of his fellow Christians.

In the spring of 410, Vandals besieged Hippo. Now 75, Augustine died after a long illness on 28 August of that year. Shortly thereafter the Vandals burned the city, destroying all of it but Augustine's cathedral and library, which they left untouched.

Augustine was canonised by popular acclaim. Almost a millennium later, on the anniversary of his death in 1373, the great Italian humanist Petrarch wrote to his friend Giovanni Boccaccio: 'No one, it seems to me, can hope to equal Augustine. Who, nowadays, could hope to equal one who, in my judgment, was the greatest in an age fertile in great minds?'

1547 After totally routing an alliance of Lutheran princes at Mühlberg, Emperor Charles V records in his diary: 'I appeared, I fought, God vanquished.'

---

25 April

'You furnish the pictures, I'll furnish the war.'

1898 Today the US Congress declared that 'a state of war exists' with Spain. Cuba was the catalyst.

Although their island had been Spanish for almost 400 years, Cubans had been fighting for independence for the last 30 of them. In 1897 the Governor-General of Cuba, General Valeriano Weyler, relocated 300,000 Cuban *campesinos* (peasant farmers) into 'reconcentration camps', to separate them from the guerrillas, but the abysmal conditions caused tens of thousands to die from starvation and disease.

Many Americans already believed that the Spanish Empire was corrupt and backward, supported by enslaved natives who laboured in misery for arrogant Spanish landowners, and the lamentable conditions in Weyler's camps seemed to prove the case.

At this time in New York, two newspaper barons, William Randolph Hearst and Joseph Pulitzer, were locked in a circulation battle. Both were quick to see in the Cuban situation the potential to sell copies through lurid stories and shocking headlines. Hearst urgently dispatched several writers and the artist Frederic Remington to cover the 'war'.

But when Remington arrived, he found plenty of misery but no combat. In January 1897 he cabled Hearst: 'Everything is quiet. There is no trouble. There will be no war. I wish to return.'

'Please remain', Hearst replied. 'You furnish the pictures, I'll furnish the war.'

Soon extravagant tales began to appear in Hearst's *New York Journal*. In one case, Spanish police arrested a Cuban woman while she was aboard an American ship. Suspected of carrying letters for Cuban rebels, she was searched by a police matron. But Hearst seized upon the incident with the headline: 'Refined Young Women Stripped and Searched by Brutal Spaniards While Under Our Flag on the *Olivette*'. Accompanying the story was a Remington sketch showing a naked woman surrounded by three glowering Spaniards.

As historian Walter Millis later wrote: 'Battles of the most sanguinary character began to take place in all the American papers; Havana, despite the insurgents' total lack of artillery, fell three or four times over, while atrocities of the most appalling kind began to be perpetrated by the Spaniards upon nearly every American front page.'

Then in 1898 came the sinking of the battleship USS *Maine*. American President William McKinley had ordered the *Maine* to Havana to reassure Americans living there. On 15 February an enormous explosion engulfed the front half of the ship, and the *Maine* settled to the bottom of Havana harbour, with 260 sailors and marines on board.

Although no one knew who had detonated the blast, both Hearst and Pulitzer had no scruples. Hearst's *Journal* headlined: '*Maine* was Split in Two by an Enemy's Secret Infernal Machine', and published drawings showing Spanish saboteurs clamping a mine to the *Maine's* hull. Many Americans came to believe that the iniquitous Spaniards had sunk the battleship in a gesture of arrogant contempt for America.

Driven by the public's patriotic fervour – pumped up by the newspapers – the US Congress demanded Spanish withdrawal from Cuba. In quick succession Spain severed diplomatic relations, McKinley ordered the Navy to blockade the island, and Spain declared war. Two days later, on 25 April, Congress declared the nation to be at war. Hearst sailed to Cuba to cover the conflict in person.

The United States won a pathetically one-sided contest, and Spain finally accepted a peace treaty by which the United States acquired Guam, Puerto Rico and the Philippines. Cuba came under US jurisdiction until it gained independence in 1902.

After the war Hearst opened more newspapers around the country, eventually owning 28, plus a string of magazines. Through his press ownership and extensive real estate dealings, he became one of the richest men in America, acquiring the movie star Marion Davies as a mistress along the way.

Over the years the public began to forget about the *Maine*. Also forgotten was the fact that no one really knew why she had blown up. But in 1976 a study by the US Navy concluded that the most likely cause was an accidental detonation in the ship's coalbunker, entirely the fault of the *Maine* and her crew.

1759 Frederick the Great writes to his brother Prince Henry of Prussia: 'Don't forget your great guns, which are the most respectable arguments of the rights of kings.'

---

26 April

'Do what you wish, provided there be no killing.'

1478 Lorenzo the Magnificent was only 29, but he was senior among the Medici and de facto ruler of Florence.

But the greatest man in Italy's grandest family had enemies. First were the Pazzi, another banking family who envied Medici dominance and who were conspiring to take over the state. Then came Francesco Salviati, whom Pope Sixtus IV had appointed as Archbishop of Pisa. But Pisa was within the Florentine Republic, and for three years Lorenzo had prevented him from taking over his bishopric, with its vast financial benefits. Finally, there was the Pope himself, who not only backed Salviati but also was at loggerheads with Lorenzo over control of cities near Florence like Imola and Città di Castello.

Francesco de' Pazzi and Archbishop Salviati met in Rome to plot the overthrow of the Medici. To add muscle, they approached the *condottiere* (mercenary leader) Gian Battista da Montesecco, but Montesecco refused to act without the Pope's blessing. Sixtus confirmed the need to cleanse Florence of the Medici, but the *condottiere* warned that any attempt 'may turn out ill without the death of Lorenzo and [his younger brother] Giuliano'.

Sixtus knew full well that no coup could succeed if the leading Medici were still alive, but how could he, the Pope, sanction the shedding of blood? 'Go, and do what you wish', he said, and then added, 'provided there be no killing.' Everyone understood that the Pope had just given his backing to murder.

Lorenzo and Giuliano had to die, and the most convenient place would be in church, when they would be together, unsuspecting, and, with luck, unarmed; so the murder was planned for Sunday, 26 April, in Florence's red-domed cathedral. The signal for the attack would be the ringing of the sanctuary bell for the Elevation of the Host. Enlisted to stab Lorenzo were two disguised priests.

On the day of the murder there was a hitch; Giuliano de' Medici was at home, sick in bed. Francesco de' Pazzi and his confederate Bernardo Bandini went to the Medici Palace and persuaded Giuliano to come to mass. On the way to the cathedral, Pazzi threw his arm around Giuliano as if for friendly support but in reality to check that he was not wearing chain mail under his tunic.

Finally, all the villains and victims were assembled inside the church. As the bell sounded, the priests struck, but they only wounded Lorenzo, slashing him across the back of his neck. Pouring blood, he spun to avoid his attackers, vaulted over the altar rail and escaped through a side door. Giuliano was not so lucky; in a frenzy of blood lust, Pazzi and Bandini stabbed him nineteen times and left him dead on the cathedral floor.

The conspirators then rushed to the Palazzo della Signoria, Florence's town hall, to seize control of the city, but there Medici supporters cornered them, while ringing the Signoria bell to summon the townspeople. Seizing Archbishop Salviati, Lorenzo's allies tied a rope around his neck and lowered him out of the Signoria window, still clad in his ecclesiastical robes. Then Francesco de' Pazzi was stripped naked and hanged from another window to dangle alongside the archbishop. Rioting citizens in the piazza below saw the archbishop fix his teeth into Pazzi's naked body as they swung choking and goggle-eyed at the end of their ropes. Three other accomplices were similarly hanged.

Some 80 conspirators were hunted down, including the two priests, who were castrated and hanged. Bandini had escaped to Constantinople, but Lorenzo's agents captured him and brought him back to Florence for execution. Medici power in Florence was now stronger than ever.

A month after the Pazzi conspiracy had been crushed, a Florentine working girl gave birth to a son, whose father was the murdered Giuliano. Although the girl and Giuliano had not been married, the Medici found a loophole in canon law – *per sponsalia de presenti* – that made the child legitimate. The infant boy was brought up in his uncle Lorenzo's household. Forty-five years later he would become Pope Clement VII.

1968 Fascist leader Sir Oswald Mosley in a letter to *The Times*: 'I am not, and never have been, a man of the right. My position was on the left and is now in the centre of politics.'

---

27 April

'From the Halls of Montezuma to the shores of Tripoli'

1805 Today a small force of American marines charged through heavy musket fire to lead an attack on the harbour fortress of Derna in present-day Libya. Within two hours Derna had fallen, bringing victory over the Ottoman province of Tripoli and adding to the Marine Corps legend.

For centuries the pirates of the Barbary Coast had been preying on ships unwise enough to sail too near the northern rim of Africa. These corsairs captured merchant ships and enslaved their crews or held them for ransom. By the end of the 18th century, Western powers, including the United States, were regularly paying vast sums in protection money to the ruling pashas.

When Thomas Jefferson became president in 1801, Yusuf Karamanli, the Pasha of Tripoli, demanded another huge payment.

Jefferson refused, and, in a show of bravado, Yusuf declared war, not by written word but using the traditional Barbary manner of chopping down the flagpole in front of the US Consulate in Tripoli.

After two years of minor skirmishes, a diplomat-turned-general named William Eaton drew up a bold plan. He enlisted the support of Hamet Karamanli, the rightful ruler of Tripoli who had been exiled by his brother Yusuf. Eaton promised to restore Hamet to power in return for help. Hamet then recruited 500 Arab and Greek mercenaries, who were reinforced by a detachment of eight American marines under the command of First Lieutenant Presley O'Bannon. With Eaton at its head, this unlikely force headed toward the Tripolitan port of Derna, which three US warships would bombard from the sea.

After a fractious 45-day trek across 600 miles of desert, in which Muslim and Christian allies threatened to fight each other, this rag-tag army arrived before Derna. Eaton's demands for surrender were abruptly refused – 'My head or yours!' replied the enemy commander – so he launched a ground attack while American warships pounded the fortress. Hamet led a contingent of mercenaries to storm the governor's palace, while Eaton led the rest of his men against the fortress, with Lieutenant O'Bannon's marines in the lead.

When hostile fire held up the attackers, Eaton ordered a charge, during which he was shot in the wrist. But O'Bannon's marines swept forward through the musket fire to seize the gun emplacements, then turned the cannon back on the city as the defenders fled. Meanwhile Hamet secured the lightly defended governor's palace to complete the victory. When O'Bannon hoisted the American flag over the harbour defences, he became the first American to raise his country's flag over a foreign battlefield.

Later Hamet presented O'Bannon with his curved Mamluk sword in recognition of his bravery. In 1835 the Mamluk sword was adopted for all future Marine Corps officers (including the writer of this book) as part of their dress uniform.

With Derna subdued, Eaton planned to march on Tripoli, but Yusuf sued for peace. In early June he guaranteed the right of passage of American ships but, to Eaton's fury, Yusuf remained in power. Yusuf's disillusioned brother Hamet was unceremoniously sent back to Egypt, and the mercenaries were dispersed, only partly paid, but Eaton and O'Bannon returned to the United States as heroes.

Soon the legend 'To the shores of Tripoli' was added to the Marine Corps battle standard. Half a century later, during the

Mexican–American War, American marines stormed Chapultepec Castle, once the palace of the Aztec emperor Montezuma. This resulted in a new legend, now reading 'From Tripoli to the Halls of Montezuma'. Then, tradition has it, a marine serving in Mexico transposed the phrases to read, 'From the Halls of Montezuma to the Shores of Tripoli' and set the words to music, taking the tune from Offenbach's opera, *Genevieve de Brabant*. In 1929 it officially became the Marine Corps 'Hymn':

> From the Halls of Montezuma,
> To the shores of Tripoli;
> We fight our country's battles
> In the air, on land, and sea;
> First to fight for right and freedom
> And to keep our honor clean:
> We are proud to claim the title
> Of United States Marine.

1980 Tony Benn is quoted in *The Observer*: 'The Marxist analysis has got nothing to do with what happened in Stalin's Russia; it's like blaming Jesus Christ for the Inquisition in Spain.'

28 April

'The Queen of Tears'

1772 Pity poor Caroline Matilda. Daughter of George II and brought up in England, at fifteen she was sent to Copenhagen to marry her seventeen-year-old cousin, Christian VII of Denmark, who, though mentally unstable, was the all-powerful king of a country still a feudal backwater.

During their short honeymoon Christian was attentive to his young wife, but their relationship soon soured. The king preferred prostitutes to his bride, and Caroline Matilda spent long hours isolated in the royal castle of Frederiksborg, treated with ignominy and often with cruelty.

Christian was eventually persuaded of the need for an heir and briefly returned to the marital bed. In January 1768 the queen gave birth to a son, the future Frederick VI, but during her pregnancy the king took up with the prostitute/actress Støvlet-Cathrine.

Later that year Christian set out to visit royal courts around Europe, but near Hamburg he fell ill and called for a doctor named Johann Friedrich

Struensee, a brilliant man of 31 who combined advanced medical skills with a passionate interest in the ideas of Rousseau and the Enlightenment.

During the eight-month tour Struensee managed to allay Christian's madness, and, to the astonishment of the king's entourage, the king was now charming and amusing at parties and state functions. Struensee was brought to Copenhagen as the king's personal physician, and Christian became increasingly dependent on him.

At first Caroline Matilda strongly disliked this intrusive German, but Struensee professed to believe that together the two of them could bring Denmark in from semi-feudal darkness to the freedoms of the Enlightenment. Then, when a smallpox epidemic ravaged Copenhagen, he persuaded her that her infant son Frederick could be safeguarded by inoculation (a daring procedure at the time – Jenner's first smallpox vaccination was still 26 years in the future). Caroline Matilda agreed and Frederick survived. Now the queen's dislike of Struensee turned to attraction, and they embarked on a passionate affair.

With the queen in his bed and the king in his pocket, Struensee began to take on increasing authority. In July 1771, the king made him Confidential Cabinet Minister, but, with Christian unfit to rule, he was in fact Denmark's dictator, with power to pass any law he pleased.

Struensee wasted no time introducing reforms modelled on the principles of Rousseau, while ignoring the strongly reactionary Danish aristocracy. Visionary in his views and intoxicated by power, in sixteen months he promulgated over a thousand ordinances, including the abolition of torture, freedom of the press, restriction of noble privileges, banishment of the slave trade in Danish colonies and distribution of farmland to peasants. The new laws touched every aspect of public life and, predictably, caused havoc. Although Danes at first welcomed Struensee's reforms, they soon learned that there was to be no democratic government. The 'will of the people' was whatever Struensee conceived it to be.

On 7 July 1771 Caroline Matilda gave birth to a daughter. By now her scandalous liaison with Struensee was becoming public knowledge, and the girl was assumed to be Struensee's child. With the nobility ripe for revolt, Christian's stepmother, Queen Dowager Juliane Marie, her son Frederick and the Commander of the Guards conspired to overthrow their German master.

After a *bal masqué* at Christiansborg Castle on 17 January, the conspirators seized Struensee and Caroline Matilda, and then persuaded the king to sign the arrest order.

Struensee was tried and convicted of *lèse majesté* (offending the dignity of the sovereign). When he admitted his illicit relations with the queen, she attempted to save him by claiming that she 'had been his temptress'. All to no avail. On this day in 1772 the state executioner first chopped off Struensee's right hand and then decapitated him.

Queen Caroline Matilda was divorced and condemned to imprisonment, but her brother George III sent an English warship to her rescue, and the Danes were only too happy to be shed of her. Sent to Celle in Hanover, she died of scarlet fever three years later without ever seeing her children again, still only 24. She is known in Danish history as 'The Queen of Tears'.

1945 '*Sparami nel petto!*' ('Shoot me in the chest!') – Benito Mussolini's plea to Italian partisans just before they summarily shoot him and his mistress near Lake Como.

---

29 April

'If you give me six lines written by the hand of the most honest of men, I will find something in them to have him hanged.'

1624 Only a year earlier Charles, duc de La Vieuville had become France's Superintendent of Finances, Louis XIII's most important advisor, but on this day this arrogant, greedy and corrupt nobleman appointed a new member to the Royal Council, Armand Jean du Plessis, aka Cardinal Richelieu. It was, to coin a phrase, a cardinal mistake. Richelieu was quite prepared to spread rumours about La Vieuville's corruption that had the virtue of being true. On 12 August Louis had La Vieuville arrested, and the next day Richelieu took his place as the king's principal minister. A month later he had La Vieuville imprisoned in the Château d'Amboise.

Richelieu would remain Louis' first minister until his death eighteen years later. Known as *l'Éminence rouge* for the red cardinal's clerical dress he wore, he was brilliant, calculating, pragmatic and unrelenting, with the clearest of visions of the greatness and glory that he thought his country deserved.

France was surrounded by inimical Habsburgs, kings of Spain as well as Holy Roman emperors who controlled Austria, today's Belgium and most of Germany, and Louis XIII was belaboured by rebellious princes. Richelieu's first task was to bring France's feudal nobility to heel.

Travelling the country with an overpowering escort of 100 horse guards and 100 musketeers, plus his household of 180, he ordered all fortified castles razed, thereby stripping recalcitrant nobles of defences they could have used in revolt. He fashioned a large spy network and had suspected conspirators imprisoned or executed. 'In the course of ordinary affairs, justice requires authentic proof', he said. 'It is not necessarily so in matters of state. There, occasions arise where one must start with an execution.' Ruthless against the king's enemies, he claimed: 'If you give me six lines written by the hand of the most honest of men, I will find something in them to have him hanged.'

Another domestic problem was religion. Since the mid-16th century, France's Protestant Huguenots had battled Catholics for religious freedom and (much the greater crime in Richelieu's eyes) for political independence from the crown. The Huguenot fortress of La Rochelle had allied itself with Protestant England. In 1628 Richelieu personally led a fifteen-month siege during which the Rochellais were reduced to eating first horses, then dogs and cats and finally rats. When they capitulated, three-quarters of the city's 27,000 inhabitants had died of starvation. The pragmatic cardinal ordered La Rochelle's walls demolished but pardoned the surviving citizens, even allowing them to remain Protestant. For his victory Louis made Richelieu a duke.

The Thirty Years' War had started in 1618 when Ferdinand II of Bohemia attempted to impose Roman Catholicism on his domains, and Protestant nobles rose up in rebellion. Eventually the Habsburg Holy Roman Empire was drawn in, pitted against Protestant forces. Richelieu, however, saw the chance to redirect the war from religious conflict to that of nationalism versus Habsburg hegemony. He subsidised the Protestant Dutch and Swedes against the Catholics, earning himself the enmity of Catholics all over Europe but forcing the Habsburg Empire to drain its resources and head toward bankruptcy. Richelieu died before the war ended, but by the time the Peace of Westphalia was signed in 1648, France had become the dominant power in Europe with an absolute monarch on the throne.

In 1642, when he was 57, Richelieu was sick and weary. After persuading Louis to appoint Cardinal Mazarin as his successor, he waited for death in the Palais Cardinal, that magnificent structure he had built on the rue Saint-Honoré (today the Palais Royal).

As death closed in, he tried one last remedy, an old peasant woman's panacea of horse dung mixed with wine. As Aldous Huxley wrote: 'It was with the taste of excrement in his mouth that the arbiter of Europe's destinies gave up the ghost.'

On hearing of Richelieu's death, the worldly old Pope Urban VIII commented: 'If there is a God, Cardinal Richelieu will have much to answer for. But if not – well, he had a successful life.'

1962 In an address at a White House dinner honouring Nobel Prize winners, President Kennedy tells his guests: 'I think this is the most extraordinary collection of talent, of human knowledge, that has ever been gathered together at the White House, with the possible exception of when Thomas Jefferson dined alone.'

---

30 April

'There is no need to pity me, for I die as a man of honour. But I pity you, because you are fighting against your king, your country and your oath.'

1524 Today in northern Italy near Lake Garda, Pierre Terrail, seigneur de Bayard was killed in battle, dying as he had lived, *le chevalier sans peur et sans reproche* (the fearless and faultless knight).

The Chevalier de Bayard was born in 1473 into a noble family, of which four family heads in the past five generations had fallen in battle. He was knighted at 22 after the French victory at Fornovo and remained almost continuously at war for the rest of his life.

Bayard was one of France's greatest soldiers, but his renown stems more from the man himself than from his battlefield success. In a time when mercenary armies lived for loot, he refused to share in plunder and was considered the ideal knight, aggressive and heroic but also chivalrous, devout and magnanimous. Although known for his courage, he preferred the name his contemporaries gave him for his cheerfulness and kindness, '*le bon chevalier*'.

When he was 31, Bayard was fighting near Naples, where French and Spanish armies occupied opposite banks of the Garigliano river. During an armed reconnaissance about 300 French soldiers began to cross the river on a bridge of boats. Told at the last moment, Bayard joined the group still dressed in a simple doublet, without time to put on his cuirass and helmet. A much larger Spanish force spotted the incursion and attacked, forcing the French to retreat back across the boat-bridge, but it was so narrow that only one soldier at a time could cross it. Bayard remained alone on the bridge, singlehandedly holding off the enemy until the French could reassemble on the other bank.

Bayard distinguished himself at Genoa, Padua, Bologna and Brescia, where he was seriously wounded with a spike in the thigh. By 1515 he had become so famous that a young King François I asked him to knight him after the Battle of Marignano. Six years later Bayard with only 1,000 men stymied an enemy force of 35,000 for six weeks at the siege of Mézières, saving central France from invasion.

In 1523 Bayard was sent to Italy in an army commanded by Amiral de France Guillaume de Bonnivet. The Holy Roman Empire forces proved too strong for the French, and Bonnivet was forced to retreat, having been defeated and wounded at Robecco. He ordered Bayard to assume command and save the army. At first Bayard repulsed the pursuers, but on this day he was wounded by a harquebus ball in the back while guarding the rear near the Sesia river.

Unable to mount his horse, Bayard had his men place him sitting against a tree facing the oncoming Imperial soldiers, with his sword thrust into the ground before him as an improvised cross. 'I have never turned my back to the enemy', he said. 'I do not want to start now, at the end of my life.' He was soon surrounded, and he saw his old comrade-in-arms, the renegade Charles, duc de Bourbon, who had fought with him at Marignano but who later deserted the French for Imperial service. (This is the same duc de Bourbon who would sack Rome in 1527.)

'I am very sad to see you in this condition', said Bourbon to his stricken friend. 'You, who were such a virtuous knight.'

'Sir, there is no need to pity me', replied Bayard, 'for I die as a man of honour. But I pity you, because you are fighting against your king, your country and your oath.' A few minutes later Bayard died.

The Chevalier de Bayard remains a hero in France half a millennium after his death. There is even a statue of him at the country's leading military academy at Saint-Cyr.

1945 At four o'clock, just before shooting himself in his Berlin bunker, Adolf Hitler issues his last communiqué: 'My wife and I choose to die in order to escape the shame of overthrow or capitulation. It is our wish for our bodies to be cremated immediately on the place where I have performed the greater part of my daily work, during twelve years of service to my people.'

1 May

'You may fire when you are ready, Gridley.'

1898 For the past three years Spain had been ruthlessly suppressing a revolution in Cuba. America's revulsion to Spanish atrocities was stoked by the 'yellow' journalism of Pulitzer and Hearst newspapers and reached a fever pitch after the sinking of the battleship *Maine* in Havana harbour in February 1898. On 25 April the US Congress declared war. The next day the government ordered Commodore George Dewey and his Hong Kong-based Asiatic Squadron to attack the Spanish fleet in the Philippines.

At dawn on 1 May, Dewey steamed his four cruisers and two gunboats into Manila Bay to confront the Spanish flotilla. His flagship was the cruiser *Olympia* commanded by Captain Charles Gridley. Inside the bay the Spanish admiral Patricio Montojo had anchored his ships close to shore but just beyond the range of the Spanish batteries in Manila, fearing that if the American ships and the batteries exchanged fire, the American bombardment would rain havoc on the city's civilians as it fired on the batteries.

At 5.15 this morning the Spanish warships took the first shots of the battle but scored no hits as the American ships were still out of range. By 5.40 the two fleets were only about 5,000 yards apart, and Dewey calmly commanded his flag captain: 'You may fire when you are ready, Gridley.' Gridley immediately passed the order to the 8-inch guns in the ship's forward turret, and the cruiser bellowed out a salvo, which was instantly repeated by the other American warships.

The American fleet steamed back and forth before the anchored Spaniards, steadily decreasing the range and firing broadside after broadside. But, due to the thick white smoke from the guns and the black smoke from the ships' funnels, it was impossible to see what damage the barrage was causing.

As it turned out, many of the American shots missed their mark, as cannon at that time were still manually sighted with the naked eye. But the Spanish fleet consisted of a variety of obsolete vessels manned by untrained crews, and the shore batteries were out of range, so the American ships were hardly touched. Before noon eight of Montojo's ships had been sunk, with casualties of 350 men, and the Spanish capitulated. Dewey lost eight wounded and one dead (due to heat stroke), and no ships. One of those injured was Captain Gridley, who was already in precarious health. While being invalided home after the battle, he was forced to stop in Kobe, Japan, where he died on 5 June.

On 3 July another American fleet destroyed the Spanish Caribbean Squadron off Cuba, and the war came to an end on 12 August, with Spain humiliated, both of her fleets at the bottom of the ocean. Cuba gained independence from Spain, and the United States acquired the Philippines, Puerto Rico and Guam, and, more importantly, took the first step in becoming a world power.

1464 Edward IV marries Elizabeth Woodville after she has told him: 'Full well I know that I am not good enough to be your queen, but, ah, dear liege lord, I am far too good to become your mistress.' (Another king, France's Henri IV, is similarly rebuffed in 1590 when the aristocratic Antoinette de Guercheville tells him: 'My rank is not noble enough for me to become your wife, but my heart is too noble for me to become your mistress.') *
1769 Arthur Wellesley, later Duke of Wellington, is born in Dublin, but he later refutes the implication that he is an Irishman: 'Because a man is born in a stable, that does not make him a horse.'

---

2 May

*'Let us pass over the river,
and rest under the shade of the trees.'*

1863 Chancellorsville, Virginia: scene of one of the American Civil War's bloodiest battles. The North suffered 17,000 casualties to the South's 13,000, but the greatest loss to the Confederates was the legendary general, Thomas Jonathan Jackson, known then and now as 'Stonewall'.

Jackson was a slight, wiry man with a high intelligent forehead and a handsome curly beard. Dour and eccentric, he was an accomplished psychosomatic who (thought he) suffered from constant indigestion, neuralgia, chilblains, tonsillitis and incipient deafness. He also had poor eyesight, for which his treatment was to immerse his head in cold water with his eyes open and remain submerged until he ran out of breath.

Stern, righteous and God-fearing, Jackson was not liked by his men, but his courage under fire, his cool head and his brilliant tactical abilities made him the kind of general that soldiers willingly follow. As one observer commented: 'He lived by the New Testament and fought by the Old.' The Northern general Ulysses Grant remembered him as a 'fanatic ... [who] fancied that an evil spirit had taken possession of him'.

Jackson had earned the nickname 'Stonewall' at the First Battle of Bull Run when, greatly outnumbered, he refused to buckle under a massive Union attack, helping the South to a major victory.

The Battle of Chancellorsville began on 1 May as the Union and Confederate armies manoeuvred for position, but with little combat. The Union commander Joseph Hooker's force of 133,000 men far outnumbered the Confederate army of 61,000, but the South was led by the brilliant general Robert E. Lee, who decided on the risky strategy of splitting his army to outflank the larger Northern force.

The next day, 2 May, the cavalry general Fitzhugh Lee (Robert E.'s nephew) led Jackson up a hill on a reconnaissance. As the two men looked down on the unsuspecting Yankees, Lee observed Jackson intent in prayer. As he later wrote: 'His eyes burned with a brilliant glow, lighting up a sad face. His expression was one of intense interest, his face was coloured slightly with the paint of approaching battle, and radiant at the success of his flank movement. To the remarks made to him while the unconscious line of blue was pointed out, he did not reply once during the five minutes he was on the hill, and yet his lips were moving.'

Now the battle started in earnest, as Jackson led the 26,000 men of his II Corps on a bold fourteen-mile march to strike the exposed Union right flank and drive it back in confusion with heavy losses. At dusk Jackson rode out on a moonlight reconnaissance. Some of his own nervous soldiers mistook him and his aides for Yankees and opened fire, hitting Jackson in the right hand and twice in the left arm. Back at the Confederate field hospital, Jackson's arm was amputated; the wound looked serious but not mortal. When General Lee heard about Jackson's injury, he sent him the message: 'You are better off than I am, for while you have lost your left, I have lost my right arm.'

The battle, considered a stunning victory for the South, continued until 6 May when both sides withdrew to lick their wounds. But the most serious Confederate wound refused to heal. The amputation gravely weakened Jackson, who contracted pneumonia. Soon he was half-delirious. On 10 May he seemed to wake from his restless sleep and clearly pronounced his last words: 'Let us pass over the river, and rest under the shade of the trees.'

Almost a century later, Jackson's enigmatic farewell found an echo in Ernest Hemingway's novel about the death of an officer entitled *Across the River and into the Trees*.

1519 Leonardo da Vinci dies in Cloux on the Loire, supposedly in the arms of King François I, after having lamented: 'I have offended God and man because my work did not achieve the quality it should have.'

---

3 May

'In Flanders fields the poppies blow/ Between the crosses, row on row'

1915 On 22 April the Germans had opened the Second Battle of Ypres with the first chlorine gas attack on the Western front, killing 1,400 Allied soldiers and wounding twice that many. In the early morning of 2 May, however, the Allied front line, composed of French, British and British Empire troops, came under attack by standard artillery. Despite the incoming fire, a 22-year-old Canadian lieutenant named Alexis Helmer of the Canadian Field Artillery climbed out of his trench to check on his battery. He had gone only a few yards when a German 8-inch shell caught him in the open, killing him instantly.

Assigned to the same unit was brigade-surgeon Major John McCrae, a fellow Canadian who had served in South Africa as a lieutenant during the Second Boer War but had later become a prominent pathologist. At the onset of the First World War, McCrae was already 42, but he quickly rejoined the army, writing home to his mother: 'I am really rather afraid, but more afraid to stay at home with my conscience.'

The day Helmer was killed, McCrae was operating from a hastily dug bunker behind the lines. They had become close friends during the opening months of the war, and on Helmer's death it was McCrae himself who performed the burial service.

The next day – 3 May – as McCrae sat in the back of an ambulance at an Advanced Dressing Station outside Ypres, he brooded over how quickly poppies grow around the graves of fallen soldiers. He then composed the most beloved poem of the First World War:

In Flanders fields the poppies blow
Between the crosses, row on row,
    That mark our place; and in the sky
    The larks, still bravely singing, fly
Scarce heard amid the guns below.

We are the Dead. Short days ago
We lived, felt dawn, saw sunset glow,
    Loved and were loved, and now we lie,
    In Flanders fields.

Take up our quarrel with the foe:
To you from failing hands we throw
    The torch; be yours to hold it high.
    If ye break faith with us who die
We shall not sleep, though poppies grow
    In Flanders fields.

McCrae's verses first appeared in *Punch* on 8 December, went on to be published throughout the English-speaking world and were translated into numerous other languages. Although blood-red poppies have been artistically associated with the graves of soldiers at least since Napoleonic times, it was McCrae's poem that transformed the poppy into the remembrance symbol of today that commemorates military personnel who have given their lives in war.

By 25 May the Second Battle of Ypres was over, an Allied loss with some 60,000 casualties versus 39,000 for the Germans. At the beginning of June, McCrae was sent to Boulogne-sur-Mer to establish a Canadian General Hospital and promoted to lieutenant colonel. But his health was frail – he had been an asthmatic since childhood – and on 28 January 1918 he succumbed to pneumonia and meningitis.

1814 Arthur Wellesley is created Duke of Wellington; nineteen days later he writes to his nephew Henry Wellesley: 'I believe I forgot to tell you that I was made a Duke.' * **1871** Prime Minister William Gladstone in the House of Commons: 'The personal attendance and intervention of women in election proceedings ... would be a practical evil not only of the gravest, but even of an intolerable character.'

4 May

*'The young lion will overcome the old/
In the field of war by a single duel'*

1555 Today in Lyon the publishing house Macé Bonhomme published a collection of enigmatic quatrains forecasting disasters such as earthquakes, wars, floods, plagues, invasions, murders and battles, all undated. Written in French, Greek, Latin and Occitan, the book was entitled *Les Prophéties* (*The Prophecies*), the creation of the French physician and astrologer Michel de Nostredame, who Latinised his name to Nostradamus.

Nostradamus was born on 14 December 1503 in Saint-Rémy in Provence. After receiving a medical degree at Avignon, he is supposed to have developed extraordinary healing powers, but he was destined to be no ordinary physician, becoming either the greatest soothsayer or the greatest charlatan in history.

When he was in his late forties Nostradamus began putting himself into a meditative state in order, he said, to experience visions of the future. He also started to dabble in the occult while producing horoscopes for rich aristocrats. In 1550 he published an almanac stuffed with cryptic divinations that was such a commercial success that he thereafter wrote one annually. Whether Nostradamus believed his own prophecies is moot.

One famous incident supposedly happened in 1553 when the seer encountered a group of Franciscan monks and threw himself on his knees, clutching at the habit of one of the monks, Felice Peretti. When asked why he had done so, he answered that he must show deference to 'his Holiness'. Nineteen years after Nostradamus' death, Peretti became Pope Sixtus V.

In the 1550s Nostradamus started writing *Les Prophéties*, which contained 942 Delphic predictions, probably purposely obscure to evade being accused of witchcraft by the Inquisition, but their opacity also meant the quatrains could be interpreted to fit numerous events. Later generations claimed they forecast everything from the Great Fire of London to Napoleon's downfall to the Second World War to the death of Princess Diana.

The most famous of *Les Prophéties'* quatrains is I.35, with its uncanny foretelling of an event that happened four years after the book was published:

The young lion will overcome the old
In the field of war by a single duel
In a golden cage, his eyes will be pierced
Two wounds in one, then he will die a cruel death

On 30 June 1559 King Henri II was jousting in the great 'Tournament of Queens' at the Palais des Tournelles in Paris. At the tournament's end the knights and spectators were on the point of leaving when Henri, now 40, decided on one more bout against a younger opponent, Gabriel de Lorges, Comte de Montgoméry, a French nobleman of 29.

The trumpet sounded and the armoured figures met with a mighty crash. The impact snapped Montgoméry's lance, and the sharp stump smashed into the king's face, penetrating his gilded helmet and driving a splinter in over his right eye.

For over a week Henri endured the tortures of 16th-century medicine, as the court surgeon Ambroise Paré tried to remove the splinter (having practised the operation on the heads of some newly decapitated criminals), but he died of septicaemia on 10 July.

For the next seven years Nostradamus continued to churn out murky forecasts, and on 1 July 1566 he offered his final prediction, to the priest at his bedside. 'You will not find me alive at sunrise', he said. The next morning he was found dead, lying on the floor next to his bed.

Since his death *Les Prophéties* has been published in many languages and hundreds of editions, including one with a title that could probably apply to all of them, *Nostradamus For Dummies*.

1702 When England enters the War of the Spanish Succession two months after the accession of Queen Anne, Louis XIV laments: 'It means I'm growing old when ladies declare war on me.' * **1904** After work begins on the Panama Canal despite Congressional bickering, President Theodore Roosevelt smugly comments: 'I took the Canal Zone and let Congress debate, and while the debate goes on the canal does too.'

---

5 May

*'You try to distract yourself from the pain,
but only death will end it.'*

1821 Today at 5.49 in the afternoon Napoleon Bonaparte, once emperor of half of Europe and lord to 70 million people, died on the remote island of Saint Helena. He had lived for 51 years, eight months and twenty days. His last words were a faintly whispered *'Tête d'armée! France! France! Joséphine!'*, a wistful final thought for his first wife who had died seven years before.

Napoleon spent his last five and a half years on Saint Helena, an island with only 2,000 inhabitants but with 1,400 British troops to guard against his escape. Bored to distraction and bitter at both the enemies who had defeated him and the supporters who had betrayed him, he kept a minor court of a few French officers and their wives who had followed him into exile. By 1818 his health had started to break down, as he suffered from extreme nausea, headaches, weakened sight, insomnia, deafness and bleeding gums. Initially his doctors diagnosed liver problems, but by the next year the centre of pain moved to his stomach, suggesting stomach cancer, the same affliction that had killed his father. Napoleon reflected stoically: 'You try to distract yourself from the pain, but only death will end it.'

By March 1821 he was refusing the drugs the doctors were giving him, telling one: 'I'm no longer fooling myself; my life is slipping away.' Nonetheless, he remained lucid, reminiscing about 'the glory we have acquired'.

On 15 April Napoleon signed his last will in which he professed 'the most tender sentiments' for his wife Marie-Louise, even though he had not seen her for seven years and she was now living happily with her lover, the Austrian count Adam Albert von Neipperg, by whom she had already borne two children. He also managed to blame France's defeat on 'the treason of Marmont, Augereau, Talleyrand, and Lafayette' while claiming that 'I die prematurely, assassinated by the English oligarchy'.

On the evening of 3 May Napoleon lapsed into unconsciousness, apparently paralysed, after taking a huge dose of calomel laxative that his doctors hoped would help him. Two days later he was dead.

When his doctors opened him up they found he had been killed by a 'stomach ulcer' (i.e. cancer) and an infected liver that, produced by the damp, cold Saint Helena climate, had aggravated the cancer, thus justifying his accusation to have been slain by the English who sent him there.

Napoleon's body was exposed in a *chapelle ardente* dressed in the uniform of the Imperial Guard, decorated with the orders of the Legion of Honour and the Iron Crown, booted, armed with his sword and wearing his tricorne hat. He then received a military funeral staged by the British garrison on Saint Helena. Covered in the cloak that he had worn at Marengo, his coffin was buried in a grave twelve feet deep, lined with stone. The ceremony concluded with three artillery salutes, announcing to his friends that they had nothing more to hope for and to his enemies that they had nothing more to fear.

There he remained for nineteen years until his body was returned to Paris for an elaborate funeral replay. Just before leaving Saint Helena his remains were disinterred and the coffin was opened for two minutes. All those present testified that, like some medieval saint, he had remained in a state of perfect preservation.

On 15 December 1840 over a million people jammed the funeral procession's three-mile route where, accompanied by a marshal and an admiral of France, sixteen black horses in splendid trappings drew the funeral carriage to the Invalides, where King Louis-Philippe awaited. The Archbishop of Paris conducted the obsequies while Mozart's Requiem was performed.

Today in the Dôme des Invalides Napoleon lies encased in seven caskets that are enclosed in a massive sarcophagus carved from red quartzite that rests on a green granite base. Every year over one and a half million people come to see it.

1941 Five years to the day since his exile, Emperor Haile Selassie enters Addis Ababa after Ethiopia is liberated from Italian occupation and tells his countrymen: 'As Saint George who killed the dragon is the Patron Saint of our army as well as of our allies, let us unite with our [British and South African] allies in everlasting friendship and amity in order to be able to stand against the godless and cruel dragon which has newly risen and which is oppressing mankind.'

6 May

'Greed is but a word jealous men inflict upon the ambitious.'

53 BC Today the richest man in Rome was killed in remote Anatolia. He was Marcus Licinius Crassus who, despite his colossal fortune and his powerful position as one of Rome's original Triumvirs, was eaten away by his craving to become a great military leader.

At 29 Crassus had fought under Sulla during his overthrow of the Roman state, playing a critical role in Sulla's final victory at the Colline Gate. Under Sulla's dictatorship, Crassus bought many properties at knock-down prices after Sulla had proscribed their owners. He also established a private fire brigade of over 500 slaves to fight Rome's frequent fires. When conflagrations broke out, he refused to let his firefighters extinguish the blaze until the owners had sold their burning houses at a trifling price. Through such methods Crassus became the richest man in Roman history (after Augustus Caesar), but he was dismissive of those who condemned his methods: 'Greed is but a word jealous men inflict upon the ambitious', he said.

When he was 44 Crassus commanded an army of 40,000 men that crushed the slave revolt led by Spartacus, who was killed on the battlefield. The next day Crassus lined the Appian Way from Rome to Capua with 6,000 crucified slaves. The Roman Senate did not award him a triumph, however; he had defeated only slaves.

Crassus twice became consul, both times sharing the consulship with Pompey the Great. He also used his vast wealth to support Julius Caesar, who was just rising to prominence. In 59 BC he joined Caesar and Pompey to form the First Triumvirate, which effectively ruled Rome.

By this time Pompey already enjoyed the reputation of a great general, and soon Caesar was winning spectacular battles in his conquest of Gaul, so Crassus found himself running well behind in standing and prestige. His solution was to mount an invasion of the Parthian Empire, which dominated modern Iran, Iraq and eastern Turkey. Crassus had boasted that 'no man should be accounted rich who could not maintain an army at his own cost', and at the end of 55 BC he headed for Syria, where he funded a force of seven legions (about 35,000 men), 4,000 horse and about the same number of auxiliaries.

Today at Carrhae (just north of today's Turkish–Lebanese border) Crassus met the vastly smaller army of the Parthian general Surena, who commanded 1,000 cataphracts (heavily armoured cavalry) armed with lances and 9,000 horse archers.

At first Surena tried to unnerve the Romans with the thunderous beating of thousands of drums and then sent his horse archers to harry the enemy. The legions repeatedly advanced to engage in the close-quarters fighting at which they excelled, only for the horse archers to fake a retreat and then swivel on their horses and fire backwards on the Romans – the famous 'Parthian shot' – while keeping themselves well clear. In feint after feint the Parthians charged the Romans, then pulled away while continuing to shoot, inflicting heavy casualties. When Crassus ordered his troops into the *testudo* (tortoise) formation with interlocking shields to protect against the arrows, Surena's cataphracts charged their lines, causing more losses. When the Romans loosened their formation to repel the cataphracts, the horse archers returned to fire again.

Desperate, Crassus sent his son Publius with eight infantry cohorts (about 4,000 men) plus 1,300 cavalry and some extra archers to drive off the enemy horse archers, but they were ambushed and destroyed, and Publius fell on his sword. His head was presented to Crassus on a spike.

The next day Surena called for a peace conference, which Crassus, unnerved by his son's death, reluctantly attended. There a fight broke out between his officers and the Parthians and, in the words of Livy, 'he was captured and killed to avoid suffering the indignity of remaining alive'.

Taking Crassus' corpse back to camp, the Parthians mocked his famous greed by pouring molten gold down his throat. His head was then used as a prop in a play put on for the Parthian king.

1946 When the US Congress threatens to integrate the Marine Corps into the Army, Marine Commandant Archie Vandegrift tells the Senate Committee on Naval Affairs: 'We do not rest our case on any presumed ground of gratitude owing us from the Nation. The bended knee is not a tradition of our Corps. If the Marine as a fighting man has not made a case for himself after 170 years of service, he must go. But I think you will agree with me that he has earned the right to depart with dignity and honour, not by subjugation to the status of uselessness and servility planned for him by the War Department.'

7 May

'The eagle has ceased to scream, but the
parrots will now begin to chatter.'

1945 For the Germans, it had been a bitter twelve days, as the Second World War headed toward its inevitable end in Europe.

On 25 April, the last Germans were expelled by the Finnish army from Finland and retreated into Norway. Three days later the Italian dictator Benito Mussolini was summarily executed near Lake Como and hung by his heels in a Milan petrol station. Then on 30 April, as the Russians bloodily advanced through Berlin, Hitler shot himself along with Eva Braun, his long-term partner whom he had married less than 40 hours before. The next evening Nazi propaganda minister Joseph Goebbels and his wife Magda poisoned their six small children before Goebbels shot first his wife and then himself. By this time some 2,500,000 German soldiers had surrendered or been captured in April alone. Then, in the early hours of 2 May, a million more in Italy and Austria surrendered to British Field Marshal Alexander, while on the same day the Russians took full control of Berlin.

After that, surrender followed surrender. On 4 May German forces in Bavaria capitulated to the Americans and those in Holland and Denmark to the British. The next day Grossadmiral Dönitz ordered all U-boats to cease offensive operations and return to their bases, and the day after that Reichsmarschall Hermann Göring gave himself up to American Air Force commander General Carl Spaatz.

By now Dönitz was trying to form some sort of government, in order to effect a German capitulation to the Americans and British. He ordered the Chief of Staff of the German Armed Forces High Command, General Alfred Jodl, to proceed to Supreme Allied Commander General Dwight D. Eisenhower's headquarters in Reims to give up all German forces fighting the Western Allies, but Eisenhower demanded an unconditional surrender on all fronts, threatening to close all Western lines to German soldiers, thus leaving them to the mercy of the Soviets. Jodl radioed Dönitz, informing him of Eisenhower's ultimatum. Bowing to the inevitable, Dönitz authorised the complete and total surrender of all German forces.

So it was that at the Allied headquarters in Reims at 02.41 on the morning of 7 May General Alfred Jodl signed the unconditional surrender documents. One day later the surrender was signed again, this time with the Russians in Berlin.

Back in London General Ismay, the British Chief of Staff, rushed to tell Prime Minister Winston Churchill that Germany had formally capitulated. But instead of reacting with joy, the PM responded in his own orotund prose: 'The eagle has ceased to scream, but the parrots will now begin to chatter. The war of the giants is over and the pigmies will now start to squabble.'

Indeed, only two months later the victorious leaders met at Potsdam to decide how to administer the defeated Nazi Germany. By then the only 'giant' left standing was Russian dictator Joseph Stalin; Hitler and Mussolini were dead, as was US President Franklin Roosevelt, replaced by Harry Truman. In the first general election since 1935 (general elections had been suspended during the war), Churchill himself was unseated by Clement Attlee, who replaced him halfway through the conference. With the Soviet Union occupying Central and Eastern Europe, the world was set for the beginning of the Cold War, even though the 'hot war' was still raging in the Pacific.

1795 As a ferocious public prosecutor for the Revolutionary Tribunal of Paris, Antoine Fouquier-Tinville has earned the nickname 'Purveyor to the Guillotine'. After the fall of Robespierre, he is convicted on charges almost as trumped up as those he previously used when prosecuting, despite his plea of criminals throughout the ages: 'It is not I who ought to be facing the tribunal, but the chiefs whose orders I have executed.' Today he is guillotined in the Place de Grève (now the Place de l'Hôtel-de-Ville) in Paris.
* **1954** At 17.50 hours, the beleaguered French soldiers in Dien Bien Phu send a last radio message before being overwhelmed: 'We're blowing up everything. Adieu.'

---

8 May

'God is always with the strongest battalions.'

1760 Throughout history, Christian warriors leading their men into battle have professed to believe that God was on their side – the very first Christian Roman emperor, Constantine, was one. In 312, after seeing a flaming cross in the sky engraved with the words 'By this sign thou shalt conquer', he triumphed at the Milvian Bridge. (Despite this miraculous intervention, Constantine delayed his own baptism until a few days before his death 25 years later.)

During the late Roman Empire, Christian soldiers used the battle cry '*Nobiscum deus*' ('God with us'), and in 1198 England's Richard the Lionheart wrote of one victory: 'Thus have we defeated the King of France at Gisors; but it is not we who have done the same, but rather God.'

In the 12th century the crusading knights of the Teutonic Order translated this idea into German as '*Gott mit uns*' ('God with us'), and in 1701 Frederick I of Prussia added the slogan to his coat of arms. '*Gott mit uns*' was also inscribed on the helmets of German soldiers during the First World War and on their belt buckles during the Second. History's most unlikely assertion of celestial intercession came from Adolf Hitler; after he had escaped an assassination attempt, he informed Mussolini that God had saved him to lead Germany's revenge on the world.

Of course there have always been those who doubted heavenly meddling in military affairs. In the early 2nd century, the worldly historian Tacitus wrote in his *Histories*: 'The gods are on the side of the stronger.' (Many centuries later the famous historian Edward Gibbon had a nautical take on this. 'The wind and waves are always on the side of the ablest navigators', he wrote.)

Tacitus of course was no Christian. But, although the great 17th-century French general Turenne certainly was, he expressed much the same view, as we know from a letter by his friend the aristocratic Marquise de Sévigné, who wrote: 'Fortune is always, as poor M. de Turenne used to say, on the side of the biggest battalions.' ('Poor M. de Turenne' because he had recently lost Bonn during the Dutch War.)

Although a good Protestant, Frederick the Great also had little truck with divine intervention. Perhaps he was pondering his worst-ever defeat during the Seven Years War at Kundersdorf when on this day in 1760 he wrote a letter to his devoted friend, Duchess Dorothea of Saxe-Meiningen, in which he expressed his weary scepticism: '*Gott ist immer mit den stärksten Bataillonen.*' ('God is always with the strongest battalions.')

In 1770 Voltaire wrote to a friend: 'One says that God is always on the side of the big battalions.' (Voltaire was a noted friend and correspondent of Frederick the Great. Had he picked up the phrase from

Frederick?) Voltaire later qualified the comment with: 'God is not on the side of the big battalions, but on the side of those who shoot best.'

Napoleon (originally an artillery officer) seemed to agree with Voltaire's second assessment when he observed: 'God is on the side with the best artillery.' Similar sentiments have even been ascribed to fictional characters; in *Gone with the Wind* Margaret Mitchell has the daring Confederate blockade-runner Rhett Butler say: 'God is on the side of the strongest battalion.'

Inevitably, in any discussion of God's intervention versus military might, there will be some who would straddle the two points of view. Most notable of these may be the Puritan but tough-minded general Oliver Cromwell, who told his men before invading Ireland: 'Put your trust in God – but keep your powder dry.'

1429 When the English fail in their siege of Orléans, their commander explains that Joan of Arc is 'a disciple and limb of the fiend, called the Pucelle, that used false enchantments and sorcery'. * **1794** French chemist Antoine Lavoisier is guillotined after a judge at his trial rules: 'The Republic needs neither scientists nor chemists.' (In 2016 British populist Michael Gove declares: 'The people in this country have had enough of experts.') * **1935** Leon Trotsky writes in his *Diary in Exile*: 'Old age is the most unexpected of all the things that can happen to a man.'

---

9 May

'No woman can call herself free who does not own and control her body.'

1960 Today the American Food and Drug Administration announced it would approve Enovid 10 mg for contraceptive use, the world's first commercially produced birth-control pill, setting in motion an epochal change in mores around the world and giving women vastly more control over their sexual and reproductive lives. It had been a long time coming.

Birth control has existed since time immemorial, at least as early as 1850 BC, as shown by the Kahun Gynaecological Papyrus from ancient Egypt. Probably the most famous case history is reported in Genesis 38:9 when in about 650 BC Onan 'spilled his seed on the ground' so as to not father a child with his dead brother's widow, Tamar. This didn't work out too well for Onan – God slew him – and people have been arguing about birth control ever since.

A couple of thousand years later two determined campaigners in the United States and Great Britain started calling for women's freedom to use contraception. They were Margaret Sanger and Marie Stopes, who had met in England in 1913 when Sanger was visiting.

In 1916 Margaret Sanger (who popularised the phrase 'birth control') established a clinic in Brooklyn, but the police closed it after nine days and she was sentenced to 30 days in the Queens penitentiary. In 1921 she founded the first birth control league in America, the same year that Marie Stopes opened a clinic in London.

By now contraception was widely practised in the United States and Britain (despite a continuing and ineffectual ban by the Catholic Church), but all known methods except celibacy were prone to failures.

A noted liberal and proto-feminist, Margaret Sanger declared: 'No woman can call herself free who does not own and control her body. No woman can call herself free until she can choose consciously whether she will or will not be a mother.' In 1951 she met the biologist Gregory Pincus and persuaded the Planned Parenthood Federation of America (which she had founded) to fund some hormonal contraceptive research. She asked Pincus to create a cheap birth control pill and introduced him to the suffragist and philanthropist Katharine McCormick, who agreed to underwrite one of the 20th century's most ambitious – and risky – scientific experiments.

Pincus recruited the professor of gynaecology John Rock, and the two started working on secret experiments in Massachusetts, where they were both based, a state where it was a felony to 'exhibit, sell, prescribe, provide, or give out information' on birth control. Risking possible jail time, they carried out tests on 50 women with progesterone, a hormone produced by the body during pregnancy, which had already been shown to prevent conception in rats and rabbits. Their success encouraged them to set up much more extensive trials in Puerto Rico starting in 1955.

By today's standards, these experiments were unethical, illegal and unsafe. Impoverished women were recruited at Puerto Rico's 67 birth control centres and told that the pill they were given would prevent pregnancy. They were not informed that it was an experimental drug, nor that they were guinea pigs in a trial. The pills contained much higher doses of hormones than modern oral contraceptives and caused significant side-effects – but they were highly effective in preventing conception.

In June 1957 the FDA approved Searle's Enovid (Enavid in the United Kingdom), a combination of oestrogen and progesterone, for menstrual disorders, and on this day three years later finally approved a slightly modified version for use as a contraceptive. By that time, at least half a million women were already using it. Unfortunately, Marie Stopes died in October 1958, three years before it was legalised in the UK, but Margaret Sanger lived to see the success of her work, dying in 1966.

In the US, puritan America continued to resist the pill's universal use; only in 1972 did the Supreme Court strike down a Massachusetts law prohibiting the distribution of contraceptives to unmarried people.

1782 Mozart decides to leave the employment of Prince-Archbishop Colloredo in Salzburg, which will give him independence, inconceivable at the time, and pave the way for the freedom of Beethoven, Schubert and Liszt after him. That evening he writes: 'My happiness starts today.' * **1969** Charles de Gaulle: 'Patriotism is when love of your own people comes first; nationalism, when hate for people other than your own comes first.'

---

10 May

'Where they burn books, /they end up burning people, too.'

1933 If you're lucky enough to stay at Berlin's Adlon Hotel, take a stroll down Unter den Linden and then turn left into an 18th-century square called Bebelplatz. There, set in the cobbles in front of the Opera House, is a glass window through which you see an underground room lined with empty white bookshelves, with enough space for 20,000 books. Beside the window are two bronze panels bearing the words of the 19th-century German poet Heinrich Heine:

> *Das war ein Vorspiel nur, dort*
> *wo man Bücher verbrennt,*
> *verbrennt man auch am Ende Menschen.*

> (This was only a prelude;
> where they burn books,
> they end up burning people, too.)

In the heady early days of Hitler's rise, many German students enthusiastically followed their new Führer, and on 8 April 1933 the German Student Union proclaimed a nationwide 'Action against the Un-German Spirit' that would culminate in a literary *Säuberung* (cleansing) by fire. Their first target was the Institut für Sexualwissenschaft (Institute of Sex Research) in Berlin, which, along with varied research into sexuality, also campaigned for gay rights and tolerance. On 6 May the students attacked the Institute, hauling out its huge library of books. Then, on this evening just four months after Hitler came to power as Chancellor, some 40,000 onlookers gathered in Bebelplatz for their incineration.

First the university students' honoured guest, propaganda minister Joseph Goebbels, enjoined the eager crowd: 'The era of extreme Jewish intellectualism is now at an end ... No to decadence and moral corruption! Yes to decency and morality in family and state!' Then, as bands played, the students and brown-shirted SA stormtroopers tossed some 20,000 books onto a huge bonfire in a torchlit Wagnerian ceremony of Nazi salutes and anthems.

The books consigned to the flames were those the Nazis considered 'un-German' – that is, subversive or counter to their ideology (like rights for homosexuals, who would soon find themselves in concentration camps). Literature by Jewish authors, regardless of the field, was included, and all books 'degrading German purity'. The first burned were by Karl Marx and the Marxist theoretician Karl Kautsky, quickly followed by the works of noted German-language writers like Thomas Mann, Stefan Zweig, Albert Einstein, Friedrich Engels, Sigmund Freud, Franz Kafka and Erich Maria Remarque. The foreign writers whose works were burnt make a sort of Legion of Honour of quasi-contemporary authors such as Joseph Conrad, Aldous Huxley, D.H. Lawrence, H.G. Wells, André Gide, John Dos Passos, Theodore Dreiser, Ernest Hemingway, Jack London, James Joyce, Romain Rolland, Fyodor Dostoyevsky, Leo Tolstoy, Victor Hugo and of course Vladimir Lenin and Leon Trotsky. That same evening in 34 university towns throughout Germany, other students joined the fun with their own book-burning parties.

Just as Heine had predicted 113 years before, the burning of books was soon followed by the burning of people. The first Nazi concentration camps had been built just two months before Berlin's infamous bonfire of books, and by the end of the Second World War about 11 million people had died in various concentration, prisoner of war and death camps.

> **1631** After Johann Tserclaes, Count of Tilly captures and pillages Magdeburg, massacring 20,000 inhabitants and burning most of the city, he modestly notes: 'Since the capture of Troy and the destruction of Jerusalem, a victory such as this has never been seen.' * **1928** David Lloyd George in the House of Commons: 'Liberty is not merely a privilege to be conferred; it is a habit to be acquired.'

11 May

'The blood of our enemies is still the blood of men.'

1745 For pure complexity, it would be hard to beat the War of the Austrian Succession, an eight-year conflict involving nineteen countries that spread as far as North America, India and Scotland.

Its putative cause was the Salic law enacted 1,200 years earlier by Clovis, the king of the Salian Franks. It stipulated that women could not inherit the throne. This law had already caused enough trouble as *casus belli* of the Hundred Years' War. Now it was causing more.

In 1713 Holy Roman Emperor Charles VI issued the Pragmatic Sanction to ensure that the immense Habsburg possessions could be inherited by a woman. When Charles died in 1740 after mistaking toadstools for mushrooms, his daughter Maria Theresa should have acceded to his various crowns, but France, Prussia and Bavaria cried foul, citing the Salic law (a disguised effort to gobble up Habsburg territories when the inexperienced Maria Theresa was just 22). But Maria Theresa was supported by Britain, the Dutch Republic, Sardinia and Saxony, which had no desire for these Pragmatic Sanction-deniers to become even more powerful.

So started the War of the Austrian Succession, now in its fifth year. On this day a French force of 50,000 men met an equal-sized army of British, Dutch, Hanoverian and Holy Roman Empire troops at Fontenoy in present-day Belgium.

The French commander was Marshal Maurice de Saxe, illegitimate son of the Elector of Saxony, Augustus the Strong, so called because he could bend horseshoes with his bare hands. (Saxe was just one of Augustus' 376 bastard offspring.)

The opposing alliance (the Pragmatic Army) was led by George II's corpulent 24-year-old son William, Duke of Cumberland. (The relationship between Saxe and Cumberland was as complex as the war;

Saxe's mother's brother had once had an affair with Cumberland's grandmother and was murdered for his pains, probably on the orders of Cumberland's grandfather, George I.)

Cumberland had set out to relieve the Dutch garrison in Tournai that Saxe was besieging. Because of a severe attack of dropsy, Saxe had to be carried on a wicker carriage, but he mounted his white palfrey in great pain to give his orders. He positioned his main force around the nearby village of Fontenoy. So sure was he of victory that he invited Louis XV, his fifteen-year-old son and his chief minister, Cardinal Richelieu, to come and watch the fun.

Cumberland sent his main force forward, determined to smash his way through. In a moment of *opéra bouffe*, at one point the English captain Sir Charles Hay and his 1st Foot Guards came face to face with the French at a distance of 30 paces. Later Voltaire recounted the incident: 'The English officers saluted the French by doffing their hats ... the French returned the greeting. My Lord Charles Hay, captain in the English Guards, cried, "Gentlemen of the French Guards, fire!" The Comte d'Auteroche, the lieutenant of Grenadiers, shouted, "Gentlemen, we never fire first; fire yourselves."'

French historians claim the English shot first, English historians claim the French did. In any event, the Pragmatic Army braved its way through heavy fire, but after nine hours of fighting were forced into retreat. The French had suffered 7,000 casualties, but the Pragmatic Army's losses were worse, at about 11,000. Surveying the carnage, Louis XV told his son: 'See how much blood a triumph costs. The blood of our enemies is still the blood of men. The true glory is to save it.'

Tournai then fell to Saxe's siege, allowing him to advance across the Austrian Netherlands, finally forcing Brussels to surrender on 12 February 1746. To honour his victories, Louis granted him the great Château de Chambord for life.

The war ended in 1748 with the Treaty of Aix-la-Chapelle, by which time Maria Theresa had long succeeded as Archduchess of Austria and Queen of Hungary.

The Duke of Cumberland withdrew to England, gained the sobriquet of 'Butcher' by shooting all the prisoners and wounded at the Battle of Culloden and, obese and unmarried, died of a stroke at 44.

Saxe died of pneumonia at Chambord in November 1750, but not before – at 50 – producing an illegitimate daughter by his eighteen-year-old mistress, who in turn was the grandmother of the celebrated writer, George Sand.

1812 When Prime Minister Spencer Perceval is shot by a failed business-man in the House of Commons, he cries out: 'I am murdered, murdered!' (He is right.)

---

12 May

'Put not your trust in princes, nor in the sons of men, for in them there is no salvation.'

1641 Today Thomas Wentworth, 1st Earl of Strafford, was beheaded at the Tower of London, abandoned by the king whom he had served so well.

Charles I had been at loggerheads with Parliament since inheriting the throne in 1625. One of his early opponents had been Wentworth, who so vigorously opposed the king's policies that he was imprisoned for six months. Despite it all, however, he was a strong supporter of the crown. 'The authority of a king', he said, 'is the keystone which closeth up the arch of order and government.' When Charles gave up his disastrous wars against Spain and France, Wentworth declared his wholehearted loyalty. As a professed supporter of the pig-headed, self-righteous king, however, he came to be seen as a 'traitor' by the largely Puritan Parliament that was bent on curbing Charles's unfettered power.

Over the next dozen years Charles gave Wentworth increasingly important positions, culminating in Lord Deputy of Ireland. There he ruthlessly supported the king's interests, but only succeeded in alienating English settlers while continuing to drive the native Irish population from their lands, earning himself the sobriquet of 'Black Tom Tyrant'. Recalled to England in 1639, he became Charles's closest advisor at a time when relations between king and Parliament were reaching a new low. In January 1640 the king created him Earl of Strafford.

The leader of Parliament's resistance was the Puritan John Pym, who thought that Charles, with his fervent belief in the divine right of kings, was intent on creating a royal dictatorship. Now Pym focused on Strafford, accusing him of attempting to help the king usurp Parliament's powers. Pym led Parliament into demanding Strafford's impeachment, specifying that he had advised the king to bring his Irish army to England to crush his opponents.

Strafford was charged with treason and brought to trial on 22 March 1641, with Pym leading the prosecution, but Strafford ably defended himself, repeatedly referring to the prosecution's principal weakness: how could it be treason to carry out the king's wishes? It soon became apparent that he was no traitor. In less than a month the trial collapsed.

But by this time Pym and his supporters had become obsessed with bringing Strafford down, no matter the means, and resorted to a bill of attainder, i.e. a summary condemnation by special Act of Parliament. Just three days after Strafford had been cleared by the trial he was sentenced to death by Parliament.

Now Strafford's fate was sealed – except that the execution required the assent of the king. Charles assured Strafford that 'upon the word of a king you shall not suffer in life, honour or fortune', but by now the mood in Parliament and among the public was growing ugly, bringing real danger of riots and bloodshed, the monarchy itself under threat. Supporting Charles to the very end, Strafford wrote to the king: 'I do most humbly beseech you, for the preventing of such massacres as may happen by your refusal, to pass the bill.' Nonetheless, he still hoped that the king would find a way to save him.

But on 10 May Charles signed the death warrant, self-piteously remarking that 'my Lord Strafford's condition is happier than mine'. When Strafford learned of the king's betrayal, he raised his eyes to heaven and, with a paraphrase of Psalm 143, bitterly addressed the secretary who had brought the news: 'Put not your trust in princes, nor in the sons of men, for in them there is no salvation.'

Two days later Strafford was brought to Tower Hill, where, before a crowd of over 100,000 onlookers, he faced death with courage. Removing his jacket, he spoke to his executioner: 'I do as cheerfully put off my doublet at this time as ever I did when I went to bed.'

On learning of Strafford's death, France's chief minister Cardinal Richelieu commented: 'The English are mad in cutting off the best head of their country.' How right he was. Just fifteen months later Charles raised his standard at Nottingham to begin the English Civil War.

> **1945** PM Winston Churchill sends a telegram to US President Harry Truman regarding his concern about Soviet actions: 'An iron curtain is drawn down upon their front. We do not know what is going on behind.'

13 May

*'God in his wisdom has provided man
with natural forks – his fingers.'*

1637 By the time of Louis XIV, dining in France was already an elaborate affair, and grand households used full sets of cutlery at table. But the progress from the simple spoon – which has been used from time immemorial – to plates, forks and table knives was surprisingly slow.

The spoon was the first eating utensil, known to the ancient Egyptians, in the Ozieri culture in Sardinia since about 3000 BC, and in most of Europe for several thousand years. But it wasn't until the reign of François I in the first half of the 16th century that the dinner plate came into use in France. Previously, Frenchmen used trenchers, which in noble households were usually wooden plates, while common people made do with flat pieces of stale bread.

Forks were the next culinary innovation, also coming to France during François' reign. They had been used in ancient Egypt and in parts of China from about 2400 BC. Their popularity spread via the Silk Road to classical Greece but didn't migrate to other European countries until 1075, when the Byzantine princess Theodora Anna Doukaina married the Doge of Venice, Domenico Selvo, and brought gold forks as part of her dowry, thus introducing them to Italy. (She also brought the napkin and the finger bowl, for which she was much mocked, probably because table cloths were already in use – to wipe your hands.)

At the time the fork was considered scandalous and even heretical. The 11th-century Italian monk (and later saint) Pier Damiani anathematised it, claiming: 'God in his wisdom has provided man with natural forks – his fingers. Therefore it is an insult to Him to substitute artificial metallic forks for them when eating.' When Theodora Anna Doukaina died of a mysterious wasting illness at only 25, Damiani claimed that 'after her excessive delicacy ... [her] body ... entirely rotted away'. (Damiani was an extreme ascetic and big on self-mortification, and in his book *Liber Gomorrhianus*, written in 1051, he excoriated fellow priests for a problem that dogs the Catholic Church to this day: priests having sex with adolescent boys.)

Outside Italy not much is heard about the fork for the next 500 years, but in 1533 a young (fourteen) Catherine de' Medici came from Florence to Paris to marry François' son, the future King Henri II.

In her trousseau she brought several dozen dinner forks wrought by Benvenuto Cellini. At first France's nobility scoffed at this Italian affectation and continued to plough through their meals with hands and knives, but before long it had become *de rigueur*. (Apparently the English were even slower than the French; only in 1633 did Charles I pronounce: 'It is decent to use a fork.' It took another century after that before common folk starting using them.)

The last major item of tableware to arrive in France was the table knife, invented by Louis XIII's wily chief minister, Cardinal Richelieu.

One of Richelieu's favourites was Pierre Séguier, whom he had promoted to Chancellor. He'd even allowed his nephew to marry Séguier's daughter. Despite their friendship, one thing about Séguier irritated him: when they dined together, he picked his teeth with the tip of his knife.

At that time in France men normally carried one or two small, pointy knives that were used to cut meat and spear food and carry it from plate to mouth. In grand houses like Richelieu's, of course, guests used forks and no longer brought their own knives, but the ones supplied by the host were equally pointed and often used in place of toothpicks. (Only the most exalted had toothpicks, which were made with precious metal and set with expensive stones.)

Good manners prevented Richelieu saying anything directly to Séguier, especially since many men had the same distasteful habit. So on this day in 1637 he summoned his butler and instructed him to grind down the points on his table knives so that they had round ends and thus were useless for picking teeth. So the table knife was born, completing the accepted tableware that remains the standard today.

1935 When future French chief of government (and traitor) Pierre Laval asks Joseph Stalin to encourage Catholicism in Russia to conciliate the Pope, Stalin replies: 'The Pope! How many divisions has he got?'

---

14 May

*'I saw the blood on my knife
and the place where I hit him ...'*

1610 On one of the blackest days in French history, today Henri IV, France's greatest king, was stabbed to death as he rode in his carriage.

Henri had inherited the crown when France was being torn asunder by savage religious wars. During his sixteen-year reign, he brought peace to his realm after nearly 40 years of conflict and gave virtually equal rights to Protestants through the Edict of Nantes. 'Those who follow their consciences are of my religion', he declared, 'and I am of the religion of those who are brave and good.'

He was straightforward, courageous and manly – so manly that he was known as *le vert galant* (the old playboy), fathering six children within marriage and at least twelve without. He contrasted dramatically with his effete predecessor, Henri III, claiming to rule 'weapon in hand and arse in the saddle' (*'le bras armé et le cul sur la selle'*). He also galvanised France's economy and restored Paris as a great city.

But many still detested Henri. Protestants felt betrayed when he converted to Catholicism and Catholics doubted his true conviction. The first attempt on his life came only nine months after his coronation, when Jesuit monks persuaded a Catholic fanatic named Jean Chastel that, since the Pope had not recognised Henri's conversion, killing him would be a service to God. Chastel's knife sliced through Henri's lip, but the king's bodyguards overwhelmed him; his sentence was to be torn apart by four horses.

There were at least a dozen more attempts to murder Henri, but none succeeded – until today.

The attacker was once again driven by religious zeal. His name was François Ravaillac, a strapping, red-bearded 32-year-old from Angoulême who had been a monk in an austere religious order but was expelled for his 'visions'.

One of these visions instructed Ravaillac to convince Henri to convert France's Huguenots to Catholicism, so he came to Paris, but he had no access to the king. Then the deluded Ravaillac fantasised that Henri was planning to make war on the Pope and 'to transfer the Holy See to Paris'. Now he decided on murder.

On the afternoon of 14 May, Henri set off in his carriage with the arch-Catholic duc d'Épernon, to visit a sick minister. At about the same time Ravaillac was walking towards the Louvre carrying a knife under his doublet. As Ravaillac reached the corner of the rue de la Ferronnerie and the rue Saint-Honoré, he saw Henri's carriage, blocked on one side by a cart filled with wine and on the other by a cart filled with hay. Henri's footmen had stepped away to move the carts aside. Seizing the moment, Ravaillac boosted himself up by a spoke of a wheel, reached into the carriage and stabbed the king. Henri tried to defend himself, only to be stabbed a second time, this thrust piercing his lung.

Guards immediately pounced on Ravaillac, who made no attempt to escape. As Henri's carriage sped for the palace, the king reassured his companions (and perhaps himself) with the words, 'It's nothing, it's nothing.'

Henri was carried into the Louvre as doctors raced to his aid, but he had lost too much blood to survive. When his death was announced, according to a contemporary account, 'the stores closed, everyone shrieked and cried and lamented, large and small, young and old, and women and girls tore their hair'.

Imprisoned in the Conciergerie, Ravaillac said: 'I know very well he is dead; I saw the blood on my knife and the place where I hit him. But I have no regrets at all about dying, because I've done what I came to do.'

Ravaillac claimed he was executing a divine mission, but he may have been manipulated by Henri's enemies, notably the duc d'Épernon, who was with Henri in the carriage and had singularly failed to prevent the assassination. It also later emerged that, during his stay in Paris, Ravaillac had lodged with Épernon's mistress.

Thirteen days later Ravaillac was unspeakably tortured and drawn and quartered, but neither the duc d'Épernon nor anyone else was ever charged with the crime.

1866 Disraeli in a speech in the House of Commons: 'Ignorance never settles a question.' * **1918** Lenin tells the Party Central Committee: 'It is not national interests we are upholding – we claim that the interests of socialism, the interests of world socialism, rank higher than national interests, higher than the interests of the state. We are defenders of the socialist fatherland.'

---

15 May

'A little learning is a dang'rous thing.' 'To err is human, to forgive divine.' 'Fools rush in where angels fear to tread.'

1711 Today, six days before his 23rd birthday, Alexander Pope published *An Essay on Criticism*, a 744-line poem written in heroic couplets (rhyming pairs of lines in iambic pentameter) that most modern readers would find heavy going both in style and content, but which includes the quotations above, three of the most famous in the English language. With the exception of publication dates for several of Shakespeare's plays, no date in history has added so many classic lines to our literary vocabulary.

Born in London in 1688, Pope had contracted Pott's disease (a form of tuberculosis that affects the spine) that so deformed his body that he was a hunchback and so stunted his growth that he reached only 4ft 6in. On top of this crippling ailment, he was also a Catholic at a time when Catholics in Britain were ineligible for public office or a position at a university. But he was sharply intelligent and studious, and, although largely self-taught, he learned to read works by English, French, Italian, Latin and Greek poets in the original.

Today Pope is best known for *The Rape of the Lock* and *The Dunciad*, and for his translation of Homer, but *An Essay on Criticism* was his first major work, one that he developed over a three-year period. In it, Pope looks to ancient Greece for guidance and sets out poetic rules regarding how writers and critics behave (or should behave). In the poem's opening couplets, he claims that bad criticism does greater harm than bad writing and later makes veiled attacks on the contemporary critic, John Dennis.

A furious Dennis responded: 'as there is no creature in nature so venomous, there is nothing so stupid and so impotent as a hunch-back'd toad. ... This little author may extol the ancients as much and as long as he pleases, but he has reason to thank the good gods that he was born a modern. For had he been born of Grecian parents, and his father by consequence had by law the absolute disposal of him, his life had been no longer than that of one of his poems – the life of half a day.'

Dennis died in impoverished obscurity in 1734, while Pope continued to amaze the literary world with his poems and satirical aphorisms, including (among many):

'Histories are more full of examples of the fidelity of dogs than of friends.'

'Blessed is the man who expects nothing, for he shall never be disappointed.'

'It is with narrow-souled people as with narrow-necked bottles: the less they have in them, the more noise they make in pouring it out.'

'I never knew any man in my life who could not bear another's misfortunes perfectly like a Christian.' (He may have borrowed this from La Rochefoucauld, who wrote: '*Nous avons tous assez de force pour supporter les maux d'autrui*.' ('We all have strength enough to endure the misfortunes of others.'))

Such was Pope's output that today he is the second-most frequently quoted writer (after Shakespeare) in *The Oxford Dictionary of Quotations*.

Always plagued by bad health, at 56 Pope was dying. On the morning of his death his doctor tried to cheer him up by telling him he was improving. 'Here am I', Pope replied, 'dying of a hundred good symptoms.' He died at eleven o'clock at night on 30 May 1744.

1479 BC Thutmose III defeats the King of Kadesh at Megiddo and later has inscribed on walls at Karnak: 'The capture of Megiddo is the capture of a thousand cities.' * **1973** Prime Minister Edward Heath comments on the Lonrho affair in the House of Commons: 'It is the unpleasant and unacceptable face of capitalism, but one should not suggest that the whole of British industry consists of practices of this kind.'

---

16 May

'The King of France would have been whipped so that he would have ejaculated out of sheer rage like a donkey.'

1770 Young Louis the groom was only fifteen, slim, shy, ignorant and, unknown to himself, just four years from becoming King of France.

The bride was Marie Antoinette, christened Maria Antonia, the fifteenth of Austrian Empress Maria Theresa's sixteen children. She was only fourteen and had just a year of French tutoring when she married on this day.

After renouncing her rights to her family's Habsburg domains, on 19 April Marie Antoinette had married Louis by proxy at the Augustinian Church in Vienna. A few weeks later she set out in a cavalcade of 48 six-horse carriages, carrying in her pocket a letter from her mother instructing her: 'Do so much good to the French people that they can say that I have sent them an angel.' Her first destination was a tent on a tiny island in the Rhine between Strasbourg and Kehl. There she was stripped naked of her Austrian garments under the watchful eye of the Comtesse de Noailles, to be reclothed in French finery. Now she had become French.

On the afternoon of 14 May in the forest of Compiègne she met her husband-to-be for the first time, accompanied by his grandfather, Louis XV. The younger Louis chastely kissed her on the cheek.

Two days later the couple were joined in the chapel of Versailles, the groom wearing a suit of silver, the bride a lilac dress dripping with pearls and diamonds. But one witness noted that Louis 'was more timid than his wife. He seemed to shiver during the ceremony and blushed up to his eyes when he gave the ring.'

In perhaps a metaphor of nature, rain fell during the afternoon, and the celebratory fireworks had to be postponed. After a light supper King Louis escorted the young couple to the royal bedchamber, where the Archbishop of Reims blessed the bed. Finally the two were alone, but the wedding night saw no pyrotechnics either, as Louis failed to perform.

And so it continued; in the evenings the royal couple would retire – and sleep. Louis' failure soon became known, and gossips wondered, if the Dauphin couldn't fulfil his duties in bed, could he fulfil his duties when he became king?

On 10 May 1774 Louis XV died of smallpox and his grandson did become king – but his marriage remained unconsummated.

Louis' failure to perform his connubial duties – and Marie Antoinette's failure to produce a child – alarmed the courts of both France and Austria. In the spring of 1777 Marie Antoinette's brother Joseph, now the Holy Roman Emperor, came to France for a six-week tour. On 18 April – a month before the king and queen's seventh wedding anniversary – he met the royal couple at the Château de la Muette. There he asked Louis frankly what the problems were. He sent home a detailed report of his astounding findings.

Describing the young couple as 'complete blunderers', he wrote: 'He has strong, perfectly satisfactory erections. He introduces the member, stays there for about two minutes without moving, withdraws without ejaculating, still erect, and begs good night ... Oh, if only I could have been there. I could have seen to it. The King of France would have been whipped so that he would have ejaculated out of sheer rage like a donkey.'

Whatever advice Joseph may have offered has not been recorded, but the couple sent him a thank-you letter, and in August Marie Antoinette wrote her mother: 'I have found the happiness most essential for my life. More than a week ago my marriage was consummated; the test was repeated, and again last night more completely than the first time … I do not think I am pregnant yet, but at least I have the hope of being so from one moment to the next.' By April of the next year she was with child, and Thérèse, the first of their four children, was born on 19 December.

1164 French nun Héloïse (Héloïse d'Argenteuil) on the day of her death: 'In death at last, let me rest with Abélard.'

---

17 May

'Speech was given to man to disguise his thoughts.'

1838 History's greatest diplomat, Charles-Maurice, Prince de Talleyrand, died in Paris at 3.35 this afternoon at 84. He had been Foreign Minister for the Directory, the Consulat, Napoleon's Empire and the Restoration. He was Europe's master intriguer. 'Speech', he claimed, 'was given to man to disguise his thoughts.' According to historian Fabienne Manière: 'He betrayed all the regimes that he served but never the more important interests of the State.'

Just 5ft 5in, Talleyrand walked with a limp due to a foot crushed by a nurse when he was an infant. (In later life he was called *le diable boiteux* – the lame devil.) Because of this infirmity he entered the Church instead of the army and rose to become Bishop of Autun, but he was defrocked for subordinating the interests of Rome to those of the French Revolution.

Talleyrand was France's chief diplomat during the beginning of Napoleon's reign, and, although he resigned in 1807, disapproving of the emperor's Spanish initiative, Napoleon retained him in the Council of State. Then he secretly connived to undermine the emperor through secret dealings with Tsar Alexander of Russia.

After Napoleon's fall, he became President of the provisional government, was France's leading negotiator at the Congress of Vienna and helped the Bourbons regain the French throne. For this Louis XVIII made him a prince (although he had already been made one by Napoleon). But when the reactionary Charles X succeeded, Talleyrand declined to serve him, memorably commenting that the Bourbons 'have learned nothing and forgotten nothing'.

Talleyrand's private life was as full of intrigue as his public one. He amassed a huge fortune by soliciting bribes, enabling him to keep a private *hôtel* off the Place de la Concorde in Paris (now owned by the American embassy). His country residence was the breathtaking Château de Valençay and the fabled Antonin Carême his personal chef. For three years he also owned Château Haut-Brion, famous for one of the greatest wines in France.

Talleyrand was also a noted seducer, whose many mistresses included his own nephew's wife – and her mother. He had several illegitimate children, one of whom may have been the painter Eugène Delacroix. Another mistress was Catherine Noele Grand, a ravishing courtesan with whom he lived for almost six years before marrying her in 1802. ('If someone gets a good wife he will be happy', he mused, 'if he gets a bad one, he can become a philosopher.')

All his life Talleyrand was the subject of gossip and calumny, but the cynical diplomat brushed it off: 'Never speak badly about yourself, your friends will do it for you.'

Talleyrand's final post was ambassador to England, where he served until he was 80. Returning to Valençay, he advised King Louis-Philippe and settled down to write his memoirs. At the last he moved back to Paris, intent on putting things straight with the Church before he died.

On the day of his death he lay in bed, surrounded by mourning nobles, including Louis-Philippe. According to one tale, the dying man murmured, 'Sire, I am suffering like a soul in Hell', to which the king replied, 'Already?'

That morning Talleyrand signed his last treaty – an agreement that renounced much of his life (including his wife of 36 years) but restored him to the Church. Ever conscious of his rank, when he was receiving the last rites, he admonished the startled priest: 'Do not forget that I am a bishop.' As the contemporary French historian Ernest Renan commented: 'He deceived both earth and heaven.'

No doubt the great diplomat hoped his deathbed pact with the Church would gain for him an influential post in heaven, but popular opinion saw him going in the other direction. The *tout Paris* joked that when he entered Hell, the Devil welcomed him with praise: 'Prince, you have even surpassed my instructions.'

When the Austrian statesman Klemens von Metternich heard that Talleyrand had passed away, he pondered: 'Died, has he? I wonder what he *meant* by that.'

1792 The New York Stock Exchange is formed under the Buttonwood Agreement, which reads: 'We the Subscribers, Brokers for the Purchase and Sale of the Public Stock, do hereby solemnly promise and pledge ourselves to each other, that we will not buy or sell from this day for any person whatsoever, any kind of Public Stock, at a less rate than one quarter percent Commission on the Specie value.'

18 May

'Scilt ende vrient'

1302 If you can't pronounce the medieval Flemish phrase '*Scilt ende vrient*', you are not alone – but had you been a French soldier in Bruges on this day, it would have cost you your life.

King Philip (IV) the Fair of France had invaded Flanders in 1299 and now controlled the whole territory. Initially many Flemings had tolerated his rule, but Philip appointed as governor Jacques de Châtillon, a pig-headed soldier who imposed a repressive government, raised new taxes and garrisoned French troops in Flemish homes. Infuriated, the Flemings rose in revolt, and on this night stormed into houses in Bruges where the French were billeted, slaughtering anyone who could not pronounce '*scilt ende vrient*' ('shield and friend'), a tongue-twisting Flemish phrase which no francophone could manage. Over 2,000 Frenchmen were slain, including virtually the entire garrison, although Jacques de Châtillon managed to escape. This night-time slaughter came to be known as the Brugse Metten (Bruges Matins) after the monastic service of Matins that takes place at night and ends at dawn.

Enraged by the rebellion, King Philip dispatched an army of 8,000 men, including 2,500 mounted knights, 1,000 Genoese crossbowmen, 1,000 spearmen and 3,500 light infantry. In command was the king's uncle, Robert d'Artois, the greatest warrior in France. Desperate, 400 Flemish noblemen gathered together a motley army of about 9,000 militarily untrained workmen and artisans, mostly from the weavers' guild, armed with staves and *goedendags* (a combination of a club and a spear).

On the morning of 11 July near Kortrijk, about 50 miles west of Brussels, the French faced the Flemings on a marshy plain, crisscrossed by numerous ditches and streams. The crossbowmen initiated the battle, but the French cavalry, eager to prove their mettle, galloped through the bowmen in a premature charge. Believing they had been betrayed, the Genoese retreated in disarray, and the French horses could make no headway as their hooves sank into the soft ground. The great mass of Flemings then swarmed over the enemy knights before their supporting infantry could come forward.

The weavers and workmen had no use for the rules of chivalry; to the cry of '*de leeuw in Vlaanderen*' ('Flanders and lion'), they massacred 75 heads of great noble houses and hundreds of knights. No prisoners were taken. At the end of the battle Robert d'Artois was knocked from his charger. Dropping his sword, he cried: '*Prenez, prenez le comte d'Artois, il vous fera riches!*' ('Take him, take the Count of Artois, he will make you rich!') He was instantly skewered by Flemish spears. Another of the French dead was Jacques de Châtillon, the man whose bullying tactics had instigated the revolt.

In all, 1,200 French knights were slaughtered. In the aftermath the Flemings gathered over 500 'golden' spurs from the field of battle and hung them in the vault of Our Lady's Church in Kortrijk. Ever since, this mighty victory by Flemish artisans over the flower of French knighthood has been known as *Guldensporenslag* (Battle of the Golden Spurs).

1835 Alexis de Tocqueville publishes *Voyage in England and Ireland*, in which he writes: 'The Frenchman constantly raises his eyes above him with anxiety. The Englishman lowers his beneath him with satisfaction. On either side it is pride, but understood in a different way.' * **1956** Nelson Algren publishes *A Walk on the Wild Side* that includes the advice: 'Never sleep with a woman whose troubles are worse than your own.'

---

19 May

'It's with baubles that men are led.'

1802 During the French Revolution all Ancien Régime decorations and awards had been abolished, leaving First Consul Napoleon Bonaparte without a symbolic way to reward his soldiers, so, on this day (28 Floréal, Year X, according to the Revolutionary calendar) he decreed the creation of l'Ordre national de la Légion d'honneur, the National Order of the Legion of Honour. Unlike most medals of the time, the Legion of Honour was open to both the military and civilians, without regard to birth or religion. 'I want to decorate my soldiers and my scholars', said Bonaparte, but during his years in power, of the 48,000 men given the Legion, only 1,200 were civilians, showing where his real intentions lay.

Two weeks earlier, a member of the Conseil d'État had challenged Bonaparte on the merits of such an award, claiming that it violated the revolutionary principles of equality and suggesting that the Roman Republic was the precedent to follow.

'Are we are still talking about the Romans!', Bonaparte retorted. 'It is rather strange to give the Romans as an example, a people in whom awards were most pronounced. The Romans had patricians, knights, citizens and slaves. Each had his own dress and customs. They were rewarded with ... mural crowns, triumphs! ... I defy you to show me an old or modern republic in which there were no awards. You may call these baubles; well, it's with baubles that men are led.'

The Legion of Honour is divided into five degrees: Chevalier, Officier, Commandeur, Grand Officier and Grand Croix (although in Bonaparte's time the Grand Croix was called the Grand Aigle, i.e. Great Eagle). It remains the highest decoration in France, and the Legion's highest-ranking member is the President of France.

Until 1851 all Legion of Honour recipients were men, but in that year Marie-Angélique Brûlon was belatedly made a Chevalier by Bonaparte's nephew, Emperor Napoleon III. Of course Marie-Angélique might as well have been a man; she had fought in Corsica from 1792–99 disguised as one, an expert, it is said, with sword and dagger in hand-to-hand combat. Today about a fifth of new Legion appointments are to women (although not all are so bellicose).

In the past two centuries the Legion of Honour has been awarded about 1,000,000 times. Membership is technically restricted to French nationals, but in fact it has been bestowed on citizens of 78 foreign countries. Foreign heads of state and their spouses are often made Grand Croix as a courtesy.

Among Brits have been vital allies like Winston Churchill but also some surprising cultural figures such as Graham Greene, Paul McCartney, J.K. Rowling and Ninette de Valois, one of the founders of the Royal Ballet. (Would she have received this eminently French award had she kept her original name of Edris Stannus?)

The only German ever given the Grand Croix was Kaiser Wilhelm I, who delayed the German bombardment of Paris during the Franco-Prussian War in order to reduce civilian casualties. Then, having just whipped the French, he sent troops to help them suppress the Paris Commune that started after the war had finished.

Romanian dictator Nicolae Ceaușescu received the reward, but it was later revoked. (Likewise, Britain's Queen Elizabeth stripped Ceaușescu of his honorary Knight of the Bath the day before his own country shot him.)

Honoured Americans include a clutch of military leaders (Eisenhower, MacArthur, Marshall, Nimitz, Patton and Colin Powell) and gallant soldiers (Audie Murphy and Alvin York). The largest group, however, comes from the movies – directors Orson Welles, Steven Spielberg and Martin Scorsese and actors Kirk Douglas, Clint Eastwood, Jerry Lewis and Arnold Schwarzenegger. Less surprising is America's foremost wine critic, Robert Parker.

Despite these international exceptions, the Legion of Honour remains steadfastly French, with over 90,000 living members. So if you see someone with a red rosette or thin red ribbon in their buttonhole, he or she will probably be French, rewarded by their government for some significant achievement.

1897 After serving two years in prison for 'gross indecency', Oscar Wilde is released carrying his long letter (later titled *De Profundis*) to his lover Lord Alfred Douglas in which he writes: 'To regret one's own experiences is to arrest one's own development. To deny one's own experiences is to put a lie into the lips of one's own life. It is no less than a denial of the soul.'

---

20 May

'I would carry him on my shoulders step by step, from island to island, from country to country, and I would not fail him, not even if it meant begging my bread.'

1217 On 15 June 1215 King John had signed the Magna Carta, but his subsequent refusal to keep its terms sparked the First Barons' War. The recalcitrant barons had not only revolted, they had also invited France's Prince Louis (the future Louis VIII) to join them. Louis and his army landed on the Kent coast on 21 May 1216, marched to London, which he entered without a fight, and he was proclaimed king at old St Paul's Cathedral. But then on 19 October King John died (it is said) of a surfeit of peaches mulled in wine, leaving the throne to his nine-year-old son Henry (III). Luckily for Henry – and for England – the realm was protected by the greatest knight in Christendom, William Marshal, Earl of Pembroke.

The younger son of a minor nobleman, Marshal had been a champion jouster, defeating over 500 knights during his tournament career. A contemporary described him as 'a man who hammered like a blacksmith on iron'. At 21 he joined the royal household as a tutor-in-arms.

In his thirties Marshal spent two years bolstering the defences of the Kingdom of Jerusalem. On his return he re-joined Henry II's court, fighting for Henry and then his sons Richard the Lionheart and John. At 43 he had married the seventeen-year-old daughter of the immensely wealthy Earl of Pembroke, with whom he had ten children.

When King John died, Marshal had been made regent during Henry III's minority. Now, with the barons in revolt and the French invading the country, Marshal thought only of protecting the boy-king: 'By God's sword, if all abandoned the king, do you know what I would do?' he said. 'I would carry him on my shoulders step by step, from island to island, from country to country, and I would not fail him, not even if it meant begging my bread.' On this day came his greatest test – when he was already 70 years old.

After Louis took London, many royal supporters defected and joined him. Soon the entire south-eastern half of England was under French control, the gravest threat to England since William the Conqueror had invaded 150 years before.

While moving with half his army to besiege Dover, Louis sent Thomas, comte du Perche with 611 knights and 1,000 infantry to the walled town of Lincoln. The town quickly yielded, apart from the castle where the castellan stubbornly held out.

Gathering a force of 400 knights, 317 crossbowmen, and several hundred infantry, Marshal now marched to Lincoln's rescue.

After Marshal's crossbowmen took the city gate, they climbed on rooftops near the castle to fire down onto the besieging forces. Then Marshal and his cavalry charged the French, completely routing the enemy. Perche refused to yield, but during the mêlée an English knight caught him with a sword thrust through his eye and into his brain. Some 300 French knights were captured, while most of the infantry was killed during the battle or as they fled. The victory had been so complete that it was dubbed 'the Lincoln Fair'. But the day ended on a less than chivalrous note, when Marshal's men sacked the town, slaughtering women and children, because the town had sided with the French.

In the wake of Marshal's victory, many of the English knights now switched their allegiance back to the boy-king Henry. After two of his fleets were sunk while trying to bring in reinforcements, Prince Louis was forced to renounce his claim to the English throne and return to France.

When William Marshal died two years later he was the richest and most respected man in England. Even his traditional enemy, King Philip Augustus of France (Prince Louis' father), said of him: 'He was the most loyal man I ever knew.' Today you can see his tomb in the Temple Church in London. King Henry, whose throne he had saved, reigned for another 53 years.

1834 Revolutionary aristocrat in France and America, the Marquis de Lafayette dies in Paris at 76 with the final comment: 'What do you expect? Life is like the flame of a lamp ... when there is no more oil ... Phut! It goes out and all is over.'

---

21 May

'Veni, vidi, vici'

47 BC '*Veni, vidi, vici*' – 'I came, I saw, I conquered' – Julius Caesar's magnificent boast that would become his motto emblazoned on placards during his triumphs in Rome. He first used it to report to the Senate his overwhelming victory in Anatolia on this day.

During Rome's civil war, King Pharnaces of the Bosporan Kingdom in the Crimea had sided with Caesar, but after Caesar's triumph, Pharnaces had invaded Cappadocia, Colchis, Lesser Armenia and Pontus, kingdoms allied to Rome, selling many of the conquered people into slavery and castrating any male Roman citizen he captured.

In the meantime Caesar had been pursuing his famous dalliance with Cleopatra in Alexandria, but finally the news of Pharnaces' depredations stirred him to action, and on 26 March he bade farewell to his pregnant mistress and headed for Pontus (now in north-eastern Turkey, bordering on the Black Sea) with his veteran but depleted 6th Legion, collecting three more legions as he moved north.

Learning of Caesar's approach, Pharnaces entreated him to come not as an enemy but as a friend. Caesar's response was to demand

Pharnaces' immediate withdrawal from Pontus, the return of all captives and loot, and an enormous sum in tribute. Meanwhile the Roman legions continued their inexorable advance, soon nearing Zela (now Zile in Turkey), where Pharnaces had built a fortified camp on a ridge three miles from the town.

Caesar camped with his troops about five miles from Zela, and before daybreak on this day (21 May by our calendar, but 2 August by the Roman calendar) he set out with his army, arriving at dawn on a hill two miles across a valley from the enemy. There he set about fortifying his position, leaving only his first line in order of battle.

When Pharnaces saw that only the Roman first line was under arms he ordered his infantry and scythed chariots into an immediate attack.

According to a report by one of Caesar's lieutenants, when Pharnaces' soldiers began crossing the valley towards the Roman position, 'Caesar at first laughed at his ostentation, in crowding his army into so narrow a place, where no enemy in his right mind would have ventured: in the meantime Pharnaces continued his march, and began to ascend the steep hill on which Caesar was posted.'

Amazed by Pharnaces' recklessness, Caesar called all his troops into action, ranging them in battle order.

Initially the enemy's chariots caused havoc among the Roman troops, but the Romans responded with volleys of *pila* (2-metre javelins), which stopped the enemy advance. Then the opposing armies closed with a shout, and Caesar's experienced 6th Legion overpowered the enemy left. After initial bitter resistance, Pharnaces' centre and right began to fold and fled back down the slope and up towards their own defences. 'Our victorious men did not hesitate to advance up the unfavourable ground and attack their fortifications, which they soon forced, despite the resistance made by the troops left by Pharnaces to guard it. Almost the whole army was cut to pieces or made prisoners.'

Pharnaces managed to escape with some cavalry, but a few months later he was captured and put to death by one of his own governors.

Zela had been a spectacular victory; Caesar had won not just a battle but also a war in just four hours. He announced his great triumph in a letter to Rome in perhaps the most famous battle report in history: '*Veni, vidi, vici.*'

1927 When Charles Lindbergh lands after making the first non-stop flight from New York to Paris, he is mobbed by well-wishers, but his first remark is about his plane: 'Are there any mechanics here?' * **1964** American psychologist B.F. Skinner writes in the *New Scientist*: 'Education is what survives when what has been learnt has been forgotten.'

22 May

'I found him a pigmy, but I lost him a giant.'

1809 The Napoleonic marshal Jean Lannes came from humble stock. The son of a Gascon stable boy, he learned to read and write from a village priest. He was immensely strong, athletic and brave (he was wounded nine times in combat). Entering the military at 23, he fought in a long list of famous Napoleonic battles, beginning with Arcole and Rivoli in Napoleon's Italian campaign and later at the Battle of the Pyramids, Abukir, Marengo, the siege of Ulm, Austerlitz, Jena, Friedland, the siege of Zaragoza and finally the Battle of Aspern-Essling just outside Vienna, where on this day he was mortally wounded.

Born on 10 April 1769, Lannes was just four months older than Napoleon and became the only marshal who was a personal friend to the emperor, calling him the familiar '*tu*' rather than the formal '*vous*'.

During the second day of the battle at Aspern-Essling, the French were defeated (up to that time, Napoleon's only loss in a major battle) and Lannes braved the hottest fire to cover the retreat to a small island in the Danube. As he was talking to his friend General Pierre-Charles Pouzet, the Austrians fired a massive cannon barrage. A ball cut Pouzet in half, drenching Lannes in blood. Dazed but not wounded, Lannes sat down at the edge of a ditch, his hand over his eyes and his legs crossed. As he sat there, plunged in gloomy meditation, a three-pound shot struck him just where his legs crossed. He was carried off to a field hospital where his left leg was amputated.

Hearing of his marshal's terrible wound, Napoleon rushed to comfort him. Dropping on his knees beside the litter, he exclaimed: 'Do you know me? It's your friend Bonaparte.'

There are two dramatically different versions of Lannes' response. According to General Petit, the marshal heroically addressed the emperor: 'I am dying for you and my country. Do not mourn my loss. Live and save the army!' However, according to Charles-Louis Cadet de Gassicourt, who was there at the time, Lannes bitterly reproached Napoleon with the words: 'I am dying for you, like so many others. You will not mourn my loss any more than the rest.' Later his other leg was amputated.

On the morning of 23 May, Lannes was moved to a house in Ebersdorf. For four days he seemed to be recovering, but during the night of 27 May he was suddenly taken by the fever and delirium of gangrene. On the 29th Napoleon visited him again, remaining half an hour at his bedside, but nothing could save the brave marshal – he succumbed to his wounds at daybreak on 31 May. On the same day the emperor wrote to Lannes' widow: 'The Marshal died this morning of wounds received on the field of honour. My sorrow is as deep as yours. I lose the most distinguished general in my armies, my comrade in arms during sixteen years, he whom I considered my best friend.' In 1810 Lannes was reinterred in the Panthéon in Paris.

Later when in exile in Saint Helena, Napoleon wrote in his memoirs: 'With Lannes, at first his courage was more important than his mind, but his mind grew every day to put the two in balance. I found him a pigmy, but I lost him a giant.'

Of Napoleon's 26 marshals, two became kings (Bernadotte and Murat), two were shot by firing squad (Ney and Murat), one (Brune) was murdered by royalists, one (Mortier) was killed by anarchists in 1835 during an assassination attempt against King Louis-Philippe, and only one other besides Lannes (Józef Poniatowski) was killed in battle, drowned crossing a river at Leipzig after having been badly wounded.

1885 Last words of Victor Hugo, who dies in Paris: 'This is the fight of day and night. I see black light.'

---

23 May

'I am Heinrich Himmler.'

1945 On 30 April Adolf Hitler shot himself in his Berlin bunker. The next day his malign propaganda minister Joseph Goebbels did the same, and on 2 May Martin Bormann swallowed cyanide. On 6 May Hermann Göring surrendered to the US Army, and on 8 May Nazi Germany formally capitulated, ending the Second World War in Europe.

Most of the top Nazi brass were now dead or captured, but where was Germany's number two man, Reichsführer Heinrich Himmler?

Himmler headed the Gestapo, the police and the SS. More than any other individual, he created the network of state terror by which the Third

Reich compelled obedience. 'The best political weapon is the weapon of terror', he claimed. 'Cruelty commands respect. Men may hate us. But we don't ask for their love; only for their fear.' (Echoing the mad Roman emperor Caligula, who said: 'Let them hate, so long as they fear.')

Himmler was also the main architect of the Holocaust. 'Anti-Semitism is exactly the same as delousing', he said. 'Getting rid of lice is not a question of ideology, it is a matter of cleanliness. In just this same way anti-Semitism for us has not been a question of ideology but a matter of cleanliness.'

Ever since Germany's defeat at Stalingrad in 1943, Himmler had realised that the war was lost. On 20 April 1945 – Hitler's birthday – he saw the Führer for the last time. After swearing total loyalty, he headed for Lübeck to betray him. There he entered into secret peace negotiations with Count Folke Bernadotte, head of the Swedish Red Cross. When Hitler learned of Himmler's treachery, he stripped him of his offices and ordered his arrest as a traitor.

But ten days later Hitler was dead, and Himmler still needed to escape the Allies. He equipped himself with a forged paybook under the name of Sergeant Heinrich Hitzinger, shaved off his moustache, ditched his infamous rimless glasses for a patch over his left eye and headed south.

On 21 May British soldiers at a checkpoint on a bridge crossing the Oste River stopped a small dishevelled figure travelling with two companions. Sent first to a POW camp at Barnstedt, two days later the three prisoners were transferred to a British interrogation centre near Lüneburg, where they were stripped and searched (the British believing that there is no better way to interrogate a man than when he is standing naked and you are comfortably seated, smoking a cigarette).

As questioning began, one of the Germans stepped forward. He removed the patch from his eye and told the astonished British officers, 'I am Heinrich Himmler'. He then demanded to see Field Marshal Montgomery to discuss a demented scheme to offer the British several SS divisions to help defend them from the Russians, who, he said, were about to cross the Elbe and attack the British.

The officer in charge gave the naked Himmler a pair of shorts and an army blanket to throw around his shoulders (Himmler refused to wear a British uniform) and sent him to the headquarters of the Second British Army in Lüneburg.

There Himmler was searched again, but when a doctor attempted to examine the inside of his mouth, he bit down on the doctor's probing fingers and on a hidden cyanide capsule fitted around a wisdom tooth. As the smell of prussic acid spread through the room, Himmler collapsed to the floor, writhing in agony. Despite desperate British efforts to save him, he was dead in twelve minutes.

In the early morning of 26 May, four British soldiers carried Himmler's body to a forest near Lüneburg and buried it in a secret, unmarked grave. Now not even Himmler's corpse would ever be found.

1701 As the rope is placed around his neck, the pirate Captain Kidd makes a last bitter comment about the rich and powerful men who he thought had betrayed him: 'This is a very false and faithless generation.'

---

24 May

'As though seated on a royal throne, the Sun governs the family of planets revolving around it.'

1543 Now seventy years old and lying comatose from a stroke, the great astronomer Nicolaus Copernicus was on the edge of death. Twenty-three years earlier he had finished his revolutionary work, *De revolutionibus orbium coelestium* (*On the Revolutions of the Celestial Spheres*), but the book had never been published. Its contentious theme – that the Earth revolves around the Sun rather than the reverse – was not only psychologically threatening, but heretical. If it was true, the Earth was no longer the constant, unmoving centre of the universe but just a planet like any other. Copernicus had challenged head-on Ptolemy's geocentric model that had been accepted for 1,400 years. His theory was also directly counter to the teachings of the Church.

Born in the small town of Torun in Poland in 1473, Copernicus was a highly educated polymath who had studied first at the University of Kraków and then in Bologna, where he lived in the same house as the university's principal astronomer. He is said to have spoken Polish, German and Latin (in which he wrote) as well as Italian and Greek. After obtaining a doctorate in canon law, he returned to Poland to become a canon, practised medicine and became deeply involved in Church finances. In his spare time he took up astronomy.

In 1530, when he was 57, Copernicus completed his immortal work, *De revolutionibus*, which laid out his theory: 'At rest in the middle of everything is the Sun. For, in this most beautiful temple, who would place this lamp in another or better position than that from which it can light up the whole thing at the same time? For, the Sun is … called by some people the lantern of the universe, its mind by others, and its ruler by still others … Thus indeed, as though seated on a royal throne, the Sun governs the family of planets revolving around it.'

Copernicus was not the first to posit a heliocentric view of the universe; 1,800 years earlier the Greek astronomer Aristarchus of Samos had theorised that the Sun was at the centre of the universe with the Earth revolving around it, but his ideas were rejected in favour of the geocentric ideas of Aristotle in the 4th century BC and Ptolemy in the 2nd century AD, and their Earth-centred views had been accepted throughout the Christian era. Copernicus was the first modern scientist to challenge the prevailing theory, but due to his works' contentious subject matter, he was unable to publish.

Finally, in 1543, a Lutheran printer in Nuremberg, free from the pressures of the Church in Rome, brought out the great work. Before seeing his book in print, however, Copernicus suffered a stroke and lapsed into unconsciousness. Then one of his colleagues placed a copy of the work, printed at last, in his unfeeling hands. Immediately before he died he regained consciousness just long enough to realise that his theories had at last been published.

Copernicus was buried in Frombork Cathedral, where his tombstone is said to have been graven with the words 'Stand, Sun, move not'. His work would eventually destroy much of the underpinning of the medieval world and change for ever our way of seeing the universe. Two and a half centuries later Johann Wolfgang von Goethe opined: 'Of all discoveries and opinions, none may have exerted a greater effect on the human spirit than the doctrine of Copernicus.'

1844 Samuel Morse sends the first telegraph message, from Washington to Baltimore: 'What hath God wrought!'

25 May

*'I have loved righteousness and I have hated
iniquity, therefore I die in exile.'*

1085 Today Gregory VII, one of the most contentious popes of the Middle Ages, died in exile in Salerno.

Prior to gaining the papal crown, Gregory had spent 24 years serving five different popes and became famous around Europe under his original name of Hildebrand. In 1073, when Hildebrand was in his late fifties, Pope Alexander II died. During Alexander's funeral in the Lateran Basilica, the assembled clergy and common people shouted in unison: 'Let Hildebrand be Pope!' Hildebrand fled from the church, only to be tracked down to the Basilica di San Pietro in Vincoli a mile away. There, amid repeated acclamations, he was duly elected by the cardinals, to become Pope Gregory VII. It was a remarkable start to a papal reign – so remarkable that there have been suspicions ever since that Hildebrand himself had orchestrated it.

In his first year as Pope, Gregory applied himself vigorously to cleansing the Church, cracking down on the selling of religious offices, and issuing draconian decrees to enforce priestly celibacy, but his great lifelong goal was to increase the power of the papacy.

Believing that all Christians owed the Pope – that is, himself – absolute and unquestioned obedience, Gregory claimed overlordship over Europe's kings and princes, including the most powerful of them all, Holy Roman Emperor Henry IV, who reigned over northern Italy, Burgundy and most of Germany.

In 1075 Gregory issued the Dictatus Papae, a list of papal powers that specified that the Pope could depose any temporal ruler, including the emperor. Thunderstruck, Henry and most of his bishops renounced their obedience to 'Frater Hildebrand', and the emperor called on Gregory to abdicate. Fuming with indignation, in February 1076 Gregory issued a new command: 'Through [God's] power and authority, I withdraw the government of the whole kingdom of the Germans and of Italy from Henry the king ... For he has risen up against the Church with unheard of arrogance. And I absolve all Christians from the bond of the oath that they have made to him or shall make. And I forbid anyone to serve him as king.' Never before had a pope deposed a king.

The result was a disaster for Henry, who was forced to back down when Germany's local rulers began to abandon him, only too glad to be free of his control. On 28 January 1077 he made his way to Canossa Castle in northern Italy to meet Gregory. Wearing a hair shirt, for three days and three nights he stood barefoot in the snow before the entrance gate, begging forgiveness for his sins. Gregory lifted the excommunication, but by then Henry's barons had revolted, claiming fealty to a rival Holy Roman Emperor. When Henry crushed this revolt, Gregory excommunicated him a second time.

Henry's response was to install a papal rival, the Antipope Clement III, and in 1081 he invaded Rome to get rid of Gregory once and for all. After two failed attempts to take the city, the emperor finally prevailed in 1084 when the Romans, including many cardinals and other clergy, opened the gates to his army. Gregory's answer was to excommunicate Henry for the third time and hunker down in the Castel Sant'Angelo after sending for his Norman allies from southern Italy.

The Normans drove off Henry and freed the embattled pope but sacked Rome while they were at it, so infuriating the citizens of Rome that they rose up and forced Gregory to flee to the castle of Salerno by the sea. There on this day he died, pronouncing just before he passed away: 'I have loved righteousness and I have hated iniquity: therefore I die in exile.' These last words (*Dilexi justitiam et odivi iniquitatem: propterea morior in exilo*) are engraved on his sarcophagus in Salerno's cathedral.

Gregory may have died an outcast, despised during his own reign for his expansive use of papal powers, but in the longer term he may have had the last laugh, as he was canonised by Pope Paul V in 1606 for his reforming zeal.

> **1916** American automotive pioneer Henry Ford: 'History is more or less bunk.'

26 May

*'There was an old bastard named Lenin/
Who did two or three million men in.'*

1922 Today in Gorki, Russian dictator Vladimir Lenin suffered his first stroke, which temporarily deprived him of his ability to speak and paralysed his right side. It was a harbinger of worse to come.

Lenin's stroke may have been caused by a revolutionary named Fanya Kaplan, who was incensed by his increasing dictatorship. In August 1918 she fired three shots as he headed for his car, hitting him in the lung and the base of the neck. (She was arrested, interrogated and summarily shot.)

Lenin's doctors thought it too dangerous to remove the bullet lodged in his neck, close to his spine, but his health started to deteriorate. Four years later the bullet finally had to be removed, but within a month he suffered the stroke.

One of his Lenin's last directives had been to order the hunting down of anti-Bolshevik priests, causing almost 20,000 executions – a fitting milestone in his first five years running the country. 'A revolution without firing squads is meaningless', he said.

According to his biographer Louis Fischer, Lenin was 'a man with iron will, self-enslaving self-discipline, scorn for opponents and obstacles, the cold determination of a zealot, the drive of a fanatic, and the ability to convince or browbeat weaker persons by his singleness of purpose'. He saw his own views as absolute truth and dismissed others with disdain, preaching: 'We can and must write in a language that sows among the masses hate, revulsion, and scorn toward those who disagree with us.' He despised the precepts of liberal democracy, saying: 'It is true that liberty is precious – so precious that it must be rationed.' Believing that the end always justifies the means, he was more than willing to shed blood for the revolutionary cause.

Apart from sanctioning the murder of Tsar Nicholas and his family, Lenin ordered the requisitioning of crops that, along with a terrible drought, killed 5 million people, and he promoted the Red Terror that killed another 200,000. He took Russia into the Polish–Soviet War, where thousands more died, and issued the famous Hanging Order to execute kulak leaders. The first gulags were set up during his supremacy.

After his first stroke, Lenin returned to Moscow, but in December he was felled by a second, causing him to ponder the future of the Bolshevik revolution without him at the helm. He dictated his 'Testament' in which he evaluated Russian leaders like Trotsky and Stalin, whom he had promoted to General Secretary in March. Lenin wrote: 'Stalin is too crude, and this defect which is entirely acceptable in our milieu and in relationships among us as communists, becomes unacceptable in the position of General Secretary. I therefore propose to comrades that they should devise a means of removing him from this job.' He considered Trotsky the most suitable replacement.

In March 1923 Lenin suffered stroke number three, which again caused partial paralysis of his right side and left him unable to speak. After making a slow and incomplete recovery, he visited the Kremlin for the last time and then returned to his Gorki mansion where, on 21 January 1924 a fourth and final stroke finished him off. (If you're into communist dictators, his embalmed corpse is still on display in his mausoleum in Red Square in Moscow.)

Despite Lenin's misgivings, during his illness Stalin had been able to retain his hold on power, which he strengthened into an iron grip that lasted until his death 29 years later. During Stalin's dictatorship, about 6 million people starved to death in the famine of 1932–33, almost 2 million more perished in the gulags, another million died as a result of forced resettlement and 800,000 were executed.

Between them, Lenin and Stalin killed more of their own people than any other dictators in history (until Mao surpassed them), prompting a lovely limerick from the British-American historian Robert Conquest:

> There was an old bastard named Lenin
> Who did two or three million men in.
> That's a lot to have done in
> But where he did one in
> That old bastard Stalin did ten in.

1632 Connecticut colonists and their Narragansett and Mohegan allies set fire to a Pequot fort near the Mystic River, massacring 650 Pequot Indians, including women, children, and the elderly. Connecticut militia leader Captain John Underhill justifies the killing: 'Sometimes the Scripture declareth women and children must perish with their parents … We had sufficient light from the Word of God for our proceedings.'

---

27 May

'Alas! You won't let me see my lord, neither dead nor alive!'

1234 Today France's devout King Louis IX and Marguerite de Provence, still just thirteen, were married in the Gothic cathedral at Sens. The marriage had been arranged by Louis' mother, the redoubtable Blanche of Castile, who dominated her son and had chosen Marguerite more for her religious devotion than her beauty, which Blanche found excessive.

When the wedding festivities had been concluded, Marguerite was led with great pomp to her nuptial chamber, where she awaited her new husband. Two hours later Louis had not appeared, so she sent one of her ladies-in-waiting to enquire, only to learn that he was in his chapel at prayer. At dawn Marguerite finally fell asleep in tears.

The next evening was another wait in vain – the king was still praying. The third night the same. Finally, on the fourth night, Louis received Blanche's permission to fulfil his conjugal duties with the stern command: 'Go, then, and think of your descendants.' She paced the corridor outside until she thought the marriage had been consummated and then strode into the nuptial bedroom, saying: 'And that's enough for this evening.' Without a word to Marguerite, she ordered the king to finish the night alone in the room next door.

Ever since her husband Louis VIII had died in 1226, Blanche had in effect ruled France, three times leading armies in battle. A woman of great resolve and courage, she was determined to retain her influence over her son but feared that he might now turn to his wife for counsel. Nothing illustrates the theme of the mother-in-law from hell better than the tale of Marguerite and Louis at the castle of Pontoise.

The castle contained a spiral staircase, with Marguerite's bedchamber at the bottom and Louis' at the top. According to the almost contemporary chronicler Jean de Joinville, the royal couple were so afraid of Blanche that 'they were wont to converse on a winding stair that went from one chamber to the other, and their affair was so well planned that when the guards spied Queen Blanche coming towards her son's chamber they would knock on the door with their staffs and the king, hearing it from the stair, would hastily run up into his room so that his mother might find him there'. (Another version says that Louis kept a dog trained to bark at Blanche's approach.)

In 1242 Marguerite nearly died in childbirth. Entering the queen's bedroom, Blanche found Louis there, holding her hand. 'What are you doing?' Blanche thundered, 'You are wasting your time here, get out!', and led him from the room. The distressed young queen cried out: 'Alas! You won't let me see my lord, neither dead nor alive!' ('*Hélas! Vous ne me laisserez donc voir mon seigneur, ni morte ni vive!*') At this she fainted, and the king rushed back to her bedside, thinking she was dying, but his presence brought her out of her swoon.

Despite Blanche's strong objections, in 1249 Louis left on crusade, taking Marguerite with him and leaving his mother in France as regent. The campaign was a disaster; Louis' army was destroyed, his brother killed and Louis captured. But then Marguerite showed her true mettle, personally negotiating his ransom and raising 400,000 livres to pay it. If only briefly, she was the only woman ever to lead a crusade.

Louis remained in the Middle East for four years, helping the Latin kingdoms there rebuild their defences. While he was there Blanche fell ill and died. Louis did not speak for two days when he heard the news.

In 1270 Louis embarked on another crusade, this one even more disastrous than his first. Six weeks after landing in Tunis he was felled by the plague. He and Marguerite had been married for 36 years and, despite Blanche's efforts to keep them apart, they had produced eleven children. Marguerite lived on as queen mother until she died at 74 in 1295. Two years later Pope Boniface VIII proclaimed Louis a saint.

1564 Despite a series of debilitating diseases, John Calvin continues to work, but when friends see that he is dying, they beg him to reduce his workload, to which he indignantly replies: 'Would you that the Lord should find me idle when He comes?' * **1955** Former president Harry Truman in a television interview: 'I have found the best way to give advice to your children is to find out what they want and then advise them to do it.'

---

28 May

'The volley fired by a young Virginian in the backwoods of America set the world on fire.'

1754 The French and British had fought each other in three separate mini-wars in North America since 1689, vying for control of this vast new continent. Today saw the first battle in what would be called the French and Indian War, another British/French conflict there, each side supported by their Indian allies.

The Ohio Territory – a roughly circular area of some 260,000 square miles directly south of Lake Erie – had long been claimed by both the British and the French. It was of particular interest to many colonials from the Colony of Virginia, who owned property there. In 1753, however, the French began to build fortifications along the Ohio River, causing Virginia's colonial administrator Robert Dinwiddie to send a written demand that the French leave the Ohio Valley. Chosen to carry the letter was a 22-year-old Virginian lieutenant colonel named George Washington.

When the demand was rebuffed, on 24 March 1754 Dinwiddie ordered Washington to return with 160 men to defend a Virginian fort at the forks of the Ohio (today's Pittsburgh). Should he meet French resistance, he should 'make Prisoners of or kill & destroy [the French]'.

Before Washington could get there, however, the British garrison had surrendered to the French, so Washington started to build a small fort about forty miles south, calling it Fort Necessity. But then on 27 May a British settler told him that a scouting party of about 50 French Canadians and allied Indians was in the area, led by Ensign Joseph Coulon de Jumonville. Picking 40 from his own colonial militia plus twelve allied Mingo warriors, Washington set out to ambush the enemy.

The next day Washington and his men concealed themselves behind rocks around the French camp, but before they could attack they were discovered. 'Whereupon', wrote Washington in his diary, 'I ordered my company to fire.'

The 'battle' lasted only fifteen minutes. The British, who lost only one man, killed nine of the enemy and captured 21. An evidently young Washington later wrote to his brother: 'I fortunately escaped without any wound, for the right wing, where I stood, was exposed to and received all the enemy's fire … I heard the bullets whistle, and, believe me there is something charming in the sound.'

There was, however, one unsettling and debated issue. Some reports say that the French commander Jumonville was killed outright during the battle while others say that he was wounded and captured – and that when Washington was trying to interrogate him, the chief of the Mingos pulled out his tomahawk, smashed his skull and scalped him. Whatever the truth, Jumonville did not survive the day.

This was the opening skirmish of the French and Indian War, which continued for nine years, finally ending with the Treaty of Paris on 10 February 1763. The winning British took over all of New France (Canada) while abandoning to France the Caribbean islands of Guadeloupe and Martinique, which had previously been occupied by the British. But this war fought out in North America was really just the beginning of a much larger conflict, the Seven Years' War, a bloody worldwide struggle spanning five continents, affecting Europe, the Americas, West Africa, India, and the Philippines and involving every European great power of the time, with France on one side and Great Britain on the other. French and British killed and wounded came to about 400,000 roughly evenly split, as well as very substantial losses for the other belligerents.

So in a very real sense George Washington's small victory on this day was a prelude to what is sometimes called the first global war. The British writer, historian and Member of Parliament Horace Walpole, who was 36 when Washington defeated the French, later wrote: 'The volley fired by a young Virginian in the backwoods of America set the world on fire.'

> **1358** In France the Jacquerie peasant uprising breaks out near Paris, where 100 peasants burn a manor house to the ground, killing the owner and his family. According to the nobles who eventually crush the uprising: '*Oignez vilain, il vous poindra, poignez vilain, il vous oindra.*' ('Spare a villain, he'll cut your throat, show a villain your steel and he'll kneel.') * **1774** Horace Walpole in a letter to a friend: 'The way to ensure summer in England is to have it framed and glazed in a comfortable room.'

29 May

'Qui m'aime me suive!'

1328 Philippe de Valois is best remembered for thwarting England's Edward III's bid to claim the French throne – and then almost losing it anyway at the Battle of Crécy. Today at age 35 he was crowned Philippe VI of France in Reims Cathedral.

During the celebrations following the formal ceremony, Philippe was approached by his vassal, Louis de Nevers, Count of Flanders, whose rapacious taxation of his subjects had sparked a peasant insurrection in 1323, a revolt that had turned into a full-blown rebellion led by a rich Flemish farmer named Nicolaas Zannekin. Chased out of his own domains, Louis beseeched his liege King Philippe to come to his aid.

Determined to crush this threat to the social order, Philippe summoned his barons, who were all in Reims for the coronation, and was soon marching north towards Flanders with 2,500 mounted knights and 12,000 light infantrymen and archers. En route he stopped in Saint-Denis to collect the Oriflamme, the king's battle standard during the Middle Ages that signalled that no prisoners would be taken. Meanwhile Louis de Nevers was raising more troops in and around Oudenaarde and Ghent.

Philippe and his army plundered and ravaged West Flanders as far as the gates of Bruges, then headed towards the town of Cassel, about 60 miles to the west, where 8,000 insurgents were entrenched on a small hill, with Zannekin in command. From there the rebels could see the smoke rising from their burning villages as the French army began to deploy before them.

Puffed up by his own importance as commander of the insurgents, Zannekin presumed the airs of a knight in sending a messenger to Philippe to propose they fix a day for the battle, as was sometimes done in medieval times. Philippe answered with contempt that the Flemish were just rabble, without a leader. His knights had such a low opinion of their adversaries that they loosened their armour to relax in camp.

Then, without warning, Zannekin's army attacked, surprising the French infantry in the middle of a nap. But Philippe and his knights were quick to recover. Dressed in royal blue embroidered with *fleurs de lys* of gold, he rode before his army crying: '*Qui m'aime me suive!*' ('Let him who loves me follow me!') and then led the charge himself, at the head of his knights.

The Flemish rebels disintegrated under the assault; over 3,000 were killed – including Zannekin – with many thousands more wounded. The French lost just seventeen knights.

In the aftermath, Louis recovered control over Flanders, fined the cities that had revolted and confiscated the property of nobles who had fought against him. In Bruges, the burghers were forced to throw themselves on their knees before him, imploring mercy. Philippe ordered the demolition of the fortifications at Bruges, Ypres, and Kortrijk.

But the Battle of Cassel was the high point in the careers of both Philippe VI and Louis de Nevers. A decade later the Flemish revolted once again, and Louis was forced to flee his Flemish lands, never to return. Philippe was dragged into the Hundred Years' War and suffered a devastating defeat in 1346 at the Battle of Crécy – in which Louis was killed. The next year he lost Calais to the English, and one year after that the Black Death struck France, killing about a third of the population, including his wife. When he died in 1350 at 57, France was a poor and divided country. But the royal dynasty he founded – the Valois – ruled France until 1589.

1453 During the last day of Sultan Mehmed's conquest of Constantinople, Emperor Constantine XI Palaeologus calls out: 'Is there no Christian to cut off my head?' His own men refuse, but Turkish soldiers dispatch him.

---

30 May

'*All they that loue not Tobacco & Boies were fooles.*'

1593 On 12 May the playwright Thomas Kyd was arrested on suspicion of posting treasonous bills around London. When his quarters were searched, there was no sign of treason, but an investigator found a tract he described as 'vile heretical conceits denying the eternal deity of Jesus Christ'. Kyd denied the papers were his, but under torture claimed they belonged to his former roommate, the playwright Christopher Marlowe. Marlowe, said Kyd, would 'jest at the divine scriptures, gibe at prayers' and was an atheist who said that Jesus was homosexual.

The authorities issued a warrant for Marlowe's arrest, but he was never interrogated because of what happened today, Wednesday, 30 May.

Marlowe spent the day in a house (sometimes described as a tavern) in Deptford with three shady characters named Ingram Frizer, Nicholas Skeres and Robert Poley. The men were sitting at a table while Marlowe was lying on a couch when he and Frizer began arguing about the bill (famously called 'the Reckoning'). In the heat of the debate, Marlowe grabbed Frizer's dagger and wounded him in the head. In the fight that followed, Frizer retrieved his dagger and stabbed Marlowe, delivering (according to the coroner's report) a 'mortal wound above his right eye to the depth of two inches and in breadth one inch'.

So died Christopher Marlowe, still only 29 but already the author of seven plays and three poems which mark him as one of England's greatest writers. Although his works such as *Tamburlaine the Great*, *The Jew of Malta*, *Edward II* and *Doctor Faustus* are testament to his genius, his life and death remain an enigma:

Was Marlowe really a heretic? By the standards of the time, probably yes, at least an atheist. Shortly after his death, an Elizabethan double agent, informer and Catholic priest named Richard Baines wrote the so-called 'Baines Note', a list of accusations claiming that Marlowe thought 'that the first beginning of Religioun was only to keep men in awe … the woman of Samaria & her sister were whores & that Christ knew them dishonestly … St John the Evangelist was bedfellow to Christ … all the apostles were fishermen and base fellowes neyther of wit nor worth'. Thomas Kyd agreed.

Was Marlowe a homosexual? Probably. His plays *Edward II* and *Hero and Leander* both focus on homosexual relationships (about Leander he writes, 'in his looks were all that men desire') and Richard Baines claimed that Marlowe avowed that 'all they that loue not Tobacco & Boies were fooles'. But he could be lyrical about women; when Faustus sees Helen of Troy, he rhapsodises:

> Oh, thou art fairer than the evening air
> Clad in the beauty of a thousand stars!

Was Marlowe a government spy? Probably. While studying at Cambridge, he was nearly denied his degree because he was absent without leave for 32 weeks, but agents of Queen Elizabeth I insisted he receive the degree, suggesting he had performed services for the state.

Was Marlowe murdered? Probably not, but there are numerous theories that he was. One is that Queen Elizabeth ordered him killed for his public proselytising of atheism. Four weeks after a jury had concluded that Ingram Frizer had killed Marlowe in self-defence, Elizabeth officially pardoned him. Another claims that the wife of Marlowe's patron Thomas Walsingham had him murdered because she thought he was sexually involved with her husband. Another theory is that some government ministers organised the assassination because they feared that, were he questioned under torture after his arrest, he might reveal them as atheists.

The most fanciful idea is that, helped by his three louche friends, Marlowe faked his own death and fled abroad to avoid questioning. From the Continent he continued to write plays, but they couldn't be produced under his own name so he found a friend who would front for him. That friend was another playwright just two months younger than Marlowe – William Shakespeare.

1431 After Joan of Arc is executed in the old market place in Rouen, an anonymous English soldier exclaims: 'God forgive us: we have burned a saint.' But the Catholic Church waits until 1920 to canonise her. * **1778** When asked to renounce Satan on his deathbed, Voltaire replies: 'Now, now, my good man, this is no time for making enemies.' * **1962** Field Marshal Bernard Montgomery in a speech in the House of Lords: 'Rule 1, on page 1 of the book of war is: "Do not march on Moscow"... [Rule 2] is: "Do not go fighting with your land armies in China."'

---

31 May

*'I used the full scope of my intelligence
to prove that I am a fool.'*

1785 Louis René Edouard, Cardinal de Rohan was perceptibly slow of wit, but he headed one of France's wealthiest families. Also living in Paris was his lover Jeanne de La Motte, an adventuress who carried royal blood in her veins (she descended from an illegitimate son of

Henri II) but no cash in her pockets. Jeanne decided that Rohan could be bilked to her advantage.

A few years earlier, a Parisian jeweller named Böhmer had crafted a diamond necklace of extraordinary value and ostentation. It contained 647 jewels with a total weight of 2,300 carats and lay on the breast fifteen inches from top to bottom. It had initially been designed at the request of Louis XV for his mistress Madame du Barry, but before this stupefying vulgarity could be finished, Louis had died of smallpox. Böhmer tried to sell it to the new queen, but even the extravagant Marie Antoinette found the asking price of 1,600,000 livres too steep, remarking that for the same money the government could buy two ships of the line.

Here Jeanne de La Motte saw her opportunity. Pretending she was acting as go-between for the queen, she gave Cardinal de Rohan a series of letters purportedly from Marie Antoinette. In fact, they were forgeries prepared by another of Jeanne's lovers. They asked Rohan to purchase the diamond necklace for the queen, who, being short of ready cash, wanted to repay in three instalments. The queen needed the Cardinal (said the letters) to act as guarantor to the jeweller for so large a sum. Jeanne de La Motte clinched the deception by having a veiled prostitute disguised as the queen meet Rohan at midnight in the gardens at Versailles.

Completely duped, the Cardinal purchased the diamonds and handed them over to Jeanne, ostensibly for delivery to Marie Antoinette. Jeanne immediately broke up the necklace and sold the stones separately in London.

A few months later the first instalment to the jeweller fell due. Jeanne knew the truth would have to come out, but calculated that the vain and rich Rohan would pay for the necklace himself rather than publicly admit to being so humiliatingly gulled. But she had not counted on the reaction of the jeweller. On learning of the sting, he went straight to the queen, who promptly informed her husband, Louis XVI.

On 15 August, the day of the Assumption, the Cardinal came to Versailles to conduct holy offices in the royal chapel, but before he could begin, he was summoned to the king's chambers. There Louis and Marie Antoinette presented him with the jeweller's contract he had signed. Disconcerted, he made a full confession.

The king and queen concluded that Cardinal de Rohan had used the queen's name in order to purchase the diamonds for himself, and the same day he was thrown into the Bastille, to await trial before the French Parlement. Jeanne de La Motte was arrested the following morning.

The trial was brief, Rohan admitting to his credulity rather than criminality. 'I used the full scope of my intelligence to prove that I am a fool', he said. Parlement believed him and, on the evening of 31 May 1785, acquitted him of all charges. (Nonetheless, Louis promptly had him exiled.)

Jeanne de La Motte was not so lucky. Sentenced to prison for life, she was whipped and branded with a 'V' for *voleuse* (thief). A year later she escaped disguised as a boy and made her way to London, where she wrote scurrilous pamphlets accusing the queen of fictitious crimes, including a passionate liaison with Rohan.

For Marie Antoinette, the whole affair was a disaster. In spite of the evidence, the French public tended to believe that somehow she had contrived to spend a fortune on diamonds, and hatred for her continued to grow. 'This diamond necklace business may well rock the throne of France', Talleyrand presciently observed at the time. Four years later a French mob stormed the Bastille, igniting the French Revolution.

1916 After two of his ships have exploded within half an hour during the Battle of Jutland, Vice Admiral Earl Beatty remarks to his Flag Captain, Ernle Chatfield: 'There's something wrong with our bloody ships today, Chatfield.'

---

1 June

'Our Empire is like the sea, yours is but a handful of sand.'

1215 Today the Mongol hordes of Genghis Khan sacked Zhongdu (modern Beijing), the capital of the Jin Empire of northern China. By his death twelve years later, the Mongol leader's conquests would reach to the Caspian Sea. His sons and successors would extend their grip over the whole of China, Persia, and most of Russia to create the greatest land empire in history.

Genghis Khan, named Temujin at birth, was born around 1162 holding a clot of blood in his hand, a sure sign of great military prowess. By 1206 he had crushed the nomadic tribes from Mongolia's steppes to create a single nation, murderously eliminating all rivals. The tribes called him Genghis Khan – universal leader.

In 1208 the Jin emperor Wanyan Yongji demanded that the Mongols submit as a vassal state, but Genghis publicly called him a coward and, on receiving Yongji's envoy, spat on the ground and rode off – a virtual declaration of war. When he heard of this contemptuous dismissal, Yongji fulminated: 'Our Empire is like the sea; yours is but a handful of sand ... Why should we fear you?' He was soon to learn.

In early 1211 Genghis spent four days praying on a holy mountain and then announced: 'The Eternal Blue Sky has promised us victory and vengeance.' Soon his army was riding for China. According to legend, even before you could see the dust or hear the drumming of hooves, their pungent stench signalled the approach of death.

Ferocious and well disciplined, Genghis Khan's formidable cavalry could fire arrows 200 yards with deadly accuracy. Although invincible in the open, they could not conquer well-defended cities, but Genghis learned from his enemies how to use siege machinery and to divert rivers to flood cities and the surrounding countryside.

After an early Mongol victory, Yongji tried to negotiate a peace, but the Khan persuaded his ambassador to defect and reveal the Jin positions. The resultant slaughter was so great that Yongji was assassinated by one of his own generals, and Genghis forced the Jin to abandon the northern half of their empire. (By 1233, his son Ögedei had overrun the rest of it.)

Genghis's next target was the Khwarazmian Empire (largely in Iran). Initially he sought a trade agreement, but a local governor executed the Khan's mission of 450 men, triggering a Mongol invasion that would destroy the Khwarazmians and butcher much of their population. The local governor was killed by pouring molten silver into his ears and eyes.

Genghis Khan told his chiefs to 'show no clemency to my enemies ... Rigour alone keeps such spirits dutiful', and ordered entire towns to be destroyed. After conquering Urgench, he gave his troops the young women and children as slaves and then ordered each of his 50,000 soldiers to execute 24 enemy civilians – 1.2 million people. He razed important cultural centres such as Bukhara and Samarkand, where he forced the inhabitants to assemble outside the city and then massacred them all, building pyramids of severed heads to celebrate his victory.

Next Genghis sent his generals on raids to Persia and Russia, where they defeated every army they met. He then attacked the Tanguts in northwest China. During the campaign he executed the entire royal family.

Genghis died during this final invasion. Some say he succumbed to illness, others that he died after falling from a horse, and some that he was killed in battle. According to the grisliest tale, he bled to death after a Tangut princess he had taken as concubine hid a knife in her sex, then drew it out and castrated him when he came to her bed.

His army took his corpse back to Mongolia, massacring anyone they met 'to serve their master in the other world'. When he was buried on a sacred mountain, forty slave girls and forty stallions were killed to accompany him in the afterlife. Then a thousand of his warriors rode over the burial site to keep it forever secret.

1813 Mortally wounded American Captain James Lawrence orders his crew: 'Don't give up the ship!' Although his ship is battered and captured by the British outside Boston Harbour, after the war Lawrence's exhortation will become the motto of the US Navy. * **1879** Son of Napoleon III and last scion of the Bonapartes, Prince Louis Bonaparte is killed while fighting for the British during the Zulu War. On hearing the news, Disraeli remarks: 'A very remarkable people, the Zulus: they defeat our generals, they convert our bishops, they have settled the fate of a great European dynasty.'

---

2 June

'There's a sucker born every minute.'

1835 Today a 24-year-old American began his first tour around the United States, his first step towards becoming the country's most flamboyant showman. Although he became legendary through the shows he staged, he was also known as the Prince of Humbugs through the hoaxes with which he fooled the public. He was P.T. (Phineas Taylor) Barnum.

Barnum's first sham was mounted at Niblo's Garden in New York. It involved a blind and almost completely paralysed black slave named Joice Heth, whom he had purchased from another promoter. Although she was in her late 70s, Barnum advertised her as George Washington's nurse, 'the first person who put clothes on the unconscious infant', and claimed that she 'was born in the year 1674, and has, consequently, now arrived at the astonishing age of 161 years'.

Over his career Barnum arranged for dozens of hoaxes, including the mummified body of the 'Feejee mermaid', a grotesque composed of the head and body of a monkey sewn to the back half of a fish. Another was a deformed black dwarf with a small, tapering head named William Henry Johnson, whom Barnum renamed Zip the Pinhead. Audiences were told that Zip came from a tribe of 'missing links' in Africa who lived on raw meat, fruit and nuts. For Barnum's shows Zip was held in a cage where, dressed in a furry suit, he would screech and rattle the bars. Barnum also promoted a weed that would turn black people white. When asked why he was so successful at milking the gullibility of the American public, Barnum explained: 'There's a sucker born every minute.'

Barnum's shows included the diminutive 'General' Tom Thumb, who was only 2ft 5in tall. He was four years old, but Barnum claimed he was eleven, billing him as 'the Smallest Person that ever Walked Alone'. Tom became a sensation after Barnum taught him how to sing, dance and impersonate famous people. He stayed with Barnum for over twenty years and never grew taller than 3ft 4in. (Barnum and Tom became close friends, and later Tom bailed out Barnum when he had financial troubles.) Also featured were the 'giantess' Anna Swan, who was 7ft 6in and weighed 413 pounds, and Jumbo the elephant, an enormous beast over thirteen feet tall. Another bizarre exhibit was Chang and Eng, the famous Siamese Twins.

Barnum's Grand Traveling Museum, Menagerie, Caravan & Hippodrome toured all over the United States and Europe and performed before Queen Victoria and Czar Nicholas I. Eventually this became the Ringling Bros. and Barnum & Bailey Circus, which Barnum advertised as 'The Greatest Show on Earth'.

In 1841 Barnum established Barnum's American Museum in New York, which became the most famous showplace of the century. Here the public could see jugglers, magicians, singers, dancers and ventriloquists, a menagerie of animals and an ever-changing 'freak show' with albinos, bearded women, morbidly obese men and midgets. Other curiosities included educated dogs and fleas, living statuary, dioramas of the Creation and the Deluge, black Americans performing an 'African war dance', flower and bird shows, and America's first aquarium, which featured a whale. All of this was offered for 'twenty-five cents, children half price'. In 1850 Barnum promoted the American tour of singer Jenny Lind, the Swedish Nightingale, paying her an unprecedented $1,000 a night for 150 nights.

Although claiming to believe that 'nobody ever lost a dollar by underestimating the taste of the American public', Barnum was actually a concerned citizen who vigorously opposed slavery, served four terms in the Connecticut legislature and in 1875 became mayor of Bridgeport. Ironically, the great hoaxer became a scourge of spiritualist mediums and published *The Humbugs of the World*, which exposed the shams that mediums used and offered $500 to any medium who could prove power to communicate with the dead.

Barnum died on 7 April 1891, having suffered a stroke during a performance the year before. Entrepreneur to the end, his last words were: 'How were the receipts today at Madison Square Garden?'

1882 On the island of Caprera, Italian patriot and anti-clerical revolutionary Giuseppe Garibaldi dies at 74, leaving his will with the instructions: 'I do not want to accept, at any time, the hateful, contemptible and wicked ministry of a priest, whom I consider an atrocious enemy of mankind and of Italy in particular. And I believe that only in a state of madness or of truly crass ignorance can an individual put himself in the care of a descendant of Torquemada.'

---

3 June

*'For seventeen years, he did nothing at all
but kill animals and stick in stamps.'*

1865 According to his biographer, he was distinguished 'by no exercise of social gifts, by no personal magnetism, by no intellectual powers. He was neither a wit nor a brilliant raconteur, neither well read nor well educated, and he made no great contribution to enlightened social converse. He lacked intellectual curiosity and only late in life acquired some measure of artistic taste.' In other words, observed historian Robert Lacey, he was 'exactly like most of his subjects'. He was George V, born today in Marlborough House in London.

The second son of Edward VII, George never expected to become king, but he saw much of the world serving in the Royal Navy (on a visit to Japan, he had a blue and red dragon tattooed on his arm). But when influenza carried off his elder brother Eddy in 1892, George became the heir not only to the throne but also to Eddy's fiancée, Mary of Teck.

George and Mary produced six children. The journalist Randolph Churchill wrote that George once commented: 'My father was frightened of his mother, I was frightened of my father, and I am damned well going to see to it that my children are frightened of me.' When Edward VII died, however, George wrote in his diary: 'I have lost my best friend and the best of fathers ... I never had a cross word with him in my life.'

During the First World War, George changed the royal family's name from the Germanic Saxe-Coburg-Gotha to Windsor and ordered his British relatives to follow suit. His cousin Louis of Battenberg simply translated his to Louis Mountbatten. Germany's Kaiser Wilhelm (who was George's cousin) claimed that henceforth in Germany Shakespeare's *The Merry Wives of Windsor* would be known as *The Merry Wives of Saxe-Coburg-Gotha*. Not that George minded the gibe; he considered Wilhelm 'the greatest criminal known for having plunged the world into war'.

Another first cousin was Tsar Nicholas II, whom he enormously resembled and liked. Nevertheless, after Nicholas had abdicated, George refused him asylum for fear of being associated with the autocratic Russian regime when British socialism was raising its head. Three months later the Bolsheviks shot Nicholas, his wife and their five children.

George was an avid stamp collector, appointing a Philatelist to the King and telling him: 'I wish to have the best collection, not just one of the best collections, in England.' He also became a passionate hunter, once shooting a thousand pheasants in a day and 21 tigers, eight rhinoceroses and a bear during ten days in Nepal. After George's death his biographer Harold Nicolson recorded in his diary: 'For seventeen years, he did nothing at all but kill animals and stick in stamps.'

In spite of his mundanity, by the end of his reign the British people both admired and loved him. George shrugged, 'I cannot understand it, after all I am only a very ordinary sort of fellow.' But, as Nicolson wrote: 'His subjects had come to recognise that King George represented and enhanced those domestic and public virtues that they regarded as specifically British virtues. In him they saw, reflected and magnified, what they cherished as their own individual ideals – faith, duty, honesty, courage, common sense, tolerance, decency, and truth.'

George died of influenza at Sandringham just after eleven o'clock on 20 January 1936. He might have lasted a few hours longer had not his doctors, with the understanding of the government, administered a fatal dose of morphine so that his death would come in time to be announced in the next day's *Times* rather than in the plebeian tabloids a few hours later.

According to *The Times*, with his final breath George asked: 'How is the Empire?' Another story, however, insists that his last comment was to his doctor. Seven years earlier George had recuperated at the seaside resort of Bognor, which had re-labelled itself Bognor Regis in his honour. Now the doctor tried to soothe his patient with the thought that once again he could convalesce at the same resort, to which the king responded: 'Bugger Bognor!'

1924 Dying of tuberculosis, Franz Kafka asks his doctors for a morphine overdose: 'Kill me, or else you are a murderer!'

---

4 June

'I have lived as a philosopher and die as a Christian.'

1798 The Italian adventurer Giacomo Casanova died today, his last years spent in genteel poverty, but he is remembered as history's greatest philanderer. In truth, however, his seductions form only a part of his extraordinary life.

Born in Venice in 1725, Casanova graduated from the University of Padua at seventeen, a year after he had lost his virginity in a *ménage à trois* with two teenage sisters. He then became an abbot in a seminary, but his indebtedness landed him in prison. Next he became a military officer for the Republic of Venice but managed to lose most of his pay playing faro and abandoned his military career – to become a professional violinist. During the years ahead he would be a diplomat, spy, financier and writer of science fiction who also wrote mathematical treatises and at least one play and translated the *Iliad*. One of history's great travellers, he criss-crossed Europe and visited at least sixteen capital cities, making and losing half a dozen fortunes while becoming fluent in five languages.

This remarkable man mingled with half the crowned heads of Europe, including George III and Queen Charlotte, Charles III of Spain, Joseph II of Austria, Catherine the Great and Frederick the Great, who offered him a job as a tutor to bright young noblemen (Casanova declined). He discussed balloon travel with Benjamin Franklin (then in Paris) and etymology with Dr Johnson in London. Others he met included two popes, Voltaire and Bonnie Prince Charlie, as well as 'Butcher' Cumberland, Goethe, Rousseau, Madame de Pompadour and probably Mozart.

Constantly in trouble with the law, Casanova was expelled from three different countries, once for wounding a Polish count in a pistol duel over an Italian actress. He was imprisoned in Venice as a suspected necromancer, but pried off the jail's lead roof tiles and escaped by gondola.

By the time he was 60, Casanova was *persona non grata* in half the cities in Europe and running dangerously low on funds. Then this notorious free liver and bon vivant settled down in the obscure Castle of Dux in Bohemia (now in the Czech Republic) as a librarian. Bored with this sedentary and secluded life, after four years he began to compose his memoirs as 'the only remedy to keep from going mad or dying of grief'. Clearly hoping for literary success, he wrote in French rather than Italian because 'the French language is more widely known than mine'.

Entitled *The Story of My Life*, Casanova's memoirs recounted his extraordinary escapades both in and out of the bedroom, commenting: 'Cultivating whatever gave pleasure to my senses was always the chief business of my life.' No doubt he would have achieved even more conquests had he not lost his potency at about the age of 50. Although Casanova's tally of 132 liaisons may seem impressive, it appears lacklustre next to Cuban dictator Fidel Castro, who allegedly slept with 35,000, or writer Georges Simenon, who claimed: 'Since the age of thirteen-and-a-half, I have had 10,000 women.' But what is sure is that none of history's other womanisers led the adventurous life that Casanova enjoyed. As he said in his memoirs: 'Whether you think my actions good or bad, no one can deny that I truly lived.'

The old reprobate died at 73 today in the Castle of Dux, his last words an unlikely 'I have lived as a philosopher and die as a Christian'.

His memoirs remained unpublished for the next quarter of a century, but he would no doubt have been pleased that, when they were published, they were immediately added to the Vatican's list of forbidden books. Today his memoirs are still in print, and the original manuscripts were acquired in 2010 by the Bibliothèque nationale de France for a handsome $9.6 million.

1940 After the last of the British and French troops are evacuated from Dunkirk, Winston Churchill makes his 'we shall fight on the landing grounds' speech but reminds the Commons: 'Wars are not won by evacuations.'

---

5 June

'He has a beautiful pair of them, and they are really hanging well, just like our figs.'

1305 Time has not been kind to Clement V, who was elected pope on this day, for he is principally remembered as a lackey to King Philip the Fair (IV) of France. But he has one more amusing distinction in the folklore of France that still lives with us today.

Clement was born Bertrand de Got in Villandraut, 35 miles south of Bordeaux, and it was in Bordeaux where he climbed the papal ladder until the bitterly fought conclave of 1304–05 at which Philip engineered his succession as pope. A true Frenchman at heart, Clement insisted on being crowned in Lyon instead of Rome, and in 1309 he settled in Avignon, bringing the whole papal court with him to start the so-called 'Babylonian Captivity' that would last for 68 years. He never once set foot in the Eternal City.

As pope, Clement led the Church and did Philip's bidding, most notoriously in helping to destroy the Templars. Such was his notoriety that he earned a place in the *Inferno*, where Dante (a contemporary) called him 'a lawless shepherd, of ugly deeds'.

This was the Clement of verifiable history. But he also played a role in one of the enduring myths of the medieval papacy.

Since the 9th century there had been tales of a female pope, the so-called 'Pope Joan', a woman who disguised herself as a man and reigned under the name of John VIII for a few months (or two years) from 855, only to be exposed when she gave birth to a little girl in the streets of Rome (or when riding on horseback).

Such a legend – widely believed in the Middle Ages – made the Church's cardinals particularly cautious when choosing a new pope. Since Clement had a somewhat feminine appearance, it was said that on his election he was subjected to a gender test by '*trône percé*' (a marble throne with a hole through the seat). The new pope was forced to lift his robes and sit on the throne, and a committee of cardinals peered through the hole from beneath. One relieved cardinal then reported to the conclave: '*Il en a une belle paire et elles sont bien pendante comme nos figues!*' ('He has a beautiful pair of them, and they are really hanging well, just like our figs!') Clement was then duly elevated.

At some point after Clement's undignified examination, figs grown in Provence became known as '*les couilles du pape*' (the pope's balls). Because of their hallowed etymology, these figs were traditionally given to beggars by worshippers leaving Midnight Mass on Christmas Eve. Even today these figs are still grown, and in the year 2000 a fig jam called Couille du Pape was awarded the title of best *confiture* in France.

> **1910** American short story writer O Henry's last words: 'Turn up the lights, I don't want to go home in the dark.'

6 June

'Women who rule only make themselves ridiculous one way or the other.'

1654 When Sweden's Queen Christina was born, her unbalanced German mother Maria Eleonora wanted a son so desperately that she exclaimed: 'Instead of a son, I am given a daughter, dark and ugly, with a great nose and black eyes. Take her from me, I will not have such a monster!'

But her father Gustavus Adolphus loved his daughter deeply, took her to military reviews and had her educated like a boy. When she was five, he was killed at Lützen fighting for the Protestants against the Catholics during the Thirty Years' War. Maria Eleonora refused to let him be buried and for a year and a half regularly visited his open coffin, often touching the decaying corpse. A regency governed the country until at eighteen, Christina began to rule in her own right.

Christina was short and pockmarked, with a humped right shoulder and unruly, uncombed hair, and she sometimes wore men's clothing.

But she had a razor-sharp mind, worked ten hours a day, learned to speak eight languages and was so passionate about philosophy and the arts that she was called 'the Minerva of the North'.

When she was 23, Christina shocked her government by announcing that 'it is impossible for me to marry. My temper is a mortal enemy to this horrible yoke, which I would not accept, even if I thus would become the ruler of the world.' Another explanation may have been the beautiful young noblewoman Ebba Sparre, with whom she may have had a sexual relationship.

While Christina was liberal and a proto-feminist, she was wildly extravagant and could be arbitrarily cruel – she once had a critic beheaded for accusing her of 'bringing everything to ruin'. In 1651 she announced that she intended to abdicate in favour of her cousin, Charles Gustavus, claiming that the country needed a king to lead the army. As she wrote in her autobiography: 'Women who rule only make themselves ridiculous one way or the other. I myself am no exception.' Secretly, she was contemplating becoming a Catholic, a religion banned in Lutheran Sweden and against which her father had fought and died.

On this day, still only 27, Christina formally abdicated in the great hall of Uppsala Castle. When the Lord High Steward Per Brahe hesitated to remove her crown, she took it off herself.

She soon departed for Rome, where Pope Alexander VII received her in splendour and, when she officially converted to Catholicism, performed the baptismal ceremonies. Within three years, however, he had soured on his famous convert, who proved too worldly for the pious pope, who kept his coffin in his bedroom and a carved skull on his writing table. Their final split occurred when she visited France in 1657.

While staying at Fontainebleau she seized some letters of her equerry, Marchese Gian Rinaldo Monaldeschi, that suggested he had betrayed her interests. Summoning him to a palace gallery, she ordered two servants to execute him on the spot, but since he was wearing a coat of mail, they chased him around the room for two hours before dealing him a fatal blow. Although the execution was legal because Christina had judicial rights over members of her court, it so shocked the French that she was forced to leave, and Pope Alexander castigated her as 'a queen without a realm, a Christian without faith, and a woman without shame'.

Christina returned to Rome twice more before she died in 1689. The writer François Maximilian Misson described her as 'very small of stature, exceedingly fat and corpulent. Her complexion and voice and face are those of a man. She has a big nose, large blue eyes, blonde eye-brows, and a double chin from which sprout several tufts of beard … she wears [her hair] powdered and standing on end, uncombed.' But she became a great art collector, founded the Accademia dell'Arcadia for philosophy and literature, opened Rome's first public opera house and made Alessandro Scarlatti her choirmaster and Arcangelo Corelli her orchestra director. Giovanni Bernini became a personal friend. At six in the morning on 19 April this androgynous intellectual dynamo succumbed to pneumonia.

1918 US Marine Sergeant Dan Daly leads a successful charge against German positions at Belleau Wood with the order to his men: 'Come on, you sons of bitches! Do you want to live forever?' * **1944** Going ashore in the first wave during the Normandy landings, American General Theodore Roosevelt Jr tells his men: 'We'll start the war from right here.'

---

7 June

'Who's your fat friend?'

1778 Thomas Carlyle defined a dandy as 'a Man whose trade, office and existence consists in the wearing of Clothes'. Today in London the ultimate dandy was born, George Bryan Brummell, known to his contemporaries and to history as 'Beau'. Like a meteor blazing through the midnight sky, when he ran out of fuel he crashed and burned.

Brummell made his first sartorial mark at Eton, where he added a gold buckle to the standard white cravat. He was still a student there when his father died, leaving him an inheritance of about £25,000 (roughly £2,000,000 today). He was also at Eton when he was first presented to the extravagant and selfish Prince George, later George IV.

After a brief stint at Oxford, Brummell purchased a commission in the Prince of Wales's Own regiment, the 10th Royal Hussars, where he made a strong impression on George and other officers through his caustic, witty repartee and his insistence on impeccable fashion (it is said that he polished his boots with champagne). Although promoted to captain, he left the regiment when it was transferred to Manchester, a city, he complained, with no society and no art.

During the next few years Brummell established himself as fashion's arbiter in London. Always immaculately bathed and shaved, he wore an impeccably tailored dark blue coat over a freshly laundered and starched shirt with an elaborately knotted cravat. He claimed that he took five hours a day to dress, and when asked how much it cost to be well-dressed, he replied: 'My dear Madam, with strict economy, it might be done for eight hundred a year.' (At the time, a craftsman made £1 a week.) Rather than the knee breeches and stockings of the time, he preferred trousers and made fashionable the modern men's suit, worn with a tie.

From 1796 to 1810 Brummell lived in Mayfair and continued to set his mark on men's fashion so that even titled aristocracy asked for advice. 'Fashions come and go', he told them, 'bad taste is timeless.'

Although sixteen years older than Brummell, Prince George, who was well on the way to becoming the 25-stone behemoth of his later years, remained in awe of him and sought his advice on his clothing, his toiletries and even his snuff. Brummell became cockier and more arrogant and began to gamble heavily.

In 1811, when George III lapsed into insanity, George became regent. With his enhanced position he began demanding more respect, but Brummell continued to treat him as an equal and protégé. Worse, he joked to some friends that he was going to cut the regent and bring the Old King back into fashion. George was infuriated, and his relations with Brummell noticeably cooled.

In July 1813 Brummell joined three other Regency bucks, Lord Alvanley, Henry Mildmay and Henry Pierrepoint, to host 'the Dandies' Ball' at Watier's Club. When Prince George arrived, he affably greeted the other three hosts but walked past Brummell, staring him in the face without a word, cutting him dead. It was an appalling display of bad manners that stung Brummell into his notorious remark: 'Alvanley, who's your fat friend?'

From that point Brummell's connection with the regent was completely severed, and money lenders and tradesmen, aware that he had been dropped from royal favour, began to cut off his credit. Brummell, always extravagant, began to lose heavily at the gaming table and was soon mired in debt.

Three weeks before his 38th birthday Brummell fled to Calais to escape debtors' prison. For the rest of his life he was kept afloat by his rich English friends. Now in a downward spiral, he neglected his clothes, seldom washed and declined mentally. When he was 59, he was moved to Le Bon Sauveur asylum outside Caen, where, penniless and insane, he died of tertiary syphilis two years later.

Despite Brummell's tawdry end, his reputation as the ultimate of dandies led to his statue being placed in London's Jermyn Street in 2002.

1777 The Marquis de Lafayette writes to his sister explaining his volunteering to fight in the American Revolution: 'The happiness of America is intimately linked to the happiness of all humanity; it will become the respectable and safe refuge of virtue, honesty, tolerance, equality and a quiet freedom.' * **1967** American writer Dorothy Parker dies; previously asked to compose her own epitaph, she writes: 'Excuse my dust.'

---

8 June

'Were women to "unsex" themselves by claiming equality with men, they would become the most hateful, heathen, and disgusting of beings and would surely perish without male protection.'

1913 Four days earlier a forty-year-old suffragette named Emily Davison had flung herself in front of a galloping racehorse and on this day died from her injuries.

The debate on women's rights had been simmering since at least 1792 when Mary Wollstonecraft wrote *A Vindication of the Rights of Woman*. Two decades later Jeremy Bentham had supported the cause, and in 1865 women in Manchester formed the first women's suffrage committee. In 1867 John Stuart Mill tried but failed to persuade Parliament to give women the vote.

In the 19th century what would later be called male chauvinism was simply a widely accepted belief, supported by an indignant Queen Victoria, who in 1870 wrote that she was 'most anxious to enlist everyone who can speak or write to join in checking this mad, wicked folly of "Woman's Rights", with all its attendant horrors on which her poor feeble sex is bent, forgetting every sense of womanly feeling and propriety ... Were women to "unsex" themselves by claiming equality with men, they would become the most hateful, heathen, and disgusting of beings and would surely perish without male protection.'

In 1903, two years after Victoria's death, a vociferous feminist named Emmeline Pankhurst founded the Women's Social and Political Union. Initially favouring non-violent protest, in frustration these suffragettes (a term coined by the press) turned increasingly militant, setting fire to unoccupied houses and churches, smashing Regent Street windows and cutting telegraph wires.

In November 1906 Emily Davison joined the Union. She had studied at Oxford but gained no degree because they were not awarded to women at that time. Described by Emmeline Pankhurst's daughter Sylvia as 'one of the most daring and reckless of the militants', Davison was first arrested in 1909 for assaulting a constable during a protest march. Two years later she was sentenced to six months in Holloway Prison for setting afire the post box outside Parliament. There she and other suffragette prisoners barricaded themselves in their cells and went on hunger strike, a move the wardens countered by flooding the cells and force-feeding the women. Davison then threw herself from a prison balcony, intending to kill herself, only to be saved by a wire netting. She told a newspaper: 'I felt that by nothing but the sacrifice of human life would the nation be brought to realise the horrible torture our women face!' In 1912 she was jailed again, for trying to horsewhip a Baptist minister whom she had mistaken for the Chancellor of the Exchequer, Lloyd George. In all, Davison was arrested nine times and force-fed 49 times.

On 4 June 1913 Davison took a train to the Epsom Downs racetrack and waited behind the guard rail at Tattenham Corner, the final bend before the home straight. As the horses galloped around the bend she ducked under the rail and ran onto the course, to be knocked senseless to the ground by King George V's horse, Anmer, which also fell in the collision.

Anmer survived, but Davison never regained consciousness. Although it was (and is) hotly debated whether she intended to die for her cause, an analysis of news camera films carried out in 2013 suggested that she was only trying to attach a suffragette flag to the horse's bridle, a view reinforced by the fact that she was carrying the return stub of her railway ticket and a ticket to a suffragette dance later that day.

Davison's sacrifice had little impact on the cause of women's rights, as a year later the country was embroiled in the First World War. Only in 1918 did the British government finally allow women over 30 with certain property qualifications to vote, and ten years later, in a society changed for ever by the war, women were at last given equal rights to men. Meanwhile Emily Davison has come to be seen as a martyr for women's rights, even though she probably died by accident.

> **68 AD** The Roman Senate declares Galba emperor; Tacitus later writes: 'He seemed much greater than a private citizen while he was a private citizen, and had he never become emperor, everyone would have agreed that he had the capacity to be emperor.'

9 June

'What an artist dies in me!'

68 AD Ever since Julius Caesar had defeated Pompey at Pharsalus in 48 BC, the Julio-Claudian dynasty had ruled the Roman world, but each ruler had died a gruesome death:

- Caesar was assassinated in the Senate, bequeathing money and troops to his great-nephew Octavian, who on becoming emperor was known as
- Augustus, who (according to Roman historian Cassius Dio but disputed by others) was murdered by his wife with poisoned figs so that her son
- Tiberius would rule. Tiberius was smothered on orders from his nephew and successor
- Caligula, who was murdered by officers of his own guard, to be succeeded by his uncle
- Claudius, who was poisoned by his wife Agrippina to gain the title for her son
- Nero, who today was driven to suicide.

Only sixteen when he came to power in 54 AD, Nero had been tutored by Seneca and for a time had been a hard-working and generous ruler, with an interest in the arts. He inaugurated competitions in poetry and music and was an avid theatre-goer.

But within five years Nero had become the monster of legend, murdering at will, especially his own family. He had his mother cut down by his soldiers and his stepbrother poisoned. He had one wife suffocated in a hot vapour bath and killed another by kicking her in the stomach while she was pregnant. He also engaged in sickening sexual conduct with both sexes. (He had a young slave named Sporus castrated and then married him, taking him to bed like a wife. This prompted a Roman joke that the world would have been a better place had Nero's father chosen such a wife.) He began to give public performances of his music and appeared on the stage, even though the Roman aristocracy considered these to be scandalous breaches of civic dignity.

By the time Nero was in his late twenties, conspiracies were rising against him for his cruelty, extravagance and greed. The early ones were snuffed out (Nero's old tutor Seneca was also snuffed out on baseless suspicion of joining one of the plots), but in March 68 Gaius Julius Vindex, the Roman governor of Gaul, revolted. At first Nero simply scoffed: 'I have only to appear and sing to have peace once more in Gaul.' Indeed, the Roman army easily crushed the rebels, but not before Vindex had been joined by Servius Galba, the governor of Spain.

Soon other provinces joined Galba, and the Senate proclaimed him emperor while condemning Nero to a slave's death, nailed naked to a cross and flogged with rods. Then Nero's own Praetorian commander Nymphidius Sabinus abandoned him. Knowing he could no longer cling to power, the emperor tried to flee Rome, but his guards refused to help him, one asking derisively, 'Is it so terrible a thing to die?'

Nero then retreated to the imperial palace, to awake at midnight to find himself alone, deserted even by his slaves. Leaving in panic, by chance he encountered one of his freedmen, Phaon, in the street. Phaon smuggled the disguised emperor to his villa outside the city where the terrified fugitive hid in a dingy room. But soon soldiers were at the door, probably tipped off by Phaon, desperately trying to save his own skin.

Seeing no way out, Nero exclaimed at the last: '*Qualis artifex pereo!*' ('What an artist dies in me!') He then stabbed himself in the throat, but, botching the job, he had to call on his private secretary Epaphroditus to finish him off. According to Suetonius, he died 'with glazed eyes bulging from their sockets'. (Epaphroditus later became Emperor Domitian's secretary but was executed on the grounds that a freedman should never help in his master's suicide.)

When news of Nero's death reached Rome, the Senate posthumously declared him a public enemy, but the terrors of his reign would be replaced by the chaos of the 'Year of the Four Emperors', peace coming only with Vespasian in July 69 AD.

1899 Although outweighed by his opponent Jim Jeffries by 55 pounds, boxing heavyweight champion Bob Fitzsimmons confidently tells reporters: 'The bigger they come, the harder they fall.' But Jeffries lifts the title in an eleventh-round knockout.

10 June

'I am as innocent as the child unborn.'

1692 Today an innocent woman was hanged in Salem in colonial Massachusetts, the first fatality of the most notorious witch hunt in American history.

During the 17th century, condemnation of witches was widespread, bolstered by both Catholic and Protestant churches. (Didn't Exodus 22:18 instruct: 'Thou shalt not suffer a witch to live'?)

In January 1692, eleven-year-old Abigail Williams triggered a witch hunt in Salem when she and her nine-year-old cousin Betty Parris started having fits. Twisting themselves into strange positions and screaming with pain, they hurled things around the house, dashing about and diving under furniture. Then Ann Putnam, also eleven, claimed to have seen 'witches flying through the winter mist'. A local doctor claimed the girls' behaviour must come from supernatural causes, and the town authorities brought them in for questioning.

The girls named three easy targets – a homeless beggar woman, a local woman who had not attended church in three years, and Betty Parris's family's Caribbean slave, Tituba. All three denied being witches, but Betty's father – a minister – whipped Tituba until she confessed: 'The Devil came to me and bid me serve him.' All three women were jailed.

Now four more 'possessed' young girls joined the accusers, denouncing more women for casting spells. The concerned colony governor William Phips established a Special Court of Oyer and Terminer (to hear and to decide). The influential Puritan minister Cotton Mather urged the judges to accept 'spectral evidence', i.e. testimony by a witness that the accused's spectre had afflicted her.

The court's first case targeted Bridget Bishop, an unpopular woman of about sixty who criticised her neighbours and was slow to pay her bills. Moreover, she owned a tavern where drink was served on the Sabbath, dressed oddly and seemed indifferent to the Puritan standards of the village.

Two magistrates conducted a preliminary examination, in which five girls declared that Bishop's spectre had tormented them. 'What do you say now you see they charge you to your face?' a magistrate asked Bridget Bishop. 'I never did hurt them in my life', she replied. 'I did never see these persons before. I am as innocent as the child unborn.'

Bishop was brought to trial on 2 June. A local farmer swore that he had seen her transform herself into a cat, and another man testified that after an argument with Bishop, his pig had been bewitched. Two confessed witches claimed that she was one of them. Convinced by such unimpeachable testimony, the jury convicted her, and Chief Justice William Stoughton condemned her to death. She was hanged on Gallows Hill today, still protesting her innocence.

Bridget Bishop was only the first casualty of the Salem witch trials. By September twelve more women and six men had been executed. One, an 80-year-old farmer named Giles Corey, was subjected to *peine fort et dure* because he refused to enter a plea. A board was placed on his chest and then stones were piled upon it until he was slowly crushed to death over two agonising days. At least five others died in prison, and two dogs were executed as accomplices of witches. In all, about 400 people were tried for witchcraft; 50 confessed and the remainder were imprisoned. Not one was found innocent.

Salem's witch frenzy abated almost as soon as the last victim was hanged. In October the colony's governor prohibited further arrests, released many accused witches, and dissolved the special court. Five years later the General Court ordered a day of fasting and repentance, and in 1702 the trials were declared unlawful, their verdicts quashed.

Many hypotheses have been put forward to explain the mass hysteria that gripped Salem. Some blame the claustrophobic strictures of Puritan society, with its teaching that human failure was the work of the Devil. In 1976, however, Professor Linnda Caporael developed an intriguing theory that the bizarre behaviour of accusers and victims alike was caused by the ingestion of ergot, a fungus found in rye and other cereals. Eating ergot-contaminated foods can lead to spasms, vomiting, delusions and hallucinations. It thrives in warm, damp climates like that of the swampy meadows around Salem, where rye was grown.

1864 In the midst of the Civil War, Abraham Lincoln replies to a delegation from the National Union League about a second term: 'I have not permitted myself, gentlemen, to conclude that I am the best man in the country; but I am reminded, in this connection, of a story of an old Dutch farmer, who remarked to a companion once that it was not best to swap horses when crossing streams.'

11 June

'If a man shall take his brother's wife, it is an unclean thing.'

1509 Today at the church of the Friars Minor in Greenwich, seventeen days before his eighteenth birthday, Henry VIII married Catherine of Aragon, now 23. It was a dynastic union, as Catherine was the daughter of Spain's Catholic Monarchs, Isabella of Castile and Ferdinand of Aragon. She was also the aunt of an eight-year-old boy who one day would become the most powerful man in Europe as Holy Roman Emperor Charles V.

Catherine had come to England in 1501 to marry Henry's elder brother Arthur, but five months later Arthur was dead of 'sweating sickness' (probably consumption or pneumonia). Catherine remained in England, mostly at the bidding of her father-in-law Henry VII, who would have had to give back her 200,000-ducat dowry should she return to Spain. He also arranged for her to marry his younger son Henry when he came of age.

Although married for political and pecuniary reasons, for many years Henry and Catherine seemed content. The one shadow that darkened their days was Catherine's failure to bear a son and heir. In her first nine years of marriage, she suffered two miscarriages, two stillborn children and two more who survived only a few days. In 1516 she delivered a healthy baby, but it was not the son Henry so much desired but a girl (the future Queen Mary).

In March 1522, however, fate took a hand when Anne Boleyn was introduced at court. At first Henry paid her little attention (perhaps because her sister Mary had been his mistress), but by 1526 he was in hot pursuit.

Henry's infatuation with Anne came just when he was beginning to realise that Catherine would never bear him a son. And Henry had come to believe he had found the cause – God.

In perusing his Bible, he came across Leviticus XX, 21 with its admonition: 'If a man shall take his brother's wife, it is an unclean thing: he hath uncovered his brother's nakedness; they shall be childless.' Had not Catherine been married to Henry's brother Arthur? Catherine had not been childless, but, perhaps for a queen, having no son was the same thing. God was showing his hand, and it was up to Henry to act.

He tried to pack Catherine off to a nunnery, but she refused to go. Then he importuned Pope Clement VII for an annulment. Meanwhile Catherine swore that she and Arthur had never consummated their union and called on her *duenna* (chaperone) as witness to her claim. Furthermore, she argued, the Pope at the time of her marriage to Henry (Julius II) had granted dispensation.

At this time most of Europe was dominated by Catherine's nephew, Emperor Charles V, whose troops had sacked Rome and made Pope Clement virtually a prisoner in 1527. Fearful of antagonising Charles, Clement refused to grant Henry an annulment.

Henry's response was to abandon Catherine; on 14 July 1531 he left her at Windsor and never saw her again. She was stripped of her title as queen, becoming 'princess dowager' as Arthur's widow, and their daughter Mary was declared a bastard. In bitterness she wrote to Charles V: 'My tribulations are so great, my life so disturbed by the plans daily invented to further the king's wicked intention … it is enough to shorten ten lives, much more mine.'

But nothing would stop Henry. On 14 November 1532 he married Anne Boleyn in a secret ceremony, even though he was still legally married to Catherine.

Desperate but determined to have his will, Henry finally ended his marriage to Catherine in the only way he could – he rejected the authority of the Pope and declared himself supreme head of a new Church of England. He then had Archbishop of Canterbury Thomas Cranmer do what the Pope had refused. On 23 May 1533, Cranmer declared the marriage illegal. Five days later he confirmed Henry's marriage to Anne.

Stricken with cancer, Catherine died at Kimbolton Castle on 7 January 1536, three weeks after her 50th birthday. Knowing death to be approaching, she wrote one last letter to Henry, saying: 'I pardon you everything, and I wish to devoutly pray God that He will pardon you also.'

1727 George I dies from a stroke in Osnabrück. Dr Johnson later summed him up: 'George the First knew nothing, and desired to know nothing; did nothing, and desired to do nothing.'

12 June

'Act, and God will act.'

1429 Joan of Arc was certain she had been sent by God to restore to France lands taken by the English and their Burgundian allies and to see Dauphin Charles crowned king. Indeed, God seemed to be siding with the French; a month earlier they had broken the English siege of Orléans under Joan's devout leadership, and now they were approaching another English stronghold, the walled town of Jargeau, twelve miles to the east. Commanding the English garrison was the Duke of Suffolk, while the duc d'Alençon led the French, with Joan once more inspiring the troops.

When the French reached Jargeau's outskirts, Alençon vacillated. It was Joan who tipped the balance, urging: 'Do not hesitate to assault the English. God conducts our work. If I had not this assurance, I would rather guard sheep than expose myself to so great perils.' The French advanced, but an English sortie from the town drove them back until Joan raised her standard and rallied the French, forcing the English back inside the walls.

During the night, as the French bivouacked in the suburbs, Joan exhorted the defenders to capitulate, calling out: 'Surrender this place to the King of Heaven, and to the noble King Charles, and go away! Otherwise He will destroy you.' The next day her holy threat would be realised.

It was a Sunday, 12 June, and many French soldiers must have wondered what Joan would do – a month earlier at Orléans she had refused to do battle on a Sunday. But now she urged Alençon on, assuring him that God would grant a victory: 'Act, and God will act.' ('*Agissez et Dieu agira.*')

Alençon ordered his primitive cannons to bombard the town, but the English soon returned fire. The duke claimed Joan's miraculous warning saved his life: 'As I stood in a certain place, Joan said to me, "Step aside from there. If you do not, that machine [cannon] will kill you". I stepped aside, and a little later the machine that Joan had indicated killed the Sire de Lude in the very place from which I had withdrawn.'

After the attackers' guns had brought down one of Jargeau's towers, the French stormed the walls. Alençon reported that 'Joan was on a ladder, her standard in her hand. The ladder was struck, and Joan herself by a stone that hit her helmet. The blow knocked her to the ground, but she sprang up and called to the soldiers, "Friends, friends, up! Up! Our Lord has condemned the English. At this moment they are ours. Have good heart!" And the next instant Jargeau was taken.'

After this triumph, the French scored quick victories at Meung-sur-Loire and Beaugency, with Joan continually assuring Alençon that God favoured their cause. Soon there would be another proof.

The army headed north, although they were uncertain where the English forces were. In fact, the English were organising for battle near Patay. As French outriders rode forward, a stag bolted from the woods and ran straight through the English lines, causing a great outcry from the startled soldiers. Now that Providence had revealed the enemy's position, the main French force thundered forward, routing the foe.

The duc d'Alençon and Joan spent the next two weeks in Orléans, where King Charles dithered, uncertain of his next move. 'Have the trumpets sounded, and take horse', Joan said to Alençon. 'It is time to go to the noble King Charles, to put him on the road to his coronation at Reims.' Just a month later, on 17 July, Charles was duly crowned in Reims Cathedral, with Joan in attendance.

1987 At the Brandenburg Gate in Berlin, President Ronald Reagan tells the crowd: 'General Secretary Gorbachev, if you seek peace, if you seek prosperity for the Soviet Union and Eastern Europe, if you seek liberalisation: Come here to this gate! Mr Gorbachev, open this gate! Mr Gorbachev, tear down this wall!'

---

13 June

'To the strongest.'

323 BC Towards evening today in Nebuchadnezzar's palace in the fabled city of Babylon died Alexander the Great, still only 32. In thirteen years as King of Macedonia he changed the Western world for ever.

Born in Pella on 20 July 356 BC, Alexander showed early promise as a teenager by singlehandedly breaking a fiery stallion called Bucephalus, which he used for hunting and later for war. From thirteen to sixteen he was tutored by Aristotle.

When Alexander was twenty, his father, Philip II of Macedon, was assassinated by the captain of his bodyguards, for reasons that are clouded by history and still debated among scholars. Whatever the cause, Alexander was proclaimed king on the spot and inherited a priceless legacy, the finest army in the world.

Alexander began his reign by eliminating potential rivals, ordering the execution of his cousin, Amyntas and two Macedonian princes. He then began pacifying restive Greek states, culminating in the razing of Thebes to curb a rebellion.

In April 334 BC Alexander set out on his fabled conquests – first Turkey, the Levant, Egypt, Syria and back through modern-day Iraq and Iran, conquering the Persian Empire. And still onwards he went, into Parthia, skirting the southern edge of the Caspian Sea into today's Afghanistan and across the Hindu Kush into India and Pakistan, where on reaching the river Hyphasis, his troops refused to go further. He founded about twenty Alexandrias, including Kandahar (a contraction of Iskandahar) in Afghanistan and Alexandria in Egypt, where he was buried.

While in the Punjab Alexander had encountered an aged Hindu holy man named Calanus, who travelled with him on his return journey. But when the army reached Susa (in the far west of today's Iran), Calanus was collapsing from fatigue and illness and decided he would take his own life. He chose to die by fire, but just before his immolation he enigmatically said to Alexander, 'We shall meet in Babylon', foreseeing Alexander's death there later that year.

As always in antiquity, when a great man died young, there were stories of plots and murders. Plutarch tells us of the bad omens that foretold a coming calamity. Alexander's pet lion was kicked to death by a donkey, and ravens attacked each other over the walls of Babylon, one falling dead at the king's feet. After Alexander's death a story grew that conspirators had given him poisoned wine. Feeling as if 'an arrow had struck him in the liver', he tried to throw up the poison by forcing a feather down his throat, but the feather, too, had been poisoned, compounding the original dose. Modern historians are sceptical, most believing that, already weakened by alcohol, Alexander was finally consumed by malaria or typhoid fever.

Alexander died without an heir, his only son born posthumously and therefore with no real chance to inherit his father's empire, but that would not have mattered to the great conqueror. When asked to whom he left his empire, he answered: 'To the strongest.'

Nonetheless, Alexander did leave behind two dynasties, not in Greece but in the Middle East, and not of his own blood but through two of his generals who had been his boyhood companions.

The first was Seleucus, who took control of Syria and Iran to form the Seleucid Empire, which lasted for 240 years. The other was Ptolemy, who became King of Egypt. His family ruled for 293 years until his descendant Cleopatra clasped an asp to her bosom in 30 BC.

Shortly before he died Alexander ordered all Greeks to worship him as a god, which he sincerely believed he was. He had been well prepared for this role; his mother had told him that Zeus rather than King Philip was his real father, and when he conquered Egypt, he became Pharaoh and thus officially the son of the greatest Egyptian deity, Amon-ra. He thus established the idea of a god-king in Europe, a concept that reached full bloom in Rome three centuries later with the Emperor Augustus and eventually transformed itself into the divine right of kings.

1953 American baseball pitcher Satchel Paige publishes 'Six Rules for a Long Life' in *Collier's* magazine, of which number 6 is: 'Don't look back. Something might be gaining on you.'

---

14 June

'God will not suffer rebels to prosper, or this cause to be overthrown.'

1645 Almost twenty years earlier, Britain's Charles I had rebuffed Parliament's attempts to rein him in by announcing: 'Princes are not bound to give an account of their actions but to God alone.' Today, after three years of civil war, he still retained his dogged belief in the Divine Right of Kings and was certain that God would bring him righteous victory as he faced a superior Parliamentarian army at Naseby.

So far in the war, neither the king nor his prime opponents, Sir Thomas Fairfax and Oliver Cromwell, had gained any clear military advantage, but by the spring of 1645 perhaps God was showing his hand. In May the Royalists had driven the enemy from the Roundhead stronghold at Leicester, and in June they had forced Fairfax to lift the siege of the Royalist capital at Oxford.

But now Fairfax and Cromwell, with an army of 6,500 horse and 7,000 foot, were heading north from Oxford to seek out Charles's smaller force. Many Royalists felt that they should turn further north to take on the rebellious Scots or strike against the unprotected

Parliamentarian heartland of the eastern counties, but instead, with only 7,500 cavalry and infantry, Charles overruled any dissention and chose to meet the Roundheads head-on. The battle would take place near Naseby in Northamptonshire, some 50 miles from Oxford. Confident that heavenly favour would bring victory, he told his cavalry commander, Prince Rupert of the Rhine: 'God will not suffer rebels to prosper, or this cause to be overthrown.'

By ten o'clock an early mist had cleared, and Rupert opened the battle with a charge against the Roundhead cavalry. Although the attack was successful, Rupert's undisciplined men rode on to plunder the enemy baggage wagons, leaving the Royalist infantry open to attack from the enemy's superior force. Assaulted by Parliamentarian cavalry on both flanks while fighting Roundhead infantry in front, Charles's army started to disintegrate. In a futile gesture, Charles prepared to charge the enemy cavalry but was held back by one of his own generals, a Scottish nobleman, the Earl of Carnwath, who seized his bridle, swore at him and said: 'Would you go upon your death?' Seeing the king hesitate, the bulk of the Royalist infantry surrendered. In all, about 4,500 – mostly infantry – were taken, including 500 officers, and about a thousand were slain. The Parliamentary army lost 400 killed or wounded. In the aftermath Parliamentarian troops also hacked to death at least 100 women camp-followers.

Naseby was the pivotal battle of the English Civil War. Charles's army had been shattered, while the Parliamentarian New Model Army had been tested in blood and won. On 10 July Fairfax and Cromwell scored another crushing victory at Langport in Somerset, destroying the last army available to the Royalists. In May the next year Charles sought shelter with a Presbyterian Scottish army, but he was eventually handed over to the English Parliament. The so-called Second English Civil War was fought in 1648, but it was really a series of failed Royalist and Scottish uprisings against Parliamentarian rule. Right up to the end Charles believed in his God-given right to rule, and he must have been sorely disappointed that Providence had not intervened on the battlefield – and perhaps even more so when he was executed on 30 January 1649.

1658 After French general Viscount Henri de Turenne defeats a Spanish force reinforced by a contingent of English commanded by the Duke of York (the future James II) at the Battle of the Dunes, he sends Louis XIV his famously terse report: 'The enemy came, was beaten, I am tired, good night.'

* **1801** American traitor Benedict Arnold dies in London; shortly before his death he once more dons his American uniform, exclaiming: 'Let me die in this old uniform in which I fought my battles for freedom. May God forgive me for putting on any other.'

15 June

'It constitutes an insult to the Holy See, a serious weakening of the royal power, a disgrace to the English nation, a danger to all Christendom.'

1215 With this ringing denunciation, Pope Innocent III utterly condemned King John of England's new pledge to his rebellious barons. It was, said the Pope, 'a shameful and demeaning agreement, forced upon the king by violence and fear'. The agreement in question had indeed been forced upon the king; it is called the Magna Carta.

During his sixteen years on the throne, John had alienated his barons by excessive taxation and exacerbated the situation by losing his possessions in Normandy. He had also infuriated Pope Innocent by refusing to accept his nominee Stephen Langton as Archbishop of Canterbury, leading to the Pope's placing all of England under interdict. When interdict failed to bring John to heel, the Pope excommunicated him.

Unfortunately for John, the Pope was not his only adversary; the French king Philip (II) Augustus was now threatening to invade England, with the Pope's encouragement. Finally, in May 1213 John yielded, accepting Langton as Archbishop and recognising the Pope as his feudal lord.

Langton now returned to England from exile in Burgundy, but John almost immediately violated his oath to repeal unjust laws and restore some of the barons' privileges (or liberties, as the barons would call them). So now the king was again faced with both rebellious barons and a defiant Archbishop of Canterbury, who provided moral leadership.

In early 1215, the barons assembled at Stamford in Lincolnshire and renounced their feudal ties to the king. Then, forming an 'Army of God', they marched south. On 17 May they occupied London, whose citizens willingly opened its gates to them. It was time for King John to eat humble pie. He asked Langton to set up peace talks with the rebels.

It was agreed to meet at Runnymede, a meadow lying on the south bank of the Thames, just a little south-east of Windsor Castle. It was here on this day eight centuries ago that the rebel barons forced this shifty, feckless and untrustworthy monarch to put his Great Seal on the Magna Carta, the foundation of British liberty.

The Magna Carta strengthened the rights of the barons and all free men (but did nothing for the serfs), and restricted the use of capricious power by the king, establishing the principle of the ruler's responsibility towards his subjects.

The most famous clause is number 39, which reads: 'No free man shall be taken, or imprisoned, or dispossessed, or outlawed, or banished, or in any way injured, nor will we go upon him, nor send upon him, except by the legal judgement of his peers, or by the law of the land.' It thus forced the king to follow legal procedures and guaranteed all citizens equal access to the courts. Other clauses protected Church rights and made new taxation contingent on baronial consent. The barons agreed to surrender London and to disband their army, but in return there would be a council of 25 nobles who would make sure that John lived up to his promises.

But as soon as the barons were headed for home, King John urgently appealed to Pope Innocent. The Pope – now firmly on John's side since he was his feudal master and England a 'papal territory' – declared the Magna Carta to be 'illegal and unjust' and excommunicated the rebels.

This excommunication – and John's obdurate refusal to abide by his sealed agreement – sparked the Barons' War, in which the future Louis VIII of France joined forces with the rebels and invaded England. During this conflict, Pope Innocent died on 16 July 1216, followed by John two months later, and the barons began to see Louis more as a threat than an ally, and the war petered out.

The following year the Magna Carta was reinstated to form the basis for future governments. It was modified over the centuries, as many of its original provisions became outdated or irrelevant. But it remains today a symbol against oppression and of freedom under the law.

1381 Fourteen-year-old Richard II faces Wat Tyler and disperses the mob at Smithfield during the Peasants' Revolt; when the revolt is finally crushed, he tells the peasants: 'Villeins [serfs tied to the land] you are and villeins ye shall remain.' * **1877** Lord Salisbury in a letter to Lord Lytton: 'No lesson seems to be so deeply inculcated by the experience of life as that you never should trust experts. If you believe the doctors, nothing is wholesome: if you believe the theologians, nothing is innocent: if you believe the soldiers, nothing is safe. They all require to have their strong wine diluted by a very large admixture of insipid common sense.'

16 June

*'The Roman Pontiff cannot and ought not
to reconcile himself or agree with, progress,
liberalism and modern civilisation.'*

1846 When wisps of white smoke drifted from the Vatican chimney on this sultry day in June, the waiting crowds knew that, through his cardinals, God had chosen another pope. The new pontiff was Giovanni Mastai-Ferretti, formerly Archbishop of Imola and now enthroned as Pius IX.

Pius was a sincere man of some sophistication, with a deep sense of humanity, a sharp intelligence and a disarming appearance of humility, although legend has it that he had the 'evil eye', the power to injure people just by looking at them. In consequence villagers would hide their children when he rode through Italy.

Initially somewhat of an ecclesiastical liberal, Pius became pope at a time when the papacy was under sharp attack on both spiritual and temporal grounds.

The revolutions of 1848 across Europe terrified him, turning him ever more conservative in his views. Then came a direct threat to the temporal power of the papacy as Italy struggled to unify itself. The Papal States at its centre blocked the creation of a single Italian state.

Pius could not imagine the papacy depending on spiritual power alone and was aghast at the idea of the Church losing its lands and secular authority. During the Risorgimento he dispatched the Papal Army to defend the papal territories, boasting: 'Give me an army saying the Rosary and I will conquer the world.' On 18 September 1860, however, his soldiers were brushed aside at Castelfidardo, in the last battle they ever fought.

From this point Pius turned his back on all progress. When Darwin published *On the Origin of Species* in 1859, he called Darwinism 'repugnant at once to history, to the tradition of all people, to exact science, to observed facts, and even to reason itself'. He also insisted that the US Constitution 'has not the right to leave every man free to profess and embrace whatever religion he may desire'.

In 1864 Pius published his doggedly reactionary *Syllabus*. Here, among 80 'principal errors of our times', came his assertion that 'the Roman Pontiff cannot and ought not to reconcile himself or agree with, progress, liberalism and modern civilisation'.

Pius is also associated with two of Catholicism's most contentious doctrines, those of the Immaculate Conception and of Papal Infallibility, both of which were defined and accepted as Church doctrine during his pontificate.

In spite of his refusal to compromise (or perhaps because of it), in the end Pius lost everything he valued most. When King Vittorio Emanuele's troops marched into Rome in 1870, the Papal States were incorporated into the Kingdom of Italy and the Papal Army was disbanded. After this, he was referred to (chiefly by himself) as the 'Prisoner of the Vatican'.

Pius IX soldiered on until he died in 1878. By that time his popularity was so low that a mob attacked his funeral procession and attempted to throw his body into the Tiber. His pontificate of 31 years, seven months and 23 days is the longest in all the twenty centuries of Church history. Perhaps as a sort of long-service award, in 2000 Pope John Paul II beatified him.

1858 Abraham Lincoln accepts the Republican nomination for the US Senate in Springfield, Illinois: '"A house divided against itself cannot stand." I believe this government cannot endure, permanently half slave and half free. I do not expect the Union to be dissolved – I do not expect the house to fall – but I do expect it will cease to be divided. It will become all one thing or all the other.'

---

17 June

'A teardrop on the face of eternity'

1631 Today India's great Mughal emperor Shah Jahan was leading a punitive raid on rebellious princes in the Deccan Plateau in central India when his army camped for the night in Burhanpur, a small city 300 miles north-east of Mumbai. With him was his heavily pregnant wife, Mumtaz Mahal, still beautiful at 37 despite bearing thirteen children during nineteen years of marriage.

At sunset the royal doctor was summoned – the queen was going into labour. The emperor's bodyguards rushed to bring hot water, and a camel brought brush and wood for a fire. During the next hours sentries heard the soft cries of the queen and then at last the squall of a newborn child. But instead of exultation from the imperial enclosure, there was only stunned silence; Mumtaz Mahal, the 'Chosen One of the Palace' and most beloved of the emperor, had died.

Although Shah Jahan had two other wives, his marriage to Mumtaz Mahal had been a true love match. According to the official court chronicler, the relationship with his other wives 'had nothing more than the status of marriage. The intimacy, deep affection, attention and favour which His Majesty had for [Mumtaz Mahal] exceeded by a thousand times what he felt for any other.'

Mumtaz Mahal played a crucial supporting role as the emperor's advisor and was his inseparable companion, accompanying him when he travelled around his empire, even on military operations. Together they established a brilliant court of splendid display and oriental grandeur.

The emperor was so stricken by grief that his hair and beard turned white in only a few months and he went into secluded mourning for a year. When he appeared again, he set out to build a monument to eternal love in her honour. Mumtaz Mahal had been buried in Burhanpur, but her body was disinterred and transported in a golden casket back to Shah Jahan's capital at Agra. There, on the banks of the Yamuna River, construction began on the most beautiful mausoleum in history.

Requisitioning over 1,000 elephants for transport, Shah Jahan had white marble brought from the quarries of Nagaur, 300 miles away, and other materials from all over India and Asia. More than 20,000 workers laboured for 21 years to build the mausoleum, at the staggering cost of 32 million rupees, finally completing it in 1652. Legend has it, probably apocryphal, that Shah Jahan was so enamoured of its splendour that he had the thumbs of all 20,000 workers cut off to prevent them from ever creating another building so beautiful. The emperor called the tomb the Taj Mahal, a shortened version of his wife's name. Almost three centuries later, the Indian writer Rabindranath Tagore termed this memorial to love and death 'a teardrop on the face of eternity'.

Five years after the Taj Mahal was finished, Shah Jahan fell ill, igniting a power struggle among his sons. His son Aurangzeb defeated and killed his eldest brother and, on Shah Jahan's unexpected recovery, locked him away in the Agra Fort, within sight of the beautiful mausoleum.

For the eight years that remained to him Shah Jahan lived in opulent confinement in his fortress prison, wistfully gazing at the magnificent monument he had constructed for Mumtaz Mahal. When he died his body was laid in the vault below the building alongside that of his adored wife.

> **1719** Just before dying, British playwright and politician Joseph Addison sends for his wastrel stepson Lord Warwick to witness how a Christian man meets death: 'See in what peace a Christian can die.'

18 June

'No nation has friends, only interests.'

1940 The situation in Europe was dire. Despite the 'miracle at Dunkirk', British losses totalled 68,000 while the French had suffered 300,000 during the short course of the war. On 10 June the French government fled Paris, on the 14th the city fell and on the 15th Marshal Pétain took over as premier.

But British Prime Minister Winston Churchill had chosen today – the anniversary of the Battle of Waterloo – to address the House of Commons, concluding: 'Let us therefore brace ourselves to our duties, and so bear ourselves that, if the British Empire and its Commonwealth last for a thousand years, men will still say, "This was their finest hour."'

Few noticed that the same evening an obscure French brigadier general named Charles de Gaulle gave a speech aimed at his own countrymen.

The previous day a British plane had flown de Gaulle to London, and Churchill had put the BBC at his disposal. As de Gaulle later wrote, in a rare moment of gratitude: 'Shipwrecked and desolate on the shores of England, what could I have done without his assistance?'

On 18 June the French government asked Germany for an armistice, and at six o'clock that evening de Gaulle addressed his nation (in French):

> This [Vichy] government, alleging the defeat of our armies, agreed with the enemy to stop the fight. But has the last word been said? Must hope disappear? Is defeat final? No!
>
> Because France is not alone! … This war is not limited to the unfortunate territory of our country. This war was not decided by the battle of France. This war is a world war. The fate of the world is here.
>
> I, General de Gaulle … invite the French officers and soldiers, [and] the engineers and the workers in the armaments industries who are on British territory, to get in touch with me … Whatever

happens, the flame of the French resistance must not be extinguished and will not be extinguished.

De Gaulle also placed posters around London urging Frenchmen to join him, with the optimistic line: '*La France a perdu une bataille, mais la France n'a pas perdu la guerre.*' ('France has lost a battle, but France has not lost the war.') However, of the 10,000 French in Britain, only 300 volunteered, and of the 100,000 soldiers on British soil, only 7,000 joined de Gaulle, the rest returning to France, quickly to be interned.

But de Gaulle's speech gave a spark of hope to the people of France and solidified him as their leader in exile – so much so that he was condemned to death for treason in Vichy France.

De Gaulle's relations with British and American leaders were frosty. He was the self-proclaimed leader in exile of a defeated nation but saw himself as equal to Roosevelt, Churchill and Stalin. Roosevelt excluded him from the strategic meetings at Tehran, Cairo and Yalta, for which de Gaulle bore a grudge for the rest of his life. Churchill derisively observed: 'He looks like a female llama who has just been surprised in her bath.' Harry Truman was more direct: 'I don't like the son of a bitch.'

De Gaulle considered himself the embodiment of France, once remarking: 'When I want to know what France thinks, I ask myself.' On one occasion he told Churchill that the French people thought he was a reincarnation of Joan of Arc, to which Churchill rejoined that the English had had to burn the last one.

When taken to task for his hauteur toward friendly powers, de Gaulle loftily replied: 'No nation has friends, only interests.' Despite the acrimony, he persevered. In September 1941 he formed the Free French National Council and guided France's Resistance. Eight days after D-Day he went to France and in August entered Paris as liberator, to become head of the government in November. Although he abruptly resigned after two months, in June 1958 he was recalled from retirement to become president. To this day most of his compatriots consider him the greatest Frenchman since Napoleon.

1815 During the Battle of Waterloo the French Guard commander Pierre de Cambronne answers a call to yield with: '*La Garde meurt, mais ne se rend pas.*' ('The Guard dies but never surrenders.') After the battle Cambronne denies the comment, claiming he made only the one-word reply, '*Merde!*' – the word since known to the French as '*le mot de Cambronne*'. The next day Wellington writes to Lady Frances Shelley: 'Nothing except a battle lost can be half as melancholy as a battle won.' * **1877** After seeing James Whistler's 'Nocturne in Black and Gold', John Ruskin writes: 'I have seen, and heard, much Cockney impudence before now; but never expected to hear a coxcomb ask two hundred guineas for flinging a pot of paint in the public's face.'

19 June

'May my blood put an end to the misfortunes of my new homeland!'

1867 On the Cerro de las Campanas in Santiago de Querétaro in central Mexico stands the Emperor Maximilian Memorial Chapel, raised in memory of the man who was executed there on this day. A three-minute walk away is a statue of Benito Juárez, once Mexico's president and the man who had him shot.

Maximilian von Habsburg was the younger brother of Austrian Emperor Franz Joseph. A well-meaning, likable lightweight, he had been persuaded by Mexican reactionaries, his ambitious wife Charlotte and French Emperor Napoleon III to accept the imperial crown of Mexico, a country mired in a ferocious civil war between extreme reactionaries backed by the Church and anti-clerical republicans. Napoleon had chosen Maximilian for his Habsburg pedigree, but another reason might have been that Maximilian was (probably falsely) rumoured to be the fruit of his mother's extramarital affair with Napoleon's cousin, the first Napoleon's son, the Duke of Reichstadt.

Napoleon had invaded Mexico in 1861 for the putative reason of collecting the debts Mexico owed to France, but his real ambition was to establish French dominance in Latin America. His timing had been ideal since the Civil War precluded American armed intervention to back up the Monroe Doctrine, which banned European powers from intervening in the western hemisphere. By 1863 the French had captured Mexico City and chased the country's president, Benito Juárez, into exile. Maximilian set sail the next year.

Maximilian knew that Mexico was a priest-ridden society of the extreme right, with few civil liberties, no religious freedom and a system of peonage that enslaved most of the peasants, but he intended to impose a 'liberal dictatorship', restore order and stop the civil war.

He learned Spanish and made himself as Mexican as possible, ignoring that his government was held in power solely by a French army.

Maximilian tried to govern fairly; he established religious freedom, reduced working hours and banned corporal punishment and child labour, but he was financially incompetent, almost tripling Mexico's debt, while the civil war continued unabated. To curb the insurgents, in October 1865 he issued the infamous Black Decree that permitted immediate execution of captured 'rebels'. Over 11,000 of Juárez's supporters were summarily shot.

In April 1865 the American Civil War ended, and within a year an American army was massed on the Rio Grande, causing Napoleon III to order his troops to sail for home. Maximilian was left with a ragtag force of Austrians, Belgians and a few die-hard Mexican reactionaries. He vacillated on whether to abdicate but was dissuaded by his wife, his mother and his ultra-conservative ministers. He took personal charge of the army and fought bravely but was soon besieged, starved and finally betrayed and captured at Santiago de Querétaro, when one of his colonels allowed a republican column to enter the city. At a military show trial he was sentenced to death. Despite strong protests from Austria, France and Great Britain – and petitions from liberals like Victor Hugo and Garibaldi – Juárez confirmed the sentence.

At dawn this morning Maximilian carefully dressed in a white shirt, dark trousers and a long black frock coat and then mounted a carriage accompanied by a priest and guards and headed for the Cerro de las Campanas. There, as a band bizarrely played his favourite song, 'La Paloma', he and two faithful generals were placed in front of a rough adobe wall facing three squads of seven soldiers shouldering rifles. After giving each soldier a gold coin not to shoot him in the head so that his mother could see his face, he addressed his executioners: 'I will die for a just cause, that of the independence and freedom of Mexico. May my blood put an end to the misfortunes of my new homeland! Viva México!'

Just 34, Maximilian had been Emperor of Mexico for three years and nine days. Napoleon III waxed philosophical about his Mexican adventure: 'God did not want it; let us respect His decrees.' Back in Austria there was mourning, and from then on, the Imperial Navy would never play 'La Paloma'.

1879 American Civil War General William Sherman at the Michigan Military Academy: 'I am sick and tired of war. Its glory is all moonshine … War is hell.'

---

20 June

'It will touch every sailor's heart to have a girl queen to fight for.'

1837 Today one of Britain's least remembered monarchs died after seven years as king. He was William IV, known mostly as Queen Victoria's uncle and predecessor.

William was George III's third son and never expected to become king. He joined the navy at thirteen, fought at Cape St Vincent, became a firm friend of Horatio Nelson and left after twelve years' service.

At 26 William set up house with Dora Jordan, a beautiful and successful actress/courtesan four years older. Dora had already borne four illegitimate children by two different men; during the 21 years she lived with William she would bear ten more. (Former Prime Minister David Cameron is a great-great-great-great-great-grandson of this liaison.)

When William left Dora in 1811, she blamed it on lack of money, but it may have been ambition. That year George III had relapsed into insanity and his first son, the future George IV, became regent. But both he and George's second son Frederick had long left their wives, and neither had children, making William the heir presumptive. But he could never be king with a courtesan mistress, and he came under pressure to find a wife and father a legitimate son to ensure the line of succession.

In 1818 he found one, Princess Adelaide of Saxe-Meiningen, when he was almost 53 and she half his age. They were a contented couple, but both their daughters died in infancy, and twin sons were stillborn. By the time George IV died and William inherited the throne, he was 64 and it was clear that he and Adelaide would not produce an heir. All eyes turned to his eleven-year-old niece Victoria who, barring a miracle or an accident, would become the nation's next monarch.

William was fond of Victoria, once commenting: 'It will touch every sailor's heart to have a girl queen to fight for. They'll be tattooing her face on their arms, and I'll be bound they'll think she was christened after Nelson's ship.' His only regret was that he rarely saw her because of her grasping mother, a German princess also named Victoria who had married William's younger brother Edward, Duke of Kent.

In 1818 the Kents had moved into Kensington Palace, where young Victoria was born. After Edward died in 1820, the duchess raised her daughter with an eye on building her own influence, position and bank account. She was extremely protective of Victoria and rarely came to Court because of the scandalous presence of William's illegitimate children, whom she snubbed. She thought William was a dissolute vulgarian and kept him and his niece apart whenever she could, even refusing to allow Victoria to attend his coronation.

The elder Victoria's airs of superiority and her quarantining of her daughter infuriated William. His one wish was to live long enough for Victoria to reach her majority and be free of her mother's control. It all came to a head during a banquet to celebrate William's 71st birthday. William warmly welcomed Victoria but turned upon her mother:

> I trust in God that my life may be spared for nine months longer, after which period, in the event of my death, no regency would take place. I should then have the satisfaction of leaving the royal authority to the personal exercise of that young lady [Victoria] ... not in the hands of a person now near me [Victoria's mother], who is surrounded by evil advisers and who is herself incompetent to act with propriety ... I have been insulted, grossly insulted, by that person, but I am determined to endure no longer a course of behaviour so disrespectful to me ... I have particularly to complain of the manner in which that young lady has been kept away from my Court ... she ought always to have been present, but I am fully resolved that this shall not happen again.

William had his wish. Victoria henceforth attended Court, and he died ten months later, 26 days after Victoria's eighteenth birthday. From this day she would reign for the next 63 and a half years.

---

451 AD After Attila the Hun boasts, 'Grass never grows again where my horse has trod', an alliance of Romans and Visigoths defeats him at the Battle of Châlons, Attila's only defeat. * **1791** Louis XVI and Marie Antoinette flee Paris, only to be caught at Varennes. The next day Louis protests: 'There is no longer a king in France.'

---

21 June

'For the days in which he was still able to speak or write, the fate of the whole Resistance hung on the courage of this one man.'

1943 Today nine Resistance leaders were secretly meeting in Caluire, a suburb of Lyon, to plan sabotage against France's German occupiers.

Unknown to them, one of their number, René Hardy, had been shadowed by the Gestapo – and now they pounced.

Among those arrested was a retired government functionary named Joseph Mercier. Hauled off to Montluc Prison in Lyon, he was unmasked as Jean Moulin, the chief of the Resistance in France.

In 1940 Moulin experienced his first brush with the Gestapo while a *préfet* in Chartres. After the Germans had caused extensive civilian casualties while bombarding the hamlet of La Taye, they demanded that Moulin verify that the deaths had been caused by French Senegalese soldiers. Moulin refused, was beaten up and imprisoned. There he tried to cut his throat with a piece of broken glass. He barely survived and was shortly released, but was left with a scar that he would hide under a scarf.

Later that year the Vichy government dismissed numerous 'unreliable' government officials, including Moulin, but before leaving his post he created false identification papers, using the name Joseph Mercier.

Mercier/Moulin now moved near Marseille and joined the Resistance, then a fractured conglomeration of differing and often competing groups, ranging from unreconstructed monarchists to fanatical communists. With a view to establishing an all-embracing single movement, in 1941 he used his false passport to travel to London via Lisbon where the Free French leader Charles de Gaulle ordered him to unify France's Resistance groups. On 2 January 1942 Moulin parachuted back into France.

According to the French writer (and Resistance hero) André Malraux: 'It was a time when, out in the countryside, we listened tensely to the barking of dogs in the depths of the night; a time when multi-coloured parachutes, laden with weapons and cigarettes, fell from the sky by the light of flares burning in forest clearings or on windswept plateaus; a time of cellars, and the desperate cries of the torture victims, their voices like those of children ... The great battle in the darkness had begun.'

Within a year Moulin had set up a radio link to London in the attic of a presbytery, begun the infiltration of public services and persuaded three prominent Resistance units – Combat, Libération and Francs-tireurs – to join forces.

In February 1943 Moulin returned to London. De Gaulle charged him with setting up the Conseil national de la Résistance that would bring five more Resistance groups into a unified front. On 21 March he again parachuted into France carrying a microfilm of his orders in the false bottom of a box of matches.

In May the next year Moulin called a secret meeting of principal Resistance leaders, and, despite intense bickering, managed to establish the Conseil, reporting to de Gaulle. But all the while the Gestapo were circling, looking for their prey.

Now came the fatal meeting in Caluire. Moulin was taken to prison and subjected to seventeen days of interrogation and torture, most of it carried out by the notorious 'Butcher of Lyon', Gestapo chief Klaus Barbie.

Moulin was brutally beaten, needles were jammed under his fingernails and his knuckles were crushed, but he remained silent. When he could hardly speak but before his hands were mangled, a Gestapo guard handed him writing materials. Moulin's response was to draw a caricature of his torturer.

Having failed to crack Moulin, Barbie sent him to Germany for further interrogation. He was placed on a train to Berlin, but when the train reached Metz on 8 July he died from the effects of his torture.

On 19 December 1964 – the twentieth anniversary of the liberation of France – Jean Moulin's ashes were formally transferred to the Pantheon in Paris, on the initiative of General de Gaulle. Addressing the hushed crowd was André Malraux, now France's Minister of Culture. In eulogising Moulin's achievements, he said: 'For the days in which he was still able to speak or write, the fate of the whole Resistance hung on the courage of this one man.'

---

217 BC Hannibal defeats the Romans at the Battle of Lake Trasimene, killing 15,000; Livy later summarises the fight: '*Pugna magna victim sumus.*' ('In a battle, a big one, the defeated were us!') * **1813** After a British/Portuguese army under Wellington defeats the French at the Battle of Vitoria, British soldiers plunder the abandoned French wagons; disgusted by this gross abandonment of discipline, Wellington writes in his dispatch: 'We have in the service the scum of the earth as common soldiers.'

---

22 June

'E pur si muove.'

1633 Today the Inquisition issued its verdict: Galileo Galilei was guilty of having 'believed and taught' the pernicious doctrines of Copernicus. The court declared that the great scientist was 'vehemently suspected by this Holy Office of heresy' because he 'held the doctrine (which is false and contrary to the Holy and Divine Scriptures) that the sun is the centre of the world, and that it does not move from east to west, and that the earth does move, and is not the centre of the world'.

Although Rome's implacable opposition to heliocentrism could be justified by Biblical references such as Ecclesiastes 1:5 ('And the sun rises and sets and returns to its place'), a more powerful reason was the steady pressure of militant Protestantism that was eroding Catholicism. The papacy was fighting back by reinforcing all its most traditional dogmas.

Almost a century previously Nicolaus Copernicus had published *On the Revolutions of the Celestial Spheres*, his seminal work on the heliocentric theory. In the early 17th century Galileo had based some of his own work on it, although it was anathema to the Church of Rome. In 1616, the Church ordered Galileo not to 'hold, teach, or defend in any manner' Copernicus' ideas, and at first he obeyed, although in private he said: 'I do not feel obliged to believe that the same God who has endowed us with sense, reason, and intellect has intended us to avoid their use.'

In 1632 Galileo published *Dialogo Sopra i Due Massimi Sistemi del Mondo, Tolemaico e Copernicano* (*Dialogue on the Two Great Systems of the World, Ptolemaic and Copernican*), comparing the two theories. In the book's preface he made it clear which should be believed, writing that he 'takes the Copernican side with a pure mathematical hypothesis'. Even worse, he wrote his unorthodox book in Italian rather than scholarly Latin, making it accessible to a wide audience of readers.

Since 1623 the Church had been led by the rich and aristocratic Pope Urban VIII, who had initially been both a supporter and personal friend of Galileo's, and the great scientist had once dedicated a book to him. But, under pressure from the Dominicans who were in charge of the Inquisition, in early 1633 Urban banned Galileo's new book and summoned him to Rome to abjure his work.

The trial began on 12 April, and a panel of Catholic theologians argued that Galileo's *Dialogo* taught the theory of Copernicus. After fierce interrogation and threats of torture, on this day Galileo was condemned to house arrest for the remainder of his life and to public and private penance for his sins.

After hearing his sentence, the 69-year-old scientist knelt before the tribunal and devoutly recanted 'the false opinion that the Sun is the centre of the world and immobile, and that the Earth is not the centre of the world and moves'. But as he rose from his knees, he muttered his celebrated denial: '*E pur si muove.*' ('And yet it does move.')

Galileo spent the remaining eight years of his life under house arrest in Arcetri on the outskirts of Florence, seeing only those visitors permitted by a watching Church. Even then, however, the great scientist could not be totally silenced, as he wrote one further book (this one on the less controversial subject of mechanics) which had to be published in Protestant Holland because of the papal ban on anything he had written or ever might write. Galileo's *Dialogo* remained on the Catholic Index of Forbidden Books until 1835.

1535 When Pope Paul III sends obdurate Bishop Fisher a cardinal's hat, Henry VIII swears: 'Mother of God! He shall never wear it on his shoulders, then; for I will leave him never a head to set it on!' Today, 23 days later, Fisher is decapitated on Tower Hill.

---

23 June

'Oh dear, I think I'm turning into a god.'

79 AD Not born to the purple but the son of a simple knight, Roman Emperor Vespasian was already 60 when he seized power. Known for his bluff, straightforward style and a sometimes coarse sense of humour, he had spent most of his life as a soldier, first coming to prominence in 43 AD during the Roman invasion of Britain. There he fought in thirty battles and subdued two enemy tribes, feats for which he was awarded *ornamenta triumphalia* (triumphal regalia).

Vespasian earned his greatest military renown while crushing the Jewish rebellion in Judea. He quashed resistance at places like Gabara and Jotapata, where, during the 47-day siege, 40,000 enemy were killed. (During this encounter an arrow wounded him in the foot.) He also destroyed the walled city of Jericho, after which he famously tested the buoyancy of the Dead Sea by throwing in some shackled prisoners to see if they would float (they did).

While Vespasian was besieging Jerusalem in June 68, the atrocious Nero had escaped execution by his own soldiers only by suicide, plunging Rome into the calamitous Year of the Four Emperors. The following January, Nero's successor Galba was brutally cut down in the Roman Forum by soldiers supporting Otho, but by April Otho was dead, another suicide after his defeat at Cremona by the army of the next claimant, Vitellius.

After only four months of power, Vitellius learnt that Vespasian's legions in the eastern provinces had acclaimed their general as emperor. Soon an army was marching towards Rome, although Vespasian himself remained in the east for another year. On 24 October 69 they crushed Vitellius' legions at Bedriacum, and in December, after furious fighting, they entered the capital. Vitellius hid himself in the janitor's quarters of the imperial palace, but the assaulting soldiers found him and frog-marched him to the Forum, where they slit his throat and threw his body into the Tiber. Now Vespasian was the only would-be emperor left standing, and the Roman Senate 'elected' him, probably saving the empire from dissolution.

Relaxed and down-to-earth, Vespasian dispensed with the usual bodyguard and mixed freely with Rome's citizens. He followed a practice of reconciliation, dispensing justice with mercy. According to the historian Suetonius (who was born the year Vespasian became emperor): 'No innocent party was ever punished during Vespasian's reign.'

After nearly ten years in power, Vespasian was nearing 70 when he caught a fever while visiting Campania. He then made matters worse by retreating to his summer residence near Reate (modern Rieti, 50 miles north-east of Rome) and bathing in cold water. Suspecting that the end was near, the old commander wryly referred to Rome's habit of deifying dead emperors with the remark: 'Oh dear, I think I'm turning into a god.' ('*Vae, puto deus fio.*')

Vespasian tried to soldier on with his imperial duties, but on this day he was seized with violent diarrhoea. Almost fainting, he struggled to remain on his feet, murmuring: 'An emperor should die standing.' ('*Decet imperatorem stantem mori.*') He then fell dead into the arms of his attendants.

During his reign, Vespasian had embarked on an ambitious recon-struction programme in a country torn by war. Now of course the Roman Empire is long gone, as are most of its buildings, but one of Vespasian's monuments is still with us, the Flavian Amphitheatre in Rome (Flavius was his original family name), which we call the Coliseum.

1789 When conservative factions want to close the National Assembly, the Marquis de Mirabeau responds: 'Go tell your master that we are here by the will of the people, and that we will only come out by the force of bayonets!' * **1961** Princeton University president Robert Goheen addresses graduating students: 'If you feel that you have both feet planted on level ground, then the university has failed you.'

24 June

'The Kingdom of France is too great for a woman to hold, by reason of the imbecility of her sex.'

1340 The problems all started in 1328 with the death of Charles IV. He was the last of three brothers who in turn had been king of France, as none could produce a male heir. When Charles died, his cousin Philippe VI took the throne, as there were simply no more brothers. There was a sister, Isabella, married to England's Edward II, but she was excluded by the Salic Law, which said that only males could inherit the throne.

Isabella's son Edward III himself conceded that 'the Kingdom of France is too great for a woman to hold, by reason of the imbecility of her sex'. But, claimed Edward, a woman could transmit inheritance, and therefore the crown of France should rightfully be his. Obviously, Philippe did not agree, and therein lie the origins of the Hundred Years' War.

During the 1330s France and England met in intermittent minor clashes, and the French raided English coastal towns, but the Hundred Years' War really began on this day when its first major battle took place at sea near the port of Sluys, north of Bruges. Although now silted up and forgotten, Sluys was then considered the best harbour in Europe. It was there that Philippe VI assembled his fleet of over 400 ships under the command of admirals Hugues Quiéret and Nicolas Béhuchet. The latter was notorious for having massacred English prisoners after the naval skirmish at Arnemuiden in 1338.

For his part, Edward ordered ships from all over England, totalling perhaps 300 sail, mostly small converted merchant vessels called cogs that were square-rigged and single-masted with sharp prows and sterns and steered by an oar or a rudder. Each had a crew of five or six, plus a fighting force of ten to fifteen archers and men-at-arms.

In 1340 Edward had himself ceremoniously crowned, formally assuming the title 'King of France and the French Royal Arms'. On 20 June he embarked on the cog *Thomas* at Ipswich and led his fleet across the Channel, being joined by more English ships on the Flanders coast. So confident was he of victory that he brought with him several ladies from his queen's household to enjoy the spectacle.

At about eleven o'clock this morning Edward launched his attack on the French fleet. The clash was essentially a land battle at sea, as the English would rain arrows down on French ships and then men-at-arms would board and engage in hand-to-hand fighting. Edward had a significant advantage in his archers, who were equipped with longbows and could fire at about twice the rate of the French crossbows.

The battle was fierce but one-sided, lasting into the evening. The English captured those enemy ships that were not destroyed in battle and inflicted over 20,000 casualties, including Admiral Quiéret, who was killed. There were only a few hundred English dead, but one was a lady of the queen's household.

It is said that the French commander Nicolas Béhuchet wounded King Edward during the fight. Either for that insult to the king's dignity or for having executed the English prisoners at Arnemuiden, Edward had Béhuchet strung up from the mast of his ship after the battle, despite his having surrendered and been taken for ransom.

After such a calamitous battle no one dared tell King Philippe the outcome. Finally his frightened courtiers pushed forward the court jester, who said: 'Oh, the cowardly English, the cowardly English!' Asked to explain, the jester continued: 'They did not jump overboard like our brave Frenchmen.'

Thus the English won the first real battle, although in the end they lost the war. The end, however, came 113 years later.

1941 Senator and future president Harry Truman: 'If we see that Germany is winning, we ought to help Russia and if Russia is winning, we ought to help Germany, and that way let them kill as many as possible.'

---

25 June

'Our response to the rulers will be dynamite, bomb, stiletto, dagger.'

1894 Of France's 25 presidents from Louis-Napoléon Bonaparte through Emmanuel Macron, three have been slain while in office, but only two were murdered. The first was Marie François Sadi Carnot, who died just before one in the morning today from an assassin's stab wound.

The previous evening Sadi Carnot had just delivered a speech in Lyon and was leaving in an open carriage when a twenty-year-old Italian anarchist named Sante Geronimo Caserio struck. As Caserio boasted at his trial: 'I heard the "Marseillaise" and the cries of "Vive Carnot!" I saw the cavalry come up. I understood that the moment had come and I held myself ready. On seeing the President's carriage I drew my dagger and threw away the sheath. Then, when the carriage was passing close by me, I sprang forward to the step, supported myself by resting my left hand on the carriage, and with my right hand buried the dagger in the President's breast.' Rushed to hospital, Sadi Carnot died the next morning.

In court Caserio refused to deny or apologise, explaining: 'If governments can use rifles, shackles and prisons against us, to defend our lives, must we anarchists have to stay locked up at home? No. On the contrary, our response to the rulers will be dynamite, bomb, stiletto, dagger. In short, we must do everything possible to destroy the bourgeoisie and the government.' He was guillotined seven weeks later, while Sadi Carnot was given an elaborate funeral in the Panthéon.

The most recent French president to die at the hands of an assassin was Paul Doumer, already 74 when he was elected in June 1931. Eleven months later, while he was at a book fair in Paris, an unhinged Russian émigré shot him three times at the base of the skull and in the right armpit because he thought that France had failed to support the White Movement in Russia against Bolshevism. This assassin, too, was guillotined. (Had Doumer lived in today's world of vociferous feminism, he probably would have been shot anyway for saying: 'The wife is a blank page on which the husband writes as he pleases.' ('*La femme est une page blanche sur laquelle l'époux écrit à son gré.*'))

The other French president slain while in office was not murdered by an assassin but killed by his mistress. He was Félix Faure, who had been elected in 1895. Two years later, when he was 56, he met Marguerite Steinheil, then 28, and soon became her lover. In February 1899 Faure suffered a fatal stroke in the Élysée Palace while being pleasured by his paramour. A delicious scandal erupted, one Parisian newspaper headlining: 'Félix Faure has sacrificed too much to Venus!' From then on Le Tout-Paris referred to Marguerite as '*la pompe funèbre*', a wicked pun for those who speak French, and much too coarse to explain here.

1876 Chief Sitting Bull to his braves just before he annihilates Custer's cavalry at the Battle of Little Big Horn: 'This is a good day to die. Follow me!'

26 June

'Sic transit gloria mundi.'

1409 The Papal Schism – that unhappy period when several pretenders simultaneously claimed to be pope – had its roots in the 'Babylonian Captivity' of the papacy when the Holy See moved from Rome to Avignon in 1310. The Captivity ended in January 1377 when Gregory XI brought the papacy back to Rome, but Gregory died the next year, and Urban VI was elected to St Peter's throne. Stubborn and dictatorial, Urban saw vice in every corner and wildly accused his cardinals of lasciviousness and simony. But to a large group of French cardinals, his greatest sin was his refusal to return the papacy to Avignon after having gained their votes by his promise to do so.

At first the 'Avignon' cardinals tried to depose Urban, calling him 'anti-Christ, devil, apostate, tyrant, deceiver' and other condemnations, but he stubbornly clung to power, prompting the enraged cardinals to hold their own conclave. On 20 September 1378 they elected Robert of Geneva as their new pope and whisked him back to Avignon. Robert styled himself Clement VII, but the problem was, Urban VI remained pope in Rome, starting the Papal Schism.

The split that started with Clement and Urban would become the most serious disruption in the Church's history, with both Roman and Avignonese popes claiming supremacy. Finally, in 1409 King Charles VI of France helped to organise the Council of Pisa, where 22 cardinals and 80 bishops agreed that the two competing popes were 'makers of schism, notorious heretics, guilty of perjury and violation of solemn promises, and openly scandalising the universal Church'. The Holy See was declared vacant, and the cardinals chose a new pope, Cardinal Pietro Filargo, who took the name Alexander V.

On this day Alexander was crowned in the old St Peter's Basilica. His coronation began with a procession from the sacristy that stopped three times. At each halt the papal master of ceremonies would fall to his knees before the new pope, holding a silver reed that bore a scrap of smouldering flax. As the flax burned to smoke, he would say in a loud and mournful voice: '*Pater Sancte, sic transit gloria mundi!*' ('Holy

Father, thus passes the glory of the world!') This was the first time that the papal coronation ceremony had included this reminder of the ephemeral nature of life and earthly grandeur.

Warned during his coronation that 'thus passes the glory of the world', Alexander experienced it first-hand. Even after he was enthroned, both the current Roman pope and the Avignonese one still refused to abdicate, so instead of the single pope, now there were three. Furthermore, after a reign of a mere nine months, Alexander died – and when the Papal Schism finally ended in 1417, he was declared an antipope.

But '*Sic transit gloria mundi*' lived on for another 553 years, used in every papal coronation service through that of Paul VI in 1963. He was the last pope to be crowned; his successor John Paul I replaced the papal coronation with a papal inauguration, and, with a less regal pontiff, the reminder of the transience of worldly glory fell out of use.

1718 Tsarevich Alexei dies in prison from torture ordered by his father, Peter the Great, who has told him: 'I will cut you off like a gangrenous member.' * **1830** George IV dies; the next day *The Times* opines: 'There never was an individual less regretted by his fellow creatures than this deceased king. What eye has wept for him?' * **1963** President John F. Kennedy tells a West Berlin crowd: 'All free men, wherever they may live, are citizens of Berlin, and therefore, as a free man, I take pride in the words "*Ich bin ein Berliner!*"'

---

27 June

'Dinna fire till ye can see the whites of their e'en.'

1743 The Battle of Dettingen, fought today about eighteen miles east of Frankfurt, was part of the complicated War of the Austrian Succession, an eight-year conflict in which Prussia, France, Spain, Bavaria, Saxony and eventually Sweden battled against Austria, Britain, Hanover, the Dutch Republic, Saxony, Sardinia, and eventually Russia.

In late spring of 1743 a multi-national army with troops from Britain, Austria and Hanover was advancing along the Main valley against the French. In command was Britain's George II, the last time in history that a reigning monarch led a British army into battle. In charge of one British regiment was the cocksure Lieutenant

Colonel Sir Andrew Agnew of Lochnaw, a 55-year-old veteran of the Marlborough campaigns.

On 27 June Agnew was dining with his officers when he was informed that the French were preparing to attack. 'The loons!' he exclaimed, 'the scoundrels will never have the impudence to attack the Scots Fusiliers!' He then ordered his men to finish their dinner, assuring them that they would fight all the better for it. He continued eating until the enemy were so close that a stray shot knocked a bone from his hand.

Assembling his men on the battlefield, Agnew formed his Fusiliers in a square and held a steady rolling fire that kept off the advancing French infantry. But when the French cavalry joined the attack, the Scot employed an unorthodox tactic. Instead of standing fast and taking the charge head-on, he ordered the two centre companies to divide and fall back from the centre, making an alleyway into which the French cuirassiers galloped. As the enemy charged, Agnew gave his famous command: 'Dinna fire till ye can see the whites of their e'en.' He then added by way of encouragement: 'If ye dinna kill them they'll kill you.' The French, as they rode through this lane of soldiers, were subjected to a withering crossfire, as the Fusiliers aimed at the horses, bringing them down in heaps so that their riders could easily be bayonetted.

(Agnew's memorable 'whites of the eyes' order was repeated at least twice. During the Seven Years' War at Prague in 1757, Frederick the Great commanded his men: 'By push of bayonets; no firing till you see the whites of their eyes.' Much more famously (to Americans), in 1775 at the Battle of Bunker Hill, American General Israel Putnam ordered his men: 'Don't shoot until you can see the whites of their eyes.')

Despite the Fusiliers' heroics, the British were forced to pull back, but the allies counter-attacked, causing the enemy line to collapse, and won the battle.

After the battle, King George rode up to Agnew and said in jest: 'So, Sir Andrew, I hear the cuirassiers rode through your regiment today.' 'Ou, ay, yer Majestee', replied the colonel, 'but they didna gang back again.'

The War of the Austrian Succession dragged on for another five years, concluding *status quo ante bellum* except for a few small exchanges in territories. Six years after it finished, the Seven Years' War broke out, this time involving Prussia, Britain, Brunswick, Sweden, Saxony, France, Austria, Russia, Portugal and Spain.

> **1848** Cardinal Newman writes in a letter to Mrs William Froude: 'We can believe what we choose. We are answerable for what we choose to believe.'
> * **1936** President Franklin D. Roosevelt in a speech to the Democratic National Convention: 'There is a mysterious cycle in human events. To some generations much is given. Of other generations much is expected. This generation of Americans has a rendezvous with destiny.' * **1954** Winston Churchill, in a speech at White House: 'To jaw-jaw is always better than to war-war.'

28 June

'The empire on which the sun never sets.'

1519 The British like to think that the phrase above refers uniquely to the glories of their Victorian heyday, but it was first used in the 16th century – '*El imperio donde nunca se pone el sol*' – for the universal monarchy of the European and American dominions under Holy Roman Emperor Charles V. Today Charles's global empire received a mighty boost when he was chosen Holy Roman Emperor.

A contemporary describes Charles as 'a lonely figure, not prone to laughter', and his portraits depict his minor deformity, the famous 'Habsburg jaw', by showing him with his mouth slightly open. But Charles was also intelligent and ambitious, and now, at just nineteen, already rich and powerful. At six he had inherited the Netherlands from his father Philip the Handsome. Then at sixteen he gathered in the Kingdom of the Two Sicilies and Spain's new colonies in the Americas on the death of his grandfather, Ferdinand of Aragon, and was proclaimed king of Castile and Aragon jointly with his mother, Juana la Loca, but he would do the ruling, as she had gone mad.

Thus Charles was in pole position to become the new Holy Roman Emperor when his grandfather HRE Maximilian I passed away on 12 January 1519. But he was not the only candidate – France's François I, England's Henry VIII and Friedrich der Weise (Frederick the Wise), Elector of Saxony were also in the running. Now it was up to the seven Kurfürsten (Prince-electors) in Frankfurt to choose the winner.

Henry VIII never seriously pushed his candidacy, and Friedrich der Weise dropped out, even though he was backed by Pope Leo X. François I, however, had serious intent. He was six years older than Charles and had proven himself in battle with his triumph at Marignano.

A century and a half later, Louis XIV would claim that cannon were *Ultima Ratio Regum* (the last argument of kings), but Charles and François fought with a less violent weapon, money. François underlined the gentlemanly nature of their rivalry when, on hearing of Charles's candidacy, he sent him the message: 'Sire, we are both courting the same lady.'

To fund his campaign, François applied for massive loans from Europe's richest man, the Augsburg merchant and banker Jakob Fugger, but Fugger had backed Charles's grandfather Maximilian, who had made him a count, and preferred Charles for his German heritage. He refused François but lent Charles two-thirds of the 851,000 guilders he distributed to the Kurfürsten to make clear his superior virtues (about £120 million today). Thus it was that Charles became the 20th Holy Roman Emperor.

Charles never stopped accumulating territories and titles, including Tournai, Friesland, Utrecht and the northern Netherlands. Six modern European nations (Spain, Italy, Belgium, Austria, Luxembourg and Holland) claim him as a past sovereign. In the Americas, Cortés added Mexico in 1521 and Pizarro Peru in 1532.

Charles was truly an emperor without nationality, as he lived in and ruled more of Europe than anyone since the Romans. A tireless traveller, he spent half his life in Germany and the Low Countries, a third in Spain and over three years in Italy. As he said in his last public speech: 'My life has been one long journey.' Born near Ghent, Charles was also multilingual; brought up in French and Flemish, he learned Spanish, German, Italian and Basque (hence his celebrated if apocryphal quip: 'I speak Spanish to God, Italian to women, French to men and German to my horse.').

Charles sought to turn the many kingdoms under his rule into a vast, universal empire united in the Catholic faith, but, thwarted by Martin Luther and the Protestant Reformation, he became so worn out and disillusioned that he took the unprecedented step of relinquishing his titles one by one, Spain and the Low Countries to his cold-eyed son Philip II, Austria, Italy and the German provinces to his brother Ferdinand. He retired to the monastery of San Jerónimo at Yuste, in the loneliness of Extremadura in Spain, where, ridden by gout, saddened and sick, he died of malaria eighteen months later at the age of 58.

1762 After Catherine the Great of Russia and her lover Grigory Orlov mount a bloodless coup d'état against her husband, Tsar Peter III, Prussia's Frederick the Great says of Peter: 'He let himself be driven from the throne as a child is sent to bed.' * **1914** On their fourteenth wedding anniversary, Austrian Archduke Franz Ferdinand and his wife Sophie are murdered at Sarajevo; his last words: 'Sophie, Sophie, don't die – stay alive for our children.'

29 June

'Power tends to corrupt, and absolute power corrupts absolutely.'

1868 This famous dictum on the corrosive effects of power has been quoted in reference to dictators like Stalin, Hitler and Mao, but its origin is far less obvious – it refers to the pope of Rome.

On this day the pope in question, Pius IX, convoked the First Vatican Council. Its most important achievement was the passing of the First Dogmatic Constitution that defined the dogma of Papal Infallibility – that is, that the Pope is infallible in decisions on morals or faith, when speaking *ex cathedra*. It was a contentious declaration, but not the first from the 77-year-old pontiff.

Elected in June 1846, Pius was initially an ecclesiastical liberal, but in 1848 Europe exploded into revolution. Pius feared for his own safety, after his Interior Minister Pellegrino Rossi was assassinated on the steps of the Papal Chancellery on 15 November. The next day crowds filled Rome's streets, demanding a democratic government and social reforms. A week later Pius fled the Vatican disguised as an ordinary priest; he remained in exile in Gaeta until April 1850.

By the time of the First Vatican Council in 1868, Pius had become a stark conservative. He felt threatened by the march of civilisation and its implied threat to the Church and its authority, so he reacted by promulgating the famous decree *Pastor aeternus* that made the Pope's infallibility Church doctrine.

The idea of Papal Infallibility was hardly new; it had been around at least since the 11th century when Pope Gregory VII (Hildebrand) had declared: 'The Roman church has never erred, nor can it err until the end of time.' But at this council it became official Church dogma, albeit controversial.

One who objected was the British historian and writer, John Dalberg-Acton, 1st Baron Acton. A Catholic himself, Acton had travelled to Rome during the Council to lobby against it. Although unsuccessful, he brooded on the issue, and nineteen years later wrote to his friend Mandell Creighton, a Church of England bishop: 'I cannot accept your canon that we are to judge Pope and King unlike other men, with a favorable presumption that they did no wrong ... Power tends to corrupt, and absolute power corrupts absolutely. Great men are almost always bad men, even when they exercise influence and not authority.'

Despite objections from men like Acton, Pius was now deemed infallible in matters of faith, but he proved only too fallible in matters of politics. A year after *Pastor aeternus* was declared, Italian king Vittorio Emanuele's troops marched into Rome during the reunification of Italy. Although a plebiscite revealed that Roman citizens were overwhelmingly in favour of incorporating the city into the new nation, Pius flatly refused. He spent the rest of his life in the Vatican, rejecting all discussion with the Italian government, and died in 1878 at the ripe age of 85, still thinking of himself as a prisoner of the 'invading' Italians.

1963 The Profumo scandal; when told at the trial of Stephen Ward that Lord Astor had denied an affair or having even met her, Mandy Rice-Davies replies: 'Well, he would, wouldn't he?'

---

30 June

'If I am to be killed, let Adolf do it himself.'

1934 In February 1920 Adolf Hitler had taken over Munich's Hofbräuhaus to harangue 2,000 avid followers, but when hecklers disrupted his speech, he called in a crew of local thugs. Armed with rubber truncheons, they forcibly ejected the agitators.

These beer-hall brawlers had been battling leftists in the streets since the early days of the Weimar Republic. They referred to themselves as the Sturmabteilung (Assault Division) or SA and sported military uniforms featuring brown shirts, after the fashion of Mussolini's Blackshirts. By 1921 Hitler was using them to protect Nazi meetings while attacking those of the Social Democrats and Communists.

By the time Hitler became Chancellor in 1933, SA membership had increased to 2,000,000, twenty times the size of the German army, restricted as it was by the Treaty of Versailles. A year later it had reached 3,000,000.

In January 1931 Hitler had made his old friend Ernst Röhm SA Chief of Staff. A 43-year-old homosexual veteran with scars on his face from a combat wound, Röhm was so close to Hitler that he addressed him as *du* (the German familiar form of 'you') and called him by his first name, a privilege awarded to no other Nazi official.

Under Röhm's leadership, SA paramilitaries continued to attack Jews and intimidate anyone resisting Nazi rule. In a single month they fought in 400 street battles, causing 82 deaths.

By now, however, the ambitious Röhm began dreaming of absorbing the German army into the SA, with himself as commander. German generals were aghast, and industrialists, who had sided with Hitler, regarded the SA as plebeian rabble. Göring and Himmler, jealous of Röhm's power, whispered in Hitler's ear that Röhm was planning a coup. President Hindenburg told Hitler that if he did not rein in the SA he would declare martial law, but on 29 June 1934 the SA went on another bloody rampage in Munich.

Hitler ordered all SA leaders to Bad Wiessee, 30 miles south of Munich, and the next day flew into Munich at dawn. At the Bavarian Interior Ministry, he tore the epaulettes off the shirt of the Munich police chief for failing to keep order and had him shot. Now protected by the SS (Schutzstaffel – Protection Squad), Hitler then left for the Hanselbauer Hotel, where Röhm and his followers were staying.

The SS stormed the hotel while the SA leaders were still asleep and found one officer in bed with a trooper. Hitler had both taken outside and shot. The SS took Röhm and other SA leaders to Stadelheim Prison, where five SA generals and a colonel were given one-minute 'trials' and then executed by firing squad, but Röhm was held overnight.

On Hitler's orders, the next day two SS officers entered Röhm's cell and handed him a pistol loaded with a single bullet, telling him he had ten minutes to kill himself. Showing a trace of backbone at the last, Röhm answered: 'If I am to be killed, let Adolf do it himself.'

The officers returned after the designated ten minutes, only to find Röhm standing defiantly, his chest bared. Without a word they shot him dead.

Everywhere in Germany Hitler's enemies and rivals were gunned down, including his predecessor as Chancellor, Kurt von Schleicher, and his wife, and Gregor Strasser, formerly second only to Hitler in the Nazi political organisation. Gustav Kahr, the commissioner who had crushed Hitler's Beer Hall Putsch in 1923, was hacked to death with pickaxes. Nazi records say that 77 people were executed, but historians put the total much higher.

The German public and the army applauded this blood-soaked orgy – the 'Night of the Long Knives' – and President Hindenburg congratulated Hitler for 'nipping treason in the bud'. Even abroad it was extolled; on 2 July the *Daily Mail* opined approvingly: 'Hitler's love of Germany has triumphed over private friendships and fidelity to comrades who had stood shoulder to shoulder with him.'

On 13 July Hitler told an applauding Reichstag: 'I was responsible for the fate of the German people, and thereby I became the supreme judge of the German people. I gave the order to shoot the ringleaders in this treason.'

1793 During the French Revolution, the populist Club des Cordeliers passes a motion: 'That the owners will be invited ... to have painted on the frontage of their houses, in capital letters, these words: Unity, Indivisibility of the Republic, Freedom, Equality, Brotherhood or death.' * **2016** In her speech declaring her bid for the Conservative Party leadership, Theresa May makes the Delphic forecast: 'Brexit means Brexit.'

1 July

'Jerusalem! Jerusalem!'

1270 Louis IX of France was the ideal king of the Middle Ages – physically strong and of immense strength of character, he was an accomplished knight, fearless in battle, heroic in adversity, unbending when sure of the justice of his cause and as dedicated to the service of God as the most devoted of monks.

In 1248–49, when he was 34, Louis had led the Seventh Crusade, only to be captured near Damietta and ransomed for the colossal sum of 400,000 livres. But crusading was in his blood, and two decades later he was mulling another effort, this time to free Jerusalem from the Mamluks, the very people who, as slave soldiers, had captured him in 1249 and who had become masters of Egypt the following year.

While Louis was making plans, his brother, Charles of Anjou, King of the Two Sicilies, urged him to sail first to North Africa where one of Charles's vassals, the Bey of Tunis, was in revolt. Charles slyly suggested that the Bey might be ripe for conversion to Christianity, and Louis duly agreed to head for Tunis before taking his crusade to the Holy Land.

On 1 July 1270 Louis sailed from France, departing from a Mediterranean port he had ordered built 30 years before, the small walled town with the ominous name of Aigues-Mortes (derived from *aquae mortuae* – dead waters – after the surrounding saline marshland). The king had chosen the date with care, for on 1 July 1097 Christian forces had scored their first victory of the First Crusade at the Battle of Dorylaeum. What he forgot was that it was at the height of the African summer.

Seventeen days later Louis landed in Tunis. Initially his army gained some painless victories, but the blistering heat scourged his men, and soon plague appeared, first ravaging the army and then striking the king himself. Camped near the ruins of Carthage, Louis instructed his son and successor Philip (III) to take special care of the poor. When he died on 25 August, his last words were: 'Jerusalem! Jerusalem!'

Louis expired at the age of 56, having reigned for 43 years. His entrails were buried on the spot where he died (you can still visit the Tomb of Saint Louis there today), but his corpse was subjected to the process of *mos Teutonicus*, in which the body is dismembered and boiled in wine so that the flesh separates from the bones. His disjointed skeleton was brought back to France in one long funeral procession, with mourners lining the roads as it passed through Sicily (where his heart was enshrined in the Duomo di Monreale in Palermo) and along the Italian peninsula, over the Alps and on to Paris. This great king was entombed in the Basilique Saint-Denis just north of Paris, historic last resting place of the kings of France. (During the French Wars of Religion in the 16th century, his sepulchre was destroyed, but one finger was rescued and is still venerated at Saint-Denis.)

From the moment of his burial Louis was thought a saint and people prayed for miracles at his tomb. At the urging of his grandson Philip the Fair, Pope Boniface VIII canonised him in 1297, only 27 years after his death. He is the only French king ever declared a saint. Bizarrely, however, tradition among the local Tunisians denies that Louis fell victim to plague, claiming that he converted to Islam under the name of Sidi Bou Said and lived on for another quarter century, to die as a saint of Islam.

1916 After General Douglas Haig's Fourth Army loses 20,000 dead and 40,000 wounded on the first day of the Battle of the Somme, the greatest one-day loss ever sustained in British history, Haig complacently writes in his diary: 'The total casualties … cannot be considered severe in view of the numbers engaged, and the length of front attacked.' * **1943** Homosexual Dutch artist and resistance fighter Willem Arondeus is shot by a German firing squad. His last words are: 'Tell the people that homosexuals are no cowards!'

---

2 July

'We are here in Rome and here we will stay!'

1871 Ever since (they say) Romulus and Remus founded it on 21 April 753 BC, Rome had always been the capital – of a city state, of the Roman Kingdom, of the Roman Republic and of the Roman Empire. Then in 286 AD Emperor Diocletian moved the capital (of the Western empire) to Mediolanum, now Milan. But in June 1871, 1,585 years after Diocletian, Rome once again became a capital, and today the man who made it happen, King Vittorio Emanuele, at last entered the city of a united Italy.

In the mid-19th century, Italy was a hodgepodge of principalities and territories. Vittorio Emanuele was King of Sardinia (but governed from Turin), Austria ruled in Venice, dukedoms such as Tuscany, Modena and Parma were independent, and the Pope ran the Papal States.

The First Italian War of Independence (1848–49) was led by Vittorio Emanuele's father, Carlo Alberto, but he was defeated and abdicated in favour of his son. The first major progress towards Italian reunification came in June 1859, when Vittorio Emanuele, allied with France's Napoleon III, slugged it out with Franz Joseph of Austria at Solferino, a few miles from Lake Garda. All three monarchs were at the battle, which was unexpectedly bloody, but in the end, Austria was the loser. Franz Joseph was forced to cede Lombardy to Napoleon III, who immediately passed it on to Vittorio Emanuele. By the next year Austria had withdrawn her troops from most of Italy, except for Venetia.

The Risorgimento continued apace, led by Vittorio Emanuele but planned by his prime minister, Camillo Benso, conte di Cavour, the great architect of Italian reunification who played the French off against the Austrians, charmed the British and used Garibaldi to do much of the fighting.

In August 1859 Modena joined the embryonic Italian state, followed by Parma, and then Tuscany. On 17 March 1861 the Kingdom of Italy was officially proclaimed and Vittorio Emanuele promoted himself from King of Sardinia to King of Italy. Now without the support of Austrian troops, the papacy was strong-armed out of Bologna, whose citizens voted to join the new kingdom. In 1866 Austria was finally forced to cede Venetia, and that left only Rome, ruled by the defensive and reactionary Pope Pius IX.

Pius had been sheltering behind the power of France, but when Napoleon III was captured by Prussia at Sedan on 2 September 1870, he was left almost defenceless. Vittorio Emanuele sent an emissary with a face-saving proposal for peaceful annexation, but Pius flung the king's letter on the table, shouting: 'You are all a set of vipers, of whited sepulchres, and wanting in faith … but I tell you, you will never enter Rome!'

Now Vittorio Emanuele dispatched an army of 50,000 men under the command of General Raffaele Cadorna. When they reached Rome, they found the city defended by only 13,000 Papal soldiers. Although he knew his position was hopeless, in a histrionic gesture of the persecuted martyr, Pius ordered his men to fight. The next day – 20 September – after a three-hour cannonade that breached Rome's Aurelian Walls, Cadorna and his army entered the city through the

Porta Pia. The price for Pius' futile grandstanding was 68 unnecessary Italian and Papal deaths.

The following June, Italy's capital was officially transferred from Turin to Rome. Then on this day Vittorio Emanuele arrived as king of a united Italy, exclaiming: '*A Roma ci siamo et ci resteremo!*' ('We are here in Rome and here we will stay!')

By now the elderly Pius had sullenly retreated to the Vatican, refusing to recognise the new Italian state. He died on 7 February 1878. During his funeral procession a group of Romans screaming 'Long live Italy! Death to the Pope!' almost succeeded in throwing his coffin into the Tiber. Vittorio Emanuele, who had died a month earlier, was honoured with a fine equestrian statue in Rome's Piazza Venezia and the astounding Vittorio Emanuele monument, sometimes called 'The Wedding Cake' for its gaudy kitsch.

1932 Presidential candidate Franklin Roosevelt at the Chicago Convention: 'I pledge you – I pledge myself – to a new deal for the American people.' * **1937** As American aviatrix Amelia Earhart disappears over the Pacific while trying to fly around the world, she radios: 'KHAQQ calling Itasca. We must be on you but cannot see you but gas is running low … we are flying at 1,000 feet … one-half hour fuel and no landfall.' * **1961** Before dawn Ernest Hemingway shoots himself with his favourite shotgun in Ketchum, Idaho; his last words, spoken to his wife Mary the night before: 'Goodnight, my kitten.'

---

3 July

'*Who made you king?*'

987 AD Back in the 10th century, the western part of Charlemagne's empire, known as West Francia, covered most of today's France. It was a time of unusual chaos – Saracens regularly raided the Mediterranean coast while Normans plundered the Atlantic coast, sailing up rivers to burn cities and devastate the countryside. In addition, parts of the country were beset by plague.

To make matters worse, in 986 King Lothair of West Francia died, leaving the throne to his twenty-year-old son Louis (V). Although the great-great-great-great-great-grandson of Charlemagne, Louis was known as *le Fainéant* (the Do-Nothing); his most notable accomplishment during his thirteen-month reign was to be thrown from his horse and killed while hunting. Dying childless, he was the last of France's Carolingian kings, who had ruled since Pepin the Short (Charlemagne's father) was crowned in 751.

Thirteen days after Louis' death, France's most important nobles gathered at Senlis where Adalbéron, the Archbishop of Reims, extolled the most powerful among them, Duke Hugues Capet: 'He is most illustrious by his exploits, his nobility, his forces. The throne is not acquired by hereditary right; no one should be raised to it unless distinguished not only for nobility of birth, but for the goodness of his soul.' By unanimous vote Hugues was elected the new King of the Franks (*rex Francorum*). (All Capetian kings were titled King of the Franks until Philip (II) Augustus started calling himself King of France in about 1180.)

And so on this day Hugues Capet, wearing a purple coat interwoven with gold, was crowned in a fitting ceremony at Noyon. The only fly in the ointment was that he had been elected king rather than inheriting the throne.

Hugues Capet played a pivotal role in French history: he moved the capital to Paris and started the long consolidation that evolved into modern France. But he ruled for only nine years, most spent trying persuade his barons to forget Adalbéron's claim that 'the throne is not acquired by hereditary right'. On one occasion when Adalbert I, Count of Périgord, was besieging Tours, Hugues ordered him to cease. As Adalbert did not obey, Hugues wrote to him saying, 'Who made you count?' 'Who made you king?' replied Adalbert, a reminder that it was the dukes and counts who had elected him.

Acutely aware of this challenge to his dynastic rights, Hugues had his fifteen-year-old son Robert (II) crowned on 30 December 987, thus preventing the nobility from electing a new king on his death. This established the hereditary principle for the Capetian dynasty, and what a dynasty it turned out to be. The direct Capetians lasted 341 years with fifteen kings, before Charles IV died without a male heir on 1 February 1328.

On Charles IV's death, Philip VI started the reign of the House of Valois, a cadet branch of the Capetians. Philip's major claims to fame lie in starting the Hundred Years' War (along with England's Edward III) and commanding the French army at the disastrous Battle of Crécy. But the Valois would rule for 261 years.

On 13 December 1533 the Valois line of monarchs came to an end after the successive reigns of three weak, neurotic and childless brothers, François II, Charles IX and Henri III, when a deranged monk stabbed the last of these to death on 1 August 1589. This brought the House of Bourbon – yet another offshoot of the Capetians – to the throne, as Henri de Navarre became King Henri IV.

The Bourbons governed France until 1848, except for the interregnum of the French Revolution and the reign of Napoleon, bringing the total of French Capetian/Capetian-related kings to 32. Since the Bourbons were also kings of Spain from 1700 to the present (even under Franco, Spain was still officially a monarchy), Hugues Capet's dynasty can be said to have lasted in one way or another for over a thousand years and is still going strong.

1940 After the British sink most of the French fleet at Mers-el-Kébir, killing 1,250 French sailors, Charles de Gaulle speaks to his countrymen by radio: 'Come what may, even if for a time one of them is bowed under the yoke of the common foe, our two peoples – our two great peoples – are still linked together. Either they will both succumb or they will triumph side by side.'

---

4 July

'We must indeed all hang together, or, most assuredly, we shall all hang separately.'

1776 Today at the Pennsylvania State House in Philadelphia the world's oldest republic came into being, as the Second Continental Congress approved the Declaration of Independence.

Although the Declaration of Independence was in force, it was not actually signed by the thirteen states' delegates until 2 August. The first to sign was the President of the Continental Congress, the diminutive John Hancock of Massachusetts. There are two versions of his comments, both full of patriotic bravado:

'There, I guess King George will be able to read that.'

'There! John Bull can read my name without spectacles and may now double his reward of £500 for my head. That is my defiance.'

Hancock then urged all the delegates to sign immediately, saying: 'We must be unanimous, there must be no pulling different ways; we must all hang together.'

'Yes', replied Benjamin Franklin, 'we must indeed all hang together, or most assuredly we shall all hang separately.' Then the 55 other delegates added their signatures.

This seismic event of 4 July should be story enough for any date, but this one had a fascinating coda half a century later.

On 4 July 1826 the United States reached its 50th birthday, firm in democracy, independence and progress. Instead of the thirteen original states, there were now 24, including two west of the Mississippi. The population had quintupled to 12 million, the country was at peace and one of its great selfless servants, John Quincy Adams, was president.

It had been hoped that celebrations in Washington would be embellished by two of the nation's surviving founders, John Adams, second president and father of the current president, and Thomas Jefferson, America's third president and greatest political thinker. But Adams was 90, living quietly in Quincy, Massachusetts, while Jefferson at 83 had long since retired to Monticello, his estate in Virginia, so Washington had to celebrate without them.

It was only two days later that the news arrived: Jefferson had died quietly at one o'clock on the afternoon of 4 July, and John Adams followed him shortly before six. A poignant aside, among Adams's last words were: 'The country is safe. Jefferson still lives.'

John Quincy Adams interpreted this strange and solemn marking of America's 50th birthday as a 'visible and palpable' indication of divine favour to the two departed founders and to the nation they had helped to create. In a further strange sequel, on the same date five years later America's fifth president, James Monroe, died.

1917 Six days after American troops have arrived in France, General Charles Stanton visits the tomb of America's great Revolutionary ally, the Marquis de Lafayette, in the Cemetery of Picpus and says: '*Lafayette, nous voici!*' ('Lafayette, we are here!')

---

5 July

'Mad, bad and dangerous to know'

1813 The two lovers had embarked on a passionate affair the previous year, but by now he had tired of her obsessive pursuit. By chance they met this evening, at Lady Heathcote's ball in London. Approaching his table, she histrionically flourished a table knife, but he taunted her with amused disdain. The lady fled, humiliated, theatrically slashing at her wrist when some ladies tried to take the knife from her. The entire shoddy episode was reported in the press, and her lover contemptuously commented that she had 'performed ye dagger scene'.

She was Lady Caroline Lamb, 28 years old, tall and waiflike, with short, curly blonde hair and hazel eyes. Eight years earlier she had married the future prime minister William Lamb, Lord Melbourne. Her lover was George Gordon, Lord Byron.

Now 25, Byron had a year earlier published the first two cantos of *Childe Harold's Pilgrimage* and, as he later recalled, 'I awoke one morning and found myself famous'. Among those captivated by the poem's Romantic pessimism was Caroline. They were first introduced in March 1812, after which she wrote, 'That beautiful pale face is my fate', then famously described him in her diary as 'Mad, bad and dangerous to know'.

They were soon enmeshed in an affair that shocked London society. He insisted that she admit she loved him more than her husband and was jealous of her waltzing with other men since, with his club foot, he could not dance. She wrote him an endless stream of letters and dramatically offered to pawn her jewellery if he needed money (he was famously profligate).

But, as historian David Cecil observed: 'It was not Byron she cared for: it was his reputation, and still more the idea of herself in love with him. Beautiful, brilliant, seared with the pains of exotic passion, and the most lionised man in England, he was everything she had all her life been seeking.'

But to Byron, Caroline was a mad, passionate obsession, one that he abandoned when his desire was sated. Within months he was struggling to end the affair, but Caroline continued to pursue him, once coming to his apartments and trying to stab herself to show her desolation. By autumn the romance had irretrievably collapsed.

Byron once described Caroline as 'the cleverest, most agreeable, absurd, amiable, perplexing, dangerous, fascinating, little being', but now he brutally wrote: 'Correct your vanity which has become ridiculous – exert your caprices on others … and leave me in peace.' But she was still torn by jealousy and regrets, becoming so emaciated that Byron remarked that he was 'haunted by a skeleton'. Then in December 1812, she resolved to put the affair behind her and melodramatically burnt his letters in a bonfire while 'some village girls dressed in white capered around the flames in a ritual dance of triumph, and a page recited verses composed by Caroline for the occasion'.

During this endless drama, Lord Melbourne showed astonishing patience. He had concluded that Caroline and Byron were just silly poseurs, both pretending a passion that neither possessed.

During the first half of 1813 Caroline continued to send Byron letters while dramatising her grand emotions, but the histrionic dagger scene was their final public confrontation. By January 1815 Byron had wed Caroline's cousin, Annabella Milbank, a disastrous marriage that crashed in four years due to his infidelity and the rumour of an incestuous liaison with his half-sister Augusta. Weighed down by debt and scandal, Byron left England in April 1816, never to return (he died in Greece in 1824). Lord Melbourne took Caroline to Paris and Brussels, where she was reputed to have seduced the Duke of Wellington. Back in England, she published *Glenarvon*, a novel that luridly portrayed her marriage and her affair with Byron, further embarrassing her husband.

In 1825 Caroline separated from Melbourne, but he was supportive of her for the rest of her life. Her mental instability, aggravated by alcohol and laudanum, so weakened her that she died of dropsy (oedema) on 26 January 1828, her estranged husband at her side. Six years later he became Queen Victoria's first prime minister, but he never remarried.

1946 Louis Réard introduces the first bikini bathing suit at the Piscine Molitor in Paris, defining it: 'It's not a bikini unless it can be pulled through a wedding ring.' An American women's magazine comments: 'It is hardly necessary to waste words over the so-called bikini since it is inconceivable that any girl with tact and decency would ever wear such a thing.' *
2005 French President Jacques Chirac about the British: 'You cannot trust people who have such bad cuisine. It is the country with the worst food after Finland.'

---

6 July

'Do not hack at me as you did my Lord Russell.'

1685 Today a royal bastard led his army against the forces of his uncle, King James II, in one last glorious roll of the dice to seize the British throne. He was James, Duke of Monmouth, now 36, the attractive, arrogant and ambitious son of Charles II.

For twenty years Monmouth had followed a highly successful military career, becoming Master of the Horse, in effect in command of the country's forces.

When Charles died in February 1685, however, he left his throne to his brother James, rather than to this illegitimate son, who at the time was in self-imposed exile in the Dutch Republic, having been accused (probably falsely) of involvement in a plot to assassinate both Charles and James.

Monmouth detested his stubborn, humourless and haughty uncle, a devout Catholic at a time when Catholicism was highly unpopular in England. Overtaken by ambition, he convinced himself that he should wear the crown, and in June 1685 he landed at Lyme Regis with 150 supporters.

On reaching Taunton, Monmouth declared himself king and his uncle James nothing but a popish usurper. He raised an army of 3,000 men, but they were mainly farmers and artisans, not soldiers (one volunteer was 24-year-old Daniel Defoe).

After a series of indecisive skirmishes, the rebel force met the royal army this evening at Sedgemoor, 135 miles west of London. King James's men were led by the Earl of Feversham and the 35-year-old Colonel John Churchill (the future Duke of Marlborough), who twelve years earlier had saved Monmouth's life at the siege of Maastricht.

At 10.00pm Monmouth launched his attack, with his limited cavalry at the front, but the better trained regular army outflanked him and started a rout. Some 1,300 rebels were killed while 500 more were captured, compared to a trifling loss of 200 royal soldiers. Monmouth escaped but a few days later was captured while sleeping in a ditch.

Monmouth was convicted of treason and condemned to death. Only nine days after the battle, he faced the axe on Tower Hill. Retaining his bravado till the end, he turned to his executioner Jack Ketch and commanded: 'Do not hack at me as you did my Lord Russell.' He then gave Ketch six guineas and laid his head on the block. But still fearing a botched job, he asked to feel the edge of the axe with his thumb and complained that it was too dull.

British 19th-century historian Thomas Babington Macaulay takes up the tale:

> The hangman ... had been disconcerted by what the Duke had said. The first blow inflicted only a slight wound. The Duke struggled, rose from the block, and looked reproachfully at the

executioner. The head sank down once more. The stroke was repeated again and again; but still the neck was not severed, and the body continued to move. Yells of rage and horror rose from the crowd. Ketch flung down the axe with a curse. 'I cannot do it,' he said; 'my heart fails me.' 'Take up the axe, man,' cried the sheriff. 'Fling him over the rails,' roared the mob. At length the axe was taken up. Two more blows extinguished the last remains of life; but a knife was used to separate the head from the shoulders. The crowd was wrought up to such an ecstasy of rage that the executioner was in danger of being torn in pieces, and was conveyed away under a strong guard.

Six weeks later most of the other rebels were convicted at the 'Bloody Assizes' in Taunton. Over 300 were hanged, a few hanged, drawn and quartered, hundreds more fined, flogged, or imprisoned and 800 transported to Barbados.

Sedgemoor was the last battle ever fought on English soil, although they were still fighting in Scotland until the Battle of Culloden in 1746.

1189 Last words of Henry II of England when he dies at Chinon in France, knowing that his son Richard the Lionheart has sided with his bitter enemy, French King Philip Augustus: 'Shame, shame; shame on a conquered king.' * **1762** When Tsar Peter III is assassinated in prison, probably with the connivance of his wife Catherine the Great, she tells her confidantes at court: 'I must walk uprightly; I must not be suspected.' She tells the public he died from haemorrhoidal colic. * **1946** When reporters suggest to Brooklyn Dodgers baseball manager Leo Durocher that rival manager Mel Ott of the New York Giants is a 'nice guy', Durocher retorts: 'Nice guys finish last.'

---

7 July

'Carry my bones before you on the march. For the rebels will not be able to endure the sight of me, alive or dead.'

1307 Today just south of the Scottish border at Burgh by Sands, death came to England's King Edward I as he moved with his army to thrash the ever-rebellious Scots.

Edward had considered Scotland a vassal state since 1278, when King Alexander III of Scotland had paid homage to him. But the Scots had long regarded themselves as independent, and Alexander claimed that he had paid homage only for lands he held of Edward in England.

Alexander died in 1286, leaving the throne to his granddaughter, Margaret, Maid of Norway, not yet three years old. When Margaret died four years later, Scotland was in leaderless turmoil, with thirteen claimants to the throne. At length Scottish leaders asked King Edward to arbitrate. Edward agreed, on the condition that the new king would recognise him as his overlord. The Scottish crown finally went to John Balliol, who swore fealty to Edward (earning for himself the derisive name 'Toom Tabard' (Scots for 'Empty Coat') among his subjects). But then John refused to send troops for Edward's wars in France, rejected his demand to cede three border castles, and renounced his pledge, provoking Edward to invade and depose him.

For the next few years, Edward was more or less continuously at war in Scotland, trying to defeat uprisings by rebels like William Wallace. By 1303 he had launched seven separate campaigns against the defiant Scots.

One of Scotland's most ambitious and bellicose barons was Robert the Bruce, who had taken part in Wallace's revolt but made peace with Edward in 1302. But when his father died two years later, he inherited his family's claim to the Scottish throne. After murdering his main rival, he had himself crowned king in March 1306 and turned against the English, fighting for Scotland's (and his own) independence.

Edward's reaction was predictable; although 68 (a great age for the time) and infirm of body, he marched north once more to punish Bruce and the Scots. One of his lieutenants routed Bruce's small army, and Bruce fled into hiding. Edward executed Bruce's brother and imprisoned his daughter and sisters, one of whom was hung in a cage at Roxburgh Castle, where she remained for four years.

Despite Bruce's defeat, there remained ample Scottish resistance, and Edward was determined to carry on his campaign, but now he was so weakened by dysentery that he had to be carried in a horse litter. Resolute, he drove himself on until he reached Burgh by Sands on 6 July, but there he could go no further. Carried to a bed, he waited for death. Still resolved to bring the Scots to heel, he gave his men his final order: 'Carry my bones before you on the march. For the rebels will not be able to endure the sight of me, alive or dead.'

When his servants came the next morning to lift him up so that he could eat, Edward died in their arms. He was buried in Westminster Abbey, where his tombstone reads: 'Here is Edward I, Hammer of the Scots' ('*Malleus Scotorum*').

With Edward gone, Bruce returned to fight Scotland's barons and resist further English attempts to impose their rule. He recaptured most of the castles in Scotland once held by the English and sent raiding parties into northern England. In 1314 he defeated Edward's son Edward II at Bannockburn. Later reflecting on the Edwards, father and son, Bruce declared: 'I am more afraid of the bones of the father dead than of the living son, and, by all the saints, it was more difficult to get half a foot of land from the old king than a whole kingdom from the son!'

1456 In Notre Dame Cathedral, Jean Juvénal des Ursins, Archbishop of Reims, delivers the ecclesiastical court's verdict: 'We proclaim that Joan [of Arc] did not contract any taint of infamy and that she shall be and is washed clean of such.' The acquittal is not much help to Joan, who had been burned at the stake five years and 38 days before.

---

8 July

'Thou, who hast conquered others, shouldst conquer thyself.'

452 AD For his brutality, cruelty and sheer destructive energy, Attila the Hun was called the Scourge of God. After fifteen years devastating the Eastern Roman Empire, in 451 he led a gigantic nomad force across the Rhine and laid waste to every town he came upon: Reims, Metz, Amiens, Beauvais, Cologne, Strasbourg. But his advance into the west was stymied not only by his only military defeat but also by intractable Christian saints who denied him city after city.

His first difficulty was the town of Tongeren, 60 miles east of Brussels. Of details we have none, but tradition tells us that the city was saved by the local bishop, Saint Servatius, who some say even baptised Attila (a commendable feat, since other records suggest that Servatius had died in 384). In any event, Attila failed to burn the city to the ground as was his wont.

If Attila was baptised, it did very little good, for we next hear of him menacing Paris. Many wanted to flee, but another saint, Geneviève, encouraged the women to resist with her famous call to action: 'Let the men flee, if they want, if they can fight no longer. We women, we will pray to God so strongly that [Attila] will hear our supplications.'

Apparently Attila heard, since he abandoned his assault on Paris and set to besieging Orléans instead. But Orléans, too, escaped destruction when its bishop Anianus (later St Aignan) restored the city's crumbling battlements by carrying holy relics around them. He then prayed to heaven while throwing sand from the River Loire from the city's ramparts. Each grain miraculously turned into a wasp, and the swarm put the Huns to flight.

Attila's next target was Troyes, 125 miles to the east. Alas, he had not counted on Troyes' redoubtable bishop, Lupus. Lupus sent several members of the clergy to treat with Attila, but the Hun massacred them all. Undeterred, after several days of prayer Lupus led another procession of churchmen to Attila's camp. Apparently Attila was so impressed by Lupus' courage that he spared the city. (After his death in 479 Lupus was buried in Troyes Cathedral; although his tomb was desecrated during the French Revolution, you can still see part of his skull there today.)

After so many disappointments, in June 451 Attila finally brought the Roman army and their allies the Visigoths to battle near Châlons, in what today is the champagne country of France. Attila was almost killed in the only battlefield defeat of his career, and he was forced to abandon his invasion.

Despite this setback, Attila returned in 452, first attacking northern Italy and then descending on Rome itself. Hoping to avoid battle, Western Roman Emperor Valentinian III sent three envoys to negotiate, of whom one was Pope Leo I.

On this day Valentinian's ambassadors reached Attila's camp at the River Mincio, near the south shore of Lake Garda. Leading the procession in great pomp was Pope Leo, who pleaded with Attila: 'We pray for mercy and deliverance. O Attila, thou king of kings … Thou hast subdued, O Attila, the whole circle of the lands which it was granted to the Romans, victors over all peoples, to conquer. Now we pray that thou, who hast conquered others, shouldst conquer thyself. The people have felt thy scourge; now as supplicants they would feel thy mercy.'

While Leo was making his plea, St Peter and St Paul appeared at the Pope's side and threatened Attila with death unless he left Rome in peace. (You can see this famous scene in Raphael's fresco in the Apostolic Palace in the Vatican.) Terrified, Attila called off his invasion, having been bested by five saints in a year.

Six months later he was dead, some say by the hand of his young wife. As for Leo, three years later he persuaded another invader, the Vandal chief Genseric, not to burn Rome or murder its people but to be satisfied with pillage. When he died in 461, he was declared Saint Leo the Great.

> **1961** British War Secretary John Profumo meets Christine Keeler at Cliveden; after the scandal breaks, Charles de Gaulle comments: 'That will teach the English to try to behave like Frenchmen.'

9 July

'I desire the good of the kingdom more than you think, because instead of only one king, I would give it six.'

1472 Louis XI of France was in a pickle. One of his putative vassals, Charles the Bold, Duke of Burgundy was thirsting for kingship and dreamt of resurrecting the ancient kingdom of Lotharingia, once part of Charlemagne's empire. To that end Charles masterminded an alliance whose members included the King of England (Edward IV), the King of Aragon, the Duke of Brittany and Louis' own brother, Charles, the Duke of Berry. Their aim was nothing less than the dismemberment of France, leaving King Louis only a rump state and with a new kingdom for each of the plotters. 'I desire the good of the kingdom [of France] more than you think', said Charles the Bold, 'because instead of only one king, I would give it six.'

But before Charles could bring his alliance into action, the king's brother died from a combination of tuberculosis and a venereal disease contracted from his mistress. The alliance promptly folded, but, undeterred, Charles assembled an army of 80,000 men and marched into France, torching villages and crops as he advanced. When the army approached the small town of Nesle, the inhabitants put up strong resistance. During a truce taken to arrange the town's surrender, the Burgundians burst in and massacred all the men, women and children who had fled to a church for refuge. Charles then published a manifesto accusing Louis of having poisoned his brother, showing that Donald Trump did not invent fake news.

Duke Charles then advanced further into France until in June he reached Beauvais, 50 miles north of Paris. Beauvais had no artillery and only 300 men-at-arms, but its walls presented a formidable barrier, manned not only by soldiers but also by Beauvais' citizens. Charles ordered an immediate assault but found that his siege ladders were too short. When his men tried to force the main gate, defenders flung torches in their faces.

Charles now settled down for a protracted siege, his artillery incessantly hammering Beauvais' walls. On this day his army launched another fierce attack, but now the women of Beauvais demonstrated unexpected courage. Led by a fifteen-year-old butcher's daughter named Jeanne Laisné, they mingled with the fighters on the ramparts, bringing munitions for the men and dropping stones, boiling water and melted fat on the besiegers.

Despite this fierce resistance, Charles' troops continued their attack until one of them reached the top of the rampart, where he started to fix the standard of Burgundy. Suddenly Jeanne Laisné, armed with her father's butcher's hatchet, cut down the flag bearer and seized the standard as her battered victim fell from the walls. She then waved the standard above her head as a trophy of victory.

The struggle lasted nine hours, but towards evening a great shout went up from inside the city: 200 lancers from the king's garrison of nearby Noyon had ridden through the south gate into the city.

Although his cause now looked hopeless, Charles the Bold believed his honour demanded that he capture the city. For the next twelve days his artillery mercilessly bombarded Beauvais, destroying a third of its wall and many of its houses, but the besieged put up stout resistance. In the midst of danger the women, led by Jeanne Laisné, continued to supply their men with stones to throw and wine to drink and to retrieve Burgundian arrows littering the ramparts. Three times the Burgundians planted their standard on the wall, and three times they were repulsed.

Finally a furious Duke Charles gave the signal for his depleted army to retreat. At three o'clock during the night of 22 July they abandoned Beauvais in profound silence and headed back towards Burgundy. Thanks to Beauvais' resistance, Louis XI now had time to prepare the defence of his realm. His crown was saved. Jeanne Laisné became a heroine whose nickname would last for centuries – Jeanne Hachette. Her statue still stands in the city's old market place.

1896 When pressed to endorse the existing gold standard, American presidential candidate William Jennings Bryan retorts at the Democratic National Convention in Chicago: 'You shall not press down upon the brow of labour this crown of thorns; you shall not crucify mankind upon a cross of gold!'

---

10 July

'That which the Prince most abhors in the world, is your Majesty. If he could, he would drink your Majesty's blood.'

1584 Today Prince William of Orange (the Silent), the founder of the Dutch monarchy, was assassinated on the orders of Philip II of Spain.

Raised a Lutheran, William converted to Catholicism while serving Holy Roman Emperor Charles V. He was rapidly promoted and became the emperor's confidant in the most secret matters of state, so discreet that he came to be called 'the Silent'.

When William was 22, Charles retired to the Monastery of Yuste. So close had the two become that the gout-afflicted emperor leaned on William's shoulder during his abdication ceremony. But then Charles's son Philip II inherited royal power. Charles had fought the spread of Protestantism, but Philip was a true fanatic, utterly determined to obliterate the Reformation in the Spanish Netherlands. (Although Charles had brought the Inquisition to the Netherlands, Philip encouraged its grisly work, proudly commenting: 'The Inquisition of the Netherlands is much more pitiless than that of Spain.')

In 1559 William was hunting near Paris with France's King Henri II, who was as extreme as Philip. Thinking that William would be aware of Philip's plans, Henri started to discuss their secret agreement for the violent extermination of 'that cursed vermin, the Protestants', in France, the Low Countries 'and the entire Christian world'.

Deeply troubled, William told Protestant leaders in the Dutch Provinces of the murderous plan and vowed to prevent the slaughter.

In 1566 zealous Protestants demolished a number of Catholic monasteries, churches and statues during the *Beeldenstorm* (Iconoclastic Fury) in the Low Countries, and the next year Philip sent the Duke of Alba and an army to destroy Protestantism with fire and sword.

For the next twelve years William – who had now abandoned Catholicism for Calvinism – and his Protestant allies battled against Alba and his replacement, Philip's half-brother, Don Juan de Austria, in a brutal conflict that began the Eighty Years' War. Don Juan informed Philip: 'The people here are bewitched by [William]; they love him, they fear him, they desire him for their lord. They inform him of everything, and take no step but by his advice. That which the Prince most abhors in the world, is your Majesty. If he could, he would drink your Majesty's blood.' The war was a story of victories and defeats, of courage and sacrifice, of suffering and grief, but finally of a Protestant victory which came more through stalemate than success on the battlefield.

On 6 January 1579 the Low Countries' southern (predominantly Catholic) provinces signed the Union of Arras to express their loyalty to Philip. (In 1830 most of this area would become part of Belgium.) Then, on 29 January, the northern, Protestant provinces agreed the Union of Utrecht, unifying an area that would form most of today's Netherlands. William became *Stadtholder*, a type of de facto hereditary head of state. In 1581 these provinces declared independence.

In 1580 Philip had promised 25,000 crowns to anyone who would kill William. On this day in 1584 an obsessive Catholic named Balthasar Gérard came to William's home in Delft. When William came downstairs to greet him, Gérard shot him in the chest and fled. William is said to have murmured, 'My God, have pity on my soul; my God, have pity on this poor people' before he died. 'Better late than never', said Philip. Gérard was caught and brutally executed.

Off and on religious conflict continued in the Netherlands until the Peace of Münster in 1648, when Dutch independence was finally recognised by the Spanish crown.

Today in the Netherlands William the Silent is known as *De Vader des Vaderlands* (the Father of the Fatherland). The Dutch flag is derived from his flag, and the Dutch national anthem, the *Wilhelmus*, was written in his honour.

---

138 AD Only 62 but suffering severely and dying from ill-health in his villa at Baiae, Emperor Hadrian dismisses all his doctors, saying: 'How miserable a thing it is to seek death and not to find it.'

---

11 July

'When the sword is once drawn, the passions of men observe no bounds of moderation.'

1804 Alexander Hamilton was the most influential American politician who never attained the presidency. As the political commentator George Will wrote in 1992: 'There is an elegant memorial in Washington to Jefferson, but none to Hamilton. However, if you seek Hamilton's monument, look around. You are living in it. We honour Jefferson, but live in Hamilton's country, a mighty industrial nation with a strong central government.' Today this illegitimate son of an itinerant Scottish trader was killed in America's most famous duel.

Born on Nevis in 1757, at fifteen Hamilton came to the American colonies, then a pastoral society of two and a half million people. During the Revolution he fought heroically at the battles of Trenton, Princeton and Yorktown and served as one of George Washington's aides-de-camp. After the war he became a lawyer, founded the Bank of New York (still existing as BNY Mellon) and was a delegate at the Constitutional Convention. A strong advocate of central government, he co-wrote *The Federalist Papers* in which he warned that conflict between individual states and the central government could lead to the dissolution of the nation: 'When the sword is once drawn, the passions of men observe no bounds of moderation.' His words foreshadowed his own death seventeen years later.

In 1789 Washington appointed Hamilton the country's first Secretary of the Treasury, and during the next six years he created a sophisticated monetary policy that saved the government from collapse, but he resigned in 1795 to make some money. Finding him working at his desk one evening, Talleyrand wrote: 'I have seen one of the wonders of the world. I have seen a man labouring all night to support his family, who has made the fortune of a nation.' Diligent he may have been, but he later caused a huge scandal when, despite his marriage vows, he enjoyed an extramarital fling with a married woman in 1791–92.

During his career, Hamilton made a bitter enemy of Aaron Burr, a man with a history strangely similar to his own. Burr was also a lawyer and New York politician who had a distinguished war record and who founded a bank (which morphed over the centuries into JPMorgan Chase & Co.). Like Hamilton, Burr had an illicit affair, fathering two children by an East Indian servant during his first marriage. On top of that, when Hamilton's mistress petitioned for a divorce, it was Burr who represented her.

Hamilton detested Burr as corrupt and 'profligate, a voluptuary in the extreme'. In 1796 he helped block Burr's bid for the vice presidency, and three years later he backed Jefferson for president, forcing Burr to settle for vice president. Then in 1804 Hamilton helped thwart Burr's hopes of becoming governor of New York. Hating Hamilton for his influence – and for his attacks on his honesty – Burr challenged him to a duel.

A few days beforehand Hamilton wrote to a friend: 'I have resolved ... to reserve and throw away my first fire, and I have thoughts even of reserving my second fire.'

At dawn on this day the two adversaries and their seconds were rowed across the Hudson River to Weehawken in New Jersey – duels were illegal in New York. By morbid coincidence, it was the same spot where Hamilton's son had been killed in a duel three years before.

Grimly they measured their positions, pistols in hand. The time was just 7.30.

Two shots broke the morning calm. Hamilton deliberately shot wide, but Burr's aim was true, and Hamilton fell, clutching his stomach, blood seeping through his fingers. The bullet had entered his abdomen above his right hip, piercing his liver and spine.

Although constantly attended by a surgeon, Hamilton died 28 hours later. Burr lived on another 32 years, the only American vice president to fight a duel (although one president, Andrew Jackson, killed a man in a duel before he became president). The dead Hamilton had vastly more influence over his nation than the man who shot him and survived.

---

711 In the first great battle in the Arab conquest of Iberia, leader of the Umayyad Caliphate Tariq ibn Ziyad inspires his men before routing the Christian Visigoths under Roderick at Guadalete: 'At the moment when the two armies meet hand to hand, you will see me, never doubt it, seeking out this Roderick, tyrant of his people, challenging him to combat, if Allah is willing … But should I fall before I reach Roderick, redouble your ardour, force yourselves to the attack and achieve the conquest of this country, in depriving him of life. With him dead, his soldiers will no longer defy you.' (The Arabs won the battle and Roderick was killed.)

---

12 July

'This is a good token for me, for the land desireth to have me.'

1346 Today an invading king tripped and fell before his army, but his quick-wittedness turned his stumble from a bad omen into a promise of victory.

England's Edward III had already added the title 'King of France' to his own, convinced that he should have inherited the realm through his mother, sister of the long-dead French king Charles IV. By 1346 he had been battling the French on and off for almost ten years, starting the Hundred Years' War. Now he was leading another invasion.

Edward's previous efforts had focused on Gascony, but a French turncoat named Godfrey de Harcourt had persuaded him to attack Normandy instead, where he could surprise the French. On this day Edward's fleet anchored off the sandy stretch of beach that lies between La Hougue and St Vaast, twenty miles east of Cherbourg.

First to disembark were 12,000 troops. Then came the king – only to trip on the sand, just catching himself with his hands. Knowing that his watching soldiers might see his fall as foretelling failure, he sprang to his feet and declared: 'This is a good token for me, for the land desireth to have me.'

Indeed, a good token it was, as Edward proceeded to sack Caen and then utterly destroy the French army at Crécy. His final victory before retiring back to England was at Calais, which surrendered after eleven months of siege. (Edward's campaign, however, did not have much effect on the Hundred Years' War, which continued spasmodically for another 107 years.)

Surprisingly, Edward was not the only conqueror to interpret a stumble as a favourable portent.

Back in 47 BC during the Roman Civil War Julius Caesar had landed in North Africa, in today's Tunisia. As he stepped from his ship, he fell on his face before his assembled troops. Spreading his arms, he kissed the ground, dramatically exclaiming: 'Africa, I hold you.' ('*Teneo te, Africa.*') After an initial defeat, Caesar, too, went on to victory over the remnants of Pompey's forces in Africa and southern Spain.

In 1066 came another fortunate slip. When William the Conqueror landed at Bulverhythe on the Sussex coast, he tripped as he came ashore before his army. Quickly regaining his feet, he opened his fist to display a handful of earth, claiming it to be a symbol of his claim to the territory. 'What astonishes you?' he asked his men, 'I have taken possession of this land with my hands, and by the glory of God, as far as it extends it is mine – and yours!' Just over two weeks later he triumphed at Hastings.

Yet another English king turned a similar mishap into a positive in 1415. When Henry V landed with his small army at Harfleur, he staggered and fell to his knees. With admirable quickness of mind, he clasped his hands together as if he had intentionally knelt to pray. Within a month he captured Harfleur and followed it up with his overwhelming victory at Agincourt.

It would seem that monarchs who slip should reinterpret their fall as a sure sign of success, but one who didn't was the Emperor Napoleon at the start of his invasion of Russia in 1812. When his horse threw him on the bank of the Niemen as he crossed into Russia, one of his soldiers cried out: 'It is a bad omen. A Roman would retire.' Six months later, three-quarters of his Grand Armée lay dead in the Russian snows while Napoleon himself was hurrying back to Paris to stop a coup d'état.

1862 In the midst of the Civil War, Congress authorises America's highest military award, the Medal of Honor: 'To such non-commissioned officers and privates as shall most distinguish themselves by their gallantry in action and other soldier-like qualities during the present insurrection.' Later made a permanent decoration, by 1915 it was also awarded to officers in all services.

---

13 July

'Since I am so ugly, it behoves that I be bold.'

1380 It was the midst of the Hundred Years' War, and the French were battling to retake territories lost to the English. Leading the attack was the Constable of France, Bertrand du Guesclin, the foremost knight of his age.

Son of a knight, du Guesclin was born ugly near Dinan in Brittany. Contemporary historians describe him as small, with short legs and overly broad shoulders, long arms, a large round head with a flat nose and 'black skin like that of a wild boar'. According to the contemporary troubadour Cuvelier, 'there was none so ugly from Rennes to Dinan'. His parents 'hated him so sore that often in their hearts they wished him dead or drowned in the river'. Such was their antipathy that they sent him to live with an uncle, even though he was developing into an athlete of formidable strength.

At seventeen, too young to compete in a jousting tournament, du Guesclin borrowed his cousin's armour and entered the lists, his face hidden by his helmet. After defeating twelve other knights, he found himself pitted against his own father, who had not recognised him. Du Guesclin refused to joust and lowered his lance in respect, and then another knight lifted du Guesclin's visor to reveal his homely visage. So moved was his father that he promised to equip him with his own armour.

From the age of 21 du Guesclin was a professional soldier. According to historian Barbara Tuchman, he was 'skilled in the tactics of ambush and ruse, use of disguise, spies, secret messengers, smoke clouds to hide movements, bribes of money and wine, torture and killing of prisoners, and surprise attacks during the "Truce of God"'.

Du Guesclin credited his success to his own inventive audacity; fully aware of his unprepossessing looks, he explained: 'Since I am so ugly, it behoves that I be bold.' He adopted as his motto: *'Le courage donne ce que la beauté refuse.'* ('Courage gives what beauty refuses.')

In May 1380 du Guesclin, now 60, was leading a small army in the Massif Central, preparing to attack Châteauneuf-de-Randon, a castle held by the English and home to many *écorcheurs*, mercenaries who acted more like brigands, pillaging every village too small to resist.

Du Guesclin arrived at Châteauneuf in June and soon encircled the citadel. The defenders, desperate in the terrible heat, promised to surrender within fifteen days if no relief arrived. But by this time du Guesclin had fallen gravely ill, having drunk too much cold water after fighting in the full sun. On 13 July he gave his final command to his men, 'Remember that whenever you are at war, the churchmen, the children and the poor are not your enemies', and died on the very day of the promised capitulation. But the English commander was good to his word. Hauling down his flag, he led his men out of the citadel to lay the keys on du Guesclin's coffin.

Du Guesclin had asked to be buried at his birthplace in Dinan, so his funeral cortege headed north with his corpse. His body was embalmed at Le Puy and his entrails entombed in the Church of St Laurent. But the embalming was botched, so when the cortege reached Montferrand, his body was boiled to detach the flesh from the bones, and the boiled flesh was buried in a church there.

Continuing on the journey, the cortege met a king's officer at Le Mans who brought the skeleton to Saint-Denis near Paris for burial, while the great warrior's heart was carried back to Dinan to be interred in the basilica of Saint-Sauveur. Thus du Guesclin has four separate tombs, one more than even the kings of France, who traditionally had three – one for the heart, one for the entrails and one for the body.

1793 To gain access to implacable revolutionary Jean-Paul Marat while he is taking a therapeutic bath, French aristocrat Charlotte Corday sends him a note saying: 'Have the goodness to receive me, I can help you to render a great service to France.' Once admitted, she stabs him to death. *
1962 British Liberal politician Jeremy Thorpe on beleaguered PM Harold Macmillan sacking half his Cabinet: 'Greater love hath no man than this, that he lay down his friends for his life.'

14 July

'Is it a revolt?' 'No, Sire, it is a revolution.'

1789 Today the infamous Bastille fell to a rioting Parisian mob. It was a fitting climax for a royal prison that had played a colourful part in French history since the 14th century.

The Bastille owed its existence to the English – initial work on its walls began in 1357 as a defence against them during the Hundred Years' War. In 1370 Provost of Paris Hugues Aubriot began transforming the walls into a fortress. Eventually it would have eight round 78-foot towers connected by walls ten feet thick, surrounded by a moat. It was first used as a prison in 1380 when Aubriot himself, who had run afoul of the Church, became its first prisoner. He managed to escape and vanished from history.

The king who made most use of the Bastille was Louis XIV, who imprisoned anyone who annoyed or resisted him with dreaded *lettres de cachet*, avoiding the inconvenience of a trial. During his reign he locked up 2,320 people there. By the time of its fall, the Bastille had accommodated over 5,000 prisoners, including Voltaire (who was incarcerated there twice), La Rochefoucauld, the English architect John Vanbrugh (arrested for suspected espionage) and the Marquis de Sade, who wrote *120 Days of Sodom* while imprisoned there. Over the centuries it became a symbol of royal repression, although France's king at its fall, Louis XVI, used it sparingly and even ordered a review to release unjustly imprisoned inmates.

In the summer of 1789 the Bastille was governed by Bernard de Launay, who commanded a force of 82 *invalides* (pensioned soldiers too old or decrepit to serve in the field) plus 32 men from a Swiss regiment. The fortress walls mounted eighteen eight-pound guns and twelve smaller pieces.

On Tuesday 14 July, Paris simmered with insurrection. Angry citizens thronged Place Vendôme, the Hôtel de Ville and Place Louis XV, convinced that conservative factions were on the verge of overthrowing recent reforms like the establishment of the National Assembly. In reaction, soldiers and cavalry tried to intimidate the mob, only to be met with stones and bricks.

Now a crowd of 800 revolutionary Parisians, armed with muskets and cannon captured in the Invalides earlier in the day, marched on the Bastille. Their initial aim was to seize the fortress's guns and 250 barrels of gunpowder. After a protester cut the chains to the drawbridge leading to the inner courtyard, the mob surged in, to be met with gunfire from the defenders. Instantly both sides were firing, but it soon became apparent that the defenders could hold out indefinitely; only one had been killed compared to 100 of the insurgents.

Although in no immediate danger, de Launay wished to avoid more bloodshed and offered to open the gates if his soldiers were spared. The attackers gave assurances of safety, and the drawbridge was lowered. Immediately the rioters rushed in and killed three of the Bastille garrison. De Launay was dragged away and severely beaten. Realising the inevitable fate that awaited him, he shouted out, 'Enough – let me die!' and kicked an assailant in the groin. He was then stabbed to death and decapitated, his head carried through the streets on a pike. And so trickery rather than force of arms took the Bastille. Inside were a mere seven prisoners.

That evening at Versailles a member of the Estates General, Frédéric, duc de la Rochefoucauld-Liancourt, told King Louis of the Bastille's fall. 'Is it a revolt?' Louis asked. 'No, Sire, it is a revolution', responded the duke.

Revolution it was, although it was another three years before the abolition of the monarchy. Bastille Day, now the nation's most famous and most French holiday, was officially established only on 6 July 1880, 91 years after the event.

1954 Historian Arnold Toynbee remarks in a BBC radio broadcast: 'America is a large, friendly dog in a very small room. Every time it wags its tail it knocks over a chair.'

---

15 July

*'Democracy is like a train; you get off once
you have reached your destination.'*

2016 Just before 11.00 this evening Turkish jets swept low over Ankara. A few minutes later army helicopters bombed the police headquarters just outside the city. In Istanbul two bridges over the Bosporus were closed, and by 11.30 soldiers had occupied Taksim Square and Turkish Radio had been commandeered. Soon broadcasts were telling shocked listeners: 'The democratic and secular rule of law has been eroded by the current government.' It was the start of a coup d'état led by renegade Turkish generals and admirals, in the great tradition of the Turkish military, which had toppled four elected governments, in 1960, 1971, 1980 and 1997.

In Marmaris on Turkey's Mediterranean Coast, President Recep Tayyip Erdoğan was enjoying a holiday. When he heard of the attempted coup he hurriedly left his hotel, just before two helicopters landed a squad of infantry who riddled the hotel with small arms fire, killing two policemen.

Erdoğan had long been a controversial force in Turkey. Early in his career the courts shut down his Islamic fundamentalist Welfare Party for threatening Turkey's secularism, established by Kemal Atatürk in 1923. After he became mayor of Istanbul in 1994, he told like-minded Muslims: 'Democracy is like a train; you get off once you have reached your destination.' He left no doubt where his interests lay: 'The mosques are our barracks, the domes our helmets, the minarets our bayonets and the faithful our soldiers.' The courts convicted him of 'incitement to violence and religious or racial hatred' for which he spent four months in jail.

Starting in 2003, Erdoğan won three straight elections for prime minister. The initial improvements he made to the economy were outweighed by his efforts to make Turkey a more Islamist state. He also became increasingly autocratic. After police forcibly removed peaceful protesters from a sit-in in Istanbul in 2013, he ominously commented on television: 'The police were there yesterday, they are there today, and they will be there tomorrow.' In 2015, a thirteen-year-old boy was arrested for criticising him on Facebook.

After twelve years as prime minister, Erdoğan was barred from seeking a fourth term, so he ran for president, previously a largely ceremonial role. Once installed, he continued to direct the country.

Then came today's coup d'état, in which the parliament and the presidential palace were bombed, over 300 people were killed and 2,000 injured. But the coup failed in less than 24 hours because many in the military opposed it, and the Turkish population in Ankara and Istanbul gathered in major squares in protest, ignoring the insurgents' orders to stay inside. Many lower-ranking rebels were conscripted soldiers, who baulked at firing on demonstrators.

Erdoğan imposed a three-month state of emergency – that ended two years later. He fingered his one-time ally Fethullah Gülen as the coup's prime instigator. Gülen was a shadowy imam and politician who had founded his own movement, which promoted a tolerant Islam that emphasised altruism, hard work and education. In 2013 Erdoğan and his party had been enmeshed in a $100 billion scandal involving bribery and fraud. He accused Gülen of using the investigation to bring him down and of infiltrating the country's police, army and security services. Denying all, Gülen fled to the United States.

Within two years, Erdoğan had ordered 50,000 people arrested and 180,000 government employees fired from their jobs. 2,745 judges and 15,000 education staff were dismissed or detained, and the licences of 21,000 teachers working at private institutions were revoked. The government also seized over 1,000 companies whose owners were suspect and shut down sixteen television channels, 23 radio stations, 45 newspapers, fifteen magazines and 29 publishing houses. Erdoğan also jailed 160 journalists, more than in North Korea, Cuba, Russia and China combined.

The one person Erdoğan failed to get was his arch-enemy Gülen. The American government refused to extradite him because there was no convincing evidence that he was involved in the coup. But Erdoğan continued to consolidate his power. In July 2018 he abolished the job of prime minister and made the president (himself) the executive head of government with vastly increased authority.

1099 As Jerusalem falls during the First Crusade, crusaders attack the Temple of Solomon where, according to an eyewitness: 'In this temple almost ten thousand [Saracens] were decapitated. If you had been there, you would have seen our feet splattered with the blood of the dead ... Not a single life was spared, not even women or children. You would have seen a wondrous sight, when our poorest soldiers, learning of the Saracens' cleverness, cut open the stomachs of the slain to take from their bowels the jewels they had swallowed while still alive.' * **1815** On the run after Waterloo, Napoleon surrenders to British Captain Frederick Maitland on HMS *Bellerophon*, hoping for political asylum: 'I come like Themistocles, to offer myself to the hospitality of the British people. I place myself under the protection of their laws.' The British send him to Saint Helena instead.

16 July

'We ought not to have more use and esteem of money and coin than of stones.'

1228 Today Pope Gregory IX proclaimed Francis of Assisi a saint less than two years after his death. Gregory had known Francis for a decade and had witnessed his devoted life, but what really convinced him of his sanctity was a dream – the second papal dream in the saint's miraculous story.

Son of a rich cloth merchant, Francis was baptised Giovanni di Pietro di Bernardone, but his father called him Francis (Francesco in Italian, meaning French one) in honour of his French mother. Francis spent a riotous youth squandering his father's money, but when he was 22, an icon of a crucified Christ in the run-down chapel of San Damiano spoke to him: 'Francis, Francis, go and repair My house which, as you can see, is falling into ruins.' Francis obeyed the call by selling his horse and some fine cloth from his father's shop.

Alarmed by his son's transformation, his father brought him up before an ecclesiastical court. The presiding bishop ordered him to return all property that came from his father. According to *The Legend of St Francis* published in 1246, Francis stripped to the skin in the courtroom. So touched was the bishop that he wrapped Francis in his own cloak.

From then on Francis forswore property altogether, and, clad in a rough garments and barefoot, he began to preach repentance, earning him the nickname '*Il poverello*' ('the little poor one').

When he was 29 Francis came to Rome with twelve followers to seek approval for his order from Pope Innocent III. At first Innocent refused, but, after dreaming that he saw Francis holding up the church of San Giovanni in Laterano, he approved, and the Franciscan order, or Friars Minor, was officially founded on 16 April 1210. Its First Rule reads: 'Let none of the brothers carry or receive money or coin in any manner ... except on account of the manifest necessity of the sick brothers. For we ought not to have more use and esteem of money and coin than of stones ...'

Despite his zeal, Francis was one of history's more likeable saints. He called animals 'brothers' and 'sisters' and famously preached to the birds. It is said that he once tamed a man-eating wolf by making the sign of the cross and ordering it to hurt no one. He is also supposed to have created the first crèche in 1220.

In 1224 Francis experienced a dramatic vision. St Bonaventure, leader of the Franciscan order later that century, describes it: 'As it stood above him, [Francis] saw that it was a man and yet a Seraph with six wings; his arms were extended and his feet conjoined, and his body was fixed to a cross.' When the seraph vanished, Francis found the wounds of the stigmata on his body.

By the time he was 45, Francis was sick, worn out by his impoverished life and almost blind from trachoma picked up in the Middle East. Knowing that he was *in extremis*, he requested his fellow monks at the monastery of Porziuncola to lay him on the bare ground to die, murmuring: 'Welcome, sister death.' He died during the evening hours of 3 October 1226 while listening to a reading of Psalm 142.

Six months later Ugolino di Segni mounted the papal throne as Gregory IX. For the past seven years he had been Cardinal Protector of the Franciscans. Although he loved Francis well, Gregory hesitated to declare him a saint, until one night when Francis came to him in a dream bearing the same stigmata that had marked him in life. When he awoke all his doubts were swept away and he canonised Francis on 16 July 1228. The very next day Gregory laid the foundation stone for the Basilica of Saint Francis in Assisi. On 18 June 1939, Pope Pius XII named Francis a joint Patron Saint of Italy along with Saint Catherine of Siena.

1964 American Senator Barry Goldwater in his speech accepting the Republican presidential nomination: 'Extremism in the defence of liberty is no vice. And ... moderation in the pursuit of justice is no virtue!'

---

17 July

'It seemed as if all of them guessed their fate, but not one of them uttered a single sound.'

1918 On 1 November 1894 Tsar Alexander III died of kidney failure, leaving the throne to his 26-year-old son Nicholas (II). Now absolute master of 125,000,000 people, Nicholas fretted: 'I know nothing of the business of ruling.' On this, at least, he was correct.

As Tsarevich, Nicholas had visited both the British Parliament and the American Congress, but, unmoved by the workings of democracy, he defined his most important duty as 'maintaining the principle of autocracy just as firmly and unflinchingly as it was preserved by my unforgettable dead father'.

In 1904 Russia's (and Nicholas') problems started to spiral out of control. During the Russo-Japanese War, the Japanese pummelled the Russians, who lost 275,000 men plus most of their Pacific and Baltic fleets.

While the war was raging, on 'Bloody Sunday' in January 1905 a huge crowd of unarmed workers, many with wives and children, marched on the Winter Palace, calling for improved working conditions and an end to the war. The Imperial Guard opened fire, killing and wounding hundreds and provoking a series of massive strikes that triggered the Revolution of 1905. Nicholas reluctantly established the first Duma (parliament) but decreed that 'the Emperor of All Russia has supreme autocratic power'.

As Nicholas dissolved Dumas and dismissed prime ministers, Russia simmered with unrest, punctuated by terrorist attacks. Meanwhile his neurotic wife Alexandra fell increasingly under the spell of the baleful monk Rasputin, who she believed could cure her haemophiliac son.

Then on 28 June 1914 Austrian Archduke Franz Ferdinand was assassinated, and Russia, tied to Serbia by treaty and the rather mystical concept of Pan-Slavism, was soon at war. In September 1915 Nicholas went to the front, leaving Alexandra in control of the country, but her relationship with Rasputin further gnawed at the tsar's authority. Although repeatedly warned about Rasputin's malign influence, Nicholas declined to remove him; in December 1916 some discontented nobles did it for him.

By now Russia had lost almost 5 million soldiers, and those still fighting lacked food, shoes, ammunition and weapons. In February 1917 strikes and rioting paralysed Petrograd, and troops mutinied. In a last desperate attempt to assert his authority, the tsar prorogued the Duma, but liberals established a Temporary Committee. Abandoned by the army, his ministers and his people, on 15 March Nicholas abdicated, ending three centuries of Romanov rule.

After returning from exile in April, Lenin overthrew the Provisional Government and established a dictatorship, plunging Russia into civil war.

Now prisoners of the state, in April 1918 the tsar and his family were sent 1,300 miles east to Yekaterinburg. Nicholas hoped that the anti-Bolshevik White Army would liberate his family, and in mid-July gunfire could be heard in the distance, but the threat that he might be rescued sealed his fate.

Just after 1.00am on 17 July the tsar, his wife and their five children, along with his doctor and three servants, were woken and herded into a basement room. Three chairs were brought for the tsar, his wife and his thirteen-year-old son and heir Alexei. According to one of the guards: 'It seemed as if all of them guessed their fate, but not one of them uttered a single sound.'

A few minutes later, a Cheka (secret police) execution squad armed with revolvers entered the room. Its leader Yakov Yurovsky, a fervent Bolshevik with a Lenin-like goatee, read aloud the sentence of death. Nicholas, facing his family, turned and said 'What? What?' as the executioners opened fire. Three of the tsar's daughters were given some protection by the diamonds sewn into their clothing, so they were finished off with bayonets.

The guard remembered: 'All the members of the tsar's family were lying on the floor with many wounds in their bodies. The blood was running in streams. The doctor, the maid and two waiters had also been shot ... the heir was still alive and moaned a little. Yurovsky went up and fired two or three more times at him. Then the heir was still.' The last alive was the tsar's youngest daughter, seventeen-year-old Anastasia, who was bludgeoned with rifle butts and stabbed with bayonets.

1453 In the last battle of the Hundred Years' War, the French defeat the English at Castillon, killing their commander, the intrepid John Talbot, Earl of Shrewsbury. French chronicler Matthew d'Escourcy writes: 'Such was the end of this famous and renowned English leader who for so long had been one of the most formidable thorns in the side of the French, who regarded him with terror and dismay.'

---

18 July

'When you tell a lie, tell big lies. This is what the Jews do.'

1925 After his comic-opera Beer Hall Putsch in 1923, Adolf Hitler had been sentenced to five years in Landsberg Prison. There he was treated more as a celebrity than a convict, permitted the freedom of the grounds and visits by friends and collaborators. He served only nine months, but to fill the idle hours he dictated to his secretary Rudolph Hess a rambling tome of over 700 pages, a mixture of idealised autobiography and toxic political ideas, with an exposition on propaganda techniques. He wanted to call the book *Four Years of Struggle against Lies, Stupidity, and Cowardice*, but his publisher opted for the snappier *Mein Kampf* (*My Struggle*) and published the first volume on this day, with Volume 2 appearing in 1926.

For anyone who could wade through Hitler's fevered prose, *Mein Kampf* revealed his plans eight years before he became dictator.

Hitler blames Jewish conspirators and political treachery for denying Germany victory in the First World War and says that the German loss must be avenged. He defines his racial theories in which fair-skinned, blue-eyed, blond-haired Aryans are members of the 'master race', and at the bottom end of the scale come the *Untermenschen* (undermen), the Slavs and – especially – the Jews.

'All the human culture, all the results of art, science, and technology that we see before us today, are almost exclusively the creative product of the Aryan', Hitler writes. But Germany's problems were all the fault of the Jews – or Social Democrats and Marxists working for Jewish interests. The Jews were conspiring to undermine Germany's Aryans: 'The black-haired Jewish youth lies in wait for hours on end, satanically glaring at and spying on the unsuspicious girl whom he plans to seduce, adulterating her blood and removing her from the bosom of her own people.'

Anticipating the Holocaust, Hitler writes: 'If at the beginning of the [First World War] and during the war twelve or fifteen thousand of these Hebrew corrupters of the nation had been subjected to poison gas ... then the sacrifice of millions at the front would not have been in vain.' He calls his stand a holy mission: 'I am convinced that I am acting as the agent of our Creator. In standing guard against the Jew, I am doing the Lord's work.'

Mein Kampf also foreshadows Hitler's own absolute rule: 'There must be no majority decisions ... The decision will be made by one man.' It explains his concept of *Lebensraum*: 'We must eliminate the disproportion between our population and our area ... We must secure for the German people the land and soil to which they are entitled.' The conquered territory would provide space for Aryans and be used to cultivate food. The Slavic inhabitants would be enslaved or eliminated.

In *Mein Kampf*, Hitler also presages future euthanasia programmes: '[The state] must see to it that only the healthy beget children.' And Hitler betrays what he really thinks about the German public: 'All propaganda must be popular and its intellectual level must be adjusted to the most limited intelligence among those it is addressed to.' He comments: 'If you wish the sympathy of the broad masses, you must tell them the crudest and most stupid things.' He also sums up the Nazi state that was to come: 'When you tell a lie, tell big lies. This is what the Jews do … in the big lie there is always a certain force of credibility.' (Hitler here may have been echoing Lenin, who opined: 'A lie told often enough becomes the truth.')

Mein Kampf sold only 9,473 copies in its first year, but as Hitler became known, sales soared to 240,000 before he became chancellor in 1933. From then on it was given to every newlywed couple and every soldier fighting at the front and was translated into eleven languages. By the end of the war, 10 million copies had been sold or distributed.

Not everyone was thrilled by Hitler's magnum opus. His ally and fellow dictator Benito Mussolini judged it 'a boring tome that I have never been able to read'.

---

390 BC The Senones under Brennus defeat the Romans at the Allia River and then occupy Rome except for the citadel. After a seven-month siege, the Romans agree to pay 1,000 pounds in gold as ransom, but Brennus flings his sword onto the scale as the gold is weighed, saying disdainfully: '*Vae victis!*' ('Woe to the vanquished!') * **1817** Jane Austen dies in Winchester at 41 after a year and a half of slow decline, probably of Addison's disease or Hodgkin's lymphoma. Her last words: 'I want nothing but death.'

---

19 July

'The great questions of the day will not be decided by speeches and the resolutions of majorities, but by blood and iron.'

1870 Today, in a magnificent example of hubris and wounded pride, the French government, under the direction of Emperor Napoleon III, declared war on Prussia. It was to be the death knell of the French monarchy.

In 1864 Prussia had occupied two German-speaking Danish provinces (Holstein and Schleswig), and two years later had defeated Austria to shift power among Germanic states away from Austria towards Prussia.

Napoleon watched the Prussian expansion with dread. France was Europe's most powerful nation, but now an increasingly militant Prussia seemed on the verge of usurping its place. Unknown to him, Prussia's 'Iron Chancellor' Otto von Bismarck was aiming to manoeuvre France into war, believing that it would induce the remaining German states to join Prussia. As Bismarck had predicted back in 1862: 'The great questions of the day will not be decided by speeches and the resolutions of majorities, but by blood and iron.'

Conveniently, the throne of Spain was vacant, so Bismarck proposed a German prince, a cousin of King Wilhelm of Prussia, as a candidate. Alarmed at the prospect of encirclement by Hohenzollerns, France protested strongly. Furthermore, Napoleon believed in the invincibility of French arms and wanted a brilliant coup that would show the world who was top dog in Europe. He sent an ambassador to Bad Ems, where Wilhelm was taking the waters, to request an immediate withdrawal of the Prussian candidate for Spain.

The meeting ended amicably, although Wilhelm declined to offer a guarantee. He then sent a telegram to Bismarck in Berlin giving an account of the meeting. But the cunning chancellor altered the telegram, making it appear as if Wilhelm had delivered a humiliating snub to the French ambassador, and released this edited version of the Ems telegram, as it is known to history, to the press. He assured his friends that the doctored message would produce 'the effect of a red flag on the Gallic bull'.

The next day, Bastille Day, French papers emblazoned the now-insulting telegram on their front pages, and 20,000 enraged Parisians, waving flags and patriotic banners, marched through the streets. And so, on this flimsy *casus belli*, France declared war against Prussia.

The French won the first engagement, a skirmish at Saarbrücken, but republican-minded newspapers smelled royal blood. 'France is running two dangers right now', declared *Le Rappel*. 'The first – and the least – is the danger of defeat … The other more serious danger is that of victory … The [French] Empire is dying. If the Prussians are beaten, it will be resurrected.'

But from then on it was all Prussia, culminating in the Battle of Sedan on 1 September, when the Prussians captured 104,000 French troops, including Emperor Napoleon himself.

On 1 January 1871 the German states proclaimed their union as the German Empire, bringing the population to 41 million, up from 25 million of Prussia alone, and leapfrogging France's 37 million. While the Prussian army was still besieging Paris, King Wilhelm of Prussia was crowned Kaiser Wilhelm of Germany in the Hall of Mirrors in the Palace of Versailles. France finally surrendered on 28 January, forced to cede Alsace and part of Lorraine, pay 5 billion gold francs in reparations and submit to a three-year occupation by enemy troops.

Napoleon III never saw France again. While he was in German captivity, the French proclaimed the Third Republic and ended monarchy in France for ever. Napoleon whiled away his days in exile in England, where he died two years later.

Kaiser Wilhelm ruled a united Germany until his death in 1888. Bismarck died just after midnight on 30 July 1898, at the age of 83. The year before his death he had presciently predicted: 'One day the great European War will come out of some damned foolish thing in the Balkans.'

1588 As the Spanish fleet is beating up the Channel, Sir Francis Drake is interrupted in his game of bowls to lead his ships in defence. 'We have time enough to finish the game and beat the Spaniards, too', he says. *
1848 The first women's suffrage convention in the US opens in Seneca Falls, New York. It ends with a 'Declaration of Sentiments' that starts: 'The history of mankind is a history of repeated injuries and usurpation on the part of man toward woman, having in direct object the establishment of an absolute tyranny over her.'

---

20 July

'Don't let it end like this. Tell them I said something.'

1923 Swarthy and moustachioed, Pancho Villa looked just like the Mexican bandit that he was. He was also a revolutionary hero and guerrilla leader with a taste for fame and a flair for self-promotion.

The son of a sharecropper who died when Villa was fifteen, he was born Doroteo Arango on 5 June 1878. According to his own account, when he was sixteen he came home from the fields to find that the owner of the hacienda where he lived had raped his twelve-year-old sister. Grabbing a pistol, he shot the *hacendado* dead and then stole a horse and fled to the mountains to join a gang of bandits.

The bandits supported themselves by rustling cattle and robbing rich gentry. In addition to selling stolen livestock, Arango worked as a miner. But it wasn't long before he added more serious crimes to his record, like robbing banks.

When he was twenty he was tracked down by the *rurales* (the rural police force), arrested for assault and stealing mules and forced to join the Mexican army. A year later, however, he killed an officer, stole his horse and deserted back to his bandit friends. He now changed his name to Pancho Villa, in honour, he said, of the noted bandit Agustín Villa, whom he claimed to have been his real father.

The first quarter of the 20th century in Mexico was a period of revolutionary chaos, as reactionary generals like Porfirio Díaz and Victoriano Huerta battled with more enlightened politicians like Francisco Madero and Venustiano Carranza. Villa had backed Madero, who made him a colonel in the revolutionary forces, and he led his troops to several victories. But when Madero was assassinated in 1913, the country descended even further into anarchy, leaving Villa as the most powerful of the bandit warlords who were duelling for control. Villa's vanity now became more apparent; he loved being photographed and even signed a contract with a Hollywood studio to have his battles filmed.

Then Carranza and the politician/general Álvaro Obregón joined forces, and Obregón crushed Villa at the Battle of Celaya, forcing Villa to go on the run, waging guerrilla war. (Obregón himself had his right arm blown off during the fighting.) Then the United States, backing Carranza for his democratic reforms, refused to sell arms to Villa. Feeling betrayed, Villa killed seventeen Americans in an assault on a train in Chihuahua and then sent 100 guerrillas across the border to New Mexico to capture arms. This time eighteen Americans were killed, and President Woodrow Wilson sent General 'Black Jack' Pershing in pursuit, but Villa avoided capture during an eleven-month manhunt.

It seemed like a lucky break for Villa when Carranza was assassinated in May 1920 and Adolfo de la Huerta became interim president. Villa received an amnesty and went into pastoral retirement in exchange for a huge hacienda in Canutillo and 500,000 gold pesos for himself and his men, but in December Obregón became president. Three years later Villa was dead.

No one knows for sure who ordered Villa's murder, but most believe it was the ruthless Obregón, an old enemy who wanted to be certain this troublesome bandit did not rejoin the revolution.

When Villa visited the nearby town of Parral, he usually came with a cohort of bodyguards, but today he brought only three. After a quick stop at the bank, he was headed back to his hacienda in his black Dodge when a pumpkin-seed seller ran towards his car and shouted 'Viva Villa!' It was a signal to seven riflemen who appeared in the middle of the road and fired 40 bullets into the automobile. Villa was hit nine times in the head and chest. As he lay mortally wounded, he murmured: 'Don't let it end like this. Tell them I said something.'

Obregón won re-election in 1928, but while dining with his friends he was shot and killed by a religious fanatic before he could begin his second term.

1944 In Rastenburg, German staff officer Colonel Claus von Stauffenberg attempts to assassinate Hitler. He is apprehended and shot the next day; his last words: '*Es lebe das heilige Deutschland!*' ('Long live our sacred Germany!') * **1957** Prime Minister Harold Macmillan declares in a speech at Bedford: 'Most of our people have never had it so good.'

---

21 July

'From the top of these pyramids, forty centuries are looking down upon you.'

1798 Revolutionary France had been at war with Great Britain since 1793, and earlier this year Napoleon Bonaparte had proposed an invasion of Egypt, now part of the Ottoman Empire. It would, he said in a letter to the Directory, not only protect French trade interests but also threaten British access to the Red Sea, a major route to India. Since he had recently returned from a series of totemic victories in his Italian campaign, government ministers were only too happy to send this over-ambitious general to an obscure front, well away from the levers of power in Paris.

In May 1798 Bonaparte embarked with his army at Toulon. After capturing Malta, he landed in Egypt and quickly overran Alexandria. But today, as he neared Cairo, he was blocked by an Ottoman force of 24,000 men, including 8,000 ferocious Mamluk horsemen.

Hoping to inspire his men for the battle ahead, Bonaparte gestured towards the pyramids faintly visible on the horizon and proclaimed: 'We will fight. Remember that from the top of these pyramids, forty centuries are looking down upon you.' ('*Nous allons combattre. Songez que du haut de ces pyramides quarante siècles vous contemplent.*')

In fact, the French needed little inspiration, as Bonaparte's impenetrable infantry squares and 47 cannon destroyed virtually the entire Egyptian force in less than two hours, at a cost of only 29 dead and 260 wounded. (In a gruesome epilogue, French soldiers stripped the enemy corpses, searching for valuables hidden in their clothing.)

The only real opposition during the battle had come from the Mamluk cavalry, superb riders and fanatic in their intent, who had come close to breaking the French squares, causing Bonaparte to comment: 'If I could have united the Mamluk horse with the French infantry, I should have seen myself as master of the world.'

Although Bonaparte had triumphed, just ten days after the battle Admiral Nelson destroyed the French fleet at Aboukir Bay, leaving the victorious army with no means to bring in more troops or to return to France.

Bonaparte settled down to rule Egypt, crushing a revolt in Cairo and winning a series of small victories against remaining resistance. Despite the demolition of an Ottoman army at Aboukir in July 1799, he realised that the glory he had won would become tarnished and that eventually his own small force would be whittled away. 'An army that cannot be reinforced is already defeated', he said. He also believed the time was ripe in France for a triumphant return. Without telling his soldiers, in August he surreptitiously slipped away to return to France, leaving his army in the hands of General Kléber.

Within three months Bonaparte had overthrown the Directory in his 18 Brumaire (9 November 1799) coup d'état, becoming First Consul of France. His army was not so fortunate. Kléber was assassinated by an Arab nationalist and the remainder of the army was finally repatriated on British ships after capitulating in September 1801. By this time 15,000 French troops had been killed in action and another 15,000 had died from disease. But the French public chose to remember Bonaparte's heroic victories rather than his losses. In November 1804, 99.93 per cent of French voters voted to establish a new French Empire with Bonaparte as emperor.

1403 Henry IV and his son Prince Harry (the future Henry V) defeat and kill Henry Percy (Hotspur) at Shrewsbury, about which Shakespeare writes: 'Ill-weaved ambition, how much art thou shrunk!/When that this body did contain a spirit,/A kingdom for it was too small a bound,/But now two paces of the vilest earth/Is room enough.' * **1969** When Neil Armstrong becomes the first person to land on the Moon, he says: 'That's one small step for a man, one giant leap for mankind.'

22 July

'Kill them all. God will know his own.'

1209 This famous command, uttered by a papal legate, triggered one of the most brutal massacres of the Middle Ages.

Five years earlier Pope Innocent III had launched the catastrophic Fourth Crusade, intended to conquer Muslim-controlled Jerusalem but resulting in the sack of Christian Constantinople instead. Now, in early 1209, he had turned his attention to heretics in south-west France, ordering a crusade to extirpate the dangerous heresy known as Catharism. (The Cathar cult was particularly strong around Albi, hence the attack became known as the Albigensian Crusade.)

'Catharism' comes from the Greek *katharos* (pure), which is what believers attempted to be. They thought that the material world was evil and man's task was to free himself from it. The most devout renounced life's pleasures, including meat and sex, in an attempt to find communion with God.

The Church in Rome could hardly find fault with such asceticism, but other Cathar doctrines were anathema. Cathars rejected the divinity of Christ and sternly criticised the Church for its nepotism, greed and corruption, but perhaps their most terrible crime was their refusal to contribute financial support to Rome.

Pope Innocent tried to bring the heretics to heel through diplomacy, but when his emissary was murdered, he abandoned negotiation for force. To gain recruits, he offered participants absolution for all sins if they served for 40 days, then gave the task of leading the campaign to a minor French noble, Simon de Montfort, who was spiritually supported by the fanatical papal legate, Arnaud-Amaury.

Soon a sizeable army of crusading knights, mercenaries, criminals seeking absolution, adventurers and religious fanatics was marauding its way through southern France, slaughtering and pillaging indiscriminately as they went.

On 21 July the army reached the walls of Béziers, six miles from the Mediterranean coast. At the city gates de Montfort declared that the town would be spared, provided it hand over the heretics; he then presented a list of 222 Cathars to be given up for execution. But the city leaders, not themselves Cathars, refused to deliver the victims, saying: 'We had rather be drowned in the salt sea than surrender our fellow citizens.'

The next day, as the crusaders were pitching camp in preparation for a siege, a small group of defenders charged out from one of the town gates, intent on harassing the mercenaries and camp followers of the crusading army. But the mercenaries chased the defenders back inside the town and then stormed the walls. Realising that Béziers was now defenceless, de Montfort ordered the crusader knights into the fray, which quickly became a brutal sack.

There was to be no mercy for the heretics, but how, Arnaud-Amaury was asked, can one tell a Cathar from the numerous devout Catholics in the population? 'Kill them all', said the Pope's representative. 'God will know his own.' ('*Tuez-les tous, Dieu reconnaîtra les siens.*')

Except for those few who managed to flee, the entire population of Béziers – 15,000 men, women and children – was put to the sword, 7,000 alone in the vast Romanesque Cathedral of Sainte-Madeleine where they had sought sanctuary.

Unlike most of the crusades to the Holy Land, the Albigensian Crusade eventually succeeded in its aims by destroying city after city in southern France, among them Carcassonne, Albi, Toulouse, Montségur and finally, in 1255, the very last Cathar stronghold, the Castle of Quéribus. With some poetic justice, de Montfort himself was killed by a boulder thrown from a trebuchet mounted on the ramparts of Toulouse. The few surviving Cathars fled where they could – Spain, Lombardy, England and Germany – or went underground. Three centuries later the Midi proved fertile ground for the Protestant Reformation.

The Church's experience with the Cathars had wider repercussions. Innocent died in 1216, but his nephew gained the papal throne as Gregory IX. Fully aware of the dangers of heresy, in 1231 the new Pope launched the Inquisition, which lasted in one form or another until 1908.

1298 Before the battle of Falkirk against Edward I in the First War of Scottish Independence, William Wallace tells his men: 'I have brought you to the ring; dance as best you can.' But the Scots are routed by the English. * **1832** Napoleon's son the Duke of Reichstadt (L'Aiglon) dies of tuberculosis at 21 at Schönbrunn Palace in Vienna, in the same room that Napoleon had slept in 22 years before. His last words: 'I am going under. Call my mother.'

23 July

'There will soon be only five kings left: the kings of England, diamonds, hearts, spades and clubs.'

1952 Today a cabal of Egyptian officers toppled their dissolute monarch, the fat and balding King Farouk.

In 1882 Great Britain had invaded Egypt when a revolt threatened the Suez Canal. Although British governance was largely benign, the country's poverty and corruption led to nationalist demonstrations and violence. In 1922 Britain made Egypt nominally independent and established a monarchy, but retained a military presence. When King Faud died in 1936, his sixteen-year-old son Farouk inherited the throne.

Farouk was the master of dozens of palaces, often travelled to Europe on shopping sprees and amassed a collection of fabulous jewellery. The British high commissioner described him as 'uneducated, lazy, untruthful, capricious, irresponsible and vain, though with a quick superficial intelligence and charm of manner'. He failed to add that Farouk had an insatiable appetite for women and assembled a huge collection of pornography while his aides kept him supplied with European prostitutes. He drove a red Bentley and decreed that no other private cars were to be red.

In 1948 a group of disillusioned Egyptian army officers formed the clandestine Free Officers movement led by Colonel Gamal Abdel Nasser. They considered Farouk a British puppet, a contemptible playboy who lived in luxury while the population remained mired in squalor. Aware that the Egyptian monarchy was fragile, Farouk grumbled: 'The whole world is in revolt. There will soon be only five kings left: the kings of England, diamonds, hearts, spades and clubs.'

While the Free Officers were still planning their moves, a bloody incident propelled them into open revolt. In January 1952 British soldiers in Ismailia attacked a police station that was sheltering Egyptian resistance fighters. Fifty Egyptian police officers were killed and 100 wounded, provoking Free Officer cells to initiate riots in Cairo in which nine Britons and sixteen Egyptians were killed and 750 buildings looted and burned.

The next day Farouk dismissed his prime minister, but the three governments he imposed during the next six months all failed to halt the country's downward spiral. (So chaotic had the country become that the CIA considered a project to overthrow Farouk, known internally as 'Project FF' (Fat Fucker).) Then the Free Officers, fearing that informers had penetrated their organisation, launched their revolution.

On 22 July 200 officers and 3,000 troops took control of army headquarters in Cairo while the king was enjoying a late champagne and caviar picnic in Alexandria. Then at 6.00 this morning, rebel air force units began circling Cairo's skies, and at 7.30 the Free Officers announced their takeover on Cairo radio. Now tanks roamed the streets, but there was no opposition.

Two days later revolutionary armoured columns occupied Alexandria while Farouk fled to the Ras El Tin palace with his loyal Sudanese Guard. Free Officer troops tried to storm the palace but were repulsed by the Sudanese, plus Farouk himself, who shot four attackers with his hunting rifle as they raced across the palace grounds. Soon a ceasefire was agreed, and the next day he was ordered to abdicate and depart the country.

With no alternatives open to him (both Britain and the United States had declined to come to his aid), Farouk tearfully agreed, and at 6.00 that evening he sailed away on his yacht with his family, seen off to the strains of the Egyptian national anthem and a 21-gun salute. Although forced to leave a thousand suits and his pornographic tie collection behind, Farouk managed to take on board crates labelled champagne that had been surreptitiously packed with gold bars.

The ex-king sailed first to Capri, then settled in Monaco and finally in Rome. Meanwhile his hoard of pornography had been discovered, making him a global object of ridicule. By now he weighed nearly 300 pounds – an acquaintance described him as 'a stomach with a head'. On 18 March 1965 he collapsed and died in the Île de France restaurant in Rome, where he had been sharing a midnight supper with a 22-year-old blonde.

1099 Besieged in Valencia by King Bucar and a vast Moorish army, El Cid is killed by a stray arrow, but following his last order, at midnight his soldiers strap his armoured body upright on his horse and ride out with it through the city gates. The *Chronica del Cid* relates: 'It seemed to King Bucar that before them came a knight of great stature upon a white horse with a bloody cross, who bore in one hand a white banner and in the other a sword which seemed of fire and he made great mortality among the Moors … And King Bucar and the other kings were so dismayed they never checked the reins until they had ridden into the sea.'

24 July

'What did the president know
and when did he know it?'

1974 Former president Harry Truman detested Richard Nixon, once declaring: 'Richard Nixon is a no good, lying bastard. He can lie out of both sides of his mouth at the same time, and if he ever caught himself telling the truth, he'd lie just to keep his hand in.' Now history was about to prove Truman right.

On 17 June 1972 Washington police caught five burglars breaking into the Democratic National Committee headquarters at the Watergate office complex. The housebreakers were quickly indicted, and the FBI launched an investigation, but voters didn't blame the break-in on the president, and Nixon was re-elected in November with a landslide 61 per cent of the vote.

Early the next year the Senate established a committee to investigate Watergate, and Attorney General Elliot Richardson named Archibald Cox as special counsel.

Now many began to believe that Nixon was somehow implicated, but his denials were fervent and there was no proof. Then, on 16 July 1973, former presidential aide Alexander Butterfield was asked if any White House conversations had been recorded. 'I was wondering if someone would ask that', Butterfield answered. 'There is tape in the Oval Office.' At Nixon's request, in 1971 Butterfield had overseen the installation of hidden microphones in Nixon's office and the cabinet room and on all telephone lines.

Both the Senate committee and Cox immediately subpoenaed the tapes, but Nixon refused to release them, citing executive privilege, and ordered Cox to drop his subpoena. Cox refused.

Nixon then demanded that Attorney General Richardson fire Cox, but Richardson resigned in protest. Nixon eventually found a compliant Solicitor General in Robert Bork, who replaced Cox with Leon Jaworski, but by then there was such a public uproar that Nixon felt forced to go on television to profess his innocence. 'People have got to know whether or not their president is a crook', he told the nation. 'Well, I am not a crook.'

As the investigation ground on, the Senate committee's vice chairman Howard Baker posed the fundamental question about the break-in: 'What did the president know and when did he know it?'

In March 1974 a grand jury indicted several former presidential aides, and Nixon agreed to release transcripts of several White House recordings but refused to release the tapes themselves, prompting an appeal to the Supreme Court.

On this day the Court made its decision; by a unanimous vote of 8 to 0, the judges ruled that Nixon's claims of executive privilege were invalid and that the tapes must be released.

The public was dismayed by the president's profanity, as well as by his rants against Jews ('an irreligious, atheistic, immoral bunch of bastards'), blacks (they live like 'a bunch of dogs'), Catholics ('The Catholic Church ... was homosexual, and it had to be cleaned out') and women ('I'm not for women, frankly, in any job ... [because they are] erratic and emotional.'). But most damaging of all was the 'smoking gun' tape, recorded just days after the break-in. In it Nixon can be heard discussing how to stop the FBI investigation, proving that he had been involved in the Watergate cover-up from the beginning.

Now even Republican congressmen turned on Nixon, and, knowing that he would be impeached by the House and removed from office by the Senate, on the evening of 8 August he announced on television that he would resign the next day, the only American president ever to do so.

The Watergate investigation resulted in 48 convictions, but the new president, Gerald Ford, pardoned Nixon for any crimes that he might have committed while in office, in order to end the national divisions created by the scandal. Americans remember Nixon as the president who could not tell the truth, as they remember George Washington, who could not tell a lie, and Donald Trump, who could not tell the difference.

1797 When a Spanish musket ball shatters his right elbow at Tenerife, Admiral Nelson tells his ship's surgeon: 'Doctor, I want to get rid of this useless piece of flesh here.' Half an hour after the amputation he is back in his cabin giving orders and writing dispatches with his left hand.

---

25 July

'He had James, the brother of John,
put to death with the sword.'

813 AD Today in Galicia, in the north-west corner of Spain, a local priest made an astonishing discovery – the tomb of Saint James the

Greater, who had been martyred in Jerusalem on the very same date almost eight centuries before.

According to legend, a Galician hermit named Pelagio saw supernatural lights emanating from a forest. Intimidated by the vision, he turned to the local priest, Theodemar of Iria, who was guided to James's tomb by following a star. Theodemar informed King Alfonso II of Asturias of this miracle, and the king had a chapel built on the site and came to the shrine as its first pilgrim. Since then the place has been called Santiago de Compostela – Saint James of the Field of Stars. It also became the goal of Europe's most famous pilgrimage.

Spanish folklore holds that in 40 AD James came to Iberia to convert the population. While he was preaching near today's Zaragoza, the Virgin Mary appeared to him upon a pillar, causing him to return to Judea to meet his martyrdom. (The pillar can still be found in the Catedral-Basílica de Nuestra Señora del Pilar in Zaragoza.)

Four years later, when King Herod Agrippa was persecuting Christians, he selected James as his first victim. As attested by Acts 12: 1–2: 'About that time Herod the king laid violent hands on some who belonged to the church. He had James, the brother of John, put to death with the sword.' Traditionally, 25 July has been accepted as the date of his execution.

Then, says Spanish myth, James's disciples took his body to Jaffa, where a miraculous stone ship transported him to Padrón in Galicia. There the disciples asked the local pagan queen Lupa for permission to bury the body, but she sent them to a sacred mountain that housed a dragon, hoping that the dragon would devour them. But the moment the dragon saw the cross, it exploded, and the disciples moved a few miles north until they found a suitable place for the martyr's tomb. Nothing more was heard of James's burial place for the next 800 years, until Theodemar of Iria's astounding discovery.

Whatever you may believe of Saint James's story, what is indisputable is that from the 9th century onwards a journey to Santiago de Compostela became Europe's greatest pilgrimage. The various routes there became known as the Way of Saint James (El Camino de Santiago), and Spanish legend holds that the Milky Way was formed from the dust raised by the trudging faithful.

Pilgrims could be recognised by the scallop shells they carried, remembrances of the Galician coast and the symbol of Saint James. (They are still called *coquilles Saint-Jacques* in French and *Jakobsmuschel* in German.) During their journey the travellers might be entertained with tales of the saint – how he appeared to Charlemagne in a dream, urging him to liberate his tomb from the Moors, or how he rode a white horse in the sky, armed with a sword and flourishing a large banner, at the Battle of Clavijo, inspiring Christians to defeat the Moors of Córdoba.

Over the centuries the pilgrimage to Santiago de Compostela gradually declined until, in 1882, the *Codex Calixtinus* was printed for the first time. This illustrated manuscript, probably authored by Pope Callixtus II in the 12th century, contained accounts of miracles associated with Saint James, descriptions of the route and advice for pilgrims. The *Codex* brought renewed interest in the pilgrimage, which was reinforced two years later when Pope Leo XIII declared that James's remains were authentic and indeed interred at Compostela.

Today about 300,000 believers take the great pilgrimage each year, most entering Spain near Roncesvalles and trekking 350 miles to Santiago de Compostela. There the lucky ones stay at the luxurious 15th-century Hostal dos Reis Católicos that was originally built to house pilgrims, and all can visit the majestic cathedral, an 11th-century masterpiece raised on the site of King Alfonso's original chapel. A particularly good time to arrive is 25 July, still celebrated as the feast day of Saint James.

1603 James I is crowned at Westminster, uniting the crowns of England and Scotland, but he will soon disappoint Parliament by declaring: 'I will govern according to the common weal, but not according to the common will.'

26 July

'Mother Earth, witness how my enemies shed my blood.'

1533 With a population of perhaps 12 million, the Inca Empire encompassed most of modern Peru and large parts of Ecuador, Bolivia, Argentina and Chile, an area five times the size of Great Britain. On this day the ruthless conquistador Francisco Pizarro brutally executed the Inca emperor Atahualpa, leading to the complete destruction of the empire.

Pizarro had heard that the empire was 'stuffed with gold', making him dream of repeating the exploits of his distant cousin Hernán

Cortés, who was subjugating the Aztecs in Mexico. In 1524–26 he mounted two expeditions, but neither produced significant booty. Then in January 1531 he set out once more.

Emperor Atahualpa was now about 30, and his command was absolute. 'In this realm, no bird flies, no leaf moves, if that is not my will', he claimed. His subjects believed that he was divine, directly descended from the Sun.

Atahualpa was then facing a rebellion led by his half-brother Huáscar. In April 1532 he destroyed Huáscar's army and put him to death. Following the victory, he went to Cajamarca, high in the Andes in northern Peru, where Pizarro now led his expedition.

Pizarro arrived on 15 November with an exiguous force of 110 foot soldiers and 67 cavalry. Atahualpa was curious to know this white intruder at first-hand, and, dismissing warnings from his entourage, he accepted Pizarro's invitation to visit him in his Cajamarca fortress. The next day he arrived in great pomp, accompanied by only 5,000 unarmed men of his 60,000-man army.

Among those who greeted Atahualpa was the Dominican chaplain, Fray Vicente de Valverde, who approached the emperor holding a crucifix and a Bible. After expounding the true faith of Christianity, Valverde called on Atahualpa to renounce all other gods.

Atahualpa scoffed at the friar's claims, noting that 'the Christ that you speak of died, the Sun and Moon never die'. Valverde claimed that his Bible would tell him the truth. 'Give me the book, so that it will tell me', Atahualpa commanded. Valverde handed him his Bible, and the emperor exclaimed, 'The book doesn't even talk to me!' and threw it to the ground.

At this Valverde turned towards Pizarro and said 'I absolve you' – implying: for all the crimes you are about to commit. At this signal, Spanish horsemen hidden behind the fort charged while cannon and harquebuses opened fire, slaughtering 5,000 unarmed Incans in just an hour. Pizarro locked Atahualpa in his fortress with a chain around his neck.

Atahualpa offered to buy his liberty by filling a room with gold and two rooms with silver, and sent messengers to the far corners of the empire for precious metals. As irreplaceable works of art poured into Cajamarca, Pizarro had them melted into ingots and sent to Spain.

The next summer Pizarro heard rumours (later proved false) that a vast horde of troops was advancing towards Cajamarca. On 26 July 1533 he charged Atahualpa with stirring up rebellion, idolatry, polygamy, incest and murdering his brother Huáscar. There was no trial – the

Spaniards simply pronounced him guilty and sentenced him to be burned alive. To Atahualpa this meant not only the cruellest of deaths but also the loss of his hopes for resurrection. The Incans believed that only if your body was embalmed could you be reborn in the afterlife.

As night was falling Atahualpa was taken from his prison and tied to a stake in the middle of the square. At the last moment Valverde offered death by strangulation if Atahualpa would consent to be baptised. The emperor agreed, was baptised and then summarily garrotted.

The Spaniards continued their conquest of the Inca Empire, although Pizarro was murdered by one of his own confederates in 1541. The last Inca emperor Túpac Amaru was beheaded by the Spanish in 1572. As he mounted the scaffold before 10,000 wailing Incans, he called out what could have been the epitaph of the whole empire: 'Mother Earth, witness how my enemies shed my blood.'

1945 The United States, Britain, and China issue the Potsdam Declaration that concludes: 'We call upon the government of Japan to proclaim now the unconditional surrender of all Japanese armed forces … The alternative for Japan is prompt and utter destruction.' When Japan fails to respond, eleven days later the American B-29 *Enola Gay* drops an atomic bomb on Hiroshima.

---

27 July

'If you think that the crown would be better
served by one of you, I agree to it and want
it most heartily and with good will.'

1214 Faced with an army almost twice the size of his own, today France's King Philip (II) Augustus offered his barons his throne. When no one accepted, he achieved a crushing victory that would change the face of Europe.

Aligned against Philip was a powerful coalition. Chief was King John of England, who was desperate to reconquer some of the vast territories in France that he had lost to Philip in the previous decade, all once part of the inheritance from his father, Henry II.

Siding with John was his nephew, Holy Roman Emperor Otto IV, who was fighting to retain his title in the face of the enmity of the Pope and his own recalcitrant barons. Otto calculated that if he could defeat Philip, he could keep his barons loyal by distributing conquered territories among them. Also joining the alliance were two of Philip's vassals, Count Renaud of Boulogne, who wished to establish independence from France, and Count Ferrand of Flanders, who had already defied his overlord so openly that Philip had sworn: 'Either France shall become Flanders, or Flanders, France!'

The alliance's plan called for John to move north from Poitou, destroying as he went, thus drawing Philip to attack. This would leave Paris open to Otto and the two counts, who would descend on the capital.

Philip's hope was to defeat his enemies piecemeal, starting with John. When the English invested the fortress at Roche-aux-Moines near Angers, the French swept down, and the English army dissolved almost without a fight.

Philip then moved north, gathering reinforcements from the local populace as he went. Many of the communal militia answered his call, doubling his strength to 11,000 foot and 4,000 cavalry, but when he reached Bouvines, ten miles south-east of Lille, he found Otto's allied force of 25,000 men preparing for battle.

Fully aware of the odds against him, on this day Philip addressed his barons: 'You are all my men and I am your lord. I have much loved you and brought you great honour, and gave freely of my own. But if you think that the crown would be better served by one of you, I agree to it and want it most heartily and with good will.' Impressed by his offer – and perhaps fearful of taking command against so strong an enemy – the assembled nobles cried out: 'We want no other king but you!'

Emperor Otto launched an immediate cavalry attack against the outnumbered French, but the fight soon descended into a wild mêlée in which Philip was dragged from his horse by Flemish pikemen but saved by some of his knights. Eventually repeated attacks by the French cavalry drove the enemy into disarray, and Otto's demoralised soldiers abandoned the fight after his wounded and terrified horse bolted, carrying him off the field.

For the losers, the Battle of Bouvines proved catastrophic. Ferrand of Flanders and Renaud of Boulogne remained French prisoners for the next twelve years, when Flanders was finally released. A year later Boulogne, still incarcerated, took his own life. Both men's territories were now firmly under French control.

Holy Roman Emperor Otto lost his imperial title, deposed by the Pope a year later. He retreated to his castle at Harzburg, where he died of dysentery in 1218.

King John lost all his French possessions except Gascony. His failure so weakened his prestige that the following year back in England his barons forced him to sign the Magna Carta, which severely limited the power of the Crown.

The Battle of Bouvines made France Europe's predominant power and established Philip as one of his country's greatest kings. It also changed the very nature of France. For the first time in history, the French nobility and army were joined by local militias of merchants and middle-class citizens, fighting together under the royal emblem of the *fleur de lys*. It marked the emergence of the French nation.

1675 While fighting the Holy Roman Empire in a minor skirmish at Sasbach, the man whom Napoleon considered the greatest military leader in history, Henri de la Tour d'Auvergne, vicomte de Turenne, is struck by a cannonball; as he lies dying he murmurs: 'I did not mean to be killed today.' * **1946** When dying of cancer in the American Hospital in Paris, Gertrude Stein asks her lover of nearly 40 years, Alice B. Toklas: 'What is the answer?' When she receives no reply, she asks: 'In that case, what is the question?' * **2003** Bob Hope's last words after his wife asks where he wants to be buried: 'Surprise me.'

---

28 July

'Terror is nothing other than justice, prompt, severe, inflexible.'

1794 Maximilien Robespierre was born of good bourgeois stock in the town of Arras, where he was once a choirboy. He was compulsively neat, righteous and ascetic, indifferent to both fine food and women. The public called him 'the Incorruptible' for his selfless revolutionary zeal. He termed himself 'a slave of freedom, a living martyr to the Republic', but he was to become the most feared man in France, who brought the Revolution's Reign of Terror to its apogee.

On 27 July 1793 Robespierre was elected to the Committee of Public Safety, formed three months earlier to 'oversee' (i.e. direct) the government. Under his leadership the Committee passed the Law of Suspects that ordered the arrest of all 'enemies of the Revolution', including nobles, relatives of émigrés, officials removed from office, and officers suspected of treason – that is, anyone thought not fully to support the Revolution. Suspects were considered guilty unless proven innocent, and the standard sentence was death by guillotine (jovially known as *Le Rasoir National* – The National Razor). By December Robespierre had established a virtual dictatorship, and the Terror reached its crescendo.

On 5 February 1794 Robespierre laid out his principles in a speech to the National Convention. 'The basis of popular government during a revolution is both virtue and terror', he said. 'Virtue, without which terror is destructive; terror, without which virtue is impotent. Terror is nothing other than justice, prompt, severe, inflexible. It is therefore an emanation of virtue … By sealing our work with our blood, we may see at least the bright dawn of universal happiness.'

The implacable Robespierre brought not only counter-revolutionaries to the guillotine but also former friends and colleagues, more for opposing his political power than for crimes against the state. He even condemned brother radicals like Georges Danton and his childhood friend, Camille Desmoulins. Both were guillotined on 5 April after a three-day trial where they had been prevented from defending themselves or having witnesses appear on their behalf. ('Pity is treason', Robespierre said.) According to fellow revolutionary François Buzot: 'Robespierre never forgave men for the injustices which he had done them, nor for the kindnesses that he had received from them, nor for the talents that some of them possessed, and he did not have.'

During the Terror almost 17,000 people were guillotined, including 2,639 in Paris, and up to 25,000 more were murdered without trial or died in overcrowded and unsanitary prisons. But eventually the Reign of Terror that Robespierre had done so much to create devoured him in its turn.

By the summer of 1794 Robespierre was losing his grip on power and shut himself in his rooms at the Hôtel de Ville. In the early hours of Monday, 28 July (Décadi, 10 Thermidor by the Revolutionary calendar), French troops seized him, and in the scuffle he was shot in the jaw. A young gendarme claimed to have fired because Robespierre was urging the citizens of Paris to rescue him, but most historians believe that the shattered jaw was a failed suicide attempt.

Later that day the Revolutionary Tribunal sentenced Robespierre to death without trial, along with 22 of his supporters, including his brother. About eight o'clock that evening he was taken to what today is the Place de la Concorde, where the guillotine waited. His face was wrapped in a bloodstained bandage, but he made no sound. Just before the final act, the executioner ripped off the bandage and his jaw fell open and blood poured from the gaping wound. A witness reported that he 'let out a groan like a dying tiger, which could be heard across the square'. And then the blade whistled down, severing his head from his body. According to legend, Robespierre was the only man to be guillotined face-up.

1540 After serving Henry VIII for seven years, Thomas Cromwell is executed, his head set on a spike on London Bridge. Two years earlier Henry had told the French ambassador that Cromwell was 'a good household manager, but not fit to meddle in the affairs of kings'. * **1988** President Ronald Reagan tells the Future Farmers of America: 'The ten most dangerous words in the English language are "Hi, I'm from the government, and I'm here to help."'

---

29 July

'The sadness will last for ever.'

1890 In Arles on Christmas Eve two years earlier Vincent Van Gogh had famously hacked off his left earlobe and given it to a prostitute. When he was hospitalised the next day, he was diagnosed with 'acute mania with generalised delirium'.

Van Gogh had shown signs of instability almost all his life. Even as a schoolboy he had felt isolated and abandoned, and his early working career had been punctuated by failure in London and Paris. At 26 he had become a missionary in Belgium but gave his room to a homeless man and lived in a hut in such squalor that his father thought he should be placed in a lunatic asylum. But the next year, at his brother Theo's suggestion, he took up painting. After a year at the Académie Royale des Beaux-Arts in Brussels, he began in earnest. 'I dream my painting, and then I paint my dream', he said as he sought to explore nature through the explosive colours that he saw in his mind.

Four months after that fateful Christmas Eve in Arles, Van Gogh committed himself to the Saint-Paul-de-Mausole asylum only a few miles away at Saint-Rémy-de-Provence, where he suffered from 'moods of indescribable anguish'. Although ravaged by loneliness and tormented by failure, he continued to work. The last painting he produced there was of a seated old man with his elbows on his knees and his head in his hands, an image of desolation and despair entitled

'At Eternity's Gate'. In May 1890, after a year in Saint-Rémy, he moved to the Auberge Ravoux in Auvers-sur-Oise to be nearer Theo, who was living in Paris. During 70 days at Auvers, he created more than 80 paintings.

On the morning of 27 July Van Gogh left the inn after breakfast and set out for a wheat field where he had been painting. That afternoon he left his easel against a haystack, placed a revolver to his breast and pulled the trigger. Deflected by a rib, the bullet passed through his chest and was stopped by his backbone. Van Gogh passed out. When he came to some hours later, he tried to find the revolver to finish the job, but, failing, he staggered back to his bedroom in the inn. When the innkeeper found him lying in bed, Van Gogh explained: 'I shot myself … I only hope I haven't messed it up.'

The innkeeper immediately called for two doctors and sent word to Theo. As neither doctor was a surgeon, the bullet could not be removed. When one doctor said that he still hoped to save his life, Van Gogh murmured: 'Then I'll have to do it over again.' But there was no need; the internal wound became infected.

The next afternoon Theo arrived and found his brother in a cheerful mood, but as the day wore on, his body systems began to close down. He died at one in the morning on this day. In a letter to his sister, Theo wrote that: 'He himself wanted to die. When I sat at his bedside and said that we would try to get him better and that we hoped that he would then be spared this kind of despair, he said, "*La tristesse durera toujours.*"' ('The sadness will last for ever.')

Within six months Theo had also died, brought down by paralytic dementia, a disease of the brain. Theo's doctors said his illness was brought on by 'heredity, chronic disease, overwork [and] sadness', but modern science suggests it was probably caused by late-stage syphilis. Theo and Vincent were buried side by side at Auvers-sur-Oise cemetery.

1759 Future president George Washington in a letter of instructions to the captains of the Virginia Regiments: 'Discipline is the soul of an army. It makes small numbers formidable; procures success to the weak, and esteem to all.' * **1918** Future president Franklin Roosevelt and future prime minister Winston Churchill meet for the first time, after which Churchill exclaims: 'Meeting Franklin Roosevelt was like opening your first bottle of champagne; knowing him was like drinking it.'

30 July

'There is no compensation for the loss of liberty.'

1683 Marie-Thérèse, Louis XIV's submissive and miserable first wife, died today after 23 years of unhappy marriage. Within a year of her wedding Louis had established his first *maîtresse en titre*, Louise de la Vallière, a court beauty of seventeen. He took at least eight more mistresses who produced thirteen children. The last was Françoise Scarron. Marie-Thérèse would have been horrified had she known that her death opened the path for Louis to marry Françoise in a *mésalliance* so great that the marriage was never revealed to the public.

Françoise was born in Niort near a prison where her father Constant d'Aubigné was incarcerated for conspiring against Cardinal Richelieu. At sixteen, with both parents dead, she married the crippled poet Paul Scarron, 25 years her senior. 'I preferred to marry him rather than a convent', she said. Scarron died nine years later, and Françoise lived quietly in Paris, devout and outwardly prudish but taking a series of lovers. Then at 33 she landed a plum job – governess to the royal bastards of Louis' mistress Athénaïs de Montespan, which gave her frequent access to the king.

Françoise was intelligent, scheming and drearily pious, but she caught Louis' roving eye, becoming his mistress in about 1673. She later denied it, boasting: 'The cleverest way is to conduct one's self irreproachably.' But about that time Louis gave her 200,000 livres, enough to buy the spectacular Château de Maintenon, and two years later he made her Marquise de Maintenon, generosity in the extreme if she were just a friend. She now styled herself simply Madame de Maintenon.

Françoise was very different from Louis' other paramours. Instead of younger, she was three years older than he, and he increasingly spent time with her not satisfying his appetites but talking about politics, religion and economics.

So it might have continued, except on 26 July 1683 Queen Marie-Thérèse complained that she was ill. No one paid much attention, but four days later she was dead. Louis simply shrugged: 'Poor woman. It's the only time she ever gave me any trouble.'

Probably on 9 October Louis married Françoise, according to the duc de Saint-Simon, 'at the dead of night in one of the king's cabinets at Versailles'. Louis bound all the participants to eternal secrecy; he had always maintained an immense distance between himself and even his most exalted subjects, but he had just married a widow without a drop of royal blood. The marriage was never officially announced, and, since it was morganatic, Madame de Maintenon was never Queen Consort of France.

Louis moved his new wife into a huge apartment in Versailles, just across from his own, and spent several hours a day with her discussing affairs of state. She listened and advised, in the words of historian Philippe Erlanger, 'with eyes still lowered, the modesty of a nun and the authority of a moralist'.

Louis now no longer had open mistresses and banned operas and comedies during Lent. Meanwhile Françoise was sanctimoniously telling her friends: 'The true way to soften one's troubles is to solace those of others.'

But she soon realised that satisfying her ambitions did not bring her happiness. As she wrote to a friend, 'there is no compensation for the loss of liberty. The king keeps me in sight, and does not leave my room. I have to get up at five to write to you. Months become moments, and I live with a speed that suffocates me.'

Françoise was disliked by the royal family and more so by Louis' courtiers, even though they incessantly sought her intervention with the king. Historians still debate her influence, most believing that she had little impact on major decisions like Louis' revocation of the Edict of Nantes.

One of Françoise's contributions was the creation of the Maison Royale de Saint-Louis in Saint-Cyr, a school for poor girls of noble families. Always the puritan, she insisted that all males except priests be banned from the school, with even priests allowed to meet the students only in the confessional. When Louis died in 1715 she moved there, and on her own death in 1719 she was buried in the school chapel.

1914 When French Socialist leader Jean Jaurès tells Undersecretary of Foreign Affairs Abel Ferry that the Socialists will continue their campaign against the war, Ferry warns: 'No, you will not dare to do that because you will be killed at the first street corner.' The next day Jaurès is shot to death in his favourite restaurant by a crazed patriot. * **1928** On his 65th birthday Henry Ford pronounces: 'Take all the experience and judgement of men over fifty out of the world, and there would not be enough left to run it.'

31 July

*'I always consider myself, my dear General, as one
of your lieutenants on a detached command.'*

1777 Today the US Second Continental Congress made a nineteen-year-old Frenchman with no military experience a major general. Although the young man had been recommended by the country's ambassador to France, Benjamin Franklin, the congressional resolution specified 'his zeal, illustrious family and connexions' – that is, the new general might be able to persuade France to support American independence. Furthermore, he offered to serve without pay.

He was Marie-Joseph Paul Yves Roch Gilbert du Motier, Marquis de Lafayette, whose family had always intended that he follow a military career. 'I was baptised like a Spaniard', he later joked, 'with the name of every conceivable saint who might offer me more protection in battle.'

An aristocrat to his fingertips, Lafayette could boast a forebear who supposedly had brought back the crown of thorns during the Sixth Crusade in the 13th century, while another ancestor had been Joan of Arc's companion-at-arms at Orléans. A marquis at two when his father had been killed in battle, he lost his mother and great-grandfather when he was twelve, leaving him an income of 120,000 livres when a labourer made 600 livres a year. At seventeen he married a duke's daughter (to whom he was devoted until her death 33 years later).

In 1775 Lafayette became interested in the American rebellion and determined to join the cause. After buying the brig *Victoire* for 112,000 livres of his own money, he sailed to South Carolina in June 1777 and became a major general the next month.

The day after receiving his commission, Lafayette was introduced to the American commander-in-chief, George Washington, then 45. The childless general and the orphaned aristocrat became friends for life. He named his son Georges Washington de Lafayette, and years later he wrote to Washington: 'I always consider myself, my dear General, as one of your lieutenants on a detached command.'

During the Revolutionary War Lafayette fought in seven battles while showing courage and leadership. During the defeat at Brandywine he was shot in the leg but rallied his troops to lead an orderly retreat, for which Washington cited him for 'bravery and military ardour'. During the bitter winter of 1777–78, when the Americans were haemorrhaging troops from desertion, he stayed at Washington's camp at Valley Forge and shared his troops' hardships.

After a trip to France to drum up support against the English (when he went hunting with Louis XVI), he returned to play a key role at the war's final battle at Yorktown.

Lafayette's life in France after the war was just as dramatic as during the revolution. As commander of the Parisian national guard, he saved Louis XVI and Marie-Antoinette from a howling mob that invaded Versailles – and also had the royal couple brought back from their flight to Varennes. He ordered the final demolition of the Bastille (and later gave its key to George Washington). He created the modern French flag by combining the blue and red of Paris with the Bourbon royal white and co-wrote the *Declaration of the Rights of Man and of the Citizen*. But he criticised growing French extremism, and in August 1792, Danton ordered his arrest. Lafayette fled to the Austrian Netherlands, only to be incarcerated for five years by the Austrians as a dangerous revolutionary.

In 1797 Napoleon Bonaparte procured his release, and he continued to fight for democracy in the face of tyranny, be it revolutionary, royal or Napoleonic, even passing up a chance to become dictator on the overthrow of Charles X in 1830.

At the invitation of his old friend from Valley Forge days, President James Monroe, in 1824 Lafayette returned to America and toured all 24 states to a rapturous reception. He visited Washington's grave, stayed with Thomas Jefferson at Monticello, dined with James Madison and John Adams and attended the presidential inauguration of John Quincy Adams. During the trip he collected some dirt from Bunker Hill and took it back to France. When he died at 76 on 20 May 1834 he was buried in the Picpus Cemetery in Paris – but in American soil.

1784 When his wife tells him not to eat so much, French philosopher Denis Diderot asks: 'Whatever harm do you think that can do me?' He dies a few minutes later. * **1798** Admiral Horatio Nelson predicts: 'Before this time tomorrow I shall have gained a peerage, or Westminster Abbey.' The next day he destroys Napoleon's fleet at the Battle of the Nile. * **1941** Obersturmbannführer Adolf Eichmann drafts a memo for Hermann Göring to Reinhard Heydrich: 'I charge you further to submit to me as soon as possible a general plan of the administrative material and financial measures necessary for carrying out the desired final solution of the Jewish question ("*Endlösung der Judenfrage*").'

1 August

*'The city must completely disappear
from the surface of the earth.'*

1944 On 27 September 1939 German soldiers had marched into Warsaw, only 26 days after they had crossed the Polish border to start the Second World War. But four years later the tide had turned: the Russian army was sweeping in from the east and the Allies had landed in Normandy.

Warsaw was held by only 15,000 German troops, while the Polish underground Home Army numbered 40,000 soldiers (including 4,000 women). As Soviet troops approached the city, Moscow radio called for the Poles to rise up against their oppressors, and the Polish government-in-exile in London ordered a revolt. Today the resistance launched the Warsaw Uprising, the largest single military effort taken by any European resistance movement during the war.

In addition to throwing out the Germans, the Poles were desperate to liberate Warsaw before the Soviets got there. They feared that if the Russians took the city, they would forcibly set up a Soviet-controlled communist regime.

In the initial brutal street fighting the Poles established control over most of central Warsaw, but then Hitler ordered in reinforcements, increasing German forces to 30,000 men – plus tanks, artillery and aircraft. And the Russians, now in Warsaw's suburbs, ignored Polish attempts to establish radio contact and refused to support the Poles with air cover, even though they occupied an airfield only five minutes' flying time away.

Both Roosevelt and Churchill pleaded with Stalin to come to Warsaw's aid, but the Soviet dictator refused. Eventually Churchill sent 200 supply drops without air clearance, and the US Air Force sent one high-level mass airdrop, but the Russians denied permission for the planes to land on Soviet airfields after dropping supplies.

As the battle for Warsaw raged, the Germans used tanks and flame throwers to clear houses, building by building. No prisoners were taken. Even those in hospitals were killed. Behind German lines SS and Wehrmacht troops went from house to house, shooting the inhabitants regardless of age or gender. In some Polish-controlled areas, German aircraft used incendiary bombs to obliterate resistance. Meanwhile the

Red Army had reached Warsaw's right bank but made no efforts to enter the city or aid the Polish rebels.

On 2 October, after 63 days of bitter fighting, the Poles – out of weapons, food, water and hope – were forced to surrender. The Polish underground Home Army had lost 16,000 dead and 6,000 badly wounded, and the 15,000 prisoners who had not been shot were sent to POW camps in Germany. About 150,000 civilians had been killed, mostly from mass executions. In addition, about 700,000 civilians were expelled, of whom 55,000 were sent to concentration camps. German casualties totalled over 8,000 killed and 9,000 wounded.

The Poles had been heroically but decisively defeated, but the destruction was not yet at an end. 'The city must completely disappear from the surface of the earth and serve only as a transport station for the Wehrmacht. No stone can remain standing. Every building must be razed to its foundation', declared Reichsführer-SS Heinrich Himmler.

During the uprising about a quarter of Warsaw's buildings had already been wrecked, but now German troops systematically levelled another 35 per cent of the city, block by block, destroying 10,455 buildings, 25 churches, fourteen libraries, 145 school and university buildings, and most of the city's monuments. Almost a million inhabitants lost all of their possessions. Together with damage from earlier in the war, some 85 per cent of the city was destroyed.

On 17 January 1945 the Russians entered what remained of Warsaw and turned Poland into a puppet state. By then only about 400,000 people remained in the city, down from 1.3 million before the war. But the Communists initiated the Bricks for Warsaw campaign, restoring many of the historic streets, buildings, and churches, and in 1989 the Poles shucked off the Russians in the first free elections since the war. Today the population has risen to 1,740,000. No wonder they call Warsaw the 'Phoenix City'.

1714: Tormented by ill health, thirteen miscarriages, the deaths of four infant children with her one surviving child predeceasing her, Queen Anne dies at 49; her court physician John Arbuthnot comments: 'I believe sleep was never more welcome to a weary traveller than death was for her.'

---

2 August

'The dead man's hand'

1876 This afternoon in Deadwood in the Black Hills of the Dakota Territory, Wild Bill Hickok was pondering his cards at a saloon poker table when a young drifter approached from behind, drew his revolver and shot him in the back of the head.

Hickok was one of the Wild West's meanest – and deadliest – characters. He looked the classic cowboy, with dark, shoulder-length hair, narrowed eyes and a droopy moustache. He carried a pair of silver-plated Colt revolvers with ivory grips.

Hickok was just as tough as he looked. When he was 22, as he was driving freight toward Santa Fe, he shot a bear blocking the road. The bear shrugged off the shot and attacked. Hickok slit the bear's throat with his Bowie knife, but was hospitalised for four months with his injuries.

A year later Hickok shot dead at least one and possibly three men who were threatening a freight company station manager. *Harper's Monthly* enthusiastically reported that he had single-handedly killed nine 'desperados, horse-thieves, murderers, and regular cutthroats in the greatest one man gunfight in history' – while suffering eleven bullet wounds.

During the American Civil War, Hickok scouted for the Union Army and during the Indian Wars for George Custer of Custer's Last Stand fame. Then he moved to Kansas, becoming sheriff in Hays City and marshal of Abilene, two untamed frontier towns. In his first month in Hays, he killed two men in gunfights, one of whom he suckered by yelling, 'Don't shoot him in the back; he is drunk!' and then shooting him when he turned to check.

In Abilene a disgruntled tavern owner tried to persuade the notorious outlaw and gunfighter John Wesley Hardin to shoot Hickok, but Hardin was wary of the redoubtable marshal and responded: 'If Bill needs killing, why don't you kill him yourself?' The tavern owner then tried to intimidate Hickok, saying that he 'could kill a crow on the wing'. Hickok sneered: 'Did the crow have a pistol? Was he shooting back?'

In 1871, however, after shooting dead a saloon owner in another brawl, Hickok accidentally killed his own deputy. He never fought in another gunfight but teamed up with his old friend Buffalo Bill Cody

385

in Cody's Wild West Show. He married a circus owner and had an affair with the frontierswoman 'Calamity Jane'.

Wild Bill then became an itinerant gambler. A contemporary recorded: 'His whole bearing was like that of a hunted tiger – restless eyes, which nervously looked about him in all directions closely scrutinising every stranger. When he played cards … he sat in the corner of the room to prevent an enemy from stealing up behind him.'

In 1876 Hickok moved to Deadwood, where he regularly played poker at Nuttal & Mann's Saloon. On the evening before his murder his opponents included the itinerant buffalo hunter, Crooked Nose Jack McCall, who lost heavily. Hickok condescendingly offered him money for breakfast, which infuriated McCall.

When Wild Bill joined the game the next afternoon, the only seat available was a chair that put his back to a door. He twice asked to change seats, but was refused. Now McCall entered the saloon, slipped up behind Hickok and shot him at point blank range, shouting 'Damn you! Take that!'

At his trial McCall was acquitted because he claimed Hickok had killed his brother, but he was subsequently rearrested after bragging about his deed and put on trial a second time (not considered double jeopardy because Deadwood was not a legitimately incorporated town). This time, when it was discovered that McCall did not have a brother, he was hanged.

In death, Hickok's legend grew. The cards he was holding when he was murdered – a pair of black aces and a pair of black eights – became known as 'the dead man's hand'.

He was buried in Deadwood, where his tombstone is marked 'Pard, we will meet again in the Happy Hunting Ground'. Although (or perhaps because) he had fatally shot 36 men, in 1979 he was elected to the Poker Hall of Fame.

---

216 BC When sceptics question his plan of crossing the Alps into Italy, Hannibal answers: 'I will find a way or make one.' Today he utterly destroys the Romans at Cannae. * **1100** When a stag bounds between King William Rufus and Walter Tirel in the New Forest, William shouts: 'Shoot, Walter, shoot, as if it were the devil.' Tirel's arrow glances off the stag's back and kills the king.

---

3 August

'I humbly beseech you in the name of the son of Holy Mary and for your own love of me to show mercy to these men.'

1347 In his endless quest to claim the crown of France, on 12 July 1346 England's Edward III landed at St Vaast-de-la-Hogue with an army of 15,000 men to start his campaign for the subjugation of Normandy. After sacking Caen he annihilated the French army at Crécy and then marched on Calais.

Calais was strongly fortified, with huge walls and a double moat. On 3 September the English army approached, and a herald rode up to the town gates with a trumpet sounding before him, calling upon Calais' governor Jean de Vienne to surrender. But de Vienne refused, saying that he held Calais for Philippe (VI) of France and that he would defend it to the last. So now the English surrounded the city, determined to starve it into submission.

For month after month the citizens of Calais resisted, devouring first their horses, then their dogs and finally their cats and rats. By June 1347 food had become so scarce that de Vienne expelled 500 'useless mouths' – women, children and elderly men – from the town. Some sources say that their sorrowful, famished looks gained pity for them, and Edward ordered that they should go safely through his camp, after offering them a hearty dinner. Others claim that the English refused to allow them through their lines, so they starved to death just outside the walls.

By July still no French army had come to the rescue, and conditions in Calais had become desperate. At length after eleven months of siege de Vienne approached under flag of truce and offered to surrender the city if its citizens were allowed to leave unmolested. At first Edward refused, but finally agreed to spare Calais' inhabitants if six of the richest burghers would present themselves to him carrying the keys of the town, with bare feet and heads and nooses around their necks.

De Vienne called together the townsmen and asked if they should all continue to starve together or sacrifice their best and most honoured for peace. In response, the richest burgher, Eustache de St Pierre, offered himself and was followed by five other prominent volunteers.

On this day the six burghers appeared as ordered, sweating from the heat and shivering in their fear of the king's wrath. But just as Edward was about to signal their execution, his wife Queen Philippa, who had accompanied her husband throughout the siege, knelt before the king. 'Gentle Sire', she begged, 'since I have crossed the sea, with much danger, to see you, I have never asked you one favour; now I humbly beseech you in the name of the son of Holy Mary and for your own love of me to show mercy to these men.'

For some time the king looked at Queen Philippa in silence and then exclaimed: 'Dame, dame, would that you had been anywhere than here! You have entreated in such a manner that I cannot refuse you; I therefore give these men to you, to do with as you please.' Thus the burghers were spared and the English took Calais, which remained in English hands until the reign of Mary Tudor.

Over half a millennium later, in 1884, the town of Calais commissioned Auguste Rodin to create a statue based on the event, one that would express the French burghers' courageous willingness to die for their compatriots. Not to be outdone, in 1908 the British government ordered another cast placed in the shadow of the Houses of Parliament, intended to illustrate the clemency of a just and merciful English king.

1650 When the Scots proclaim Charles II as king, Oliver Cromwell writes to the General Assembly of the Church of Scotland: 'I beseech you, in the bowels of Christ, think it possible you may be mistaken.' * **1914** When Germany declares war on France, British Foreign Secretary Sir Edward Grey observes: 'The lamps are going out all over Europe; we shall not see them lit again in our lifetime.' * **1936** When Jesse Owens wins the first of four Olympic Gold Medals in Berlin, Hitler comments: 'The Americans ought to be ashamed of themselves for letting their medals be won by Negroes.'

---

4 August

'I am tasting the stars!'

1693 The ancient abbey of Saint-Pierre d'Hautvillers was situated about twenty miles south of Reims in the old province of Champagne. There Benedictine monks not only followed their religious duties but also cultivated wine. But in this northern region, grapes had to be harvested early, resulting in a pleasant but undistinguished pink wine rather than the deep reds produced further south in Burgundy. To make matters worse, the chilly winters temporarily halted the fermentation process, but warmer days in the spring 'reawakened' the fermentation after the wine had been bottled. The result was the formation of bubbles that caused wine bottles to explode or to pop their corks (which at the time were not corks at all but wooden stoppers).

This was a particular problem for one of the monks, 55-year-old Dom Pierre Pérignon, who for five years had been the abbey's cellar master. In an attempt to reduce the bubbles, Pérignon started blending several types of grapes – mostly pinot noir and pinot meunier – and removing their skins. He also introduced thicker, stronger bottles and imported cork from Spain to replace the wooden stoppers, fastening them with oil-soaked hemp.

On this day in the summer of 1693 Pérignon decided to test a bottle of his new wine to see how it had developed. On sipping the effervescent liquid, he excitedly called to his brother monks: 'Come quickly! I am tasting the stars!' Champagne had been invented.

It may not surprise the reader that glum historians pour scorn on this charming story, insisting that sparkling wine was invented in France in 1531 – or by a 17th-century English scientist named Christopher Merret (who did produce the first lists of British birds and butterflies). Some even maintain that Pérignon's famous quotation about tasting the stars originated in a 19th-century advertising campaign.

What is certain is that Pierre Pérignon really was the wine master at the Abbey of Saint-Pierre d'Hautvillers – he died there in 1715 and his tomb can still be found in the abbey's church. He was one of history's first oenophiles, probably the first to blend wines and to make white wine by discarding the skin of black grapes. According to cellar master Richard Geoffroy: 'Dom Pérignon was the entrepreneur of champagne. He made it happen.'

Such is the appeal of Pérignon's story that in 1936 the French champagne house Moët & Chandon named their first *cuvée de prestige* (top-of-the-range brand) after him, calling it Dom Pérignon. Today it is still one of the world's best and most prestigious champagnes. As James Bond said of the villain in the film *The Spy Who Loved Me*: 'Maybe I misjudged Stromberg. Any man who drinks Dom Pérignon '52 can't be all bad.'

1265 As Prince Edward's army crushes the forces of England's virtual dictator Simon de Montfort at the Battle of Evesham, de Montfort tells his soldiers: 'Commend your souls to God, for our bodies are our foe's.' He is killed in the battle.

5 August

'I have slain the English; I have mortally opposed the English King; I have stormed and taken the towns and castles which he unjustly claimed as his own.'

1305 Ever since 1297, when he had killed the English High Sheriff of Lanark, William Wallace had been fighting the English for Scottish independence. Four months later he secured a major victory at Stirling Bridge, where, although heavily outnumbered, he slaughtered 5,000 English as they crossed the river, but the next year Edward I of England led a 25,000-man army into Scotland and annihilated Wallace's force at Falkirk. At the close of the battle, Wallace fled into the nearby forest of Torwood, where he personally killed Sir Brian de Jay, master of the English Templars, during his escape.

Wallace spent the next seven years alternately hiding from the English and keeping his revolt alive through sporadic guerrilla raids. On this day he was in Robroyston, near Glasgow, when he was betrayed by the Scottish nobleman John de Menteith, who had earlier fought for the Scottish cause but had changed loyalties after Edward had captured and imprisoned him. There are two versions of Menteith's treachery. The first says Wallace's servant revealed where Wallace was staying, and Menteith seized him in bed during the night. The story we like better has Menteith spotting Wallace in a tavern and picking up a loaf of bread and turning it end to end as a signal to English soldiers, who surrounded Wallace before he could draw his sword. In any event, now Wallace was carried away to London at the pleasure of the king.

Eighteen days after his capture Wallace was tried in the great hall at Westminster, charged with treason and the murder of civilians ('he spared neither age nor sex, monk nor nun'). During his trial Wallace strenuously objected: 'I cannot be a traitor, for I owe [King Edward] no allegiance. He is not my sovereign; he never received my homage; and whilst life is in this persecuted body, he never shall receive it. To the other points whereof I am accused, I freely confess them all. As Governor of my country I have been an enemy to its enemies; I have slain the English; I have mortally opposed the English King; I have stormed and taken the towns and castles which he unjustly claimed as his own. If I or my soldiers have plundered or done injury to the houses or ministers of religion, I repent me of my sin; but it is not of Edward of England I shall ask pardon.'

The trial was just a formality – although five judges were in attendance, Edward had determined the result long before it started. Within an hour after the sentence was read, Wallace was taken to Smithfield, where first he was hanged but cut down while still alive. He was then emasculated and disembowelled, and his entrails were burned before his eyes. Finally, he was decapitated and his body cut into parts, to be hung in public places as a reminder of the fearsome wrath of the king. His left leg was displayed in Aberdeen, his right one in Perth, and his left arm in Berwick, his right one in Newcastle. His head was impaled on a spike at London Bridge.

So died the man the English considered a treacherous outlaw and the Scottish a national hero. With Wallace dead, Edward believed he had cowed the Scots, but in fact, by his barbarous method of execution he had turned Wallace into a martyr. By the time of his own death in 1307 Edward was already facing a new and far more dangerous enemy, Robert the Bruce, who totally destroyed the army of Edward's son Edward II at the Battle of Bannockburn seven years later. It took four more centuries before England and Scotland were formally brought together under the name of Great Britain.

1864 During the American Civil War, Union Admiral David Farragut leads his ships through a minefield to destroy a Confederate fleet at Mobile Bay on the Alabama coast of the Gulf of Mexico with the order: 'Damn the torpedoes! Full speed ahead.'

---

6 August

'His kindred flew from Florence to Rome like so many bees … to suck the honey of the Church.'

1623 Pope Gregory XV had succumbed to fever at the beginning of a sweltering July, so now 54 cardinals huddled in the heat to select his successor. As they were deliberating, a swarm of bees entered the conclave, perhaps a sign from Heaven indicating God's choice. On this day wisps of white smoke drifted from the Vatican chimney – a new pontiff had been elected. He was a blue-blooded 55-year-old Florentine named Maffeo Barberini, whose family coat of arms featured three golden bees on a field of blue. He would take the name Urban VIII.

According to a Venetian ambassador: 'His Holiness is tall, dark, with regular features and black hair turning grey. He is exceptionally elegant and refined in all details of his dress; has a graceful and aristocratic bearing and exquisite taste. He is an excellent speaker and debater, writes verses and patronises poets and men of letters.'

Urban's passionate interest in the arts is best exemplified through his friendship with and patronage of the 17th century's greatest sculptor, Gian Lorenzo Bernini, who created majestic pieces like Rome's Triton Fountain (appropriately in Piazza Barberini) and even more spectacular work in St Peter's Cathedral, where he designed the immense gilt-bronze baldachin to go over the high altar, which took twelve years to complete. To make the huge baldachin, Urban authorised the seizure of the massive bronze girders from the portico of the Pantheon. When the public learned of this vandalism, one anonymous wit left a famous message: '*Quod non fecerunt barbari, fecerunt Barberini.*' ('What the barbarians did not do, the Barberini did.')

Today Urban is best known for his relationship with Galileo. He had been an early friend and supporter of the scientist, who dedicated his 1623 work on comets, *Il Saggiatore*, to him. But when Galileo insisted that the Earth revolves around the Sun, Urban summoned him to Rome and then condemned him to live the rest of his life under house arrest.

In the 17th century, however, Urban had an even more famous distinction: nepotism. He created a brother, a cousin and two nephews cardinals and made another nephew, Taddeo, a prince. The 19th-century German historian Leopold von Ranke calculated that during Urban's reign his family amassed 105 million scudi in personal wealth, more than twice the papacy's annual income, fully justifying the criticism of Urban's contemporary, the Canterbury Cathedral canon John Bargrave, who wrote: 'Upon his elevation, his kindred flew from Florence to Rome like so many bees (which are the Barberini's arms), to suck the honey of the Church, which they did excessively.' Not surprisingly, under Urban's stewardship Vatican debt almost tripled and more than four-fifths of papal revenues was being spent on interest payments.

Urban's final years were darkened by a war around the ancient city of Castro, a complicated conflict between Urban and the Pamphili family caused largely by pride and greed on both sides. Urban not only lost the war but spent a fortune doing it, leading to immense unpopularity among his subjects. Dejected by the loss and now 76, he died on

29 July 1644. No doubt he would have been even more despondent had he known that his successor would be the detested Giovanni Battista Pamphili, elected as Innocent X. Soon after his accession, Innocent accused Urban's three nephews of embezzling public funds, forcing them to flee to Paris. Only with the intercession of Cardinal Mazarin were they able to return to Rome.

1890 William Kemmler, who killed his common-law wife in a drunken rage, becomes the first person ever executed by electric chair. The chair was designed by Thomas Edison. The 2,000 volts scorch his hair and skin, causing an unbearable stench that nauseates the witnesses. Edison's competitor George Westinghouse, who has designed a different electrical system, comments: 'They would have done better using an axe.'

---

7 August

'The Turks and the Frenchmen took three assaults to breach the Peyrolière bastion, past the tower of Cinq Quayre or Quinquangle, where Ségurana fought.'

1543 The quotation above comes from *Le Journal authentique du Siège de Nice*, written in 1543, just after the bloody siege of Nice that began on this day. In it is the name 'Ségurana', the only historical reference we have to one of France's most legendary heroines, Catherine Ségurane.

Today nothing could be more French than Nice, rising along an idyllic sweep of coastline romantically called La Baie des Anges on the Côte d'Azur. But in the 16th century Nice was not part of France but controlled by Charles II of Savoy, who had unwisely allied himself with Holy Roman Emperor Charles V, who was at war with French King François I.

In his desperation to combat Emperor Charles, François had cemented the unholiest of alliances – with Suleiman the Magnificent's Ottoman Empire. Into the fray Suleiman sent his famous admiral/corsair Hayreddin Barbarossa.

Barbarossa's 110 galleys joined the 50 commanded by Prince François de Bourbon at Marseille. Their first target was Villefranche, four miles east of Nice, which they sacked and destroyed. They then moved up the coast to Nice itself, starting a month-long siege.

As the Niçois hunkered down behind the city's walls, the attackers brought up their artillery. After five days of incessant cannonade, they finally breached the Peyrolière bastion on 15 August. But just as the Turks were about to enter Nice, two very different women came to the defenders' aid. First, the Virgin Mary appeared, giving heart to the besieged (most appropriately, it was Assumption). Then, according to Niçois folklore, came Catherine Ségurane, an earthy washerwomen who was bringing food to soldiers manning the ramparts.

During the assault some Turkish Janissaries reached the top of the wall, one waving a red banner with a golden crescent. Just as he was planting the banner as a sign of victory, Catherine attacked him with a wild scream, killing him with a blow to the head with her laundry beater. After throwing several more attackers off the wall, she grabbed the banner, tore it in pieces and hurled it into the sea. Then, standing on the wall, she turned her back on the enemy with scorn, lifted her skirt and bared her bottom, a gesture so fiendishly inflammatory to Muslims that the Turks began pulling back in panic.

Despite Catherine's heroics, Barbarossa bombarded Nice's walls for another week, opening two new breaches and forcing the city to surrender. Only the city's castle, the Château de Cimiez, held out because the French galleys ran out of gunpowder to supply the Turks. 'Are your seamen to fill your casks with wine rather than powder?' complained Barbarossa. He was further disgusted when the French attackers protected the fleeing Niçois, whom he had expected to enslave. On 7 September Charles of Savoy arrived with a relief army, and the next day the besiegers started to break camp. The last night before leaving, Barbarossa plundered the city, putting parts of it to the torch.

For reasons perhaps only the French can understand, Catherine Ségurane has remained in Nice's collective memory as a mystical figure that somehow embodies the city's identity, to the point that the Niçois are sometimes called 'Séguran'. They have placed a plaque near the remains of the Sincaïre bastion that shows her brandishing the banner taken from the Turks, and the city still boasts a rue Catherine Ségurane, where you can see a mounted cannonball fired by the Turkish fleet.

1815 When Napoleon is exiled to St Helena, Goethe comments: 'They have chained down another Prometheus. For the sake of a great name he knocked half the world into pieces.'

8 August

'The black day of the German Army'

1918 It was still well before sunrise today when almost 1,000 British and French guns fired the first deafening salvo towards the German lines near Amiens. At the same moment British tanks and infantry units from Britain, Canada and Australia moved forward through a no-man's-land obscured by darkness, a heavy mist and smoke laid down by the Royal Air Force. Forty-five minutes later the French would start their attack on the first day of the Hundred Days' Offensive that would ultimately end the First World War.

In the bloodbath of the preceding four years, the Allies had lost 17 million killed, wounded or missing, but preying on British minds was the Battle of the Somme in 1916. They had planned for months, but their preparations were visible to German reconnaissance planes. Then the pre-assault artillery bombardment had lasted ten days, supposedly smashing enemy defences but in reality only warning the Germans of an imminent attack, and the British had suffered 60,000 casualties on the first day alone.

Now at Amiens surprise was the key. Moving troops and equipment only at night, the British had put over 500 tanks, 2,000 artillery pieces and several divisions of infantry into attack position without alerting the Germans.

The Allied force was heavily weighted towards the British Empire, with ten British divisions, five Australian and five Canadian, but France also provided twelve divisions, and there was one American division which had only arrived in France earlier in the year. In overall command was Supreme Allied Commander Ferdinand Foch, who had been made a Marshal of France just two days before the battle. (Foch was nothing if not enthusiastic. 'I shall fight without ceasing', he said to a group of officers. 'I shall fight in front of Amiens. I shall fight in Amiens. I shall fight behind Amiens. I shall fight all the time.' He also had clear ideas on command structure: 'A committee should have an odd number of members', he said, 'and three is already too many.')

But the mind behind the Allied plan at Amiens was an Australian major general named John Monash. An engineer in civil life, Monash was initially suspect because he was not a professional soldier, he was a Jew, and both his parents were German. He fervently believed that the key to battle success was surprise and that 'mechanical means', i.e. artillery and tanks, should be used extensively and primarily to protect the infantry. Monash had already proven his theories at Hamel in July, where infantry supported by tanks and artillery achieved their objectives in less than two hours.

At Amiens there was no pre-assault artillery barrage; instead the coordinated artillery and tank-supported infantry attacks caught the Germans completely by surprise. Many surrendered immediately, and some German divisional officers were captured while eating breakfast. More and more Germans now threw down their arms, as the Allies punched a fifteen-mile gap in the German line, and the Canadian Corps advanced over eight miles, one of the greatest advances in a conflict characterised by static trench warfare.

The Germans lost about 27,000 men that day, one that their commander General Erich Ludendorff called 'the black day of the German Army' ('*Der Schwarzer Tag des deutschen Heeres*'). Here he referred not to territory lost but to the collapse of German morale that led to large numbers of troops surrendering almost without firing a shot.

The battle lasted for three more days, bringing total German losses to 75,000 men, of whom 50,000 were prisoners.

When Ludendorff told Kaiser Wilhelm about the catastrophe at Amiens, the Kaiser gloomily concluded: 'We have reached the limits of our capacity. The war must be terminated.' During the next three months the Allies pushed the Germans behind the Hindenburg Line and almost out of France. Just 93 days after the first assault at Amiens, Kaiser Wilhelm abdicated and fled to Holland, and on 11 November Germany signed the armistice in Marshal Foch's railway carriage at Compiègne, bringing the First World War to an end.

1588 On the critical day against the Spanish Armada, Drake's fleet sinks or damages eleven enemy ships and kills 2,000 Spaniards, which forces the Armada to sail north around Scotland, but a severe gale causes 24 more ships to founder and the invasion to be abandoned. On hearing of the defeat, Spanish King Philip II complains: 'I sent my ships against men, not against seas.'

9 August

'We are dancing on a volcano.'

1830 When France's Louis XVIII died in September 1824, his younger brother inherited the throne as Charles X. Already 66, Charles was a harsh reactionary who detested the idea of parliamentary supremacy, once claiming that 'I would rather hew wood than be king after the English fashion'.

Charles passed a series of laws that bolstered the power of the nobility and clergy and appointed a succession of ever more reactionary prime ministers, culminating with the ultra-royalist Jules de Polignac in 1829. Charles seemed determined to return, in fact and in spirit, to the Ancien Régime. The next March he dissolved the liberal government and called for new elections to get representatives more to his taste. The result was a bitterly resentful population simmering with revolutionary anger.

On the evening of 31 May, Charles's distant cousin Louis-Philippe, duc d'Orléans gave a grand ball in the Palais Royale in honour of the King of Naples. As the 2,000 guests disported themselves in the lantern-lit garden, the former French minister to Naples, Narcisse-Achille de Salvandy, remarked to his host: 'You are giving us quite a Neapolitan fête.' Then he added in reference to the Italian peasants who were given to dancing on the slopes of Vesuvius: 'We are dancing on a volcano.' Less than a month later, he was proved right.

In June, when the elections Charles had called for did not produce results he wanted, he suspended the constitution, hobbled the press and dissolved the newly elected Chamber of Deputies. The result was the July Revolution, three days that the French still call '*Les Trois Glorieuses*'.

On 27 July unruly crowds milled around Paris as troops positioned themselves on the Place du Carrousel, the Place Vendôme, and the Place de la Bastille. At twilight violence exploded, as Parisians hurled roof tiles and flowerpots from their windows at the soldiers in the streets. The soldiers opened fire, killing 21 civilians. Rioters then paraded the corpse of one of their fallen throughout the streets, shouting '*Mort aux Ministres! À bas les aristocrates!*'

Fighting continued throughout the night and into the next day. All business ground to a halt as rioters tilted with soldiers and police, shouting '*À bas le roi!*' In mid-afternoon Charles received a note from Marshal Auguste Marmont, who had been charged with suppressing the riots: 'Sire, it is no longer a riot, it is a revolution.' The king asked Prime Minister Polignac for counsel; his advice was to continue the fight.

By dawn of the third day the revolutionaries had thrown up over 4,000 barricades, and they now hoisted the tricolour over important buildings and occupied the Louvre and the Hôtel de Ville. The Swiss Guard deserted, as did many soldiers and police. That evening members of the dismissed parliament began establishing a provisional government.

On 2 August Charles X abdicated, and Louis-Philippe, duc d'Orléans seemed just the man to replace him; he was a Bourbon, a liberal royal and France's richest capitalist to boot. Backed by Lafayette and future French president Adolphe Thiers, he was offered the crown by the French legislature and sworn in on this day, 9 August.

Charles X had hunkered down with his family at Rambouillet, but, after learning that a mob 14,000 strong was preparing to besiege him, he fled to Great Britain on packet steamers provided by Louis-Philippe. After living briefly in Lulworth Castle in Dorset, he moved to Edinburgh, then Prague, then Teplice in Austria and finally to Gorizia (now in north-east Italy) where he died of cholera on 6 November 1836.

Meanwhile Louis-Philippe had fashioned himself as the Citizen King, ambling about Paris in a large three-cornered hat, with an umbrella in his left hand and his right hand extended to shake the hands of passing Frenchmen. At heart, however, he was still too reactionary for his times, and in 1848 when revolutionary fever seized most of Europe, he was forced to flee from France, to end his days an exile in Surrey at the age of 76.

---

48 BC When Pompey and his allies refuse to compromise, Julius Caesar defeats him at the Battle of Pharsalus, afterwards remarking bitterly: '*Hoc voluerunt.*' ('This is what they wanted.')

---

10 August

'An Establishment for the increase and diffusion of knowledge'

1846 On this day American President James Polk signed into law the act that established the Smithsonian Institution, which would eventually become a conglomeration of museums housing 138 million works of art, artefacts and specimens. This unrivalled complex owes its existence to a gift from an illegitimate English aristocrat who never set foot in the United States.

Back in 1740, when Hugh Smithson married Lady Elizabeth Seymour, an heiress of the mighty Percy family, he changed his name to the more prestigious Percy. On the death of his father-in-law, he inherited the title of Earl of Northumberland and was later elevated to duke.

Hugh (Smithson) Percy may have owed his social advancements to his wife, but not his fidelity as, after almost a quarter-century of marriage, he embarked on an affair with a rich and handsome widow named Elizabeth Macie.

As liaisons often do, the affair led to a pregnancy, and on 5 June 1765, Elizabeth secretly gave birth to a son in Paris. The boy was named James Macie. A year after James graduated from Oxford (1785), his natural father died, without ever seeing or acknowledging his son. Nonetheless, James changed his name from Macie to Smithson, his father's pre-marriage surname.

Leading a peripatetic life, Smithson travelled endlessly through Europe; he was in Paris during the French Revolution, and after Napoleon came to power, he was briefly imprisoned as a suspected spy. But his real interest was science.

While still a student, Smithson had sailed to the Hebrides on a geological expedition, and he spent the remainder of his life conducting research in chemistry, mineralogy, and geology. He published 27 papers on subjects ranging from mineral analyses to improvements to the blowpipe and the windmill, as well as essays on a better method for making coffee and the composition of snake venom. Among his many eminent friends were scientists Henry Cavendish, Joseph Priestley, Antoine Lavoisier and Joseph Banks.

In 1800 Smithson's mother died, leaving him half her ample fortune. Then in 1829 Smithson succumbed to a long illness. Rich but unmarried and childless, he passed his inheritance on to his only nephew, with a peculiar footnote. In the event that his nephew should die without heirs, the whole of his estate would go to 'the United States of America, to found at Washington, under the name of the Smithsonian Institution, an Establishment for the increase and diffusion of knowledge'. Apparently he had concluded that this nascent democracy was the most likely place to make good use of his money.

In 1835 Smithson's nephew obligingly died childless, and President Andrew Jackson dispatched a diplomat to England to collect the bequest, which turned out to be 105 sacks containing 104,960 gold sovereigns, worth about $500,000, or 1.5 per cent of the United States' entire federal budget at the time.

The US Congress spent eight years haggling over how to interpret Smithson's vague mandate 'for the increase and diffusion of knowledge'. Eventually ex-president John Quincy Adams persuaded the government to use the money for an institution of science and learning. It was only then, on this day in 1846, that President Polk signed the necessary legislation.

Today the Smithsonian Institution comprises nineteen museums and galleries, including a zoo. The most famous are the National Museum of Natural History, the National Portrait Gallery, the National Museum of American History and the National Air and Space Museum, which alone attracts almost 7 million visitors annually (about a million more than the British Museum but fewer than the Louvre's 10 million). In total, 30 million people visit the Smithsonian's various museums each year.

Smithson's magnificent gift was surely inspired by his belief that, as he wrote: 'It is in his knowledge that man has found his greatness and his happiness, the high superiority which he holds over the other animals who inhabit the earth with him.' But perhaps he was also making a statement against the father who had ignored him when he predicted: 'My life will live on in the memory of men when the titles of the Northumberlands are extinct or forgotten.'

---

955 Otto I the Great, King of East Francia, annihilates a Hungarian army at the Battle of Lechfeld, definitively ending Hungarian incursions into western Europe; contemporary Saxon chronicler Widukind of Corvey reports: 'Never was so bloody a victory gained over so savage a people.'

---

11 August

'Now we are in the power of the wolf.'

1492 Today the papacy moved into its most worldly, cynical and corrupt period with the election of Rodrigo Borgia, the Spanish-born cardinal who became Pope Alexander VI. Borgia's triumph was all the greater because his opponents had been so well-connected. Of the 27 living cardinals, ten had been created by popes to whom they were related, and eight were the nominees of European crowned heads. One of these was Giuliano della Rovere, whose uncle Sixtus IV had been the last pope but one, and who was backed with huge sums by Charles VIII of France, King Ferrante of Naples and the Republic of Genoa.

Borgia also had a papal uncle, Calixtus III, who had died in 1458, but his victory in the conclave was assured not by the papal blood in his veins but by bribes greater than even della Rovere could offer. Chief among Borgia's bribees was Cardinal Ascanio Sforza, whom he rewarded with the Vice-Chancellorship of the Holy Roman Church, a castle at Nepi, the Bishopric of Eger (worth 10,000 ducats a year – £10 million today), the Palazzo Borgia, a couple of canonries and four mule-loads of silver.

Many in the Church's higher echelons were shocked by Borgia's elevation – the young Cardinal Giovanni de' Medici (later Leo X) lamented: 'Now we are in the power of the wolf, the most rapacious perhaps that this world has ever seen; and if we do not escape, he will inevitably devour us.' Giuliano della Rovere was truly aghast – he hated Borgia for being chosen over him and had opposed his election so vigorously that Borgia – now Alexander VI – began plotting his assassination.

In fear for his life, della Rovere fled to the court of Charles VIII. In 1494 Charles invaded Italy to lay claim to the Kingdom of Naples. En route he entered Rome with his army, with della Rovere riding at his side. But Charles had no interest in deposing Alexander, and after his army returned to France, Alexander deprived della Rovere of his benefices as an enemy of the Apostolic See.

Charles died in 1498, succeeded by Louis XII, who invaded Italy a year later, once again with della Rovere in his retinue. Now Alexander dispatched his secretary and another cardinal to kidnap della Rovere and bring him back to Rome, but their plot failed – perhaps luckily for della Rovere because in 1502–03 one cardinal died in the Vatican Palace and another in the Castel Sant'Angelo, both rumoured poisoned on Alexander's orders.

Alexander died in 1503, and after the 27-day reign of Pius III, on 1 November della Rovere finally managed to buy enough votes to assure his own election, taking the name of Julius II. One of his first acts was to declare that any future papal election won by simony would be invalid.

When Julius, as he now was, moved into the Vatican Palace, he refused to occupy the same rooms where Alexander had lived. 'He desecrated the Holy Church as none before', he said. 'He usurped the papal power by the devil's aid, and I forbid under the pain of excommunication anyone to speak or think of Borgia again. His name and memory must be forgotten. It must be crossed out of every document and memorial. His reign must be obliterated. All paintings made of the Borgias or for them must be covered over with black crepe. All the tombs of the Borgias must be opened and their bodies sent back to where they belong – to Spain.' Julius' tirade served only to make Alexander even more famous than he was before. His body was removed from St Peter's and installed not in Spain but in Rome's Spanish national church of Santa Maria in Monserrato degli Spagnoli.

1918 Lenin issues his Hanging Order against Russia's kulaks (affluent peasants): 'The insurrection of five kulak districts should be pitilessly suppressed ... Hang (absolutely hang, in full view of the people) no fewer than one hundred known kulaks, filthy rich men, bloodsuckers. Publish their names. Seize all grain from them. Designate hostages ... Do it in such a fashion, that for hundreds of *verst* [roughly, kilometres] around the people see, tremble, know, shout: "strangling (is done) and will continue for the bloodsucking kulaks". Telegraph the receipt and the implementation. Yours, Lenin.' * **1867** Otto von Bismarck, in letter to Meyer von Waldeck: *'Die Politik is die Lehre von Möglichen.'* ('Politics is the art of the possible.')

---

12 August

'Other women cloy/The appetites they feed, but
she makes hungry/Where most she satisfies.'

30 BC Today the last pharaoh of Egypt died by her own hand, still only 39. She was Cleopatra, the original *femme fatale* and lover of Julius Caesar and Mark Antony. She would be extolled by poets, classic and modern, for the next 2,000 years.

Shakespeare praised her 'infinite variety' with the ultimate compliment: 'other women cloy/The appetites they feed, but she makes hungry/Where most she satisfies.' Swinburne agreed: 'Her mouth is fragrant as a vine,/Her charms a vine with birds in all its boughs.'

Pharaohs had ruled Egypt since Menes 3,000 years before, but in 323 BC Alexander the Great's general Ptolemy established the Ptolemaic dynasty, of which Cleopatra was the last. Her first language was Greek, but she spoke eight other languages as well, her voice 'an instrument of many strings', according to Plutarch.

Cleopatra had first captivated Mark Antony sailing up the Cydnus River in her opulent barge that (says Shakespeare) 'like a burnished throne, burned on the water'. During eleven years they produced three children and lived in oriental splendour, but, as Edmund Spenser wrote, 'so did warlike Antony neglect the world's whole rule for Cleopatra's sight'. Ever since Caesar's death, however, his heir Octavian (the future Emperor Augustus) had laid claim to imperial power and resolved that Egypt should be a Roman province rather than an independent kingdom.

In 31 BC Octavian crushed Mark Antony's and Cleopatra's fleets at Actium, and within a year his legions were marching towards Alexandria. On their approach, Cleopatra secreted herself in her new mausoleum and had the rumour spread that she was dead. When Mark Antony heard, he attempted suicide but succeeded only in stabbing himself in the stomach. When Cleopatra's servant informed him that she was not dead after all, he was carried by litter to her mausoleum and hoisted through a window by her serving women, who were too frightened to open the gates. There, stretched out on his lover's couch, he died.

When Octavian arrived, Cleopatra refused him entry, so he sent soldiers in through the windows to disarm her before she could kill herself. He allowed her to arrange a splendid funeral for Mark Antony but kept her surrounded with guards.

In a last desperate attempt, Cleopatra dressed in her most transparent garments and threw herself at her conqueror's feet, but he was immune to her allure. Now, says the Roman poet Horace, who was 24 at the time and later Octavian's friend, she was 'resolved to die: scorning to be taken by hostile galleys, and, no ordinary woman, yet queen no longer, be led along in proud triumph' through the streets of Rome.

Historians (and poets) still debate the manner of her death. Some say she ordered a basket of figs in which was secreted an asp (the deadly Egyptian cobra, a symbol of divine royalty). Then, according to Horace, 'she dared to gaze at her fallen kingdom with a calm face, and touch the poisonous asps with courage, so that she might drink down their dark venom, to the depths of her heart'.

Many ancient historians like Strabo, Cassius Dio and Suetonius were sceptical, particularly given the difficulty of smuggling a large cobra in a basket of figs. Some suggested she might have pricked (or bitten) her arm and introduced poison from a smuggled container, from which the American poet Conrad Aiken takes his cue: 'She poured cold poison into a cup/And watched the thick foam wink and seethe:/ One black bubble upon her tongue/And she would cease to breathe.'

Whatever her method, just prior to her death Cleopatra wrote to Octavian, pleading to be buried with Mark Antony. He instantly sent soldiers to prevent her suicide, but they found her lying dead on her golden bed, two of her servant girls expiring at her feet.

On his return to Rome, Octavian proudly announced to the Senate: 'I have added Egypt to the Empire of the Roman people.' His achievement lasted over six centuries, until the Arab conquests in 639, but through the magnificent drama of her life and death Cleopatra became immortal, the most famous of all the queens of history.

1974 President Gerald Ford to the US Congress: 'Government big enough to supply everything you need is big enough to take everything you have.'
* **2005** World Wide Web inventor Tim Berners-Lee in *The Guardian*: 'Legend has it that every new technology is first used for something related to sex or pornography. That seems to be the way of humankind.'

---

13 August

*'We Spaniards know a sickness of the
heart that only gold can cure.'*

1521 Today Hernán Cortés' Spanish conquistadors and his Tlaxcalan allies destroyed the Aztec capital of Tenochtitlán, bringing an end to the Aztec Empire.

In March 1519 Cortés had landed on the Mexican coast with 500 soldiers, 100 sailors, a few cannon and sixteen horses. Inland lay the immensely rich Aztec Empire, more than twice the size of England, with a population of 25 million. Cortés burned his ships to show his men it was conquest or death.

The Aztec Empire was composed of subjugated tribes held in check by force and alienated by Aztec demands for thousands of sacrificial victims, whose living hearts would be ripped from their chests on Aztec priests' altars.

Aware of the discontent, Cortés allied himself with the Tlaxcalan tribe and set off for Tenochtitlán, a huge city built on islands in the middle of a lake and connected to the mainland by causeways. There

Emperor Moctezuma warily waited for his arrival. When the emperor's envoys came to Cortés' camp, they gave him a Spanish helmet filled with gold nuggets. Accepting the gift, Cortés warned the envoys: 'We Spaniards know a sickness of the heart that only gold can cure.'

Initially Moctezuma welcomed Cortés, believing him to be an emissary of the god Quetzalcoatl, but Cortés realised that at any moment Moctezuma could order his guards to put them all to death, so he seized and shackled the emperor and took an enormous ransom. When the Aztecs revolted, Cortés forced Moctezuma to plead for peace, but his warriors jeered and hurled rocks. Three days later Moctezuma died, the Spanish claiming from a head wound from a thrown rock and the Aztecs insisting that the Spaniards had murdered him.

Faced by thousands of hostile warriors, on 30 June – *la Noche Triste* (the Night of Sorrows) – Cortés' tiny force and 3,000 Tlaxcalan allies fought a desperate battle and broke out of the capital, but two-thirds of the Spaniards were slain or captured, while the Tlaxcalans lost 2,000 men. Spanish prisoners were literally disheartened on Aztec altars. The Spaniards had melted down 11 tonnes of gold objects, but most was lost during their escape.

Then virulent smallpox broke out in the Aztec capital, probably contracted from an African slave who was part of the Spanish expedition. The people had no resistance and no idea how to treat it. Within a year it killed a third of the population.

For ten months Cortés and his allies blockaded Tenochtitlán, while more Spaniards arrived from Cuba. Then in June 1521 Cortés launched his attack with 700 infantry plus 150,000 Tlaxcalans.

After Spanish cannon had sunk the Aztec war canoes on the lake, for ten gruelling weeks the Spaniards and Tlaxcalans made their way street by street, destroying buildings as they slaughtered Aztecs. Cortés was wounded in the leg and dragged from his horse but was saved by one of his soldiers. During the fighting the Spaniards could see Aztec priests on the Great Pyramid cutting out and eating the living hearts of 70 captured comrades and then throwing body parts at the attackers.

The battle continued until on this day Cortés' massive final attack killed the last 15,000 defenders, while a handful of survivors fled in canoes. Only then did the new emperor, Cuauhtémoc, surrender. About 100,000 Aztecs had been slain.

Cortés demanded the return of the gold lost during *la Noche Triste*. When burning oil was poured on his feet, the captured emperor confessed to dumping it into the lake. Most was irretrievably lost, but the

Spanish sent three caravels of what remained back to Spain, intended for the Spanish King Carlos I (Holy Roman Emperor Charles V). En route, however, the ships were intercepted by a French privateer, who gave the gold to the French king, François I.

Cortés became Mexico's ruler for the next three years and renamed Tenochtitlán Mexico City. He banned the Aztec religion while summoning Franciscan missionaries to convert the tribes to Christianity. Within a generation the Aztec religion and language had virtually ceased to exist, and by 1580 only 2 million Aztecs were left alive.

1704 John Churchill, Duke of Marlborough, defeats the French at the Battle of Blenheim; almost a century later Robert Southey pens his satirical lines: '"Now tell us all about the war,/And what they fought each other for." … "And everybody praised the Duke,/Who this great fight did win."/"But what good came of it at last?"/Quoth little Peterkin./"Why that I cannot tell", said he,/"But 'twas a famous victory."' * **1728** Charlotte Aïssé writes in a letter: 'No man is a hero to his valet nor Fathers of the Church among their contemporaries.'

---

14 August

'The war situation has developed not necessarily to Japan's advantage.'

1945 The last two months of the Second World War were a catalogue of disasters for the Japanese:

On 22 June General Mitsuru Ushijima, the commander of Japan's 32nd Army, committed *hara-kiri* after his force at Okinawa had been annihilated by American soldiers and marines; 110,000 Japanese had perished, and the *Yamato*, the largest battleship ever built, had been sunk with 3,000 aboard.

On 26 July at Potsdam, Allied leaders Harry Truman, Winston Churchill and Chiang Kai-shek demanded that the Japanese government proclaim 'the unconditional surrender of all Japanese armed forces'. The declaration warned: 'The alternative for Japan is prompt and utter destruction.'

On 6 August an American B-29 dropped an atomic bomb on Hiroshima, killing 70,000 people.

On 8 August the Soviet Union declared war on Japan.

On 9 August the Soviet Union invaded Manchuria and, on the same day, 74,000 Japanese died at Nagasaki under a second atomic bomb.

During this period, American aircraft had continued to fire-bomb Japanese cities so relentlessly that by now 325,000 civilians had been killed and 5 million more made homeless – in addition to over 2 million Japanese soldiers, sailors and airmen who had lost their lives during the war.

And yet even on the day that Nagasaki was obliterated, surrender was unthinkable to the Japanese high command – Japan had never been invaded or lost a war in its history. Led by War Minister Anami, they argued that the fight should continue. Finally, on 10 August, Emperor Hirohito intervened, telling his cabinet and military chiefs that he favoured accepting Allied terms. Doggedly, Anami insisted that they should fight on, 'even if we have to eat grass, chew dirt and sleep in the fields'.

After four more days of debate, the deadlocked military and cabinet finally agreed to surrender. (Anami committed *hara-kiri*.)

Now Hirohito took the unprecedented step of broadcasting to his nation. This evening around eleven o'clock he recorded his radio address, known as the *Gyokuon-hōsō* (Jewel Voice Broadcast), but it was a speech of exaggeration, evasion and euphemism. Never mentioning 'surrender', he said: 'We have ordered Our Government to communicate to the Governments of the United States, Great Britain, China and the Soviet Union that Our Empire accepts the provisions of their Joint Declaration ... We declared war on America and Britain out of Our sincere desire to ensure Japan's self-preservation and the stabilisation of East Asia, it being far from Our thought either to infringe upon the sovereignty of other nations or to embark upon territorial aggrandisement ...'

Then, in one of history's greatest understatements, the emperor proclaimed: 'The war situation has developed not necessarily to Japan's advantage, while the general trends of the world have all turned against her interest.'

He went on to suggest that continuing to fight would not only destroy Japan but also 'lead to the total extinction of human civilisation'. Therefore, 'we have resolved to pave the way for a grand peace for all the generations to come by enduring the unendurable and suffering what is unsufferable'.

Just before midnight a statement of surrender signed by every member of the cabinet was sent to Switzerland and Sweden for forwarding to the Allied powers.

Many in Japan's military remained radically opposed to surrender, believing it dishonourable. That night several hundred officers tried to raid the Imperial Palace to destroy the recording, but it was smuggled out of the palace in a basket of women's underwear and broadcast to the nation at noon the next day.

Although the broadcast was, in historian Max Hastings' words, 'a self-serving caricature of Japan's recent history', somehow it worked. There was no military coup, and the civilian population received the news with both sadness and relief. The war that Japan had started and paid so dearly for was over at last.

1952 French economic historian Alfred Sauvy coins the phrase 'Third World' ('*Tiers Monde*') in *L'Observateur*: 'Because at the end, this Third World, ignored, exploited, despised like the Third Estate, wants to become something too.'

---

15 August

'The count Rolland, though blood his mouth doth stain,/And burst are both the temples of his brain,/ His olifant he sounds with grief and pain.'

778 AD The Battle of Roncevaux, fought on this day, was really just a skirmish between Charlemagne's rear guard and a few Basque guerrillas, but from it sprang *The Song of Roland*, a so-called *chanson de geste* (song of heroic deeds) and the oldest surviving major work of French literature.

At this time the Moors ruled most of Spain, but now some of them were fighting each other, and one leader, Sulayman al-Arabi, came to Charlemagne's headquarters at Paderborn to ask for help. Believing this might give him the chance to relieve Christians oppressed by Moorish rule – and to extend his growing empire into northern Spain – Charlemagne agreed to come with his army.

In 777 Charlemagne crossed the Pyrenees but found that, although heavily taxed, the Christians living under Moorish rule were well treated and prosperous – and actually preferred the Moors to Charlemagne's Franks. No chance, then, for heroic liberation of beleaguered Christians, so Charlemagne turned his army around and headed back towards France.

While recrossing the Pyrenees, his men had to march in single file through a high mountain pass near the town of Roncesvalles (Roncevaux in French), five miles from the Spanish–French border. There his rear guard was ambushed by Basque brigands – Christian ones at that. Among the few casualties was the rear guard's commander, Count Roland. After looting the Frankish baggage train, the guerrillas slipped away before Charlemagne could bring in reinforcements.

This minor encounter somehow remained alive in folklore, until three centuries later an unknown poet composed *The Song of Roland*, an epic that exalts the virtues of chivalry – honour, valour, fidelity and defence of the faith. Some 4,004 verses long, it was written in the *langue d'oïl*, the dialect that would one day become the French language, and sung by itinerant minstrels. It became the most celebrated poem of the Middle Ages, but it bears scant relation to the actual battle.

Charlemagne's Spanish campaign lasted only a few months, but *The Song of Roland* has him in Spain for 'full seven years'. The *Song* also gives him a snow-white beard, although Charlemagne was only about 35 at the time of the battle. It describes the enemy as 400,000 Moors, i.e. Muslims, rather than several hundred Christian Basques, and Roland has become Charlemagne's nephew.

The epic relates that Roland volunteers for the rear guard but is betrayed by his stepfather Ganelon, who secretly informs the Moors so that they can ambush the Franks at Roncevaux Pass. Even though heavily outnumbered, Roland refuses to signal for help by blowing on his olifant (a hunting horn). But finally, with his men dead all around him, he realises that he has waited too long and raises his olifant to his lips so that Charlemagne can avenge his death, but in his zeal he blows so hard that his temples burst:

> The count Rolland, though blood his mouth doth stain,
> And burst are both the temples of his brain,
> His olifant he sounds with grief and pain.

Then, after slaying innumerable Moors, Roland 'joins his hands: and so is life finish'd'.

Because he has died fighting the Moors, Saints Michael and Gabriel take his soul straight to Heaven. Charlemagne then returns with his army and defeats the Moors. Ganelon's treachery is revealed and he is torn limb from limb by galloping horses. The poem ends with Charlemagne mourning:

'God!' said the King: 'My life is hard indeed!'
Tears filled his eyes, he tore his snowy beard.

The Song of Roland continued to inspire French soldiers over the centuries. During William the Conqueror's invasion of England, it was sung to galvanise the Norman troops. During the 11th and 12th centuries, French soldiers regularly sang it before going into battle. It is said that King John of England once asked his soldiers: 'Why should we sing of Roland if today there are no more Rolands?' To which one of his men replied: 'There would still be Rolands if there were any Charlemagnes.'

1811 French philosopher, writer and diplomat Joseph de Maistre writes in *Lettres et Opuscules Inédits*: 'Every country has the government it deserves.'

---

16 August

'The strong make war, but you, happy Austria, make marriages. What Mars grants to others, Venus gives to you.'

1477 Today in Ghent the eighteen-year-old Habsburg, Archduke Maximilian, married the charming duchess, Mary of Burgundy, two years his senior. It was the first in a series of dynastic marriages that would culminate in Habsburg dominance of Europe.

Four centuries earlier the Habsburgs had established themselves in their fortress perched high among the crags in what today is Switzerland – the Habichtsburg or Hawk's Castle. For two more centuries they had remained a minor power, even though a Habsburg became Holy Roman Emperor for the first time in 1273. By then 'Habichtsburg' had evolved to 'Habsburg'.

The Habsburgs remained relatively poor, even when another of the family, Frederick III, gained the imperial title in 1440. According to future pope Pius II, the emperor 'possesses but a precarious sovereignty; he has no power ... no revenues, no treasure'.

Elsewhere in Europe the immensely powerful, rich and headstrong Charles the Bold, Duke of Burgundy, whose lands included most of modern Belgium and Holland and parts of France, was determined to elevate his duchy to a kingdom – and only the Holy Roman Emperor, that is, Frederick III, could bestow that royal title. For that alone

Charles agreed to accept Frederick's son Maximilian as prospective husband for his only child, Mary.

Before the marriage could take place, however, Charles embarked on a titanic struggle to carve out a kingdom by force of arms, and in 1477 was hacked to death in battle. His daughter Mary, although now the ruling duchess, was alone and vulnerable, and the French were preparing to invade.

Mary desperately needed support, and a husband to lead her armies, so on this day seven months after her father's death, she wed her erstwhile fiancé Maximilian, bringing her vast lands with her. As the Hungarian king Matthias Corvinus wrote at the time: '*Bella gerant fortes: tu, felix Austria, nube. Nam quae Mars aliis, dat tibi regne Venus.*' ('The strong make war, but you, happy Austria, make marriages. What Mars grants to others, Venus gives to you.') How right he was, as the future would show.

Although Maximilian's marriage to Mary was political, it turned into a love match. In a letter to a friend, he eagerly wrote: 'She has skin as white as snow, brown hair, a little nose, a small head and face, greybrown eyes, beautiful and light. Her lower eyelid droops a little, as if she had just been asleep, but you hardly notice it. Her lips are a little strong, but pure and red. She is the most beautiful woman I have ever seen.'

Sadly, five years later Mary was thrown from her horse and killed while falconing. She left behind a three-year-old son, Philip, who succeeded to her Burgundian possessions.

Fourteen years later, on 20 October 1496, Philip made the next dynastic union when he married the Infanta Juana, daughter of Ferdinand and Isabella of Spain. The marriage was a miserable one, marred by Philip's numerous infidelities and his wife's possessive insanity, but the laws of inheritance brought the Low Countries, Austria and Spain (including Spanish possessions in Italy) under Habsburg control.

Ten years later Philip died of typhoid fever, leaving behind a six-year-old son named Charles. Charles would inherit the throne of Spain, and in January 1519 his grandfather, Emperor Maximilian, died. Contenders for the imperial title included François I of France and England's Henry VIII, but Charles outbribed them both to become Holy Roman Emperor on 28 June 1519.

Now the greatest emperor in history, Charles ruled Austria, Germany, Belgium, parts of Italy, the Netherlands and Spain, including all its vast territories in the New World. His empire spanned 1.25 million square miles.

Even now there was still one more dynastic marriage to come. On 8 July 1521, Charles's brother Ferdinand von Habsburg married Anne of Hungary, leading to the incorporation of Hungary into the Austrian Empire. Matthias Corvinus certainly got it right: 'The strong make war, but you, happy Austria, make marriages.'

1776 Horace Walpole in a letter to the Countess of Upper Ossory: 'The world is a comedy to those that think, a tragedy to those that feel.' * **1925** The *New York World* first prints the 17th-century French proverb: '*Bonjour lunettes, adieu fillettes.*' ('Hello glasses, goodbye girls.')

---

17 August

'Her Royal Highness had heard of the enormous size of his machine and sent for him by courier.'

1820 On 5 July, the Pains and Penalties Bill 1820 was introduced in Parliament at the request of George IV, its aim to dissolve George's marriage to Caroline of Brunswick and deprive her of the title of Queen. On this day six weeks later the debate was opened in the House of Lords; it was in essence a public trial of the king's wife, charging her with adultery, with the members of Parliament acting as judge and jury.

Although Caroline was George's first cousin, they had never met until 5 April 1795, when he was 32 and she 26. On that day she landed at Greenwich and then travelled on to London in preparation for her marriage, which took place three days later.

According to the Earl of Malmesbury, '[Caroline's] figure was very bad, short, very full-chested and jutting hips. She was stockily built, dressed dowdily, lacked moral reticence and good sense, and washed so seldom she was malodorous.' Upon meeting his bride, George appealed to his valet: 'I am not very well, Harris; pray get me a glass of brandy.'

As soon as the wedding ceremonies were over, George resorted to the bottle to give him fortitude for the night ahead. Blind drunk, he managed to make love that night and again the next evening. Later he wrote to a friend: 'It required no small [effort] to conquer my aversion and overcome the disgust of her person.' Caroline claimed George was so drunk that he 'passed the greatest part of his bridal night under the grate, where he fell, and where I left him'. They never slept together again.

In 1811, after becoming regent for his mad father, George III, George banished Caroline from court, and she decamped to Montague House. Three years later she agreed to leave England in exchange for an annual allowance of £35,000 (£3 million today); the moment she was gone George had Montague House demolished as one might burn a mattress infested with fleas.

Caroline moved to Italy where she appointed a dark, moustachioed Italian named Bartolomeo Pergami as her secretary and purchased the Villa d'Este on Lake Como. Pergami, who apparently had a stronger stomach and emptier purse than Prince George, soon became her lover, and together they travelled around Europe. Society was shocked by their liaison, and lurid rumours abounded. Caroline was reputed to have enjoyed a fling with the Dey (ruler) of Algiers, which prompted the Irish judge Lord Norbury's celebrated pun: 'She was as happy as the Dey was long.'

On 29 January 1820 George III died, bringing his son to the throne. That June Caroline returned to London to assert her rights as queen, but George wanted only divorce. Since divorce was not then possible unless one of the parties was guilty of adultery, George hoped that Parliament would convict her and annul the marriage. When Caroline's 'trial' opened today, Pergami was named as co-respondent and damned as 'a foreigner of low station'. Witnesses testified that the couple had slept in the same room, kissed, and been seen together in a state of undress. When asked how Caroline had met Pergami, a servant attested that 'Her Royal Highness had heard of the enormous size of his machine and sent for him by courier'.

The debate was widely reported in the press in all its salacious detail. On 10 November the Lords passed the bill by 108–99, but Prime Minister Lord Liverpool, only too aware of George's own feckless character, let the bill drop, knowing that it was unlikely to pass in the Commons.

George's final rejection of his wife came at his coronation on 19 July 1821 when he banned her from the ceremony in Westminster Abbey, although she caused a scandal by pounding on the church door demanding to be let in.

This last denial may have finally done Caroline in, as she fell ill and died nineteen days later. Shortly before her death she had ordered engraved on her coffin: 'Caroline of Brunswick, the injured Queen of England.'

1661 French *surintendant des finances* Nicolas Fouquet gives so lavish a housewarming at his new château of Vaux-le-Vicomte that Louis XIV imprisons him in Pigneroles, from which he never emerges. Voltaire later writes: 'On 17 August at six in the evening, Fouquet was King of France; at two in the morning, he was nobody.' * **1786** Knowing death is imminent, Frederick the Great speaks to his valet Strutzki for the last time: '*La montagne est passé, nous irons mieux.*' ('We're over the hill, we'll be better now.')

18 August

*'I am coming, I am coming.
It is right. Just wait a moment.'*

1503 With these final words addressed to the God he had so often ignored, Rodrigo Borgia passed away today at 72. He had been Pope for eleven scandalous years under the papal name of Alexander VI. Even his death was shrouded in controversy and suspicions of murder, and his funeral provided an appropriately grisly finale.

Alexander had been born Spanish in the town of Játiva but had easily progressed through the ranks of the Church through the patronage of his uncle, Pope Calixtus III, who created him a cardinal when he was 25. He became pope at 61, largely through stupendous bribes, and, although he was a great patron of the arts, he was more famous for his treachery, simony, nepotism and lust for power. His three mistresses provided him with nine illegitimate children, including the murderous Cesare, whom Alexander made a cardinal at eighteen, and the notorious Lucrezia.

During the week before his death, Alexander was feeling ill and feverish. On 15 August he was bled but the fever intensified. Then, on the morning of the 18th, he made his last confession and, after receiving Extreme Unction, he died that evening.

On hearing of his father's death, Cesare dispatched his villainous henchman Michelotto and his thugs to grab the Pope's treasure. According to the eyewitness Johann Burchard, the Papal Master of Ceremonies, 'the intruders closed all the doors that gave access to the Pope's room. One of the men took out a dagger and threatened to cut Cardinal Casanova's throat and to throw him out of the window unless he handed over the keys to all the Pope's treasure. Terrified, the cardinal surrendered the keys, whereupon the others entered the room next to the papal apartment and seized all the silver that they found, together with two coffers containing about a hundred thousand ducats [worth today about $135 million].' Only then was Alexander's death announced to the public.

That evening the Pope's bier was first placed in the Sistine Chapel and then carried into St Peter's, where it remained overnight. By four o'clock the next afternoon, Burchard wrote, Alexander's face 'had changed to the colour of mulberry or the blackest cloth and it was covered in blue-black spots. The nose was swollen, the mouth distended where the tongue was doubled over, and the lips seemed to fill everything. The appearance of the face then was far more horrifying than anything that had ever been seen or reported before.' According to another witness, the 'blackened corpse ... [exhaled] an infectious smell', and was so gruesome that 'no fanatic or devotee dared to kiss his feet or hands, as custom would have required'.

Later that evening Alexander's swollen body was carried into the Chapel of Santa Maria della Febbre, where eight workmen attempted to put it into a coffin. According to Burchard: 'The carpenters had made the coffin too narrow and short, and so they placed the Pope's mitre at his side, rolled his body up in an old carpet, and pummelled and pushed it into the coffin with their fists.'

Such a gruesome finish inspired instant rumours that Alexander had been poisoned. One was that he had accidentally been dosed with arsenic by Cesare, who had intended it for a rival cardinal, but the most dramatic (and improbable) is that Caterina Sforza, whom Alexander had once imprisoned, had sent him a bamboo cane inside which was a secret letter that had been rubbed with the shirt of a man who had died of plague. In all likelihood, however, Alexander died of what the Italians called *mal aria* (bad air – they had no idea the disease was borne by mosquitoes), a constant menace of Roman summers 500 years ago.

1572 Henri de Navarre (the future Henri IV of France) marries Marguerite de Valois (la Reine Margot); Marguerite later writes: 'We were thus married, but fortune, which never gives complete happiness to humans, soon changed this happy state of triumph and marriage into something totally the opposite.' (The marriage is plagued by infidelities and unhappiness and is annulled after seventeen years.)

---

19 August

'I know I have the body of a weak,
feeble woman; but I have the heart and stomach
of a king, and of a king of England too.'

1588 Today at Tilbury, as she awaited Spanish invasion, Queen Elizabeth I addressed her troops in an iconic speech that would, over time, help establish her legend as the Virgin Queen and Gloriana, the monarch who brought a Golden Age to England.

Half a century earlier Henry VIII had built five coastal blockhouses to protect the River Thames and hence the route to London. One stood at Tilbury, across the river from another at Gravesend, just where the river narrows. During Henry's time no threat had come, but now Elizabeth faced the might of the Spanish Armada.

Fearing that the Spaniards might take control of the English Channel, the queen had sent an army of 4,000 men to the Tilbury blockhouse, under the command of Robert Dudley, Earl of Leicester.

On 8 August the English fleet had miraculously routed the Spanish at Gravelines, but even with this victory, the danger persisted, for the Duke of Parma waited in the Spanish Netherlands with 30,000 soldiers, ready to invade. So Elizabeth made her way to Tilbury to raise the spirits of her men.

On this morning she dressed in white velvet, over which she wore a silver cuirass. Mounted on a white horse, she dispensed with her bodyguard and rode among her subjects with an escort of only six men. Ahead of her rode the Earl of Ormonde carrying the sword of state, followed by a page bearing her white-plumed silver helmet on a cushion. Then, as her soldiers gathered round, she spoke:

My loving people

We have been persuaded by some that are careful of our safety, to take heed how we commit ourselves to armed multitudes, for fear of treachery; but I assure you I do not desire to live to distrust my faithful and loving people. Let tyrants fear. I have always so behaved myself that, under God, I have placed my chiefest strength and safeguard in the loyal hearts and goodwill of my subjects; and therefore I am come amongst you, as you see, at this time, not for my recreation and disport, but being resolved, in the midst and heat of the battle, to live and die amongst you all;

to lay down for my God, and for my kingdom, and my people, my honour and my blood, even in the dust.

I know I have the body of a weak, feeble woman; but I have the heart and stomach of a king, and of a king of England too, and think foul scorn that Parma or Spain, or any prince of Europe, should dare to invade the borders of my realm; to which rather than any dishonour shall grow by me, I myself will take up arms, I myself will be your general, judge, and rewarder of every one of your virtues in the field …

Elizabeth of course did not have to fight, let alone lay down her life, since the mighty Armada was to sail north around Ireland to be dispersed and destroyed by severe North Atlantic gales, leaving Parma and his soldiers with no means to cross the Channel. But, as historian Susan Frye has written: 'The Queen's review of the troops proved a brilliant stroke, which grew more brilliant in the succeeding weeks, years, and centuries because it provided a moment through which generations could cast Elizabeth I as the powerful political icon she remains.'

---

14 AD Just before Roman Emperor Augustus dies after 41 years in power, he tells those around him: 'If I have played my part well, clap your hands, and dismiss me with applause from the stage.'

---

20 August

'It is impossible to displace him except by assassination.'

1940 Today a Soviet NKVD (secret police) killer buried an ice axe in the back of the head of Leon Trotsky, once one of the USSR's top leaders but now in exile in Mexico. Soviet despot Joseph Stalin had personally ordered the hit.

In establishing Russia's communist dictatorship, Trotsky was almost as malignant as Stalin. He led the Red Army to victory during the Russian Civil War but also set up brutal labour camps and ordered summary executions. As he said in 1918: 'Root out the counter-revolutionaries without mercy, lock up suspicious characters in concentration camps … Shirkers will be shot, regardless of past service.' He approved of the mass killings during the Red Terror, commenting: 'Terror can be very efficient against a reactionary class …

Intimidation is a powerful weapon of policy, both internationally and internally.'

With views like these, you would think Trotsky would have found a soulmate in Stalin; instead he found a mortal enemy.

In 1923 an ailing Lenin recommended that Trotsky replace Stalin as the Communist Party's General Secretary, but Stalin clung to power, biding his time to destroy his rival. Lenin died the next year, and within four years Trotsky had been expelled from the Politburo, the Central Committee and the Communist Party. In January 1928 he was exiled to Kazakhstan and in 1929 thrown out of the USSR altogether.

First he lived in Turkey but then moved to France, where he set up the Fourth International to rival the Soviet Comintern in overthrowing global capitalism and establishing world socialism through international revolution.

When Hitler took dictatorial power in Germany in 1934, Trotsky abandoned France for Norway, but in 1936 pressure from Stalin forced him to seek asylum in Mexico. There he moved into a fortified compound at Coyoacán near Mexico City. Meanwhile, back in Russia he was convicted *in absentia* on fabricated charges of treason. He no doubt fuelled Stalin's paranoia when he stated: 'Inside the Party, Stalin has put himself above all criticism and the State. It is impossible to displace him except by assassination.' But it was Stalin who would do the assassinating.

Stalin's first strike came on 24 May 1940 when he sent an NKVD death squad to Trotsky's compound. Armed with machine-guns, the attackers subdued Trotsky's guards, entered the compound and fired 300 rounds into his house, riddling the bedroom where Trotsky and his wife were hiding under the bed. Miraculously, no one was hit, and the gunmen, certain that no one could have survived the fusillade, left without entering the house.

Their first attempt had failed, but the NKVD had a second string to their bow. They had recruited the fanatical 27-year-old Spanish communist Ramón Mercader, who had seduced a lonely American communist named Sylvia Ageloff so that she would introduce him into the Trotsky household. He assumed the name of Frank Jacson.

At 5.20 on the afternoon of 20 August 'Jacson' entered the compound and found Trotsky alone in his study, reading at his desk. Standing behind him, Jacson pulled an ice axe from under his folded raincoat and brought it down savagely on Trotsky's skull. Trotsky fell to the floor, screaming, and his bodyguards rushed in and beat Jacson to the ground. Bloodied but not dead, Trotsky called to his guards, 'Do not kill him. This man has a story to tell', saving Jacson's life.

Trotsky was rushed to a hospital where he remained conscious for several hours but died the next day.

Making no attempt to deny his guilt, Jacson was sentenced to twenty years in prison. Released in May 1960, he flew directly to Castro's communist Cuba. He later moved on to the USSR, to be decorated as a Hero of the Soviet Union and made a general in the KGB ('grandson' of the NKVD). His true identity as Ramón Mercader was revealed to the outside world only after the collapse of the USSR. When he died on 18 October 1978, his last words were: 'I hear it always. I hear the scream. I know he's waiting for me on the other side.'

---

480 BC As he prepares to fight the Persians at Thermopylae, Spartan King Leonidas has a last meal with his men, telling them: 'Breakfast well, for we shall have dinner in Hades.' All the Spartans are killed in the battle.*
1119 At the Battle of Brémule, French King Louis the Fat fights so close to the enemy that a Norman knight seizes his bridle and shouts, 'The king is taken!', to which Louis shouts back, 'The king cannot be taken, neither at war, nor at chess!' and downs his opponent. (Louis lost the battle anyway.)

---

21 August

'Though I now sink out of view, and shall be forgotten,
I believe I have made some marks which will tell for
the cause of civil liberty long after I have gone.'

1858 They had arrived all morning by riverboat, railroad, wagon and carriage; on horseback and on foot. By midday 12,000 people jammed the main square of Ottawa, Illinois. Shortly after one o'clock, to loud cheering, the two candidates arrived. It took them another half an hour, pushing through the packed assemblage, to reach the speakers' platform.

It was the first of the Lincoln–Douglas debates, part of the contest for the Illinois seat in the US Senate. The two-term incumbent, Frederick Douglass, long a force of national stature in the Democratic Party, faced a Republican challenger, Abraham Lincoln, an ambitious lawyer, leader of his state's party, but virtually unknown outside Illinois.

The campaign had started in the early summer, with both candidates travelling around the state, often speaking at the same place only a day, or even hours, apart. When Lincoln proposed a series of face-to-face debates, Douglass's supporters were sure, as historian Allan Nevins phrased it, 'the champion of mighty Senate debates would shake this provincial attorney, in full sight of the nation, as a mastiff shakes a terrier'.

Today in Ottawa, Douglass began by asserting that his opponent's party, the Republicans, was a sectional – northern – rather than a national organisation and that its essential aim was the abolition of slavery. Citing Lincoln's recent statement that the Union 'cannot endure permanently half free and half slave', Douglass said that the Union had existed that way since its founding 70 years ago. Why, he asked, should it not continue? One result of abolition, he claimed, was that Illinois would be flooded with newly emancipated slaves from Missouri, looking for work and wanting to become 'citizens and voters, on an equality with ourselves'.

Lincoln replied that Douglass's argument was 'as thin as the homeopathic soup that was made by boiling the shadow of a pigeon that had been starved to death'. He had 'no purpose to interfere with the institution of slavery where it exists'. But Negroes had a natural right to 'life, liberty, and the pursuit of happiness'. The founding fathers had put slavery on a course towards eventual extinction by banning it in the national territories and halting the slave trade, but now Douglass and the Democrats were attempting to perpetuate it.

When the debate was over, after three hours under a broiling sun, cheering Republicans carried Lincoln off on their shoulders. The newspaper reports were highly partisan. The Chicago *Times*, supporting Douglass, headlined: 'Lincoln's Heart Fails Him! Lincoln's Legs Fail Him! Lincoln's Tongue Fails Him!' The Chicago *Journal*, supporting Lincoln, reported that 'since the flailing Senator Douglass received at Ottawa, his friends should now address him as "the late Mr Douglass"'.

On election day, 2 November, the results were close. The ballots cast by voters were for a new state legislature, which in turn would elect a senator. Lincoln won the popular vote 125,275 to 121,090, but the legislators elected Douglass over Lincoln 54 to 46.

The results were a disappointment but no surprise to Lincoln. He had written to a friend that the contest 'gave me a hearing on the great and durable question of the age, which I could have had in no other way; and though I now sink out of view, and shall be forgotten, I believe I have made some marks which will tell for the cause of civil liberty long after I have gone.'

But in defeat, there was victory. He had won the people's vote. He had gained a strong reputation well beyond the borders of his state. And in the not too distant future lay the presidential election of 1860.

1810 Napoleonic marshal Jean-Baptiste Bernadotte becomes Sweden's crown prince, taking the name of Charles John; just before he dies after 26 years as king, he smugly remarks: 'No one living has made a career like mine.'

---

22 August

'I will not budge a foot, I will die king of England.'

1485 England's Richard III had been king for only two years and two months, having usurped the throne from his twelve-year-old nephew Edward V, whose murder in the Tower of London he may have ordered. But now a rival was raising arms in France, claiming that the crown should rightfully be his. This was 28-year-old Henry Tudor, but he, too, had only the flimsiest of claims. Although of royal blood, only through his mother could he trace his ancestry back to a king, and that was to Edward III five generations back, and his bloodline on his father's side was even thinner. His paternal grandfather had (perhaps) been married to Catherine de Valois, the widow of Henry V.

But Henry Tudor was the only living male member of the House of Lancaster and so became its champion in the Wars of the Roses, that bloody rivalry for the English crown that had afflicted the country for 30 years. Gathering an army in France composed primarily of French mercenaries, Henry landed at Milford Haven in Pembrokeshire on 7 August.

Attracting more supporters as he made his way through Wales (his father had been Welsh), Henry led 5,000 men by the time he met Richard's forces on this day at a field near Market Bosworth, twelve miles west of Leicester. Richard commanded 8,000, but these included contingents from three vacillating barons, Henry Percy, 4th Earl of Northumberland, and the brothers William and Thomas Stanley.

Richard positioned his force on Ambion Hill and then brought them down to attack the enemy, calling on Percy for reinforcements. But Percy held his soldiers back, and Thomas Stanley also remained uncommitted.

Desperate, Richard took the initiative; surrounded by several hundred mounted men of his household, he charged past the Stanleys to strike directly at Henry Tudor himself.

He succeeded in dispersing Henry's personal bodyguard and bringing down his standard bearer, but Henry was saved by the intervention of the other Stanley brother, William, who turned his coat and ordered his men into battle, not for Richard his king but for Henry.

Now Richard's cause was all but lost, but even when defeat was certain, he challenged his fate. 'I will not budge a foot', he swore to his lieutenants, 'I will die king of England.' Surrounded by Stanley's soldiers, he was unhorsed (giving rise to Shakespeare's famous if invented line, 'A horse, a horse, my kingdom for a horse!'), and killed by a blow to the head from a Welsh axe. Stripped by Lancastrians eager for plunder, Richard's naked body was carried off the battlefield on a donkey's back. For centuries the location of his grave was a mystery, until, in 2012, his remains were discovered under a car park that covered the ruins of the Grey Friars monastery in Leicester.

Richard was the last English king to die in battle. According to tradition, the crown that he had worn on his helmet was found dangling from the branches of a hawthorn bush. Retrieved by a Lancastrian soldier, it was placed on Henry's head to shouts of 'Long live King Henry VII!'

Today's Battle of Bosworth Field ended the Wars of the Roses, except for a final battle against resurgent Yorkists at Stoke. It also brought to an end the great Plantagenet dynasty that had supplied every English king for the past 332 years, starting with Henry II. And when Henry Tudor took the crown as Henry VII, he began his own 118-year dynasty that included such notables as Henry VIII, Bloody Mary and Elizabeth I.

1961 American poet Robert Frost in the *Muscatine Journal*: 'A bank is a place where they lend you an umbrella in fair weather and ask for it back when it begins to rain.'

---

23 August

'The greater part convinced that there were now no gods at all, and that the final endless night of which we have heard had come upon the world.'

79 AD For Romans today was Vulcanalia, the festival honouring Vulcan, the god of fire, including that from volcanoes (a word that itself derives from the god's name). Pious citizens lit bonfires into which live fish or small animals were thrown as a sacrifice, to be consumed in the place of humans.

Perhaps this year the offerings had been insufficient, because the next morning Mount Vesuvius began to develop small fissures that released ash and smoke. Then, at around one o'clock, the mountain violently exploded, throwing up a deadly cloud of volcanic gas, stones and ash twenty miles high. According to the Roman writer Pliny the Younger, who witnessed the event, it looked like a massive umbrella pine, probably not dissimilar to the mushroom cloud of a nuclear explosion – except that Vesuvius' eruption released 100,000 times the thermal energy of the Hiroshima bombing, spewing molten rock and pulverised pumice at 1.5 million tons per second. Below, at the south-eastern base of the mountain, the city of Pompeii was buried in pumice and ash – and worse was yet to come.

Pliny, then just seventeen, observed the eruption from the port of Misenum, across the Bay of Naples. Of the second morning he tells us: 'Though it was now morning, the light was still exceedingly faint and doubtful; the buildings all around us tottered … The chariots, which we had ordered to be drawn out, were so agitated backwards and forwards, though upon the most level ground, that we could not keep them steady, even by supporting them with large stones. The sea seemed to roll back upon itself, and to be driven from its banks by the convulsive motion of the earth … the shore was considerably enlarged, and several sea animals were left upon [the beach]. On the other side, a black and dreadful cloud, broken with rapid, zigzag flashes, revealed behind it variously shaped masses of flame: these last were like sheet-lightning, but much larger.'

Misenum was in danger, even though it was nineteen miles from the volcano. As Pliny reports: 'The ashes now began to fall upon us, though in no great quantity … a dense, dark mist seemed to be following us, spreading itself over the country like a cloud … night came upon us, not such as we have when the sky is cloudy, or when there is no moon, but that of a room when it is shut up, and all the lights put out. You might hear the shrieks of women, the screams of children, and the shouts of men; some calling for their children, others for their parents, others for their husbands, and seeking to recognise each other by the voices that replied; one lamenting his own fate, another that of his family; some wishing to die, from the very fear of dying; some lifting their hands to the gods; but the greater part convinced that there were now no gods at all, and that the final endless night of which we have heard had come upon the world.'

In fact, Misenum escaped the worst effects of Vesuvius' eruption, but pyroclastic surges of 250°C rolled over Pompeii's walls, knocking down all structures in their path and incinerating the inhabitants who had survived the ash and volcanic debris of the day before. Among the dead was Pliny's uncle, the admiral and naturalist Pliny the Elder, who perished from the fumes after he crossed the bay to assist evacuation attempts. By the time the eruption was over, Pompeii and some 20,000 of its citizens were covered with over twenty feet of pumice and the nearby town of Herculaneum had been overwhelmed by a gigantic pyroclastic surge, formed by a mixture of ash and hot gases.

Vesuvius has erupted many times since the year 79 and is still active today, having last erupted in 1944. Its crater now measures 2,000 feet across and 1,000 feet deep, and on its slopes is grown a wine known as Lacrima Christi, the Tears of Christ.

1628 John Felton, an army officer who believes that Buckingham has blocked his promotion, stabs George Villiers, Duke of Buckingham at the Greyhound pub in Portsmouth; Buckingham lives just long enough to chase his murderer but falls down crying: 'The villain hath killed me!'

---

24 August

'A race much dipped in their own blood.'

1113 Today Ermengarde, Countess of Anjou gave birth to a strapping son, whom she would call Geoffrey. He grew to be a handsome lad with a taste for riding, hunting and women. One day he would become the thirteenth Count of Anjou and his family would become England's greatest royal dynasty – but he had an ill-omened background. Legend has it that he was descended from the fairy Melusine, who was half-serpent.

Anjou centres on the fine old town of Angers near the River Loire. In springtime the land is yellow with a type of broom called *planta genista*, and young Geoffrey so much enjoyed wearing a sprig of this cheerful bloom in his hat that he came to be known as Geoffrey Plantagenet.

When he reached a precocious sixteen, Geoffrey married Matilda, ten years his senior and daughter of Henry I of England, in a grand dynastic marriage. Although they intensely disliked each other, they produced three sons, the eldest of whom was Henry II, who became the first of fourteen Plantagenet kings. Two of Henry's sons also wore the crown, Richard (I) the Lionheart and John. According to the contemporary chronicler Gerald of Wales, Richard liked to boast of his ancestor Melusine, claiming that the Plantagenets 'came from the devil and would return to the devil'.

Many Plantagenets came to sticky ends, often at the hands of their own relations. Henry II 'died of shame' in his castle at Chinon in 1189, harried by his rebellious sons Richard and John in league with his arch-enemy Philip Augustus of France. Ten years later Richard died of gangrene after being hit by an arrow in a pointless siege in France, bringing John to the throne. John expired on the run from his own barons, but not before murdering his nephew Arthur.

The next Plantagenet king done in by his family was the homosexual Edward II, whose ignored wife Isabella took Roger de Mortimer as her paramour, took over England and imprisoned Edward in Berkeley Castle. There in 1327 his keepers thrust a red-hot spit up through his anus, burning out his internal organs, allowing Isabella to rule as regent for her son Edward III (who later had Mortimer hanged, drawn and quartered).

Another Plantagenet king to die at the hands of his own family was Richard II, who in February 1400 was (probably) starved to death in Pontefract Castle on orders of his cousin, the usurper Henry IV.

In 1422 yet another Plantagenet monarch, Henry V, bit the dust at the Château de Vincennes, apparently from dysentery, which he had contracted fighting against the French at the siege of Meaux.

1455 saw the start of the Wars of the Roses, pitting the Plantagenet houses of Lancaster and York against one another. During it Henry VI (probably) had his skull crushed on orders of a cousin, Edward IV, while locked up in the Tower of London. Edward also had his rebellious brother George, Duke of Clarence, drowned in a butt of Malmsey.

In 1483 the twelve-year-old Edward V was killed in the Tower of London, probably by his uncle, Richard III. Then Richard was cut down at Bosworth Field in 1485, for once not by his own family but by Henry Tudor, ending the Plantagenet hold on the throne of England. (The male line of the Plantagenets became extinct in 1499 when Edward, the son of George, Duke of Clarence, was beheaded for treason.)

As well as fighting each other, the Plantagenets also fought their own barons (think Magna Carta and King John), the Welsh (conquered by

Edward I), the Scots (again Edward, who died while fighting them in 1307), and the French from Edward III's declaration of war in 1339 to the Battle of Castillon in 1453 during the Hundred Years' War.

Although they were 'a race much dipped in their own blood', as the medieval philosopher Roger Bacon described them, the magnificent Plantagenet dynasty ruled England for 331 years, longer than any other English dynasty before or since. The line's founder Geoffrey Plantagenet never once visited England.

---

410 When Alaric and his Visigoths sack Rome, he asks for 5,000 pounds of gold, 3,000 pounds of silver, 4,000 silk tunics and 3,000 pounds of pepper. A Roman senator asks: 'Will you leave us with nothing?' Alaric responds: 'If you give us what we want, you can keep your lives.' * **1572** France's Charles IX orders the St Bartholomew's Day massacre: 'Kill all the Huguenots in France, that there may not be left one of them to reproach me with it afterwards.'

---

25 August

'Paris outraged! Paris broken! Paris martyred! But Paris liberated!'

1944 At 3.30 on this Friday afternoon, Free French general Philippe Leclerc and Henri Rol-Tanguy, Resistance leader for the Île-de-France, stood before the Montparnasse railway station to receive the German surrender of Paris. An hour later Charles de Gaulle arrived to see Leclerc sign the document. Paris was free at last, after four years and 72 days of German occupation.

Fifteen days earlier the city's railway workers had gone on strike, followed by Métro workers and postmen, while Rol-Tanguy's fighters placed posters around the city calling on the population to rise (a call that cost the lives of 1,500 Parisians). Meanwhile Leclerc's 2nd French Armoured Division was advancing with the American Third Army under the command of George Patton.

On 19 August German troops started to retreat from Paris, and a day later Resistance fighters occupied the Hôtel de Ville. The Resistance could field tens of thousands of men but lacked heavy weapons, while the few remaining Germans were backed up by 80 tanks and armoured vehicles. Neither side had a clear advantage, so a truce was agreed, but incidents of vicious fighting broke out, and Rol-Tanguy's men constructed barricades in the streets.

The Allied Supreme Commander Dwight Eisenhower was wary of attacking Paris; he could spare neither the troops nor the time in his push for the German border, and he was acutely aware that the Germans might destroy the great city before pulling out. (Fortunately, the German commander, General Dietrich von Choltitz, would ignore Hitler's order to raze it.) But on 22 August de Gaulle and his chief of staff Pierre Koenig convinced Eisenhower of the need to seize the capital, not only to defeat the Germans but also to prevent a possible communist takeover. De Gaulle insisted that the honour of liberating Paris must go to a French combat unit.

Now Leclerc's 2nd Armoured Division was pushing forward from the west. Two days later Leclerc sent a plane over the city dropping leaflets encouraging the insurgents: 'Hold on, we're coming!' At 8.30 on the evening of 24 August Captain Raymond Dronne became the first Allied officer to enter Paris when he led 150 men through the Porte d'Italie.

The rest of Leclerc's division entered the next morning, wiping out small pockets of German resistance as they went. Meanwhile the American 4th Division attacked Paris from the east, meeting little resistance.

At the German headquarters in the Hôtel Meurice on the rue de Rivoli, the 200 remaining defenders capitulated, and von Choltitz was brought to Leclerc's control centre at the Montparnasse train station. In the meantime, Ernest Hemingway, now a war correspondent, led two truckloads of French irregulars to the Ritz Bar and asked the bartender: 'How about 73 dry martinis?'

The next day de Gaulle led a military procession down the Champs-Élysées and was received in Notre Dame by the Committee of Liberation. There a brisk firefight broke out between recalcitrant Vichy supporters and Resistance fighters. Without flinching, he marched down the aisle as bullets flew, until the last of the attackers had been swept away. Then, standing in brilliant sunshine outside the Hôtel de Ville, he addressed a huge, wildly cheering crowd.

'Paris', he said, 'stood up to liberate itself and succeeded in doing this with its own hands ... Paris! Paris outraged! Paris broken! Paris martyred! But Paris liberated! Liberated by itself, liberated by its people with the help of the French armies, with the support and the help of all France, of the France that fights, of the only France, of the real France, of the eternal France!'

De Gaulle then offered token thanks to the Allies ('with the help of our dear and admirable Allies'), virtually ignoring that Leclerc's troops had advanced from Normandy with Patton and were dressed in American uniforms with American armoured vehicles. He went on to warn that the enemy was not yet beaten but promising that the French army 'will keep fighting until … the day of total and complete victory'. After a call for national unity, he closed with a ringing '*Vive la France!*'

1924 Benito Mussolini: 'God does not exist – religion in science is an absurdity, in practice an immorality and in men a disease.'

---

26 August

'*Let the boy win his spurs.*'

1346 Today one of England's greatest medieval knights fought in his first major battle. He was Edward of Woodstock, first son of King Edward III and known to history as the Black Prince.

It was at the opening stages of the Hundred Years' War. Asserting the flimsiest of claims to the throne of France, Edward III had been challenging France's Philippe VI since the late 1330s, and in 1346 Edward had invaded, accompanied by his son, then only sixteen.

On this day the English army of 11,000 men, including 7,000 longbowmen, met a far larger French force just beyond Abbéville near the small town of Crécy, with Prince Edward in command of the vanguard.

The battle began when Philippe sent his Genoese crossbowmen forward. They were at an inherent disadvantage, having a shorter range than the English longbows and capable of firing only two arrows a minute versus five for the English. Before the Genoese came within effective range, the English archers launched a murderous shower of arrows, forcing them to retreat. At this moment Prince Edward ordered his men to attack the French line.

Almost immediately, however, the Count of Alençon led a counterattack, blunting Edward's charge and putting him in deadly danger. The prince was thrown to the ground and saved only by his standard bearer, who fought off the French while he scrambled to his feet. Now young Edward sent a messenger to ask his father for help. According to the contemporary chronicler Jean Froissart, the king answered: 'Go back to him and to those who have sent you and tell them not to send for me again today, as long as my son is alive. Give them my command to let the boy win his spurs, for if God has so ordained it, I wish the day to be his and the honour to go to him and to those in whose charge I have placed him.'

The prince and his men rallied, and meanwhile the French knights were riding down their own retreating crossbowmen in their haste to attack, but a deadly shower of English arrows brought down men and horses in thousands. Once the knights had been unhorsed, English men-at-arms finished them off with swords and maces.

The battle had one pathetic moment of 'honour'. Allied to the French was John the Blind, King of Bohemia, who had lost his sight ten years earlier. Froissart relates that John's aides urged him to flee the developing debacle, but John refused, answering: 'As I am blind, I request you to lead me so far into the engagement that I may strike one stroke with my sword.' He then charged into battle with a French knight guiding him on each side; 'intent that they should not lose him in the press, they tied all the reins of their bridles each to other … they adventured themselves so forward, that they were there all slain, and the next day they were found in the place about the king, and all their horses tied each to other.'

Eventually darkness brought the grisly slaughter to a close. Fewer than 100 English had lost their lives, but 15,000 French and Genoese soldiers lay dead on the field and a further 1,500 French knights had been captured or killed. After the battle Prince Edward is said to have gone to John the Blind's body and taken his helmet with its ostrich feather crest, afterwards incorporating the feathers into his coat of arms and adopting John's motto, '*Ich dien*' ('I serve') as his own. It is still used today by Princes of Wales.

Edward of Woodstock remained England's foremost knight until his death 30 years later, his most storied victory at Poitiers in 1356, where he captured King Jean II, who had inherited the throne on Philippe's death. But he is perhaps most remembered for his epithet, the Black Prince, which he was never called in his lifetime. It did not come from his colouring (he was blond and blue-eyed) but probably from the black armour he wore.

1920 The Nineteenth Amendment to the United States Constitution is adopted: 'The right of citizens of the United States to vote shall not be denied or abridged by the United States or by any State on account of sex.'

27 August

*'All the Britons dye themselves with woad,
which produces a blue colour, and makes their
appearance in battle more terrible.'*

55 BC Just after midnight today, Julius Caesar sailed from today's Boulogne with 8,000 men of the Seventh and Tenth Legions in 80 transports, plus a few war-galleys. His purpose: to make a reconnaissance in force of a mysterious island to the north.

The island was Britain, then known only by the reports of traders and so remote that many doubted its existence. Caesar knew better; for three years he had been campaigning in adjacent Gaul. He told the Roman Senate that military necessity drove him to invade because 'in almost all the Gallic campaigns the Gauls had received reinforcements from Britain'. In fact, he believed the island was rich in tin, gold and pearls, and its conquest would burnish his reputation.

At nine o'clock the Roman fleet approached the British coast near Dover, but the Britons had gathered at the top of the White Cliffs, javelins at the ready, forcing Caesar to sail seven miles north to an open beach at Walmer. But waiting there were massed enemy cavalry and war chariots, which had shadowed the fleet up the coast, leaving the slower infantry behind.

Caesar's soldiers eyed the enemy with fear, until a standard bearer leaped into the water, shouting: 'Jump down, soldiers, unless you want to give up our eagle to the enemy.'

The Romans attacked, but, as Caesar described in *Commentarii de Bello Gallico*: 'The size of the ships made it impossible to run them aground except in fairly deep water; and soldiers, unfamiliar with the ground, with their hands full, and weighed down by the heavy burden of their arms, had at the same time to jump down from the ship, get a footing in the waves, and fight the enemy.'

In the end the Britons gave way because their chariots and cavalry, unsupported by infantry, were unsuited for defensive fighting, and Roman catapults and slings fired from the warships eventually drove them back.

The Romans established their camp, but, as a native of the non-tidal Mediterranean, Caesar was caught unawares when the British high tide filled his beached warships with water, and his anchored transports were driven against each other, threatening his return to Gaul.

The Britons then renewed their attacks, hoping to keep Caesar in Britain over the winter and starve him into submission, but the Romans fended off the enemy while repairing their ships. After only about three weeks in Britain, they re-embarked and returned to Gaul.

In truth, Caesar's expedition achieved little. No treasures were found, few slaves were captured, and Caesar was lucky to have escaped disaster. Nonetheless, when his favourably doctored reports reached Rome, the Senate declared twenty days of *supplicatio* (thanksgiving).

A year later Caesar invaded again, now with five legions and 2,000 cavalry, and marched inland as far as London, winning several small engagements. But after obtaining hostages and a peace treaty that theoretically made some tribes subservient to Rome, he retired back to Gaul, leaving not a single Roman soldier in Britain to enforce his settlement.

In *Commentarii de Bello Gallico*, Caesar vividly described this strange and alien land: 'Most of the islanders do not sow corn, but live on milk and flesh and clothe themselves in skins. All the Britons dye themselves with woad, which produces a blue colour, and makes their appearance in battle more terrible. They wear long hair, and shave every part of the body save the head and the upper lip.'

These tales of war chariots and blue-painted barbarians gained highly favourable public attention in Rome, cementing Caesar's reputation. But his adventures in Britain were far from subjugation, which had to wait until Emperor Claudius invaded in 43 AD. As the historian Tacitus commented: 'It was, in fact, the deified Julius who first of all Romans entered Britain with an army: he overawed the natives by a successful battle and made himself master of the coast; but it may be said that he revealed, rather than bequeathed, Britain to Rome.'

1808 Emperor Napoleon: 'In war, three-quarters turns on personal character and relations; the balance of manpower and materials counts only for the remaining quarter.'

---

28 August

'I have a dream'

1963 In 1863, President Abraham Lincoln had issued the Emancipation Proclamation to free America's slaves, yet a century later

African-Americans still suffered monumental injustices, especially in the south, where Jim Crow laws ensured that they remained second-class citizens. Blacks were forced to ride in the back of buses, and there were separate restrooms, restaurants, hotels and drinking fountains for whites and blacks. In the north there was no legal discrimination, but ancient prejudices still held the black man down.

During the 1950s the Supreme Court had declared segregated buses and separate public schools for black and white students unconstitutional. (In 1957 President Dwight Eisenhower used 101st Airborne troops to protect black students entering desegregated schools in Little Rock, Arkansas.) Freedom Riders – civil rights activists both black and white – rode interstate buses into segregated states where local government had defied Federal anti-segregation rulings.

In December 1962 two staunch civil rights activists, A. Philip Randolph and Bayard Rustin, began planning a massive march on Washington. Today would be the day of protest.

The capital was placed on high alert, with 12,000 policemen, soldiers and national guardsmen on duty. Over 2,000 chartered buses, 21 trains, ten airliners, and uncounted cars converged on Washington from all over the country. Some 250,000 people, black and white, came to bear witness.

Gathering at the Washington Monument, the immense crowd marched to the Lincoln Memorial. Randolph gave a short address and was followed by other luminaries, including Josephine Baker, the black American *vedette* who had so enthralled Paris in the 1920s. Mahalia Jackson, Bob Dylan, Joan Baez and Marian Anderson all sang. The sixteenth speaker was a 34-year-old Baptist minister named Martin Luther King Jr. On this day he cemented his place among great Americans with the defining speech of the era.

In cadences reminiscent of the Bible and of Negro spirituals, King said that 'the life of the coloured American is still sadly crippled by the manacle of segregation and the chains of discrimination ... Now is the time to rise from the dark and desolate valley of segregation to the sunlit path of racial justice. Now is the time to lift our nation from the quicksand of racial injustice to the solid rock of brotherhood ...

'There will be neither rest nor tranquillity in America until the coloured citizen is granted his citizenship rights ... we will not be satisfied until justice rolls down like waters and righteousness like a mighty stream.'

Towards the end of King's speech, Mahalia Jackson called out: 'Tell them about the dream, Martin!' King departed from his prepared text for what turned into the most famous part of his address:

'I still have a dream … I have a dream that one day out in the red hills of Georgia the sons of former slaves and the sons of former slave-owners will be able to sit down together at the table of brotherhood … I have a dream that my four little children will one day live in a nation where they will not be judged by the colour of their skin, but by the content of their character. I have a dream today …'

King concluded: 'When we let freedom ring, when we let it ring from every tenement and every hamlet, from every state and every city, we will be able to speed up that day when all of God's children, black men and white men, Jews and Gentiles, Protestants and Catholics, will be able to join hands and sing in the words of the old spiritual, "Free at last, free at last. Thank God Almighty, we are free at last."'

After the march, King and other civil rights leaders met with President John F. Kennedy at the White House. Although Kennedy was committed to passing a civil rights bill, he was gunned down in Dallas on 22 November. But on 2 July the next year the new president Lyndon Johnson signed the Civil Rights Act that banned discrimination based on 'race, colour, religion, sex or national origin' in employment practices and public accommodations.

1957 Zsa Zsa Gabor says in *The Observer*: 'I never hated a man enough to give him his diamonds back.'

---

29 August

'I've gone from saint to whore and back
to saint again all in one lifetime.'

1915 & 1982 She was called radiant. Or luminous. Or incandescent. She was Ingrid Bergman, a natural Swedish beauty who refused to wear makeup except for lipstick and hated high heels. She also caused one of Hollywood's greatest scandals that threatened to end her career.

Bergman was born on this day in 1915 in Stockholm, to a Swedish father and a German mother. She studied acting at Stockholm's Royal Dramatic Theatre School, where Greta Garbo had gone a decade earlier, but left after a year to act. The first time she visited a film studio, she recalled, 'it felt like walking on holy ground'.

At 21 Bergman married Petter Lindström and the next year bore him a daughter. She made a string of Swedish films, including *Intermezzo*, which so impressed producer David O. Selznick that he brought her to Hollywood for an English-language remake. It made her an overnight star.

In 1942 Bergman played her most iconic role, that of Ilsa Lund in *Casablanca*, opposite Humphrey Bogart. Shot in only six weeks, *Casablanca* won the Oscar for best film and has remained on almost everyone's list of all-time greatest films.

The next year Bergman was nominated for Best Actress in *For Whom the Bell Tolls*, inspired, perhaps, by her co-star Gary Cooper, with whom she had an affair. Then she won the Oscar for *Gaslight*, after which she complained: 'I made so many films which were more important, but the only one people ever want to talk about is that one with Bogart.'

In 1945 she starred in *Spellbound* opposite Gregory Peck (who briefly became her lover) and later that year, after Nazi Germany surrendered, she toured Europe entertaining American troops. There she fell in love with the photographer Robert Capa. Meanwhile she played a nun in *The Bells of St Mary's*.

In 1946 Bergman played opposite Cary Grant in Hitchcock's *Notorious*. Hitchcock later commented that 'Ingrid took films more seriously than life'. With her wholesome Swedish beauty, she was widely admired for her integrity and moral decency, an image reinforced by her next role as Joan of Arc. Again nominated for Best Actress, she was suddenly embroiled in scandal. While shooting *Stromboli* in Italy, she began a romance with the married director Roberto Rossellini and was expecting his child. It was a *cause célèbre* that whipped the puritanical American public into a moralistic frenzy, and she was even denounced in the Senate as 'an assault upon the institution of marriage' and 'a powerful influence for evil'.

After a bitter and highly publicised divorce from Petter Lindström, Bergman married Rossellini, and for the next six years she would shun Hollywood, make four further films with him and bear two more children, one the actress Isabella Rossellini. But while shooting in India Rossellini impregnated a 27-year-old Indian actress, bringing his union with Bergman to an ignominious end.

But Bergman said that acting always came first: 'If you took acting away from me I would stop breathing.' After making a French language film for Jean Renoir, she won her second Oscar in *Anastasia*. She finally returned to Hollywood in 1958 to a rapturous reception, causing her to comment: 'I've gone from saint to whore and back to saint again all in one lifetime.'

Bergman continued to star in films, plays and television (she won an Emmy for *The Turn of the Screw*) and married producer Lars Schmidt (this marriage, too, would eventually fail). In *Murder on the Orient Express* in 1974, she won the Oscar for Best Supporting Actress, although fellow cast member John Gielgud waspishly remarked: 'She speaks five languages and can't act in any of them.' Four years later, at 63, she made her final film, *Autumn Sonata*, in Swedish, for which she received her seventh Academy Award nomination.

Although by this time Bergman had breast cancer, in 1982 she completed the TV mini-series *A Woman Called Golda*. She died in London on her 67th birthday. She was posthumously awarded a second Emmy.

1786 When Shays' Rebellion begins in Massachusetts, Thomas Jefferson writes to a friend: 'The tree of liberty must be refreshed from time to time with the blood of patriots and tyrants. It is its natural manure.'

---

30 August

'There is no merit in conquering people forsaken by their own god.'

70 AD Today Jerusalem fell to the might of Rome after a six-month siege. The price of Jewish resistance was several hundred thousand dead, a hundred thousand enslaved and the destruction of the Jews' most sacred building, the Temple.

Judea had been a Roman province for 60 years, but the rapacity of Roman governors and the intransigence of some fanatical Jewish groups in the city had led to armed revolt. In 66 AD Jewish Zealots triggered the Jewish War when they attacked the Roman garrison in Jerusalem, leading to insurrection across the province.

Emperor Nero despatched future emperor Vespasian, who crushed the uprising in the north. By 70 only Jerusalem and a few isolated fortresses like Masada remained defiant. But within Jerusalem itself bloody civil war erupted. The Zealots demanded a Jewish king descended from King David, who had reigned a thousand years before, and the terrorist *Sicarii* ('dagger-men') stabbed anyone advocating peace with Rome.

Despite the turmoil within, Jerusalem's three massive stone walls remained impervious to Roman attack. In 69 Nero committed suicide and Vespasian returned to Rome to struggle for power, leaving his son Titus in charge.

In April of 70 Titus marched on Jerusalem and built a five-mile wall around the city, as high as the city walls it faced. To exhaust the food supply, he allowed Jews to enter the city to celebrate Passover but refused to let them out. Twice he attempted to negotiate with Jewish leaders but was almost killed in a sudden attack.

Now Titus instituted more draconian measures; anyone caught attempting to leave would be crucified between the walls. Soon thousands of bodies ringed the city, while the population began to starve. According to the Jewish historian Josephus, who was there: 'The terraces were crowded with exhausted women and little children, the alleys with dead old men; boys and young men wandered about like ghosts, their bodies swollen.'

In May Titus brought his battering rams to bear, and by midsummer he had breached the first two walls. Then, late in the night of 29 August twenty legionaries launched a surprise assault over the third wall, killing the Zealot guards in their sleep. Then the Romans charged towards Temple Mount, where Jerusalem's Second Temple stood, a massive structure raised by King Herod in 19 BC.

Titus had intended to rededicate the Temple to the emperor, but a legionary started a raging fire that engulfed it and spread to other parts of the city. According to Josephus: 'Passion alone was in command ... As [the Roman legions] neared the Sanctuary they pretended not even to hear [Titus'] commands and urged the men in front to throw in more firebrands ... everywhere was slaughter and flight. Most of the victims were peaceful citizens, weak and unarmed, butchered wherever they were caught. Round the altar the heaps of corpses grew higher and higher, while down the Sanctuary steps poured a river of blood and the bodies of those killed at the top slithered to the bottom.'

A few Jews escaped through secret tunnels while others mounted a final stand in the upper city, but by nightfall all resistance was crushed. Titus then ordered the wholesale destruction of the city.

Josephus relates that 'the [city] wall was so thoroughly laid even with the ground by those that dug it up to the foundation, that nothing was left to make those that came thither believe [Jerusalem] had ever been inhabited ... Those places which were adorned with trees and pleasant gardens were now become desolate country every way, and its trees were all cut down. Nor could any foreigner who had formerly seen Judea and the most beautiful suburbs of the city, and now saw it as a desert, but lament and mourn sadly at so great a change.' The only section of the Temple wall to survive Titus' wrath is today called the Wailing Wall.

The Romans had stamped out the revolt, and Jerusalem was once more under imperial control. But Titus declined a victory wreath for his triumph because, he said, 'there is no merit in conquering people forsaken by their own god'.

1918 When the Socialist Revolutionary Party wins the most votes in Russia's first-ever democratic elections in November 1917, Lenin's Bolsheviks disband the Constituent Assembly. Today SRP member Fanya Kaplan shoots Lenin three times but fails to kill him. Arrested the same day, she says: 'I did it on my own. I will not say from whom I obtained my revolver. I will give no details. I had resolved to kill Lenin long ago. I consider him a traitor to the Revolution.' She is executed four days later.

---

31 August

'We are in a chamber pot and about to be shat upon.'

1870 Today a 120,000-strong French army found itself surrounded by an overwhelmingly powerful Prussian army. Leading the beleaguered French was Napoleon III, the last emperor ever to command in the field, while his wife Empress Eugénie ruled as regent in Paris.

For 22 years Napoleon had been the master of France, first as president, then as emperor, but now France's position in Europe was threatened by the potential unification of the German states. In July 1870 the crafty Prussian chancellor Otto von Bismarck, who wanted the conflict as a means of drawing together some reluctant German principalities, had cunningly manoeuvred Napoleon into war.

The Prussian forces were commanded by Generalfeldmarschall Helmuth von Moltke and accompanied by Crown Prince Wilhelm Friedrich, soon to become emperor of the combined German states as Kaiser Wilhelm I, and Bismarck, here to see the final victory in the war he had engineered.

After some early French successes, the larger and better-trained Prussian army quickly got the measure of the French, defeating them six times within a month. Although Napoleon was nominally France's commander, Marshal Patrice de MacMahon made most of the military decisions. The emperor was in poor health; a heavy smoker, he was suffering a urinary tract infection and often had to walk with a cane. Knowing that he was of little help to his generals, he thought of returning to Paris, but Eugénie telegraphed him: 'Don't think of coming back, unless you want to unleash a terrible revolution. They will say you quit the army to flee the danger.'

On 30 August Moltke thrashed the French again, forcing them to retreat to Sedan in the Ardennes, a small town with a 16th-century fortress at its centre. The next day the Prussian army of 200,000 men completely encircled the town, cutting off all hope of reinforcements. 'Now we have them in the mousetrap', Moltke exulted.

Before dawn on 1 September, Prussian artillery positioned on the heights around Sedan began a merciless bombardment, causing panic among the French, while transport carts, artillery and refugees clogged the streets. Desperate to break the Prussian grip, Napoleon ordered MacMahon to attack, but at five o'clock an enemy shell seriously wounded him in the hip. Command now passed to General Auguste-Alexandre Ducrot, who famously summed up the situation: 'We are in a chamber pot and about to be shat upon.' ('*Nous sommes dans un pot de chambre, et nous y serons emmerdés.*')

Ducrot's prediction proved precise. Prussian artillery continued to reduce French forces, and Napoleon knew that he could never continue as emperor after such a disastrous loss. He spent the day riding where the action was hottest, hoping for a stray shell to end his reign in dignity. He survived unscathed, but his army was shattered, with 17,000 casualties against half as many for the Prussians. At one o'clock the next afternoon he ordered a white flag hoisted above the citadel and sent a message to Crown Prince Wilhelm: '*Monsieur mon frère*; Not having succeeded in dying in the midst of my troops, nothing remains for me but to deliver my sword into Your Majesty's hands.' He thus became one of 104,000 French prisoners of war.

When news of his surrender reached Paris, Empress Eugénie cried out: 'No! An emperor does not capitulate! He is dead! ... Why didn't he kill himself?' When convinced that Napoleon had indeed been taken, she slipped out of Paris with the help of her American dentist and sailed to England in the yacht of a British official.

Two days after the defeat, while republicans in Paris were overthrowing Napoleon's empire, Napoleon's captors took him to Prussia, never to see France again. He spent a few months in regal confinement with Crown Prince Wilhelm Friedrich and then went into exile with Eugénie in Chislehurst in Kent, where he died two years later at 64. His last words, addressed to his doctor, were a plaintive: *'N'est-ce pas que nous n'avons pas été des lâches à Sedan?'* ('We were not cowards at Sedan, were we?')

1974 Woody Allen: 'The lion and the calf shall lie down together but the calf won't get much sleep.'

---

1 September

*'You are about to see one king in his
tomb and another in his cradle.'*

1715 This evening, after 72 years, three months and seventeen days as King of France, Louis XIV died four days short of his 76th birthday. His reign was (and remains) the longest of any European monarch. In the millennium between Charlemagne and Louis-Philippe, of 49 French kings – Carolingians, Capetians, Valois and Bourbons – only Louis reached the age of 70.

Louis had been monolithic and unchanging throughout his life, embodying the idea of the divine right of kings. As he wrote in his memoirs: 'God, who has given kings to men ... [reserved] to Himself alone the right to examine their conduct.'

He cared only for the glory of France and for his own, and could sometimes not distinguish between them. He kept his country almost constantly at war, his cannon inscribed with the motto *'Ultima Ratio Regum'* (the last argument of kings), but with varying degrees of success. But his cultural achievements were of a high order. He founded the Comédie Française and backed France's two greatest classical playwrights, Racine and Molière. He initiated the three great French academies – of Painting and Sculpture, of Architecture, and of Science. He also turned Paris into Europe's grandest city by razing the old city walls and building the Invalides and the Champs Elysées.

Now, although he had been suffering for weeks from gangrene in one of his legs and the fever that attended it, he seemed remarkably composed. 'I have always thought that dying would be more difficult', he said to his wife, Madame de Maintenon, five days before his death. 'But now that I am on the point of this moment that men fear so much, I do not find it so hard.'

The king had nominated his nephew Philippe d'Orléans as regent for the heir to the throne, Louis' great-grandson, another Louis, now just five years old. 'You are about to see one king in his tomb and another in his cradle', he told Philippe. 'Always cherish the memory of the first and the interests of the second.'

The king then called for his great-grandson. *'J'ai trop aimé la guerre'*, he said ('I loved war too much'). 'Do not imitate me in that, nor in my too great expenditure ... Relieve your people as much as you can, and do for them that which I have had the misfortune not to be able to do for them myself.'

For weeks Louis' doctors had searched for a means to save him, but now all despaired for his life. In desperation they summoned a quack from Marseille, who spoon-fed the king a few drops of his magic elixir, to no effect. Abandoning all hope, Louis asked his confessor for a general absolution. His last recorded remark was: 'I depart, but the State will always remain.' (*Je m'en vais, mais l'État demeurera toujours.*') Then, at 7.45 this Sunday evening, he passed away in the great palace he had built at Versailles.

Louis' great-grandson now became Louis XV. As king he was an enduring failure, in the words of one historian, 'a perpetual adolescent called to do a man's job'. France, the greatest power in Europe on his ascension, was weakened both militarily and financially during his reign, while he discredited the monarchy by an endless stream of illicit affairs (including the four Mailly sisters, one after the other). Perhaps his greatest accomplishment, if such it can be termed, was taking Madame de Pompadour as his official mistress. She was a great patron of the arts and advised him on government policy. (She warned him: '*Après nous, le déluge.*' ('After us, the deluge.'))

By the time that Louis XV died in 1774, he had been king for almost 59 years, and he and his great-grandfather had reigned for 131 consecutive years between them. This extended period of absolute monarchy and the social petrification that accompanied it were major causes of the French Revolution that broke out just fifteen years after the younger Louis' death.

1939 As Germany invades Poland to start the Second World War, Hitler lies to the Reichstag: 'Last night, Polish soldiers opened fire for the first time on German soil. This morning Germany retaliated. From now on, bombs will be met by bombs.'

---

2 September

*'All the skie was of a fiery aspect, like
the top of a burning oven.'*

1666 Next time you're in London, walk east from the Tower of London for half a mile until Monument Street. There stands a 202-foot Doric column of Portland stone topped with a gilded urn of fire. Designed by Christopher Wren and Robert Hooke, it is 202 feet from the site in Pudding Lane where the Great Fire of London began today.

Although a city of half a million people, London was still medieval in character, with wood and pitch houses crowded cheek by jowl, the upper storeys overhanging the lower ones, blocking out the sun. The cobble-stoned streets were narrow and foul, doubling as the city's sewers. To make matters worse, a plague epidemic had just killed 100,000 people.

The long, dry summer, exacerbated by high winds from a storm, now ensured perfect conditions for a fire.

At one o'clock on the morning of 2 September, a servant in Thomas Farynor's bakery in Pudding Lane woke to find the house ablaze. The baker and his family were awakened by choking smoke and escaped through a window onto their neighbour's roof, but a panicky maid perished in the flames.

Alerted to the fire, citizen firefighting brigades tried to stem its progress with buckets of water from the river, but, fanned by the wind, it continued to spread. By eight o'clock it had reached the Thames and started to burn the houses on London Bridge. Meanwhile, diarist Samuel Pepys and his wife had retreated to an ale-house on the Bankside: 'We saw the fire as only one entire arch of fire from this to the other side the bridge, and in a bow up the hill for an arch of above a mile long: it made me weep to see it. The churches, houses, and all on fire and flaming at once, and a horrid noise the flames made, and the cracking of houses at their ruine.'

On the second day the fire roared unabated through London's medieval lanes and reached its peak on the third day, spreading from the Temple to near the Tower of London. Even the great 13th-century cathedral of St Paul was caught by the flames. According to another eyewitness, the writer John Evelyn, 'ye melting lead [from the roof] running downe the streetes in a streame, and the very pavements glowing with fiery rednesse, so as no horse nor man was able to tread on them'. As the cathedral collapsed, refugees fled the city to Hampstead, Highgate and Moorfields while others piled their possessions onto boats in the Thames. Evelyn describes the scene: 'All the skie was of a fiery aspect, like the top of a burning oven, the light seen above forty miles round … 10,000 houses all in one flame; the noise and cracking and thunder of the impetuous flames, ye shrieking of women and children, the hurry of people, the fall of Towers, Houses, and Churches, was like an hideous storme.' By now half of London was burning, and even King Charles joined the firefighters, passing buckets of water, as fire brigades began blowing up houses with gunpowder to make firebreaks.

By 6 September, the inferno had at last been extinguished, but, as Evelyn reported, 'the people who now walk'd about ye ruines appear'd like men in a dismal desert, or rather in some greate citty laid waste by a cruel enemy; to which was added the stench that came from some poore creatures bodies'. Only one fifth of London was still standing. The fire had destroyed most of the civic buildings, 13,000 houses, 52 guild halls and 89 churches. Luckily, it had spared the Tower of London and especially the White Tower, where the army's powder magazine was kept. Amazingly, only six people had died.

One positive to come from the fire was the mass incineration of the rats that harboured plague-infected fleas. The other was the rebuilding of London. King Charles chose six commissioners to redesign the city with wider streets and buildings made of brick instead of timber. Most importantly, the great architect Christopher Wren built almost 50 churches, including a new St Paul's Cathedral, the masterpiece we can still visit today.

1901 About to become president, Theodore Roosevelt at the Minnesota State Fair: 'There is a homely adage which runs, "Speak softly and carry a big stick; you will go far."'

---

3 September

'The sea! The sea!'

401 BC This afternoon at Cunaxa, on the left bank of the Euphrates River about 50 miles west of Baghdad, a fierce battle triggered one of the great adventures in military history.

There, an expeditionary force of 50,000, led by Cyrus, governor-general of Asia Minor, confronted the army of his older brother, Artaxerxes II, King of Persia, whom he sought to dethrone and succeed. In the course of the action, a Greek mercenary force holding Cyrus' right wing routed the Persians on their front; but elsewhere disaster unfolded: the left wing was soon outflanked, and Cyrus himself was slain. Only the Hellenic contingent – some 13,000 strong – managed to close ranks and escape destruction. But the Greeks were now alone, outnumbered, and stranded deep in enemy country. How would they survive and reach the safety of their now-distant homeland?

Hoping to negotiate a peaceful retreat homeward, a group of four Greek generals and twenty captains accepted the invitation of one of Artaxerxes' satraps to a feast in the Persian camp, but on arrival they were brought before the king and decapitated.

Without leadership, the fate of the mercenaries looked bleak, but at a meeting of under-officers to discuss their perilous situation, a young Athenian named Xenophon addressed their plight, urging them to take bold measures: 'Here's a grand enterprise!' he told them. 'Let us take the lead and show the others how to be brave! Show yourselves the best of officers, and as worthy to be captains as the captains themselves!' He was elected one of five commanders.

And so began the March of the Ten Thousand, a slog of over a thousand miles to reach the Black Sea and the safety of Trapezus, a Greek colony there.

For over five months the Greeks force-marched northwards through hostile territory: up the Tigris valley, through Kurdistan, and into Armenia, crossing trackless deserts, fording deep rivers, and struggling up snow-clogged mountain passes, suffering from frostbite, snow-blindness, and starvation, all the time facing raids and ambushes by elements of the Persian army and by local tribes resentful of what the Greek force requisitioned from their countryside.

Eventually, however, there came a supremely revitalising moment. As the force neared the top of a ridge, Xenophon, commanding the rear guard, heard shouting from the head of the column. Fearing it meant the enemy was attacking the front, he raced forward with cavalry to give support. It was then that he heard what the men were shouting: 'The sea! The sea!' ('*Thalatta! Thalatta!*') They had reached the Black Sea.

Their numbers by now reduced to fewer than 9,000, the Hellenes arrived at Trapezus a few days later, where they stayed for a month, welcomed as fellow countrymen and provided with food and safety. There they made sacrifices to the gods for their good fortune and held a contest of games and sports near their encampment.

Then the Greeks made their way slowly westward by land and sea, past Byzantium and the Bosporus, finally to the sea coast of Asia Minor, where Xenophon departed for home and the expeditionary force, now only 6,000 soldiers, but with a new commander, embarked on another campaign against the Persians.

Some twenty years later, Xenophon wrote his famous account of the trek, *Anabasis* (*The March Up Country*).

1650 Oliver Cromwell cries out: 'Let God arise, let his enemies be scattered!' as English Parliamentarian forces attack a Scottish army loyal to Charles I at Dunbar. On the same date eight years later he dies at Whitehall of septicaemia, having told his retainers: 'It is not my design to drink or to sleep, but my design is to make what haste I can to be gone.' The diarist John Evelyn records: 'The joyfulest funeral that I ever saw, for there was none that cried but dogs.'

---

4 September

'Odoacer was the first barbarian who reigned in Italy, over a people who had once asserted their just superiority above the rest of mankind.'

476 AD Today the last Roman emperor in the West resigned his office. Italy now had a king, Flavius Odoacer, a professional soldier from a Germanic tribe called the Thuringii.

History – or at least tradition – tells us that Romulus and Remus founded Rome on 21 April 753 BC. It was a monarchy until 509 BC, when the city's nobility revolted against the tyrannical Tarquinius Superbus and established the Roman Republic. Rome gradually grew in power with conquests of neighbouring kingdoms and for the next five centuries was an empire without an emperor, governed by the Roman Senate, which annually elected two consuls to serve for a single year.

In times of crisis the Senate appointed dictators to rule for six months, although later ones, notably Sulla and Julius Caesar, forced the Senate to accept them on a more or less permanent basis. Caesar's adopted son Octavian gained dictatorial control after his defeat of Mark Antony in 30 BC. On 16 January 27 BC the Roman Senate gave Octavian the new title of *Imperator Caesar Divi Filius* [Divine Son] *Augustus*, giving official sanction to the fact that the Roman Republic had now become a dictatorship under the rule of an emperor.

Today, 503 years and 231 days after Augustus' elevation, the last Roman emperor abdicated his imperial office, bringing to an end the Roman Empire (although its eastern half continued as the Byzantine Empire for another 977 years). He was a fourteen-year-old boy called

Romulus Augustulus, his name a happy combination of Rome's alleged founder and its first emperor.

By the time of Romulus Augustulus' resignation, the empire had long been under attack by marauding bands of barbarian tribes such as the Vandals, Alans, Sueves, Huns, Goths and Visigoths. In 410 the Visigoths led by Alaric had sacked the imperial capital, the same year in which all Roman troops were withdrawn from England, leaving it to the depredations of the Scoti, Saxons, and Picts. In 455 the Vandals under Genseric sacked Rome again.

Romulus Augustulus' father was a Roman aristocrat from the Balkans named Orestes, who for a time had served in the court of Attila the Hun. After Attila's death Orestes reached high rank in the Western Roman Empire. In 475 he revolted against the Western emperor Julius Nepos and took de facto control of the West.

On 31 October 475 Orestes placed his son on the imperial throne, while remaining the power behind it. But Orestes had made a fatal miscalculation. His army was largely composed of German mercenaries, to whom he had promised land in Italy. When Orestes backtracked on his promises, the mercenaries revolted under their leader Flavius Odoacer, whom they declared their king.

Orestes rallied the few units of Roman troops stationed in northern Italy, but he stood no chance against the savagery of Odoacer's barbarian army. Orestes was captured near Piacenza on 28 August 476 and swiftly executed. Five days later Odoacer easily defeated the remnants of Orestes' army at Ravenna and seized Romulus Augustulus.

On 4 September Romulus Augustulus was deposed as emperor, and Odoacer took the title of King of Italy. In the words of Edward Gibbon: 'Odoacer was the first barbarian who reigned in Italy, over a people who had once asserted their just superiority above the rest of mankind.'

But what to do with Romulus Augustulus? Rather than executing the boy emperor, in an act of remarkable clemency for the time, Odoacer exiled him to a villa in Campania, where he fades from history.

It was an exceptionally kind fate for Roman emperors, of which there were 92, most of whom came to unpleasant ends. Five committed suicide, eleven were executed, twelve were killed in battle, three more were killed after having been captured in war, and 36 were murdered. One, Petronius Maximus, was stoned to death by a Roman mob, but perhaps the unluckiest was Carus, who was struck by lightning.

> **1823** Former president Thomas Jefferson writes to former president John Adams: 'To attain all this [universal republicanism], however, rivers of blood must yet flow, and years of desolation pass over; yet the object is worth rivers of blood, and years of desolation.'

5 September

'Place Terror on the order of the day!'

1793 The year had started badly for France's revolutionaries. Austria and Prussia were already trying to invade the country, and by February Great Britain and the Dutch Republic had joined the coalition, followed by Spain in March. Their aim was to prevent this virulent strain of republicanism from infecting other parts of Europe and to restore the monarchy in France. Furthermore, counter-revolutionary efforts that were rampant around France would culminate in bloody insurrection in the Vendée by the end of the year.

Meanwhile, the French government was growing increasingly despotic. On 21 January Louis XVI had been fed to the guillotine, and in April the National Convention created the Committee of Public Safety to protect the country against foreign attacks and internal rebellion. By July the Committee had become the de facto executive government, and on the 27th, they made the fatal step of electing the fanatical Maximilien Robespierre to join its ranks.

Besieged by foreign powers outside its borders and traitors real and imagined within, the French Revolution now moved into its bloodiest and most notorious phase. Today (19 Fructidor by the Republican calendar) the Committee of Public Safety, led by Robespierre, proclaimed: 'It is time that equality bore its scythe above all heads. It is time to horrify all the conspirators. So legislators, place Terror on the order of the day! Let us be in revolution, because everywhere counter-revolution is being woven by our enemies. The blade of the law should hover over all the guilty.' For the first time in history, terror became official government policy.

So began the Terror, that frenzy of republican butchery with which the rabid revolutionaries cleansed the state with blood. Later the ferocious Joseph Fouché offered this heartless justification: 'The blood of criminals fertilises the soil of liberty and establishes power on sure foundations.'

The very epicentre of the Terror was the great open square on the Seine that today we know as the Place de la Concorde, now one of

Paris's most spectacularly beautiful. But in 1793 its beauty was over-shadowed by the sight of the guillotine, raised on a platform to give the spectators a better view, where 1,343 victims were beheaded.

Thousands of people congregated here daily to see the tumbrels of the condemned arrive. Seated around the scaffold with wine and bread bought from enterprising grocers, the spectators enjoyed the sight and smell of running blood. The notorious *tricoteuses* sat knitting to the swish of the blade and the cries of terror from those waiting their turn on the scaffold. Here the Revolution devoured its first victims and eventually itself. Not only Louis XVI, Marie Antoinette, Philippe Égalité and Charlotte Corday but also Danton, Saint-Just and Madame Roland were all beheaded here.

Beyond today's Place de la Concorde (renamed Place de la Révolution), another 1,200 people were executed in other parts of Paris, and the Terror spread inexorably across all of France. About 15,000 victims were guillotined, but in Lyon Joseph Fouché decided that beheading was too slow and had over 300 mown down by cannon fire. In Nantes 2,000 were towed out in barges into the middle of the Loire and drowned. Around the country at least another 10,000 died in overcrowded and unsanitary prisons awaiting trial, bringing total deaths during the Terror to something like 40,000.

Among the last to die were sixteen Carmelite nuns who had refused to give up their monastic vows. Executed on 17 July 1794, they mounted the scaffold singing hymns. Just eleven days later the Terror bled to a close with the beheading of Robespierre, the man who had done most to create it.

1914 During the Battle of the Marshes of Saint-Gond (part of the First Battle of the Marne), General Ferdinand Foch reports to General Joffre: 'My centre is giving way, my right is in retreat; situation excellent. I shall attack.'

---

6 September

'In the most naked way an assault not on power, not on wealth, but simply and solely upon free government.'

1901 Two American presidents had already been shot dead in the last 36 years – Abraham Lincoln in 1865 and James Garfield in 1881. Today would see a third, President William McKinley.

Raised in a small town in Ohio, McKinley rose from private to major during the American Civil War, fighting in several ferocious battles, including Antietam. First a Republican congressman, then governor of Ohio, in 1896 he scored a massive victory to become the nation's 25th president at 53.

The most important event in McKinley's presidency was war with Spain. Since the 1860s Cubans had been striving for independence from Spanish colonial rule, but revolutionary violence was met with savage repression. In January 1898 McKinley ordered the battleship USS *Maine* to Havana to reassure Americans living there. Three weeks later the *Maine* exploded in Havana harbour, causing outrage in the United States and putting pressure on the government to intervene. When McKinley first tried diplomacy rather than war, the bellicose Assistant Secretary of the Navy Theodore Roosevelt claimed: 'McKinley has no more backbone than a chocolate éclair.' In April the US did finally go to war and handily defeated Spain in just three months. The island became an American protectorate, and the US annexed Puerto Rico, Guam and the Philippines.

McKinley easily won a second term in 1900, with Roosevelt, who had become a national hero during the war, as his vice president.

Early in his second term McKinley came to Buffalo to attend the Pan-American Exposition. Round-faced, chubby and balding, on this day he was standing confidently in the receiving line when a young man with a white handkerchief wrapped around his right hand approached him. Thinking the man was injured, McKinley reached out to shake his left hand when suddenly two shots rang out from a .32 revolver concealed under the handkerchief. The first bullet was deflected by a button on McKinley's suit but the second buried itself deep in his stomach and his assailant cried out: 'I done my duty.' Bystanders over-powered the shooter as he was preparing to fire a third shot; he was saved from mob violence when the stricken president called out to his bodyguards: 'Be easy with him, boys.' McKinley was driven to a nearby hospital (thus becoming the first American president to ride in an automobile).

Rushed into surgery, McKinley at first seemed to be on the mend, but six days later his condition deteriorated; unknown to the doctors, the gangrene that would kill him was growing on the walls of his stomach, slowly poisoning his blood. He died on 14 September, killed as much by bungled surgery as by the bullet, which the surgeons were unable to find in his stomach because he was so fat.

McKinley's assassin was a deranged anarchist named Leon Czolgosz, who claimed that he had murdered the president because he was the head of a corrupt government. The new president Theodore Roosevelt, who had been sworn in on McKinley's death, called the murder 'in the most naked way an assault not on power, not on wealth, but simply and solely upon free government'.

At his trial Czolgosz refused to testify. Despite claims by the defence that he was mentally ill, he was judged legally sane and convicted. When strapped to the electric chair on the morning of 29 October – only 45 days after McKinley's death – he claimed: 'I killed the President because he was the enemy of the good people – the good working people. I am not sorry for my crime.' Three jolts of 1,800 volts finished him off.

1519 France's philandering King François I gives orders for work to begin on the Château de Chambord, 170 yards long with 440 rooms and 356 sculpted chimneys. With his diamond ring he engraves on a window in his study: '*Souvent femme varie/Bien fol qui s'y fie.*' ('A woman is very fickle/He who trusts her is a fool.')

---

7 September

'To the meaningless French idealisms, Liberty, Equality, and Fraternity, we oppose the German realities, Infantry, Cavalry, and Artillery.'

1914 Ever since Germany had routed France in the Franco-Prussian War, the Germans had maintained a disdainful superiority, best expressed by one-time German chancellor Fürst Bernhard von Bülow's contemptuous remark: 'To the meaningless French idealisms, Liberty, Equality, and Fraternity, we oppose the German realities, Infantry, Cavalry, and Artillery.' These realities were now to be put to the test at the First Battle of the Marne.

On 4 August German cavalry units had swept over the frontier into neutral Belgium in the first fighting of the First World War. Following the plan of the late German Field Marshal Alfred von Schlieffen (he had died in January 1913), the Germans were to storm past Brussels and down into France at Lille and along the coast, then swing around below Paris to catch the main French army from the rear, defeating France in 40 days, before the Russians had a chance to fully mobilise.

'Exterminate first the treacherous English', ordered Kaiser Wilhelm II, 'and annihilate the despicable little army of General French.'

After an unexpected delay around Liège, the Germans advanced inexorably against ineffectual resistance by French armies and the British Expeditionary Force. The French Fifth Army was almost destroyed at Charleroi, and the BEF was forced to retreat after Mons. German forces were now within 30 miles of Paris. But then came the Marne.

In command of the French (who fielded 39 divisions versus six for the BEF) was Marshal Joseph Joffre, who had confidently told his superiors, 'I would tear up the Boches in less than two months', but ordered his men: 'A soldier who can no longer advance must, cost what it may, keep the conquered ground and be killed where he stands rather than retreat.'

But the man who saw the way to stop the enemy was not Joffre but General Joseph-Simon Gallieni, once Joffre's superior but now military governor of Paris. Seeing the German First Army wheeling before Paris, Gallieni realised that their right flank was exposed and convinced Joffre to attack.

On 6 September French and British units moved forward to exploit the gap between German armies. The next day Gallieni ordered one of the most extraordinary moves of the war. Realising that the French front-line units needed reinforcements, he commandeered 600 Paris taxis, brought them together at Les Invalides and loaded them with five infantry battalions, five soldiers per taxi plus a driver. That evening and through the night of 7–8 September the taxis made their way towards the front lines, with only their tail lights lit, each driver following the taxi ahead. Watching his taxi convoy depart, Gallieni remarked: 'Well, here at least is something out of the ordinary!' ('*Eh bien, voilà au moins qui n'est pas banal!*') The drivers were paid 70,000 francs for their work.

On 8 September the reinforced French Fifth Army launched a surprise attack, forcing the Germans to retreat to the Aisne, while the Ninth Army was also advancing against determined German resistance.

French and British troops continued the attack but made little further progress, missing the best opportunity of the war to rout the enemy. The Battle of the Marne was now effectively over, but so was Germany's Schlieffen Plan. The Allies had stalled the enemy onslaught and forced them back into positions that would not change much over the next four years. Stalemated in the west, the Germans' hope of knocking France out of the war had vanished, and they now had to fight on two fronts, assuring their eventual defeat.

1814 Napoleon fights a bloody draw against the Russians at Borodino, losing 30,000 dead, wounded and captured. On hearing the news, a prescient Talleyrand remarks: '*Voilà le commencement de la fin.*' ('There is the beginning of the end.') In a memorial service 27 years later to the day, Tsar Nicholas I tells his army: 'God punished the foolish; the bones of the audacious foreigners were scattered from Moscow to the Niemen – and we entered Paris.'

8 September

'*I have not written even half of what I saw.*'

1298 Today about 100 miles from Dubrovnik near the island of Korčula a Genoese fleet of 75 galleys utterly destroyed a larger Venetian fleet, sinking or capturing 83 galleys, killing 7,000 and capturing 5,000 more. Among those taken was a well-travelled Venetian adventurer who had commanded one of his city's galleys. He was Marco Polo.

The prisoners were taken to Genoa where Marco shared his cell with a writer of chivalric romances named Rustichello da Pisa. During his ten months in prison, Marco dictated a detailed account of his travels that two years later would be published in Old French as *Livre des Merveilles du Monde* (*Book of the Marvels of the World*), better known to most of us as *The Travels of Marco Polo*. In Italian the book's title would be *Il Milione* (*The Million*), deriving from Polo's nickname 'Emilione'.

In the preface, Marco tells of his father Niccolò's and his uncle Maffeo's earlier travels to Bolghar (now in Russia), Bukhara (in modern Uzbekistan) and present-day Beijing, where they met Kublai Khan, the Mongol ruler of China, who treated them munificently and asked them to carry a letter for the Pope and return with 100 Christians who could teach grammar, rhetoric, logic, geometry, arithmetic, music and astronomy. The Polo brothers arrived back in Venice in 1269. Two years later they set off on their return to China, this time accompanied by Marco, who was then about seventeen. Their journey would be an amazing feat today, let alone in the 13th century.

The Polos sailed to Acre (now in Israel) and then rode on camels past Baghdad to Hormuz on the Persian Gulf, a distance of about 1,500 miles. On they went, following the Silk Road through Afghanistan and then across the vastness of Cathay (China). In Marco's telling, this three-year trip was filled with perilous adventure with merchant caravans, sandstorms and bandit attacks, finally ending in Shangdu, 125 miles from Beijing, where Kublai Khan had built a magnificent summer palace. (Five hundred years later Samuel Taylor Coleridge would feature this palace in his poem beginning 'In Xanadu did Kubla Khan/A stately pleasure-dome decree …')

Kublai Khan was fascinated by Europeans and took a shine to Marco, an intelligent young man who already spoke four languages and probably learned Chinese. Marco remained at the royal court for seventeen years, often sent on fact-finding missions to distant parts of the empire. Kublai so valued the Polos' contributions that he declined their requests to return to Venice. Finally in 1292 they were allowed to join a flotilla of fourteen junks that sailed to Hormuz on a hair-raising two-year voyage. They stopped at Ciamba (modern Vietnam), Singapore, Sumatra, Sri Lanka, the west coast of India and the southern reaches of Persia. Of the 600 passengers aboard, only eighteen survived the trip (including all three Polos).

The Polos travelled overland to Constantinople and at last reached Venice in 1295, carrying a large fortune in gemstones (but not the pasta that Marco supposedly introduced to Italy. It had already existed since Roman times).

Three years later came Marco's capture, imprisonment and release. He then moved into his father's palazzo, became a wealthy trader and raised a family. Meanwhile, *The Travels of Marco Polo* was astonishing Europeans with its tales of his odyssey in the Far East and telling of China's emperor, court, palaces and wealth, its paper money, postal service, coal burning, gunpowder, eyeglasses and porcelain, things that had not yet appeared in Europe. He also reported on the geography, warfare and commerce of Kublai's empire – and the sexual practices of the Chinese. Many doubted that he had actually seen all these fantastic things, some even claiming that the Italian title, *Il Milione*, stood for the million lies in the book.

In 1324 Marco was about 70, old and ill. On his deathbed he was urged to retract some of the seemingly incredible stories he had told. *'Non ho scritto neppure la metà delle cose che ho visto'*, he answered – 'I have not written even half of what I saw.'

1560 Amy Robsart, the wife of Queen Elizabeth's favourite Robert Dudley, is found dead with a broken neck at the foot of the stairs at Cumnor Place. Elizabeth's deadly enemy Mary, Queen of Scots says: 'The Queen of England is going to marry her horse keeper who has killed his wife to make room for her.' * **1858** Presidential candidate Abraham Lincoln during a speech in Clinton, Illinois: 'You can fool all the people some of the time, and some of the people all the time, but you can not fool all the people all the time.'

9 September

'I was bred to arms from my childhood and am stained with rivers of blood that I have shed.'

1087 At daybreak today William the Conqueror died at the Convent of St Gervais near Rouen of an injury inflicted in battle a month before. A few days later he received a gruesome burial in the Abbaye aux Hommes at Caen.

William had been a brutal overlord in his conquered English territories. To suppress rebellion, during the winter of 1069–70, he reduced the north of England to a desert, causing widespread famine and a death toll of 100,000. He punished rebels with mutilation, variously depriving them of hands and feet, and a contemporary chronicle reports that 'whoever slew a hart or hind was to be blinded'. Further: 'If a man lay with a woman against her will, he was forthwith condemned to forfeit those members with which he had disported himself.'

For twenty years before his death William's main concern had been his subjugated kingdom in England, but he had not forgotten his original patrimony, the Duchy of Normandy. Thus when a French army started to pillage his lands in the summer of 1087, he quickly crossed the English Channel with his own troops. (Legend has it that William, who had grown fat over the years, was further enraged on hearing that France's King Philippe I had scoffed that he looked like a pregnant woman.)

On 15 August William captured and burned Mantes, a town 30 miles west of Paris. As flames consumed the buildings, William's horse shied away from a fiery ember and threw him violently against the pommel of his saddle, causing internal injuries so severe that peritonitis soon set in.

The injured king was moved by litter to the Convent of St Gervais on the outskirts of his Norman capital of Rouen, where he lay in pain, his abdomen filling with fluid. On Thursday morning, 9 September, the tolling of the bells of Rouen Cathedral awakened him. Construing this as a divine signal, he bitterly repented the brutal repression he had visited upon England: 'I was bred to arms from my childhood and am stained with rivers of blood that I have shed', he said. 'I've persecuted the natives of England beyond all reason, whether gentle or simple. I have cruelly oppressed them and unjustly disinherited them, killed innumerable multitudes by famine or the sword.' After commending himself to God, he died at age 59. The moment he was dead, his servants stole his rings, jewellery and even his clothing, leaving his swollen body lying naked on the floor.

William's corpse was taken to the Abbaye aux Hommes at Caen, which he had founded years before. His macabre funeral was held on a day of blazing heat. Just as the funeral procession reached the church, a fire broke out, and the pallbearers were forced to put the coffin on the ground to fight the fire. Once it had been doused, they reclaimed the coffin and continued into the church.

By now William's body had become grotesquely bloated by the heat, and when the pallbearers tried to transfer it to a stone sarcophagus, it was too big to fit. As they struggled to cram it in, it burst, drenching his funeral clothing and creating a putrid stink that sent the mourners running from the church.

Eventually William was interred, but 500 years later rioting Huguenots dug him up and scattered his bones around the town of Caen. Some were found and replaced, but republicans desecrated his grave again during the French Revolution. It is said that only his left femur now remains in his tomb.

1942 After failing to persuade his father-in-law Benito Mussolini to quit the Second World War, Foreign Minister Galeazzo Ciano comments: 'Victory has a hundred fathers, but defeat is an orphan.'

---

10 September

'Fate closes its eyes for a long time, but one day it finds us anyway.'

1898 This afternoon Empress Elisabeth of Austria – known to friends and to history as Sisi – was stabbed to death on the shore of Lake Geneva.

Born on Christmas Eve in 1837, Sisi developed into a radiant beauty – the lustful Franz Liszt termed her 'a celestial vision'. At sixteen she married her 23-year-old cousin, Emperor Franz Joseph, but what looked to be a fairy-tale marriage was blemished by Sisi's neurotic restlessness, her domineering mother-in-law and the demands of empire.

This unhappy union lasted 44 years and produced four children, but right from the beginning troubles multiplied. Franz Joseph's mother Sophie, a domineering woman derisively called 'the only man in the Hofburg', constantly interfered, bringing up the first two children herself rather than letting Sisi do it. Meanwhile Franz Joseph was a slave to duty, and the marriage was further weakened by his infidelities.

Sisi, an undisciplined free spirit, never adapted to the role of empress, a failing suggested even before the marriage, when she told her nanny: 'Yes, I do love the Emperor – if only he weren't the Emperor!' She claimed she would rather marry a butcher.

Sisi could be gay and vivacious but remained at heart a child, incessantly complaining, moping and bearing grudges for life. She found court life oppressive and her husband unresponsive, and after six years of marriage she repeatedly left her family to live in seclusion on Madeira, on Corfu and in Venice. She was fixated with being beautiful – she spent two hours a day just doing her hair. After age 32, she refused to sit for portraits in order to preserve her public image of youthful beauty. Eventually Franz Joseph's infidelities made her seek her own, and she entered an affair with her handsome Magyar secretary, Count Imri Hunyadi.

But neither Sisi by her travels nor Franz Joseph by his work could escape the tragedies that dogged them. In 1857 their two-year-old daughter died of typhus. Ten years later Franz Joseph's younger brother Maximilian, briefly Emperor of Mexico in a disastrous colonial venture, was shot by a Mexican firing squad. In 1889, in one of the great scandals of the century, their son Crown Prince Rudolf killed his mistress and himself in the royal hunting lodge at Mayerling.

In her diary Sisi once wrote: 'All men must meet their fate at a given hour. Fate closes its eyes for a long time, but one day it finds us anyway.' In 1898 fate found Sisi on a trip to Switzerland.

In the early afternoon today, Sisi, now an elegant 60, and her lady-in-waiting left their hotel on foot to catch the steamship for Montreux. As they idled along the promenade, a 25-year-old Italian anarchist named Luigi Lucheni approached. Pretending to stumble, he made a movement with his hand as if to maintain his balance but in fact to screen the sharpened file with which he stabbed Sisi above the left breast.

Sisi was knocked to the ground but because she was so tightly corseted she was unaware that she had been wounded. After walking a few yards and boarding the steamer, she collapsed. Carried to the top deck, she asked plaintively: *'Was ist mit mir geschehen?'* ('What happened to me?') She died a few moments later.

At his trial the assassin revealed that he had not originally targeted Sisi – he had planned to kill the duc d'Orléans but finding him absent from Geneva, had settled on the empress. 'I am an anarchist by conviction', he said. 'It did not matter to me who the sovereign was whom I should kill.' Given a life sentence, after ten years he hanged himself in his cell.

Even after Sisi's murder, tragedy continued to stalk the Habsburgs. Franz Joseph's nephew and heir Franz Ferdinand was shot with his wife at Sarajevo in 1914. With most of his family dead and the empire he was meant to preserve crumbling around him, Franz Joseph, dutybound to the last, died at the age of 86 on 21 November 1916, having spent most of the previous night at his desk signing wartime orders.

1419 When Jean Sans Peur, Duke of Burgundy, is treacherously assassinated on a bridge at Montereau with an axe blow to the head, the Burgundians sign an alliance with Henry V of England, which lets England invade France. A French prior from Dijon famously sums up the result: 'The English entered France through the hole in the Duke of Burgundy's head.' * **1608** When Captain John Smith is chosen president of the British colony of Virginia, he tells the colonists: 'You must obey this now for a law – that "he that will not work shall not eat".' * **1813** American Admiral Oliver Hazard Perry defeats the British at the Battle of Lake Erie. He reports: 'We have met the enemy and they are ours.'

---

11 September

'Quintilius Varus, give me back my legions!'

9 AD Today in the Teutoburg Forest, 60 miles from Hanover, the Roman army suffered its worst defeat since Cannae over two centuries before. The victors were a coalition of Germanic tribes led by a prince of the Cherusci named Arminius, the Latinised version of his German name, Hermann.

Arminius had lived in Rome as a hostage and had served in the Roman army for six years. Granted Roman citizenship and equestrian rank, he was now a trusted advisor to General Quintilius Varus, whose army was pacifying the area east of the Rhine. But secretly Arminius was betraying his masters, leading them into a cataclysmic ambush.

Arminius guided the Romans into the Teutoburg Forest and then left camp in order, he said, to assemble allied forces, promising to return. But the 'allied forces' were in fact German rebels, who were already killing Roman soldiers stationed in local towns.

The next day Varus marched deeper into the forest with 18,000 infantry and cavalry. Most were trained only to fight from set formations that could not be used in the dense woodland. Furthermore, they were accompanied by unwieldy wagons and numerous camp followers.

According to Roman historian Cassius Dio, 'the mountains had an uneven surface broken by ravines, and the trees grew close together and very high'. As a violent storm broke out, the Roman column stretched more than ten miles along a narrow, muddy track, and Varus failed to send out reconnaissance patrols.

Suddenly from the dark woods came the scream of enemy warriors, who banged their shields and rained down javelins. Darting in and out, they surrounded the column in a murderous assault. The Roman soldiers, who were mixed in haphazardly with the wagons and camp followers, could not form in order of battle and suffered heavy casualties.

Somehow the Romans managed to establish an armed camp, where 'they either burned or abandoned most of their wagons and everything else that was not absolutely necessary to them'. The following day the survivors broke out, as torrential rains continued. Weighed down with waterlogged shields and unable to use their bows with drenched strings, they took further heavy casualties.

Then, on this day, the third day of battle, the Romans fell into the main ambush that Arminius had prepared. A sandy track led between surrounding swampland and the Kalkriese Hill, where the Germans had built an earthen wall from behind which they hurled their javelins. According to the historian Velleius Paterculus, when a desperate Roman attempt to storm the wall was repulsed with heavy losses, one cavalry commander 'left the infantry unprotected … to reach the Rhine with his squadrons of horse. But … he did not survive those whom he had abandoned, but [overtaken by German cavalry] died in the act of deserting them.'

The German warriors now charged the disintegrating Roman forces en masse. With most of his men now dead, the Roman commander Varus fell on his sword. The Germans crucified or buried alive some captured soldiers, while enslaving others. Officers were tortured to death, sacrificed to Germanic gods. Arminius sent Varus' severed head to the king of another tribe with the offer of an anti-Roman alliance, but the king declined and sent the head to Rome, where it was buried with honour.

When news of the catastrophe reached Rome, Emperor Augustus neither ate nor drank for days and, according to Suetonius, 'for several months in succession he cut neither his beard nor his hair, and sometimes he would dash his head against a door, crying "Quintilius Varus, give me back my legions!"' ('*Quintili Vare, legiones redde!*')

Although Arminius was killed thirteen years later by his own squabbling relatives, over the centuries he gained totemic status among Germans, who saw him as a hero who had saved his nation, his culture and his language from Roman annexation. In 1875 Germans erected an 87-foot statue of 'Hermann der Cherusker' in the Teutoburg Forest.

The battle marked a critical juncture in European history; Augustus' successor Tiberius accepted that the empire had reached its limits, its frontier fixed on the Rhine rather than the Elbe. Roman forces never again set foot in the German heartland.

1649 Oliver Cromwell crushes all resistance at the Siege of Drogheda in Ireland, when his men slaughter 2,700 Royalist soldiers plus 800 civilians, prisoners and priests. He calls the massacre 'the righteous judgement of God on these barbarous wretches'. * **1783** Benjamin Franklin in a letter to Josiah Quincy: 'There never was a good war, or a bad peace.' * **1906** William James in a letter to H.G. Wells: 'The moral flabbiness born of the bitch-goddess SUCCESS. That – with the squalid cash interpretation put on the word success – is our national disease.'

---

12 September

'It is the great battle of the Cross and the Quran which is now to be fought.'

1565 As the sun rose on 18 May, the horizon filled with white sails emblazoned with the red crescent of Ottoman sultan Suleiman the Magnificent. The Great Siege of Malta had begun.

Back in 1522 Suleiman's forces had kicked the Knights Hospitaller (a Catholic military order) out of Rhodes, but in 1530 Holy Roman Emperor Charles V had given Malta to the Knights for an annual fee of a single Maltese falcon. Now Malta had become the key to Christian defences against Ottoman expansion in the Mediterranean.

On Malta there were fewer than 700 Knights Hospitaller, backed up by 4,500 Spanish, Italian, Greek and Sicilian soldiers. After arming some Maltese civilians, the defence force came to 9,000 men. Their leader was the Grand Master of the Knights, the 71-year-old Jean de La Valette, a veteran of the siege of Rhodes, who had survived a year as a slave in a Muslim galley.

The Ottoman armada of 180 ships was commanded by the corsair admiral Turgut, the so-called 'drawn sword of Islam'. Suleiman's grand vizier Mustafa Pasha headed an army 40,000 strong, including contingents of Sipahi (elite cavalry) and fanatical Janissaries, kidnapped Christian boys who had been forcibly converted to Islam.

As the Muslim fleet anchored close to Malta's Grand Harbour, La Valette encouraged his knights: 'It is the great battle of the Cross and the Quran which is now to be fought … We, for our part, are the chosen soldiers of the Cross, and if Heaven requires the sacrifice of our lives, there can be no better occasion than this.'

On 25 May Turkish artillery – including an enormous cannon that fired a 160-pound shot – began hammering the fortress of St Elmo, defended by only 850 men. Despite 19,000 artillery rounds and several direct assaults, the Christians held out for 35 days, killing 9,000 attackers before being wiped out to a man. During the fighting Admiral Turgut had been felled by a cannonball.

Mustafa Pasha had the dead defenders' heads hacked off and their headless corpses nailed to crosses and floated across the harbour. When the bodies washed ashore, La Valette executed his prisoners and used their heads as cannonballs to bombard the enemy. La Valette told his men: 'It would be better to die in battle than terribly and ignominiously at the hands of the Muslims.'

For the next month exchanges of cannon fire were punctuated by brief assaults, but, apart from St Elmo's, the defenders' fortifications were still largely intact, as the garrison laboured round the clock to repair breaches in the walls. The Turkish troops were now suffering from dysentery while ammunition and food were running out.

On the morning of 15 July, Mustafa ordered a land and sea assault led by 1,000 Janissaries, but the attack foundered when the defenders sank all but one of the transport boats. Another effort with two huge siege towers failed when Maltese engineers tunnelled out through the rubble and destroyed the towers with salvos of chain shot.

On 23 August Mustafa Pasha ordered another major attack, but the Christians held their ground, even the wounded taking up arms. By now both Christians and Muslims were reeling from losses and beginning to despair.

Then, on 7 September, 95 Spanish galleys arrived with 9,500 reinforcements. In a brief assault the next day the relief force slaughtered 3,000 Muslims, and Mustafa Pasha started to raise camp, his army close to mutiny. As the Turkish fleet set sail, La Valette rushed cannon to the remains of St Elmo to fire on the retreating fleet. Finally, on 12 September, the last Ottoman sail disappeared over the horizon.

Over four brutal months the Turks had fired 130,000 cannonballs, destroyed most of Malta's houses and killed 6,000 civilians, 2,000 soldiers and almost half of the Hospitallers. But they had failed to take Malta, while losing 30,000 men.

On hearing of the defeat, Suleiman the Magnificent swore to mount another expedition, but within a year he was dead. After the Great Siege, La Valette laid the first stone of a new city with his own hands. It is called Valletta and is now the capital of Malta.

1683 After Christian forces destroy the invading Turkish army outside Vienna, Polish King John Sobieski reports to the Pope: 'I came, I saw, God conquered.' * **1819** When General Gebhard Leberecht von Blücher dies at 76, he says to an aide: 'You have learned many things from me. Now you are to learn how peacefully a man can die.'

---

13 September

'God, who has given me so many kingdoms to govern,
has not given me a son fit to govern them.'

1598 Next time you are in Madrid, be sure to visit the old town's stately Plaza Mayor. At its centre you will find a fine equestrian statue of Philip III, who built the square and who today inherited the throne of Spain.

Earlier in the day Philip's austere father Philip II, in great pain from gangrene of the leg caused by gout, had died of cancer in the Escorial, the palace-cum-monastery he had built.

Heir to half of Europe and much of South America, Philip II had seen his father, Holy Roman Emperor Charles V, retire to a monastery in an age when kings abdicated only with death. Philip, however, had worked right up to the end, dying at 71 after 42 years of unremitting labour as king.

Philip had been married four times (once to the fanatical Mary Tudor) and outlived all his wives, spending his last eighteen years with neither wife nor mistress. But his greatest sorrow was his four sons.

His first-born, Don Carlos, revolted against him, certainly was a sadist and was probably insane. In 1568 Philip locked him up in the Alcázar in Madrid, where he died mysteriously the same year.

Ten years later Philip's second son, Fernando, died of dysentery at six, while his third son, Diego, succumbed to smallpox at seven in 1582, leaving Philip inconsolable, for the only remaining heir to the throne was the small and sickly five-year-old Philip.

The young Philip developed into an excellent linguist (French, Portuguese and Latin) but was so devout that he became known as Philip the Pious. Although pleasant and respectful, he was indolent and incurious, with neither intelligence nor drive, causing his father to bemoan: 'God, who has given me so many kingdoms to govern, has not given me a son fit to govern them.'

Philip III, as he now was, was twenty when he inherited the throne. His first move was to appoint Francisco Gómez de Sandoval y Rojas as his chief minister and create him duque de Lerma, thus establishing the system of *validos* – royal favourites – who ruled in the king's stead. Lerma enjoyed unfettered power and enriched himself through influence peddling, corruption and the sale of public offices.

During the twenty years of Lerma's ascendancy, Spain and its empire were largely rudderless. One of Lerma's worst decisions was to expel the Moriscos in 1609, Muslim Spaniards who had been publicly converted but who may have secretly retained their allegiance to Allah. They continued to speak Arabic and wear Arabic clothing and were thought to spend too little, work too much, and multiply too quickly. Lerma (and probably Philip as well) feared that they might rise up in revolt. By 1614, 275,000 Moriscos had been forced to leave the country, causing unrest and a labour shortage – Moriscos had accounted for almost 5 per cent of the population.

Lerma finally came to grief in 1618, ousted in a plot by his own son and the courtier and royal advisor, the Count of Olivares (who would become the *valido* of Philip's son, Philip IV). Ensnared in corruption scandal, Lerma escaped with his life only because he asked Rome to make him a cardinal.

During his last years Philip brought Spain into the Thirty Years' War, but he died in Madrid on 31 March 1621, a month shy of his 43rd birthday, 27 years before the war's end.

Spanish monarchs have a long history of patronising great artists. Charles V and Philip II both sat for Titian, Philip IV became a noted backer of Velásquez, and Charles IV appointed Goya as court painter. Philip III was also a patron of the arts, but his taste was lacking. He commissioned two paintings by El Greco but did not like either of them, and he also rejected a sculpture by Benvenuto Cellini. His one successful association with a great artist was with Velásquez, who painted a fine portrait of Philip on horseback in 1635 – when Philip had been in his grave for fourteen years.

---

81 AD Emperor Titus dies; contemporary historian Suetonius relates: 'All people mourned for him as for the loss of some near relation.'

---

14 September

'I want to wash my hands and swim in French blood.'

1516 On this sultry Friday, while the Christian world celebrated the Feast of the Holy Cross, France's King François I led 39,000 French and Venetian troops to a hard-fought victory over half that number of Swiss mercenaries at Marignano, twelve miles south-east of Milan.

François coveted Milan, which would give him control of Lombardy, and based his demands on his predecessor Louis XII's wafer-thin claim that his grandmother had been a member of Milan's previous ruling family, the Visconti. But now Duke Massimiliano Sforza ruled the duchy, buttressed by (and largely under the thumb of) the Swiss, who had put his family back in control.

François' campaign started with a remarkable Alpine passage in which the French army carved a new route through the Alps over the Col d'Argentière and descended into Italy with 50 large cannons. Admiring contemporaries compared it to Hannibal's crossing seventeen centuries before.

Caught by surprise, the main Swiss force holed up in Milan and asked for terms. But then fresh troops from the Swiss cantons arrived, determined to keep Milan under Sforza (and their own) rule – otherwise they would receive no financial rewards. On 13 September the

Swiss cardinal Matthäus Schiner, a sworn enemy of King François, feverishly harangued his countrymen in front of Milan cathedral: 'I want to wash my hands and swim in French blood.' Swayed by Schiner's fiery rhetoric, the Swiss vowed to fight and take no prisoners except François himself. They then marched out of Milan, banners flying and Alpine horns blaring, towards the French camp at Marignano.

The Swiss attack caught the French by surprise. François was in his tent admiring himself in his new German armour but quickly rallied his men, but the Swiss were the most feared soldiers in Europe – Machiavelli called them 'brutal, arrogant and victorious'. Some carried eighteen-foot pikes, others huge two-handed swords.

The real fighting started around sunset, fierce attack and counter-attack by both sides. At first the Swiss seemed to have the advantage, but furious French cavalry charges, often led by the king himself, succeeded time and again in reversing Swiss gains. Night fell and the fighting went on by moonlight, but eventually dust, smoke and darkness made it impossible to see, and both sides pulled back, too exhausted to continue.

The battle resumed at dawn the next morning, with the Swiss pikemen attacking even more fiercely than the day before. Once again King François led his cavalry into action, dramatically crying out, '*Qui m'aime me suive!*' ('Let him who loves me follow me!'). (He had borrowed the line from his 14th-century predecessor Philip VI at the battle of Cassel.) François would later boast to his mother that he had led 'thirty brave charges' that tipped the balance.

In truth, the tide was finally turned about eleven o'clock by the arrival of the *condottiere* (mercenary leader) Bartolomeo d'Alviano with allied Venetian forces. The Swiss now knew they were beaten; 400 pikemen from Zurich stayed to hold back the enemy and were wiped out by cannon fire, allowing the main Swiss army to retreat unmolested to Milan. But, writes historian Desmond Seward: 'Those strange men, as venal as they were brave, at once asked Duke Massimiliano for three months' pay. When he announced he had no money, they told him that their contract was broken. On ... the day after the battle they marched back to their valleys.' The duke quickly agreed to François' demands.

François had celebrated his 21st birthday only the day before the battle. On the last day he theatrically had himself knighted by one of his generals and sent his mother this modest appraisal: 'There has not been so fierce and cruel a battle these last two thousand years.' He then ordered struck a victory medal graven with the words: 'I have vanquished those whom only Caesar vanquished.'

His triumph at Marignano gave François both the duchy of Milan and an unquenchable thirst for military glory. In the next 30 years he would fight three more wars for the control of Milan – and lose them all.

1852 The Duke of Wellington dies at age 83 at Walmer Castle; his last words are: 'Do you know where the apothecary lives? Then send and let him know that I would like to see him. I don't feel quite well and will lie still till he comes.' *The Times* reports: 'The Duke of Wellington has exhausted nature and exhausted glory. His career was one unclouded longest day.'

---

15 September

'My poor land battleships have been let off prematurely, on a petty scale.'

1914 & 1916 The Allied victory during the so-called 'Miracle of the Marne' in 1914 forced German forces to retreat 40 miles to a point north of the Aisne River, where today they began to dig trenches that would remain there until the end of the First World War. The German commander Helmuth von Moltke was so shaken by the defeat that he reported to the Kaiser: 'Your Majesty, we have lost the war.'

Sadly for both sides, the war was hardly over. Sir John French, British Expeditionary Force commander, ordered his own men to start digging, and on this day the British began to create their own trench system (because his soldiers had so few entrenching tools, they scoured nearby farms and villages for pickaxes, shovels and spades). Thus the war moved from a brief period of classic attack and manoeuvre to static trench warfare, eventually with 35,000 miles of trenches, protected by barbed wire, that stretched from the North Sea coast of Belgium southward through France to the southernmost point in Alsace, at the Swiss border.

The advent of trench warfare immediately brought new challenges for attackers. What was needed was something that could trample barbed wire and roll over wide trenches. In January 1915 Winston Churchill wrote to Prime Minister Asquith about developing armoured caterpillar tractors, promising that 'forty or fifty of these machines prepared secretly and brought into position at nightfall could advance quite certainly into the enemy's trenches, smashing away all the obstructions and sweeping the trenches with their machine-gun fire and with grenades thrown out of the tops'. By June a prototype vehicle had been put together, and by September 1916 the British had produced about 50 armed and armoured tracked vehicles, which for security reasons were codenamed 'tanks'.

The urgent need for such weapons was vividly illustrated on 1 July 1916, the first day of the Battle of the Somme, in which 20,000 British soldiers perished charging German trenches, with another 40,000 wounded, the heaviest day of casualties in British history. But then, during the Battle of Flers-Courcelette on 15 September 1916 – two years to the day since trench warfare had been introduced – 32 tanks rumbled heavily out of the British lines heading towards the German entrenchments. They were steel brutes seven feet high and 32 feet long with an eight-man crew and a rarely achievable top speed of 3.7 miles per hour. Most broke down before reaching the objective, but thirteen of them, with British infantry close behind, managed to advance 3,500 yards, punching a gaping hole in the enemy line, whose defenders fled to the rear after taking one look at the monstrous machines moving inexorably towards them over trenches and barbed wire, invulnerable to machine-gun fire.

The triumph was momentary, for there was no way for the British to exploit the sudden breakthrough, and the Germans regained the lost territory through stubborn counter-attacks, so the long tragedy of the Somme resumed, unaffected by the brief intrusion of technology. Churchill lamented: 'My poor land battleships have been let off prematurely, on a petty scale.' There were those, however, including the British commander-in-chief General Haig, who saw in tanks a new weapon that could win the war.

After their Somme début, tanks with improved design fought in several battles on the Western Front, and at Cambrai in November 1917 about 437 Mark IV tanks led eight infantry divisions against the Hindenburg Line, passing through barbed wire defences, which the Germans had thought impregnable. They advanced five miles through the enemy's front until they were stopped at a canal when, ironically, a bridge collapsed under the weight of a tank. Even though the British attack then stalled, the battle fulfilled Churchill's promise that even the strongest trench defences could be overwhelmed with the aid of tanks. Like the stirrup, the bow, and gunpowder, the tank had transformed the practice of warfare.

1935 The Reichstag passes The Law for the Protection of German Blood and German Honour that starts: 'Moved by the understanding that purity of German blood is the essential condition for the continued existence of the German people, and inspired by the inflexible determination to ensure the existence of the German nation for all time, the Reichstag has unanimously adopted the following law …' Among the clauses are: 'Marriages between Jews and citizens of German or related blood are forbidden … Extramarital relations between Jews and citizens of German or related blood are forbidden … Jews are forbidden to fly the Reich or national flag or display Reich colours.'

16 September

'The Cry of Sorrows'

1810 At 2.30 this morning the people of Dolores in central Mexico were awoken by the clamour of ringing church bells. When they arrived outside the church they found their priest Miguel Hidalgo giving an impassioned speech urging them to join him in revolt against Spain. It was the first step towards Mexican independence.

Mexico had been under the Spanish heel since 13 August 1521, when the brutal conquistador Hernán Cortés had conquered the Aztec capital. In 1535 the territory had formally become part of the Spanish Empire under the name of New Spain. For the next three centuries resistance to the hated *Gachupines* (Spanish-born Mexicans) smouldered, only occasionally bursting into flame.

A strong believer in a free Mexico, 57-year-old Miguel Hidalgo had already demonstrated his rebellious spirit by reading prohibited books and fathering children. For these peccadillos the Church had exiled him to Dolores. There he joined a pro-independence group, but when Spanish authorities arrested several of its members, he decided to act.

On this September morning first he sent his brother and some armed volunteers to the local prison to free 80 revolutionary inmates. He then set the bells tolling in his church and made his famous call for revolution. Within minutes a mob of some 600 men were ready to join him.

Now the defiant priest marched across Mexico, gathering an army as he went, mostly farmers and poor from the cities. Hidalgo was proclaimed general and supreme commander, but his army increasingly resembled a mob, looting the towns they captured. By 28 September this unruly horde that now totalled about 30,000 had reached Guanajuato. There the Spanish and *Criollos* (Mexicans of pure Spanish descent) barricaded themselves in the Alhóndiga de Granaditas, a fortified granary, but Hidalgo's insurgents overwhelmed the defenders, killing about 500 men, women and children.

Soon Hidalgo had enlisted almost 90,000 volunteers, but they were undisciplined and poorly armed. Nonetheless they headed for Mexico City. On 30 October they encountered professional troops for the first time at Monte de las Cruces. The revolutionaries overpowered the government forces by sheer weight of numbers, but they suffered 2,000 dead and many more wounded.

Next came the climactic battle of the insurrection. On 17 January 1811 Hidalgo's army met 6,000 well-trained and armed Spanish troops at the Battle of Calderón Bridge. Hidalgo could field almost 90,000 men; 20,000 were on horseback and adequately armed, but only 3,000 others had rifles, while the rest fought with spears, slings, and bows and arrows. The battle was a catastrophe for the revolutionaries, who lost 13,000 men, compared to just 1,000 for the enemy.

In the wake of this defeat, Padre Hidalgo led 1,000 men to the Wells of Baján, thought to be in the hands of the rebels. There the turncoat royalist officer Ignacio Elizondo greeted the revolutionary leaders with an honour guard but then arrested them after a brief gunfight.

Hidalgo was taken to Chihuahua with 27 other rebel leaders. After being defrocked and excommunicated by the Bishop of Durango, he was found guilty of treason by a military court. As he faced the firing squad on 30 July 1811, he told his executioners: 'Though I may die, I shall be remembered for ever; you will all soon be forgotten.' After the firing squad had done its work, his head was struck from his corpse and publicly displayed in the Alhóndiga de Granaditas, where it remained for ten years.

Mexican independence did not come quickly but was finally achieved on 27 September 1821, when a reactionary army general named Agustín de Iturbide completed the revolt against Spain, to become Emperor of Mexico.

Even today, however, Miguel Hidalgo is considered the father of his country. The incendiary speech he made in Dolores that sparked the revolution is called '*El Grito de Dolores*' – 'The Cry of Dolores'. But *dolores* means 'sorrows', so Hidalgo's call also means 'The Cry of Sorrows', appropriate for this priest who gave his life for his country's freedom. Today Mexicans celebrate 16 September as Independence Day in remembrance of Father Hidalgo's cry.

1824 Suffering from gout and gangrene in his legs, the immensely fat Louis XVIII tells his courtiers: 'A king of France may die, but he is never ill.' He tries to rise from his bed, whispering: 'A king should die standing up.' He falls back, dead at 68. * **1973** Waspish American writer Gore Vidal writes in the *Sunday New York Times*: 'Whenever a friend succeeds, a little something in me dies.'

---

17 September

'Fight on and fly on to the last drop of blood and the last drop of fuel, to the last beat of the heart.'

1916 Flying over Cambrai this morning in an Albatross biplane, a young German pilot, only 24 years old and on his first combat patrol over the Western Front, encountered a British FE-2 fighter armed with a .303 machine-gun. He recounted the incident this way: 'My Englishman twisted and turned, flying in zig-zags. I was animated by a single thought: "The man in front of me must come down, whatever happens." … I gave a short burst of shots with my machine-gun. I had gone so close that I was afraid I might dash into the Englishman. Suddenly I nearly yelled with joy, for the propeller of the enemy machine had stopped turning. Hurrah! I had shot his engine to pieces; the enemy was compelled to land, for it was impossible for him to reach his own lines.'

The British pilot managed to put his plane down at a German airfield at Flesquières, close to the German lines. The German followed him to the ground, where he discovered that the pilot was mortally wounded and his observer already dead.

This was the first official kill in a career that would see the German become the leading ace on either side in the First World War, with a tally of 80 enemy planes. He was the legendary Red Baron, Manfred von Richthofen, a Freiherr (Free Lord), a noble title often translated as 'baron'. He became a squadron commander who would instruct his men: 'Aim for the man and don't miss him. If you are fighting a two-seater, get the observer first; until you have silenced the gun, don't bother about the pilot.'

Born into a prominent Prussian aristocratic family, Richthofen initially became a cavalry reconnaissance officer, seeing combat in Russia, France, and Belgium. But trench warfare and machine-guns soon made cavalry obsolete, and he ended up in a supply unit. Desperate to return to action, he is said to have written to his superiors: 'I have not gone to war in order to collect cheese and eggs.' He was transferred to the Luftstreitkräfte (Air Forces). He was not a natural pilot and crashed during his first flight at the controls, but he became a master tactician, preferring to swoop down on the enemy from above with the sun behind him.

Richthofen's path was that of a skyrocket, bursting into glory before tumbling to earth. From his first victory to his death was less than 600 days. By the end of 1916 he had downed fifteen enemy planes. In January 1917 he was promoted to squadron commander and awarded the Pour le Mérite (the Blue Max), the highest German military honour. It was then that he flamboyantly had his plane painted bright red in tribute to his old cavalry regiment. Later he switched to a Fokker triplane, also painted red, for which he gained the sobriquet, the Red Baron.

While leading his squadron, Richthofen continued to scourge enemy aircraft, downing 22 British planes in April, including four in a single day. Three months later, however, he was almost killed when he was knocked out by a blow to the head, regaining consciousness just in time to land his plane. Surgeons had to remove bone splinters from his head. While convalescing, on orders from the Luftstreitkräfte he wrote a sketchy autobiography entitled *The Red Fighter Pilot* (*Der Rote Kampfflieger*) in which he enthused: 'Fight on and fly on to the last drop of blood and the last drop of fuel, to the last beat of the heart.'

Richthofen himself did exactly that. On the morning of 21 April 1918 he was attacking an enemy plane near the Somme, and he may never have noticed another British fighter closing in behind. One burst of fire and a single bullet caught him in the chest. The Red Baron's triplane began a mile-long slide toward the ground, finally crashing behind Allied lines. When British troops came up to the wreckage, he was still barely alive. His last word was a discouraged '*Kaputt*.' ('Finished.')

1796 George Washington tells Congress in his 'Farewell Address': 'It is our true policy to steer clear of permanent alliance with any portion of the foreign world.'

---

18 September

'Holding a wolf by the ears'

14 AD On this day, 29 days after the death of the emperor Augustus, the Roman Senate confirmed his adopted son Tiberius as Rome's Princeps ('First Citizen'), the official title of the emperor. Tiberius only reluctantly accepted the title, claiming that he was too old (he was 54) and wanted only to serve the state. The Roman historian Suetonius relates: 'The cause of his hesitation was fear of the dangers which threatened him on every hand and often led him to say that he was "holding a wolf by the ears".'

Tiberius was the son of Tiberius Claudius Nero and Livia Drusilla. It was his fate – for good or ill – that when he was two, Augustus fell desperately in love with his mother, forced Claudius Nero to divorce her, divorced his own wife and married Livia.

Tiberius thus became the emperor's stepson, but he lacked the vital ingredient to make him heir to power – imperial blood.

Tiberius became a highly successful general, fighting the Parthians and rebellious tribes in the Alps and directing Roman operations in Austria and Germany. In the meantime, the heir to the throne was Augustus' faithful friend and foremost general, Marcus Agrippa, who also had no imperial blood in his veins but had married the emperor's daughter Julia. But in 12 BC Agrippa died, and Augustus forced Tiberius to divorce his own wife to marry Julia, Agrippa's widow.

The marriage made Tiberius the empire's most powerful man after Augustus, but he detested Julia, who was debauched and flagrantly unfaithful, publicly humiliating him with night-time escapades in the Forum. Meanwhile Augustus adopted Julia's children by Agrippa, Lucius and Gaius, raising them to the succession, which meant that when his grandsons came of age, Tiberius would be swept aside.

For six years Tiberius continued his successful military career, but in 6 BC, miserably unhappy with his adulterous wife and disillusioned about his chances of becoming emperor, he retired to Rhodes, where he remained for eight years.

But Lucius died in 2 AD and Gaius followed him two years later, making Tiberius practically the only candidate left to take the reins on the emperor's death. Augustus, who had never liked Tiberius, reluctantly made him his heir, announcing coldly: 'This I do for reasons of state.' He feared that Tiberius' measured deliberation and distant manner would ill prepare him for ultimate power, lamenting: 'Poor Roman people, to be ground by those slow-moving jaws.'

After Augustus' death in 14, Tiberius became a hardworking and productive ruler, believing that 'it is the duty of a good shepherd to shear his sheep, not to skin them'. But he faced intractable problems abroad and agitators, vested interests and aristocratic disdain at home. After thirteen years in power he abruptly moved to his magnificent villa on Capri. He never visited Rome again, delegating progressively more authority to the commander of his guard and leaving the squabbling Senate – 'Men fit to be slaves', he called its members – to its own devices.

Over time, Tiberius became increasingly murderous and vindictive. According to Suetonius, 'Every day brought a new execution'. He slowly descended into paranoia and paedophilia, importing a troop of young boys and girls to take part in imperial orgies.

When he was 71, Tiberius made an error that cost him his life, when he brought his eighteen-year-old great-nephew Caligula to Capri, eventually naming him as heir. Initially Caligula was docile and obsequious, but he already showed signs of the sadism that would mark his years as emperor.

In early 37 AD, Tiberius travelled to Campania to take part in military games. At 77, he was worn and emaciated, and he fell seriously ill. Returning to his villa on Capri, he lapsed into unconsciousness.

Believing Tiberius to be dead, Caligula slipped the seal ring from the imperial finger to show himself to the waiting crowd as the new emperor. But suddenly Tiberius awoke and demanded food. Caligula was petrified with terror, but his ally Macro, the quick-thinking commander of the Praetorian Guard, rushed in and stifled the old emperor with a blanket.

---

96 AD In a plot orchestrated by his wife Domitia Longina, the tyrannical Roman emperor Domitian is stabbed to death; earlier he had written: 'All emperors are necessarily wretched, since only their assassination can convince the public that the conspiracies against their lives are real.'

---

19 September

'Compared to them, Auschwitz was just child's play.'

1940 Today during a round-up in the streets of occupied Warsaw, a 39-year-old Polish officer dressed in civilian clothes was picked up by

German soldiers, along with 2,000 civilians. Three days later he was sent to the Auschwitz concentration camp and would henceforth be known as inmate number 4859. He had deliberately set out to be arrested; he was on a secret mission to get into Auschwitz and smuggle out reports. His name was Witold Pilecki.

Pilecki had first seen combat during the First World War and the Polish–Soviet War that followed. Fighting in both set-piece battles and partisan warfare behind Soviet lines, he was twice awarded the Krzyż Walecznych (Cross of Valour).

Later he settled down in his family's estates in Sukurcze, where he became a community leader, founded an agricultural cooperative, chaired a local milk-processing plant and ran the local fire brigade. In his spare time, if he had any, he became a talented painter. But, living in a country wedged between Hitler's Germany and Stalin's USSR, he foresaw the dangers of invasion.

Then in September 1939 Germany and the USSR did invade. Pilecki took part in heavy fighting against the Germans, and when Poland surrendered he continued as a partisan, hiding in Warsaw and helping to found the Secret Polish Army.

On 21 September, even before the Polish surrender, Gestapo chief SS-Obergruppenführer Reinhard Heydrich ordered that Polish Jews be rounded up, and in May 1940 the Germans converted a former army barracks at Auschwitz into a detention camp. But because Polish resistance leaders had no information source inside Auschwitz, Pilecki volunteered to get himself interned there.

Suffering from typhus, malnutrition, lice and brutal guards, Pilecki stayed in the camp for 950 days, organising intelligence gathering with other inmates and building a secret transmitter to send reports to the Polish underground. And what explosive reports they were; on 1 September 1941 the first prisoners were gassed, as Auschwitz was turned from concentration camp into extermination camp. Pilecki radioed that 'the number of people gassed on arrival reached 1.5 million', remarkably close to the actual number of 1.1 million. The Polish underground forwarded his reports to London, but the British government refused to believe them.

By early 1943 the Gestapo at Auschwitz were ruthlessly seeking members of Pilecki's clandestine cell, and Pilecki knew he had to get out. On the night of 26 April he and two accomplices overpowered a guard, cut telephone and alarm wires, unlocked the front door with a duplicate key and escaped. That night they swam across the Vistula before reaching a nearby forest. Pilecki then made his way back to Warsaw to rejoin the resistance.

During the Warsaw Uprising in 1944 Pilecki fought against the Germans but was captured and sent to a POW camp. Seven months later he was liberated by troops of the US 12th Armored Division.

In July 1945 Pilecki joined Polish military intelligence in Ancona, Italy and was ordered to return to Soviet-occupied Poland to report on the military and political situation. After he set up an intelligence-gathering network, the Communist authorities began homing in, but he refused to leave. On 8 May 1947 he was arrested.

For ten months Pilecki was imprisoned and tortured, but he refused to name his comrades. Before his trial he told his wife: 'I can't live anymore, they've killed me. Compared to them, Auschwitz was just child's play.'

Pilecki's show trial started in March 1948; inevitably, he was condemned to death. On 25 May, in true KGB fashion, his jailers shot him in the back of the head at the Mokotów Prison.

Just after he had been sentenced, Pilecki had told the court: 'I've been trying to live my life so that in the hour of my death I would feel joy, rather than fear.' No doubt his shade would have been pleased when in 2006 the Polish government awarded him his nation's highest honour, the Order of the White Eagle.

1926 American journalist H.L. Mencken writes in the *Chicago Tribune*: 'No one in the world ... has ever lost money by underestimating the intelligence of the great masses of the plain people.' Commonly misquoted as: 'No one ever went broke underestimating the intelligence of the American public.' * **1946** Winston Churchill in a speech at Zurich University: 'We must build a kind of United States of Europe.'

---

20 September

'The Church says that the Earth is flat, but I know that it is round. For I have seen the shadow of the Earth on the Moon and I have more faith in the shadow than in the Church.'

1519 The quotation above, long attributed to the Portuguese explorer Ferdinand Magellan, may be apocryphal, but it accurately represents his faith that he could reach the Spice Islands by sailing west from Spain rather than south around Africa.

Born around 1480, as a youth Magellan was a page in the Portuguese court. At 25 he enlisted in the Portuguese fleet in India, fought in several battles and was wounded twice, resulting in a limp that lasted for the rest of his life. In 1517, after Portugal's King Manuel had twice declined to back expeditions, Magellan decided to try the Spaniards, whose king was future Holy Roman Emperor Charles V, grandson of Ferdinand and Isabella who had financed Columbus. Although only eighteen, Charles was a man of imagination and intelligence and agreed to underwrite five ships but insisted that three of the captains be Spanish, something Magellan would have cause to regret.

On this day, Magellan's fleet with 270 men aboard set sail from Sanlúcar de Barrameda, the port city of Cádiz, headed for West Africa and then across the Atlantic to Brazil. During the voyage one of the Spanish captains, Juan de Cartagena, challenged Magellan's choice of route and refused to obey further orders. Magellan had him confined until the ships reached South America in December.

The fleet now sailed south along the coast of Patagonia, searching for a way through to the Pacific. In March 1520, the expedition set up winter quarters, but on Easter Sunday the Spanish captains, egged on by Cartagena, mutinied. Magellan killed one captain through a ruse, then forced the others to back down. He then had one captain beheaded and marooned Cartagena and a mutinous Spanish priest on a small island, never to be heard of again.

Although one ship was lost, run aground on a sandbar, finally, on 21 October, Magellan discovered the straits that today bear his name, but before he could send his fleet through, he lost a second ship, when another mutinous captain reversed course to sail back to Spain.

On emerging from the straits after 38 difficult days, Magellan faced the Pacific, which he had imagined to be a small sea, perhaps only a week's sail from the Spice Islands (now the Maluku Islands in Indonesia). In fact, he spent 99 days on a crossing so calm that he named the sea *Mar Pacífico* (Peaceful Sea). During the voyage his men were racked by scurvy and starvation, reduced to eating putrid and worm-infested biscuits, sawdust and grilled rats.

In March 1521 the expedition reached the Philippines, and Magellan began the time-honoured Iberian practice of forcibly Christianising the natives and making them swear allegiance to the Spanish king. (At the same time Cortés was attacking the Aztec capital and Pizarro was preparing to destroy the Incas.)

When natives on the small island of Mactan refused his demands, Magellan burnt their huts. When that didn't work, on 27 April he landed with 60 crewmen, only to be attacked by 1,500 enraged warriors. Magellan tried to cover the retreat of his men but was cut down by spears and poisoned arrows. Four days later the chief of a nearby island, who claimed he had converted to Christianity, invited 30 of the remaining sailors to a feast but murdered 28 of them at dinner.

By now there were only 119 survivors of those who had sailed from Spain, insufficient to man three ships, so one ship was emptied and burned.

The two remaining ships spent the next six months searching for the Spice Islands, finally reaching them in November. Magellan's erstwhile flagship *Trinidad* had to be refitted and then tried to return to Spain via the Pacific but was wrecked in a storm.

After bartering for massive quantities of cloves, in mid-December the remaining ship, the *Victoria*, set sail for Spain via the Cape of Good Hope, but rations began to run out and a number of crewmen starved to death before she finally reached Cádiz on 6 September 1522. Of the 270 men who had started the historic voyage three years earlier, only eighteen were aboard at the end.

1777 Samuel Johnson: 'When a man is tired of London, he is tired of life; for there is in London all that life can afford.' * **1792** After revolutionary French forces defeat the Prussians at the Battle of Valmy, Wolfgang von Goethe, who was there as a sightseer, exclaims: 'From this place, and from this day forth begins a new era in the world's history, and you can all say that you were present at its birth.'

---

21 September

'You have acted like a man who has cut off his right hand with his left.'

454 AD By the middle of the 5th century the Roman Empire had long been split between East and West, and the latter had only a few years to run. But in the East, one man above all came to be seen as the empire's protector. Called 'the last of the Romans', he was Flavius Aetius.

During his youth at the imperial court, Aetius was an occasional hostage, first at the court of the Visigoths and later with the Huns.

In 423, when Aetius was about 27, Western Emperor Honorius died. A high-ranking officer named Joannes claimed the title, but Eastern Emperor Theodosius II sent an army to put his four-year-old cousin Valentinian on the throne. Aetius sided with Joannes, who sent him to ask the Huns (whom Aetius knew from his years as a hostage) to intervene on his side.

Aetius was soon headed for Rome accompanied by a Hunnish army, but when he arrived he found that Joannes had been defeated and executed, and Valentinian (III) installed as emperor, with his formidable mother Galla Placidia as regent. After confronting Galla Placidia's army, Aetius managed to do a deal by which he bribed the Huns to return home while he became the Roman army commander in Gaul.

During the next quarter-century Aetius defeated the Salian Franks twice, the Visigoths three times, and also the Burgundians, Suebi and Alans. Elevated to patrician rank, he became the ex-officio protector of the young Valentinian and Galla Placidia. His moment of supreme triumph came in 451, when Attila the Hun invaded western Europe. Turning to his former enemies the Visigoths, Aetius persuaded their king Theodoric to join him, and together they routed the Huns at Châlons, the only defeat of Attila's career.

The next year Attila was back, ravaging Italy before marching on Rome. Faced with a hugely superior foe, Aetius could not afford a pitched battle, but he brilliantly managed to harass and slow Attila's advance with only a shadow force. In the end, Attila withdrew, some say at the miraculous intervention of Pope Leo I, or, others maintain, due to plague breaking out in his camp.

Aetius was now at the height of his powers, having effectively ruled the Western Empire as head of the military for two decades. The next year (453) he was granted his fourth consulship and betrothed his son to Valentinian's daughter. But all this success had earned Aetius the enmity of the Roman senator Petronius Maximus and Valentinian's eunuch chamberlain Heraclius. Worse, Emperor Valentinian – who, in Gibbon's words, 'had reached his thirty-fifth year without attaining the age of reason or courage' – had never forgotten Aetius' attempt to make Joannes emperor 30 years before. Together, the emperor, Maximus and Heraclius formed a plot to rid themselves of their most capable general.

On this day in Ravenna, Aetius was called to the throne room to present some financial accounts. Gibbon relates that suddenly Valentinian drew his sword and 'plunged it into the breast of a general who had saved his empire; his courtiers and eunuchs ambitiously struggled to imitate their master; and Aetius, pierced by an hundred wounds, fell dead in the royal presence'.

Afterwards the emperor tried to justify himself to one of his courtiers, Sidonius Apollinaris. 'Aetius's death was no happy thing for me', he said, to which Apollinaris replied: 'I am ignorant, sir, of your motives or provocations; I only know that you have acted like a man who has cut off his right hand with his left. Who is now to save Italy from the Vandals?'

Indeed, in the words of historian J.B. Bury, Valentinian 'thought he had slain his master; he found that he had slain his protector'. Six months later Maximus masterminded another palace coup in which Valentinian and Heraclius were assassinated. Two months after that, on hearing that the Vandals were approaching Rome, Maximus attempted to flee, but an angry mob stoned him to death. Three days later the Vandals sacked the city.

---

19 BC Virgil dies in Brindisi; his epitaph: 'Mantua bore me; the people of Calabria carried me off; Parthenope [Naples] holds me now. I have sung of pastures, of fields, of chieftains.'

---

22 September

'I only regret that I have but one life to lose for my country.'

1776 The United States was only two and a half months old, and the war against Britain was not going well. In the first major battle since the Americans had declared independence, on 27 August British forces under General William Howe had routed George Washington at the Battle of Long Island. Desperate to learn Howe's next move, Washington needed a spy to slip behind enemy lines, an extremely hazardous mission that could easily end in death. There was only one volunteer, a 21-year-old Yale graduate and former schoolteacher, Captain Nathan Hale.

On 12 September Hale disguised himself as a Dutch schoolmaster and surreptitiously crossed the East River to British-controlled Long Island, but before he could learn much about Howe's intentions, on 15 September Howe landed at Kip's Bay, in what today is midtown Manhattan, and seized control of New York, forcing Washington's Continental Army to withdraw north to Harlem Heights.

Having discovered what he could about British troop strength, Hale planned to return to American lines, but fires started by Washington's soldiers blocked his route, so he took refuge in a local tavern. There his luck ran out. By chance a British officer saw him there and recognised him despite his schoolteacher disguise.

Seized and hustled off to Howe's headquarters, Hale readily admitted his mission, and the British found sketches of fortifications and notes on troop numbers and positions on his person. Howe sentenced him to hang the next day, without further trial (as was customary with spies in that age).

Hale was locked in the headquarters' greenhouse for the night and denied both a Bible and a clergyman. Then, according to an eyewitness, British Captain John Montresor: 'On the morning of his execution, my station was near the fatal spot, and I requested the Provost Marshal to permit the prisoner to sit in my marquee, while he was making the necessary preparations. Captain Hale entered: he was calm, and bore himself with gentle dignity, in the consciousness of rectitude and high intentions. He asked for writing materials, which I furnished him: he wrote two letters, one to his mother and one to a brother officer.'

Hale's execution today took place on what now is the corner of 63rd Street and 3rd Avenue in Manhattan. Remarkably composed, just as he was led to the gallows he pronounced his celebrated quote: 'I only regret that I have but one life to lose for my country.' He then climbed the ladder that would be pulled from beneath his feet.

Hale became much more famous after the Revolution than he ever was during it, so it is possible that his famous last words have been embellished by history. They bear a remarkable resemblance to the hero's speech in Joseph Addison's 1713 play *Cato*: 'What a pity is it that we can die but once to serve our country!'

1792 Yesterday the French monarchy was abolished after the revolutionary priest Abbé Grégoire told the National Convention: 'Kings are in morality what monsters are in the world of nature. The royal courts are a workshop for crime, the foyer for corruption and the den of tyrants. The history of kings is a catalogue of the martyrdom of nations!' Today the French Republic is founded.

23 September

*'The wooden wall only shall not fail, but
help you and your children.'*

480 BC Twelve years earlier Persian King Darius I had invaded Greece, but the Athenians had routed his army at Marathon. Darius died in 486 BC, and now his son Xerxes was readying a huge force to crush the insolent Athenians.

The contemporary historian Herodotus puts the Persian army at 2,641,610 men, but modern estimates suggest 200,000 to 300,000, still dwarfing anything the Greeks could field.

To cross from Asia Minor into Greece, Xerxes constructed two boat bridges across the Hellespont. When waves destroyed them during a storm, he ordered the sea scourged with 300 lashes and pronounced: 'Ungracious water, your master condemns you to punishment for having injured him without cause. Xerxes the king will pass over you, whether you consent or not!' By then the storm had abated, and his army easily crossed on new bridges.

Although the Greek city-states formed a defensive league, the Persians rolled irresistibly forward, defeating the Spartans at Thermopylae in August of 480, which opened the route to Athens. The Athenians abandoned their city, and to help the evacuation, the Greek fleet moved to Salamis, an island a mile off-coast from the Athenian port of Piraeus. A few brave soldiers remained on the heavily fortified Acropolis, but soon that too had fallen, with all defenders slain.

The assembled Greek generals bickered interminably over how to meet the Persian onslaught. Some wanted to withdraw to Corinth, while the Athenian leader Themistocles argued for a naval battle. At length they met at the Temple of Apollo at Delphi to ask for the oracle's guidance. Her pronouncement was suitably enigmatic: 'Zeus the all-seeing grants Athene's prayer that the wooden wall only shall not fail, but help you and your children.'

Some thought she was referring to the palisade that once fenced the Acropolis, but Themistocles argued that 'the wooden wall' meant their wooden ships. Eventually he won the dispute only by threatening to withdraw his 200 galleys, more than half the Greek fleet.

On 22 September another debate erupted, and this time Themistocles took an even greater gamble. He sent a slave with a secret message to Xerxes: Themistocles is on your side, and the rest of the

Greeks are ready to run away. Attack now and you shall have a great victory. Having heard from his own spies about dissension in the Greek camp, Xerxes believed Themistocles' message and attacked. The Greeks suddenly had no choice but to stay and fight, even though the Persian fleet of 800 galleys was twice the size of the Greek one.

Themistocles' plan was to lure the Persian fleet into the narrow straits between Piraeus and Salamis, where enemy ships would have no room for manoeuvre but the heavier Greek galleys could ram the enemy. On this day Xerxes fell into the trap.

Xerxes had placed his golden throne ashore on Mount Aigaleos to watch his inevitable victory, but he witnessed his own fleet being destroyed. Only his ally Artemisia, Queen of Halicarnassus, seemed to succeed, as she rammed and sank a trireme. The king lamented: 'My men have become women, my women, men.' Unknown to him, she had actually sunk a Persian galley while trying to escape.

For seven long hours Greek triremes ran up alongside enemy galleys, shearing off their oars, and then returning to ram or board. By evening 300 Persian galleys lay shattered on the seabed, against only 40 for the Greeks. Thousands of Persians had gone down with their ships because most did not know how to swim.

Xerxes scuttled back to Persia, leaving behind an army to achieve on land what he had failed to do by sea, but in August the following year that army was destroyed at the battle of Plataea.

Along with the victory at Plataea, Salamis ended the Persian threat, until Alexander the Great conquered the Persian Empire in 331 BC. It prevented Greece from being crushed by Oriental despotism, leaving it free to develop its systems of democracy and the philosophical ideals that have pervaded Western civilisation ever since. In the words of historian Will Durant: 'It made Europe possible.'

1779 When a British captain asks him to strike his colours at the sea battle of Flamborough Head, American Captain John Paul Jones responds: 'I have not yet begun to fight!' He wins the battle. * **1907** Mark Twain in a speech: 'I have been complimented many times and they always embarrass me; I always feel that they have not said enough.'

24 September

'You are the Messenger of God.'

622 AD Born in the then pagan city of Mecca in modern-day Saudi Arabia in about 570 AD, the prophet Muhammad showed early signs of the destiny that God held in store for him. As a young child, he came close to death but God sent two angels who opened his chest, took out his heart and removed a blood clot from it. Then, when he was about twelve, a Christian monk in Syria prophesied that he would become a prophet.

At first Muhammad's life was a prosaic one; he became a merchant and at 25 married a wealthy widow fifteen years his senior, who bore him six children. But when he was about 40 he began receiving direct revelations. One evening as he rested in a secluded cave, the voice of the Angel Gabriel called out to him: 'You are the Messenger of God.' Thus began a lifetime of religious revelations, which he and others collected as the Quran.

From that time on, Muhammad began preaching submission to God, that is, Islam. Living in a pagan, polytheistic society, he insisted on the oneness of God as the all-powerful controller of the universe. He told of the Last Judgement at which all men would be judged and some rewarded in Paradise. He also introduced the world to the concept of *jihad*, holy war against infidels.

After Muhammad had spent four years teaching his family and close friends in Mecca, God commanded him to promulgate his faith to the world at large. In 621 he sent some of his followers north to the small town of Yathrib, but Mecca's pagan leaders reacted in fury to this upstart who would turn their world upside down and plotted to eliminate him.

On the evening of 9 September the next year, tribal chiefs besieged Muhammad's house, planning to kill him in the morning. But during the night Muhammad slipped from the house and threw a handful of dust at the besiegers, causing them to be unable to see him. Then he stole away with his future father-in-law Abu Bakr and hid in a cave outside the city.

After sheltering there for three days, Muhammad and Abu Bakr started the long trek of 210 miles to Yathrib, pursued by a tribal war party determined to bring them back, dead or alive, but each time the pagan chief closed in on Muhammad, his horse stumbled, and he was finally forced to abandon the chase.

After following back roads for eight days, Muhammad and Abu Bakr reached Quba', where they established a mosque. They then continued to Yathrib, which they entered on this day, completing the epic journey known as the Hegira. The day would mark the beginning (Year I) of the Muslim calendar. The history of Islam had begun.

Yathrib was soon renamed Madīnat an-Nabī, literally 'the City of the Prophet', but the name morphed over the centuries to simply Medina. There Muhammad set about building the followers of Islam into an organised community and an Arabian power. He constructed a theocratic state, conquered most of the Arabian peninsula and proselytised with sermons and force of arms. Unlike most religious figures, Muhammad was known as a womaniser, with thirteen wives and many concubines.

After several days of headaches and fever, on 8 June 632 Muhammad died with his head on his wife's lap, but Islam continued to spread. Within twenty years the Byzantine and Persian empires had fallen to the prophet's successors, and during the next two centuries vast Arab conquests continued, stretching from India across the Middle East and Africa, and up through western Europe's Iberian peninsula.

By 1900 there were about 200 million Muslims worldwide, a number that has now ballooned to over 2 billion and is still growing at almost 2 per cent a year.

---

768 King of the Franks Pépin the Short dies. According to Abbé Suger, at his request he is buried 'at the [Basilica of Saint-Denis'] doorstep, prostrate and not lying on his back, because of the sins of his father Charles Martel', so that the faithful entering the church would trample his tomb. His sons Charlemagne and Carloman inherit his kingdom.

---

25 September

'The lion in them turned to timid hare.'

1396 A mission to save the Holy Land from Muslim domination had first been proposed in 1095 with Pope Urban II's impassioned call to join the First Crusade. During the next three centuries Europeans launched seven more major campaigns, gradually ceding the Middle East to the Turks. Today another crusade, even more futile than its predecessors, reached its unhappy denouement at Nicopolis in Bulgaria in the last battle of the last crusade.

By the late 14th century the Ottoman Turks had reduced the once mighty Byzantine Empire to little more than the city of Constantinople, and now the fearsome Turkish Sultan Bayezid, called the Thunderbolt for his sudden and devastating attacks, was determined to extend his rule. In 1395 he besieged and captured Nicopolis, a Bulgarian fortress on the banks of the Danube, killing the Bulgarian Tsar Ivan Shishman in the process. Nicopolis' fall led Pope Boniface IX to call for another crusade.

In July 1396 the Duke of Burgundy's 25-year-old son, the squat and ugly Jean de Nevers, set out with 10,000 Frenchmen, 2,000 Germans, 1,000 Englishmen and assorted soldiers from Poland, Austria, Lombardy and Croatia, as well as a contingent of Knights Hospitallers. They were joined at Buda by 30,000 Hungarians under the command of their king, Sigismund. The crusaders' ambition was nothing less than to throw the Turks out of the Balkans and then to march through Anatolia and Syria to recapture Jerusalem. Their first target would be Turkish-occupied Nicopolis.

Throughout the centuries, crusader courage and determination had been far stronger than their planning and preparation. The crusade of 1396 was no exception; the crusaders arrived before Nicopolis on 12 September but they had brought no siege equipment and so were forced to encircle the fortress rather than overpower it.

Hearing of the siege, Bayezid the Thunderbolt was soon on the march. Joined by Serbian allies, the sultan's force took up positions on the Nicopolis road, with its flanks protected by deep gullies.

Lusting for blood, the impatient French knights immediately launched an attack, in spite of pleas for caution from King Sigismund. They routed the Turkish infantry and light cavalry, but suddenly the French cavalry were forced to halt; they had charged into a field planted with sharpened stakes and had to dismount or disembowel their horses. But even on foot they were formidable fighters, breaking the enemy line while killing thousands.

Now the French and their allies charged up a small hill hoping to loot the Sultan's quarters, only to find the Ottoman heavy cavalry massed there. Cut off, they panicked and were surrounded and slaughtered or captured. As described by a contemporary chronicler, the French monk Michel Pintoin: 'The lion in them turned to timid hare.' One of the few who fought bravely was Jean de Nevers, who was captured (but later ransomed for the exorbitant sum of 200,000 florins). For his courage he was thereafter known as Jean sans Peur (John the Fearless).

The crusaders' Hungarian infantry initially routed the Turkish force before them, but Bayezid's Serbian allies emerged from ambush to stampede them into panicky retreat.

Only a few crusaders escaped. Sigismund fled to the Danube and got away in a fisherman's boat. Incensed by his heavy losses, Bayezid ordered several thousand prisoners, including 300 knights, to stand naked before him and give their names and financial resources. Those without the means to pay ransom were immediately killed, either by decapitation or by severing their limbs from the body. A few survivors were given to Muslim soldiers as slaves. Jean de Nevers and other noble captives were forced to stand beside the sultan and watch the executions.

Once again, Islam was triumphant. For five centuries the Bulgarians would remain under the oppressive Turkish yoke. The Bulgarian nobility was destroyed – aristocrats were coerced either to accept Islam or face execution. Peasants were turned into serfs and thousands of young boys were pressed into the Turkish Janissary corps. Only in 1878 did the Bulgarians regain their freedom.

1066 King Harold defeats his brother Tostig and Norwegian King Harald Hardrada at Stamford Bridge. After Tostig asks Harold what reward would be offered to Harald Hardrada if he pulled back his army, Harold replies: 'He shall have seven feet of good English soil, or a little more perhaps, as he is so much taller than other men.'

---

26 September

'No, Philadelphia has captured Howe!'

1777 'Well! Here are the English in earnest!' recorded Mrs Henry Drinker in her journal, as a British column entered Philadelphia this morning. 'About 2 or 300 came in through Second Street without opposition ...'

The British army's commander, Sir William Howe, was confident that by seizing the rebel capitol he could bring the war in America to an end. It would be a far less costly action than pursuing the destruction of the Continental Army in pitched battle. In fact, he had come close to achieving the latter just two weeks earlier at the Battle of the Brandywine, but George Washington, though badly outmanoeuvred, managed to extricate his forces to safety.

Howe, like his superiors in London, believed that with a British army on the scene, Pennsylvania loyalists were sure to rally to Britain's cause, helping his troops to put down rebel resistance and restore the king's rule. Loyalists indeed flocked to the city but in numbers that were nowhere near British expectations.

When Benjamin Franklin, then in Paris, received the news that Howe had captured Philadelphia, he countered: 'No, Philadelphia has captured Howe!' Franklin was right. As the fighting season ended, Howe and his 15,000 troops occupied the city but not much more, while from nearby Valley Forge Washington's battered army lay in watch, a fighting force still to be reckoned with.

The British spent the winter of 1777–78 in urban comfort, well fed and entertained by a steady flow of theatrical performances and concerts. Howe acquired a mistress, the wife of a prominent loyalist, Joshua Loring, and their liaison prompted these famous lines:

> Sir William, he, snug as a flea,
> Lay all this time a-snoring;
> Nor dreamed of harm, as he lay warm
> In bed with Mrs Loring.

In the months after Howe's capture of Philadelphia, the British government in London grew increasingly dissatisfied with the state of operations in North America. In October had come news of the American victory at Saratoga. Then, in February, France announced it would join the war on the side of the Americans. In May Howe was recalled, replaced by Sir Henry Clinton, who bore orders to evacuate the city and return to New York.

On 18 June 1778 the British left Philadelphia. It was a quiet departure. In the words of one resident: 'They did not go away, they vanished.'

1938 Adolf Hitler in a speech in Berlin: 'The Sudetenland is the last territorial claim I have to make in Europe, but it is one on which I shall not yield.' * **1952** Democratic presidential candidate Adlai Stevenson in a speech in Indianapolis: 'In America any boy may become President, and I suppose it's just one of the risks he takes.'

27 September

'Here I am, a strong man defeated by an even stronger one.'

52 BC In 58 BC Julius Caesar embarked on his conquest of Gaul. For six years he skilfully played off one tribe against another, crushing all who opposed him and bringing most of Gaul under Roman control. But in 53 BC, while he was temporarily back in Rome, a young warrior from the Arverni named Vercingetorix began making alliances to liberate Gaul: 'When we in Gaul act with a single will, the whole world will not be able to resist us.'

Given supreme command, Vercingetorix ruthlessly imposed his authority, executing and even burning alive tribesmen who wavered. Soon Roman settlements were under attack throughout Gaul.

Seeing all his conquests in danger, Caesar rushed back to rejoin his legions, about 60,000 men. During the next nine months of brutal slog, the Romans won fixed battles but Vercingetorix harassed every movement, hunting down stragglers and foragers and denying the enemy food through a draconian policy of burnt farms and villages. His one victory in the field was at his home village of Gergovia, but Gallic casualties were so great that he was forced to retreat with 80,000 men to Alesia, a strongly fortified town near Dijon.

Since Alesia stood on a hill and was almost impregnable to direct assault, Caesar encircled it with nine miles of siege fortifications, with a palisade fifteen feet high. In front the Romans dug a 20-foot-wide trench studded with sharpened stakes and *stimuli* (wood blocks fitted with iron hooks).

Just before the Romans completed their ramparts, however, Vercingetorix sent a cavalry detachment to summon the main Gallic army. Soon a force of (according to Caesar) 250,000 was on the march.

Meanwhile Vercingetorix was completely cut off in Alesia. When food began to run out, he drove out the town's women and children. When these hapless souls approached the Roman line, Caesar ordered that none should be allowed through, so they perished of starvation between the town and the Roman fortifications.

Anticipating the approach of the Gallic army, Caesar then constructed a second wall, this one facing outward, with his army in between. When the huge enemy force arrived in mid-September of 52 BC, the Roman besiegers became the besieged.

Three times the Gauls organised simultaneous attacks, the main army assaulting the outer Roman wall while Vercingetorix stormed the inner wall, but, largely thanks to Roman cavalry, all three efforts failed, although during the last attack Caesar himself, wearing his distinguishing scarlet cape, had to lead the counter-attack.

Next the Gallic army nearly broke through the outside wall, but Caesar ordered his last cavalry reserve to ride around the enemy and attack from the rear, while his legionaries held them from the front. Caught in a pincer movement, the Gauls broke and ran. Vercingetorix was now without hope of deliverance.

The defeated commander then addressed an assembly of his allies: 'I did not undertake the war for private ends, but in the cause of national liberty. And since I must now accept my fate, I place myself at your disposal. Make amends to the Romans by killing me or surrender me alive, as you think best.'

Then, as Caesar wrote in his *Commentarii de Bello Gallico*: 'I took my place on the fortifications in front of the camp and the chiefs were brought to me there. Vercingetorix was surrendered, and the weapons were laid down before me.'

Wearing his best armour, Vercingetorix rode to the dais where Caesar was seated, dismounted, threw off his armour and placed it with his sword, spear and helmet at Caesar's feet. 'Here I am', he said, 'a strong man defeated by an even stronger one.' He then sat silent and motionless on the ground until he was led away.

The siege of Alesia was the last organised resistance; Gaul became a Roman province, while Vercingetorix was imprisoned in Rome. Then, on 26 September 46 BC, six years minus one day after his surrender at Alesia, he was marched through the city in Caesar's triumph and on the same evening ritually garrotted in his prison cell. His body was thrown into the Tiber.

1938 Days before Hitler's takeover of the Sudetenland, Prime Minister Neville Chamberlain in a radio broadcast: 'How horrible, fantastic, incredible, it is that we should be digging trenches and trying on gas-masks here because of a quarrel in a far-away country between people of whom we know nothing.'

28 September

'A dead man does not bite.'

48 BC The Roman Senate had elected him consul at 35 and then twice more over the next twenty years. The public had hailed him as Rome's *Primus inter pares* (first among equals), and the Senate had awarded him three triumphs for his victories. Yet now, after Julius Caesar – who had once been his ally and even his father-in-law – had crushed his army at Pharsalus seven weeks earlier, Pompey the Great was fleeing for his life.

After Pharsalus, Pompey set sail for Egypt, where he hoped for support from Ptolemy (XIII), whose father he had helped regain the Egyptian throne. Accompanied by his wife Cornelia, he left from Cyprus on a trireme and headed across the Mediterranean towards Pelusium (an ancient port twenty miles from Port Said) where Ptolemy and his army were encamped.

On this day Pompey brought his ship to anchor and sent a messenger to the pharaoh to ask for his aid. Ptolemy, who was only fourteen, called a council of his advisors, including his tutor Theodotus of Chios, the eunuch Pothinus, who was Egypt's regent, the Egyptian general Achillas and Lucius Septimius, a Roman soldier who had once been a tribune in Pompey's army.

As the council debated, Theodotus argued that if they helped Pompey they would make an enemy of Caesar, but if they refused to let him land, Pompey might later take revenge while Caesar would blame them for letting him go. Therefore, he urged, the best course would be to kill Pompey, which would both gratify Caesar and leave them without fear of Pompey's vengeance. Plutarch tells us that Theodotus 'smilingly added': 'A dead man does not bite.'

Persuaded, the council ordered Achillas and Septimius to carry out the deed. According to Plutarch, these two and a few servants 'put out towards the ship of Pompey. Now, all the most distinguished of Pompey's fellow-voyagers had come aboard of her to see what was going on. Accordingly, when they saw a reception that was not royal, nor splendid … just a few men sailing up in a single fishing-boat, they viewed this lack of respect with suspicion, and advised Pompey to have his ship rowed back into the open sea … But meanwhile the boat drew near, and first Septimius rose up and addressed Pompey in the Roman tongue as Imperator. Then Achillas saluted him in Greek, and invited him to come aboard the boat, telling him that the shallows were extensive, and that the sea, which had a sandy bottom, was not deep enough to float a trireme.'

After embracing his wife, Pompey stepped into the small boat as Achillas grasped his hand in greeting. Seeing Septimius, Pompey happily exclaimed: 'Surely I am not mistaken, and you are an old comrade of mine!' But, as Cornelia and Pompey's friends stood watching from the deck of the trireme, Septimius slipped behind him and thrust his sword into his back. Then Achillas stabbed him with his dagger. 'Pompey, drawing his toga down over his face with both hands, without an act or a word that was unworthy of himself, but with merely a groan, submitted to their blows, being sixty years of age less one, and ending his life only one day after his birthday.' Septimius finished the job by cutting off Pompey's head.

When Caesar arrived two days later, Pothinus presented him with Pompey's head and seal ring. But 'from the man who brought him Pompey's head he turned away with loathing, as from an assassin; and on receiving Pompey's seal-ring, he burst into tears'. Later, Plutarch reports, Caesar had both Achillas and Pothinus put to death, and 'the king [Ptolemy] himself, moreover, was defeated in battle along the river, and disappeared. Theodotus ... however, escaped the vengeance of Caesar; for he fled out of Egypt and wandered about in wretchedness and hated by all men. But Marcus Brutus, after he had slain Caesar and come into power, discovered him in Asia, and put him to death with every possible torture. Pompey's remains were taken to Cornelia, who gave them burial at his Alban villa.'

1921 As he sees an attractive young woman while walking down the Champs-Élysées on his 80th birthday, former prime minister Georges Clemenceau remarks to a friend: 'Oh, to be seventy again!' * **1964** On her 30th birthday, Brigitte Bardot says: 'When you're thirty you're old enough to know better, but still young enough to go ahead and do it.'

---

29 September

'An appeaser is one who feeds a crocodile
– hoping it will eat him last.'

1938 Since becoming Reichskanzler in 1933, Hitler had surreptitiously built up German armaments until the Wehrmacht had grown to 600,000 men, six times the limit allowed by the Treaty of Versailles. When the other European powers took no action, he illegally sent German forces into the demilitarised Rhineland. In 1938 he marched into Austria. The lack of response from Britain and France paved the way for his next move, the destruction of Czechoslovakia.

Formed from the ruins of the Austrian Empire in the wake of the First World War, Czechoslovakia was home to 14 million people, but over 3 million were German-speakers, mostly living in the Sudetenland, where three-quarters of the inhabitants were ethnic Germans. There the Sudeten German Party agitated for integration into Hitler's Third Reich.

Hitler protested at what he claimed was the repression of Czechoslovakia's ethnic Germans and in 1938 began threatening to 'liberate' them. On 30 May he signed a secret internal directive for war against Czechoslovakia to begin no later than 1 October.

That summer German newspapers published fabricated accounts of atrocities against Sudeten Germans, and Hitler claimed that the Czechs had forced 600,000 from their homes and left them to starve. He then sent 750,000 troops on 'army manoeuvres' along the Czech border. The Czech government led by Edvard Beneš started to buckle under the pressure, while Britain and France, wanting to avoid war at any cost, urged the Czechs to give more ground.

In September Prime Minister Neville Chamberlain flew to Berchtesgaden, then to Cologne and finally to Munich to meet Hitler, but the Führer was implacable. He demanded that the Sudetenland be absorbed into Germany, convincing Chamberlain that refusal meant war. Chamberlain and French Prime Minister Édouard Daladier leaned on Beneš to cede all territory with a German majority, warning that if he refused, he would stand alone. This meant that Czechoslovakia would lose 3.5 million citizens, much of its industry and its defences in the west.

Dismayed by Hitler's intransigence, the British began mobilising troops and readying home defences. Then on this day – a Thursday – Chamberlain, Daladier and Mussolini met Hitler in Munich, where they agreed to German annexation of the Sudetenland, while Hitler promised to make no further territorial claims. No Czech representative was invited, and Beneš, betrayed by his allies, was forced to accept Hitler's demands. The Munich Agreement was formally signed at 1.30 the next morning.

Chamberlain flew back to England, brandishing his hard-won agreement. Speaking to an anxious crowd outside 10 Downing Street, he made his infamous claim that 'I believe it is peace for our time'.

Most in Britain breathed a long sigh of relief – who cared about some contentious Germanic lands if the world remained at peace? But one who had long opposed Hitler's ultimatum was Winston Churchill, who told the House of Commons: 'Britain and France had to choose between war and dishonour. They chose dishonour. They will have war.' On 2 October he further disparaged Chamberlain's claim to be a peacemaker: 'An appeaser is one who feeds a crocodile – hoping it will eat him last.'

Germany immediately occupied the Sudetenland, and just six weeks later the new German citizens there had their first taste of how things would go in a Nazi state, when the anti-Jewish pogrom called Kristallnacht exploded in Germany, and Sudetenland Germans enthusiastically joined in. Then, the following March, the Wehrmacht occupied the rest of what once had been Czechoslovakia.

On 1 September Germany invaded Poland, and the next day Great Britain declared war. A distraught Chamberlain told the House of Commons: 'Everything that I have worked for, everything that I have hoped for, everything that I have believed in during my public life has crashed into ruins.' In May 1940, he was replaced as prime minister by Winston Churchill. On 9 November the frail and aged ex-PM succumbed to bowel cancer.

1829 British Home Secretary Robert Peel founds the Metropolitan Police Service; among his General Instructions is: 'The police are the public and the public are the police.'

---

30 September

'Dieu et mon droit'

1198 More than a decade earlier, Richard Lionheart had sworn fealty to France's King Philip Augustus for the vast English-held lands in France, but since inheriting the throne of England in 1189, he had insisted that he owed his sovereignty to no power other than God and his own heredity, and was therefore subject to no other monarch. In fact, Richard spent the last five years of his reign (and his life) battling Philip for control of this territory.

Ever since war had broken out in 1194, the conflict had been bitter. Both kings invaded and pillaged each other's lands with extraordinary savagery. According to Roger of Hoveden, a chronicler who had served both the English crown and Philip: 'The King of France, finding a new method of venting his rage against the people, caused the eyes to be put out of many of the subjects of the King of England whom he had made prisoners, and thus provoked the King of England, unwilling as he was, to similar acts of impiety.'

In the early autumn of 1198, Richard moved deep into French territory, capturing the town of Courcelles, only 50 miles north-west of Paris. When Philip learned of Richard's advance he marched to the town's relief with 300 knights and a small army of foot soldiers. When Philip reached the town of Gisors, three miles east, Richard resolved to attack, although he had only a small fraction of his army with him. It was, according to a letter he wrote after the battle, 'the day after the Feast of Saint Michael', that is, 30 September.

Before joining battle, to enable his troops to tell friend from foe, Richard set as the day's watchword, *Dieu et mon droit* ('God and my right'), a phrase underlining his claim that he owed his kingdom, including his French territories in Normandy, Aquitaine and Anjou, to God and his right alone. (He used a French rather than an English password since French was the language of the English court, as well as his own first language. Moreover, most of his troops came from his French territories.)

Richard's assault shattered the enemy, and he later boasted of having unhorsed three knights with a single lance. The French took flight in panic and raced for the fortified castle of Gisors, but, as Richard exultingly wrote to the Bishop of Durham, a bridge 'broke down beneath them, and the King of France, as we have heard say, had to drink of the river, and several knights, about twenty in number, were drowned'. Philip was pulled by his leg from the water to escape the fray. 'Thus have we defeated the King of France at Gisors', Richard reported, 'Yet it is not we who have done this but God, for we are fighting in a just cause.'

After the victory Richard adopted *Dieu et mon droit* as his royal motto, but he had scant time to use it – six months later he was killed at an insignificant siege at Châlus. In the 14th century Edward III adopted it, and at the beginning of the next century Henry V made it the official motto of the English monarch, which it remains to this day, appearing on a scroll beneath the shield of the coat of arms of the United Kingdom.

1891 After French far-right general and would-be dictator Georges Boulanger shoots himself in the head on the grave of his mistress, future prime minister Georges Clemenceau comments: 'He died as he has lived: a second lieutenant.'

1 October

'Le congrès ne marche pas, il danse.'

1814 The great intriguer Charles Maurice de Talleyrand once commented: 'What are politics, if not women?' It was the perfect description of the Congress of Vienna, to which he was France's delegate, representing the restored French monarchy. Among the many beautiful women there, none could match the Russian princess Catherine (Ekaterina) Bagration, called *'le Bel Ange Nu'* for her impressive décolletage and *'la Chatte Blanche'* for her unrestrained sensuality. On this day she gave the first ball of the Congress in honour of Tsar Alexander I, her confidant and likely lover.

Katya, as she was known, had become a princess almost by accident. When she was seventeen, Tsar Paul (Alexander's father), who was known for acting on a whim, suddenly announced that he would attend Catherine's marriage to Prince Pyotr Bagration, an aristocratic major general who was having an affair with Paul's daughter. The prospective bride and groom were both shocked, but no one dared to argue with the tsar, so on 2 September 1800 they were wed.

Bagration was twice Katya's age, and after five years she left him to travel the capitals of Europe. During the Napoleonic wars he fought at Austerlitz, Eylau, Heilsberg and Friedland, but at Borodino he took a shell splinter in the leg and died of gangrene seventeen days later. Now Katya could play the merry widow with all her heart.

A truly emancipated woman, Katya took many lovers, including Prince Louis Ferdinand of Prussia, Saxon diplomat Count Friedrich von der Schulenburg, Austrian foreign minister Klemens von Metternich (by whom she had a daughter when he was married to someone else) and probably Tsar Alexander.

Katya's closest rival was Princess Wilhelmine, Duchess of Sagan, a 33-year-old German beauty who at eighteen had enjoyed a secret affair with her mother's lover and borne an illegitimate child. After two unsuccessful marriages, in 1813 she, too, began a liaison with Metternich, but it ended during the Congress because she refused to be an unacknowledged mistress – he was still married. These two lionesses established themselves in the luxurious Palais Palm, each taking half and holding salons filled with Europe's most illustrious leaders and diplomats. Katya boasted that she knew more political secrets than all the envoys put together.

The Congress was the greatest gathering of political power in history. It was hosted by Emperor Franz II of Austria at a cost in today's terms of $50 million. Two emperors, five kings, 209 reigning princes and about 20,000 officials attended it. In the cast were Castlereagh and Wellington from Great Britain, Russian foreign minister Nesselrode and the two greatest masters of diplomacy and intrigue of the century, the wily Talleyrand and the arrogant Metternich.

The Congress lasted six months, marked by a brilliant succession of entertainments, including a concert of Beethoven's Seventh Symphony conducted by Beethoven himself. But most of all it is remembered for its endless series of balls, which made some question that any progress was being made. As the Austrian field marshal the Prince de Ligne famously punned: '*Le congrès ne marche pas, il danse.*' ('The congress doesn't walk [i.e. work], it dances.') He also remarked to Talleyrand: 'There is still one thing missing at the Congress: the burial of a field marshal – I'll take care of that.' Which he did, dying on 13 December 1814 at a ripe 79.

It was with bemusement that the delegates learned that Napoleon had escaped from Elba on 26 February the next year, but work continued and the last comprehensive treaty was signed on 9 June, nine days before Waterloo. Distracted by waltzes as it may have been, the Congress accomplished its stated task of carving up Europe and inaugurating a peace that lasted for nearly 40 years, until the Crimean War. Most of the boundaries established in 1815 remained for almost a century, until the First World War.

After the Congress Katya moved to Paris, living in luxury in the rue du Faubourg Saint-Honoré and taking more lovers. She married an English baron fifteen years her junior, divorced him and sold a 51-carat diamond to make ends meet. She finally died during a trip to Venice at 73.

---

331 BC Having portentously pronounced, 'Heaven cannot support two suns, nor the earth two masters', Alexander the Great utterly defeats King Darius III to destroy the Persian Empire at Gaugamela (now in northern Iraq). * **1939** Winston Churchill during a radio broadcast: 'I cannot forecast to you the action of Russia. It is a riddle wrapped in a mystery inside an enigma.'

2 October

'I wasn't really naked. I simply didn't have any clothes on.'

1925 This evening in Paris a cast of black musicians and dancers exploded on the stage of the Théâtre des Champs Élysées in a show called *La Revue Nègre*. Its star was nineteen-year-old Josephine Baker, who performed the *'Danse Sauvage'*. According to *New Yorker* correspondent Janet Flanner: 'She made her entry entirely nude except for a pink flamingo feather between her limbs; she was being carried upside down and doing the splits on the shoulder of a black giant ... She was an unforgettable female ebony statue.' Josephine shrugged off her nudity. 'I wasn't really naked', she said. 'I simply didn't have any clothes on.'

Josephine was born illegitimate in St Louis, Missouri. By fifteen, she had run away from home, supported herself by waiting on tables and street-corner dancing, and married and discarded two husbands. Then she headed for New York.

Meanwhile in Paris, André Daven, the artistic director of the Théâtre des Champs Élysées, was searching for a new type of show. His friend, the painter Fernand Léger, suggested a revue played entirely by blacks. Daven's contact in New York recruited twenty black musicians, singers and dancers, including Josephine, to come to Paris. Josephine had no regrets, later writing: 'I realised I was living in a country where I was afraid to be black ... I had been suffocating in the United States.'

La Revue Nègre created a fashionable *'négrophilie'*, as Josephine titillated audiences by dancing the Charleston wearing only her trademark skirt of artificial bananas. The writer Pierre de Régnier describes her: 'She is in constant motion, her body writhing like a snake or more precisely like a dipping saxophone. Music seems to pour from her body.'

An irrepressible free spirit, Josephine shared her dressing room with a goat, kept a pet pig and introduced a cheetah into her act, fitting it with a diamond choker. She also added singing to her repertoire, including her signature song, *'J'ai deux amours'*.

Pablo Picasso described her as, 'tall, coffee skin, ebony eyes, legs of paradise, a smile to end all smiles'. Other admirers included Coco Chanel, Ernest Hemingway, Georges Rouault, Gertrude Stein and Georges Simenon, with whom she had an affair. (Simenon was not the only lucky one; she had numerous liaisons, some with women, including the writer Colette and the Mexican painter Frida Kahlo.)

After a triumphant ten years in Europe, Josephine went back to New York, but there success eluded her, so in 1937 she returned to Paris, married her third husband and became a French citizen.

When France entered the war, Josephine showed that beneath the sex, songs and celebrity was a woman to be conjured with. The Deuxième Bureau (French military intelligence) recruited her to gather information from officials she met at parties. Then, with the fall of France, she became a spy for Charles de Gaulle's France Libre, hiding clandestine messages in her musical scores. She settled in Morocco and for three years entertained Allied soldiers while collecting all the intelligence she could. She finished the war back in France, singing for soldiers just behind the lines. She was awarded the Croix de Guerre and the Rosette de la Résistance, and de Gaulle made her a Chevalier of the Légion d'honneur.

In 1947 Josephine wed her fourth husband and moved into her château in the Dordogne, where they raised twelve adopted children, but by 1957 the marriage was effectively over.

While continuing to entertain, Josephine also became such an important figure in the American civil rights movement that in 1963 she spoke at the March on Washington at the side of Martin Luther King, Jr.

In the spring of 1975, Josephine – now approaching her 69th birthday – went on stage for the last time, in a Paris retrospective financed by Princess Grace of Monaco and Jacqueline Kennedy Onassis. Four days later, she was found lying peacefully in her bed surrounded by newspapers with glowing reviews of her performance. She had suffered a stroke after, it is said, attempting to seduce a man several decades younger than she was. Her purported last comment was: 'Oh, you young people act like old men. You have no fun.' Taken to Pitié-Salpêtrière hospital, she died on 12 April.

1780 Wearing civilian clothes and carrying a forged passport, British Major John André is caught behind American lines with plans to an American fort in his boot. Asked if he has a last request just before he is hanged as spy, he says on the gallows: 'None, but that you bear witness to the world that I die like a brave man.'

3 October

'Dulce et decorum est pro patria mori.'
('It is sweet and honourable to die for your country.')

42 BC The man who wrote this famous line was the Roman poet Horace, who today in Greece fought at the first battle of Philippi with Brutus' and Cassius' forces against Octavian (the future Augustus) and Mark Antony. Cassius committed suicide, and Brutus later killed himself, but Horace, a supremely unlikely soldier, survived, to write for another 32 years.

A surprising number of writers and artists have seen combat. In 490 BC Aeschylus fought the Persians at Marathon, and two centuries later Socrates was a hoplite in the Peloponnesian War, saving the life of Alcibiades at Potidaea. Thucydides also fought until he caught the plague (he survived).

Jewish historian Josephus witnessed the destruction of Jerusalem in 70 AD, while Greek historian Polybius went on campaign in the Third Punic War and was present at the sack of Carthage in 146 AD.

Dante Alighieri was a dashing cavalryman at the Florentine victory at Campaldino in 1289, and Leonardo da Vinci was Cesare Borgia's chief military engineer. Niccolò Machiavelli commanded the Florentine army that defeated Pisa in 1509. Another Italian, Benvenuto Cellini, fought for the Pope when Rome was sacked in 1527 and claimed to have fired the shot that killed the enemy commander, Charles de Bourbon.

When the Holy League defeated the Turks at Lepanto in 1571, Miguel de Cervantes was shot in the left hand, forcing him to abandon the military in favour of writing. Fifteen years later, English poet Sir Philip Sidney was slain at the battle of Zutphen, offering his water to a dying comrade with the famous words: 'Thy necessity is yet greater than mine.'

In the 17th century the French aphorist François de La Rochefoucauld ('If we resist our passions, it is more through their weakness than our strength') was thrice wounded during six years as a soldier.

Another writer-warrior was Leo Tolstoy, who saw action in the Crimean War, while Lew Wallace, the author of *Ben-Hur*, was a Union major general during the American Civil War, fighting at Shiloh (where Ambrose Bierce also fought). The painter Frederic Remington witnessed Teddy Roosevelt's charge on San Juan Hill in the Spanish–American War.

Winston Churchill won the Nobel Prize in Literature for *The Second World War* but had an exciting military history of his own – in 1898 he shot three Dervishes at Omdurman during the last British cavalry charge in history.

Siegfried Sassoon single-handedly captured a German trench in during the First World War. J.R.R. Tolkien, Robert Graves and A.A. Milne all fought at the Somme, where both Graves and Milne were wounded. On the German side, Erich Maria Remarque was hit by shrapnel in the leg, arm and neck in Flanders.

Also during that war Ernest Hemingway served as an ambulance driver in northern Italy, where he was wounded by mortar shell shrapnel. (During the Spanish Civil War he had been a war reporter, as was Arthur Koestler. George Orwell was shot in the throat by a sniper while fighting for the Republicans.)

Hemingway also claimed to have 'liberated' the Ritz Bar in Paris in 1944, but Roald Dahl was an authentic Second World War fighter pilot ace, while Evelyn Waugh was a commando in West Africa and Crete. J.D. Salinger (*The Catcher in the Rye*) landed at Utah Beach and fought at the Battle of the Bulge – where Kurt Vonnegut was captured. Imprisoned in Dresden, Vonnegut hid in an underground meat locker to escape the city's destruction. *Lord of the Flies* author William Golding served on the destroyer that sank the *Bismarck* and participated in the D-Day landings. Joseph Heller (*Catch 22*) flew 60 combat missions as a B-25 bombardier on the Italian front. Ronald Searle was captured when Singapore fell and worked on the Siam-Burma Death Railway as a prisoner.

Most writers and artists have considered their artistic achievements more important than their military ones. As Edward Bulwer-Lytton wrote in his play *Richelieu*: 'The pen is mightier than the sword.' Military men would disagree; Douglas MacArthur riposted: 'Whoever said the pen is mightier than the sword obviously never encountered automatic weapons.' Horace would have scoffed at the debate but would have said (and did): '*Carpe diem*' ('Seize the day') and '*Nunc est bibendum*' ('Now is the time for drinking').

1574 The Dutch fleet enters Leiden to save it from a long Spanish siege after Burgomaster Pieter Van der Werff convinces its citizens to hold out, telling them: 'Take my body to appease your hunger, but expect no surrender so long as I remain alive.'

---

4 October

'A dreadful plague of Saracens ravaged France with miserable slaughter, but they not long after in that country received the punishment due to their wickedness.'

732 AD Today the rampaging Moors were riding toward Tours, a wealthy city ripe for plunder, but suddenly they saw a massed Frankish army blocking their path. The stage was set for the forces of Allah to meet the forces of Christ in a pivotal battle that would decide the fate of western Europe.

In the 8th century the most aggressive power in the world was militant Islam, intent on endless conquest for the glory of Allah. In 711 the Arabs had crossed from North Africa, and now their kingdom of al-Andalus covered all the Iberian peninsula except the northern rim. Twenty years later, the Umayyad Caliphate was again on the march.

The Umayyad governor Abd al-Rahman first led his cavalry into Aquitaine, where he routed Aquitaine's Duke Odo near Bordeaux and looted the area's rich monasteries. Then he headed for Tours.

Desperate, Odo fled to Paris to beg for support from his one-time enemy, Charles, the de facto ruler of the Franks. Charles welcomed him with caution but agreed to help only after the duke had sworn fealty. The Franks were Europe's last line of defence – beyond were only the scattered tribes of Germany and Italy ruled by the Lombards, none a match for the Moors.

Assembling an army 30,000 strong, Charles and Odo marched south. Somewhere between Tours and Poitiers, Charles positioned his force at the top of a wooded hill, hoping the slope and the trees would disrupt the Moorish cavalry. When Abd al-Rahman arrived with about 80,000 mounted men, he hesitated, fearing Charles's army might be larger than his own.

For six days the two armies nervously watched each other, each reluctant to attack. The Moors trotted on their horses, magnificent with lances and scimitars but without body armour, depending on the will of Allah and their own ferocious courage to defeat their enemies. The Franks were primarily on foot but lightly armoured and armed with axes, swords and javelins.

At last Abd al-Rahman ordered the attack, and several thousand horsemen galloped toward the waiting Franks. But the uphill slope slowed their horses, and Charles had formed his men into impenetrable squares that, in charge after charge, the Muslim cavalry could not break. According to the *Mozarabic Chronicle*: 'In the shock of battle the men of the North seemed like a sea that cannot be moved. Firmly they stood, one close to another, forming as it were a bulwark of ice.'

The Moors knew no battle tactic other than the wild cavalry charge, and their casualties began to mount under the rain of javelins and thrown axes. Suddenly a cry went up: their treasure – all they had plundered since leaving Spain – was under attack. Several squadrons of cavalry turned to protect their goods but discovered that the cry was false. By then it was too late. The Franks had cut down Abd al-Rahman, and the Arab horsemen started deserting the field.

Charles's soldiers rested in place through the night, believing the battle would resume at dawn, but when they reconnoitred the enemy camp they found only empty tents – the Moors had vanished during the night. The contemporary English monk, the Venerable Bede, explained: 'A dreadful plague of Saracens ravaged France with miserable slaughter, but they not long after in that country received the punishment due to their wickedness.'

As Edward Gibbon memorably concluded, had the Moors won the battle, 'Perhaps the interpretation of the Koran would now be taught in the schools of Oxford, and her pulpits might demonstrate to a circumcised people the sanctity and truth of the revelation of Mahomet.'

After this battle Charles became known as Charles Martel – Charles the Hammer – for his hammering defence that broke the Moorish onslaught. Ruler of the Franks and now overlord of Aquitaine, he died in 741, leaving behind a virtual kingdom that was to be enlarged into an empire by his grandson, Charlemagne. Charles's great victory at Tours ended the Muslim threat to western Europe until Suleiman the Magnificent marched into Austria in the 16th century.

1953 Frank Lloyd Wright in the *New York Times Magazine*: 'The physician can bury his mistakes, but the architect can only advise his client to plant vines.'

---

5 October

'We'll give them a whiff of grapeshot.'

1795 Today was 13 Vendémiaire, An IV, according to the French republican calendar. Both Louis XVI and Robespierre had already been fed to the guillotine, but hard-eyed monarchists and fanatical revolutionaries still roamed the streets of Paris. The previous evening a mob of 30,000 armed and excited protesters had surrounded the Tuileries, where the Convention was meeting. The government must fall, no matter who was there to pick up the pieces.

In charge of government security was vicomte Paul Barras, a brawny provincial nobleman who had helped bring about the executions of both Louis XVI and Robespierre. As commander of the Army of the Interior and the police, he was one of the most powerful men in the country. He had recently begun a new affair with a tempting 32-year-old widow from Martinique named Joséphine de Beauharnais.

Realising that only military force could quell the revolt, Barras called on an unknown 26-year-old brigadier general named Napoleon Bonaparte and asked him to take over the republican defences. 'I agree', Bonaparte replied, 'But I warn you that once I take my sword from its scabbard, I will put it back again only after restoring order.'

As an ex-artillery officer, Bonaparte recognised the need for cannon and ordered Major Joachim Murat, whom he now met for the first time, to commandeer 40 guns and place them at key points around the Tuileries.

At five that morning the royalists launched a probing attack, which was easily repulsed, but at ten o'clock they began a major assault, during which Bonaparte's horse was shot from under him. Outnumbered six to one, the republican forces were in danger of being overrun.

When the attackers reached point-blank range, Bonaparte is traditionally supposed to have said: 'We'll give them a whiff of grapeshot.' His cannon opened fire, instantly cutting down over 200 and wounding twice as many more, causing the royalist attack to falter. Now the young general ordered Murat's squadron of cavalry to counter-attack, and the insurgents fled in panic.

(Although Bonaparte is usually credited with the 'whiff of grapeshot' phrase, the Scottish historian Thomas Carlyle may have coined it to describe the event.)

In an uncanny way, the lives of many of the principal players from 13 Vendémiaire would be intertwined in the years to come. A year later Bonaparte married Barras' lover, Joséphine de Beauharnais, whom he had met at Barras' house. Barras went on to even greater power in the government but was precipitously driven from office and eventually exiled from France by Bonaparte, the general he had drafted. Murat became one of Bonaparte's most successful marshals, ultimately becoming the King of Naples. And of course in his coup d'état of November 1799 Bonaparte also destroyed the republican government that he had so well protected.

1789 When a French mob marches on Versailles to protest at a shortage of bread, Marie Antoinette supposedly comments: 'Let them eat cake!' (*'Qu'ils mangent la brioche!'*) * **1945** When awarding US Marine Hershel Smith the Medal of Honor for destroying eight Japanese pillboxes on Iwo Jima with a flamethrower, President Harry Truman says: 'I would rather have this medal than be president of the United States.'

---

6 October

'Lord, open the eyes of the King of England.'

1536 William Tyndale was the sort of religious fanatic whom religious fanatics hate. Ordained a Catholic priest but, while on the faculty at Cambridge University, he was converted to the idea that the Bible rather than the Church hierarchy should be the authority for religious doctrine. He also became committed to providing a Bible that was accessible to all worshippers, and his life's work became its translation from 4th-century Latin to English.

When he was 25 Tyndale became a chaplain in Gloucestershire and started translating the New Testament. When a priest fumed against the project, he retorted: 'I defy the Pope and all his laws. If God spares my life, I will cause the boy that driveth the plough to know more of the scriptures than thou dost.'

Tyndale's views were too hot for England to hold. In 1524 he left the country for Germany, never to return.

Tyndale would have known that Martin Luther had published his German translation of the New Testament in 1522. In 1525 Tyndale completed his English version, the first ever to be published. Within a year 3,000 copies had been printed in Worms, a total that grew to over 50,000 within a decade.

Tyndale continued to move around Germany and the Low Countries, aware that Church agents were keen to track him down. Meanwhile, back in England his enemies threatened booksellers and publicly burned copies of his Bible. Cardinal Wolsey denounced him as a heretic and that other religious fanatic, Thomas More, condemned his beliefs. Tyndale made matters worse for himself by publishing *The Practyse of Prelates* in which he opposed Henry VIII's annulment of his marriage to Catherine of Aragon. Henry became so incensed that he asked Holy Roman Emperor Charles V to send Tyndale back to England, but Charles – no friend to Protestants after his confrontation with Luther at Worms in 1521 – refused, possibly because Catherine was his aunt.

Tyndale eventually made the fatal error of trying to hide in Antwerp, then part of the Holy Roman Empire. There he made another mistake, befriending the English cleric Henry Phillips, whom Tyndale met in a safe house, taking his flattery for friendship. Phillips became Tyndale's guest at meals and was one of the few allowed to look at his papers.

In May 1535, Phillips lured Tyndale away from the safety of his quarters into the arms of waiting Imperial soldiers, to be locked up in the Castle of Vilvoorde, the state prison six miles from Brussels.

During eighteen months of incarceration, Tyndale worked on his translation of the Old Testament while managing to find printers bold enough to continue printing his New Testament and smuggling it into England in wine casks and bales of wool.

But Tyndale had been convicted of heresy and the implacable authorities condemned him to death. On this day he was brought forth from his cell and led to the scaffold. As he was roped to the stake he prayed with a fervent zeal and a loud voice: 'Lord, open the eyes of the King of England.' Then he was strangled, but the hooded executioner failed to kill him, so he was burned.

Tyndale was dead but his work was very much alive. He had translated the New Testament and the first five books of the Old Testament, and, according to the English broadcaster and author Melvyn Bragg, 'He gave the English people the liberty to think rather than the duty to believe.'

Tyndale's translation forms the basis for the King James Bible, one of the English language's greatest works of literature. It has been estimated that over 80 per cent of the King James version is his work, with familiar phrases such as:

> Let there be light
> Am I my brother's keeper?
> Judge not that ye be not judged
> The salt of the earth

Filthy lucre
Eat, drink and be merry
Blessed are the meek for they shall inherit the earth
Fight the good fight

He even wrote, 'the spirit is willing, but the flesh is weak', but he may have nicked this from Luther, who wrote: '*der Geist ist willig, aber das Fleisch ist schwach.*'

1889 When the Moulin Rouge opens in Paris, the Société Générale de protestation contre la licence des rues (General Society of Protest against Public Licentiousness) calls it '*un fait d'une gravité extrême et d'une inadmissible impudeur*'. ('An event of extreme gravity and unacceptable indecency.')
* **1927** When Mexican General Alfredo Quijano is about to be shot for revolting against the government, he orders the firing squad: 'You are too far away; come closer … You are still too far away; you had better come closer still.'

---

7 October

'I spend my time building castles in the air, but in the end, all of them, and I, blow away in the wind.'

1571 Today the Christian forces of Spain, Venice and the papacy combined to destroy the Turkish fleet at the Battle of Lepanto. It was a stunning triumph for the Christian flotilla's commander, Don Juan de Austria, but it proved to be a pinnacle that he would not reach again.

Juan was the dashing illegitimate son of retired Holy Roman Emperor Charles V and thus half-brother to Spain's King Philip II. In 1546 Charles had enjoyed a brief fling with a nineteen-year-old singer named Barbara Blomberg when he was visiting Regensburg. Juan was born the next year and immediately taken away from his mother, to be raised in Valladolid. He would see his mother only once more, when he was 29. He was occasionally visited by Charles, but never told that he was Charles's son.

Charles died when Juan was eleven, and the next year Juan was summoned to a hunt. There he met his half-brother Philip (now King Philip II) for the first time. Philip embraced him and explained that they had the same father.

Although Emperor Charles had intended him for the Church, Juan became a fine admiral/soldier, crossing swords with pirates and sub-duing rebellious Moriscos around Granada, once being shot in the head. Meanwhile he was involved with a string of high-born women, despite his puritanical brother's warning against philandering.

Then came Lepanto. Still only 24, Juan was designated commander-in-chief and ordered instant attack. When his captains urged caution, he insisted: 'Gentlemen, it is no longer the hour for advising, but for fighting.'

During the four-hour battle, the Holy League's firepower proved decisive. When his galley was overrun, the Turkish commander dropped to his knees, offering a huge ransom in return for his life, but a Spanish soldier lopped off his head as he knelt, then displayed it on the end of his pike. Over 8,000 Christians had perished, but almost 30,000 Turks had been cut down or drowned and 15,000 Christian galley slaves had been set free. (During the battle, a 24-year-old Spanish soldier named Miguel de Cervantes was wounded in the left hand.) The battle marked the end of Turkish domination of the seas and destroyed the myth of Turkish invincibility, ending for ever the danger of Islamic conquest of Europe.

In 1577 King Philip made his half-brother governor-general of the Spanish Netherlands, then in revolt against Spain. Initially Juan scored victories at Namur and Gembloux, but then he became bogged down in his efforts to crush the rebellion, suffering from lack of funds, as Philip had by now almost bankrupted Spain. In addition, Philip had appointed Juan de Escobedo as Juan's secretary, intending that he should keep in check both Juan's political ambitions and his constant womanising. But Escobedo fell under Juan's spell, began to disobey orders from Madrid and in March 1578 was murdered on orders from Philip. Then in July Juan was defeated by the rebellious Netherlanders at the Battle of Rijmenam.

Juan was now despondent, his power in the Spanish Netherlands slipping away as well as his support from Philip. 'I spend my time building castles in the air', he mused, 'but in the end, all of them, and I, blow away in the wind.' Now even his health began to deteriorate, and two months after Rijmenam he died in Namur, probably of typhoid, still only 31.

1849 At 5.00am Edgar Allan Poe dies in Baltimore four days after having been found in the gutter outside a saloon. His aunt claims his last words are an unlikely 'Lord help my poor soul'. His tombstone epitaph is the refrain from his own poem: 'Quoth the Raven, "Nevermore".' * **2002** Future prime minister Theresa May at the Conservative Party conference: 'You know what some people call us – the nasty party.'

8 October

'The public be damned.'

1882 Cornelius Vanderbilt had been one of America's great self-made men, quitting school at eleven to work on his father's ferry in New York harbour and eventually amassing a fortune of $100 million through ships and railroads. Because of his involvement with ships he became known as 'the Commodore'. His son Billy, however, was a disappointment. Frail and apparently without ambition, he suffered a nervous breakdown in his teens and then at nineteen married against his father's wishes.

But Billy Vanderbilt clearly had more in him than Cornelius appreciated. When he was 36, he convinced his father to put him in charge of the bankrupt Staten Island Railroad, which he quickly returned to profit. Over the next twenty years Billy became progressively involved with his father's railroads, and on the Commodore's death in 1877, he inherited Cornelius' whole empire. Within six years he had doubled his family's wealth to $200 million (today worth about $3 billion), making himself the richest man in America – and he might have made even more, had not poor health forced him to retire.

Billy not only amassed a great fortune, he also gave much of it away, supporting a wide range of charities, including Vanderbilt University (which his father had generously endowed), the YMCA and the Metropolitan Museum of Art. Moreover, he accumulated for himself the finest collection of paintings and sculpture in private hands in the United States.

Despite these accomplishments, however, Billy Vanderbilt is today best known for a single retort he made when he was 60.

On Sunday afternoon, 8 October 1882, Billy was riding in his own private car on his own railroad, the New York Central. As the train neared Chicago, two newspaper reporters entered the car to interview him. One asked him if the New York Central would launch an express service as the competing Pennsylvania Railroad had recently done.

Vanderbilt demurred – such a service would be sure to lose money. But, the journalist insisted, how about the interests of the public? 'The public be damned', answered Vanderbilt shortly, ending the interview.

The next day Chicago newspapers headlined Billy's retort, and soon it was picked up all over the nation. Vanderbilt always denied he had ever made the remark. 'Both my words and ideas are misreported and misrepresented', he said. Indeed, there are enough variations of the story to give his denials some credibility. But the accusations stuck in the public mind, and for the remaining three years of his life he was seen not as the great businessman and philanthropist that he was, but, in the words British prime minister Ted Heath used in another context, 'the unpleasant and unacceptable face of capitalism'.

1918 During the Meuse–Argonne Offensive in the First World War, American Corporal Alvin York, a backwoodsman from the Tennessee mountains, single-handedly puts 35 German machine-guns out of action, kills over twenty machine-gunners and captures 132 enemy soldiers in a single morning. That evening he writes in his diary: 'I had orders to report to Brigadier General Lindsey, and he said to me, "Well, York, I hear you have captured the whole damned German army." And I told him I only had 132.'

---

9 October

'The distance is nothing; it's only the first step that is difficult.'

251 AD (or thereabouts) The man who would become the patron saint of France, St Denis, was put to death on (or near) this date. His martyrdom has inspired Frenchmen for 1,800 years. The cathedral built on the spot where he was executed was for centuries the burial place of the kings of France, his name became a war-cry for French armies, and the battle standard of the kings of France, the Oriflamme, was consecrated upon his tomb. We don't know the exact date of Denis' death, but the Church has designated 9 October as his feast day, so that is as close as we can come.

Sometime before 250 AD Pope Fabian ordered seven bishops from Rome to Gaul to convert the still largely pagan population. One of these was Denis, who, accompanied by his two companions, Rusticus and Eleutherius, was sent to Lutetia, the town centred on the Île de la Cité in what today is Paris. There they built a small church and converted hundreds to Christianity. Denis is still considered the first Bishop of Paris.

In the 3rd century, however, the Roman Empire was coming under threat from barbarian hordes beyond the Rhine. When Decius became emperor in 249, he was determined to bolster the *Pax Romana* and reassure the empire's citizens. For this purpose he attempted to suppress Christianity, then still a troublesome but growing sect. In 250 he issued an edict that required all inhabitants of the empire to make a sacrifice and swear an oath of allegiance to the emperor, on pain of death. This included Christian bishops and officers of the Church, many of whom refused, including Pope Fabian, who was one of the first to die, executed on 20 January 250.

In Gaul Christianity was still in fierce competition with the Druids, and when Denis refused to comply with Decius' decree, Druid priests called on the Roman governor Fescenninus Sisinnius to prosecute the bishop and his followers.

Denis and his acolytes Rusticus and Eleutherius were seized and subjected to terrible tortures on the highest hill in Lutetia, Mons Mercurius (subsequently known as Mons Martyrum – Martyrs' Mount – today's Montmartre), which was probably a druidic holy place. The victims were scourged, stretched on the rack, burnt at the stake and finally beheaded.

But Denis was made of sterner stuff than his two companions; after his head was chopped off, he picked it up and, placing it under his arm, marched north along today's rue des Martyrs, all the while preaching a sermon. He continued for six miles until he reached the village of Catolacus, now a suburb just north of Paris, where he was buried in the cemetery.

The site immediately became a destination for Christian pilgrims, and, two centuries later, Saint Geneviève had a small chapel built on Denis' tomb. In the early 7th century Dagobert I, King of the Franks, died in the abbey that had grown from Saint Geneviève's chapel and was buried there. From then on, almost all French kings were interred at Saint-Denis, as the abbey and the town surrounding it were now called.

By the 8th century Denis' cult was well established in France, and then, in 754, Pope Stephen II (who was French) brought veneration of Denis to Rome, whence it gradually spread all over Europe. In the 12th century, on the site of Denis' tomb, the famous Abbot Suger constructed the first Gothic cathedral, the basilica of Saint-Denis, which you can still visit.

509

Although many a God-fearing Frenchman believed in Denis' miraculous perambulation, some had reservations, most memorably recorded by the 18th-century letter-writer and art patron, the Marquise du Deffand. Commenting on the legend that the saint had walked six miles carrying his head, she wrote to the French scientist d'Alembert: '*La distance n'y fait rien; il n'y a que le premier pas qui coûte.*' ('The distance is nothing; it's only the first step that is difficult.')

1967 On orders from Bolivian president René Barrientos, Che Guevara is summarily executed after having been wounded and captured during a firefight with Bolivian forces. When Bolivian sergeant Mario Terán enters the hut where Guevera is held, Guevera tells him: 'I know you have come to kill me. Shoot, coward. You are only going to kill a man.'

---

10 October

'Every damn thing you do in this life, you have to pay for.'

1963 Today in her villa on the Côte d'Azur, Édith Piaf died from liver failure at age 47. Born to poverty and raised in a brothel, she had become a French icon, with a voice that her friend Jean Cocteau described as 'like black velvet'. Despite her fame and success, her life was filled with sorrow and ill fortune.

Piaf was born Édith Gassion in a Paris slum, and her mother abandoned her at birth. Her father, an itinerant street-performer and acrobat, joined the French army during the First World War and took her to his mother, who ran a brothel in Normandy, where she was cared for by prostitutes.

When Piaf was fourteen she joined her father's troupe as a singer, but she soon left to wander the streets of Paris, singing for tips. At seventeen she gave birth to a daughter, who died two years later of meningitis.

A month after her daughter's death, chance changed Piaf's life. While she was singing near the Champs-Élysées, she was noticed by the Parisian nightclub owner Louis Leplée, who asked her to sing at his club. It was Leplée who gave her the stage name 'Piaf', meaning 'sparrow', because she stood only 4ft 8in tall. Her career was almost cut short, however, when Leplée was found tied up on his bed with a bullet in his head. The police thought she was involved because her lover Albert Valette was a suspect. She was soon cleared, but her association with gangsters and Parisian lowlife had been splashed across the newspapers.

By 1939 Piaf had become one of Paris's top entertainers with her songs of love and longing. 'Even when we have lost it, the love you have known leaves you with a taste of honey', she said. She had numerous affairs, including one with a young Yves Montand, while her fame grew with songs like '*La Vie en Rose*'. But the great love of her life was the married French boxer Marcel Cerdan, with whom she started an affair in the summer of 1948. But then came tragedy – he was killed in a plane crash while flying from Paris to New York to meet her. She wrote '*Hymne à l'amour*' to his memory.

In the 1950s Piaf was France's most celebrated singer both at home and abroad, especially in the United States, where she sang at Carnegie Hall. 'I want to make people cry even when they don't understand my words', she said. During these years she helped launch the career of Charles Aznavour, who had become her assistant, confidant and chauffeur. But this, too, brought its problems when she was injured in a car he was driving, breaking her arm and two ribs. She also became increasingly dependent on morphine and alcohol.

Piaf married twice, in 1952 to singer Jacques Pills for four years and in October 1962 when, worn out and sick at age 46, she wed Théo Sarapo, a hairdresser-turned-singer twenty years her junior.

Despite her chaotic love life, Piaf gave a number of sell-out concerts at the Paris Olympia, where in 1961 she debuted her most famous ballad, '*Non, je ne regrette rien*'. Few realised that she was in severe arthritic pain and could sing only thanks to a heavy dose of morphine.

At the beginning of 1963 Piaf recorded her last song, '*L'Homme de Berlin*'. Worn out by excesses of alcohol and morphine and the sufferings of a lifetime, she died at one o'clock this afternoon in Plascassier, just outside Grasse in the south of France. Her last words were a bitter: 'Every damn thing you do in this life, you have to pay for.'

On hearing the news, her old friend Jean Cocteau remarked: 'I have never known anyone to be less thrifty with her soul. She did not spend it, she lavished it, she threw gold through the windows.' Cocteau died the very next day.

1980 Prime Minister Margaret Thatcher reacts to doubt over her economic policies at a Conservative Party conference: 'To those waiting with bated breath for that favourite media catchphrase, the U-turn, I have only one thing to say: You turn if you want to. The lady's not for turning.'

11 October

'They can kill the body but they cannot kill the soul.'

1531 The Swiss pastor Huldrych Zwingli was ready to fight for his beliefs – and he had plenty of them.

He taught that priests should marry (and did so himself) – that churches should have no pictures, stained glass or sculpture – that monasteries should be transformed into hospitals – that dead saints cannot intercede for the living – that there is no Purgatory – that mendicant orders like the Franciscans should be abolished to give money to the poor – that unbaptised children are not damned – that bread and wine are not changed into the body and blood of Christ – that Christ alone, not the Pope, is at the head of the Church – and that fasting is not necessary during Lent, a point he dramatised in the famous *Wurstessen* (Affair of the Sausages) in 1522 when he and a dozen followers distributed smoked sausages to parishioners on the first fasting Sunday before Easter, a protest so famous that it is considered the start of the Reformation in Switzerland.

Born on 1 January 1484 in St Gallen, Zwingli became a Catholic priest at twenty, and before he was 30 was acting as chaplain to a group of Swiss mercenary soldiers. He fought for the winners against the French in the battle of Novara in 1513 and was on the losing side at Marignano against France's François I. But by now his firm Catholicism was mutating into fervent Protestantism.

When he was 34 he moved to Zürich, where a year later he nearly died of plague. Here his preaching – now strongly Protestant – was welcome, although he made an enemy of Martin Luther by his denial of transubstantiation and another of Erasmus by his rejection of Catholicism.

Zwingli's brand of Protestantism now dominated Zürich to such a degree that in 1529 five Catholic member states of the Swiss confederacy allied themselves with Austria to stop its spread in Switzerland. That same year there was a minor confrontation at Kappel on the border between the cantons of Zürich and Zug.

Two years later, however, the Catholic states felt so threatened by Zürich's (and Zwingli's) militant Protestantism that they again resorted to force of arms. On this day, once more at Kappel, their 7,000-man army met 2,000 hastily raised troops from Zürich, led by the redoubtable Zwingli. After brief resistance, the Protestants broke and fled, leaving 500 dead. Seriously wounded during the mêlée, Zwingli professed his faith with the stoic remark: 'What does it matter? They can kill the body but they cannot kill the soul.' A few minutes later he was dead. Catholic soldiers scooped up his corpse and burned it as a heretic.

On hearing of his death, arch-Protestant Luther concluded: 'It was a judgement of God. That was always a proud people. The others, the papists, will probably also be dealt with by our Lord God.' Catholic Erasmus agreed: 'We are freed from great fear by [his] death ... This is the wonderful hand of God on high.'

1963 French artistic polymath Jean Cocteau dies at 74; among his last words: 'Since the day of my birth, my death began its walk. It is walking towards me, without hurrying.'

---

12 October

'It is well that war is so terrible, otherwise
we should grow too fond of it.'

1870 Two weeks after suffering a stroke, today Robert E. Lee died of pneumonia in Lexington, Virginia. He was the great Confederate general who – almost – brought the North to its knees during the American Civil War. His last words were the perfect parting line for an expiring general: 'Strike the tent!'

Born in 1807, Lee went to West Point (where he later became commandant) and distinguished himself during the Mexican War. Although an honourable and thoughtful southern gentleman, he was ambivalent about slavery. Before the Civil War he wrote to his wife: 'slavery as an institution, is a moral & political evil in any Country ... I think it however a greater evil to the white man than to the black race ... The blacks are immeasurably better off here than in Africa, morally, socially & physically.' He owned slaves, energetically pursued runaways and is believed to have had some of them whipped.

Such was Lee's reputation as a soldier and a man that days before the war started he was offered a role as commander of Washington's defences. But rather than serving the nation to which he had sworn his loyalty, he resigned his commission and replied: 'I look upon secession as anarchy. If I owned the four millions of slaves in the South, I would sacrifice them all to the Union; but how can I draw my sword upon Virginia, my native State?'

After a year as an advisor to Confederate president Jefferson Davis, Lee took command of the Army of Northern Virginia. Although defeated in his first battle, over the next three years, through his brilliant tactics and leadership, he lost only four battles of the fifteen in which he fought, almost always commanding a smaller army than his opponents. While scoring a massive victory at Fredericksburg he remarked to his subordinate General Longstreet: 'It is well that war is so terrible, otherwise we should grow too fond of it.'

Twice Lee led armies into northern territory, believing that seeing the depredations of war on their own land would force the Northerners into a negotiated peace, but each time he was defeated, first at Antietam, the bloodiest single-day battle in American history, with a combined tally of 22,717 casualties, and later at Gettysburg, where Lee ordered 'Pickett's Charge', a massive frontal assault that resulted in the loss of 6,500 Confederates. Gettysburg's total losses over three days – almost 50,000 – were the largest of the war. It was in effect the South's death knell, although the war continued for another twenty months before Lee's (and the South's) final surrender at Appomattox.

After the war Lee became president of a small university in Virginia, which he vastly improved and enlarged. (After his death it changed its name to Washington and Lee College to honour him and that other great Virginian, George Washington.) He stoutly defended his primary adversary of the war, Union general Ulysses S. Grant. When a faculty member spoke insultingly of Grant, Lee rounded on him: 'Sir, if you ever presume again to speak disrespectfully of General Grant in my presence, either you or I will sever his connection with this university.'

Lee was resolute in making the nation whole again in the aftermath of the war, advising one Confederate war widow: 'Don't bring up your sons to detest the United States government. Recollect that we form one country now. Abandon all these local animosities, and make your sons Americans.'

Over time Lee became a heroic symbol of the defeated Confederacy, a dignified and stoic figure lionised by North and South alike. Few remember that he failed at most of his objectives – to prevent secession of the South, to defeat the North, to protect his native Virginia and to retain slavery until it gradually faded away.

For 30 years before the Civil War, Lee had lived in a beautiful pillared mansion in Arlington, Virginia, which sits just across the Potomac two miles from the White House. Seized by the Union during the war, his estate is now the Arlington National Cemetery for prominent members of the armed services.

1492 After two months and eight days of sailing, Christopher Columbus logs: 'At two hours after midnight appeared the land at a distance of two leagues.' He has discovered the New World. * **1915** Charged with helping 200 British and French prisoners of war and Belgian civilians to escape to neutral Holland, English nurse Edith Cavell is executed by a German firing squad in Brussels the day after she resolved: 'Patriotism is not enough. I must have no hatred or bitterness towards anyone.'

---

13 October

'Soldiers! Do your duty! Straight to the heart but spare the face. Fire!'

1815 With these words, today the Napoleonic marshal Joachim Murat gave his last order – to the firing squad facing him.

Murat was a courageous and charismatic cavalry officer, but vain and impetuous and an irresponsible risk-taker. As Napoleon mused in exile: 'I loved Murat because of his brilliant bravery, that's why I forgave him so much nonsense.'

Intended for the church, when he was nineteen a regiment of cavalry passed near his seminary and he ran away and enlisted. Three years later he first met Napoleon, then an obscure general trying to restrain violent mobs in revolutionary Paris. After Murat led his cavalry to chase away the crowd, he was made *chef de brigade* (colonel).

During Bonaparte's Italian campaign of 1796, Murat's daring charges earned him promotion to general. Then, at Abukir in Egypt, he led the attack that scattered the Turks, personally galloping behind the Ottoman line and plunging into the commander's tent. The Turk got off a pistol shot, wounding him in the jaw, but Murat dashed the pistol from his hand with his sabre, slicing off two of his fingers, and captured him.

When Bonaparte failed to persuade the government to make him consul during the coup d'état of 18 Brumaire (9 November 1799), Murat stormed into the council chamber with 60 grenadiers, forcing its members to flee through the windows.

In 1800 Murat's meteoric rise was given an extra boost when he married Napoleon's sister, Caroline. After playing an important role at

Marengo, on the day that Napoleon became emperor he was made a Marshal of France, with the title of 'First Horseman of Europe'.

Except for Waterloo, Murat fought in almost all of Napoleon's major battles, including Austerlitz, Ulm, Jena and Eylau, in which he attacked with 12,000 horse and saved the beleaguered French army with one of history's greatest cavalry charges.

In 1808 Murat was in charge of French-occupied Madrid when the *Dos de Mayo* uprising exploded. He ruthlessly crushed the insurgents, killing several hundred and executing 100 more.

Napoleon then named his dashing brother-in-law King of Naples and Sicily, but, lest anyone doubt who was really in charge, the emperor told him: 'I made you king that you should reign in my way, but not in yours.'

Murat remained loyal to his master, joining Napoleon's invasion of Russia and his catastrophic defeat at Leipzig in 1813. But It was now clear that Napoleon's days were numbered (he abdicated 174 days later), and Murat signed an alliance with Austria in a bid to save his throne. Napoleon scathingly called it 'Murat's betrayal'.

Murat changed sides again when the emperor escaped from Elba. He declared war on Austria, making the Allied powers determined to return his kingdom to its pre-Napoleonic ruler, King Ferdinand. He offered to join Napoleon during the Hundred Days, but the emperor spurned him, a decision he may have bitterly regretted at Waterloo when one of Murat's heroic cavalry charges might have won the battle.

In May 1815 an Austrian army encircled Murat's at a village near Assisi. After two days of fighting, Murat fell back on Naples, whence he fled to Corsica disguised as a Danish sailor. Dreaming of reconquering his kingdom, he sailed to the little Calabrian port of Pizzo, but instead of welcoming him, the hostile crowd took him prisoner and locked him up in the port's castle.

Certain of his fate, Murat refused to attend his court martial. Without waiting for a verdict, King Ferdinand decreed: 'The condemned man will be given only a half hour to receive the support of his religion.'

Murat walked with a firm step to the castle's courtyard, where the firing squad waited, as calm and unmoved as if he had been going to a military review. 'I have braved death too often to fear it', he said, refusing a chair or a blindfold. Standing facing his executioners, he kissed a cameo engraved with his wife's portrait and, vain to the end, ordered: 'Soldiers! Do your duty! Straight to the heart but spare the face. Fire!'

Murat's body was pitched into a common grave, a tawdry end for a man whom the French called 'The king of the brave and the bravest of kings'.

1307 Philip (IV) the Fair of France orders the arrest of the Templars; the arrest warrant starts: 'God is not pleased. We have enemies of the faith in the kingdom.' * **1660** Major General Thomas Harrison, who had signed the death warrant for Charles I, is executed for regicide. Samuel Pepys records in his diary: 'I went out to Charing Cross, to see Major-general Harrison hanged, drawn, and quartered; which was done there, he looking as cheerful as any man could do in that condition.'

---

14 October

*'We're eyeball to eyeball, and I think
the other fellow just blinked.'*

1962 This Sunday morning American Air Force major Richard Heyser climbed to 72,500 feet in his U-2 spy plane and headed for Cuba. He flew over the island for a mere seven minutes, as his cameras rolled, and then returned to base in Florida. His film was rushed to Washington, where intelligence experts made an alarming discovery: a Soviet SS-4 ballistic missile was being assembled for installation. With a range of 1,300 miles, such a missile could strike as far north as the American capitol. So began the Cuban Missile Crisis.

Since first taking power in Cuba in 1959, Fidel Castro had been ranting against the United States, cosying up to the Soviet Union and attempting to export communist revolution throughout Latin America. Then on 17 April 1961 American president Jack Kennedy launched the disastrous Bay of Pigs invasion that failed to dislodge Castro but outraged the Soviet Union. In that same year the US placed Jupiter missiles in Turkey, well within range of Moscow.

In May 1962 Soviet supremo Nikita Khrushchev started secretly deploying nuclear missiles in Cuba. Russian technicians disguised as 'agricultural specialists' prepared launch sites, and missiles were unloaded from Soviet cargo ships under cover of darkness, to be camouflaged by palm trees. Khrushchev believed that Kennedy had been so shaken by the Bay of Pigs fiasco that, once the missiles were in place, he would shy away from confrontation and accept them as a *fait accompli*.

But now, alerted by the spy plane's photos, America's top leaders huddled in Washington. They considered bombing the sites, and the Joint Chiefs of Staff unanimously recommended a full-scale invasion, but Kennedy faced a dilemma – if he authorised an attack, it might trigger a nuclear war, but if he did nothing, the US would be threatened by nuclear weapons only 90 miles from the Florida coast.

First, on 22 October Kennedy ordered a 'quarantine' around Cuba to prevent the Soviets from delivering more missiles. The initial ring of ships included an aircraft carrier, twelve destroyers and an anti-submarine group. Anti-submarine squadrons flying from Bermuda and Puerto Rico were also deployed.

Then, at seven o'clock that evening he sombrely spoke to the nation on television. After condemning the secret Soviet build-up, he proclaimed the quarantine and delivered an ultimatum that the Soviets remove the missiles.

The next day, however, American planes reported that 27 Soviet ships were still headed towards Cuba, some carrying crates containing more missiles. If the Soviets tried to breach the blockade, it could spark a showdown that could quickly escalate to a nuclear exchange.

But at 10.25 on the morning of 24 October, while the National Security Council were grouped to study new photos, a staffer delivered a note – the Soviet ships had stopped dead in the water and were turning back. 'We're eyeball to eyeball', exulted Secretary of State Dean Rusk, 'and I think the other fellow just blinked.'

Despite Rusk's optimism, however, the crisis was not over. Although no new missiles were arriving in to Cuba, work was continuing on the missiles already there, and Khrushchev remained belligerent. On 26 October, for the only time in history, nuclear-armed B-52 bombers went on continuous airborne alert, and 145 intercontinental ballistic missiles were readied for blast-off. Meanwhile, unknown to Washington, Castro was urging Khrushchev to launch a pre-emptive nuclear strike if the US invaded.

The next day the world came closer to nuclear Armageddon than at any other moment in history. Cornered by US destroyers at the blockade line, a Soviet submarine failed to fire a nuclear torpedo only because one of the three officers aboard refused to agree.

But on 28 October the Cuban crisis was finally defused by a more conciliatory Khrushchev, who offered to remove the missiles from Cuba if the US promised not to invade. Kennedy agreed and also secretly committed to eliminate American missiles from Turkey.

As a result of the crisis, a telephone 'hotline' was established between the White House and the Kremlin, and, having come within a whisker of nuclear war, the two superpowers also took the first steps towards a nuclear Test Ban Treaty, which was signed in August 1963.

1787 In a letter to writer Hannah More, English man of letters Horace Walpole displays an English prejudice still alive today: 'I do not dislike the French from the vulgar antipathy between neighbouring nations, but for their insolent and unfounded airs of superiority.' * **1944** After forcing German field marshal Erwin Rommel to commit suicide because of his knowledge of the von Stauffenberg plot, Hitler writes to Rommel's wife: 'Accept my sincerest sympathy for the heavy loss you have suffered with the death of your husband.'

---

15 October

'Do not be afraid, sister. I know how to die.'

1917 Today one of history's most famous spies was shot by firing squad. She was Mata Hari, now 41, a fading courtesan who had found fame but not fortune as an exotic dancer.

Mata Hari was born Margaretha Zelle, a dark-haired, olive-skinned Dutch girl who moved to Java with her dissolute husband, whose beatings and philandering eventually drove her to divorce.

She relocated to Paris and invented a mysterious new identity, claiming that she came from India, daughter of a temple dancer, and had been raised in the service of the god Shiva. Calling herself Mata Hari, she landed a role at the Guimet cabaret and found instant notoriety through her risqué routine. According to the writer Colette, 'She could undress gradually and move a long tawny body, slim and proud'. Shortly she was triumphantly touring Europe, titillating audiences and taking lovers along the way.

By the time she was in her late thirties, Mata Hari's body was thickening with age, and she progressively earned her keep as a *demimondaine*, with dozens of rich partners, including a Rothschild baron and Giacomo Puccini. Now, on the eve of the First World War, she began her career as a spy.

The extent of Mata Hari's espionage remains murky. She was enlisted by the Deuxième Bureau (French military intelligence) to seduce

German officers to learn their secrets, but the French intercepted a coded German message referring to her as 'agent H 21' and believed she had become a double agent. A squad of soldiers was sent to her hotel to arrest her; she emerged naked from the bathroom and, having dressed, offered them chocolates before being led away.

In April 1917 France was badly shaken by army mutinies, and the government desperately needed a distraction, so Mata Hari was prosecuted as 'the greatest woman spy of the century' who had caused the death of 'at least 50,000 soldiers'. She was convicted in a travesty of justice that was held *in camera*, during which the defence could not cross-examine witnesses. The jury of six French officers predictably condemned her to death.

At daybreak today Mata Hari was driven to the Caserne de Vincennes outside Paris. There in an internal courtyard twelve Zouaves stood preparing to fire.

Mata Hari met her fate bravely, telling an attendant nun: 'Do not be afraid, sister. I know how to die … Death is nothing, nor life either, for that matter. To die, to sleep, to pass into nothingness, what does it matter? Everything is an illusion.' Refusing a blindfold and unbound, she stood facing the firing squad and blew them a kiss just before the fusillade ended her life.

According to eyewitness reporter Henry Wales:

She did not move a muscle.

[The officer's] sword was extended in the air. It dropped. The sun – by this time up – flashed on the burnished blade as it described an arc in falling. Simultaneously the sound of the volley rang out. Flame and a tiny puff of greyish smoke issued from the muzzle of each rifle …

At the report Mata Hari fell. She did not die as actors and moving picture stars would have us believe that people die when they are shot. She did not throw up her hands nor did she plunge straight forward or straight back.

Instead she seemed to collapse. Slowly, inertly, she settled to her knees, her head up always, and without the slightest change of expression on her face. For the fraction of a second it seemed she tottered there, on her knees, gazing directly at those who had taken her life. Then she fell backward, bending at the waist, with her legs doubled up beneath her. She lay prone, motionless, with her face turned towards the sky.

A non-commissioned officer … drew his revolver from the big, black holster strapped about his waist. Bending over, he placed the muzzle of the revolver almost – but not quite – against the left temple of the spy. He pulled the trigger …

Such was the end of the famed Mata Hari, whose body was given to a French medical school so that student doctors could practise their dissecting skills.

---

202 BC Prior to his victory at the Battle of Zama, Scipio tells Hannibal when they meet briefly before the battle: '*Bellum parate, quoniam pacem pati non potuistis.*' ('Prepare for war, since you have found peace intolerable.') *
1888 Mark Twain in a letter to George Bainton: 'The difference between the almost right word and the right word is really a large matter – 'tis the difference between the lightning-bug and the lightning.'

---

16 October

'We shall this day light such a candle by God's grace in England, as I trust shall never be put out.'

1555 Today in Oxford two bishops were burnt at the stake for clinging to their Protestant beliefs in the face of implacable Catholicism. But behind the religious condemnation lurked the fanatical queen, Bloody Mary Tudor, taking her revenge.

Hugh Latimer and Nicholas Ridley had supported the English Reformation and Archbishop of Canterbury Thomas Cranmer in his efforts to modernise the Church. Latimer had risen to become Bishop of Worcester and Ridley Bishop of London.

But while Latimer and Ridley were ascending the Church hierarchy, they also strongly backed Henry VIII's break with Rome – and the fracturing of the king's family life that had triggered it. Latimer first rose to prominence in 1533 by championing Henry's attempts to annul his marriage to Catherine of Aragon, Bloody Mary's mother.

Twenty years later, on the death of Henry's son Edward VI, Ridley mortally offended Mary by signing the letters patent that gave the English throne to Lady Jane Grey, and three days later he told his congregation in St Paul's that both of Henry VIII's daughters, Mary and Elizabeth, were bastards. Lady Jane was officially proclaimed Queen of England – only for the Privy Council to change its allegiance nine days later, affirming Mary as queen.

Bloody Mary's vengeance was immediate; Cranmer was charged with treason and condemned to death, and within two months Lady Jane Grey, her father and husband had all been executed. Then the zealously Catholic queen turned her attention to Church reformers, most specifically Latimer and Ridley.

In March 1554 Cranmer, Ridley, and Latimer were locked up in Bocardo Prison in Oxford. In April, when the two bishops were tried for heresy, the trial focused on the minutiae of the Roman Catholic faith versus Protestantism. Latimer, who was in his late sixties, was too frail to answer vigorously, so he wrote down many of his replies, suggesting that Catholic doctrines such as transubstantiation were nowhere found in the Bible.

The younger Ridley was more defiant; he refused to remove his cap when he heard the words 'the cardinal's grace', and 'the Pope's holiness', and said he could not honour the Pope since the papacy was seeking its own glory, not the glory of God. After both men refused to recant such heresies, they were condemned to death by fire.

On this day the two bishops were brought to the place of execution just outside Oxford's city walls and were chained back to back to the stake. Ridley's brother had brought some gunpowder, to tie around the bishop's neck to bring his death more quickly.

As the executioner brought his torch to the pyre, Latimer encouraged Ridley with the famous words: 'Be of good comfort, Mr Ridley, and play the man! We shall this day light such a candle by God's grace in England, as I trust shall never be put out.'

As the fire rose, Latimer leaned towards the flame as if embracing it; and after he had stroked his face with his hands, he sank down, and soon died, as it appeared, with very little pain.

Ridley was not so lucky. The wood on his side of the pyre was green and burned low, so that only his lower body was in the flame. He cried with pain: 'Lord have mercy upon me! I cannot burn ... Let the fire come unto me, I cannot burn.' Trying to shorten his agony, Ridley's brother-in-law heaped more logs on the fire, but these only choked off the flame. Eventually one of the guards pulled away some of the faggots with a pike staff. When Ridley saw the fire flame up, he leaned towards it, touching off the gunpowder.

Thomas Cranmer had been forced to witness this barbarous execution. In December Pope Paul IV gave permission to the secular authorities to carry out their sentence, and Cranmer was burned on 21 March 1556 on the same spot where Latimer and Ridley had been burnt five months before.

1793 When a priest at the foot of the scaffold whispers to Marie Antoinette, 'Courage, madame! Now is the time for courage', she responds: 'Courage! The moment when my troubles are going to end is not the moment when courage is going to fail me.'

---

17 October

'I will return and I will be millions.'

1945 Juan Perón had been riding high. Now 50 and a colonel in the Argentine army, he had played a key role in the officers' coup of 1943 and had become Labour Minister, improving working conditions and establishing a strong alliance with the country's trade unions. Then on 15 January 1944 a massive earthquake struck San Juan Province, and Perón mounted a highly successful relief and reconstruction pro-gramme that transformed him into one of the most prominent men in the country. Then, at a charity ball in aid of earthquake victims, he met a glamorous 24-year-old blonde dancer, radio personality and *demi-mondaine* named Eva Duarte with an adventurous past (one of her lovers had been the notorious playboy Porfirio Rubirosa). He bedded her the same evening, establishing a relationship that would transform Argentinian politics.

But by mid-1945 Perón had become too successful. Six foot tall, a crack skier, boxer and fencer, he looked too much like a president in waiting. After he made a stirring speech on 18 September, rival army and navy officers arrested and imprisoned him.

Immediately his paramour Eva Duarte – known as Evita – took to the airwaves to defend him and, working with the labour unions, brought out 2 million people in protest. Today he was released. This evening, with Evita at his side, he addressed a crowd of 300,000 cheer-ing supporters from the balcony of the presidential palace, promising to lead them to victory in the upcoming presidential election. Five days later he married Evita.

As promised, Perón swept the election, helped by Evita's appeal to the masses on her radio show, and took office on 4 June 1946.

Perón established an anti-American, populist government, nationalising the central bank, public transport, utilities and universities in a frenzy of right-wing socialism aimed at helping the working class. He also helped himself and his cronies by taking bribes on public contracts.

Meanwhile Evita was laying the groundwork for her reputation as secular saint. As the impoverished illegitimate daughter of a cook and a married landowner, she was snubbed by the conservative Sociedad de Beneficencia not only for her illegitimacy but also for her rise as a courtesan. In response, she set up the Fundación Eva Perón that eventually employed 14,000 workers, awarded scholarships, built houses and hospitals and gave away millions of sewing machines, cooking pots and pairs of shoes.

Evita never held a government post, but in her charitable work she was dedicated and sincere, sometimes working twenty-hour days. She often met with the poor, sometimes kissing them and touching the wounds of the sick. She also used her radio show to support women's suffrage, which was written into law in September 1947. Although her deep concern for the working class was genuine, she was also acutely conscious of her image. When *Time* put her on its cover in 1947, it became the first publication to mention that she had been born out of wedlock. In retaliation, she had the magazine briefly banned from Argentina.

Perón was easily re-elected in 1951, but by then Evita was dying of cancer of the uterus. On 4 June the next year she rode with him in a victory parade through Buenos Aires but was so weak and in such pain that she had to be supported by a frame hidden beneath her coat. A few days later she was given the title of Jefa Espiritual de la Nación (Spiritual Leader of the Nation).

Evita's death on 26 July 1952 released an explosion of grief, and nearly 3 million people came to her funeral. On her tombstone are the words embodying her populist vision and faith: '*Volvere y seré milliones* ...!' ('I will return and I will be millions ...!')

After taking a thirteen-year-old mistress (he was 59), in 1955 Juan Perón was overthrown by a cabal of generals and fled abroad. While in exile in Madrid he married another dancer, this one 35 years his junior, and returned to Argentina in 1973, to be elected president for the third time, with his wife Isabel as vice president. He died in office in 1974 at the age of 78.

1346 Just before joining battle against the English at Neville's Cross, King David II of Scotland tells his lieutenants: 'In England are no men of war, but mere clerks … we shall take all these Englishmen as the fowler taketh fowls with his birdlime.' The battle ends with the Scots routed, David captured and most of his lieutenants dead.

18 October

'From the sublime to the ridiculous is only a step.'

1812 Today Napoleon's Grande Armée trooped out of Moscow to begin the most famous retreat in history.

Thirteen years earlier Napoleon had become First Consul, and then in 1804 Emperor of the French. By 1811 he dominated all of continental Europe, from Spain to Poland, from Denmark to Italy, all either parts of his empire, satellite countries or allied states. Now, in 1812, he was intent on taming Russia as well.

On 24 June Napoleon had crossed the Niemen River with over 400,000 men to begin his calamitous invasion. His intent was to annihilate the Russian army, but the wily Russian commander, Field Marshal Mikhail Kutuzov, had continuously avoided battle, preferring to chip away at the invaders through small, guerrilla-type raids.

For two long months the French plodded across 500 miles of empty and desolate Russian countryside, laid waste by Russian peasants before they abandoned it. Finally, on 7 September, the two armies clashed 80 miles west of Moscow at Borodino, where each side suffered 40,000 casualties but neither could claim victory. At the close of the battle Kutuzov's generals urged him to launch another attack, hoping to finish Napoleon off, but the field marshal knew that Russia's great hope was attrition: 'Napoleon is a torrent which as yet we are unable to stem. Moscow will be the sponge that will suck him dry.'

On 14 September the French army at last reached the Russian capital, but Moscow was ominously quiet. Only 15,000 of its quarter of a million inhabitants remained, mostly foreigners, vagabonds and criminals. The rest had deserted the city on orders from its governor.

Then came the fires, deliberately set by the Russians, which razed four-fifths of Moscow. No word came from Tsar Alexander I, no surrender, no discussion of terms. Each day food became scarcer; each day there was less left to burn to fight the cold.

Recognising that his plight was becoming desperate, Napoleon appealed to Alexander for a truce, but the tsar refused even to answer, later writing to an ally: 'We would rather be buried beneath the ruins of the empire than make terms with the modern Attila.' Finally, Napoleon understood that his only hope was withdrawal, and he gave the order to abandon the city.

Now the Grande Armée tramped 600 miles in retreat, numbed with fatigue and frozen by the terrible Russian winter, with regular frosts of −25° centigrade. It was encumbered with sick and wounded soldiers, overburdened with artillery and loot, its ragged columns stretching out over 50 miles in length, with thousands of stragglers and camp followers in its wake. Never far away was the enemy in pursuit: a Russian corps menaced the army's northern flank, while the main Russian army – 65,000 troops under Kutuzov's command – dogged close behind. On all sides, Cossacks and armed peasants waited out of musket range for any opportunity to harass the vulnerable columns. As described by future American president John Quincy Adams, who was in Moscow as his country's ambassador: 'The invader himself was a wretched fugitive and his numberless host was perishing by frosts, famine, and the sword.'

On 5 December the emperor left his soldiers to return to Paris to block an attempted coup d'état. The surviving elements of his command continued their slogging retreat, the numbers of effectives declining each day, as the numbers of stragglers behind them increased. When they passed out of Russia into Poland on the 14th, there were fewer than 12,000 soldiers marching with the colours. When Napoleon heard the calamitous news, he could only repeat his now famous observation: 'From the sublime to the ridiculous is only a step.' ('*Du sublime au ridicule il n'y a qu'un pas.*') The days of the empire were numbered.

1685 Louis XIV revokes the Edict of Nantes that gave freedom of religion in France: 'We have judged that we could do nothing better than to erase the entire memory of disorder, confusion and pain that following this false religion has caused in our kingdom … and fully revoke the Edict of Nantes.' * **1865** One tale has Prime Minister Lord Palmerston dying two days before his 81st birthday as he rogers a housemaid on a billiard table. Equally apocryphal, as he is dying at Brocket Hall, his doctor tells him to prepare himself for death, to which he answers: 'Die, my dear doctor, that's the last thing I shall do!'

19 October

'The Colossus fell like an oak tree in a storm.'

1813 Today, after three days of bitter fighting, Emperor Napoleon was forced to withdraw from the Battle of Leipzig, the bloodiest battle in Europe until the First World War. With only 198,000 men, Napoleon had confronted 370,000 troops from Russia, Prussia, Austria and Sweden.

The battle had all-star casting. Napoleon's marshals Oudinot, Ney, Marmont, MacDonald, Poniatowski, and Augereau led the main bodies of troops while Joachim Murat commanded the cavalry. The enemy coalition was headed by Russian Tsar Alexander I. Field Marshal Karl von Schwarzenberg commanded the Austrian contingent and Napoleon's future nemesis at Waterloo, Gebhard von Blücher, led the Prussians. Heading the Swedish army was Crown Prince Charles-John, who three years earlier had been a Napoleonic marshal named Jean Bernadotte.

During the past dozen years Napoleon had conquered one European nation after another, but in 1812, a year before Leipzig, the flower of his Grande Armée had perished in the snowy wastes of Russia. The emperor himself had barely escaped. He reached Paris before news of the Russian catastrophe, and immediately put together a new army, composed mostly of unblooded but enthusiastic conscripts with a leavening of veterans from Spain. But his foes were now working for his final destruction.

Napoleon's aim was to defeat his enemies piecemeal, before they had time to combine their forces. During the spring and summer of 1813, he and his marshals engaged the Allies in half a dozen battles, losing only two small ones when Napoleon himself was absent. In late August the emperor triumphed at Dresden, inflicting 38,000 casualties against 10,000 of his own, but none of these battles achieved his overreaching objective, to drive the enemy nations apart and out of the war.

Then came Leipzig. After two days of bitter but even conflict, on 18 October the Allies attacked with more than 300,000 men. After nine hours of assaults, the French were pushed back into the city's suburbs. At two o'clock this morning Napoleon ordered a retreat westward over the single bridge across the Elster River, with Oudinot's corps still in Leipzig to protect his rear. All went well until a frightened corporal blew up the bridge in the afternoon while it was still crowded with retreating French troops. The explosion and subsequent panic caused a rout that resulted in the deaths of thousands and the capture of tens of thousands more, including the 30,000 rear guard and injured soldiers trapped in Leipzig, who were taken prisoner the next day.

In all, Napoleon lost 73,000 men, reducing his force to just over 100,000, too small to challenge his enemies. Since he had been appointed commander-in-chief seventeen years before, Leipzig was the first battle in which he was defeated in the field. (His loss at Aspern-Essling in 1809 had really been a stalemate, and six weeks later he had destroyed his enemy at Wagram.) Even his colossal reversal in Russia owed more to freezing weather and vast distances than it did to Russian military intervention.

From Leipzig Napoleon retreated to Paris and, despite the odds, in January he took to the battlefield once again, in one last glorious roll of the dice to keep his throne. He fought eleven pitched battles in just 50 days, but despite his tactical genius – and the stoic heroism of the French troops – he had no real hope of stopping the coalition. On 30 March the Allies entered Paris, and, after having been deposed by the French Senate, on 11 April Napoleon finally abdicated as his generals demanded. As the great Prussian general Blücher remarked: 'The Colossus fell like an oak tree in a storm.'

1216 King John of England dies of dysentery at the Abbey of Swineshead. The contemporary chronicler Roger of Wendover writes that he was ill from having lost his treasure in the Wash and 'surfeited himself with peaches and drinking new cider, which greatly increased and aggravated the fever'.

---

20 October

'Is it a book that you would even wish your wife or your servants to read?'

1960 Today at the Old Bailey in London, an eminent publishing house was put on trial for publishing a book written 32 years earlier by an author now dead for three decades.

Two months before, Penguin Books had issued the first unexpurgated English edition of *Lady Chatterley's Lover* by D.H. Lawrence. Previously, Lawrence had published the full text only privately in Italy and in a paperback edition in Paris. But in 1959 the US Court of Appeals had overturned a ban on the book, judging it of 'redeeming social or literary value', and now it was to be tested in Britain under the 1959 Obscene Publications Act.

Lady Chatterley's Lover tells the story of a young married woman, Constance (Lady Chatterley), whose cold, upper-class husband Clifford has been paralysed from the waist down by a war injury. Frustrated physically and emotionally, she embarks on a passionate affair with the gamekeeper.

The prosecution was headed by Mervyn Griffith-Jones, an Eton- and Cambridge-educated barrister who, according to legend, when asked how he knew when legal action should be taken over an obscene book, replied: 'If I get an erection, we prosecute.' *The Guardian* described him as 'the incarnation of upper-middle-class morality, obsessed with the book's danger to the social order'. He believed that *Lady Chatterley's Lover* glorified adultery and was obscene in its graphic descriptions and indecent language. His outrage was heightened by the plot featuring an upper-class woman having an affair with a working-class man. The Penguin edition was particularly dangerous: an inexpensive paperback, it was within easy reach of the working classes – and Penguin had printed 200,000 copies.

Griffith-Jones first focused on Lawrence's use of Anglo-Saxon expletives, but his most heartfelt attack was against the explicit sexual descriptions and the adultery – with a servant. With the patronising class consciousness inherent in the British establishment, he said: 'Would you approve of your young sons, young daughters – because girls can read as well as boys – reading this book? Is it a book that you would have lying around in your own house? Is it a book that you would even wish your wife or your servants to read?'

Penguin's defence was led by Gerald Gardiner, ably supported by Michael Rubinstein. Old Bailey juries then were composed solely of property owners, i.e. middle-class folk likely to uphold the status quo. The law permitted the defence to select an entirely male jury, lest the obscene details prove too shocking for frail and innocent females, but Gardiner not only agreed to have two female jurors but also used his right of challenge to add a third one, reasoning that the prosecution's condescension might offend female jurors, to the benefit of the defence.

Michael Rubinstein recruited 35 expert defence witnesses, including E.M. Forster and Rebecca West, Cecil Day-Lewis and John Robinson, Bishop of Woolwich. The bishop testified: 'Archbishop [of Canterbury] William Temple once said that Christians do not make jokes about sex for the same reason that they do not make jokes about

Holy Communion – not because it is dirty, but because it is sacred …
[Lawrence] was always straining to portray it as something sacred, in a
real sense as an act of Holy Communion.'

Gardiner suggested to the jury that they (and not the arch-
conservative judge) were best fit to reach the proper verdict. In his
closing address he gently chided Griffith-Jones: 'I do not want to upset
the prosecution by suggesting that there are a certain number of people
nowadays who as a matter of fact don't have servants …'

Most importantly, Gardiner hammered home the basic principle of
the Obscene Publications Act, that a book had to be 'taken as a whole'
and should not be judged obscene if its publication 'is justified in the
interests of science, literature, art and learning'.

After three hours of deliberation, on 2 November the jury unanimously acquitted Penguin Books of all charges.

The trial's result set off an orgy of sales that would have pleased (and
enriched) D.H. Lawrence. Two million copies were sold in the last two
months of 1960 and a further 1.3 million the next year.

1930 Winston Churchill publishes *My Early Life*, in which he writes: 'It is
a good thing for an uneducated man to read books of quotations.'

---

21 October

*'The angel of death has been abroad throughout the
land; you may almost hear the beating of his wings.'*

1854 Today 38 nurses headed off to war. At their head was a 34-year-
old woman from a wealthy British family who at sixteen thought she
had heard God's voice telling her she had a serious mission in life and
so became a nurse, no fit occupation at the time for someone of her
station. She was Florence Nightingale.

In May 1853 Tsar Nicholas I had invaded the Danubian principalities (now in Romania) of the Ottoman Empire with an army of
80,000. His putative purpose was to protect the Orthodox Christian
populations, but to others it looked like a land grab. France, Austria
and Great Britain protested loudly, and by September crowds were
rioting in Constantinople. On 4 October the Turks declared war, and
in March 1854 Britain and France threw their lot in with the Turks.
The Crimean War was now in full swing.

An expeditionary force of French, British, and Turkish troops landed in the Crimea on 14 September. Six days later they clashed with the Russians at Alma, where the allies prevailed but took 4,000 casualties, half of them British. But the British had a woeful shortage of medical supplies and took two days to take the wounded from the battlefield, trundled on carts. They were ferried across the Black Sea to the British Barrack Hospital at Scutari in Constantinople, where they languished in appallingly unsanitary conditions.

Back in England the public exploded with rage about the treatment (or lack of it) of the wounded. In response, Secretary of War Sidney Herbert turned to his friend Florence Nightingale, who, as superintendent for the Hospital for Invalid Gentlewomen in London, could recruit the nurses so desperately needed.

On 5 November the nurses arrived at the British Barrack Hospital and found wounded soldiers in the hallways lying on stretchers in their own filth. Infested with rats and bugs, the hospital sat on a large cesspool, which contaminated the water. Even bandages and soap were in short supply, and far more patients were dying of disease and infection than of battle wounds.

At first both resented and ignored by male doctors, who thought a theatre of war no place for a woman, Nightingale set about tending the sick and wounded and improving the abysmal level of hygiene. She scrounged hundreds of scrubbing brushes and asked the walking wounded to scour the hospital from floor to ceiling. Among her innovations were bells for patients to summon nurses, dumb-waiters to move food up from the kitchens, and hot water piped to all floors.

Reflecting the stern morality of the day, no nurses were allowed in the wards after eight in the evening, the only exception being Nightingale herself. Every night she made her rounds carrying a lantern and chatted with the wounded, earning the nickname of 'The Lady with the Lamp'. Thanks to her tireless efforts, the hospital mortality rate was reduced by two-thirds.

Despite Nightingale's improvements, stories of death, disease and military mismanagement flooded into England. In February 1855 the Liberal MP John Bright rose in the House to denounce British participation in the war: 'The angel of death has been abroad throughout the land; you may almost hear the beating of his wings.'

But the war dragged on for another year, a nightmarish bloodbath with a quarter of a million casualties on each side. Britain suffered 2,800 killed in action, 1,800 dying of wounds and almost 18,000 dead from disease. Russia finally sued for peace, and the treaty ending the war was signed on 30 March 1856.

Florence Nightingale returned to London, still only 35, famous and widely beloved for her heroic deeds, but she refused all honours. Within three years, however, she became a bed-ridden invalid, apparently suffering from some kind of post-traumatic stress disorder. She continued to receive official visitors and to write, but as she grew older she started to lose her sight, and when she passed 80 she became completely blind. She died at 90 on 13 August 1910. Just prior to her death she had declined the offer of burial in Westminster Abbey.

1769 Voltaire in a letter to Pierre-Joseph François Luneau de Boisjermain: 'Life is bristling with thorns, and I know no other remedy than to cultivate one's garden.' * **1805** Closing with the French fleet at Trafalgar, Admiral Nelson signals to his ships: 'England expects that every man will do his duty.' * **1940** Ernest Hemingway publishes *For Whom the Bell Tolls*. Chapter 13 includes the line: 'But did thee feel the earth move?'

---

22 October

'Une foi, une loi, un roi'

1685 When the arch-Catholic duc de Guise and his men killed 30 Huguenots and wounded 100 more during a Catholic–Protestant confrontation at Vassy in 1562, it triggered the French Wars of Religion. From then on, France's Protestants suffered calamitous persecution, and both Catholics and Protestants resorted to murder and mayhem in defence of God's true faith, as they saw it. But in 1594 Henri IV became king, a nominal Protestant who outwardly turned Catholic to consolidate his power.

In 1598 Henri signed the Edict of Nantes, which gave France's 900,000 Huguenots religious freedom. The religious wars that had torn the nation apart for 36 years had come to an end at last.

Or had they? After Henri's assassination in 1610, France's Catholics once again began restricting the freedoms of the Huguenots. Then, in 1629, after several Protestant revolts, Henri's son Louis XIII issued the Edict of Grace which, while confirming the legality of the Protestants' faith, also suppressed their political rights and forced them to dismantle all 38 Huguenot-controlled fortresses. The restrictions would probably have been even heavier had not Cardinal Richelieu, who was unofficially running the country, feared offending his Protestant allies.

Richelieu's rule, however, had one pernicious effect: he moved France ever closer to absolute monarchy. And when Louis died in 1643, his four-year-old son Louis XIV inherited the throne. No one was more absolute than the Sun King.

Louis XIV resented Protestantism as a disgraceful reminder of royal weakness. He was well aware of the principle of '*Cuius regio, eius religio*', the idea that a monarch's religion should be his country's religion, a concept accepted in the Holy Roman Empire since 1555. As a king who embodied royal absolutism, Louis lived by the catchphrase coined a century earlier in the time of Catherine de' Medici, '*Une foi, une loi, un roi*' ('One faith, one law, one king').

In 1681 Louis urged all Huguenots to convert to Catholicism, but did not make Protestantism illegal. But he also introduced the *Dragonnades*, a system of terrorising recalcitrant Huguenots by billeting dragoons in their homes while exempting households that converted. The dragoons were ordered to harass and intimidate the occupants to spur their conversion.

For Protestants, the situation got even worse in 1683 when Louis married Madame de Maintenon, a pious widow of 48. She had converted from Protestantism and was under the sway of the Jesuit priest, François de la Chaise, who prodded her to prod the king to revoke the Edict of Nantes.

On this day in 1685 Louis did just that, issuing the Edict of Fontainebleau that withdrew the privileges and toleration that Huguenots had been guaranteed for the past 87 years, and made Protestantism illegal. Louis ordered the destruction of Huguenot churches and the closure of Huguenot schools, requiring children to be educated as Catholics. All who attempted to leave France would be sentenced to the galleys.

Defying royal decrees, in the years that followed about half a million Huguenots left for the more welcoming regimes in Holland, England and Prussia, where their talent, wealth and industry helped their new homelands to the detriment of France. Some 4,000 immigrated to the United States.

Under the reign of Louis' grandson, Louis XV, the law became even more repressive, but by now the general public – and even most of the clergy – were fed up with fanatical persecution of Huguenots, and the laws were increasingly ignored.

Then in 1787 Louis XVI issued the Edict of Versailles that retained Catholicism as the state religion but gave non-Catholics the right to practise their religions, as well as legal and civil status.

The relationship between State and Church see-sawed repeatedly over the next 200 years (during the French Revolution the Church was banned), but on 9 December 1905 state religion was abolished once and for all, making France a secular nation.

Finally, in October 1985 President François Mitterrand issued a fatuous public apology three centuries too late to the descendants of Huguenots around the world.

1964 French philosopher and author Jean-Paul Sartre refuses the Nobel Prize in Literature, later explaining: 'a writer who adopts political, social, or literary positions must act only with the means that are his own – that is, the written word'; and 'a writer should not allow himself to be turned into an institution.'

23 October

'They may ring their bells now, but they
will soon be wringing their hands.'

1739 Great Britain declared war against Spain today, thus launching a colonial conflict that would last nine years and become known to history as the War of Jenkins' Ear.

Back in 1713 Great Britain had signed an unedifying agreement with Spain that gave the British the right to supply the Spanish colonies in the Americas with an unlimited number of slaves, and 500 tons of goods, per year. British traders and smugglers, however, regularly exceeded the allowance on goods, so in 1729 the British had reluctantly agreed to let Spanish warships stop their trading vessels to inspect their cargo.

Two years later a Spanish captain named Julio León Fandiño carried out his inspection duties with admirable vigour but regrettable lack of restraint. Sailing off the coast of Florida, on 9 April he spied the brig *Rebecca*, which was returning to England from the West Indies. Suspecting the British of smuggling, he boarded the *Rebecca* and put the crew to torture in his search for contraband. Fandiño then had the *Rebecca's* captain Robert Jenkins bound to a mast and sliced off one of his ears with his cutlass. Fandiño told Jenkins: 'Go, and tell your king that I will do the same to him, if he is caught doing the same.'

The Spanish then released the *Rebecca*, which sailed for England, arriving at the mouth of the Thames in June. Jenkins reported this outrage to the Secretary for the Southern Colonies, but it received little attention.

During the next few years England and Spain continued to eye each other warily but avoided open conflict, but by 1738 British public opinion was strongly calling for action against the Spanish, with West India merchants leading the outcry. Captain Jenkins was summoned to the House of Commons, where he repeated his story, exhibiting his severed ear preserved in a pickle jar. Prime Minister Robert Walpole strove to maintain the peace but was opposed by the House of Commons, the king (George II) and a faction in his own cabinet. Despite his efforts to avoid war, an outraged Parliament voted to ask King George to demand redress from Spain. When diplomatic efforts brought no result, Great Britain formally declared war on this day in 1739.

A bellicose British public wildly cheered the news, lighting bonfires in the streets of London and ringing church bells as if the country had scored a great victory. 'They may ring their bells now', said Walpole sadly, 'but they will soon be wringing their hands.'

Walpole's pessimism proved prescient. The so-called War of Jenkins' Ear (a name given to it more than a century later by Thomas Carlyle) was fought mainly in the Caribbean; in 1742 it was subsumed into the major War of the Austrian Succession. It ended without a victor, although the Spanish had suffered almost 10,000 casualties – half of them killed – while the British lost 20,000 dead, wounded, missing, or captured, plus 409 ships. Among the casualties might be included Prime Minister Walpole, whose downfall was hastened by the disastrous British attack on Cartagena de Indias in 1741.

Britain had been the biggest shippers of slaves across the Atlantic during the 18th century, and, despite the war, British slavers continued to ply their trade until Parliament passed the Slave Trade Act on 25 March 1807.

1642 Before leading an infantry charge in the first battle of the English Civil War at Edgehill, Royalist major general Sir Jacob Astley falls to his knees and prays: 'O Lord, Thou knowest how busy I must be this day; if I forget Thee, do not Thou forget me!' The battle is a draw. * **1949** Hollywood producer Darryl Zanuck: 'If two men on the same job agree all the time, then one is useless. If they disagree all the time, then both are useless.'

24 October

'In ten years' time I will have become another Saint Olaf.'

1945 Back in the early 11th century Norway's quasi-mythical King Olaf II was slain in battle by an army of his own disaffected nobles and peasants, but a year after his death, he was declared a saint for his supposed Christianisation of Norway and miracles occurring at his tomb. On this day another Norwegian leader – Vidkun Quisling – was killed by his own people, but not before predicting that he, too, would one day be revered as his nation's saviour.

In 1933 Quisling had founded the Nasjonal Samling (National Unity Party) that, with the concurrent rise of Hitler, soon became fervently pro-German and anti-Semitic. Then, on 9 April 1940, Germany launched a surprise attack on Norway, quickly overwhelming sporadic resistance. On that same day Quisling staged his own coup, declaring himself Norway's leader, as King Haakon VII fled Oslo to exile in London.

Despite Quisling's previous toadying to the Nazis, his independent government lasted only five days, until Hitler installed Josef Terboven over his head as Gauleiter. (Terboven was a fervent Hitler acolyte who had participated in Hitler's abortive Beer Hall Putsch and had later married Goebbels' former mistress, with Hitler as guest of honour.) Terboven had little use for Quisling, but Quisling managed a quick trip to Berlin, where he got Hitler's backing. He returned to Norway as acting prime minister in a puppet regime reporting to Terboven, who announced that the Nasjonal Samling would be the only political party allowed.

Quisling later claimed – perhaps correctly – that many of his most Nazi-like decrees came from his determination to prevent Germany from fully annexing Norway. But what shameful decrees they were. Contraception was severely restricted to bolster the Nordic genotype, volunteers were enlisted to fight with the Waffen-SS, trade unionists were intimidated (two strike leaders were shot), and Norwegian Jews were rounded up and shipped to concentration camps abroad. On 1 February 1942 Quisling was promoted to Minister-President, although German troops continued to occupy the country. But in September 1943 he finally persuaded Hitler to promise a free post-war Norway.

In February 1943 the German 6th Army surrendered at Stalingrad and in June the next year the Allies landed in Normandy. Even a collaborator like Quisling realised that Germany would lose the war. He spent the war's final months trying to prevent Norwegian deaths in the fight that was developing between German and Russian forces. In his last meeting with Hitler in January 1945 he refused to sign the execution order of thousands of Norwegian saboteurs.

Three months later Hitler shot himself, and on 8 May the 400,000 German troops in Norway surrendered, the same day that Terboven committed suicide by detonating 50 kilos of dynamite in his own bunker. The next day Quisling and his ministers turned themselves in to the police. It was then that he made his deluded remark: 'The easiest course for me would be to take my own life. But I want to let history reach its own verdict. Believe me, in ten years' time I will have become another Saint Olaf.'

Quisling was locked up in the medieval fortress at Akershus. At his trial he was accused of assisting the enemy, theft, embezzlement and murder, as well as conspiring with Hitler over the occupation of Norway. He continued to insist that his actions had all been motivated by his fight for Norwegian independence from Germany, a defence that few of his accusers believed. On 10 September he was convicted on all but a handful of minor charges and sentenced to death.

Quisling was executed by firing squad at Akershus at 2.40 in the morning of 24 October 1945. His last words were: 'I am convicted unfairly and I die innocent.'

In April 1940 *The Times* had first used the word 'quisling' to denote a person who collaborates with the enemy: 'To writers, the word Quisling is a gift from the gods. If they had been ordered to invent a new word for traitor … they could hardly have hit upon a more brilliant combination of letters. Aurally it contrives to suggest something at once slippery and tortuous.'

1537 Henry VIII's third wife, Jane Seymour, dies twelve days after the birth of Edward VI; when she is in labour, doctors tell Henry VIII that either she or the child will probably die and ask which to save. 'The infant by all means, for another wife is easily got, but not so another child', Henry answers.

25 October

'C'est magnifique, mais ce n'est pas la guerre.'

1415 & 1854 On this date over four centuries apart British soldiers fought in two iconic battles, one a stirring triumph marred by atrocity, the other a shattering defeat illuminated by foolhardy courage.

The first was during the Hundred Years' War at Agincourt, where Henry V defeated a French army three times the size of his own. After embedding sharpened stakes in a cornfield heavy with mud from rain, he decimated the charging French with longbow fire. Then, according to eyewitness Jehan de Wavrin, when the stakes forced the enemy to dismount and flounder in the mire, the archers 'threw away their bows and quivers and took their swords, hatchets, mallets, axes, falcon-beaks and other weapons, and … struck down and killed these Frenchmen without mercy'. Then, fearing a counter-attack, Henry ordered his prisoners massacred. 'In cold blood', wrote Wavrin, 'all the nobility of France was beheaded and inhumanly cut to pieces.' It was a tawdry and dishonourable finish to a famous victory.

The second battle on this date was at Balaclava during the Crimean War.

Since September, British and French troops, plus a small contingent of Turks, had been besieging the Russians. Early action included a Russian cavalry attack on the British 93rd Regiment of Foot, whose firm stand was memorably described by William H. Russell in *The Times* as a 'thin red streak tipped with a line of steel', later popularised as 'the thin red line', symbolising British fortitude in battle. But Balaclava's most famous moment was the Charge of the Light Brigade.

Positioned on a high ridge to watch the battle, the British commander Lord Raglan saw that on the Causeway Heights the Russians had chased away a few Turkish defenders and were making off with nine 12-pounder guns that the British had positioned there. To save the guns, he sent Captain Louis Nolan with orders for his cavalry leader, Lord Lucan (the great-great-grandfather of scapegrace 'Lucky' Lucan, who murdered his children's nanny and vanished for ever in 1974).

Leaping from his horse, Nolan gave Lucan his orders, which read: 'Lord Raglan wishes the cavalry to advance rapidly to the front, and try to prevent the enemy carrying away the guns … Immediate.' Nolan, who detested Lucan, then commented: 'Lord Raglan's orders are that the cavalry should attack immediately.'

'Attack what?' demanded Lucan. 'What guns, sir?' From his position in a valley, the guns on the Causeway Heights could not be seen. The only enemy in view was a Russian redoubt at the end of the valley.

'There, my Lord!' answered Nolan with an ambiguous sweep of his arm. 'There is your enemy! There are your guns!' He then galloped away, leaving Lucan still mystified.

Now Lucan summoned his brother-in-law, the Earl of Cardigan, and instructed him to lead his brigade, armed only with lances and sabres, straight into the valley, even though the Russians were positioned on both sides and at the end, with 76 guns and twenty battalions of infantry. Cardigan tried to question the confused order, but then ordered the charge.

> Theirs not to reason why,
> Theirs but to do or die,
> Into the valley of death
> Rode the six hundred.

So wrote Alfred, Lord Tennyson of this famous charge. With Cardigan at their head, the British horse swept forward over a mile of open ground.

Moving at a trot, the brigade advanced in a line 100 yards wide and immediately came under fire from the flanks. Minutes later the Russian guns at the end of the valley scythed down the attackers, but the brigade charged on, now at the gallop. Reaching the Russian position, they cut down any gun crews that had not fled and galloped back down the valley, harassed by Russian cavalry. Of 673 attackers, 118 had been killed and 161 wounded, with a loss of 517 horses. It was such a traumatic defeat that the allies broke off the action.

The Charge of the Light Brigade remains one of the most senseless and horrifying displays of proud courage in all of military history, famously summed up by the General Pierre Bosquet, who witnessed the heroic debacle: '*C'est magnifique, mais ce n'est pas la guerre. C'est de la folie.*' ('It's magnificent, but it's not war. It's madness.')

1983 Having just been informed that the United States in a coalition with six Caribbean nations will invade Grenada after Prime Minister Maurice Bishop is executed in a coup, Margaret Thatcher tells Ronald Reagan: 'This action will be seen as intervention by a Western country in the internal affairs of a small independent nation, however unattractive its regime … You asked for my advice. I have set it out and hope that even at this late stage you will take it into account before events are irrevocable.' Reagan orders the invasion to proceed anyway.

26 October

'You sons of bitches, you have been looking for a fight and now you can have it!'

1881 Never in the colourful history of America's Wild West have so many mythic icons come together in a single tale: Tombstone, Wyatt Earp, Doc Holliday, Boot Hill – they all were part of the West's most famous gunfight, which happened today at the OK Corral.

Tombstone was a prosperous but unruly town in the Arizona Territory boasting about 10,000 residents, mostly young, single men hoping to make a fortune in the nearby silver mines. Scattered with honkytonk saloons and brothels, it was a magnet for violence – three deputy marshals had been gunned down in the past three years. Finally, the city council prohibited anyone from carrying a deadly weapon in town and hired a new marshal, a 38-year-old Kentuckian named Virgil Earp, to enforce the law.

Outside Tombstone were ranches that doubled as headquarters for 200 to 300 cattle smugglers and horse-thieves known as 'The Cowboys'. Virgil Earp had recently arrested two Cowboys for robbing a stagecoach, causing fellow Cowboys Ike Clanton and Tom McLaury to vow to get even. Sensing trouble, Virgil swore in his brothers Morgan and Wyatt as deputies.

On the morning of 25 October, Clanton and McLaury rode into Tombstone for supplies. Over the next 24 hours, the two men had several near-violent run-ins with Virgil, his brothers and their friend Doc Holliday, an itinerant dentist who gambled for a living and never ducked a gunfight.

The next day Ike's brother Billy joined them, along with Tom McLaury's brother Frank and another Cowboy, Billy Claiborne. All but Claiborne were armed. Warned by nervous citizens, Virgil Earp summoned Morgan, Wyatt and Doc Holliday, whom he deputised.

Around three o'clock, the Earps and Holliday spotted the Cowboys in a vacant lot behind the OK Corral. 'Throw up your hands', Virgil commanded, 'I want your guns!' Ike Clanton fled, screaming that he was unarmed. Billy Claiborne also turned and ran. There was a pause, then the click of a gun – or guns – being cocked. Wyatt Earp snarled: 'You sons of bitches, you have been looking for a fight and now you can have it!'

No one knows who pulled the trigger first, but suddenly gunfire erupted. Billy Clanton and Frank McLaury opened fire while Tom McLaury ducked behind his horse and shot over its back. Virgil Earp was shot in the calf and Morgan through the shoulder blades. Then Doc Holliday's shotgun blast felled Tom McLaury, and Virgil shot Billy Clanton point-blank in the chest. Wyatt Earp hit Frank McLaury in the stomach, but he staggered away and fired a shot that struck Holliday's holster and grazed his hip. Holliday and Morgan Earp returned fire, hitting Frank in the head.

About 30 rounds had been fired, and three of the lawmen had been wounded, but three Cowboys lay dead. The entire gunfight had lasted just 30 seconds. The dead Cowboys were carted away to be buried in Tombstone's famous graveyard, Boot Hill.

This should have been the end of it, but other Cowboys thirsted for revenge. Two months later three men ambushed Virgil, hitting him in the back and left arm with buckshot. A doctor saved his life, but his arm was permanently crippled. Then the following March, as Morgan Earp was playing billiards in a saloon, the Cowboys shot him dead through the glass door.

When the suspected killers all furnished alibis provided by fellow Cowboys, Wyatt Earp took matters into his own hands. Forming an eleven-man posse (including two more Earp brothers and Holliday), he caught up with and shot dead four of the Cowboy killers.

The gunfight at the OK Corral is so embedded in American culture that it has been depicted countless times in film and television. Wyatt Earp has become equally iconic; actors who have played him include Randolph Scott, Henry Fonda, Joel McCrea, Burt Lancaster, James Garner, James Stewart, Kevin Costner and Kurt Russell. In 2014 Earp's Colt .45 was auctioned for $225,000.

1769 Dr Johnson: 'It matters not how a man dies, but how he lives. The act of dying is not of importance, it lasts so short a time.' * **1939** President Franklin Roosevelt in a broadcast address to the Forum on Current Problems: 'A radical is a man with both feet firmly planted in the air.'

---

27 October

*'I will burn, but this is a mere incident. We shall
continue our discussion in eternity.'*

1553 The fact that bigotry knows no borders was perfectly demonstrated today when the unorthodox Christian theologian Michael Servetus was burned at the stake, not by the Catholic fanatics of his native Spain but by the obsessive Calvinists of Switzerland.

Servetus (Miguel Servet in Spanish) had been born in Villanueva in 1511 and studied medicine at the University of Paris, where both John Calvin and Ignatius Loyola had studied only a few years before. Loyola went on to found the Jesuits to spearhead the Counter-Reformation while Calvin launched the joyless, militant brand of Protestantism that the 20th-century journalist H.L. Mencken defined as 'the haunting fear that someone, somewhere, may be happy'.

Servetus had been raised a Catholic, but at nineteen he attended the coronation of Holy Roman Emperor Charles V at Bologna, where he was deeply shocked by the worldly ostentation of Pope Clement VII and his retinue. This led him to doubt the whole faith in which he was brought up, and two years later he published his own views, denying the concept of original sin and the Trinity, which he mocked: 'not only the Mohammedans and the Jews but the beasts of the field would make fun of us if they heard tell of our preposterous belief.'

Later Servetus became a physician in Vienne, near Lyon, where he made his discovery of the pulmonary circulation of the blood. Here he continued his religious explorations and wrote several books stating his convictions. In 1546 he began writing to Calvin, perhaps hoping for a kindred spirit who challenged the established beliefs of the Catholic Church. In his correspondence he included a copy of his book *Christianismi Restitutio* (*The Restoration of Christianity*), a work that sharply denied the idea of predestination. But Calvin had replaced Catholicism with a dogmatic belief in his own ideas, of which predestination was a central tenet. He wrote to Servetus that 'I would be as hard as iron when I behold you insulting sound doctrine with so great audacity'. He also wrote to his colleague, the equally intransigent Guillaume Farel: 'Servetus has just sent me a long volume of his ravings ... if he comes here, if my authority is worth anything, I will never permit him to depart alive.'

Unfortunately for Servetus, some of his letters were sent to the inquisitor general of Lyon, who immediately imprisoned him and the printers of his books on charges of heresy. Terrified of what penalty the French inquisitors might impose, he managed to escape, leaving the ecclesiastical authorities with the small satisfaction of burning him in effigy. Under the delusion that Calvinist Puritanism would be more understanding than inquisitorial Catholicism, he fled across the border to Calvin's City of God in Geneva.

Upon his arrival, one of Servetus' first acts was to go to church. During the service he was seized once more, this time by uncompromising Calvinists. Again he was tried for heresy. Calvin did not appear against him, but his secretary Nicholas de la Fontaine supplied most of the condemning testimony. Foreseeing his fate, Servetus told his judges: 'I will burn, but this is a mere incident. We shall continue our discussion in eternity.'

Convicted for having 'gone out of your way to infect the world with your stinking heretical poison', Servetus was sentenced to death. Calvin suggested decapitation, but his sterner co-religionists demanded a more draconian end. When Servetus was led to the stake, he refused to recant, causing Guillaume Farel to exclaim: 'See what power the devil has over one who has fallen into his hands!' Servetus was cremated alive atop a pyre of his own books.

---

312 Emperor Constantine defeats rival Maxentius at the Milvian Bridge for sole control of the Roman Empire after seeing in the sky a flaming cross inscribed with the words 'Εν Τουτω Νικα' (often rendered in Latin as '*In hoc signo vinces*' – 'By this sign thou shalt conquer'). Inspired, the next year he issues the Edict of Milan that makes Christianity the empire's favoured religion. * **1930** Benito Mussolini addresses a Roman crowd from the balcony of the Palazzo Venezia: 'The struggle between the two worlds [fascism and democracy] can permit no compromises. It's either Us or Them!'

---

28 October

*'All the gods and goddesses will give him the breath
of life, so that he breathes, eternally rejuvenated.'*

130 AD Today a beautiful young man of about nineteen drowned in the River Nile. Two days later Roman Emperor Hadrian, acting in his role as Pontifex Maximus, declared that he was a god, with life eternal. The young man was Hadrian's lover Antinous, born to a Greek family in Claudiopolis in the Roman province of Bithynia, now in Turkey.

In the year 123, Hadrian turned 47 and had been emperor for six years. Now he was once again on one of his endless peregrinations around the empire. After checking the Roman defences in Parthia, he wintered in Nicomedia, Bithynia's main city. In June he visited Claudiopolis, and there he first met Antinous, then about twelve. Struck by the boy's beauty, Hadrian sent him to Rome, to be schooled at the imperial *paedagogium*. In 125 Hadrian returned to the capital, and sometime during the next three years he and Antinous became lovers. When the emperor left for Greece in 127, he brought Antinous with him.

By that time Hadrian had been married for 27 years but had no children. It was known, moreover, that his marriage was unhappy and that he was sexually attracted to young men.

For the next three years the emperor continued his travels to inspect his empire – to North Africa, Greece, Anatolia, Syria, Arabia, and Judea – with Antinous continuously at his side. In August 130 they arrived in Alexandria to pay homage at the grave of Alexander the Great. A month later Hadrian saved Antinous' life when he was almost killed during a lion hunt. One of the hunting party later romanticised that red lotus flowers miraculously sprang from the lion's blood.

In autumn 130, Hadrian and his retinue joined a flotilla to sail up the Nile. They stopped at the ancient city of Hermopolis Magna in time for the celebration of Osiris, a god who had been drowned in the river and then arose from the dead.

On 28 October Antinous drowned in the Nile, for reasons that still elude us – accident, suicide, murder and religious sacrifice have all been suggested. The most compelling story is that, knowing the emperor to be in poor health, Antinous asked an oracle whether Hadrian would live to see old age. The augur replied that unless someone were to sacrifice his life for him, the emperor would soon die. Deeply devoted to Hadrian, Antinous walked into the river and drowned. Whatever the cause, the *Historiae Augustae*, written more than a century later, relates that 'for this youth, [Hadrian] wept like a woman'.

Hadrian in his grief ordered that Antinous be deified, identifying him with Osiris due to the manner of his death. On 30 October he announced the founding of the city of Antinopolis, to be built on the east bank of the Nile, near where Antinous drowned. He publicly declared that Antinous had conquered death and risen up to dwell among the stars, even identifying a specific star as Antinous. Proclamations were sent to every corner of the empire inaugurating the religion of the New God Antinous, and Hadrian established a festival to be held in his honour each October, the Antinoeia.

In Antinopolis Hadrian erected the Obelisk of Antinous (now in Rome). On its southern face is written in hieroglyphics: 'He heals the needy ill by sending them a dream.' The column also promises: 'All the gods and goddesses will give him the breath of life, so that he breathes, eternally rejuvenated.'

Hadrian built at least 28 temples for Antinous' worship, and some 2,000 statues of him were produced, over 100 of which survive. Traces of the cult of Antinous have been found in more than 70 cities.

Antinous' cult was attacked both by pagans who followed more traditional deities and by Christians, who destroyed many of his statues, but many memorials remained until the official prohibition of pagan religions under the reign of Emperor Theodosius in 391.

1919 After Congress passes the Volstead Act stipulating that 'No person shall … sell, barter, transport, import, export, deliver, furnish or possess any intoxicating liquor', Prohibition begins in the United States. It remains in force until 5 December 1933. * **1922** After Mussolini threatens, 'Either the government will be given to us or we shall seize it by marching on Rome,' 30,000 Fascist Blackshirts descend on the city. The next day King Vittorio Emanuele asks Mussolini to form a government.

---

29 October

'Wall Street lays an egg.'

1929 On this Tuesday, for the second day in a row, shares plummeted on Wall Street. According to the contemporary reporter Jonathan Leonard: 'In the first half hour 3,259,800 shares were traded, almost a full day's work for the labouring machinery of the Exchange. The selling pressure was wholly without precedent. It was coming from everywhere. The wires to other cities were jammed with frantic orders to sell. So were the cables, radio and telephones to Europe and the rest of the world. Buyers were few, sometimes wholly absent. Often the specialists stood baffled at their posts, sellers pressing around them and not a single buyer at any price.' At the close a record 16.4 million shares on the New York Stock Exchange had changed hands, with prices collapsing; the Dow Jones index dropped 12 per cent to 230.07 in a day that became known as Black Tuesday. The next morning the showbiz magazine *Variety* published a banner headline across its front page, using an old vaudeville expression meaning to fail wretchedly in front of the audience: 'Wall Street lays an egg.'

The Roaring Twenties in America had been a booming, freewheeling period famous for jazz, speakeasies, flappers, easy sex and financial wheeling and dealing. The Dow Jones index had started the decade at a modest 119.62 but tripled to reach an all-time high of 381.17 on 3 September 1929. Many punters, in their determination not to miss the bandwagon, bought on margin, borrowing money from their brokers, using other securities as collateral. Leverage rates of 90 per cent debt were common. It was, said England's Chancellor of the Exchequer Philip Snowden, 'a speculative orgy'.

On 24 October, heavy trading drove the US market to an 11 per cent drop at the opening bell, causing America's premier banks to step in to stop the rot. The market rallied, but it was still down by 6 per cent at the close. The following Monday the Dow Jones plunged by a record 13 per cent. Then came Black Tuesday, with its unprecedented volume that kept the ticker running until eight o'clock that evening. Financial giants like General Motors' founder William Durant and the Rockefeller family purchased huge quantities of shares to buoy prices, but not even their muscle could stem the tide. Losses on Black Tuesday came to $14 billion (an inflation-adjusted $470 billion today). Few realised that this was only the beginning of the crash.

During the next six months the Dow gradually regained lost ground, in April 1930 rallying to almost 300, higher than it had been in October. But then came a prolonged fall that bottomed at 41.22 on 8 July 1932. Values had dropped by 89 per cent since the high of September 1929. It took 25 years for the market fully to recover; only in November 1954 did the Dow Jones surpass the 1929 peak.

It is only an urban myth that Wall Street's crisis caused an epidemic of bankers leaping from tall buildings after having lost their fortunes. New York's suicide rate was actually higher during the boom before the crash, but the crash did generate a lot of jump-related gags. Will Rogers joked that 'you had to stand in line to get a window to jump out of', and Eddie Cantor quipped that hotel clerks asked guests if they wanted a room 'for sleeping or for jumping'.

The stock market has suffered precipitous falls numerous times since 1929, most famously on 19 October 1987, when the Dow Jones fell by almost 23 per cent, the largest single-day percentage retreat in its history. Then on 16 May 2020, it fell 2,997 points, the largest point fall ever. As the mutual fund pioneer John Templeton once said: 'The four most dangerous words in investing are, it's different this time.'

1618 Standing with the masked executioner in the yard of the Old Palace at Westminster, Sir Walter Raleigh touches his axe and puns: ''Tis a sharp remedy, but a sure one for all ills.' He addresses the witnesses: 'I have a long journey to take, and must bid the company farewell.' He then calls to the executioner: 'Strike, man, strike!'

---

30 October

'Spain has no foolish dreams.'

1975 'The Leader' has always seemed a modest title for a dictator, suggesting guidance and example rather than raw despotism. Perhaps for this reason in 1939 Europe's newest dictator, Francisco Franco, took the title El Caudillo, Spanish for 'The Leader', emulating Benito Mussolini, who had become Il Duce in 1925 and Adolf Hitler, who had styled himself Der Führer from 1934.

Although a mere 5ft 3in, Franco had been a professional soldier, scrupulously honest, painfully earnest, aloof and totally dedicated to his men, first seeing combat in the Riff War in Spanish Morocco in 1913, where he was severely wounded by machine-gun fire. At 22 he became Spain's youngest captain, at 25 its youngest major and at 33 its youngest general. In 1935 he was appointed Chief of Staff at 42.

By this time, however, Spain was disintegrating, as fervid monarchists clashed with hard-left Bolsheviks while a weak republican government tried to maintain control. Franco was consigned to an obscure command in the Canary Islands, but as Spain's political system crumbled, he joined right-wing rebels. On 18 July 1936 he broadcast a *pronunciamento* calling for the Spanish army to rise against the government. In city after city, garrisons seized public buildings and arrested left-wing leaders, while workers took to the streets, called for a general strike and threw up barricades, igniting the Civil War.

The rebels needed a commander to head their cause and chose Franco because of his prestige as a general, his military ability, and Hitler's decision to channel all of Germany's aid through him.

The war lasted almost three years, until Madrid fell in March 1939, after 28 months of siege. Now that the Nationalist cause had triumphed, there was no question of what sort of regime would follow. 'We do not believe in government through the voting booth', Franco said. 'The Spanish national will was never freely expressed through the ballot box. Spain has no foolish dreams.'

Depicting himself as the defender of Catholic Spain against atheist communism, Franco established a military dictatorship. But Spain was exhausted and impoverished, and only five months after Madrid's fall the Second World War began. Although sympathetic to the Nazis, Franco carefully preserved Spain's neutrality. He met Hitler only once, but his demands for extensive German aid provoked Hitler to pronounce that rather than negotiate with him again, he'd 'rather have three or four teeth pulled out'. As a sop to Hitler, Franco allowed Spanish volunteers (the División Azul) to fight on the Eastern Front. He also compiled a list of Jews for Heinrich Himmler, but no Jews were ever handed over to Germany.

After the war Franco found himself despised by most of the Western world; his regime had executed 20,000 civilians and Spain remained a dictatorship, intensely Catholic, with no legal divorce, contraceptives or abortion, while women's roles were severely restricted (a woman could not have a bank account without her father's or husband's permission until the 1970s). Only in 1955 was Spain finally admitted to the United Nations.

In 1959 Franco began to liberalise the economy, igniting an economic boom known as 'the Spanish miracle', as the country became the second fastest-growing economy in the world, just behind Japan.

In 1947 Franco had proclaimed Spain a monarchy, but failed to designate a monarch, effectively making himself regent for life. 'I am responsible only to God and history', he said. In 1969 he named Prince Juan Carlos de Borbón as heir-apparent.

During his last years Franco suffered from Parkinson's disease. Frail and ghostly, on this day in 1975 he fell into a coma and was put on life support. Eventually his family agreed to have the machines switched off, and El Caudillo died just after midnight on 20 November at 82.

Franco was buried at the Valle de los Caídos (Valley of the Fallen), a colossal Civil War memorial outside Madrid. But Spanish autocracy died with Franco, as Juan Carlos encouraged the revival of political parties within a constitutional monarchy. In 2007 the government ordered the removal of all memorials of Franco; the last to go was an equestrian statue in Santander on 17 December 2008.

1956 When Hungary's communist government shackles the country's Catholic Church and confiscates some of its property, Cardinal József Mindszenty makes clear that 'the Church asks for no secular protection; it seeks shelter under the protection of God alone.' He is arrested, tortured and show-tried on the ludicrous charges of planning to steal the Crown of Saint Stephen in order to crown Otto von Habsburg as King of Hungary, scheming to overthrow the Communist Party and re-establish capitalism, planning a third world war, and, once this war is won by the Americans, assuming supreme political power himself. Today, during the Hungarian Revolution, he is released after eight years in prison.

---

31 October

'As soon as the coin in the coffer rings,
the soul into heaven springs.'

1517 Today, on the eve of All Saints' Day, the 34-year-old Augustinian monk Martin Luther nailed his famous 95 theses to the door of the Schlosskirche at the Saxon city of Wittenberg.

What triggered Luther's historic challenge to the Church of Rome was Pope Leo X's decision to complete the rebuilding of Rome's ancient and crumbling St Peter's Basilica – or rather, how Leo proposed to pay for the work.

Reconstruction on St Peter's had begun in 1506 during the pontificate of Julius II, but when Leo became pope in 1513, the great building was still only partly finished. Leo resolved to continue the project, but he had a problem – where to find the money. So, to raise the cash for the new basilica, he took to selling indulgences to deliver souls from Purgatory.

Leo's call went out to bishops throughout Europe, urging them to find buyers. One particularly energetic salesman was Johann Tetzel, a German Dominican friar who was assigned by the Archbishop of

Mainz to get to work. (The Archbishop himself was deeply in debt and encouraged the sale of indulgences in order to get a cut of the proceeds.) Soon Tetzel was doing a thriving business, despite the practice being banned in several German principalities. To drum up trade, he summed up his promise in a catchy slogan: 'As soon as the coin in the coffer rings, the soul into heaven springs.' ('*Sobald der Gülden im Becken klingt, im huy die Seel im Himmel springt.*') He also offered salvation for the faithful's dead relations: 'If you give me your money, then your dead relatives no longer burn in Hell but go to Heaven.'

The Church had been awash with corruption for a century, but the sale of indulgences seemed to Luther like the worst form of venality. He thought that it was a desecration of confession and penance, and that Tetzel and his like were gulling Christians into believing that they could buy absolution. In reaction to this impiety, he struck back at the offending Church, starting with Tetzel, about whom he swore: 'God willing, I will beat a hole in his drum!' Then on this day he nailed his famous 95 theses to the Wittenberg church door.

On the same day, Luther sent a hand-written copy of his theses (which he called '*Disputatio pro declaratione virtutis indulgentiarum*') to his superior, the Bishop of Brandenburg, and to the Archbishop of Mainz, the very man responsible for the German sales programme.

Luther's famous complaint targets Church abuses such as simony, nepotism and of course the sale of indulgences, singled out in Thesis 86, which asks: 'Why does the Pope, whose wealth today is greater than the wealth of the richest Crassus, build the basilica of St Peter with the money of poor believers rather than with his own money?' When Pope Leo heard about Luther's protest, he dismissed it as 'a quarrel among friars'.

Two months after Luther's defiant posting, friends translated his complaint from Latin into German, and, thanks to the developing art of printing, circulated it first throughout Germany and subsequently across much of Europe. It was the first major act in splintering the Catholic Church and, in the years to follow, igniting an orgy of violence that raged across Europe. The day he nailed his theses to the Schlosskirche door is often called the first day of the Reformation.

1987 Margaret Thatcher: 'There is no such thing as Society. There are individual men and women, and their families.' * **1971** Former president Lyndon Johnson on devious FBI chief J. Edgar Hoover: 'I'd rather have that fellow inside my tent pissing out, than outside my tent pissing in.'

1 November

'A man paints with his brains and not with his hands.'

1503 & 1512 Today – All Saints' Day – in 1503 Cardinal Giovanni della Rovere was elevated to the papal throne as Julius II a month short of his 60th birthday. He had been helped along by his uncle, Pope Sixtus IV, who had made him a cardinal twenty years before. While enjoying his riches and generally ignoring his flock, the headstrong and irascible Julius managed to father three illegitimate daughters while achieving the worldly greatness of a Renaissance prince.

Julius personally led papal armies in the field, becoming a sort of warrior-pope whose war-cry was 'Drive out the barbarians'. But he also followed his uncle's example in patronising the arts – Sixtus' greatest contribution had been the rebuilding of the Cappella Maggiore in Rome and having it decorated by masters such as Botticelli, Perugino, Pinturicchio and Ghirlandaio. The chapel came to be known as the Sistine Chapel in Sixtus' honour.

In 1508 Julius decided to add more splendour to his uncle's chapel by redoing the ceiling, then painted blue and studded with gilt stars. For this task he selected Michelangelo Buonarroti, who started work in May on what is often considered the greatest masterpiece – or collection of masterpieces – the world has yet known.

At first Michelangelo wanted to decline the commission because he considered himself a sculptor, not a painter, and had done little painting since he was an apprentice in Ghirlandaio's studio in his teens. He suspected that the Pope had chosen him on the cunning recommendation of the architect Donato Bramante, who, jealous of Michelangelo's talents, had proposed him only because his lack of experience painting frescoes would doom him to failure. But Michelangelo knew that, if he declined the commission, he might never get another from Julius, and he undoubtedly thought his own genius would carry him through. As he explained: 'A man paints with his brains and not with his hands.'

Julius wanted the ceiling to feature scenes from the New Testament, but Michelangelo doggedly insisted on the Old Testament, believing it more dramatic, and proved his point with the work's centrepiece, 'The Creation of Adam', where God, surrounded by a red cloak, reaches out his hand to give Adam the touch of life. (Only centuries later did scientists notice that the red cloak is an anatomically correct rendering of the human brain – perhaps signalling that God created the brain – or perhaps the reverse.)

It took almost four and a half years to complete this great work (although Michelangelo downed brushes for almost a year in 1510–11 when no payments were forthcoming). The painting covers some 10,000 square feet, where 343 individuals are depicted. Critics have noted that Michelangelo's women are as sturdy and muscled as his men, possibly because his models for all the figures were men.

Contrary to the popular legend, however, Michelangelo did not paint the ceiling lying on his back. According to the near-contemporary painter and art historian Giorgio Vasari: 'The work was carried out in extremely uncomfortable conditions, from his having to work with his head tilted upwards.' The job demanded intense effort, causing the earthy Michelangelo to complain: '*Nelle mie opere caco sangue.*' ('In my works I shit blood.')

On another All Saints' Day, this in 1512, the Sistine Chapel was officially reopened, on the ninth anniversary of Julius' elevation to the papacy. According to Vasari: 'The whole world came running when the vault was revealed, and the sight of it was enough to reduce them to stunned silence.'

Even then Michelangelo's work in the chapel was not done. Julius died in February 1513, and the great painter took a 24-year rest. But in 1536 he returned to create 'The Last Judgement' and in 1542 the 'Crucifixion of St Peter' and the 'Conversion of St Paul' under the patronage of Pope Paul III.

As Johann Wolfgang von Goethe opined some two and a half centuries later: 'Without having seen the Sistine Chapel one can form no appreciable idea of what one man is capable of achieving.'

1700 When Louis XIV's grandson Philip V inherits the Spanish throne on the death of the weak-minded Charles II of Spain, Louis exclaims: '*Il n'y a plus de Pyrénées.*' ('The Pyrenees have ceased to exist.') * **1755** After an earthquake on a Sunday morning destroys two-thirds of Lisbon in fifteen minutes, killing 80,000 people, Voltaire writes: 'Why would a benevolent God send an earthquake on one of Europe's most Catholic cities at precisely the hour when most were at Mass?'

2 November

'No better friend, no worse enemy.'

82 BC Today, for the second time, one of the Roman Republic's generals bloodily conquered Rome, overthrowing his own government. He was a louche outsider from a decayed patrician family who preferred the company of actors and prostitutes but rose from poverty to absolute power. He was Lucius Cornelius Sulla.

Dubbed 'Sulla Felix' – the fortunate – Sulla's first stroke of luck was to inherit a small fortune from his stepmother and then another from his mistress. Rumours circulated that he had had a hand in their demises.

In 106 BC, Sulla served under Gaius Marius during the campaign against King Jugurtha of Numidia. After a year of inconclusive fighting, Sulla captured Jugurtha by persuading his father-in-law to betray him, making people think that he, not Marius, had really won the war. Marius felt deeply humiliated, spawning a bitter feud that would define the fate of Rome.

Twenty years later the Senate placed Sulla in command of the war against the Kingdom of Pontus. By now Marius was almost unbalanced in his jealous hatred. While Sulla was busy organising his army, Marius bullied the Senate into switching the command to him instead.

In fury, Sulla marched on Rome with six legions. With no standing army, Marius was forced to draft in gladiators, but they were no match for Sulla's legions, and Marius fled to Africa. For the first time in the Republic's 422-year history, a Roman general had overthrown the government.

Sulla then headed back to the war with Pontus. His army had scarcely left when Marius joined forces with Lucius Cornelius Cinna, retook Rome and began a reign of terror, slaughtering Sulla's supporters wholesale. But Marius shortly died, and three years later Cinna was stoned to death by his own troops.

Sulla now began his second march on Rome. In November 82 he fought another army at the Colline Gate in Rome's northern outskirts. On the first day Sulla was in retreat when one of his officers, Marcus Licinius Crassus, routed the enemy's right wing, turning the tide. Early the next morning – 2 November – Sulla induced several enemy cohorts to switch sides and completed his victory.

Sulla often claimed of himself, 'No better friend, no worse enemy'. Now he was about to prove it. He herded 6,000 prisoners into the Circus Maximus and gathered the Senate in the nearby temple of Bellona. According to Plutarch, 'just as he commenced speaking to the Senate, [he] proceeded to [have the prisoners] cut down ... The cry of so vast a multitude put to the sword, in so narrow a space, was naturally heard some distance, and startled the senators. He, however, continuing his speech with a calm and unconcerned countenance, bade them listen to what he had to say, and not busy themselves with what was doing out of doors ... This gave the most stupid of the Romans to understand that they had merely exchanged, not escaped, tyranny.'

Sulla butchered his opponents on an unmatched scale, proscribing 40 senators, 1,600 knights and many others without trial. Most were executed, their property confiscated and sold for a pittance to his supporters.

Sulla also flooded the Senate with his cronies, who elected him dictator. In the early years of the Republic, a dictator could be appointed when the state was in imminent danger, but for only six months. However, no dictator had ruled Rome for 120 years, and no dictator had refused to step down after his term. Sulla did. But two years later he voluntarily relinquished power and retired to his country estate in Puteoli, where he died the next year (78 BC).

Sulla's meteoric ascent from down-and-out patrician to absolute ruler was such a cause for wonder that 'Sulla did it – why can't I?' became a catchphrase in the Roman language. One who took the phrase to heart was another impoverished patrician who was eighteen when Sulla seized power. He knew the bloody politics of the day at close hand; Marius was his uncle and Cinna his father-in-law. His name was Julius Caesar. Thirty-three years after Sulla's coup he, too, would lead an army to attack his own country and become its dictator.

1859 American abolitionist John Brown is sentenced to hang for leading a raid on a federal armoury in Harper's Ferry (now West Virginia). On his way to the gallows he slips a final note to one of his supporters in which he accurately prophesies: 'the crimes of this guilty land will never be purged away; but with Blood.'

---

3 November

'A woman has the right to mount the scaffold. She must possess equally the right to mount the speaker's platform.'

1793 Today a beautiful 45-year-old proto-feminist was guillotined in Paris. An eyewitness recorded the terrible event: 'At seven o'clock in the evening, a most extraordinary person called Olympe de Gouges, who held the imposing title of woman of letters, was taken to the scaffold … She approached the scaffold with a calm and serene expression on her face, and forced the guillotine's furies, which had driven her to this place of torture, to admit that such courage and beauty had never been seen before.'

Olympe de Gouges was born in a *petit bourgeois* family near Toulouse and at seventeen was forced to marry a man 30 years her senior. As she later wrote in a semi-autobiographical novel: 'I was married to a man I did not love and who was neither rich nor well-born. I was sacrificed for no reason that could compensate for the repugnance I felt.' Five years later her husband died, but the experience left her committed to improving the rights of women.

After moving to Paris, she devoted herself to writing. She took lovers but refused to remarry, both because of her feminist ideas and because French law forbade women to publish without the consent of their husbands.

Her output was prodigious – 43 plays, 31 novels, memoirs and other writings and 68 revolutionary pamphlets – but she was harshly criticised by people who thought a woman's place was in the home, not the theatre. She was overjoyed when the French Revolution broke out and continued to agitate for equality between the sexes, replacement of marriage by a contract signed by both spouses, and women's right to manage their own property and to divorce.

In 1789 the Assembly published its *Declaration of the Rights of Man and of the Citizen*, which defined citizens as men over 25. Olympe responded with a *Declaration of the Rights of Woman and of the Female Citizen*, which espoused all the same rights while adding 'woman' or '*citoyenne*' in place of '*citoyen*'.

Olympe opens her *Declaration*: 'Man, are you capable of being fair? A woman is asking: at least you will allow her that right. Tell me? What gave you the sovereign right to oppress my sex?' She claims that 'the only limit to the exercise of the natural rights of woman is the perpetual tyranny with which men oppose it'. She points out that under French law women are fully punishable yet denied the right to participate in government: 'A woman has the right to mount the scaffold. She must possess equally the right to mount the speaker's platform.'

But as the Revolution careened toward fanaticism, Olympe became progressively disenchanted. Originally a strong republican, she sided with the moderate Girondins against the Jacobin dictatorship of Robespierre, claiming that Louis XVI should be exiled rather than executed. Even after he was guillotined, she wrote that French *départements* should vote on whether they wanted a republic or a constitutional monarchy, ignoring that the law of 29 March 1793 made advocating a return to monarchy a capital crime.

Olympe was arrested and incarcerated for three months in harsh conditions, a policeman always present in her cell. Even then she smuggled out her last work, *Une patriote persécutée*, in which she condemned Robespierre and the Terror.

While she was imprisoned, the Jacobin government convicted the Girondin leadership of treason, and on 31 October 1793, 22 of them were guillotined in 36 minutes. Three days later Olympe was subjected to a mock trial and sentenced to death for sedition and attempting to reinstate the monarchy. She was only the second woman (after Marie Antoinette) to be guillotined during the Revolution. (Charlotte Corday had been executed, but not for treason but murder.)

Two weeks later, the revolutionary newspaper *La Feuille du Salut Public* found her guilty of what many thought was her real crime: 'She wanted to be a statesman, but the law has punished this conspirator who forgot the virtues that belong to her sex.' Not until 1945 did French women receive the right to vote.

1868 General Ulysses S. Grant is elected America's eighteenth president. In his inaugural address he comments: 'I know no method to secure the repeal of bad or obnoxious laws so effective as their stringent execution.' * **1936** Franklin D. Roosevelt is elected for his third term as president after using his last public speech to excoriate big business interests who had financed his opponents: 'Government by organised money is just as dangerous as Government by organised mob.'

4 November

*'Now this is not the end. It is not even the beginning of
the end. But it is perhaps, the end of the beginning.'*

1942 Twenty-one months earlier Erwin Rommel had taken command
of the newly created Panzerarmee Afrika. With his somewhat reluctant Italian allies, Rommel drove eastwards along the North African
coast towards Egypt, aiming to seize the Suez Canal. After defeating
the British at Gazala, he captured Benghazi and then Tobruk, earning
himself the nickname 'the Desert Fox' among his enemies and '*Der
Wüstenfuchs*' among the Germans. On 22 June Hitler promoted him
to Generalfeldmarschall.

Meanwhile the British had retreated into Egypt but rallied their battered army to make a stand at El Alamein, 150 miles west of Cairo. On
1 July 1942 Rommel attacked, with only 96,000 men against 150,000
for the British, but the following day General Claude Auchinleck
ordered a spirited counter-attack, and the fight developed into a battle
of attrition, ending in stalemate. But for the British it was a victory in
that it stopped Rommel from overrunning Egypt and taking the Canal.

Despite his defensive success, Churchill sacked Auchinleck, and
ordered General Bernard Montgomery to take command of Britain's
Eighth Army. The vain but highly intelligent Montgomery was respected
by his men, who saw him as 'quick as a ferret and about as likeable'.

By mid-October 1942 Montgomery had built his force to
195,000 men, 1,000 tanks and 900 guns, approximately double what
Rommel could field. The British also enjoyed air superiority, and British
troops were well fed and in good health while Rommel's battle-weary
soldiers were short on food as well as ammunition.

Under a full moon on the calm, clear evening of 23 October
Montgomery opened the action with a massive artillery barrage, followed by an infantry attack. Progress was painfully slow as Rommel's
force mounted determined counter-attacks, knocking out a large number of British tanks. The battle see-sawed for the next ten days, but the
British numerical superiority, especially in artillery and tanks, finally
began to turn the tide. Bold attacks by Australian and New Zealand
units opened up the German–Italian defences, and Rommel could see
that his weakened army was crumbling.

On 2 November Rommel telegraphed Hitler that 'the army's
strength is so exhausted after its ten days of battle that it is not now

capable of offering any effective opposition to the enemy's next break-through attempt'. But Der Führer was unyielding: 'There can be no other thought but to stand fast, yield not a yard of ground and throw every gun and every man into the battle … As to your troops, you can show them no other road than that to victory or death.'

By the afternoon of 4 November British armour had punched a twelve-mile hole in the enemy front, and, with huge numerical superiority, was threatening to encircle large segments of the German–Italian line. By now Rommel had committed every available man and gun but was determined to save what was left of his army. Despite Hitler's command to stand and die, at 5.30 that evening he ordered a retreat.

Basking in victory but too cautious to order an energetic pursuit, Montgomery allowed Rommel's army to escape annihilation, as about 56,000 slipped away. Nonetheless, El Alamein was a major British triumph; at the cost of 15,000 dead and wounded, the Eighth Army had killed 9,000 Germans and Italians, with a further 15,000 wounded and 30,000 captured.

The following January Montgomery declared with typical modesty: 'This is probably without parallel in history.' But only six days after the battle an exultant Churchill had a more realistic assessment, when he proclaimed at the Mansion House in London: 'Now this is not the end. It is not even the beginning of the end. But it is perhaps, the end of the beginning.' Indeed, El Alamein marked a turning of the tide of war, a shift that would be confirmed three months later by the German defeat before Stalingrad.

1576 In Antwerp, 6,000 Spanish soldiers, furious because they have not been paid, start the three-day Spanish Fury, shouting '*Santiago, Santiago! España, España! A sangre, a carne, a juego, a sacco.*' ('St James, St James! Spain, Spain! Blood, flesh, fire, sack!') They burn 1,000 buildings, sack the city and kill 7,000 civilians. * **1952** After losing the presidential election, Democratic candidate Adlai Stevenson is asked how he feels; he says that he 'was too old to cry, but it hurt too much to laugh'.

5 November

'Après nous, le déluge.'

1757 Recently, life had been difficult for Louis XV, now 47 years old, 41 of them on the throne of France. The Parlement continued to encroach on the monarchy's absolute power, the king was beset by the debt run up by his own extravagance and since 1754 France had been mired in the Seven Years' War against Prussia and England. To top off his troubles, on 5 January 1757 a crazed religious fanatic named Robert-François Damiens had attempted to assassinate him at the Palace of Versailles, to be thwarted only by Louis' thick winter clothing that prevented the killer's knife from penetrating to any vital organ. (Two months later Damiens had been publicly tortured, drawn and quartered, the last ever victim of such gruesome executions in France.)

But today things got even worse. In Rossbach in Saxony a French and Austrian army of 41,000 men under the French commander Charles, Prince of Soubise was utterly routed by Frederick the Great's force of just half that number. Frederick had sent seven regiments of cavalry in a surprise attack that crushed the French and Austrians, losing only 550 men compared to 10,000 casualties for his enemies. (Frederick later remarked: 'I won the battle of Rossbach with most of my infantry with their muskets on their shoulders.') It was the first time that a German Protestant king had inflicted such a humiliating defeat on Catholic France and Austria. Voltaire claimed that German nationalism had been born that day.

When the calamitous news of the battle reached Versailles, Louis' *maîtresse-en-titre* Madame de Pompadour was in her boudoir, sitting for the court painter, Maurice Quentin de La Tour. The king entered the room, clearly in distress; the defeat at Rossbach only added to his feeling that he was carrying all the kingdom's woes on his shoulders.

Without changing her pose, Madame de Pompadour lightly bade her royal lover to keep up his spirit. The debacle at Rossbach, she said, was of little consequence to them: *'Après nous, le déluge.'* ('After us, the deluge.')

Louis brightened and nodded: 'Things will last our time.' But, according to the French historian Charles Sainte-Beuve, from that time forward, the king and his mistress were haunted by 'a vague and sinister foreboding like anticipated remorse'.

The Seven Years' War ended with a stronger Prussia, a weaker Austria and various colonial territories in different hands, but European boundaries were returned to their *status quo ante bellum*, emphasising the pointlessness of the war from France's point of view. In the end, the battle of Rossbach was indeed of little consequence.

Madame de Pompadour died in 1764, her royal lover ten years after that, escaping the *déluge* – the French Revolution – that came in 1789.

1605 After being captured while about to blow up Parliament, Guy Fawkes explains to his captors, 'A desperate disease requires a desperate remedy.'

---

6 November

*'I shall be an autocrat, that's my trade. And
the good Lord will forgive me, that's his.'*

1796 In 1744 Sophia von Anhalt-Zerbst, the fourteen-year-old daughter of a minor German prince, had come to St Petersburg to wed Grand Duke Peter, heir to the throne of Russia. In August the next year she married him, after being received by the Russian Orthodox Church and changing her name to Catherine. History would know her as Catherine the Great.

Peter became tsar in 1762, but the marriage was a disaster from the start, perhaps never consummated. Catherine had taken a series of lovers, of whom the first, a court chamberlain, was probably the father of her son Paul, born in 1754.

Six months into Peter's reign, Catherine orchestrated a coup with the help of another lover, Grigory Orlov. Peter was imprisoned, only to be strangled in his cell by Orlov's brother, if not on Catherine's orders, at least with her connivance. Although Paul should have inherited, he was only eight, and Catherine made sure he would never threaten her grip on Russia, becoming the most absolute monarch in Europe.

Since marrying Peter, Catherine had taken a succession of increasingly younger lovers, 22 in all, whom she lavishly rewarded when she tired of their services. It was rumoured that she had them put through their paces by ladies of the court before being invited to her boudoir. No doubt the candidates needed both stamina and imagination, since the licentious Catherine grew increasingly fat. Her last paramour, Platon Zubov, must have been particularly resolute: he was 22 when the corpulent empress engaged him at the age of 60.

Although a scandal across Europe (Frederick the Great called her the Messalina of the North), Catherine changed Russia for ever. She gained 200,000 square miles of territory (more than twice the size of Great Britain), built more than 100 new towns and greatly expanded trade. She also held a brilliant court to which the greatest minds of Europe were drawn, and corresponded with Diderot and Voltaire. The Hermitage Museum began as Catherine's personal art collection.

Although liberal in spirit, politically Catherine was reactionary. Of Russia's 35 million people, 23 million were serfs, of whom 500,000 belonged to Catherine herself, while the Russian state owned almost 3 million more. She stripped the serfs of any state protection, prohibited appeals to the sovereign and increased the power of landowners. She also imposed serfdom on Ukrainian peasants, who had hitherto been free. When the writer Alexander Radishchev warned of possible uprisings because of the serfs' deplorable living conditions, Catherine exiled him to Siberia.

By 1796 Catherine was 67 and had been empress for 34 years. Early in her reign she had declared: 'I shall be an autocrat, that's my trade. And the good Lord will forgive me, that's his.' She had lived up to her part and was now about to find out if the good Lord would live up to his.

At nine o'clock this morning Catherine's chamberlain peeked into her bedroom, having not been summoned at the usual hour, but she was not there. He found her lying unconscious on the floor in her privy closet. Like George II before her and Elvis Presley after, she had been felled by a stroke while sitting on the commode.

It took six men to carry Catherine to her bedroom, where, too heavy to be lifted onto her bed, she was laid on a leather mattress on the floor. Despite her doctors' efforts, she never regained consciousness, dying at 9.45 the following evening. (The canard that she was crushed while having sex with a horse when the harness holding the horse above her broke is pure myth, but it indicates her reputation for unbridled promiscuity.)

No sooner was Catherine dead than her son Paul had the body of Tsar Peter, the man he thought was his father, exhumed. He then turned Catherine's state funeral into a double ceremony, the still fresh corpse of the bloated empress lying beside the desiccated remains of the husband murdered 34 years before.

1730 When Prussian King Frederick William I discovers that his son Frederick (afterwards Frederick the Great) has plotted with his friend (and possible lover) Hans Hermann von Katte to escape his tyrannical rule by fleeing to England, he orders Katte to be executed in front of his son.

Katte's last words are: 'Death is sweet for a Prince I love so well.' * **1938**
Mao Zedong publishes *Problems of War and Strategy*; in chapter 5 he writes:
'Every Communist must grasp the truth, political power grows out of the
barrel of a gun.'

7 November

'Ocian in view! O! the joy.'

1805 Today an expedition of some 30 men came within sight of the
Pacific Ocean after an historic trek of 4,000 miles, the first white
Americans to cross the United States. Led by 32-year-old US Army
Captain Meriwether Lewis, they had left St Louis a year and a half
before.

In 1803 the United States had doubled in size with the Louisiana
Purchase, a deal that brought a huge swathe of land running from
today's Montana and North Dakota all the way south to Louisiana.
Anxious to explore this new territory, President Thomas Jefferson commissioned the 'Corps of Discovery' and appointed Lewis as leader.
Lewis recruited his old friend Lieutenant William Clark as second in
command.

Jefferson personally briefed Lewis: the expedition should make contact with the Indian tribes they encountered, note the region's flora and
fauna and find 'the most direct & practicable water communication
across this continent'.

The Corps embarked at St Charles, Missouri on the Missouri River
in a 55-foot keelboat and two smaller pirogues. As they laboriously
toiled upstream, Lewis often went ashore to study plants and animals
while Clark stayed on board mapping the journey and keeping his
journal.

They continued north through the Great Plains and into Sioux territory in South Dakota, an area inhabited only by Indian tribes and
rich in deer, buffalo and beaver that no white American, except for a
few intrepid trappers, had ever seen. By December they were about
100 miles from today's American–Canadian border, where they built
a fort in which to winter.

In early 1805 the explorers sent back a report on their discoveries,
along with 176 botanical and mineral specimens and Clark's map of the
area they had passed through. Then in April the expedition followed

the Missouri west into Montana. In mid-June they came to the Great Falls of the Missouri, a formidable barrier – five separate falls over a twelve-mile stretch, which required a month to portage around. When they reached the Missouri's headwaters, they had to abandon their boats and find horses – ahead lay the Rocky Mountains.

Crossing these mountains was an arduous test of endurance. As autumn snow fell, food became so scarce that the men had to eat three of their colts. When they finally emerged, they had reached branches of the Columbia River. In five hollowed-out canoes, they sped west with the river's swift current, stopping to trade with Indians or to portage around the most difficult passages. Sometimes they covered 30 miles a day.

On the morning of 7 November, the expedition set off in heavy fog, but when the sky cleared, the men gave a joyous shout – there before them was the Pacific. In his notebook Clark scribbled: 'Ocian in view! O! the joy.' In his journal for the day he wrote: 'We are in view of the Ocian, this great Pacific Octean which we been So long anxious to See. and the roreing or noise made by the waves brakeing on rockey shores (as I suppose) may be heard distictly.'

The men were still twenty miles from open ocean. Forced by the atrocious weather to camp, they finally reached a sandy beach on the Pacific a week later.

The Corps remained near the Columbia for the next four months, waiting for spring weather. The return to St Louis was almost as adventurous as the trip out – moving by boat and horse and confronting Indian tribes, one of which stole most of their horses.

Although they had been given up for dead, on 23 September 1806 they disembarked at St Louis, two years, four months, and ten days after they had left. They had lost only one man – to appendicitis. (Lewis, however, had had two close calls; he had been attacked by a grizzly bear and accidentally shot by one of his own men.)

The Lewis and Clark expedition had been an astonishing success. They had succeeded in crossing the country, brought back samples of hundreds of unknown natural specimens and established diplomatic and trade relations with two dozen Indian nations. Their only disappointment was in not finding a water route across the continent, because none exists.

1783 At Tyburn (at the north-east corner of what is now Hyde Park, near Speaker's Corner) murderer John Austin becomes the last man ever to be publicly hanged there; standing under a beam with a noose around his neck, he tells the crowd: 'Let my example teach you to shun the bad ways I have followed. Keep good company, and mind the word of God.'

8 November

'How long, Catilina, will you abuse our patience?'

63 BC Today in the Roman Senate Marcus Tullius Cicero poured scorn on his rival Lucius Sergius Catilina, exposing his traitorous plans. It was Cicero's finest hour, saving Rome from a conspiracy to overthrow the state.

Catilina was a charismatic 46-year-old patrician driven by ambition and delusions of his own self-worth. Although an able military commander, dark rumours swirled about his past. He was said to have murdered his brother-in-law and later his first wife and son so that he could marry a rich and beautiful heiress. He was also tried for seducing a Vestal Virgin (a capital offence) but was acquitted.

In 66 BC Catilina was barred from running for consul and tried for corruption (but cleared), and two years later he stood as a candidate but was thwarted when Cicero and Antonius Hybrida won the election. Now Catilina began to plot his coup.

First he enlisted others to his cause – disaffected aristocrats who, like himself, had failed in their political ambitions and nursed an envious hatred for those in power. He also set out to build support among the masses by promising to cancel all debts.

While his agents fomented revolt throughout Italy, Catilina sent a retired centurion, Gaius Manlius, north to Faesulae (modern Fiesole) to assemble an army. Meanwhile in Rome the conspirators planned to murder a large number of senators and then join Manlius' army to seize power.

The plot was to be triggered by the assassination of Cicero on the morning of 7 November, but the consul had been warned and posted guards outside his house, who scared the assassins away. One of the conspirators had bragged to his mistress about his forthcoming rise to power – only to have her report everything to her best friend, Cicero's wife.

By now Cicero had ample evidence of Catilina's conspiracy, and on this morning he convened the Senate at the temple of Jupiter Stator, chosen because it was easier to guard than the Senate House. There senators edged away from Catilina, leaving him sitting in lonely defiance, as Cicero launched a bitter attack: 'How long, Catilina, will you abuse our patience? How long is that madness of yours still to mock us? When is there to be an end of that unbridled audacity of yours, swaggering about as it does now?'

Cicero taunted Catilina: 'Do you not see that your conspiracy is already arrested and made powerless by the knowledge which everyone here possesses of it?' He then urged his fellow senators to act: '*O tempora, o mores*! ['Oh, the times! Oh, the customs!'] The senate is aware of these things; the consul sees them; and yet this man lives. Lives! Yes, he even comes into the Senate. He takes a part in public deliberations; he is watching and marking down and checking off for slaughter every one among us.'

As the senators hurled abuse and called him traitor, Catilina fled from the chamber and left Rome, claiming to be going into exile but in fact joining Manlius' rebel army.

Granted emergency powers, Cicero now collected further damning evidence, letters from the conspirators attempting to enlist the Allobroges (a Gallic tribe) into joining the revolt. Cicero condemned to death without trial five chief plotters named in the letters. Despite vigorous protests from Julius Caesar on the illegality of the executions, they were strangled in the Tullianum prison on 5 December. (Five years later Cicero was exiled for having ordered the killings, and in a strange twist of fate, he, too, would be summarily executed – exactly twenty years and two days after the conspirators were put to death.)

Catilina's coup was now doomed. When the rebel soldiers heard of the executions, two-thirds deserted, leaving Catilina with only 3,000 men. In February he fought a much larger Roman army near modern-day Pistoia. The rebels battled bravely but were cut down to a man. Catilina had led from the front; according to the historian Sallust, his corpse 'was found far in advance of his men amid a heap of slain foemen, still breathing slightly, and showing in his face the indomitable spirit which had animated him when alive'.

1793 Bowing in mockery in front of a giant statue of liberty next to the guillotine, the condemned Girondin Madame Roland apostrophises: '*O Liberté, que de crimes on commet en ton nom!*' ('O Liberty! What crimes are committed in thy name!') * **1838** American philosopher Ralph Waldo Emerson: 'Let me never fall into the vulgar mistake of dreaming that I am persecuted whenever I am contradicted.'

9 November

'Either the German revolution begins tonight or we will all be dead by dawn!'

1923 Adolf Hitler's histrionic rant to 3,000 thirsty burghers in a Munich beer hall yesterday evening was intended to launch a putsch against the government, but instead it led to failure, humiliation and prison.

Germany was in turmoil. French and Belgian troops had occupied the Ruhr Valley to force the country to pay war reparations, unemployment was spiralling, violent strikes were endemic and agitators howled for a communist state. The German mark was in free fall (in 1919, a loaf of bread cost 1 mark; now it cost 100 billion), and the Berlin government had imposed a state of emergency. But Bavarian prime minister Eugen von Knilling had declared his own state of emergency, giving near-dictatorial powers to the triumvirate of state commissioner Gustav von Kahr, Bavarian state police head Hans von Seisser and army general Otto von Lossow.

For months, a young (34) Adolf Hitler had been preparing plans to overthrow the Berlin government and punish the 'November criminals' who had 'stabbed Germany in the back' by signing the Treaty of Versailles. Now he sought to gain the triumvirate's support, enlisting the help of the hero of the Battle of Tannenberg, General Erich Ludendorff.

But Kahr, Seisser and Lossow had little interest in Hitler and intended to install a nationalist dictatorship without him. To announce their plans, they organised a meeting for 8 November in the Bürgerbräukeller, an enormous beer hall in the centre of Munich. Hitler decided to force them to join him in a march on Berlin.

After ordering SA stormtroopers to surround the building, Hitler pushed forward to the speaker's platform, pistol in hand. Firing a shot into the ceiling, he shouted: 'The national revolution has broken out! The hall is filled with six hundred heavily armed men. No one may leave the hall.'

Hitler then herded Kahr, Seisser and Lossow into a back room, where, holding them at pistol point, he tried to browbeat them into joining his putsch. He then returned to the hall and announced (falsely) that the Bavarian government had ceded to Nazi demands. Mouthing banalities about 'saving the Fatherland', he concluded: 'Either the German revolution begins tonight or we will all be dead by dawn!'

Hitler then returned to the back room with Ludendorff, who convinced the triumvirate into grudging acceptance of Hitler's putsch. The next morning, however, he discovered that Kahr had only feigned to agree; during the night he had put up placards around Munich saying: 'The declarations extorted from myself, General von Lossow and Colonel Seisser at the point of a revolver are null and void.' Suddenly Hitler's putsch was no putsch at all. The Nazi leader desperately needed to regain the initiative.

Flanked by acolytes like Hermann Göring and Rudolf Hess, at 11.00 this morning Hitler and Ludendorff led 3,000 stormtroopers towards the centre of Munich, intent on seizing the Bavarian Defence Ministry. But at the end of the narrow Residenzstrasse, 100 armed policemen barred their way. It looked to be a stand-off until someone – either Hitler or the Jew-baiter Julius Streicher – opened fire. In seconds three policemen lay dead – as well as fifteen Nazis. Among the wounded were Göring, with a bullet in his thigh, and Hitler himself, who had dislocated a shoulder as he dived for cover. As reported by another Nazi at the scene, Hitler 'was one of the first to get up and turn back', running to a waiting car and leaving his dead and wounded supporters lying in the street. Only Ludendorff had stayed on his feet, contemptuously walking straight through the police lines, certain that no one would fire on a national hero.

Such was Hitler's notorious Beer Hall Putsch, comic except for the loss of life. Hitler was arrested two days later, but his trial for treason was a sham because Bavaria's minister of justice was an ardent supporter. Ludendorff was found not guilty and Hitler was sentenced to five years but served just nine months in Landsberg Prison, treated as an honoured guest and given a private room with a splendid view. He occupied his time by dictating *Mein Kampf* to Rudolf Hess.

1799 Napoleon starts his 18 Brumaire coup d'état to become First Consul; he justifies his overthrow: 'I did not usurp the throne. I found the crown of France in the gutter and placed it on my head.' * **1923** Lord Chief Justice of England Lord Gordon Hewart: 'It … is of fundamental importance that justice should not only be done, but should manifestly and undoubtedly be seen to be done.'

---

10 November

'Dr Livingstone, I presume?'

1871 For five long years there had been no word from Africa's most famous explorer, Dr David Livingstone, who had seemingly vanished – and perhaps perished – in the Dark Continent. The mystery was just the sort of subject for the *New York Herald*, whose founder had proclaimed that the function of a newspaper 'is not to instruct but to startle'. The *Herald's* most celebrated reporter, Henry Stanley, was dispatched to find him.

Leading an expedition of 200 men, Stanley headed into the African interior on 21 March 1871. He tramped through the bush for nearly eight months, encountering disease and hostile tribes along the way. Today he approached Ujiji, on the shores of Lake Tanganyika (now in Tanzania), and later reported:

> We are now about three hundred yards from the village of Ujiji, and the crowds are dense about me. Suddenly I hear a voice on my right say, 'Good morning, sir!'
>
> Startled at hearing this greeting in the midst of such a crowd of black people, I turn sharply around in search of the man, and see him at my side, with the blackest of faces, but animated and joyous, – a man dressed in a long white shirt, with a turban of American sheeting around his woolly head, and I ask, 'Who the mischief are you?'
>
> 'I am Susi, the servant of Dr Livingstone,' said he, smiling, and showing a gleaming row of teeth.
>
> 'What! Is Dr Livingstone here?'
>
> 'Yes, Sir.'
>
> ... I pushed back the crowds, and ... walked down a living avenue of people until I came in front of the semicircle of Arabs, in the front of which stood the white man ... As I advanced slowly toward him I noticed he was pale, looked wearied, had a gray beard, wore a bluish cap with a faded gold band around it, had on a red-sleeved waistcoat and a pair of gray tween trousers. I would have run to him, only I was a coward in the presence of such a mob, would have embraced him, only, he being an Englishman, I did not know how he would receive me; so I did what cowardice and false pride suggested was the best

thing, – walked deliberately to him, took off my hat, and said, 'Dr Livingstone, I presume?'

'Yes,' said he, with a kind smile, lifting his cap slightly.

I replace my hat on my head and he puts on his cap, and we both grasp hands, and I then say aloud, 'I thank God, Doctor, I have been permitted to see you.'

He answered, 'I feel thankful that I am here to welcome you.'

Dr Livingstone had seen no other white man for five and a half years – and after meeting Stanley, would never see another.

For the next four months the two men explored parts of Lake Tanganyika together, but Livingstone resolutely refused to return to England. Instead he continued to wander through the heart of Africa, eventually almost deserted by his guides and bearers, sick and feeble from dysentery, malaria and skin ulcers. Finally, unable to walk and in too much pain to be carried, he camped at a place called Chitambo on Lake Bangweulu (now in Zambia). On 1 May 1873, in the hope of clearing his system he asked his servant Susi for a dose of calomel and then told him: 'All right, you can go out now.' When Susi returned a few hours later, he found him kneeling as if in prayer, dead at the age of 60.

Two of Livingstone's native followers buried his heart and viscera beneath a tree on which they carved his name and then carried his corpse out to civilisation. Eventually it was shipped back to England where in 1874 it was interred with great ceremony beneath the floor of Westminster Abbey.

David Livingstone had spent 33 years in Africa and was widely recognised as its greatest explorer, yet he had failed in the three tasks he had set himself: to find the source of the Nile, to stop the slave trade and to convert to Christianity black Africans whom he called 'these sad captives of Sin and Satan'.

1938 Turkish leader Kemal Atatürk dies, having erroneously predicted: 'My body will become dust one day, but the Turkish republic and her principles will live for ever!'

---

11 November

*'No dumb bastard ever won a war by going out
and dying for his country. He won it by making
some other dumb bastard die for his country.'*

1885 Born today near Los Angeles was one of America's greatest –
and most controversial – Second World War generals. He was George
Patton.

Patton's grandfather and great-uncle had both been killed fighting
for the South during the American Civil War, while a family friend was
the renowned Confederate cavalry leader, John Singleton Mosby. This
ignited in Patton an interest in military history, but, bizarrely, he also
came to believe that in previous lives he had been a Roman centurion
or a Napoleonic officer.

After graduating from West Point, Patton became a cavalry officer
so expert in riding, fencing and pistol shooting that he finished fifth in
the modern pentathlon in the 1912 Olympics. He was also an expert
sailor and qualified as a pilot.

He first saw combat chasing the elusive Mexican bandit/revolution-
ary Pancho Villa in 1916, and it was then that he took to wearing his
trademark ivory-handled revolvers. But during the First World War he
found his true calling – tanks. He often rode on top of a tank during
attacks and was shot in the left leg while leading an assault against a
German machine-gun position. In only eighteen months, he was promoted from first lieutenant to colonel.

During the Second World War Patton, now a major general, headed
the 2nd Armored Division, fighting first in Morocco against the Vichy
French. To enhance discipline, he became a stickler for military protocol and ordered his soldiers to wear clean, pressed uniforms and
to shave every day. He also constantly addressed his troops to build
morale, telling his men: 'No dumb bastard ever won a war by going
out and dying for his country. He won it by making some other dumb
bastard die for his country.' His men called him 'Old Blood and Guts',
although some sniped, 'our blood, his guts'.

In Sicily Patton commanded the Seventh Army, supposedly supporting Bernard Montgomery's British Eighth Army, but he upstaged
Montgomery by beating him to Messina, killing or capturing
113,000 enemy troops on the way.

'May God have mercy upon my enemies, because I won't', Patton once said. He had little mercy on his own weaker soldiers either, igniting a huge storm when he slapped two soldiers who were hospitalised for shell-shock, cursing at one: '[You] goddamned coward, you yellow son of a bitch.' Eisenhower forced the famously profane general to apologise publicly but refused to sack him because 'Patton is indispensable to the war effort'. (Patton claimed that 'an army without profanity couldn't fight its way out of a piss-soaked paper bag'.)

After the Normandy landing Patton led the US Third Army on a legendary armoured advance across France and into Nazi Germany. In continuous combat for 281 days, they inflicted 1,500,000 German casualties, five times their own strength. Patton claimed he could have taken Berlin if his tanks hadn't run out of fuel. His most famous exploit occurred during the Battle of the Bulge, when he disengaged six divisions from front-line combat in the middle of winter and wheeled 90 degrees to rout the Germans surrounding Bastogne. (When heavy snow denied him air cover, he ordered an army chaplain to pray for good weather; when the weather cleared, Patton awarded him a Bronze Star.)

After the German surrender, Patton continued to court trouble by telling reporters that he did not see the need for 'this denazification thing' but claimed about the US ally, 'the Russian has no regard for human life and is an all-out son of a bitch, barbarian, and chronic drunk'. This caused Eisenhower to relieve him, even though he thought that 'Patton was the most brilliant commander of an army in the open field that our or any other service produced'.

Patton's final assignment was commanding occupation troops in Germany. On 8 December 1945 his car crashed into an American army truck, breaking his neck. Paralysed from the neck down, he died in the hospital thirteen days later.

1850 American essayist and philosopher Henry David Thoreau writes in his journal: 'Some circumstantial evidence is very strong, as when you find a trout in the milk.' * **1918** When the armistice is signed ending the First World War, French writer Jean Giraudoux records: 'The armistice has just been signed by Lloyd George who looks like a poodle, by Wilson who looks like a collie and by Clemenceau who looks like a mastiff.'

12 November

*'This is farewell. I shall wait beneath the moss/
Until the flowers are fragrant/
In this island country of Japan.'*

1948 Today seven top Japanese military leaders and six high-ranking government officials were sentenced to death for war crimes committed during the Second World War. The most prominent was Hideki Tojo, a professional soldier who was Japan's prime minister from 1941 to 1944.

With his balding pate, brush moustache and round spectacles, Tojo was the subject of countless cartoons and anti-Japanese propaganda during the war. Now dressed in a baggy uniform without badges or rank insignia, he still retained his composure.

Accused of enacting 'a conspiracy to wage wars of aggression … in violation of international law', the defendants were charged with 'murdering, maiming and ill-treating prisoners of war [and] civilian internees … plundering public and private property, wantonly destroying cities, towns and villages beyond any justification of military necessity … [propagating] mass murder, rape, pillage, brigandage, torture and other barbaric cruelties upon the helpless civilian population …'

Early in the trial Tojo had told the judges: 'It is natural that I should bear entire responsibility for the war in general, and, needless to say, I am prepared to do so.' The judges agreed – he was sentenced to hang.

Born at the end of 1884, Tojo was the son of a samurai turned army officer and educated to become a soldier, taught that war was a holy duty and that the emperor was a living god. When he entered the army, he was noted for his dedication and relentless work ethic, a stern and cold man with no known sense of humour. He was a fervent nationalist nicknamed 'Razor' (*kamisori*) for his sharp, legalistic mind and quick decision-making.

After serving in Japan's brutal invasion of China, Tojo was recalled to Japan in 1938 as Vice-Minister of War. Then in July 1940 he rose to Army Minister under Prime Minister Fumimaro Konoe and vigorously supported the Tripartite Pact between Imperial Japan, Nazi Germany, and Fascist Italy.

By autumn 1941, however, Konoe was forced to resign, and Emperor Hirohito chose Tojo to replace him. He took office on 18 October, less than two months before Japan's infamous attack on Pearl Harbor.

In giving the go-ahead for the attack, Tojo had little fear of meaningful American resistance. When he was 38, he had ridden by train across the United States and concluded that Americans were soft and undisciplined, interested only in money, sex and partying.

Eager to amass even more power, by the end of 1943 Tojo was serving as Prime Minister, Army Minister, and Chief of the Imperial Japanese Army General Staff, taking personal charge of the army. But now the Americans were advancing across the Pacific, and when their conquest of Saipan put bombers within range of the Japanese homeland, he was forced to resign on 22 July 1944.

With or without Tojo at the helm, Japan had no chance of avoiding total defeat and surrendered on 15 August 1945. Within a month General Douglas MacArthur ordered the detention of 40 war criminals including Tojo, but when soldiers arrived at his house to arrest him, Tojo shot himself in the chest in an attempted suicide. As he bled, he apologised for his poor aim: 'I am very sorry it is taking me so long to die.'

But Tojo didn't die; he recovered and was held in prison until the war crimes trial started on 29 April 1946. Seen as the personification of ruthless Japanese militarism, he was held responsible for the murder of millions of civilians in China and the Far East and of thousands of Allied prisoners of war. Today he was condemned to death, and 41 days later he was hanged in the Tokyo's Sugamo Prison with six other war criminals. Wearing American army work clothes, in his final statement before his execution this austere and brutal man chose to recite a haunting poem of his own devising:

> This is farewell. I shall wait beneath the moss
> Until the flowers are fragrant
> In this island country of Japan.

1793 French astronomer and politician and former Mayor of Paris Jean Sylvain Bailly is guillotined on the Champ de Mars in Paris; the previous day he reflected: 'It's time for me to enjoy another pinch of snuff. Tomorrow my hands will be bound, so as to make it impossible.'

13 November

*'All the Danes who had sprung up
in this island, sprouting like cockle amongst
the wheat, were to be destroyed.'*

1002 In 2008 workmen excavating in Oxford made a gruesome discovery – skeletons of about 35 men, all aged sixteen to 25, the remains from 11th-century Vikings. All had been brutally slaughtered. One had been decapitated, and attempts at decapitation had been made on five others. They had been beheaded from the front, facing the blow, which came from a sword, not an axe, a method used on high-ranking warriors. All the skeletons bore numerous stab marks, and 27 had shattered skulls. The bones had signs of charring, showing that the bodies had been burned.

What the workmen had found was grisly evidence of the St Brice's Day massacre, which happened on this day in 1002.

At the end of the 10th century England was constantly harried by Danish raiders, who really did 'rape and pillage' on a large scale. In addition, substantial areas of England were occupied by (moderately) peaceful Danes. King of England since he was twelve years old in 978 was the unready Aethelred.

The first years of Aethelred's reign were relatively quiet, but by the mid-980s the Danes began to raid in earnest, winning a famous victory at Maldon in Essex in 991. Fearing for his kingdom, Aethelred tried everything but fighting – he bribed the Danes to stay away (the famous 'Danegeld'), made an alliance with Duke Richard of Normandy, and buttressed the pact by marrying his daughter, Emma.

In 1002 Aethelred paid the then colossal sum of £24,000 in Danegeld, but instead of peace, he received reports that the Danes were plotting to murder him and his councillors and take over his kingdom. His answer was to organise a wholesale massacre of 'all the Danish men who were among the English race'. (In fact, he could hardly have killed all the Danes then living in England, so his decree probably referred to recent arrivals and any Danish raiders.)

We do not know the extent of the slaughter, but when his men attacked Oxford, Danish families fled to St Frideswide's church for sanctuary. After cutting down any Danish fighters they could find, the English burned the church and the Danes within. Those who escaped were slaughtered as they fled. Because it happened on the feast day of a 5th-century French bishop named Brice, the event was called the St Brice's Day massacre.

Aethelred justified his actions in a royal charter of 1004, explaining that 'all the Danes who had sprung up in this island, sprouting like cockle [weeds] amongst the wheat, were to be destroyed by a most just extermination, and thus this decree was to be put into effect even as far as death'. What Aethelred had not counted on, however, was that among those slain would be Gunhilde, the sister of the Danish King Sweyn Forkbeard. She was forced to witness the execution of her husband and son ('pierced by four lances') and bravely declared that 'the shedding of her blood would cost all England dear' before she was beheaded.

Determined to avenge his murdered sister, the next summer Sweyn Forkbeard sacked Exeter and laid waste much of Wessex, causing Aethelred to complain of 'the anger of God raging with ever increasing savagery against us'.

For a while Aethelred held his own through military resistance and large bribes, but in 1013 Sweyn invaded and forced him into exile in Normandy.

On Christmas Day 1013 Sweyn was declared King of England, but he died only five weeks later, his son Cnut inheriting the throne. At the request of some leading English barons, Aethelred returned and, with the help of his wayward son Edmund Ironside, managed to force Cnut back to Denmark, but it was not to last. In 1016 Cnut returned and subjugated most of the country. Aethelred died on 23 April 1016, and three months later Cnut married his widow Emma to complete his conquest.

The scene of the massacre, the destroyed St Frideswide's church, was first rebuilt as a monastery and starting in 1160 recreated as the Gothic masterpiece, Christ Church Cathedral of Oxford.

1789 Benjamin Franklin writes in French to French physicist Jean-Baptiste Le Roy: '*Notre constitution nouvelle est actuellement établie, tout paraît nous promettre qu'elle sera durable; mais, dans ce monde, il n'y a rien d'assure que la mort et les impôts.*' ('Our new Constitution is now established, everything seems to promise it will be durable; but, in this world, nothing is certain except death and taxes.')

14 November

*'I may be a blockhead, but I am unable to understand
how a man can use thirty pages to describe how he
tosses and turns in his bed before falling asleep!'*

1913 Today – at last – a Paris firm published *Du côté de chez Swann*
(*Swann's Way*), the first part of Marcel Proust's magnum opus, *À la
recherche du temps perdu* (translated as *Remembrance of Things Past* or
In Search of Lost Time). Working continuously until he died nine years
later, Proust would add six more volumes to create the longest book in
the French language. He spent seventeen years writing this massive masterpiece, producing 75 drafts that resulted in a narrative of 3,200 pages
featuring over 2,000 characters. One sentence alone comes to 414 words.

Born in 1871 and raised a Catholic by a Catholic father and a rich
Jewish mother, Proust was plagued by ill-health most of his life and
suffered severely from asthma. He lived in Paris's Boulevard Haussmann
with his parents until they died, and during the last three years of his
life he stayed largely in bed in his cork-lined room, with closed shutters
and drawn curtains, sleeping during the day and working at night. Yet
he continued to frequent *le beau monde*, the combination of aristocracy
and haute bourgeoisie that he portrays in his novel. When he ventured
out to join his friends, this closet homosexual with liquid, heavy-lidded
eyes and a pointed fop moustache wore a fur-lined coat indoors and
out, even at dinner parties.

Proust's first attempt to find a publisher ended in failure in 1909
when the French literary magazine *Mercure de France* declined to
publish his seminal short(er) work called *Contre Sainte-Beuve*. More
revisions and new titles fared little better. One editor lamented: 'At
the end of seven hundred and twelve pages of manuscript … you have
absolutely no idea of what it is about.' He would not be the last to
recoil before this indecipherable hand-written manuscript, with neither
chapters nor paragraphs and covered with erasures.

Du côté de chez Swann begins: 'For a long time I used to go to bed
early. Sometimes, when I had put out my candle, my eyes would close
so quickly that I had not even time to say "I'm going to sleep". And half
an hour later the thought that it was time to go to sleep would awaken
me …' Such an opening prompted a rejection from another editor who
complained: 'I may be a blockhead, but I am unable to understand
how a man can use thirty pages to describe how he tosses and turns in

his bed before falling asleep!' Even the great novelist André Gide could bring himself to read only a few pages before recommending to the *Nouvelle Revue Français* not to accept it (although he later repented his decision and humbly apologised to Proust).

Finally Proust persuaded the publisher Bernard Grasset to take his book – but Grasset did so only on the condition that Proust himself would pay the printing costs. Drawing on money inherited from his parents, he underwrote the publication, and *Du côté de chez Swann* appeared on this day in 1913.

Proust continued to labour on his work until he died of pneumonia in 1922. At his death the last three of the seven volumes existed only in advanced draft form, but his brother Robert oversaw their completion. Ever since it appeared, *À la recherche du temps perdu* has received extravagant praise and is now considered a classic. Somerset Maugham even called it 'the greatest fiction to date'. It is regularly listed among 'the greatest novels of the 20th century', sometimes even ranked number one. How much it is still read, however, invites speculation. As Mark Twain memorably noted: 'A classic is something that everybody wants to have read and nobody wants to read.'

1916 British writer Saki (H.H. Munro) is killed by a German sniper at the Battle of the Ancre immediately after having told a fellow soldier: 'Put that bloody cigarette out.' * **1965** Ronald Reagan during his 1965 campaign for Governor of California: 'Government is like a baby. An alimentary canal with a big appetite at one end and no responsibility at the other.'

---

15 November

'I have often thought that I am the cleverest woman that ever lived.'

1908 Today died the Empress Dowager Cixi, who was once a royal concubine but rose to hold supreme power in China for almost half a century.

Cixi was only sixteen when she became a concubine of the Xianfeng emperor of the Qing dynasty. But competition was tough: Xianfeng had an empress, two consorts and ten other concubines. Whenever Xianfeng wanted her, court eunuchs would present her naked before him, within a red robe.

577

At twenty, Cixi gave birth to the emperor's only surviving son. Then in 1861 Xianfeng died, only 30 but worn out by a dissipated life, and her son, now six, became the Tongzhi emperor. This put Cixi in a position of strength, but Xianfeng had noticed her insatiable ambition and on his deathbed had set up an eight-man regency.

Teaming up with Xianfeng's widow, Empress Dowager Ci'an, and Prince Gong, the dead emperor's brother, Cixi falsely accused the regents of forging the emperor's will and forced two to commit suicide, while another was beheaded in the public vegetable market. This was not the last blood she would shed.

Cixi and Ci'an became co-regents for the Tongzhi emperor, but Cixi called the shots, even though she was forced to sit behind a screen during imperial audiences. She squandered money on luxuries and lavish entertainment, drank from a jade cup, ate with golden chopsticks and amassed 3,000 ebony boxes stuffed with jewellery.

When Tongzhi came of age in 1873, the regency was dissolved and Cixi's control was threatened, but she encouraged his use of concubines and opium, and he died two years later at eighteen, from smallpox or possibly syphilis. A dark rumour swirled around the court that she had poisoned her son to cling to power.

Now Cixi and Ci'an became regents for Cixi's three-year-old nephew, whom she adopted. (He would become the Guangxu emperor when he came of age.) Six years later Ci'an suddenly died, leaving Cixi with unfettered authority.

Guangxu formally took control in 1889, and Cixi moved to her magnificent summer palace but continued to pull the strings behind the scenes. Such was her influence that during the First Sino-Japanese War, officials often ignored Guangxu and sent their reports to Cixi.

In 1898 Guangxu began a series of sweeping political and social changes that Cixi opposed. Learning of an assassination plot against her, she staged a military-backed coup and forced Guangxu to retire to the Forbidden City, isolated from the rest of the court. His servants were either executed or banished and his favourite concubine thrown down a well. 'Whoever makes me unhappy for a day, I will make suffer for a lifetime', she said. Guangxu was allowed to see only four guards and his wife, who was spying for Cixi. Nominally he remained emperor, but she held the reins. Her first act was to reverse his reforms.

In 1900 Cixi allied herself with the anti-Christian, anti-foreign Boxer cult, but widespread attacks on missionaries and diplomats led to foreign intervention and the occupation of Beijing. Disguised as a peasant woman, she fled in an ox cart with Guangxu, and China was forced to accept a humiliating peace.

In 1902 Cixi and Guangxu made a ceremonious return to Beijing, and she sent him back to his isolated palace, where he spent his time tinkering with watches and clocks. With the emperor effectively under house arrest, Cixi had good reason to gloat. 'I have often thought that I am the cleverest woman that ever lived, and others cannot compare with me', she said. 'Although I have heard much about Queen Victoria … [She had] really nothing to say about the policy of the country. Now look at me. I have 400,000,000 people dependent on my judgement.'

Cixi continued in power until 1908, when she suffered a stroke, but she had one more card to play. On 14 November she deposed Guangxu and replaced him with his nephew Puyi, who became the last Qing emperor. That same day Guangxu suddenly died, still only 37. Knowing her death was near, Cixi had poisoned him with arsenic to ensure that he made no comeback after she was gone. The next afternoon Cixi died, two weeks short of her 73rd birthday.

1954 When told he is about to die, celebrated American actor Lionel Barrymore responds: 'Well, I've played everything but a harp.'

---

16 November

'His playing is like the sighing of a flower, the whisper of the clouds, or the murmur of the stars.'

1848 Today at London's Guildhall, Frédéric Chopin, gaunt and drawn, gave his final public concert. Weighing less than seven stone (98 pounds), he was ill with tuberculosis from which he would die eleven months later. He knew his condition was terminal but had decided to perform one more time, for the benefit of Polish refugees.

Like his compositions, Chopin's life was brilliant in success, wistful in tone and brief in duration. He was born Fryderyk Franciszek Szopen in 1810 in Zelazowa Wola, 29 miles from Warsaw. Despite his name and birthplace, he was Frenchified from the start: his father was a French émigré who sent him to the local French lycée.

Chopin's genius showed itself at an early age: he gave his first concert at eight at the palace of Polish Prince Radziwill. After he had moved

579

to France in 1831 the same prince presented him to Parisian society at the home of Baron de Rothschild. He would never return to Poland.

Chopin soon became celebrated as a composer and virtuoso. He wrote some 200 pieces, and the aristocracy and rich middle class of Paris paid lavishly to hear him play and teach their daughters the piano. 'His playing', rhapsodised the music magazine *Le Ménestral*, is 'like the sighing of a flower, the whisper of the clouds, or the murmur of the stars.'

In 1836 Chopin was introduced by Franz Liszt to the Parisian baroness Aurore Dudevant, who had become famous under the pseudonym of George Sand for writing about the anguish and exultation of women in love. Six years older than Chopin and still married, she was already the focus of Parisian gossip about her turbulent liaisons with Alfred de Musset and Prosper Mérimée. Now she pleaded with Chopin to become her lover. In 1838 the two retreated to Mallorca, but the hostility of the traditionally Catholic local people to an unmarried couple forced them to move to an abandoned Carthusian monastery, where they stayed for two months.

Returning to France, Chopin and his mistress lived first in Sand's country house at Nohant, and then moved to Paris. But after nine years, their affair was over, broken by lovers' quarrels and the composer's deteriorating health.

Free but unhappy, in 1848 Chopin organised a desultory seven-month tour of Great Britain, but he found the English perplexing. 'They are kind people', he wrote, 'but so weird.' By the time of today's final concert, he had already been ill for some time, and a few days later he returned to Paris.

Moving into 12 Place Vendôme, Chopin saw only a few of his closest friends, although the celebrated mezzo-soprano Pauline Viardot waspishly commented: 'all the grand Parisian ladies considered it *de rigueur* to faint in his room.' Fearing the worst, he wrote in his last letter to his sister: 'The earth is suffocating. Swear to make them cut me open, so I won't be buried alive.'

Chopin died on 17 October 1849, a few weeks short of his 40th birthday. On the morning of his death a doctor asked him if he was in pain, to which he replied, '*Plus*' ('No more'), his last word. Shortly before his death he had requested: 'Play Mozart in memory of me, and I will hear you.' Mozart's *Requiem* was played at his funeral as he had asked.

Chopin's life had been a classic of 19th-century Romanticism: his dreamy music, his doomed affair with George Sand, and his final wasting illness. As Hector Berlioz uncharitably commented: 'He was dying all his life.'

Chopin's heart was stored in a jar of cognac and sealed in a pillar in the crypt of the Holy Cross church in Warsaw. During the Warsaw uprising in 1944, a high-ranking Chopin-admiring SS officer filched the heart and kept it in the local German headquarters before it was returned to the church at the end of the war.

The rest of Chopin's body had been interred in Paris's Père-Lachaise cemetery, but he is buried in Polish soil, scattered over his coffin from a supply the far-sighted composer had brought with him from his native country twenty years before his death.

1920 Russian baron Peter Wrangel withdraws his White Russian army at Sevastopol, ending the Russian Civil War. He later explains the cause of the counter-revolutionary failure: 'We had not brought pardon and peace with us, but only the cruel sword of vengeance.' * **1941** Reichsminister for propaganda Joseph Goebbels writes in *Das Reich*: 'The prophecy that the Führer made … that should international finance Jewry succeed in plunging the nations into a world war again, the result would not be the Bolshevization of the world … but the annihilation of the Jewish race in Europe. We are in the midst of that process … Compassion or regret are entirely out of place here.'

---

17 November

'Domestic policy? I wage war. Foreign policy? I wage war. I wage war all the time.'

1917 Today 76-year-old Georges Clemenceau was named Prime Minister of France for the second time. In a war-weary and divided country, he became an indomitable foe to the Germans, also taking the job of Minister of War.

Born in the Vendée, Clemenceau trained to be a doctor but, growing up during the reign of Napoleon III, he became a passionate republican and an atheist. He protested against the monarchy to such a degree that at 24 he fled to the United States when the government began sending dissidents to Devil's Island.

While in New York Clemenceau married Mary Plummer, with whom he had three children, despite his flagrant infidelity. After

Napoleon III was deposed, the Clemenceaus returned to France. He later voiced a judgement common among the French ever since: 'Americans have no capacity for abstract thought, and make bad coffee.'

The couple separated in 1876, but when he discovered that Mary had taken her children's tutor as a lover, he was so incensed that he had her jailed for two weeks, stripped of her French nationality and sent back to the United States. (Perhaps a reflection of his marital troubles, years later he wrote that if women were given the vote, 'France would return to the Middle Ages'.)

By 1876 Clemenceau had become a member of the Chamber of Deputies. Along with government duties, he practised as a journalist and established the newspaper *L'Aurore*, which in 1898 published Émile Zola's '*J'Accuse*', an article damning the government over the Dreyfus Affair. Hated by the establishment, Clemenceau shrugged: 'Never fear making enemies, if you don't have any, you haven't done anything.'

Although still a staunch republican, Clemenceau lurched to the right when he thought France's interests were threatened. He deserted the socialist party and, now Minister of the Interior, ordered in the military against striking miners and vineyard workers.

Clemenceau first became Prime Minister in 1906 but resigned three years later. After war broke out in 1914, he savagely attacked President Raymond Poincaré for not doing enough to win: 'There are only two perfectly useless things in this world. One is an appendix and the other is Poincaré.' By 1917 France was reeling after the bloodletting at Verdun and the Somme, and on 6 November allied Russia withdrew from the war. Reluctantly, Poincaré asked his old antagonist to become Prime Minister.

Clemenceau rapidly imposed his authority on the army, claiming: 'War! It's too serious a thing to entrust to the military.' But as well as reviewing strategy with the generals, he also went to the trenches to see the *poilus*. According to the contemporary author André Maurois: 'On the front, the soldiers saw an old man in a felt hat, who brandished a club and brutally pushed the generals to victory. It was Georges Clemenceau.' When queried in the Chamber of Deputies about his policies, Clemenceau heatedly replied: 'Domestic policy? I wage war. Foreign policy? I wage war. I wage war all the time.' His determination was rewarded when Germany surrendered in November 1918. On hearing the news, the man now known in France as *Le Père la Victoire* broke down in tears.

At the subsequent Paris Peace Conference, Clemenceau found himself seated between America's high-minded Woodrow Wilson and Britain's bellicose David Lloyd George, which he acidly described as sitting 'between Jesus Christ and Napoleon Bonaparte'. During the conference a French anarchist fired several shots at him as he was leaving his house. One bullet hit him between the ribs, just missing his vital organs. Never short of an ironic put-down, the old warrior remarked: 'We have just won the most terrible war in history, yet here is a Frenchman who misses his target six out of seven times at point-blank range.'

France at peace no longer needed her great war leader, and Clemenceau's government fell in 1920. He took no further part in politics, spending the rest of his life travelling and writing (one book a biography of his friend Claude Monet). But he never lost his old combative spirit; just before he died on 24 November 1929 he said: 'I wish to be buried facing Germany.'

1558 When courtiers ride out to Hatfield House to tell Elizabeth Tudor that she is now Queen of England because her half-sister Queen Mary has died earlier that day, she responds by quoting the 118th Psalm: 'This is the Lord's doing; it is marvellous in our eyes.'

---

18 November

'Now I am living in France, in the Babylon of the West.'

1302 Since his election in 1294, Pope Boniface VIII had been man-oeuvring against France's Philip IV (the Fair) for control of Church revenues in France. In 1296 he issued a papal bull forbidding taxation of the clergy, to which Philip retaliated by outlawing the export of money from France to Rome. Five years later, Philip imprisoned a French bishop on trumped-up charges of treason in an attempt to gain control of the clergy.

Incensed, Boniface informed Philip that 'God has set popes over kings and kingdoms', announced that he would depose him if need be, and on this day in 1302 issued the broadest declaration of power of any pope in history. The bull *Unam Sanctam* stated that 'it is absolutely necessary for salvation that every human creature be subject to the Roman Pontiff'. Even this, however, failed to rein in Philip but ultimately triggered the move of the papacy to Avignon in what is known as the 'Babylonian Captivity' for a period of 67 years.

In September 1303 Philip confronted Boniface directly by sending his councillor Guillaume de Nogaret to the Pope's summer residence at Agnani, where he accused Boniface of heresy, idolatry, nepotism, simony, sorcery and sodomy and slapped him across the face. A month later Boniface died 'of shame and rage'.

Boniface's successor Benedict XI succumbed after only eight months, rumoured to have been poisoned on Philip's orders. Then in 1305, a papal conclave in Perugia elected Philip's favourite, Bertrand de Got, a Frenchman from Aquitaine, who took the name of Clement V.

Clement refused to travel to Rome (chaotic in the extreme at the time) and chose Lyon for his coronation, where Philip could be present. His enthronement seemed an unlucky omen – Clement was knocked off his horse by a collapsing wall that killed one of his brothers, and a second brother was killed in a fight between his servants and retainers from the College of Cardinals.

Clement moved to Poitiers and then to Toulouse, acting as much for the interests of France as for the Church. To show his gratitude to Philip, he created nine French cardinals and annulled Boniface's *Unam Sanctam*. He also helped Philip to destroy the Templars in 1307. Then in 1309 he took up residence in the Dominican monastery in Avignon, where he remained until his death in 1314.

Six more popes reigned at Avignon; all were French. Most lived in regal splendour, particularly Clement VI, who smugly claimed: 'My predecessors did not know how to be pope.' He and his successors built the imposing Palais des Papes, the largest Gothic building of the Middle Ages.

One of Avignon's residents was the Italian scholar and poet Petrarch (Francesco Petrarca), who moved there in 1326. He was appalled by the uxorious lifestyle of the papal court and felt that the papacy had been abducted from Rome. In reference to the 6th-century BC exile of the Jews to Babylon, he wrote: 'Now I am living in France, in the Babylon of the West ... Instead of holy solitude we find a criminal host and crowds of the most infamous; instead of soberness, licentious banquets; instead of pious pilgrimages, preternatural and foul sloth.' Most historians believe the term 'Babylonian Captivity' of the papacy comes from Petrarch's critique.

The last Avignon pope was Gregory XI, who finally yielded to the pleas of Saint Catherine of Sienna. On 13 September 1376 he abandoned Avignon and four months later entered Rome, with Catherine at his side.

Thus the Babylonian Captivity came to an end, but not the papal conflict that it engendered. Gregory died fourteen months after his return, and the next conclave produced yet more chaos. The French cardinals were determined to return the papacy to Avignon but the Italians were equally adamant that it should remain in Rome. When the bitterly anti-French Archbishop Bartolomeo Prignano was elected (as Urban VI), the French scurried back to Avignon and elected an antipope, a Frenchman who took the name Clement VII. So began the Papal Schism that split Christendom into rival camps, with two and sometimes three 'popes' claiming legitimacy. The schism lasted until the Council of Constance in 1417.

1777 A fierce opponent of using force against the colonies in North America, William Pitt the Elder declares in Parliament: 'If I were an American, as I am an Englishman, while a foreign troop was landed in my country, I never would lay down my arms – never – never – never!' * **1783** William Pit the Younger in the House of Commons: 'Necessity is the plea for every infringement of human freedom. It is the argument of tyrants; it is the creed of slaves.'

---

19 November

'… that government of the people, by the people, for the people, shall not perish from the earth.'

1863 Today, in the midst of America's Civil War, President Abraham Lincoln gave the most famous speech ever delivered by an American.

In July, Union and Confederate armies had met head-on in a ferocious three-day battle around Gettysburg, Pennsylvania. It was the climax of Southern General Robert E. Lee's campaign to move the fighting from war-ravaged Virginia, in the hope that invading the North might make Northern politicians abandon their prosecution of a war that had already torn the country apart for two years.

The first two days of the battle were bloody but indecisive, but on the third day Lee ordered an infantry assault on the aptly named Cemetery Ridge. After a massive but ineffectual artillery bombardment, 12,500 Confederates advanced over open fields for three-quarters of a mile under heavy Union artillery and rifle fire. Charging the last several hundred yards, the Southerners were scythed down, over half their number killed or wounded. It was a decisive defeat, and Lee was forced to retreat back into Virginia, never again to fight on Northern soil.

Gettysburg had been a massive bloodletting. Each side suffered over 23,000 casualties, the bloodiest battle in American history. It was also the war's turning point; from now on the Confederacy would be on the defensive, as the North's greater manpower and industrial output would batter the South into submission.

After the battle Pennsylvania governor Andrew Curtain allocated seventeen acres of pasture for a cemetery for the dead and invited Edward Everett, congressman, governor and ambassador in an illustrious career, to deliver the memorial speech. Almost as an afterthought, President Lincoln was also asked to make a few remarks.

Everett addressed the crowd for over two hours, followed by Lincoln, who spoke for less than three minutes. An eyewitness wrote that 'with a manner serious almost to sadness, he gave his brief address'.

Four score and seven years ago our fathers brought forth on this continent, a new nation, conceived in Liberty, and dedicated to the proposition that all men are created equal.

Now we are engaged in a great civil war, testing whether that nation, or any nation so conceived and so dedicated, can long endure. We are met on a great battlefield of that war. We have come to dedicate a portion of that field, as a final resting place for those who here gave their lives that that nation might live. It is altogether fitting and proper that we should do this.

But, in a larger sense, we can not dedicate – we can not consecrate – we can not hallow – this ground. The brave men, living and dead, who struggled here, have consecrated it, far above our poor power to add or detract. The world will little note, nor long remember what we say here, but it can never forget what they did here. It is for us the living, rather, to be dedicated here to the unfinished work which they who fought here have thus far so nobly advanced. It is rather for us to be here dedicated to the great task remaining before us – that from these honored dead we take increased devotion to that cause for which they gave the last full measure of devotion – that we here highly resolve that these dead shall not have died in vain – that this nation, under God, shall have a new birth of freedom – and that government of the people, by the people, for the people, shall not perish from the earth.

In just 271 words the president had reminded a war-weary public that the Civil War was not only about saving the Union but also a battle for freedom and equality. The long-winded Edward Everett told Lincoln afterwards: 'I should be glad if I could flatter myself that I came as near to the central idea of the occasion, in two hours, as you did in two minutes.'

Lincoln's Gettysburg Address is still familiar to virtually all Americans and is carved into the interior wall of the Lincoln Memorial in Washington. In the sincerest form of flattery, in 1958 the French adopted their current constitution, which defines the French Republic as '*gouvernement du peuple, par le peuple et pour le peuple*', a literal translation of Lincoln's iconic phrase.

1873 Benjamin Disraeli at a banquet in Glasgow: 'An author who speaks about his own books is almost as bad as a mother who talks about her own children.'

---

20 November

'*Our bells are worn threadbare with ringing for victories.*'

1759 Today Admiral Sir Edward Hawke's fleet decisively defeated the French near the coast of Brittany at Quiberon Bay. It was Britain's closing triumph in 1759 that changed the course of the Seven Years' War.

During the early years of the war, despite the occasional defeat, the French had gained numerous victories around the globe, like capturing Menorca, thwarting the British attack on Fort Duquesne and thrashing them at the Battle of Carillon, inflicting over 2,000 casualties in the bloodiest battle of the American theatre of the war. Now the French were planning to invade Britain itself.

Then came 1759.

In February a British naval squadron bringing in 600 reinforcements finally broke the three-month French siege of the British fort at Madras in India. Then in May, after failing to take Martinique, an army of 6,000 British forced the French to surrender Guadeloupe. Further north, in today's Canada, in July British forces captured French-held Fort Niagara. Even more satisfying, later that month General Sir Jeffery Amherst took his artillery to high ground overlooking Fort Carillon – the same fort captured by the French the previous year – and forced the 400-man French garrison to evacuate. (The British promptly dispensed with the French name 'Carillon' and replaced it with the Iroquois word 'Ticonderoga'.)

On the Continent, on 1 August an Anglo–Hanoverian army of 37,000 under the command of Field Marshal Ferdinand of Brunswick whipped a slightly larger French force at Minden, causing 7,000 casualties. (In this battle the French colonel the Marquis de Lafayette was killed by a cannonball, leaving behind a two-year-old son who would make such a heroic contribution to the American cause twenty years later during the Revolutionary War.) That same month a British fleet destroyed or captured five French ships-of-the-line off the Portuguese coast at the Battle of Lagos. Then, on 13 September, in one of history's most noted encounters, the British conquered Quebec in the Battle of the Plains of Abraham, with both commanders – James Wolfe and the Marquis de Montcalm – falling in battle.

Despite the British victories, the French continued to plan for invasion, collecting a fleet of flat-bottomed transports that would ferry an army of 100,000 troops across the Channel to land on England's southern coast. Through their secret agents, however, the British learned of the French plans and ordered Admiral Hawke to blockade major French ports.

On 15 November a French fleet set out from Brest and headed down the coast to Quiberon Bay, where the invasion army was waiting. But an unexpected storm slowed down the French, allowing Hawke to catch them on this day and attack. The results were disastrous for the French – one ship captured, three shipwrecked trying to escape and two destroyed, plus the loss of 2,500 men, most drowned. The victors lost just two ships and about 400 killed.

The Battle of Quiberon Bay crippled the French fleet, put paid to any French thoughts of invasion and established British naval supremacy that would last until the 20th century. No wonder the British called 1759 the *Annus Mirabilis* (year of wonders). As the writer and man of letters Horace Walpole reported: 'Our bells are worn threadbare with ringing for victories.'

1910 At 82, Leo Tolstoy dies of pneumonia at Astapovo railway station; spurning a hovering priest, he says: 'Even in the valley of the shadow of death, two and two do not make six.' * **1945** As the Nazi war crime trials begin at Nuremberg, Reichsmarschall Hermann Göring tells the court: 'We weren't a band of criminals meeting in the woods in the dead of night to plan mass murders. The four real conspirators are missing: the Führer, Himmler, Bormann and Goebbels.'

21 November

*'And what good
is a new-born baby?'*

1783 On 4 June the brothers Joseph and Étienne Montgolfier had conducted an experiment in their home town of Annonay, a few miles from
Lyon. Before an intrigued crowd in the town's marketplace, they lit a
fire of wool and straw under the opening of a huge paper balloon. As
it filled with hot air, the balloon gently rose from the ground, eventually reaching 3,000 feet. After ten minutes aloft, it drifted to earth a
mile away. This was the first public demonstration of the brothers' new
invention, the hot air balloon.

In the crowd that day was the 29-year-old physics teacher Jean-
François Pilâtre de Rozier, who three months later helped the brothers
with another experiment, a balloon carrying a duck, a rooster and a
sheep, to test the dangers of high altitude. All landed safely after eight
minutes in the air.

Then, on 15 October, Étienne Montgolfier became the first human
being to ascend with a balloon, but the balloon was tethered to the
ground and rose a mere 90 feet. On the same day Pilâtre de Rozier also
took a tethered flight.

Pilâtre de Rozier now planned a free flight, but such an ascent was
considered so hazardous that King Louis XVI decreed that only criminals sentenced to death should be aboard. Only the intervention of
Pilâtre de Rozier's friend, Gabrielle, Duchess of Polignac, persuaded the
king that the honour of making the first flight should go to someone
of higher rank. Into the breach stepped the intrepid infantry officer
François, Marquis d'Arlandes, who earlier had almost killed himself
while trying to parachute. (The first successful parachute jump was still
fourteen years in the future.)

After several tests with a tethered balloon, Pilâtre de Rozier and
d'Arlandes planned to take off on this day from the garden of the
Château de la Muette in the Bois de Boulogne in Paris before a crowd
of eminent spectators, including America's ambassador to France,
Benjamin Franklin, and Louis XVI himself.

Their new balloon was an elaborately decorated globe of blue taffeta
75 feet high and 50 feet in diameter decorated in gold with garlands,
fleurs de lys, signs of the zodiac and images of the king's face, but their
first attempt to take off was almost their last – as the balloon began to

rise, the wind caught it while still tethered, and the ropes began to rip the fabric, bringing it to the ground.

Immediately some of the ladies among the spectators offered to repair the gashes in the balloon, and after an hour and a half of work, it was ready to fly. According to an eye-witness: 'The machine having been filled [with hot air] in eight minutes, it was promptly ballasted with the straw necessary for the fire during the flight, and the Marquis d'Arlandes on one side and M. de Rozier on the other took up their posts with unparalleled courage and eagerness.'

As the balloon rose, Pilâtre de Rozier and d'Arlandes tipped their hats to the cheers of spectators. They floated for 25 minutes above Paris at 3,000 feet, crossing the Seine and finally landing without incident six miles away at the Butte-aux-Cailles (now in Paris's 13th *arrondissement*). For the first time in history, man had flown.

Not everyone was impressed; a M. Marion worried that 'honour and virtue are in permanent danger if balloons are allowed to descend at any hour of the night into gardens and through windows'. But when Benjamin Franklin was asked what good a balloon flight would do, he replied: 'And what good is a new-born baby?'

The tale of the first flight has a unhappy coda. In June 1785 Pilâtre de Rozier and a friend tried to cross the English Channel in a hot-air balloon tucked under a hydrogen balloon. When the fire used to heat the air reached the hydrogen, the balloon exploded, and Pilâtre de Rozier and his companion were killed in the fall, becoming the first air crash fatalities.

1943 During the amphibious landing at Tarawa in the Pacific, future US Marine Corps commandant Colonel David Shoup reports: 'Casualties many; Percentage of dead not known; Combat efficiency: we are winning.'

22 November

'Always be more than you appear and never appear to be more than you are.'

2005 Today a 51-year-old German *hausfrau* was sworn in as her country's chancellor. With her round face, warm smile and short-cut auburn hair, she looked like someone's mother, with little magnetism, eloquence or style. Indeed, her first comment to waiting reporters was an anodyne 'I feel good, and I am very content, and I am happy'. She was Angela Merkel, who would lead Germany for the next fifteen years in such a reassuring, uncharismatic way that her countrymen would know her as '*Mutti*' ('Mummy') and the rest of the world would recognise her as Europe's foremost statesperson.

Although Merkel was born in Hamburg, her Lutheran pastor father moved his family to Perleberg in what was then the Deutsche Demokratische Republik (East Germany) when she was an infant. Raised in a Communist world, she learned to speak fluent Russian and received a doctorate in quantum chemistry from Karl Marx University in Leipzig. She was once approached by the Stasi (secret police) to become an informer but she managed to worm her way out of it by claiming that she could not keep secrets well enough to be a spy. As she later said: 'Always be more than you appear and never appear to be more than you are.' It was a maxim she would follow for the rest of her career.

When Merkel was 35 the Berlin Wall fell, propelling her into politics for the first time when she joined the new Demokratischer Aufbruch (Democratic Awakening) party. It was just the start. As she later said: 'Freedom does not mean being free of something, but to be free to do something.' And do something she did. Upon German reunification, her party merged with the Christlich Demokratische Union Deutschlands (CDU) of which Helmut Kohl was the leader. In 1982 Kohl became Germany's chancellor, a post he would hold for a record sixteen years.

The avuncular Kohl took a shine to the young East German and brought her into his cabinet as Minister for Women and Youth and then Minister for the Environment and Nuclear Safety, affectionately calling her '*mein Mädchen*' ('my girl').

By 1998, however, Germany's economy was stalling, with unemployment over 9 per cent. During the election Kohl's CDU was drubbed by the leftish Sozialdemokratische Partei Deutschlands (SPD), whose leader Gerhard Schröder became chancellor. Then, in late 1999, the *Schwarzgeldaffäre* (Black Money Affair) exploded; under Kohl's leadership, the CDU had been running a secret slush fund in foreign banks to finance the party. Forced to admit he knew of the fund, Kohl refused to name donors, discrediting himself with the public and within his party. Then on 22 December Merkel wrote an article in the *Frankfurter Allgemeine Zeitung* calling for the CDU to ease Kohl out of the party so that it could make a fresh start. Shortly Kohl was out, and Merkel became its leader – no small achievement. She was a young female Protestant from East Germany in a male, patriarchal, right-of-centre party with a strongly Catholic sister party in Bavaria.

Before the next election in 2002, Merkel was outmanoeuvred by Edmund Stoiber to lead the CDU effort, but Stoiber narrowly lost, leaving Merkel the dominant figure in her party.

Then came the election of 2005. The results were so close that the CDU and SPD formed a grand coalition with Merkel as chancellor. During the next fifteen years she would win three more elections.

In 1990 Merkel had made a breakthrough in becoming Helmut Kohl's youngest cabinet minister. Then in 2000 she made another when she became the first female leader of a major German party. In 2005 she became Germany's first female chancellor. She was also the country's youngest chancellor and the only one born after the Second World War. Repeatedly named the most powerful woman in the world, since 2016 many have seen her as the leader not only of Germany but of the free world, after the nativist Donald Trump abdicated that role. Not bad for a pastor's daughter raised in a Communist dictatorship.

1963 President John F. Kennedy is shot just after noon during a motorcade in Dallas after telling his wife that morning: 'Jackie, if somebody wants to shoot me from a window with a rifle, nobody can stop it, so why worry about it?'

---

23 November

'The devil tempted me.'

1407 This evening a murder in the dark streets of Paris unleashed a civil war between the two most powerful feudal houses in France and opened the country for the invasion of England's Henry V.

France was nominally ruled by King Charles VI, once known as *le Bien-Aimé* for his kindly nature but now subject to fits of insanity and called Charles *l'Insensé* (Charles the Mad). Although he had occasional lucid periods, his irrational spells rendered him unfit to govern and thus loosed a bloody power struggle for control of France.

The first contender was the king's dashing and handsome 35-year-old brother Louis, Duke of Orléans, now regent. His rival was the king's first cousin, the squat and ugly Duke of Burgundy, Jean sans Peur

(John the Fearless), a year older. Behind the scenes was Charles's wife, the debauched Isabeau of Bavaria, still seductive at 37 despite having borne eight children.

The enmity between Louis and Jean was palpable. Louis' efforts to drive the English out of their remaining territories on the Continent had threatened the trade between Flanders, ruled by Jean, and the English, and, as regent, Louis was siphoning off a fortune from the royal treasury, receiving about five times as much royal largesse as did Jean. In addition, Louis was conducting an affair with his sister-in-law Queen Isabeau that Jean felt insulting to the king.

Almost since the onset of King Charles's madness, Isabeau had maintained separate quarters in the Hôtel Barbette in the Marais quarter of Paris. On the evening of this day she invited Louis to sup with her and then led him to her bedchamber. Around eight o'clock the enraptured couple were disturbed by the arrival of the king's valet carrying an urgent summons from the king requiring Louis' immediate presence on the other side of Paris. He hurriedly dressed and left to ride through the darkened streets, accompanied only by two outriders, half a dozen pikemen and several pages carrying torches.

Louis had ridden only a few hundred yards on the rue Vieille du Temple when he was suddenly attacked by fifteen masked cut-throats.

'I am the Duke of Orléans!' he cried desperately. 'He's the one we wanted', shouted one of the attackers.

One hatchet blow severed Louis' right hand as he held the reins, and another knocked him from the saddle to the ground. A final swing of the hatchet cleft his skull so that his brains spilled out on the road. His small guard was scattered, one of his pages slain.

At first no one knew who had ordered the assassination. The next day Jean sans Peur sprinkled Louis' body with holy water as it lay in state and declared with apparent indignation: 'A more traitorous murder has never been committed.' He then set about changing the public's perception of the crime into a justified execution.

Four months later in the great hall of the royal residence, the Hôtel Saint-Pol, Jean's creature Jean Petit, a professor from the Sorbonne, defended the murder, claiming that Louis was an unprincipled tyrant who practised witchcraft. After such public support, Jean sans Peur could openly avow the crime. He explained to the king that Louis' death had been necessary for the well-being of the realm and admitted to his uncle, the Duke of Berry: 'I am the one who ordered the strike. The devil tempted me.'

This murder sparked off a bloody civil war between Louis' supporters (the so-called Armagnacs) and Jean's Burgundians that lasted for 28 years. Into the chaos it created stepped England's Henry V to defeat and then control the French state. Jean sans Peur did not survive long; Louis' supporters had neither forgotten nor forgiven, and in 1419 they murdered him during a diplomatic parley on a bridge in Montereau, about 50 miles from Paris.

Isabeau remained a power behind the throne. In 1420 she pushed her addled husband into signing the notorious Treaty of Troyes that made Henry V the heir to the French crown, with Isabeau's own son Charles (VII) disinherited. Thirteen days after the treaty was settled, she gave her daughter Catherine to Henry in marriage.

1918 Prime Minister Lloyd George in Parliament: 'What is our task? To make Britain a fit country for heroes to live in.' * **1959** French president Charles de Gaulle: 'Yes, it is Europe, from the Atlantic to the Urals, it is Europe, it is the whole of Europe, that will decide the fate of the world.'

---

24 November

'To feel oneself a martyr, as everybody knows, is a pleasurable thing.'

1922 A spy thriller par excellence, *The Riddle of the Sands* tells of two Englishmen who stumble on a secret rehearsal for a German invasion of England while sailing a small yacht through the Frisian Islands in the North Sea. Published in 1903, it has never gone out of print. Its author was Erskine Childers, who writes on the first page: 'to feel oneself a martyr, as everybody knows, is a pleasurable thing.' On this day Childers would achieve his own martyrdom, shot by an Irish Free State firing squad.

Born in London in 1870, Childers came from a comfortably affluent family with a British father and an Anglo-Irish mother. After his father's death when he was six, he was brought up in Ireland.

Childers became a junior clerk in the House of Commons, but when the Boer War broke out in 1898, he volunteered and distinguished himself in combat. On his return to civilian life he gained national prominence with *The Riddle of the Sands* but also began to evolve from a firm imperialist to a critic of British policy in Ireland.

By the eve of the First World War Childers had become an impassioned supporter of Irish freedom, so much so that in June 1914 he used his sailing yacht *Asgard* to smuggle 900 Mauser rifles and 29,000 cartridges from Germany to Irish nationalists in Dublin.

Despite his dedication to Irish independence, Childers became an intelligence and aerial reconnaissance officer in the First World War and was awarded the Distinguished Flying Cross.

Mustered out after four years' service, by 1919 he had become a hard-line republican and returned to Ireland. This was just when the Irish War of Independence broke out, a bitter guerrilla conflict that ended with a partitioned Ireland, the north still part of the United Kingdom but the south the quasi-independent Irish Free State, where the Governor General was a representative of the British crown and members of the government still had to declare fidelity 'to His Majesty King George V, his heirs and successors'.

Many Irish republicans bitterly resented these last vestiges of British control and monarchy. In mid-1922 they (mainly the IRA) rose against the new Irish Free State in an eleven-month civil war. Among them was Erskine Childers.

But Childers found himself ostracised by the rebels as 'that bloody Englishman' and considered by the new government a traitor to the Irish cause or even an English *agent provocateur*. The embattled government put a price on his head, while back in England that arch-imperialist, Home Secretary Winston Churchill, intoned: 'No man has done more harm or shown more genuine malice or endeavoured to bring a greater curse upon the common people of Ireland than this strange being, actuated by a deadly and malignant hatred for the land of his birth.'

In an increasingly pernicious conflict, the civil war degenerated into atrocity, and the Free State began executing prisoners as well as any Irish citizen found in possession of firearms or ammunition. On 10 November, Free State forces captured Childers, who was carrying a small Spanish-made 'Destroyer' .32 calibre pistol. Ten days later he was sentenced to death.

Before his execution Childers spoke one last time with his sixteen-year-old son, also called Erskine. 'I want you to shake the hands of every minister in the Provisional [Irish Free State] Government who's responsible for my death. I forgive them and so must you', he said.

On this day Childers met his death at the Beggars Bush Barracks in Dublin. With remarkable equanimity he shook hands with each member of the firing squad. Then, standing to meet the volley, he spoke his final words: 'Take a step or two forward, lads, it will be easier that way.'

Future Irish president Éamon de Valera, who had fought with Childers in the civil war, said: 'He died the prince he was. Of all the men I ever met, I would say he was the noblest.'

Fifty-one years later Childers' son would become President of Ireland.

1774 English man of letters Horace Walpole, Fourth Earl of Oxford in a letter: 'The next Augustan age will dawn on the other side of the Atlantic. There will, perhaps, be a Thucydides at Boston, a Xenophon at New York, and, in time, a Virgil at Mexico, and a Newton at Peru. At last, some circus traveller from Lima will visit England and give a description of the ruins of St Paul's, like the editions of Balbec and Palmyra.' * **1857** General Sir Henry Havelock defeats Sepoy armies eight times in a month but at the close of the siege of Lucknow he is struck down by dysentery. Just before he dies he tells his commander, General Outram: 'For more than fifty years I have so ruled my life that when death came I might face it without fear.'

---

25 November

'Are you now, or have you ever been, a member of the Communist Party?'

1947 Today at New York's Waldorf-Astoria Hotel 48 motion picture executives agreed to issue a draconian decree called the Waldorf Statement, in which they announced: 'We will forthwith discharge or suspend without compensation those in our employ, and we will not re-employ any of the 10 until such time as he is acquitted or has purged himself of contempt and declares under oath that he is not a Communist.'

The '10' to which the executives were referring were a group of eight screenwriters and two directors who the previous day had been found guilty of contempt of Congress for refusing to testify before the House Un-American Activities Committee (HUAC).

HUAC had been established in 1938 to burrow into the American soul for traces of disloyalty. One witness, a former Communist Party member named John Leech, fingered 42 film professionals as communists (including Katharine Hepburn, James Cagney, Frederick March and Humphrey Bogart). All were cleared except one minor actor, who was fired by his studio.

In 1945, as the Cold War was just beginning, the US Congress charged HUAC to investigate communists in positions of influence in the United States. By 1947 they were again probing the film industry. The committee subpoenaed more than 40 people and grilled them about their past and present allegiances, asking each: 'Are you now, or have you ever been, a member of the Communist Party?' This question was invariably followed by a demand to name anyone they knew in Hollywood with communist ties.

Some sought leniency by spilling the beans on their left-wing acquaintances, but ten denounced the investigators, comparing the committee's intimidating tactics to Nazi Germany and claiming that the hearings were an egregious violation of the First Amendment to the Constitution's right to freedom of speech.

While HUAC was investigating Hollywood, directors John Huston and William Wyler, actress Myrna Loy and screenwriter Philip Dunne founded the Committee for the First Amendment and enrolled superstars such as Humphrey Bogart, Lauren Bacall, Joseph Cotten, Bette Davis, Henry Fonda, John Garfield, Judy Garland, Sterling Hayden, Katharine Hepburn, William Holden, Lena Horne, Danny Kaye, Gene Kelly, Burt Lancaster, Groucho Marx, Edward G. Robinson, Frank Sinatra and Billy Wilder. (Bogart derisively commented: 'They'll nail anyone who ever scratched his ass during the National Anthem.')

These glamorous protesters descended on Washington but the HUAC Committee were unimpressed and charged the 'Hollywood Ten' with contempt of Congress and sentenced them to short jail terms and a $1,000 fine. (The most famous was Bertolt Brecht, who fled to East Germany on the day following the inquest.)

Then the Motion Picture Association of America, whose members included Louis B. Mayer (MGM), Harry Cohn (Columbia Pictures), Spyros Skouras (20th Century Fox), Samuel Goldwyn (Samuel Goldwyn Company), Albert Warner (Warner Bros.) and Dore Schary (RKO Pictures), issued the Waldorf Statement and blacklisted the Hollywood Ten. By the early 1960s they had boycotted more than 300 supposedly communist actors, directors and screenwriters.

HUAC had singled out Hollywood screenwriters as a particular target, believing that some were insidiously inserting communist propaganda into mainline movies. In a perfect illustration that even a stopped clock is right twice a day, the committee did discover that Hollywood Ten writers John Howard Lawson, Adrian Scott and Albert Maltz had indeed tried to manipulate films to express communist views.

Another convicted screenwriter was Dalton Trumbo, who later co-wrote *Roman Holiday* under an assumed name, as well as *The Brave One*, both of which won Oscars for the screenplay. He was later rehabilitated and wrote the 1960 film *Spartacus*. Years later he recalled his conviction for contempt of Congress: 'As far as I was concerned, it was a completely just verdict. I had contempt for that Congress and have had contempt for several since. And on the basis of guilt or innocence, I could never really complain very much. That this [refusing to testify – belonging to the Communist Party was not illegal] was a crime or misdemeanour was the complaint, my complaint.'

1864 Five years after Darwin publishes *On the Origin of Species*, when Disraeli is asked after a speech to the Oxford Diocesan Society what his views are, he replies: 'Is man an ape or an angel? I, my lord, I am on the side of the angel.' * **1936** In discussing the new Soviet Constitution that will go into effect a week later, cementing the complete control of the country by the party and its leader, Joseph Stalin tells doubting Politburo members: 'If you are afraid of wolves, keep out of the woods.'

---

26 November

'Do not weep for me, nor waste your time in fruitless prayers for my recovery, but pray rather for the salvation of my soul.'

1504 After relatives, courtiers, and priests had prayed fruitlessly for 50 days, Queen Isabella of Castile and Aragon knew her time was up. With these sombre and dispiriting instructions she addressed a few courtiers just before her death this Tuesday morning at the Medina del Campo Royal Palace. Her arms and legs swollen by oedema, she was perspiring with fever and tormented by insomnia and thirst. Now as her end drew near, she resigned herself to prayer.

Perhaps Isabella expected good results when she prayed; when she was fifteen, her half-brother King Henry IV of Castile had betrothed her to Pedro Girón Acuña Pacheco, 28 years her senior. Horror-struck, she had supplicated God to prevent the marriage. Just when Pedro was travelling to Madrid to meet her, he suddenly fell ill and died.

Now Isabella tried to put things right with God before her demise. According to historian Richard Cavendish: 'She feared the vengeance of the Devil for his minions – Muslims, Jews, heretics – to whom she had given no quarter all her life.' Therefore she urged her successors to confirm the Spanish Inquisition in their repression ('depraved heretics', she called them) and begged the Virgin Mary, St Michael and the saints to intercede for her in Heaven. She had already added a codicil to her will requesting that the natives in the New World be treated kindly.

Still only 53, Isabella had been Queen of Castile for 30 years and joint ruler of Castile and Aragon for 25. At eighteen she had married her second cousin, Ferdinand II of Aragon, with the help of the Valencian Cardinal Rodrigo Borgia, who ingeniously found a five-year-old papal bull issued by Pius II (now dead) that authorised Ferdinand to marry within the third degree of consanguinity, making their marriage legal. Afraid that Henry IV might prevent their union, Isabella eloped with the excuse of visiting her brother's tomb in Ávila and then headed north to Valladolid. Meanwhile Ferdinand was secretly making his way to Valladolid disguised as a servant. On 19 October 1469 they married in the Palacio de los Vivero, having (according to legend) previously signed the prenuptial agreement *Tanto monta, monta tanto* (roughly, 'As much as the one is worth, so too is the other') that meant they would share power equally.

On 11 December 1474 King Henry died, bringing Isabella to the throne of Castile. Four years later Ferdinand inherited the crown of Aragon. Borgia (now Pope Alexander VI) granted the two monarchs the title of *Reyes Católicos* (Catholic Monarchs).

Isabella and Ferdinand had a transformative effect on the world in which they lived. They formed a dynastic union of the crowns of Aragon and Castile rather than a unitary state, but in effect they created Spain. In January 1492 they completed the *Reconquista* of Spain from the Muslims, the same year they financed Columbus' historic voyage (a later myth claims Isabella pawned her jewels to do it). This set in motion the Spanish conquests in the New World and the indescribable riches that would come with them, making Spain Europe's most powerful nation for a century. They also founded the Spanish Inquisition, a loathsome institution that lasted until 1824, and expelled the Jews from Spain.

Despite her many achievements, Isabella had reason to be sombre as she neared death. Her son Juan had died at eighteen, by rumour from sexual over-exertion, so now her heir was her 25-year-old daughter

Juana, who was already showing signs of the insanity that would shortly overwhelm her. But she and Ferdinand had established marriage alliances with Portugal, Habsburg Austria, and Burgundy that would flower during the reign of their all-powerful grandson, Holy Roman Emperor Charles V.

1812 Napoleon escapes the Russians at Berezina after losing almost his entire army in the retreat from Moscow. Later Tsar Nicholas I comments: 'Russia has two generals in whom she can confide – Generals Janvier and Février.' * **1961** Truman Capote as quoted in *The Observer*: 'Venice is like eating an entire box of chocolate liqueurs at one go.'

---

27 November

'As for those who depart for this holy war, if they should perish, either during the journey on land, or crossing the seas, or fighting the idolaters, all their sins will be forgiven at that instant.'

1095 Today Muslim jihadists believe that if they are slain while fighting unbelievers they will go directly to paradise. As Muhammad himself supposedly said: 'Allah guarantees him who strives in His cause and whose motivation for going out is nothing but jihad and belief in His word, that He will admit him into paradise if martyred.'

But Muslims have no monopoly on this belief in heavenly rewards; in 879 Pope John VIII declared: 'Those who fall on the battlefield by fighting valiantly against the pagans and the infidels, who have within themselves the love of the Catholic religion, will enter the repose of eternal life.'

Today in Clermont Cathedral in France another pope, Urban II, made yet another such offer. It was the launch of the First Crusade.

At 53, Urban had now been Pope for seven years. Europe was plagued by violence, and he wanted to put an end to the brutal and incessant private wars between feudal lords by harnessing the moral forces of chivalry – that is, get the knights fighting Muslims rather than fellow Christians. Moreover, the time was now ripe for his call.

Jerusalem had been conquered by Arab armies in 638, just six years after the death of Muhammad, but for centuries Muslims and Christians there had rubbed along peacefully. In 1009, however, the fanatical El-Hakim, Muslim Sultan of Egypt, destroyed the Holy Sepulchre – the tomb of Christ. During the years that followed, the Seljuk Turks overran the Middle East and much of the Byzantine Empire, in 1071 capturing the Byzantine emperor at the Battle of Manzikert. Two years later they occupied Palestine, took Jerusalem and introduced a period of slaughter and vandalism among the Christian population. It became almost impossible for Christian pilgrims from Europe to visit the Holy Land.

Now inside Clermont's cathedral some 310 bishops and abbots waited for Urban's address, while outside a huge crowd shivered with cold, wept with religious fervour and smiled inwardly with greedy anticipation.

'Jerusalem is the navel of the world', declared the Pope, 'a land more fruitful than any other, a paradise of delights. This is the land that the Redeemer of mankind illuminated by his coming, adorned by his life, consecrated by his passion, redeemed by his death, and sealed by his burial. This royal city, situated in the middle of the world, is now held captive by his enemies ... It begs unceasingly that you will come to its aid.'

And then, like prophets and popes before him, Urban offered salvation for those who gave their lives: 'As for those who depart for this holy war, if they should perish, either during the journey on land, or crossing the seas, or fighting the idolaters, all their sins will be forgiven at that instant; this precious favour I grant by virtue of the authority with which I am invested by God Himself.'

Urban's appeal provoked an immediate and overwhelming response. Soon a massive force of some 4,000 mounted knights and 25,000 infantry, principally from France, Italy and the Germanic states, was en route to the greatest Christian adventure in history.

Wearing the symbolic white cross on their breasts, the crusaders were soon pillaging and sacking their way to the Holy Land, encouraged by their battle cry of '*Dieu le volt!*' ('God wills it!').

In June 1099 the Christian army, which had dwindled to perhaps 1,500 mounted knights and 12,000 foot soldiers, reached Jerusalem. On 15 July the great walled city fell to the crusaders for a triumphant massacre and sack. The First Crusade had reached its jubilant conclusion.

Urban died on 29 July 1099, two weeks after Jerusalem's fall but before news of the Christian victory made it back to Europe. Jerusalem remained in Christian hands for less than a century, falling to Saladin in 1187.

There were eight more crusades fought over the next three centuries aimed at retaking Jerusalem. None succeeded.

1950 When an enormous Chinese force surrounds three US Marine regiments near the Chosin Reservoir during the Korean War, Colonel Chesty Puller quips: 'They're on our left, they're on our right, they're in front of us, they're behind us … they can't get away this time.'

---

28 November

'I was Chairman Mao's dog. What he said to bite, I bit.'

1938 Today a stunning 24-year-old Chinese actress married the 20th century's greatest murderer. The groom was Mao Zedong, at 45 almost twice her age. She was Jiang Qing, who acted under the innocent-sounding stage name 'Lán Píng' ('Blue Apple'). The couple's love affair was controversial from the start because Mao was still married to He Zizhen, a lifelong Communist who had endured the Long March with him, and who had borne him five children. But He Zizhen was in a hospital recovering from a wound sustained during the Long March, so Mao divorced her *in absentia* to marry his paramour.

Jiang Qing came from humble stock – her mother had been a domestic servant, perhaps a part-time prostitute – but Jiang had a colourful history of her own. At seventeen, she had raced through a quick marriage and divorce. A year later, while at Qingdao University, she began living with a physics student named Yu Qiwei. Then she abandoned her studies for an acting career and took up with actor/director Tang Na, whom she married in 1936. Her second marriage unravelled when her husband discovered that she was still bedding Yu Qiwei on the side. Soon, however, she was being consoled by another director, Zhang Min. Then she met Mao.

For the first 30 years of her marriage Jiang remained in Mao's shadow, but that changed with Mao's Cultural Revolution. She was already the most hard-line of Maoists – 'Peaceful coexistence corrupts', she said. In 1969 she became a Politburo member and led a faction of ambitious radicals, the 'Gang of Four', that egged on the cultural revolutionaries to their most extreme.

Dissatisfied students, formed into Red Guard groups, rampaged around the country in a massive purge of traditional elements in

Chinese society. They broke into homes to destroy books, art and even Western-style clothing, targeting professionals and scholars, who were sent to re-education centres, sentenced to hard labour or even tortured and beaten to death.

Jiang enlisted the help of the most radical of the Red Guards in attempts to destroy her political rivals, including Deng Xiaoping, then deputy premier. She also attacked premier Zhou Enlai by using the Red Guards once again, this time to torture and murder his adopted son and daughter.

Over the years Jiang had been so caught up in her quest for power that she and Mao had drifted apart. In 1973 they secretly divorced. 'Sex is engaging in the first rounds,' she said. 'What sustains interest in the long run is political power.'

By then Jiang's scheming and grasping for control had taken its toll; she became a severe hypochondriac whose nerves were shot, requiring her to take uppers during the day and downers at night. To eliminate noise, she had the birds and cicadas chased away from her villa and ordered house servants to remove their shoes.

On 9 September 1976 Mao died, and Jiang's enemies were quick to strike – she was arrested the next month and sent to Qincheng Prison, where she remained until the trial of the Gang of Four began in 1980.

Among the charges were sedition, persecution of Communist Party leaders, suppression of the masses, persecuting to death 34,380 persons during the Cultural Revolution, and plotting to murder Mao.

Jiang refused to confess – a sure sign of her guilt, according to Communist orthodoxy. She denounced the court and the country's leaders while declining a lawyer. She claimed that she was just taking orders from her husband. 'I was Chairman Mao's dog. What he said to bite, I bit', she said.

But no one believed her, and she was condemned to death, but in 1983 her sentence was commuted to life imprisonment.

While in prison, Jiang was diagnosed with throat cancer, but she refused an operation. She was released on medical grounds in 1991. She then returned to hospital, but on 14 May she hanged herself in a hospital bathroom. In her suicide note she began with that standard Communist accusation: 'Today the revolution has been stolen by the revisionist clique …' She ended it with spirit: 'Chairman, your student and fighter is coming to see you!'

1956 The French film *And God Created Woman* (*Et Dieu créa la femme*) comes out; afterwards its star Brigitte Bardot says: 'My life was totally turned upside down. I was followed, spied upon, adored, insulted. My private life became public.' * **1990** Margaret Thatcher leaves Downing Street in tears two weeks after her former Foreign Secretary Geoffrey Howe has characterised her leadership as 'rather like sending your opening batsmen to the crease only for them to find, the moment the first balls are bowled, that their bats have been broken before the game by the team captain'.

29 November

'It is better to eat the dog than be eaten by the dog.'

1330 Today Roger Mortimer, once de facto ruler of England, was hanged for treason and the murder of the ineffectual, homosexual Edward II.

The darkly handsome, arrogant Mortimer was one of England's premier villains. A powerful baron who joined a minor rebellion against Edward II in 1322, he was imprisoned in the Tower of London but shortly escaped, probably helped by Edward's wife, Queen Isabella, with whom he was having an affair.

Mortimer fled to France, and Isabella manoeuvred herself into a diplomatic mission to the French court, where her brother Charles (IV) was king. Her real motive was to flee her husband, his advisor Hugh Despenser the Elder and his son Hugh the Younger, who was Edward's new favourite. There Mortimer and Isabella openly resumed their liaison – and started planning Edward's destruction.

Isabella and Mortimer raised an army and on 24 September 1326 landed on the Suffolk coast. London rose for the queen, and Edward fled to Wales, but he was captured on 16 November and forced to abdicate in favour of his fourteen-year-old son, now Edward III. Isabella and Mortimer immediately formed a regency to rule the country while locking up the former king in Berkeley Castle. The Despensers were brutally executed.

Edward II was imprisoned but still dangerous as a focal point for rebellion. On 21 September 1327 that threat was eliminated. Three of Mortimer's henchmen entered his cell while he slept and pinned him to the bed with a table. Then, according to the king's jailer, Thomas, Lord Berkeley, Edward was killed 'with a hoote brooche [red hot meat-roasting spit] putte thro the secret place posterialle'. This indescribably agonising method of execution both served as an evil parody of Edward's homosexuality and left his body outwardly unmarked so that it could be laid out in state for inspection. His death was explained as due to sudden illness.

Mortimer and Isabella reigned supreme for the next three years, but his condescension and insatiable avarice turned his fellow barons against him, and young Edward III began planning revenge on the man who had seduced his mother and probably murdered his father.

When Mortimer heard rumours of conspiracies, he interrogated Edward and some of his companions, including the nobleman William Montagu. Mortimer's probing revealed to Montagu the deadly danger of their position, and he urged Edward to strike: 'It is better to eat the dog than be eaten by the dog.'

Edward seized his chance on 19 October 1330 when he, Mortimer and Isabella were all staying in Nottingham Castle. Although the castle was securely guarded, unknown to Mortimer, centuries earlier a secret tunnel had been dug from the keep to a cave in nearby woods, providing an avenue for escape. The tunnel had not been used in years, but the castle's constable showed Montagu its entrance.

That evening Montagu and several accomplices entered the castle through the tunnel and met Edward inside. The men crashed into Mortimer's chamber as Edward smashed in the door with an axe. There Mortimer was arguing with four of his lieutenants. After a short fight in which two of Mortimer's men were killed, Mortimer was forced to yield. Hearing the clash of arms, Queen Isabella ran to the room, pleading, 'Good son, have pity on noble Mortimer'.

Edward had pity not on Mortimer but on his adulterous and murderous mother, sending her into retirement with the Poor Clares order of nuns. He brought Mortimer before Parliament, where he was accused and sentenced but not allowed to make a defence. Today the once supreme Mortimer was hanged at Tyburn before an assembled multitude of ghoulish onlookers. His corpse was left swinging from the gallows for two days and nights to edify the public.

1530 Henry VIII's former favourite Cardinal Thomas Wolsey dies at Leicester while travelling under arrest to face trial; the previous day he says to the abbot: 'Had I but served my God with but half the zeal as I served my king, He would not in mine age have left me naked to mine enemies.'
* **1780** When the dying Empress Maria Theresa is urged to take a sleeping potion, she replies: 'I could sleep but must not give way to it. Death is so

> near; he must not steal upon me unawares. For fifteen years I have been
> ready for him and must meet him awake.'

30 November

'Monsieur le Curé, I am going to die and
you're playing guessing games.'

1921 Today France's 'Bluebeard from Gambais' was condemned to death for murdering ten women and one man. He was Henri Landru, a 52-year-old Parisian petty crook with ice water in his veins.

Although a choirboy in his youth, at eighteen Landru seduced, impregnated and eventually married his cousin and produced four children. After three obligatory years in the French army, he became a low-level *fonctionnaire*, changing jobs fifteen times in eight years. Meanwhile he had started his career of embezzlements and frauds that netted him three prison sentences.

When he was 45 Landru took the first step that would lead to the scaffold. By now estranged from his wife, he would pretend to be a rich widower and place 'lonely hearts' ads to find single women with money. (He used over 90 pseudonyms and contacted almost 300 women.) He would tempt his prey with talk of marriage, invite them to his isolated villa, find a way to get his hands on their money – and make them disappear.

Landru's first known murders were in February 1915, the victims a 39-year-old widow whom he had picked up in the Luxembourg Gardens and her teenage son. By January 1919, at least nine more women had disappeared, but the police weren't even sure they were dead, much less victims of a single murderer.

But in April 1919 a neighbour of one of his victims recognised Landru in a Paris pottery shop and alerted the police. A salesman told detectives that the man was Lucien Guillet with a delivery address in the rue de Rochechouart. At 6.00am on 12 April they arrested 'Guillet' and found a driver's licence in the name of Henri Désiré Landru. While being driven to police headquarters, Guillet/Landru pulled a small black notebook from his pocket and tried to throw it out of the window. Seized by the police, it contained the names of eleven missing women.

The police searched Landru's Paris flat and two villas he rented. At the villa in Gambais they discovered partially burned women's buttons and pieces of corsets, plus 47 teeth and two kilos of calcined human bone debris, which, to the excited horror of the public, the medical examiner said came from three heads, five feet and six hands. Most damning were train ticket receipts; Landru had bought round trips (for himself) and one-way tickets for his companions when going to his villas.

Landru's trial began in November 1921. When charged with murdering ten women, he insouciantly told the court: 'If the women I have known have something to reproach me for, they have only to file a complaint.' When told that the women listed in his notebook were all missing, he scoffed: 'Well, then! If you believe everything you read in the newspapers!' His repartee kept the onlookers so amused that the Court President threatened: 'If this laughter continues, I will send you all home.' Landru instantly answered: 'For my part, Monsieur le Président, I wouldn't refuse.'

The prosecution had no corpses as evidence but convinced the jury that Landru had dismembered them, buried the torsos in the woods and burned the heads, hands and feet in the stove at the Gambais villa. As Landru was sentenced to the guillotine, he remained impassive, his eyes calm, his pale fingers idly tapping on the bar as if he were gently playing a piano.

Landru's case had been a major sensation all over France; from his jailing in 1919 until his execution in 1922, he received over 4,000 letters from admirers, including 800 requests for marriage.

At dawn on 25 February Landru was led to the guillotine at a prison in Versailles. When offered a glass of rum to calm his nerves, he politely declined: 'It's not good for your health.' At the last the prison chaplain asked, 'My son, do you believe in God?', to which Landru replied: 'Monsieur le Curé, I am going to die and you're playing guessing games.'

At 6.10 the blade of the guillotine cleanly lopped off his head. If you like the macabre, you can see it today on display in The Museum of Death in Hollywood.

1689 Sixty-three-year-old French aristocrat and letter-writer Madame de Sévigné writes to her daughter: 'I have been dragged against my will to the fatal period when old age must be endured; I see it, I have attained it; and I would, at least, contrive not to go beyond it, not to advance in the road of infirmities, pain, loss of memory, disfigurements, which are ready to lay hold of me.' * **1900** As Oscar Wilde dies in the shabby Hôtel d'Alsace in the rue des Beaux Arts in Paris, his last words are: 'My wallpaper and I are fighting a duel to the death – one or the other of us has to go.'

1 December

'Death solves all problems – No man, no problem.'

1934 Joseph Stalin had been top dog in the USSR for ten years, but now he had a problem – his one-time protégé Sergei Kirov, a dashing figure when most Communist apparatchiks were squat peasants in boxy suits. Now 48, Kirov was a dedicated Marxist who had been jailed during the Revolution of 1905, fought in the Russian Civil War and had steadily climbed the ladders of power until he joined the Politburo in 1930.

But now Kirov had begun to show independence. Worse, many Party members saw him as more humane and moderate than Stalin, who had caused the Soviet famine of 1932–33 through forced collectivisation of farms, causing 7 million deaths.

Then came the 17th Congress of the All-Union Communist Party of 1934. Although Kirov gave a fawning speech praising Stalin, several delegates urged him to stand for the leadership, overtures that Kirov unwisely reported to his boss.

When the 2,000 delegates chose new Central Committee members, three voted against Kirov, but 292 voted against Stalin, not enough to change the outcome but sufficient to feed Stalin's paranoia. But, as Stalin later said, 'Death solves all problems – No man, no problem'. Ten months later, on 1 December, Kirov was shot dead.

Six weeks earlier the NKVD (secret police) had arrested Leonid Nikolaev, a diminutive man of 30, for loitering around Leningrad's Smolny Institute where Kirov had his office. Disgruntled and unstable, Nikolaev nursed a grudge against the leadership for having expelled him from the Party. Although the guards had discovered a loaded revolver in his briefcase, he was quickly released and allowed to keep his weapon.

On the afternoon of 1 December Nikolaev paid another visit to the Smolny Institute. Finding that the NKVD had withdrawn the guards at the security desk, he made his way to the third floor. Seeing Kirov in a corridor, he fired a bullet into the back of his neck (the NKVD's favourite execution method).

Kirov's bodyguard, Borisov, and another man quickly subdued Nikolaev. The next day the NKVD picked up Borisov, but en route to NKVD headquarters he was killed in a car crash in which no one else was harmed. Meanwhile Kirov was given a state funeral with the bereaved Stalin as one of the pallbearers.

On 28 December Nikolaev and thirteen alleged members of his 'counter-revolutionary group' were tried in camera, after, it was said, Stalin had personally interrogated Nikolaev. Soon news leaked out that Nikolaev had confessed to acting under orders from a 'fascist power'. At 5.45 the next morning he and all the other defendants were found guilty and an hour later shot. Then Nikolaev's 85-year-old mother, brother, sisters, cousin and a few friends were shot, as well as 104 political criminals who were found guilty of complicity although they were already in prison when Kirov was killed. A few months later Nikolaev's wife was also put to death, after authorities announced that she had been having an affair with Kirov, thereby providing a convenient motive for his murder.

These judicial murders were just a foretaste of what was to come. Stalin used Kirov's killing as a pretext to launch the Great Purge, proclaiming monstrous plots tied to the assassination. About 1.6 million 'traitors' were tortured and convicted. Some 830,000 were executed, most of the rest sent to Gulags in Siberia. Included among the victims were more than half of the 2,000 delegates at the Congress where Kirov had praised Stalin so fulsomely. Stalin personally signed death warrants for 40,000 people with the comment: 'Who's going to remember all this riff-raff in ten or twenty years' time?'

Ever since Kirov's murder there had been whispers about who was really responsible. Stalin continued to act the innocent, naming a class of warship the Kirov-class cruiser and encouraging the Soviet Ballet to be renamed the Kirov Ballet (today the Mariinsky Ballet). But in 1956 Nikita Khrushchev strongly hinted in his Secret Speech to the Party that it was indeed Stalin. Most historians believe that Stalin ordered NKVD Commissar Genrikh Yagoda to arrange Kirov's death. Yagoda himself was convicted of treason and conspiracy and shot in 1938, along with his wife and sister.

1521 The son of Lorenzo de' Medici, Pope Leo X has first-hand experience with the murderous intrigues of Renaissance Italy – his own uncle was murdered, and in 1517 some rebellious cardinals tried to poison him. Thus, when he dies today, his last words are: 'I have been murdered. No remedy can prevent my speedy death.' Historians are unanimous, however, that he died of pneumonia.

2 December

'History repeats itself, first as tragedy, then as farce.'

1851 As Karl Marx famously noted, history seemed to be repeating itself today, as Louis Napoleon Bonaparte seized dictatorial power in France, just as his uncle Napoleon had done 52 years before.

In 1799 the first Napoleon was just back from his battles in Egypt. Seen as a national hero, and backed by a few powerful members of government (notably Talleyrand), he launched his bid for supreme authority. Wearing his splashiest general's uniform – white breeches, blue coat with gold-embroidered lapels and a flamboyant red, white and blue sash at the waist – he paraded through the streets of Paris to tumultuous applause. He then entered the Tuileries to swear allegiance to one chamber of the government (the Elders) and next promptly sent 300 soldiers to 'protect' the other chamber, the Council of the Five Hundred. In revolutionary France, the date was 18 Brumaire (9 November by the Gregorian calendar).

The next day Napoleon boldly addressed each group, but the Council of the Five Hundred turned on him savagely, and a pale and stammering Napoleon had to be accompanied from the chamber by four soldiers.

Having failed to charm the government with words, Napoleon did what he always did best. He sent in troops. His soldiers charged into the Orangerie, forcing the 500 members to flee through the windows.

On the evening of 10 November Bonaparte was declared First Consul; the republican government known as the Directory was over, and five years later he would promote himself to emperor.

By 1851 the first Napoleon had been dead for 30 years, but his nephew Louis was president of France. Louis' term was limited to four years, and the constitution forbade him from succeeding himself. In July he failed to persuade the Assembly to revise the constitution, so he, too, resolved to seize by force what he could not gain by persuasion.

Working closely with his half-brother the duc de Morny, Louis launched his coup d'état on 2 December, chosen because on that date in 1804 his illustrious uncle had famously crowned himself emperor in Notre Dame, as the powerless Pope looked on.

On the previous evening Louis' men had placed posters throughout Paris proclaiming him emperor, and then his confederate Maupas, the Prefect of Police, secretly arrested 78 troublemakers at dawn on 2 December.

Later in the day Louis rode through the streets of Paris accompanied by a glittering troop of splendid soldiers, including most of France's generals. There was no bloodshed and little resistance. Louis Napoleon was now the nation's dictator.

At the time, Karl Marx was living in London. Louis' coup inspired him to write his pamphlet *The 18th Brumaire of Louis Bonaparte*, a clear reference to the first Napoleon's earlier seizure of power.

It was here that Marx made his famous observation about history repeating itself, of which the exact wording is: 'Hegel remarks somewhere that all facts and personages of great importance in world history occur, as it were, twice. He forgot to add: the first time as a tragedy, the second time as farce.' ('*Hegel bemerkte irgendwo, dass alle großen weltgeschichtlichen Tatsachen und Personen sich sozusagen zweimal ereignen. Er hat vergessen, hinzuzufügen: das eine Mal als Tragödie, das andere Mal als Farce.*')

When it came to Napoleons, however, Marx had actually understated the repetition. Again on 2 December (this time in 1852), the Senate passed a resolution confirming that the French Empire was restored and Louis its emperor, with the title of Napoleon III. Indeed, even the two emperors' ultimate downfalls echoed one another, Napoleon I stripped of power by the Battle of Waterloo and Napoleon III by the Battle of Sedan.

1814 French writer and pornographer the Marquis de Sade dies, leaving a will stating: 'The ground over my grave shall be sprinkled with acorns so that all traces of my grave shall disappear so that, as I hope, this reminder of my existence may be wiped from the memory of man.'

---

3 December

'His eyes must always be open so that the others may sleep.'

1469 Ever since Cosimo de' Medici had become de facto ruler of the Florentine Republic in 1434, the Medici had been kings in all but name. After Cosimo's death in 1464, his son Piero took over, but Piero succumbed to gout and lung disease on 2 December 1469, leaving Florence without a head. The day after Piero's death 700 Medici supporters gathered in the convent of Sant' Antonino, where they chose a young man, just short of 21, to assume the role previously played by his father and grandfather. He was Lorenzo de' Medici, known to history as Lorenzo the Magnificent.

Lorenzo agreed to the task because, he wrote, 'it fares ill in Florence with anyone who is rich but does not have any share in government'. According to the almost contemporary historian Francesco Guicciardini, Lorenzo became a 'benevolent tyrant in a constitutional republic'. He cared intensely for Florence and its people, once telling his children how a ruler should act: 'His eyes must always be open so that the others may sleep.'

For 23 years Lorenzo was Italy's shrewdest balancer of power, juggling the interests of Milan, Venice, Naples, Bologna, the Papal States and France to the benefit of Florence. He held the unfashionable view that war was undesirable, preferring shrewd diplomacy to armed conflict.

Lorenzo's greatest test came after the Pazzi conspiracy of 1478, when he was nearly assassinated. Pope Sixtus IV, who hated Lorenzo for thwarting the consolidation of papal rule over the Romagna, had backed the conspiracy and on its failure seized all the Medici assets he could find, excommunicated Lorenzo and put the entire Florentine city-state under interdict. He then allied himself with King Ferdinand I of Naples, whose son, Alfonso, Duke of Calabria, led an invasion. But after two years of desultory fighting, Lorenzo travelled to Naples and stayed as a virtual prisoner for several months but finally persuaded Ferdinand to make peace. The disgruntled pope was forced to absolve Lorenzo and remove the interdict.

Lorenzo's greatness was not only as a ruler or deal-maker or even a banker (during his supremacy the London and Bruges branches of the Medici bank both failed), but as a man of the arts.

Andrea del Sarto painted the walls of his villa at Poggio a Caiano, while Ghirlandaio, Filippino Lippi and Botticelli decorated the one at Spedaletto. Sandro Botticelli was virtually Lorenzo's 'court painter' as well as frequent dinner companion. Other artists Lorenzo patronised included Perugino, Verrocchio (who sculpted the famous terra cotta bust of Lorenzo and eventually made his death mask) and Antonio Pollaiuolo. He met and helped Leonardo da Vinci when Leonardo was only twelve and later recommended him to Lodovico il Moro in Milan, where he painted his Last Supper. Lorenzo surrounded himself with poets and intellectuals and was an outstanding vernacular poet in his own right. He opened a school of sculpture where he 'discovered' Michelangelo at the age of thirteen. Michelangelo lived in the Medici Palace for three years, and, according to the contemporary painter-historian Giorgio Vasari, he 'always ate at Lorenzo's table with the sons of the family'. Every year on 7 November Lorenzo gave a banquet in honour of Plato's birth.

Ruler, diplomat, banker, lover of women and loving husband, philosopher, patron, poet, Lorenzo died at his villa in Careggi on 9 April 1492 at the age of 43.

Lorenzo's son Giovanni became Pope Leo X, whose selling of indulgences to finance the rebuilding of St Peter's provoked Luther into igniting the Reformation. His nephew became Pope Clement VII, who refused Henry VIII's request to annul his marriage to Catherine of Aragon, sparking England's withdrawal from Catholicism. His great-grandson Alessandro Ottaviano de' Medici also became pope (as Leo XI) but gained the name Papa Lampo ('Lightning Pope') because he died after 27 days. Another great-grandchild was Catherine de' Medici, who ruled France for 30 years through the destructive incompetence of three dismal sons. Marie de' Medici, another French queen, was Lorenzo's distant cousin.

1894 Robert Louis Stevenson dies at 44 in Samoa; on his tombstone is engraved his 'Requiem' that ends: 'Home is the sailor, home from sea,/And the hunter home from the hill.'

---

4 December

'Thou hast conquered, O Galilean'

250 AD Today the Christian soldier Mercurius was martyred by Roman Emperor Decius, but a century later he will return to slay another pagan emperor, Julian the Apostate.

Mercurius was born about 225 AD in Cappadocia in modern Turkey. At seventeen he joined the Roman army, became famous as a swordsman and showed such prowess in the field that Decius made him supreme commander.

While Mercurius was fighting the Berbers, the Archangel Michael appeared holding a shining sword and said to him: 'Take this sword from my hand by which you will achieve victory.' With this celestial help, Mercurius quickly smote the enemy and became known as Abu-Seifein – 'the holder of two swords': a military sword and a divine sword.

But then, on 3 January 250, Decius decreed that everyone in the empire (except Jews) should demonstrate their loyalty to Rome by sacrificing to Roman gods and to the emperor, in the presence of a magistrate. One of the first to refuse was Pope Fabian, who was executed on 20 January. Then Mercurius also refused, despite a personal plea from Decius.

The furious emperor ordered Mercurius bound in iron fetters and imprisoned, but once again Archangel Michael miraculously appeared and said to Mercurius: 'Have courage and win. Do not worry about these temporary tortures.' Decius had Mercurius slashed with knives and stretched between four pillars with a fire beneath him, but so much blood flowed from his wounds that it put out the fire, and the next day Mercurius was found completely healed. Since torture didn't work, Decius then had him beheaded, but his corpse emitted a fragrance like myrrh and incense, and a year later his body was found, white as snow and still fragrant.

That's the last we hear from Mercurius for 113 years, but on 26 June 363, Rome's last pagan emperor, Julian the Apostate, was slain while fighting near Samarra in modern-day Iraq.

Fifty years earlier, Julian's uncle, Constantine the Great, had declared Christianity the empire's religion of choice, so Julian had been raised a Christian, but he had converted to Hellenism and referred contemptuously to Christians as 'Galileans'. He believed (like Decius) that Christianity weaned men's loyalty away from the state and the emperor, so he reopened many pagan temples, proscribed the veneration of Christian relics and had two of his bodyguards executed for opposing the ban. He never prohibited Christianity, but he revoked its legal primacy and made all religions equal before the law.

In 363 the Sassanid (Persian) Emperor Shapur II launched a campaign against the Romans. Julian marched east and utterly destroyed the Sassanid army before their capital Ctesiphon (near modern Baghdad), but with no siege equipment, he could not take the city and withdrew.

On 26 June, as Julian's army was retreating along the Tigris, Sassanids attacked his rear guard. Julian plunged into the mêlée, so eager to fight that he neglected to don his armour. When the Romans began to drive off the enemy, Julian led the pursuit, only to be struck in the side by a thrown spear, which pierced his liver. His soldiers carried him to his tent, where his physician washed the wound with wine and attempted to suture the gash, but he died just before midnight.

At exactly the same time, Saint Basil of Caesarea was languishing in prison for his faith, praying to Mercurius (now considered a saint) to stop Julian's persecution of Christians. Miraculously, Mercurius appeared in his cell in a vision, holding a bloody spear, and revealed that with this spear he had slain Julian, whose final words were a mournful '*Vicisti, Galilæ*' ('Thou hast conquered, O Galilean'), as he recognised that Christianity would triumph after his death.

1563 Eighteen years and one day after the Council of Trent has begun, Pope Pius IV closes the final session with the denunciation of Protestants: 'Anathema to all heretics, anathema, anathema.' * **1679** Philosopher Thomas Hobbes dies; his last words: 'I am about to take my last voyage, a great leap in the dark.' * **1700** Philippe, duc d'Anjou, grandson of Louis XIV, leaves Versailles to become Spain's first Bourbon king as Felipe V; Louis' final word of advice: 'Never form an attachment for anyone.'

---

5 December

'Many persons of both sexes, unmindful of their own salvation and straying from the Catholic Faith, have abandoned themselves to devils, incubi and succubi.'

1484 Witches have been condemned since the dawn of history. In both Greece and Rome, they were occasionally put to death, a practice that continued sporadically in Europe through the Middle Ages. But in general, Europeans tolerated witches, considering them more annoying than criminal. In the 8th century, for example, Charlemagne made it a capital offence to execute supposed witches. But that was to change today, when Pope Innocent VIII issued *Summis desiderantes*, a papal bull in which he recognised the existence of witches and described their terrible deeds:

> Many persons of both sexes, unmindful of their own salvation and straying from the Catholic Faith, have abandoned themselves to devils, incubi and succubi, and by their incantations, spells, conjurations … have slain infants yet in the mother's womb … have blasted the produce of the earth, the grapes of the vine,

the fruits of the trees ... they blasphemously renounce that Faith which is theirs by the Sacrament of Baptism, and at the instigation of the Enemy of Mankind they do not shrink from committing and perpetrating the foulest abominations and filthiest excesses to the deadly peril of their own souls.

Before Innocent's bull, one could be possessed by the Devil and not responsible for one's actions, but now Innocent had redefined witches as those who had signed a pact with the Devil (and often worshipped him), which was heresy and meant damnation. Therefore witches now became the prey of the Inquisition.

The Pope had issued his bull in response to the urgings of the Dominican inquisitor Heinrich Kramer, a German from Alsace. In 1474 Kramer had been appointed Inquisitor for the Tyrol, Salzburg, Bohemia and Moravia, and his obsession with witches soon gained approval in Rome, taking its cue from Exodus 22:18: 'Thou shalt not suffer a witch to live.' When Innocent came to power on 29 August 1484, he agreed to support Kramer and three months later issued his bull, sometimes referred to as the 'Witch-Bull of 1484'. (In 1487 Innocent cemented his place in the history of noxious popes by confirming the notorious Tomás de Torquemada as Grand Inquisitor of Spain.)

The year after persuading Innocent to issue his bull, Kramer made another contribution to the anti-witch crusade with his treatise, *Malleus Maleficarum* (*The Hammer of Witches*), that recommended torture to obtain confessions and the death penalty as the only sure remedy. At that time, heretics were burned alive at the stake, and Kramer pressed for the same punishment for witches.

Although Kramer's work was condemned by some Inquisition theologians, it was too late – the genie was now well out of the bottle. During the next two centuries some 60,000 victims (the vast majority women) were burned, with persecution particularly severe in Germany and Switzerland. In the Vaud canton alone, a total of 1,700 immolations took place, with 25 in a single year. The execution of witches continued until 1782, when Switzerland's last witch, a maidservant named Anna Göldi, was beheaded for using supernatural means to put needles in the bread and milk of her employer's daughter. (England was a century ahead of the Swiss – in 1682, a senile woman from Bideford named Temperance Lloyd became the last witch ever executed there. But the crime of witchcraft was abolished only in 1736. In North

America, British colonists tried, convicted, and hanged some nineteen witches during the Salem witch trials in 1692–93.)

Although witches have long disappeared in the Western world, they still live elsewhere. The *New York Times* has reported that in 2013 two housemaids in Saudi Arabia were sentenced to 1,000 lashes and ten years in prison for casting spells against their employers.

1791 The previous day, when his still unfinished Requiem is sung at his bedside, Mozart remarks: 'Didn't I tell you that I was writing this Requiem for myself?' Today he dies at five minutes to one o'clock in the morning. *
1962 During a speech at West Point, American diplomat Dean Acheson declares: 'Great Britain has lost an Empire and has not yet found a role.'

---

6 December

'I stopped believing in Santa Claus when I was six.'

343 AD Today in the small town of Myra on the Mediterranean coast of Lycia (now Demre in Turkey) a popular local bishop named Nicholas died, whose legend would enthral millions for centuries to come.

Nicholas had been born in the Lycian seaport of Patara and had early shown signs of religious devotion. While still in the baptismal font, he stood on his feet for three hours to honour the Holy Trinity. He must have been something of a prig: on Wednesdays and Fridays he would not accept milk from his mother until his parents had finished their evening prayers.

As a young man he journeyed to the Holy Land and then returned to become Bishop of Myra, only 50 miles from his birthplace. There he was imprisoned during Emperor Diocletian's ferocious persecution of the Christians but released when Constantine came to power in 306.

One legend has Nicholas travelling to the Council of Nicea in 325, where he attacked the heresy of Arius (who denied the full divinity of Christ) by slapping him across the face. (Sadly, extant records of the council make no mention of Nicholas.)

Nicholas gained a saintly reputation by generous deeds for the poor and despondent, including the miraculous reassembling and reviving of three small children who had been carved into pieces by a greedy butcher trying to pass them off as spring lamb.

His most famous charitable act concerned three sisters who were on the point of being forced to sell themselves into prostitution because their father could not afford dowries. Hearing of their plight, Nicholas dropped bags filled with gold coins down their chimney, one of which landed in a stocking that had been hung up by the fireplace to dry.

When Bishop Nicholas died in 343, he was buried in Myra, where his tomb quickly became a shrine. We do not know if he was ever officially canonised, but nonetheless he was soon considered the patron saint of some seemingly conflicting groups: prisoners and judges, sailors and virgins, pirates and merchants, and charitable guilds and pawnbrokers. So celebrated was he that in 1087 some Italian sailors filched his bones and transported them to Bari on Italy's Adriatic coast. There they remain, enshrined in the Basilica di San Nicola, built especially to house them. (In 1957 the Italian professor Luigi Martino X-rayed and measured the bones, which showed Nicholas to have been about 70 at his death and 5ft 4in in height, with a slender build. He may well have looked a bit like Santa Claus, with a short, wide face and a broad forehead.)

During the Middle Ages the cult of St Nicholas was widespread in Europe, where he was depicted with a full beard, wearing the red robes of a bishop. The cult gradually died away except in Holland, where he was known as Sinterklaas (a Dutch corruption of Saint Nicholas). The Dutch in turn took the tradition with them to the New World when they colonised New Amsterdam (New York) in the 17th century. There Sinterklaas soon evolved into Santa Claus.

Today Santa Claus still wears red and is still full-bearded. In Great Britain and America he is known to drop down the chimney on Christmas Eve to fill deserving children's stockings hung by the fireplace, while in much of continental Europe he appears on his feast day on 6 December, the anniversary of his death, when children put their shoes outside their bedroom doors in the hope that they will be filled with fruit and sweets.

In spite of the evidence from millions of small children around the world, some remain sceptical. As the famous child actress Shirley Temple once remarked: 'I stopped believing in Santa Claus when I was six. Mother took me to see him in a department store and he asked for my autograph.' In 1969 Pope Paul VI had the Feast of St Nicholas dropped from the Catholic calendar, citing the lack of documentation of St Nick's life and deeds.

1865 The US Congress ratifies the 13th Amendment to the Constitution: 'Neither slavery nor involuntary servitude, except as a punishment for crime whereof the party shall have been duly convicted, shall exist within the United States, or any place subject to their jurisdiction.'

7 December

'At least make sure you cut my head off properly.'

43 BC 'At least make sure you cut my head off properly', he said to the centurion seconds before his death, and then leaned out of the litter in which he was being carried to offer his throat to his executioner. So on this day died 63-year-old Marcus Tullius Cicero, the Roman world's greatest orator, sometime philosopher, occasional poet, senator, consul and backer of wrong horses.

Cicero had been born in the Roman provinces of a rich and influential family. During his early years in Rome he became one of the city's greatest trial lawyers, perfecting his rhetorical style. When he was 27, he left for Greece to study philosophy and history. 'To be ignorant of what happened before you were born is to be ever a child', he later wrote.

A senator at 31, then consul at 43, Cicero was a strong believer in the old values of the Roman Republic at the very time when the expansion of the state was making its labyrinthine systems of checks and balances an unworkable way to run an empire.

As consul he thwarted the Catiline conspiracy to overthrow the government and summarily executed some of the plotters, dramatically proclaiming their death to the waiting crowd with the single word *'vixerunt'* ('they have lived'). But some of the conspirators came from exalted families, and their relations never forgave Cicero for executing them without trial. (Although a political idealist, Cicero was also a realist, observing: *'Silent enim leges inter arma.'* – 'Laws are silent in times of war.')

When Caesar invaded Italy in 49 BC, Cicero fled Rome to back Pompey as representative of the legitimate government and survived Caesar's triumph only because Caesar spared all his opponents. But after Caesar's assassination, in which he took no part, Cicero praised the murderers, while repeatedly haranguing the Senate against the unrestrainedly ambitious Mark Antony, who claimed to be Caesar's political heir. In one fiery speech he called him an embezzler and a criminal, a drunken lecher who spent his time with outlaws and prostitutes.

Cicero also seriously underestimated Octavian (the future Augustus), suggesting to his colleagues that 'the young man should be praised, honoured and got rid of'. When his remarks were reported, Cicero had gained another mortal enemy.

In 43 BC Mark Antony, Octavian and Lepidus formed an alliance against Caesar's assassins, taking the opportunity to cleanse the state of other undesirables as well. Cicero's name was added to the proscribed list, which stripped him of all property and meant that any Roman citizen could kill him without fear of state reprisal.

Cicero refused to flee from Italy, dramatically vowing: 'I will die in the country I have so often saved.' He headed south by boat to his estate in Formiae, down the Mediterranean coast about 90 miles south from Rome, but his servants, aghast at seeing him in so much danger, forced him into his litter to escape. They were too late. A force of Roman soldiers caught up with him on the road and dispatched the venerable statesman. According to the 2nd-century historian Appian, a centurion struck three times, cutting off his head and 'the hand with which [he] had written speeches against [Mark] Antony as tyrant ... The head and the hand were suspended for a long time from the Rostra in the Forum' – but not before Mark Antony's wife Fulvia had pierced his tongue with a long hairpin, symbolising the lies he had told about her husband. Appian concludes with one final grisly vision: 'It is said that even at his meals Antony placed Cicero's head before his table, until he became satiated with the horrible sight.'

Many grieved at the great statesman's death – his son, his childhood friend Atticus, his faithful manumitted slave Tiro, who collected and published Cicero's work after his death. But the sceptical Cicero would have been unimpressed; 'Nihil lacrimâ citius arescit', he once wrote – 'Nothing dries sooner than a tear.'

1815 Condemned to death by Louis XVIII for having returned to help Napoleon at Waterloo, Marshal Michel Ney tells the firing squad in the courtyard of the Palais Luxembourg in Paris: 'Don't you know that for 25 years I have learned to face both cannonballs and bullets? Come on, soldiers, straight to the heart.' * **1837** After being shouted down by the opposition during his maiden speech in the House of Commons, Disraeli replies: 'Though I sit down now, the time will come when you will hear me.' * **1941** After leading the Japanese attack on Pearl Harbor,

> Admiral Yamamoto confesses: 'I fear we have only awakened a sleeping giant, and his reaction will be terrible.'

8 December

'She dishonoured the scaffold as she dishonoured the throne.'

1793 She was a remarkable beauty with thick golden ringlets and almond-shaped, violet eyes. She was also a prostitute who became the King of France's *maîtresse en titre* and died by the guillotine. She was Madame du Barry.

Madame du Barry was born Jeanne Bécu in 1743, the illegitimate daughter of a seamstress and a defrocked monk inappropriately called Frère Ange (Brother Angel). After a brief convent education, she found work as a milliner in Paris, but was soon moonlighting in Madame Quisnoy's casino-cum-brothel. Now nineteen, she was noticed by a louche aristocrat named Jean du Barry, who took her as his mistress and launched her career as a courtesan in the highest circles of Parisian society.

In 1768 du Barry brought Jeanne to Versailles, where, with the complicity of the king's valet, she was placed in the path of the ageing (58) Louis XV. Louis had been brooding over the death of Madame de Pompadour the previous year, consoling himself with the young prostitutes he kept in his private bordello. He was immediately captivated, and Jeanne quickly found herself living in the king's apartments.

By the bizarre etiquette of the time, however, Jeanne could not become Louis' official mistress unless she was married to a noble. Jean du Barry was already married, but he swiftly orchestrated a '*mariage blanc*' (marriage in name only) between Jeanne and his brother Guillaume. Thus Madame du Barry was born.

Although the ladies at court mocked this low-born courtesan, Jeanne never complained, never sought power in the wake of the king, and never took vengeance on those who held her in contempt. But her wild extravagance – she was always in debt despite a monthly allowance of 300,000 livres – made her even more unpopular.

In 1774 Louis died of smallpox, bringing his grandson Louis XVI to the throne. Louis' wife Marie Antoinette loathed Jeanne, who was banished to the Abbey du Pont-aux-Dames and never again received at court. After three years among the nuns (many of whom she charmed, despite her scarlet past), she moved to her château at Louveciennes. Still in her mid-thirties, she embarked on several aristocratic love affairs.

When the Revolution exploded in France, Jeanne hunkered down in her château, patronising the arts, supporting local causes and enchanting her lovers. (One of whom, however, the duc de Brissac, was massacred by a drunken mob, his head tossed through an open window, where it landed at her feet.)

In 1792 Jeanne made three trips to London to help French émigrés, oblivious to the Revolutionary spies who watched her every move. The next January Louis XVI was guillotined, and then on 22 September Jeanne was arrested – her trips to England had been interpreted as treason. Tried and convicted, she fainted in court when the death sentence was pronounced.

During the few days left to her, this insouciant, pleasure-loving doxy had but one thought – somehow, anyhow – to save her life. She gave all her treasures to the nation, revealing where she had hidden her money and jewels. All to no avail.

On the frosty morning of 8 December Jeanne was loaded in a tumbrel and driven to the Place de la Révolution (now Place de la Concorde) where the guillotine waited, crying: 'Life! Life! Life for my repentance! Life for all my devotion to the republic! Life for all my riches to the nation!'

Other members of the Ancien Régime had faced execution with stoic courage, but she was dragged to the scaffold shrieking with terror. Even bound to the plank, she had one last plea to her executioner: '*Encore un moment, monsieur le bourreau, un petit moment …*' In less than a year her Svengali Jean du Barry met the same fate in Toulouse.

The French writer and politician Alphonse de Lamartine later pronounced this uncharitable verdict on one of history's most naive and harmless courtesans: 'She died a coward, because she died neither for opinion, for virtue, nor for love, but for vice. She dishonoured the scaffold as she dishonoured the throne.'

1976 American writer Gore Vidal defines ambition in America: 'It is not enough to succeed. Others must fail.'

---

9 December

'I will back the masses against the classes.'

1868 Today, three weeks before his 59th birthday, William Gladstone began the first of his four terms as prime minister, an office he would hold for fifteen years. When he resigned for the last time in 1894, he was 84 years old, the oldest person to occupy the premiership. By then he had been a Member of Parliament for almost 62 years.

Born in Liverpool, Gladstone was sent to Eton, a school that has produced twenty British prime ministers, including the first, Robert Walpole, and the most recent, Boris Johnson. (Other Old Etonian PMs include Pitt the Elder, Wellington, Balfour, Eden, Macmillan and Cameron.) After Eton, Gladstone studied at Oxford, another prime-ministerial breeding ground – 29 of the country's 55 PMs to date have gone there.

Gladstone was first elected to Parliament as a Tory but eventually became a Liberal, claiming towards the end of his career that 'I will back the masses against the classes'. Although a man of lofty principles and stern moral probity, he was seen by his enemies as humourless and sanctimonious. His great rival Benjamin Disraeli once commented: 'He has not a single redeeming defect.' It was the irreverent Disraeli who defined the difference between a misfortune and a calamity: 'If, for instance, Mr William Gladstone were to fall into the river, that would be a misfortune. But if anyone were to pull him out, that would be a calamity!'

With age, Gladstone became increasingly insufferable with his ponderous air of noble rectitude, causing fellow Liberal Henry Labouchère to remark: 'I don't object to Gladstone always having the ace of trumps up his sleeve, but merely to his belief that the Almighty put it there.'

Among those who disliked Gladstone was Queen Victoria, who complained to her private secretary: 'He speaks to me as if I was a public meeting.' When Gladstone's Liberals won the election in 1892, she wrote to Lord Lansdowne: 'The danger to the country, to Europe, to her vast Empire, which is involved in having all these great interests entrusted to the shaking hand of an old, wild, and incomprehensible old man of 82½, is very great.'

Despite his detractors, Gladstone was on the right side of history, espousing a long list of liberal causes commonly accepted today. He fought for free trade, better working conditions for London dock workers, the admission of Jews to Parliament, reduced defence spending, Irish home rule, women's right to own their own property, free elementary education and the secret ballot, and bitterly condemned the British opium trade in China. He was also highly influential in broadening the franchise to include a much wider range of working men. His reforming zeal extended to his private life. He and his wife established a 'rescue' home for prostitutes, and at night he would occasionally trawl London streets for fallen women in an attempt to persuade them to take up a different life.

His views on women's suffrage, however, were anything but liberal, as he told the Commons in 1871: 'The personal attendance and intervention of women in election proceedings ... would be a practical evil not only of the gravest, but even of an intolerable character.'

In contrast to his progressive views, Gladstone was such a dogmatic believer in the Church of England that he thought Catholics should be excluded from government. When Pius IX pronounced the doctrine of papal infallibility in 1870, Gladstone called the Catholic Church 'an Asian monarchy: nothing but one giddy height of despotism, and one dead level of religious subservience'.

During his last term as prime minister, the House of Lords rejected Gladstone's Irish Home Rule bill by a vote of 419 to 41, the greatest majority ever recorded. He then found himself at odds with his own cabinet over the navy's budget and resigned, using his failing hearing and eyesight as an excuse. But by now, in or out of office, he was affectionately known as the 'G.O.M.' ('Grand Old Man'). The mischievous Disraeli insisted it stood for 'God's Only Mistake'.

1967 French President Charles de Gaulle: 'Men can have friends, statesmen cannot.'

---

10 December

'My dynamite will lead to peace sooner than a thousand world conventions.'

1901 Today in Stockholm the first five Nobel Prizes were awarded to winners ranging from famous men such as Henri Dunant, who founded the Red Cross, and Wilhelm Röntgen, the discoverer of the X-ray, to the now obscure French poet Sully Prudhomme. Exactly five years earlier the Swedish scientist Alfred Nobel had died of a stroke on the coast of Italy, leaving his money to a trust that made (and still makes) the Nobel prizes possible.

Nobel's family's company manufactured explosives for use in torpedoes and mines, but when Nobel was 31 his younger brother was killed in an accidental nitro-glycerine explosion, prompting him to search for a way to make explosives safer to handle.

At length he discovered that nitro-glycerine combined with kieselguhr (a soft, powdered rock) would form a stable substance. His invention, patented in 1867 as 'Dynamite' or 'Nobel's Safety Blasting Powder', quickly established his fame and fortune.

Although a genius as an inventor (at least of explosives – in addition to dynamite he invented gelignite and ballistite, a predecessor of cordite), Nobel was a flop as a prophet, famously claiming that: 'My dynamite will lead to peace sooner than a thousand world conventions. As soon as men will find that in one instant, whole armies can be utterly destroyed, they surely will abide by golden peace.'

When Nobel died, he left $9,000,000 (worth $275 million today) in a fund from which the interest would be 'annually distributed in the form of prizes to those who, during the preceding year, shall have conferred the greatest benefit on mankind'. There were awards in chemistry, literature, peace, physics and medicine. A sixth discipline, economic sciences, was added in 1969.

Four people have won the Nobel Prize twice, but Linus Pauling, with the Chemistry Prize in 1954 and the Peace Prize in 1962, is the only winner in two different categories. The first woman to win was Marie Curie, for Physics in 1903 with her husband, Pierre, and again in 1911. Then in 1935 the Curies' daughter Irène Joliot-Curie won the Chemistry Prize, making four awards for the family. Perhaps the most unfortunate candidate was Indian statesman Mohandas Gandhi, who was nominated for the Peace Prize five times but never selected.

The United States leads with 383 winners, while Great Britain ranks second with 132, starting with Ronald Ross in 1902 for his work on malaria. The first American winner was President Theodore Roosevelt in 1906 for his help in settling the Russo-Japanese War. Other honoured presidents were Woodrow Wilson, Jimmy Carter (for humanitarian rather than presidential achievements) and Barack Obama after only eight months in office for 'extraordinary efforts to strengthen international diplomacy and cooperation between peoples' – but probably in reality for becoming America's first black president.

One of the most controversial Peace Prizes was awarded to US Secretary of State Henry Kissinger, who received it jointly with Lê Đức Thọ for negotiating a ceasefire between North Vietnam and the United States in 1973. But the war actually continued until 1975, and Lê Đức Thọ declined the award. Similarly, in 1978 Israeli Prime Minister Menachem Begin and Egyptian President Anwar Sadat were jointly given the Peace Prize, although the Middle East cauldron continues to simmer.

Twelve Americans have won the prize for Literature: Sinclair Lewis, Eugene O'Neill, Pearl Buck, William Faulkner, Ernest Hemingway, John Steinbeck, Saul Bellow (a transplanted Canadian), Isaac Singer (a transplanted Pole), Joseph Brodsky (a transplanted Russian), Czezlaw Milosc (another transplanted Pole), Toni Morrison, and Bob Dylan for his poetic lyrics.

British Literature prize-winners include Rudyard Kipling in 1907, followed by John Galsworthy, the American-born T.S. Eliot, Bertrand Russell, Winston Churchill, William Golding, Harold Pinter (although many believe Pinter's simian rages against America rather than his literary talents were the reason he was chosen by left-leaning Swedish judges), Doris Lessing and Kazuo Ishiguro.

The Nobel Foundation has ignored some outstanding writers. In 2001 literary critics around the world nominated James Joyce and Marcel Proust as the two greatest 20th-century writers, but neither received a Nobel Prize. Other overlooked authors include Tolstoy, Chekhov, Zola, Jorge Luis Borges, Ezra Pound, Arthur Miller and Mark Twain.

Perhaps the greatest accolade the Nobel organisation itself ever received was in 1937, when Adolf Hitler forbade German citizens to accept Nobel awards.

1918 In a speech at Cambridge, Conservative politician Sir Eric Geddes promises reparations: 'The Germans, if this Government is returned, are going to pay every penny; they are going to be squeezed, as a lemon is squeezed – until the pips squeak.'

11 December

'I have found it impossible to carry the heavy burden of responsibility and to discharge my duties as King, as I wish to do, without the help and support of the woman I love.'

1936 These words, delivered in a thin voice at 10.00 this evening on BBC radio, were those of the former King Edward VIII – the man who would not be king – speaking from Windsor Castle to inform a stunned nation that he was giving up the British crown. The day before the broadcast he had signed the instrument of his abdication in favour of his younger brother, who was now King George VI. Edward's reign had lasted 326 days, since the death of his father, George V, who had predicted: 'After I am dead, the boy will ruin himself in twelve months.'

For well over a decade Edward's womanising and reckless behaviour had worried not only his father but also the government. His private secretary Alan Lascelles opined that 'for some hereditary or physiological reason his normal mental development stopped dead when he reached adolescence'.

In 1931 Edward's former mistress, Thelma, Lady Furness, introduced him to Wallis Simpson, a glamorous American divorcee still married to her second husband. They became lovers sometime in 1934, and after Edward had inherited the throne, they holidayed together in the Mediterranean, an interlude widely covered in the European and American press but not in Britain, where newspapers loyally maintained a self-imposed silence.

Those who knew of the relationship – and by now that included the king's mother, the Archbishop of Canterbury, Prime Minister Stanley Baldwin, the cabinet ministers, and the prime ministers of the largest dominions in the British Empire – were horrified. At last it became clear to Edward that if he persisted in his plan to marry Mrs Simpson, the government would resign, bringing on elections in which the main issue would be the king's personal affairs, with all the attendant damage to the monarchy such a debate would create. At the end, he had to choose between marriage and the throne. He chose Wallis Simpson.

Some hours after his startling broadcast, HMS *Fury* slipped out of Portsmouth harbour bearing the Duke of Windsor, as Edward would now be known, to France where Wallis waited. Of that moment of departure from crown and country, he later said: 'So far as I was concerned, love had triumphed.'

For many, however, what love had triumphed over was duty, responsibility and national tradition. In Britain, where the press had kept the public ignorant of the events leading up to the abdication, the reaction was restrained, the mood one of regret, of shame for some. Among many people, there was resentment, not only towards the woman who had wooed away their king, but also towards the king who had deserted them for her.

Edward married Wallis in France on 3 June the next year, shortly after her second divorce became final. It was a small ceremony, held in the Château de Candé in the Loire valley, with only sixteen guests. Wallis became Duchess of Windsor, but in their displeasure at the marriage the British royal family withheld from her the expected title of Her Royal Highness. Snubbed, the Windsors chose thereafter to live abroad, glamorous irrelevancies in luxurious exile.

Edward died of throat cancer in 1972, just before his 78th birthday. Suffering from dementia and unable to speak, Wallis died fourteen years later at 89. Both are buried near Windsor Castle, where Edward had made his abdication speech all those years before.

1880 Prussian field marshal Helmuth von Moltke in a letter to Dr J.K. Bluntschli: 'Everlasting peace is a dream, and not even a pleasant one; and war is a necessary part of God's arrangement of the world ... Without war, the world would slide dissolutely into materialism.' * **1891** Former and future prime minister William Gladstone: 'Until society is able to offer to the industrious labourer at the end of a long and blameless life something better than the workhouse, society will not have discharged its duties to its poorer members.'

---

12 December

'...'

1901 If you're proficient in Morse code you'll have spotted that the quotation above is simply the letter 'S'. Today the Italian inventor Guglielmo Marconi picked up this signal sent by his team from 2,200 miles across the ocean. It was the first-ever transatlantic wireless transmission.

Born in Bologna in 1874, Marconi grew up both privileged and bilingual, his father a wealthy landowner and his mother the daughter of an Irish peer. When he was twenty, he first started experimenting at his family's villa near Venice with the help of his butler. His goal was to find a way to transmit messages without connecting wires.

Transatlantic telegrams had been possible since 1858, but they required a massive and expensive cable to cross the ocean. Then in the 1880s radio waves were discovered, and Marconi was determined to find a way to use them.

Marconi started small – in the summer of 1894 he used radio waves to make a bell ring across the room. By the next year he had increased the range to a mile and a half.

For two years Marconi continued to improve his system, but he failed to find Italian backers to develop it commercially. Luckily, a family friend introduced him to the Italian ambassador in London, so, still only 22, he travelled to England. After patenting his ideas, he quickly found investors, including the British Post Office, which allowed him to set up The Wireless Telegraph & Signal Company (eventually rebranded as the Marconi Company). Within a year he increased the range of his broadcasts to twelve miles, and a year later he set up a station on the Isle of Wight so that Queen Victoria could send messages to her son Prince Edward aboard the royal yacht.

After a brief but much publicised stint using his wireless telegraph to report on the America's Cup yacht races, Marconi returned to England and began investigating how to send Morse signals across the Atlantic. To many this seemed like an impossible task, arguing that since radio waves travelled in straight lines, they could go only as far as the horizon. Marconi insisted that they would follow the curve of the earth and ploughed ahead with his experiments, little knowing that waves do travel in straight lines but bounce off the ionosphere.

Stationing himself in St John's in Newfoundland, on this day Marconi attached his antenna to a 500-foot tether while another team stationed in Cornwall broadcast the most powerful radio signal they could produce. Marconi later described the momentous day: 'Shortly before midday I placed the single earphone to my ear and started listening. The receiver on the table before me was very crude – a few coils and condensers and a coherer – no valves, no amplifiers, not even a crystal … The answer came at 12.30 when I heard, faintly but distinctly, pip-pip-pip. I handed the phone to [my assistant]: "Can you hear anything?" I asked. "Yes," he said. "The letter S."' It was the starting point of the vast development of wireless telegraphy, radio and navigation services that took place in the next 50 years, in much of which Marconi played a crucial role. (In 1912 his company placed two radio operators aboard the *Titanic*. When the ship struck an iceberg, they were able to summon the *Carpathia* to pick up 700 survivors.)

Marconi continued refining his inventions and improving transmission distances aboard his 700-ton steam yacht, *Elettra*, and honours and riches flowed in.

He was awarded the Nobel Prize for Physics, the British government made him an Honorary Knight Grand Cross, the Italian Senate made him a senator and King Vittorio Emanuele III made him a *marchese*. Perhaps unsurprisingly, this rich, aristocratic entrepreneur joined the Italian Fascist Party, and in 1930 Mussolini made him a member of the Fascist Grand Council. He and his wife toured around the world promoting Fascist values and defending Mussolini's invasion of Abyssinia.

When Marconi died in Rome of a heart attack on 20 July 1937, Italy held a state funeral for him and radio stations in America, England and Italy fell silent for two minutes. The biggest wreath at his funeral came from Adolf Hitler.

1826 In the House of Commons, Foreign Secretary George Canning defends his policies towards France, Spain and Latin America: 'I called the New World into existence to redress the balance of the Old.' * **1932** When asked what are the most beautiful words in the English language, Dorothy Parker replies: 'The ones I like ... are "cheque" and "enclosed."' * **1945** In Hollywood to work on screenplays, detective story writer Raymond Chandler writes to editor Charles W. Morton: 'If my books had been any worse, I should not have been invited to Hollywood, and if they had been any better, I should not have come.'

---

13 December

'Behold the beast that comes from the sea.'

1250 Today Frederick II died thirteen days short of his 56th birthday. He had been Holy Roman Emperor for 30 years, most of them spent vying with various popes for temporal power in Italy. Short, stout, bald and, according to a contemporary, not worth 200 dirhams in a Muslim slave market, he was nevertheless the most remarkable monarch of the Middle Ages.

Frederick was born in Palermo, a prince of the Hohenstaufen dynasty that had provided Holy Roman emperors since 1138. At two he inherited the throne of Sicily and two years later became King of the Germans. A month before his 26th birthday he was crowned Holy Roman Emperor by the Pope in Rome.

An intellect of the highest order, Frederick spoke seven languages, including Arabic. He invited Muslim and Jewish sages to his court in Palermo (where he also kept a harem guarded by black eunuchs). Insatiably curious, he was both a patron of the arts and a scientist. In his most famed experiment he ordered some nurses to raise a group of foundlings without talking to them, to discover what language they would 'naturally' speak. According to a contemporary chronicle, 'he laboured in vain, for the children all died, unable to live without the loving words of their mothers'.

Frederick was a strong believer in education and founded the University of Naples. At 36 he personally wrote *The Constitutions of Melfi*, a new legal code for the Kingdom of Sicily, which emphasised the monarch's God-given right to rule and warned that 'heretics try to tear the seamless robe of God'.

A fine horseman and swordsman, Frederick wrote the first comprehensive book on falconry, *De arte venandi cum avibus* (*The Art of Hunting with Birds*). He was also the father of Italian poetry, being the first to write love songs in the vernacular. No wonder his contemporaries called him *stupor mundi* (wonder of the world).

In theory a God-fearing Christian, Frederick was eternally at loggerheads with the Church, largely because his territories impinged upon papal lands. He also supposedly described Christ, Moses and Muhammad as mountebanks. When he initially baulked at going on crusade Pope Gregory IX excommunicated him, so he set out for the Holy Land, but, rather than attacking, he negotiated the liberation of Jerusalem, Bethlehem and Nazareth without spilling a drop of Saracen blood. This so enraged Gregory that thereafter he referred to Frederick as 'Christ's foe, the serpent'. He further infuriated Rome by his demand for the Church to renounce its wealth and return to apostolic poverty. In 1239 Gregory called on the faithful to renounce their allegiance to Frederick, starting his letter, 'Behold the beast that comes from the sea', referencing Revelation 13:1: 'And I saw a beast rising out of the sea, with ten horns and seven heads, with ten diadems on its horns and blasphemous names on its heads.'

Early in December 1250 Frederick suffered a fierce attack of dysentery that confined him to his hunting lodge of Castel Fiorentino, a hundred miles up the coast from Bari. There he died on this day.

Although excommunicated at the time, on his deathbed he had himself dressed in the robes of a Cistercian monk, symbolising the relinquishment of all worldly goods.

His son Manfred reported the news to his brother Conrad: 'The sun of justice has set, the maker of peace has passed away.' But Frederick's final show of piety had not impressed the Church. One priest, Nicholas of Carbio, wrote that 'the tyrant and son of Satan ... died horribly, deposed and excommunicated, suffering excruciatingly from dysentery, gnashing his teeth, frothing at the mouth and screaming ...' Pope Innocent IV gloated: 'Let heaven exult and the earth rejoice.'

> **1914** Future Italian Duce Benito Mussolini in a speech in Parma: 'It is blood that moves the wheels of history.'

14 December

'This German prince has governed England for twenty-one years with a wisdom and energy such as none of our kings have ever shown.'

1861 Today at Windsor Castle, Queen Victoria's consort Prince Albert succumbed to typhoid fever, probably contracted from the castle's faulty drains. He was only 42.

Victoria and Albert were cousins; born in Bavaria, Albert was three months younger than his wife. Their births were attended by the same midwife, the German physician Charlotte von Siebold.

At his death the royal couple had been married for over 21 years, their relationship passionate and faithful, in a flowery 19th-century sort of way (on the day of their engagement, Albert had written: 'I ... can only believe that Heaven has sent down an angel to me, whose radiance is intended to brighten my life.').

An indefatigable worker, Albert had become Victoria's chief advisor, obsessed with doing his duty. He was liberal and progressive for his time and led reforms in university education, welfare and slavery. He had been the leading light in the creation of the Great Exhibition of 1851, which 6 million people had visited and which had turned a healthy profit, used to build several museums.

A month before his death, in spite of the chill November damp, Albert had visited Sandhurst to inspect some new buildings at the

Military Academy. Now he began to suffer from pains in his back and legs, but he insisted on continuing his work and travelled on to Cambridge. Only then did he agree to return to Windsor, tired and feverish.

Although his condition worsened, the royal doctor James Clark assured the queen that he would soon be well. Albert himself was less sanguine. 'I have no tenacity for life', he told Clark.

On 14 December Victoria and five of their nine children gathered in the Blue Room at Windsor Castle, where Albert lay in bed, clearly nearing his end. He nodded when Victoria offered him '*ein Kuss*' ('a kiss' – they privately spoke to each other in German), but, as Victoria later wrote in her notebook, at 10.45 that evening 'two or three long but perfectly gentle breaths were drawn, the hand clasping mine, and (oh! It turns me sick to write it) all, all was over – the heavenly Spirit fled to the World it was fit for, and free from the sorrows and trials of this world! I stood up, kissed his dear heavenly forehead and called out in a bitter and agonising cry: "Oh! My dear Darling!" and then dropped on my knees in mute, distracted despair, unable to utter a word or shed a tear!'

Prostrate with grief, Victoria wrote to her uncle Leopold, King of Belgium: 'My life as a happy one is ended!' She never relinquished her widow's weeds in the 40 years that remained to her.

Although Albert was dead, his work was not. He had proposed the creation of facilities for the enlightenment of the public in the area near the site of the Great Exhibition. The Victoria & Albert Museum had been opened in 1857, the same year the Science Museum was founded. After Albert's death, the Albert Hall was built, opening in 1871, a year before the completion of the Albert Memorial, a 175-foot neo-Gothic spire decorated with mosaics and pinnacles with a 14-foot bronze statue of a seated Albert at its centre.

The British public had for years scorned Albert as a 'foreigner', but now began to appreciate his many contributions to the nation. As future prime minister Benjamin Disraeli wrote: 'With Prince Albert, we have buried our sovereign. This German prince has governed England for twenty-one years with a wisdom and energy such as none of our kings have ever shown.'

1542 When James V of Scotland dies, leaving his throne to his week-old daughter Mary (Queen of Scots), he sighs with resignation: 'It came wi a lass, it'll gang wi a lass', referring to the Stewart dynasty's accession to the throne through Marjorie Bruce and its likely end through his infant daughter. * **1745** About to lead his army into battle against the Saxons at Kesselsdorf, Prussia's 70-year-old Generalfeldmarschall Leopold I, Prince of Anhalt-Dessau prays: 'O Lord God, let me not be disgraced in my old days. Or if Thou wilt not help me, do not help these scoundrels, but leave us to try it ourselves.' He won the battle.

15 December

'For not by numbers of men, nor by measure of body, but by valour of soul is war to be decided.'

533 AD Today near ancient Carthage (now Tunis) the last great Roman general defeated Gelimer, the King of the Vandals, regaining North Africa for the Eastern Roman Empire.

It was the seventh year in the reign of Justinian. Upon his ascension he had appointed a promising officer from the previous emperor's bodyguard to command his army. He was a Thracian named Flavius Belisarius, who soon proved his mettle by defeating the Persians as well as crushing the Nika riots in Constantinople that had threatened Justinian's throne.

The Eastern and Western empires had been split in 476, but Justinian had dreams of reuniting them under his own rule. The first step was to conquer the Kingdom of the Vandals, which extended across North Africa. Nominally the Vandal kingdom was a Roman vassal state, but in 530 a noble named Gelimer had overthrown his cousin to grab the throne, giving Justinian an excuse to invade. The man he chose to do the job was Belisarius, then around 30.

In mid-June 533 Belisarius led his army down to 500 transport ships moored in front of Constantinople's Imperial Palace. The logistics alone would have stopped most armies – apart from thousands of sailors, there were 10,000 infantry and 5,000 cavalry, men and horses, plus weapons, military stores, water and provisions to last for a three-month voyage of over 1,000 miles. When all were embarked, the fleet, protected by 92 brigantines, set sail for North Africa.

Early on 13 September the Roman force reached Ad Decimum, the road marker ten miles from Carthage, and there they encountered Gelimer's army. Initially the Vandals gained the upper hand, but Gelimer's brother Ammatus was slain early in the fight. When Gelimer came across his brother's body he became completely unmanned, expressing loud lamentations. Instead of consolidating his attack, he could think only of burying his brother's corpse. This allowed Belisarius to rally his troops and drive the Vandals from the field.

Belisarius now moved unopposed to Carthage, where he was welcomed by its Roman citizens, and dined with his officers on a lunch prepared for Gelimer. According to the historian Procopius, who was in Belisarius' entourage, 'we feasted on that very food, and Gelimer's domestics served it and poured the wine and waited upon us in every way'.

The Romans had taken the capital, but Gelimer was still in command of a huge army about triple the size of the Roman one. Belisarius decided to march from the city to attack but first called his men together for a pre-fight pep talk. Procopius tells us that he inspired his soldiers by telling them: 'For not by numbers of men, nor by measure of body, but by valour of soul is war to be decided.'

On 15 December the two forces met at Tricamaron, 30 miles west of Carthage. Belisarius' cavalry immediately charged the enemy, followed by an infantry assault. During the third cavalry charge another of Gelimer's brothers, Tzazon, was killed. As had happened at Ad Decimum, Gelimer lost heart, and the Vandal lines began to crumble. Without a word to his men, the Vandal chief now galloped from the field, his panicked army close behind.

Belisarius' victory was complete, having lost only 50 men to some 800 enemy dead and 2,000 taken prisoner. In March the next year Gelimer finally surrendered to Belisarius, who took him back to Constantinople.

Belisarius was given a triumph on his return, the last ever in Roman history. Gelimer was forced to march in the wake of the victorious Roman troops, but rather than being ritually strangled at the end, as was the case in former times, he was given vast estates in Galatia, where he lived until his death in 453 at the advanced age of 73.

Now that he controlled North Africa, Justinian could launch his invasion of the Western Empire. With Belisarius and the eunuch general Narses leading his forces, he conquered the Ostrogoths and took Italy, Dalmatia, Sicily and parts of Spain, temporarily reuniting the Eastern and Western Roman Empire.

1917 British economist and sometime Treasury official John Maynard Keynes in a letter to Duncan Grant on David Lloyd George's government: 'I work for a Government I despise for ends I think criminal.'

16 December

*'When a man knows he is to be hanged in a
fortnight, it concentrates his mind wonderfully.'*

1969 Today the British Parliament abolished capital punishment,
343 in favour, 185 against, with Labour PM Harold Wilson and
Conservative leader Edward Heath both supporting the bill. Hanging
was retained for espionage, treason, piracy with violence, causing a
fire in a naval ship or dockyard and a few military offences such as
mutiny. Thirty years later Great Britain signed the sixth protocol of
the European Convention on Human Rights that ended the death
penalty altogether.

Capital punishment is as old as human society. The earliest known
law code, that of King Ur-Nammu of Ur in Mesopotamia, written
about 2100 BC, specified death for murder, robbery and deflowering
the virgin wife of a young man.

Execution has been accomplished by dozens of imaginative techniques. Apart from hanging, beheading, shooting, lethally injecting and
electrocuting, victims have been burnt, gassed, flayed, crucified, tied
to the mouth of a cannon, and that old British favourite, drawn and
quartered (like Scottish rebel William Wallace in 1305). The Romans
tossed traitors off the Tarpeian Rock, fed criminals to the lions and
buried unchaste Vestal Virgins alive. Spain favoured garrotting, and in
India convicts could be trampled by elephants. Some Muslim countries
still like the idea of stoning adulterous wives.

The first known ban on capital punishment was in China in 747.
Over a millennium later Finland banned it in 1826, followed by the
Netherlands, Portugal, Norway, and Sweden. Italy gave it up in 1890,
reintroduced it under Mussolini (who may have regretted it when he
was summarily executed), and banned it again. Hitler's regime executed 40,000 people (plus 6 million concentration camp victims),
but Germany abolished it in 1949. French revolutionaries guillotined
16,000 people and summarily executed another 25,000, but in 1981
François Mitterrand ended capital punishment. During Stalin's 'Great
Purge' in Russia, 681,692 people were shot, but capital punishment
has been suspended since 1996 (excluding extracurricular hits on anti-
Putin dissidents).

Today only 54 of the world's 195 countries still execute. China leads
with 1–2,000 annually – a trifle compared to the 800,000 that Mao

boasted had been shot after the Communist takeover. Iran is first per capita with 6.5 per million inhabitants (84 times the US rate, where 23 people were put to death in 2017). In Saudi Arabia you can be beheaded for 23 different reasons, including witchcraft.

In Great Britain victims have ranged from royalty (Mary, Queen of Scots; Charles I) to pirates (Captain Kidd) and highwaymen (Dick Turpin). The luckiest was Oliver Cromwell, who was dug up and decapitated for regicide in 1661, having already been dead for two years.

About 72,000 were executed during the reign of Henry VIII, including two of his own wives. One capital crime was buggery; the first to be charged under the Buggery Act 1533 was Nicholas Udall, the headmaster of Eton (would you believe it?). Udall was spared and became headmaster of Westminster School. Buggery remained a capital offence until 1861.

Henry VIII's daughter Mary specialised in burning people at the stake, 280 in all, most famously Thomas Cranmer.

18th-century Britain favoured hanging. In 1777 clergyman William Dodd was convicted of forgery. Samuel Johnson secretly wrote a pro-Dodd address that was presented in court as coming from Dodd himself. When a friend expressed doubt that Dodd could have written it, Johnson responded: 'Depend upon it, Sir, when a man knows he is to be hanged in a fortnight, it concentrates his mind wonderfully.' Dodd was hanged anyway.

Executions in Britain continued full steam throughout the 19th century – in 1820 there were 160 capital crimes, and one hangman, a cobbler named William Calcraft, finished off 450 people.

In 1955 Ruth Ellis was the last woman executed, and on 13 August 1964 the British gave a fond farewell to hanging when two murderers became the last people executed.

Britain's foremost hangman Albert Pierrepoint helped over 600 people out of this world (a trifle compared to the French executioner Charles-Henri Sanson, who put nearly 3,000 people to death over a 40-year career, including Louis XVI). After his retirement Pierrepoint concluded: 'All the men and women whom I have faced at that final moment, convince me that in what I have done, I have not prevented a single murder.'

1945 Before launching an initial 90-minute artillery barrage using 1,600 artillery pieces to start the Battle of the Bulge, Marshal Gerd von Rundstedt declares: 'The time has come when the German Army must rise again and strike.' (Although bitterly contested, the attack failed.) * **1965** Just before he dies, British writer Somerset Maugham tells his son Robin: 'Dying is a very dull, dreary affair. And my advice to you is to have nothing whatever to do with it.'

17 December

'A sudden dart when out about 100 feet from the end of the tracks ended the flight. Time about 12 seconds.'

1903 With this entry in his diary, Wilbur Wright recorded his brother Orville's first flight in the primitive aircraft they had built. For the first time ever, a powered flying machine with a human being in control had taken off from level ground and travelled through the air.

The earliest known example of man-made flight was in about 400 BC when the Chinese invented the kite, but, as far as we know, there was no attempt to carry a passenger. Over the centuries men made innumerable efforts to fly, and the first means discovered was the glider. Four glider flyers on record are a 9th-century Moor from Cordoba whose feathery-winged glider flew but crashed; the 11th-century English monk Eilmer of Malmesbury, who glided from his abbey's roof but broke both legs on landing; the 17th-century Pole Tito Burattini, whose glider flew with a cat on board; and Englishman George Cayley, who built the first glider to carry a human being without crashing, when his biplane carried a ten-year-old boy aloft in 1804. Meanwhile in 1783 Pilâtre de Rozier and the Marquis d'Arlandes had become the first men to fly, when they drifted over Paris in a hot-air balloon.

In 1852 another Frenchman, Henri Giffard, became the first to make an engine-powered flight. He flew seventeen miles, not in a plane but in his hydrogen-filled dirigible, with a propeller powered by a small steam engine.

Although Leonardo da Vinci had designed but never built a flying machine in about 1488, it was engineer/inventor Clément Ader four centuries later who flew for 150 feet only eight inches above the ground in his steam-powered propeller-driven 'plane' with bat wings. Ader was more passenger than pilot since his craft had no steering mechanism.

In 1896 Samuel Langley launched an unpiloted, engine-driven craft from a catapult mounted on a houseboat on the Potomac River, which flew for three-quarters of a mile before crashing into the river.

About the same time the brothers Wilbur (32) and Orville (28) Wright from Dayton, Ohio began to develop an aircraft. Although not formally trained, they owned a bicycle repair shop and had gained an invaluable knowledge of mechanics.

The brothers first experimented with gliders, which they tested at Kitty Hawk, a town on a tiny island off the coast of North Carolina, chosen because of its frequent winds and soft, sandy landing surfaces. Their last glider, a boxy biplane with a 32-foot wingspan, led directly to the design of their first powered aircraft, the Wright Flyer.

The Wright Flyer was a biplane built of spruce, with muslin surface covering and a wingspan of 40 feet. The brothers carved wooden propellers and powered them with a petrol engine made in their bicycle shop. The plane used two ski-like runners to slide along a wooden track of 2×4s for take-off.

On 14 December 1903 the brothers were ready to attempt powered flight. After tossing a coin to see who would pilot their craft, Wilbur lay on his stomach on the lower wing with his head facing forward. With the primitive motor at full power, the Wright Flyer lurched forward on its track – and stalled in less than three seconds. Fortunately, there was only minor damage.

Three days later, on Tuesday, 17 December, the brothers were ready to try again.

The day dawned cold and windy, with gusts reaching 27 miles an hour. At 10.35, with Orville stretched out in the pilot's position, the Wright Flyer began to move down the track into a strong headwind, Wilbur running along at wingtip to balance the machine. After a few seconds the plane lifted into the air, but, as Wilbur recorded: 'A sudden dart when out about 100 feet from the end of the tracks ended the flight. Time about 12 seconds.' The actual distance was 120 feet, less than half the wingspan of a modern Airbus A380.

The Wright brothers flew three more times that day, culminating in Wilbur's flight of 852 feet that lasted 59 seconds. The age of the aeroplane had begun.

1830 Hounded from his offices by bitter political disputes, tubercular and broke, South American liberator Simón Bolívar dies in Colombia, remarking bitterly: 'The people send me to the tomb, but I forgive them.' * **1991** When former New Zealand prime minister Robert Muldoon resigns from Parliament, he closes his valedictory speech: 'There was a lady walking down the pavement and as we passed, she stopped and she said: "I know you, don't I?" … I said: "My name's Muldoon." She said: "You're not related to that bastard in Parliament, are you?" And on that salutary note Mr Speaker, I say goodbye.'

18 December

'As one small candle may light a thousand, so the light here kindled hath shone unto many, yea in some sort to our whole nation.'

1620 Today 102 Pilgrims, including a new-born baby, came ashore from the merchant ship *Mayflower* on the Atlantic coast of present-day Massachusetts. Near the spot where they debarked lay a granite boulder fifteen feet long and three feet wide that they dubbed Plymouth Rock in honour of the town in England from which they had set sail 103 days before.

On 11 November the *Mayflower* had anchored off what is now Provincetown Harbor, but after exploring the area for six weeks, the Pilgrims came across the sheltered waters of Plymouth Harbor, where they decided to build their colony.

The voyage had been a rough and crowded one, the passengers crammed in with about 30 crew in a ship only 100 feet long. During this perilous journey storms had cost the life of one passenger and one seaman, but, as recorded by William Bradford, the future governor of the colony they would found: 'Being thus arived in a good harbor and brought safe to land, they fell upon their knees & blessed ye God of heaven, who had brought them over ye vast & furious ocean, and delivered them from all ye periles & miseries therof.'

In the early 17th century, King James I had insisted that his subjects follow the Church of England, but these 'Separatist' Pilgrims denied the supremacy of the Crown over Church affairs and were determined to organise their own congregations under their own ministers. In 1606 they had fled to the Netherlands, after James had declared: 'I will make them conform, or I will harry them out of the land.' After twelve years of unrewarding struggle to make a living, however, they set out to found a colony in the New World. On 6 September 1620 they crowded onto the *Mayflower* to begin the long, hard journey to a new life.

The Pilgrims' first year on land was even rougher than their passage across the Atlantic. During the winter they remained on board ship, and in spring they built huts and moved ashore. On 5 April the *Mayflower* and its crew left to return to England.

The Pilgrims suffered from pneumonia, scurvy and tuberculosis as well as the harsh conditions of a New England winter, and by November 1621 only 53 remained alive. Even with their terrible losses, the remaining Pilgrims celebrated a harvest feast with the nearby Wampanoag Indian tribe, which Americans today consider to be 'The First Thanksgiving'.

Over the next years more settlers made the long sail across the Atlantic to the Plymouth Colony, and within two decades it had a population of 26,000. As Governor Bradford wrote: 'As one small candle may light a thousand, so the light here kindled hath shone unto many, yea in some sort to our whole nation.' How right he was.

Of the original 73 male passengers aboard the *Mayflower*, 24 fathered children. Many an American has proudly claimed his *Mayflower* lineage, and known descendants include ten presidents (John and John Quincy Adams, Abraham Lincoln, Ulysses Grant, James Garfield, Zachary Taylor, Calvin Coolidge, Franklin D. Roosevelt and the Bushes father and son). Other descendants range from poets (Henry Wadsworth Longfellow) and painters (Grandma Moses) to movie stars such as Humphrey Bogart, Clint Eastwood, Katharine Hepburn, Orson Welles and Marilyn Monroe. The actor Richard Gere is said to be descended from no fewer than six *Mayflower* passengers. There are also some risible *Mayflower* posterity, like Hugh Hefner and Sarah Palin.

But claiming ancestral lineage to the *Mayflower* is hardly an exclusive club; somewhere between 25 and 35 million Americans are estimated to be descendants.

1816 President John Tyler to the House of Representatives: 'Popularity, I have always thought, may aptly be compared to a coquette – the more you woo her, the more apt is she to elude your embrace.' * **1863** Prussian Minister of Foreign Affairs Otto von Bismarck tells the Prussian parliament: '*Die Politik is keine exakte Wissenshaft.*' ('Politics is not an exact science.')

---

19 December

'Each one then stood firm, thinking in his heart that the men he saw coming towards him were not Spanish, English or Italian, but Frenchmen, and of the bravest, among whom were some of his own companions, kinsmen or friends.'

1562 Since the death of her husband Henri II in a jousting accident, Catherine de' Medici had been regent for her son, Charles IX. She had tried to moderate hostility between Catholics and Huguenots (Protestants), in a country of 18 million people, of whom 90 per cent were Catholics, but where more than half the nobility were Huguenots. Despite her efforts, France was now on the brink of the religious wars that would tear the nation apart.

The leaders of the religious factions were all closely and confusedly connected. Leading the Catholics was the ageing Anne de Montmorency, Constable of France and commander-in-chief of the royal armies, and François, duc de Guise, a powerful noble (he was the uncle of the late King François II's wife, Mary, Queen of Scots). The Huguenots in turn were headed by Louis I, Prince de Condé, once Guise's close ally – Guise's mother was Condé's aunt – and Gaspard de Coligny, Admiral of France, who was Condé's uncle and Montmorency's nephew.

The first major violence came on 1 March when Guise ordered some Huguenots to abandon their Protestant service outside the town of Vassy. The Huguenots responded by throwing rocks, triggering an attack by Guise's men that killed 30 and wounded over 100 more. To top it off, the enraged duke hanged the Protestant minister.

Today, nine months later, came the first battle of France's religious wars. Coligny and Condé were leading an army towards Le Havre when a Catholic force intercepted them at Dreux, 50 miles west of Paris. With 8,500 infantry, the Huguenots had only half as many as the Catholics, but they had 4,500 cavalry, twice that of the enemy.

After observing each other for two hours, the armies began to advance. 'Each one then stood firm, thinking in his heart that the men he saw coming towards him were not Spanish, English or Italian, but Frenchmen, and of the bravest, among whom were some of his own companions, kinsmen or friends; which gave some horror to the deed but did not diminish the courage', reported Huguenot captain François de la Noue.

Then the Huguenot cavalry swept across the field, Condé and Coligny driving their enemy before them. Coligny captured his uncle Montmorency after his horse had been killed under him and his jaw broken by a pistol shot. But just as the Huguenots were congratulating themselves on an easy victory, Guise's cavalry charged, overran the Huguenot artillery, routed their disorganised infantry and captured Condé. What had looked like a Huguenot triumph had been transformed into a shattering defeat.

Montmorency and Condé were soon exchanged, but bitterness and hatred now festered among these closely related leaders, all of whom came to bloody ends. On Coligny's orders, two months later one of Coligny's spies in Guise's forces, Jean de Poltrot de Méré, ambushed Guise as he was riding back to his headquarters, shooting him in the back. Guise died six days later, bled to death by his surgeons. (Poltrot was apprehended and sentenced to be torn apart by four horses tied to his arms and legs. When the horses failed, soldiers finished the job with swords.)

In November 1567 Montmorency was fatally wounded while leading the Catholics to victory at Saint-Denis, and sixteen months later Condé was captured and murdered when the Huguenots were defeated at Jarnac. Finally, in 1572 Catherine de' Medici instigated the massacre of St Bartholomew, during which Guise's son Henri and his henchmen attacked Coligny at his home in Paris, killing him with daggers. (In this never-ending cycle of violence, in 1588 Catherine's third son, Henri III, had Henri de Guise murdered at the château of Blois. The next year Henri was stabbed to death by a fanatical Catholic monk.)

The French Wars of Religion continued until, on Henri's death, Henri IV inherited the throne, pragmatically abjured Protestantism for Catholicism, and in April 1598 issued the Edict of Nantes that gave citizens freedom of conscience regarding religion and reinstated Huguenot civil rights.

1776 Thomas Paine publishes *The American Crisis* in the *Pennsylvania Journal*, including the lines: 'These are the times that try men's souls. The summer soldier and the sunshine patriot will, in this crisis, shrink from the service of their country; but he that stands it now, deserves the love and thanks of man and woman.'

20 December

'Yet I was once your emperor.'

69 AD Today, after a mere eight months in power, Emperor Vitellius was brutally murdered in Rome, his body thrown into the Tiber. He had been the third emperor since Nero's suicide eighteen months before and the third to die violently during this so-called Year of the Four Emperors. Despite their ultimate failures, all three died with dignity.

The first of the four emperors was Nero's immediate successor, Galba, a frail 72-year-old nobleman who was almost completely bald. Galba raised taxes and refused to reward the Praetorian Guards who had helped him become emperor, causing a military revolt led by the second of the four emperors, Otho.

On 15 January 69 the Praetorian Guards, who had been bribed by Otho, captured Galba and brought him to the Roman Forum, so feeble that he had to be carried in a litter. According to Plutarch, just before he was cut down, he said: 'Strike, if it be for the good of Rome!'

Suetonius tells us that Galba's corpse was left there 'until a common soldier, returning from a distribution of grain, threw down his load and cut off the head. Then, since there was no hair by which to grasp it, he put it under his robe, but later thrust his thumb into the mouth and so carried it to Otho. He handed it over to his servants and camp-followers, who set it on a lance and paraded it about the camp with jeers.' Galba had ruled for seven months.

Otho's reign was even shorter, just 95 days, as he committed suicide on 16 April, after his army had been defeated at Cremona by the third of the four emperors, Vitellius. After the battle Otho called the remains of his army around him and declared: 'It is far more just to perish one for all, than many for one.' Retiring to his tent, he stabbed himself in the heart with a dagger.

Vitellius was a cruel, vindictive man who was reputed to have had his own rebellious son put to death. Immensely fat, he often ate four times a day, while relieving himself with emetics between meals. According to Tacitus, 'he was the slave and chattel of luxury and gluttony'.

Vitellius soon learned that the legions in the eastern provinces had abandoned him, acclaiming their general Vespasian, who would become the fourth emperor that year. An army supporting Vespasian was now on the march towards Rome, although the general himself remained in the east for another year. On 24 April they crushed Vitellius' legions at Bedriacum and then advanced on the capital.

On this day Vespasian's troops arrived at the gates of Rome and, after furious fighting, entered the city. Realising that his cause was hopeless, Vitellius put on a girdle filled with gold pieces and hid himself in the janitor's quarters of the imperial palace, but the assaulting soldiers quickly discovered him. According to Suetonius, 'they bound his arms behind his back, put a noose about his neck, and dragged him with rent garments and half-naked to the Forum. All along the Sacred Way he was greeted with mockery and abuse, his head held back by the hair, as is common with criminals, and even the point of a sword placed under his chin, so that he could not look down but must let his face be seen. Some pelted him with dung and ordure, others called him incendiary and glutton.' Standing at the top of the Gemonian Stairs, Rome's place of execution, he retorted to a tribune who was mocking him: 'Whatever you may say, yet I was once your emperor.' He was put to the torture of the little cuts and then his throat was slit.

Now, as this calamitous Year of the Four Emperors came to a close, Vespasian was the only would-be emperor left standing, and a fine ruler he turned out to be. He ended the civil war, ruled for ten years and probably saved the empire from dissolution.

1812 The last soldier to quit Russian soil during Napoleon's catastrophic retreat, Napoleonic marshal Michel Ney rejoins the French at Gumbinnen, telling the sentry on duty: 'Here comes the rear guard of the Grand Army!' * **1991** President George H.W. Bush: 'I count my blessings for the fact I don't have to go into that pit that John Major stands in, nose-to-nose with the opposition, all yelling at each other.'

---

21 December

'First you take a drink, then the drink takes a drink, then the drink takes you.'

1940 It is an irony of literary history that an author whose works are now regarded among America's finest died a failure, not only as a man, a husband, and a father but also as a writer. This was the fate of F. Scott Fitzgerald, who suffered a fatal heart attack today. He was only 44 years old, an alcoholic, and virtually forgotten. His royalty statement for the previous year was $33.00.

Yet this was the same man who had burst upon the American scene in 1920 with *This Side of Paradise*, a semi-autobiographical novel based on his years at Princeton. It ushered in the Jazz Age and captured the imagination of a generation seeking liberation from the mores of its elders. Fitzgerald was, as an observer put it, 'a kind of king of American youth'. And his wife Zelda, once described as 'a young goddess of spring', became its flapper-queen.

Their hedonistic, fast-living lifestyle was an endless round of 'gleaming, dazzling parties', held in fashionable spots along America's East Coast, or in places like Paris, Rome, Capri, and the French Riviera, and always in the company of the social and artistic avant-garde. In his novels and short stories, Fitzgerald faithfully recounted the life he and Zelda led, for he was the chronicler as well as the symbol of his age. Ultimately, their life proved destructive to them both. 'First you take a drink', he wrote, 'then the drink takes a drink, then the drink takes you.'

Even in his heyday, Fitzgerald's novels never produced the income he needed to support their desperate extravagances. *The Great Gatsby* sold fewer than 23,000 copies in his lifetime. To pay the bills, he wrote a steady stream of short stories for magazines like *The Saturday Evening Post*, for $4,000 a story. The titles suggest the spirit of the times: 'Bernice Bobs Her Hair', 'The Diamond as Big as the Ritz', and 'The Rich Boy'.

The 1929 crash and the depression that followed put an end to the Jazz Age. His generation – the 'Lost Generation', as Gertrude Stein christened it – had grown up; the new one had very different tastes. His last completed novel was *Tender is the Night* in 1934, about which he commented in his notebook: 'Show me a hero and I will write you a tragedy.' Although now considered a classic, it received mixed reviews and disappointing sales.

Meanwhile Zelda had begun to suffer schizophrenic breakdowns, and the cost of sanatoriums almost bankrupted Fitzgerald. Deeply in debt, he moved to Hollywood in 1937 to try his hand at screenwriting for MGM. In three years, his lone credit, shared with another writer, was for the script of *Three Comrades*.

After Fitzgerald's first heart attack, in November 1940, his lover of three years, gossip columnist Sheilah Graham, installed him in her apartment. On 20 December he experienced a dizzy spell while leaving the theatre. The next evening, he rose from his armchair, grabbed the mantelpiece, gasped and fell to the floor, dead.

Fitzgerald's body was laid out in a Hollywood funeral parlour. Among the few who came by was the tart-tongued writer, Dorothy Parker, who said, 'The poor son of a bitch', echoing words uttered at Jay Gatsby's funeral in *The Great Gatsby*.

Fitzgerald died a writer without an audience, but a few saw value behind the sad waste of a once promising life. His rehabilitation began with his half-finished novel, *The Last Tycoon*, published in 1941. By the 1950s, a gathering force of critics, editors, and biographers had awoken public interest in Fitzgerald's writing. By 2013 *The Great Gatsby* had sold over 25 million copies and still sells 500,000 each year.

Fitzgerald's success bore out the vision he had once expressed, with the airy confidence of a young man at the beginning of his career: 'An author ought to write for the youth of his own generation, the critics of the next, and the schoolmasters of ever afterward.'

Fitzgerald is buried in Rockville, Maryland, beside his wife Zelda, who died when a fire broke out in her mental hospital in 1948. Their gravestone is inscribed with the final elegiac sentence of *The Great Gatsby*: 'So we beat on, boats against the current, borne back ceaselessly into the past.'

1945 After an American army truck crashes into his car, America's most aggressive Second World War general George Patton is paralysed from the neck down; he dies twelve days later, saying: 'This is a hell of a way to die.'

---

22 December

*'Music should strike fire from the heart of man,
and bring tears from the eyes of woman.'*

1808 Even in Vienna there can sometimes be too much music, and today was such a day, according to many who attended a concert in the Theater an der Wien that lasted over four hours, with all the work written by a single composer.

Yet in the hindsight of history, today was one of music's most important days, as that composer (and pianist in three of the pieces) was Ludwig van Beethoven, now 38 and approaching the apogee of his career.

Born in Bonn, Beethoven came from a highly musical family, his grandfather (also named Ludwig) a prominent *Kapellmeister* (music director), his father an alcoholic tenor who gave keyboard and violin lessons (and often beat his son).

Beethoven was a child prodigy on the piano, giving his first public performance at seven. By thirteen he had already composed three piano sonatas. At 22 he moved to Vienna to study under Haydn, but, sadly for the history of music, Mozart had died the previous December, so the two never met, except perhaps once, when Beethoven visited Vienna when he was sixteen.

Three years after his arrival in Vienna Beethoven gave his first public performance, playing one of his piano concertos, while he gave piano lessons to raise extra cash. He also began to hire concert halls to premiere his new compositions, his First Symphony at the Burgtheater and his Second Symphony at the Theater an der Wien.

Although he was anxious to earn money (he was only intermittently sponsored by various Viennese nobles), he developed a highly Romantic view of music, claiming that 'Music should strike fire from the heart of man, and bring tears from the eyes of woman'. About his own Third Symphony, which he wrote in his early thirties, he rhapsodised: 'From the glow of enthusiasm I let the melody escape. I pursue it. Breathless I catch up with it. It flies again, it disappears, it plunges into a chaos of diverse emotions. I catch it again, I seize it, I embrace it with delight ...'

In 1808 Beethoven decided to stage another event at the Theater an der Wien. It was to be an extraordinary evening in the music he brought to the public, arguably the most important single presentation of new work in history.

With himself as conductor, that night Beethoven premiered his Fifth Symphony (with its unforgettable four-note opening motif, '*dit-dit-dit-dah*'), his Sixth Symphony (Pastoral), his Choral Fantasy and his Fourth Piano Concerto, both with Beethoven himself at the piano. He also played an improvised piano fantasia that he published the next year as the Fantasia in G minor.

With other works like 'Ah! Perfido', the concert lasted over four hours, interrupted by the restarting of the Choral Fantasy because of a mix-up among the performers. On top of this, in the midst of a Viennese December, the concert hall was unheated. At the end the audience was shivering with cold and exhausted, and the *Allgemeine musikalische Zeitung*, the leading music publication of the day, complained that: 'To judge all these pieces after only one hearing ... with so many performed one after the other, most of them so grand and long, is downright impossible.'

And yet, by any standard, it was a remarkable concert by one of music's very greatest composers (in 1977 Beethoven's Fifth Symphony would be sent into outer space aboard the Voyager probes). It helped Beethoven pay some bills while adding to his published repertoire and probably his self-esteem. Sometime later he told an Austrian noble: 'Prince, what you are, you are by accident of birth; what I am, I am by myself. There are and will be a thousand princes; there is only one Beethoven.'

1790 In a war against the Ottoman Empire, Russian General Alexander Suvarov completes the siege of Ismail by letting his soldiers run riot, killing 33,000 Turks inside the town, then mildly reports to Catherine the Great: 'Glory to God and Your Excellency; the town is taken, I am in it.'

---

23 December

'God grant you have not made yourself king of nothing.'

1588 Should you ever visit the château at Blois, you can still see a dark stain on the floor, which is said to have been made by the blood of the duc de Guise, murdered there on this day on the orders of King Henri III.

Cultivated and intelligent but weak, neurotic and effeminate, Henri III had spent his fourteen-year reign dominated by his mother, Catherine de' Medici. France's Wars of Religion had been festering since 1562, as fervent Catholics of the so-called Holy League had endeavoured to repress all Protestantism while French Huguenots bitterly fought back with no holds barred.

Heading the Holy League was the country's most powerful noble, the huge (6ft 6in) and muscular Henri, duc de Guise, called *Le Balafré* – Scarface – because his face had been distinctively scarred by a war wound. The haughty duke claimed to be so brave that 'even if I were to see death enter by the window, I would not go out by the door to escape her'.

King Henri had tried to soothe Catholics by cracking down on Protestantism, but his ineffectual efforts were taken by the Holy League to signify a lack of proper zeal. On 12 May 1588 – called the Day of the Barricades – the Catholic citizens of Paris, egged on by Guise, rose against the king, killing 60 soldiers and chasing him from the city. Guise and the League took control of Paris.

Henri fled first to Saint-Cloud, then to Chartres, then Rouen and finally to the royal château at Blois on the Loire. Now he resolved to rid himself of the arrogant duke, but Guise's position was so strong that he could not be arrested. The only solution was murder.

In December the Estates-General – representatives of the French nobility, clergy and the Third Estate (the ordinary people) – met at Blois. The king knew the hated Guise was sure to appear.

Henri was attended by Les Quarante-Cinq – 45 guards drawn from the poorer nobility, men with little more than a horse and a sword who were paid a lavish wage to be on call day or night. On the morning of the 23rd Henri summoned twenty of them to his bedroom, accompanied by two priests who were to pray for a successful murder. The king then sent word for Guise to join him and hid behind a curtain.

When the duke entered the room, eight guards threw themselves at him, swords drawn. The immensely strong Guise threw off several assailants, wounding four of them, but at length fell to the floor, pierced 30 times by swords and daggers. Henri then stepped out from behind the curtain and nudged the corpse with his foot, exclaiming: 'My God, he's big! He looks even bigger dead than alive.'

Henri then rushed downstairs to announce proudly to his mother: 'Madam, I am once more King of France. I have killed the King of Paris!' But, only too conscious of her son's precarious hold on power, she replied: 'What, you have killed the duke? God grant you have not made yourself king of nothing.' Ignoring her concern and untroubled by conscience, Henri left her to go to Mass.

Henri's triumph was short-lived. On 1 August the next year, a fanatical Dominican friar named Jacques Clément gained entry to his bedroom under pretext of having an urgent secret message to deliver. As he leaned over to whisper in the king's ear, Clément stabbed him in the stomach.

Henri died the next day, bringing an end to the Valois dynasty that had ruled for 261 years, giving thirteen kings to France. His death brought another Henri to the French throne, Henri de Navarre, who, as Henri IV, was the country's first Bourbon king. He would finally bring an end to France's religious wars.

1793 French Republicans under General François Westermann crush royalist insurgents in Savenay during the insurrection in the Vendée; during the next eight days 2,000 people are shot and 1,700 women and children are sent to Nantes, to be shot or drowned. Westermann reports to Robespierre's Committee of Public Safety: 'Mercy is not a revolutionary sentiment.' Indeed not – a year later Robespierre has him guillotined.

24 December

"Twas the night before Christmas, when all through the house/Not a creature was stirring, not even a mouse.'

1823 For almost two centuries parents have been reading the same delightful poem to their small children on Christmas Eve:

> 'Twas the night before Christmas, when all through the house
> Not a creature was stirring, not even a mouse;
> The stockings were hung by the chimney with care,
> In hopes that St Nicholas soon would be there.

Who would imagine that it first appeared in an obscure small-town newspaper in northern New York State? But so it was, on the night before the night before Christmas (23 December) in 1823 that the *Troy Sentinel* published 'A Visit from St Nicholas'.

The poem's composer was a 44-year-old professor of Greek literature named Clement Moore, who had written it to entertain his children the previous Christmas. Without Moore's knowledge, a house guest beguiled by the verses gave it to the *Sentinel*.

Initially the poem was published anonymously, as Moore considered himself a scholarly professor and did not wish to be known as the creator of doggerel, however charming. He finally publicly acknowledged authorship 21 years after the poem first appeared, when he included it in an anthology of his works.

'A Visit from St Nicholas' did much to standardise Americans' conception of Santa Claus (a morph of Saint Nicholas used in the American press since 1773), including his arrival by sleigh, the names and number of his reindeer, and scheduling his visit bearing presents on Christmas Eve (rather than Christmas Day).

The legend of Santa Claus originated with the real-life bishop Saint Nicholas who lived in Myra on the Mediterranean coast of Lycia (now Demre in Turkey) in the early 4th century, but the version we know today – a big, jolly man in a red suit with a white beard – stems largely from Haddon Sundblom's depiction of him for the Coca-Cola Company's Christmas advertising in the 1930s. (Some thought that Santa wore red and white because they were Coca-Cola's colours, but the true origin seems to be that bishops like Saint Nicholas wore red.)

Today some critics maintain that 'A Visit from St Nicholas' is the most famous poem ever written by an American, and it is certainly one of the most valuable – in 2006 a signed copy hand-written by Clement Moore sold for $280,000. Each year before Christmas, St Nicholas/Santa Claus can be found in innumerable shop windows, and millions of boys and girls still await his visit, enthralled by Moore's poem that concludes:

> But I heard him exclaim, ere he drove out of sight,
> "Happy Christmas to all, and to all a good-night!"

1818 In Oberndorf bei Salzburg in Austria, Father Joseph Mohr shows church organist Franz Gruber a poem he has written two years earlier. Gruber composes some music and the two men sing at Christmas Mass their new carol that begins: '*Stille Nacht! Heilige Nacht!/Alles schläft; einsam wacht.*' ('Silent night, holy night,/All is calm, all is bright.') * **1888** In Arles, Vincent Van Gogh attacks his friend Paul Gauguin with a razor (but fails to wound him), returns to his little yellow house and hacks off his own left earlobe to give to a favourite prostitute. A few days later he writes to his brother Theo: 'I hope I have just had simply an artist's freak, and then a lot of fever after very considerable loss of blood, as an artery was severed, but my appetite came back at once. My digestion is all right, and so from day to day serenity returns to my brain.'

25 December

*'Would that I had not entered
St Peter's on Christmas day.'*

800 AD Today, Christmas, Charles, King of the Franks, attended High Mass in the basilica of St Peter's in Rome. As he bowed before the altar in prayer, Pope Leo III lifted a crown that had been hidden behind the candlesticks and placed it on the king's head, proclaiming him Emperor of the Romans (*Imperator Romanorum*). According to the *Liber Pontificalis* (*Book of the Pontiffs*), the fervent crowd in the congregation 'cried aloud with one accord, "To Charles Augustus, crowned by God, the great and peace-giving Emperor, be life and victory"'.

Charles was now the divinely appointed supreme secular authority within most of Christendom. An emperor rather than a mere king, he had papal recognition as ruler over all the territories he had subjugated, which included all of modern France, Belgium and Holland, virtually all of Germany and Austria, half of Italy, part of Hungary and a few north-eastern provinces of Spain, an area of 462,000 square miles, about six times the size of Great Britain.

Thus began a sort of revival of the Roman Empire that had lapsed in the 5th century. The new emperor would be known to history as Carolus Magnus, Charles the Great, Charlemagne (or, if you're German-speaking, as Charles was, Karl der Grosse).

You would think that Pope Leo's surprise crowning would have been cause for celebration, but Charlemagne's contemporary biographer reports that the new emperor had been totally unaware of the Pope's intention and later lamented: 'Would that I had not entered St Peter's on Christmas day.'

Historians have long debated why Charlemagne might have made such a complaint. One theory is that, by being crowned by the Pope, he was implicitly recognising papal authority over his own. But most believe it was really smoke and mirrors, a 9th-century PR effort to demonstrate his own humility. In all likelihood the event had been carefully planned and stage-managed.

Leo had been elected to the papal throne in 795, following the death of 95-year-old Adrian I, who had reigned for a (then) record 23 years. But Leo was highly unpopular among Rome's nobles, particularly Adrian's relations. The problem had reached a climax in April 799, when he was set upon in the streets of Rome, thrown from his mule and almost blinded and battered to death. He was rescued and found shelter in a monastery, but his enemies in Rome accused him of murder, adultery and simony.

That summer Leo fled to Paderborn (about 250 miles west of Berlin), where King Charles received him with honour. During his three months' stay, the Pope survived an enquiry into the charges (the verdict was 'unproven'), after which Charles sent him with an armed escort back to Rome, where another inquiry declared him not guilty. In November Charles came to Rome to pay his respects to the now vindicated Pope. It seems all but certain that, during Leo's stay in Paderborn, he and Charles had cemented a deal by which Charles would reinstate Leo and Leo would proclaim Charles emperor.

Charlemagne was the first Roman emperor to be crowned by the Pope. (Another Charles, the V, would be the last in 1530.) The empire he founded (or revived) would last over 1,000 years until the abdication of Franz II in 1806. His empire would first be described as 'Holy' by Emperor Frederick Barbarossa in 1157, and the full title, *Sacrum Romanum Imperium*, was first used in 1254.

Charlemagne died in 814, leaving his empire to his son Louis I, but his Carolingian dynasty lasted only until 887. Although he had been a loyal supporter of the Church and spreader of the faith, he was canonised only in 1165 because, in the words of historian Norman Davies, 'the process was obstructed for 351 years by reports that his sexual conquests were no less extensive than his territorial ones'. Sadly for the Great Charles, he never became a proper saint because he was canonised by Paschal III, an antipope set up by Holy Roman Emperor Frederick Barbarossa in competition with the legitimate popes of the Catholic Church in Rome.

1941 American crooner Bing Crosby gives the first public performance of Irving Berlin's 'White Christmas' on the NBC Kraft Music Hall radio show, singing: 'I'm dreaming of a white Christmas.' * **1946** During his last illness American comic actor W.C. Fields tells friends: 'I have spent a lot of time searching through the Bible for loopholes.' Today he dies; his grave marker reads: 'On the whole, I would rather be in Philadelphia.'

---

26 December

'The biggest thing that has happened in the world in my life, in our lives, is this: by the grace of God, America won the Cold War.'

1991 Formed on 30 December 1922, the Union of Soviet Socialist Republics became the world's largest country, at 8.6 million square miles over 100 times the size of Great Britain. Its population of 293 million was only about half Russian. It became a byword for tyranny, ruled by a series of repressive dictators who sent millions to labour camps, starved millions and executed millions more.

At the end of the Second World War the Soviet Union swept into Eastern Europe and imposed communist regimes subservient to Moscow in seven countries. Cut off from the West by what Churchill dubbed the 'Iron Curtain', the Soviet bloc was hostile to democracy, the market economy and individual liberty, and Kremlin leaders were determined to expand communism even further. As American presidential advisor Bernard Baruch declared: 'We are today in the midst of a cold war.'

The Soviets and the West sparred in a series of proxy wars and confrontations.

In April 1949 the USSR imposed the Berlin blockade, abandoned after 407 days after President Harry Truman instigated the Berlin Airlift. Also in April, the West initiated NATO. (The NATO Secretary General, British General Hastings Ismay, joked that its goal was 'to keep the Russians out, the Americans in, and the Germans down'.)

In the early 1950s the West fought in Korea, while in 1953 Soviet tanks put down an uprising in East Germany.

In 1955 the communist bloc countered NATO with the Warsaw Pact. A year later the Soviets crushed a revolt in Hungary, and Nikita Khrushchev threatened the West: 'History is on our side. We will bury you.'

In 1957 the USSR launched the world's first ICBM, and in 1961 Khrushchev ordered the construction of the Berlin Wall. ('Berlin is the testicles of the West', he said. 'Every time I want to make the West scream, I squeeze on Berlin.')

In 1961 Jack Kennedy launched the disastrous Bay of Pigs invasion of communist Cuba, and the next year a Soviet attempt to install missiles there almost brought on full-scale atomic war. Meanwhile the United States was fighting the ultimately futile Vietnam War, and in 1968 Soviet troops crushed liberalisation in Czechoslovakia.

The 1970s brought '*détente*', but the Soviet bloc economy was collapsing, exacerbated by ruinous Soviet intervention in Afghanistan.

Ronald Reagan defined his policy towards the Soviet Union: 'It is this: We win and they lose.' He backed anti-communist insurgents in places like Afghanistan, Angola, and Nicaragua and predicted that communism would be left 'on the ash heap of history'. He initiated 'Star Wars', a defence system so costly that copying it would bankrupt the Soviet Union.

In 1985 Mikhail Gorbachev introduced *perestroika* and *glasnost* and eased relationships with the West, but the Soviet economy continued to stagnate and its alliance system neared collapse.

In 1989 a revolutionary wave of mass protests swept across Soviet satellite states in Eastern Europe, unseating entrenched despots. (Only in Romania was there real violence, where dictator Nicolae Ceauşescu was shot by firing squad.) On 9 November the East Germans breached the Berlin Wall.

In August 1991 hard-line communists attempted to overthrow Gorbachev, but the coup was crushed and the Communist Party was banned. Now the Soviet Union itself began to crumble. On 21 December eleven Soviet republics withdrew from the USSR. Four days later, when Gorbachev resigned, his Soviet pen didn't work; a CNN producer gave him the Mont Blanc with which he signed himself out of history.

At 7.32 that evening the Soviet flag was lowered from the Kremlin for the last time. The next day – 26 December – the USSR ceased to exist, after 68 years, 362 days. According to former US Secretary of Defence Robert Gates: 'There is no precedent in all of history for the collapse of a heavily armed empire without a major war.' According to historian Norman Davies: 'It could not stand the oxygen of reform … It was struck down by the political equivalent of a coronary.'

A month later President George H. W. Bush reported in his State of the Union address: 'The biggest thing that has happened in the world in my life, in our lives, is this: by the grace of God, America won the Cold War.'

1476 Conspirators stab the sadistic murderer Galeazzo Maria Sforza, Duke of Milan, to death in the Church of San Stefano. Apprehended and tortured before being executed, one of the assassins says: 'Death is bitter, but glory is eternal, the memory of my deed will endure.'

---

27 December

'I have vanquished thee, O Solomon!'

537 AD In January 532 the Nika riots had exploded in Constantinople; nearly half the city was burned or destroyed and tens of thousands killed. Among the incinerated buildings was the city's foremost church, Hagia Sophia (Holy Wisdom), founded by the Emperor Constantine two centuries before and rebuilt by Theodosius II in 415 after the original had burned down.

Now that the church lay in ruins, the current emperor, Justinian, resolved to erect an even more glorious replacement, 'like nothing seen before since the day of Adam or can be seen in the future'. This time the basilica would be of brick and stone, without the wood roof that had doomed its predecessors.

Justinian chose the renowned mathematician Isidore of Miletus and a professor of geometry and physics, Anthemius of Tralles. Although neither was formally trained as an architect, they were both *mechanikoi* – masters of the science of mechanics. The emperor was sure they could provide a durable structure and organise the logistics of drawing thousands of workers and unprecedented loads of rare raw materials from around the empire.

The materials included green marble from Thessaly, purple porphyry from Egypt, yellow stone from Syria and black stone from the Bosporus region. The 'architects' also raided the ruins of the Temple of Artemis in Ephesus for its columns.

Initial planning began at the end of February, just a month after the riots had destroyed the old church. During the five years and ten months needed for construction, more than 10,000 workers toiled at the building site.

The completed basilica featured a magnificent dome, with a huge cross in a medallion at the summit, above a vast oblong interior 265 feet long. The interior surfaces were sheathed with polychrome marbles with ornamental stone inlays encrusted upon the brick core of the structure. (The walls' stunning mosaics were created a few decades later, during the reign of Justin II.)

On Christmas Day 537 the new basilica was completed. Two days later Justinian and Menas, Patriarch of Constantinople, led the inauguration. During the extravagant ceremony the emperor gazed at his work with wonder. 'Glory to God, who has judged me worthy to accomplish this task', he murmured, and then, remembering the fabled Temple of Solomon in ancient Jerusalem, he exclaimed with pride: 'I have vanquished thee, O Solomon!'

As spectacular as the new Hagia Sophia was, it was not as solid as Justinian had hoped. On 7 May 558 a massive earthquake struck

Constantinople and the main dome collapsed. Undaunted, Justinian called in Isidore the Younger, the nephew of Isidore of Miletus, to create a new dome.

Isidore elevated the dome by 20 feet 6 inches, bringing it to its current height of 182 feet, with a width of 105 feet. It includes a corona of 40 arched windows that floodlight the basilica's interior. No wonder Justinian's subjects saw the dome of Hagia Sophia as the dome of heaven itself.

Today, 1,500 years later, the dome remains the fifth largest in the world, after the Duomo in Florence (with a width of 144 feet), the Pantheon in Rome (142 feet), St Peter's in Rome (136 feet), and St Paul's in London (112 feet). (The US Capitol's rotunda is a mere 96 feet.)

The basilica remained the centre of the Orthodox Church until 29 May 1453, when Mehmed the Conqueror subjugated Constantinople. On that bloody day hundreds of women and children fled to Hagia Sophia for sanctuary, but the Turks stormed through the portals and murdered them all, except for a few pretty girls to be sold as slaves. When Mehmed entered the church, he stopped the slaughter and then sent his *ulema* (a Muslim holy man) to the altar to proclaim: 'There is no god but Allah, and Mohammed is his Prophet!' He added four minarets around the perimeter of the building complex and covered the Christian mosaics with whitewash. The greatest church in Christendom had become a mosque.

In 1934, however, the Turkish government secularised the building, converting it into a museum, and restored the original mosaics, but on 24 July 2020 the government reconverted it to a mosque. It remains today one of the great buildings in the world and the supreme example of Byzantine architecture.

1944 In the critical days of the Second World War, when Montgomery Ward chairman Sewell Avery for the third time refuses to comply with an agreement negotiated with the unions, President Franklin Roosevelt orders the seizure of Montgomery Ward's plants and facilities, warning: 'Strikes in wartime cannot be condoned, whether they are strikes by workers against their employers or strikes by employers against their Government.'

28 December

*'This apparatus, a mere scientific curiosity,
has no commercial future.'*

1895 If you're near the Opéra in Paris, take a stroll to the nearby Hôtel Scribe, which boasts that here 'the Lumière brothers presented the world's first cinema screening'. It happened today.

In 1895 the flank of the hotel on Boulevard des Capucines featured the Grand Café, where in the basement in a large billiard room called Le Salon Indien, Louis and Auguste Lumière demonstrated their new invention, the *cinématographe*. Some 35 onlookers paid a franc apiece to see a boxy machine made of wood projecting ten short films onto a wall. The first was *La Sortie des Usines Lumière* (*Workers Leaving the Lumière Factory*), a film only 46 seconds long. Among those impressed by the spectacle was theatre director and magician Georges Méliès, who offered the brothers 10,000 francs for their machine. But Auguste Lumière refused to sell, telling Méliès: 'You should thank me, I have just stopped you from ruining yourself, for this apparatus, a mere scientific curiosity, has no commercial future.'

Louis and Auguste had been born in 1862 and 1864 respectively and during their schooldays in Lyon had exhibited both a taste and a talent for still photography. When Louis was only eighteen, he persuaded his father Antoine to bankroll him in establishing a photographic plate factory. Within a decade the brothers were manufacturing 15 million plates a year.

In 1894 Antoine took a trip to Paris, where he saw a showing of Thomas Edison's Kinetoscope, a machine with which viewers could see a moving film, but only through a peephole. Returning home, he urged his sons to find a way to project a moving image.

The brothers combined two existing ideas, the projection of successive images, a concept already developed by Emile Reynaud, and Edison's use of sprocket-wound film, giving their machine several advantages over Edison's: it could be used for both shooting film and projecting it, was quieter, smaller and lighter, and used less film. Furthermore, Edison's Kinetoscope showed images at 46 frames per second, but the Lumières understood that the human brain's illusion of continuous movement is created by images shown at any speed of more than fifteen images per second. Therefore they reduced the rate of exposure to sixteen frames a second, the rate still used today.

After patenting their invention, during the next four years the brothers made 1,422 motion pictures, each about 50 seconds long, which they showed in cities around the world. At the World's Fair in Paris in 1900 they projected some clips onto a giant 3,600-square-foot screen, comparable to today's largest ones. Eighty thousand spectators enjoyed the show. Their *cinématographe* was so successful that we have used its first three syllables – cinema – ever since. The Lumières took the name from the Greek *kinema* – 'movement'. Edison's 'Kinetoscope' derives from the same source.

Despite their success with films, the brothers attached less importance to their invention than to improvements they had made in colour photography. By 1902 they had stopped producing films, but their competitor Thomas Edison predicted: 'Cinema will become one of the pillars of human culture.'

Louis Lumière died in 1948, Auguste in 1954, too soon to witness the implementation in 1958 of the Hollywood Walk of Fame with stars embedded in the sidewalk to honour high achievers in the entertainment industry, but no doubt the brothers would be pleased that Louis' star can be found at 1529 Vine Street and Auguste's at 6320 Hollywood Boulevard.

1918 Daughter of an Anglo-Irish baronet, the aristocratic but fanatical Irish nationalist Constance Markievicz, who was imprisoned, sentenced to death for shooting a Dublin policeman during the Easter Rising and amnestied, becomes the first woman ever elected to the British Parliament. As a Sinn Féin candidate, she never takes her seat but perhaps would have been unwelcome anyway with her fashion advice: 'Dress suitably in short skirts and strong boots, leave your jewels in the bank and buy a revolver.' *
1935 Winston Churchill in *Collier's*: 'A free Press is the unsleeping guardian of every other right that freemen prize; it is the most dangerous foe of tyranny.'

29 December

'Will no one rid me of this turbulent priest?'

1170 In 1154 Henry II had become King of England at 21. The next year he appointed as Chancellor a tall, lean man with dark hair and a sallow complexion, fifteen years his senior. He was Thomas Becket.

The king and Becket worked in harmony in court and enjoyed each other's company while hunting or in the taverns of London. With his resourceful mind and astute understanding of Henry's will, Becket helped concentrate power in the king's hands at the cost of the feudal barons and the Church. So pleased was Henry that in 1162 he appointed him Archbishop of Canterbury, second in power only to the king himself.

But then Becket began to change. His public style became more imperious, his arrogance more pronounced, his ostentation more insufferable. But privately he also changed, spending hours in prayer and becoming a vegetarian. Most critically, he increasingly supported the old, medieval powers of the Church, especially when they ran counter to the claims of the Crown.

Becket infuriated Henry by excommunicating one of his barons, but the greatest dispute involved trials of miscreant priests. Becket was adamant that clerics be tried exclusively by canonical trial, but Henry insisted that they be subject to secular law. He also banned the excommunication of court officials without royal consent.

So vehement were the arguments, so bitter the quarrel, that, after Becket had been archbishop for just over two years, he fled to France but still maintained his ecclesiastical authority, excommunicating various churchmen and nobles who supported the king. Henry continued bitterly to denounce him. The clash reached its apogee in June 1170 when Henry had his son crowned the Young King by the Archbishop of York, even though only the Archbishop of Canterbury had the right to crown English monarchs. Becket responded in fury, laying all of England under interdict, which finally forced Henry into an uneasy truce.

On 1 December 1170 the archbishop returned to England, but he immediately rekindled the fire by excommunicating three bishops appointed by the king. Henry was in Bayeux when he heard the news. Incensed, he roared: 'What cowards have I about me. Will no one rid me of this turbulent priest?' (Or, '*N'y aura-t-il personne pour me débarrasser de ce prêtre turbulent?'* – this famous line, if said at all, was said in French, Henry's only language.)

Henry had spoken in a moment of fury with no intention of ordering a murder, but in court were four impatient barons, Reginald Fitzurse, Hugh de Morville, William de Tracy and Richard le Breton. Immediately they were riding hard for England.

On the afternoon of 29 December, the barons reached the archbishop's palace at Canterbury. Dressed in white cloaks over chain mail, they confronted Becket and demanded that he abandon England for ever. Scornfully he replied: 'Not for living man, not for the king, will I fly!'

At the hour of vespers, the archbishop went to his cathedral. As he stood in the north transept, the four armed knights strode in, accompanied by an excommunicated knight named de Brock. As the men approached, Becket moved to the altar, crying out: 'I am prepared to die for Christ and for His Church.' At these, his last words, de Tracy struck at him with his sword, wounding one of the few clerics supporting the archbishop but only grazing Becket's forehead. Then de Tracy and le Breton both hacked at the archbishop, knocking him down, and de Brock placed his foot on his neck and sliced through his skull so that his brains spread out on the stone floor.

The arrogant archbishop was finally dead. After the barons had fled, cathedral priests recovered the corpse and discovered that under his robes Becket was clothed in sackcloth and his body was scourged with the marks of a penitent.

Becket's tomb instantly became a place of worship, and in less than three years he was canonised. King Henry came to Canterbury publicly to confess his sins and receive absolution.

For four centuries Becket's shrine remained a goal of pilgrimage, but in the 16th century Henry VIII had it ripped from the cathedral and destroyed. He had no patience with the priest who would defy a king.

1990 British footballer George Best: 'People say I wasted my money. I say 90 per cent went on women, fast cars and booze. The rest I wasted.' (Possibly cribbed from American actor George Raft's explanation to his bank manager: 'Part of the $10 million I spent on gambling, part on booze and part on women. The rest I spent foolishly.')

30 December

'To get closer to God, you must commit many sins.'

1916 It was late in the evening of 29 December in the Moika Palace in St Petersburg when, accompanied by the jolly beat of 'Yankee Doodle' playing on the gramophone, Prince Feliks Yusupov offered his guest two cakes laced with cyanide, along with a similarly doctored glass of Madeira, but the intended murder victim, a bearded and brooding holy man, showed no ill effects and continued to chat with his host. He was the notorious Rasputin.

At two in the morning, as Rasputin was examining a beautiful ebony cabinet, Yusupov murmured, 'You would do better to look at the crucifix and pray to it', and then raised a revolver and shot him.

Believing Rasputin dead, Yusupov and his fellow conspirators drove to the monk's apartment, one plotter wearing his coat and hat, to make it look as though Rasputin had returned home. On returning to the Moika Palace, Yusupov went to check on the dead body – but suddenly the victim rose to his feet, attacked Yusupov and charged out into the courtyard.

There another assassin waited. He shot the holy man twice, and then the murderers rolled him up in a blue rug and pushed their grisly package through a hole in the frozen surface of the Malaya Nevka River. When the body was recovered three days later, water was found in the lungs. Rasputin had finally drowned, after surviving both poison and bullets.

Such was the end of the sinister '*staretz*', or self-styled mystic christened Grigory Yefimovich Novykh but universally known as Rasputin, Russian for 'debauched one'.

Born a peasant in Siberia in 1872, at eighteen Rasputin had converted to the Khlysty flagellant sect and developed the theory that he could achieve a state of grace through 'holy passionlessness', a condition best reached through the exhaustion of prolonged debauchery. Although illiterate, unkempt and unclean (he bathed but once a month), he found women susceptible to his sexually charged message from God.

For over a decade Rasputin wandered through Russia preaching and seducing and finally arrived in St Petersburg in 1903. There his reputation as a mystic grew until Tsar Nicholas and his neurotic wife Alexandra summoned him to attend their four-year-old son Aleksey, the Tsarevich, whose life was threatened by haemophilia. Miraculously,

Rasputin seemed to help the boy, possibly through his hypnotic powers, but more likely because he forbade giving him medicines, including aspirin, although at the time it was not known to be an anticoagulant. In any case, his place at court was assured.

For the next ten years Rasputin continued his drunken orgies and faith-based seductions, claiming that any woman who had sex with him would purify her soul. 'To get closer to God', he told them, 'you must commit many sins.'

Nicholas and Alexandra considered lurid reports about him to be malicious and unfounded gossip, and his baleful influence grew, much to the distress of the country's nobility. Then, in 1914, came war.

In August 1915 the feckless Tsar Nicholas left for the front to take personal command of his armies, leaving the government in the hands of Alexandra, whose spiritual advisor Rasputin had become. Now the *staretz* could influence the choice of cabinet ministers and even manipulate critical military decisions.

This finally provoked Prince Yusupov, who was married to the tsar's niece, and four other extreme conservatives to intervene. One, Vladimir Purishkevich, was a member of the Duma (parliament) while another, Grand Duke Dmitry Pavlovich, was the tsar's cousin. Seeing the tsar and tsarina impervious to reason, they resolved to murder the sinister holy man.

Hearing rumours of his impending assassination, on 7 December Rasputin sent a last letter to Alexandra that may have proved him a psychic after all. 'I shall depart this life before the first of January', he wrote. 'If one of your relatives causes my death, then no one in your family, that is, none of your children or relations, will live for more than two years. They will be killed by the people of Russia.'

Nineteen months later, on 16 July 1918, communist insurgents shot Nicholas and Alexandra and their five children in a cellar at Yekaterinburg.

1794 Edmund Burke in a letter to Whig Secretary of War William Windham about Englishmen sympathetic to the French Revolution: 'If your hands are not on your swords, their knives will be at your throats.' *
1902 Mark Twain in his *Notebook*: 'What is the difference between a taxidermist and a tax collector? The taxidermist only takes your skin.'

31 December

'A befuddled drunkard shall not outwit a woman deadly sober.'

192 AD Today Emperor Commodus' favourite concubine led a palace conspiracy to murder him, bringing a year of chaos to the Roman Empire.

Commodus had inherited the throne at eighteen on the death of his father, Marcus Aurelius, but after five years in power, he began to show signs of megalomania. He put to death one chief minister to placate the army, and allowed the Roman mob to lynch another, and once at the Roman baths he had an attendant thrown into an oven when his bath water wasn't hot enough. He began to think he was an incarnation of Hercules, wore a lion skin and wielded a club.

Commodus also started fighting in gladiatorial contests, grossly inappropriate for an emperor since only condemned criminals and other dregs of society fought as gladiators. He would not kill his gladiatorial opponents, but he would have wounded soldiers and amputees put in the arena and kill them with his sword. He brooked no rivals, once putting another gladiator to death merely for having skilfully killed a lion with a javelin.

Commodus had married at seventeen, but his wife Crispina produced no children and after four years he accused her of adultery, ordered her exiled and then executed.

In 182 Commodus had taken as concubine a woman named Marcia. At first, he treated her almost like a wife and allowed her considerable influence over Roman affairs, but he continued a lifestyle of depravity, revelling in luxuries and organising drunken orgies with his harem of 300 women and 300 boys.

In December 192 Commodus planned to celebrate the coming new year by addressing the people from the gladiators' barracks, dressed as Hercules, rather than from the palace in traditional purple. On the last afternoon of the year he told Marcia of his intentions. Dismayed, she told him it would bring shame on the empire. Dismissing her, he told his plan to his chamberlain, Eclectus, and to Laetus, the prefect of the Praetorian Guard, only to find them equally appalled.

Infuriated, Commodus went to his bedroom for his habitual nap, but first he scratched on a wax tablet the names of those to be executed that night. Heading the list were Marcia, Eclectus and Laetus.

As the emperor slept, one of his catamites wandered into his bedroom and picked up the tablet as a plaything. On leaving, the boy ran into Marcia in the hallway.

Seeing her own name at the top of the list, Marcia cried out: 'So, Commodus, this is my reward for my love and devotion, after I have put up with your arrogance and your madness for so many years. A befuddled drunkard shall not outwit a woman deadly sober.'

She called for Eclectus and Laetus, who saw they must act at once – delay could mean only death. The contemporary historian Herodian takes up the tale: 'They decided to poison Commodus, and Marcia assured them that she could administer a potion with the greatest ease. For it was her custom to mix the wine and give the emperor his first cup, so that he might have a pleasant drink from the hand of his beloved. When Commodus returned from his bath, she poured the poison into the cup, mixed it with a pungent wine, and gave it to him to drink ... he became drowsy and stupefied and fell asleep ... but, when the poison spread through his stomach and bowels, he became nauseated and began to vomit violently.'

Terrified that Commodus might regurgitate the poison and recover, the conspirators sent for his wrestling partner, Narcissus, who, for an enormous reward, strangled him in his bed.

Fearful of public reaction, the murderers had the emperor's body secreted out of the palace and buried, but when the Senate learned of their crime, instead of condemning the killers, they had the corpse dug up and dragged around Rome like a common criminal's.

But the conspirators could not escape their fate. Commodus' death ushered in the chaos of the 'Year of the Five Emperors', four of whom were assassinated or executed. The second, Didius Julianus, had Marcia and her co-plotters put to death – not for murdering Commodus, but for supporting one of his rivals.

1793 Bon viveur Armand-Louis de Gontaut, duc de Biron, a noted sophisticate and accomplished philanderer who had fought on the republican side in both the American and French revolutions, is guillotined for being an aristocrat; as he positions himself beneath the blade, he says: 'I shall arrive in the other world in time to wish my friends a Happy New Year.'

Index